A DICTIONARY
OF ENTOMOLOGY

By the same author

A DICTIONARY OF ZOOLOGY

A DICTIONARY
OF ENTOMOLOGY

A. W. LEFTWICH

B.Sc., F.Z.S., M.I.Biol.

CONSTABLE · LONDON

CRANE RUSSAK · NEW YORK

First published in Great Britain 1976 by
Constable and Company Limited
10 Orange Street London WC2H 7EG
ISBN 0 09 460070 8

Published in the United States of America 1976 by
Crane Russak & Company, Inc.
347 Madison Avenue, New York, N.Y. 10017
ISBN 0–8448–0820–2
Library of Congress Catalog Card No. 75–27143

Printed in Great Britain by
REDWOOD BURN LIMITED
Trowbridge & Esher

TO HAROLD OLDROYD

Whose immense knowledge and love of insects have been
a source of inspiration and encouragement to the author

PREFACE

While this dictionary may be regarded as a companion volume to the author's *Dictionary of Zoology* and to George Usher's *Dictionary of Botany*, it is primarily intended for amateur entomologists, for naturalists with an interest in insects and for students of zoology who may have a special leaning towards this branch of their studies. The author has omitted definitions of general biological terms that may be found in other dictionaries, except where these have a special significance in relation to insects; anatomical terms such as *abdomen, heart, eye* etc. have been defined only in terms of the body of an insect.

As in the *Dictionary of Zoology* the author has included a large number of orders, suborders and families but he has endeavoured to define these in rather less technical language in order that they may be better understood by the amateur naturalist. The number of individual species of insects is so great, probably over a million, that it is obviously only possible to include a very small proportion of these. The author has, however, defined nearly 3,000, including many of agricultural, medical or veterinary importance and others with interesting habits or other special features. It is inevitable that many of the species defined are British and European insects. The author hopes his readers will pardon this bias. A fair number of American species and many of the better known tropical insects are, however, also included. Where possible individual species will be found under their English names but in some cases under the Latin generic name.

About 700 definitions of families and larger groups have been given and about an equal number of terms relating to the anatomy and physiology of insects, making a total of more than 4,000 definitions in all.

An outline classification is added at the end together with a short explanation of several alternative systems that are in common use.

The author would particularly like to thank Mr. Harold Oldroyd of the British Museum (Natural History) for his invaluable help. Not only has he checked the entries with meticulous care, but has also made numerous suggestions for improvements and additions; his help and advice have added greatly to the value and reliability of a work such as this.

A. W. LEFTWICH

A

ABDOMEN. The hind part of the body of an insect consisting of eleven segments behind the thorax, though several segments are usually concealed. Usually without any jointed appendages other than cerci and genitalia. Many larvae, however, have false legs on the abdomen.

ABRAXAS. Genus of the common Magpie Moth or Currant Moth (*Abraxas grossulariata*), a black, white and yellow moth having a looper (geometrid) caterpillar that feeds on currant and gooseberry bushes as well as other fruits.

ACALYPTERAE. A group of cyclorrhaphous Diptera differing from the house fly etc. by reason of the fact that the wings do not have posterior lobes covering the halteres. They include many families of small flies such as the fruit fly *Drosophila*. The adults are generally small, soft-bodied and inconspicuous; the larvae live in decaying materials or in plant-tissues.

ACANTHOPSYCHE. A South African bagworm pest that does severe damage to acacia and other trees. The caterpillar makes a large case or bag from fragments of leaf, twig, grass etc. and spends the winter in it, as well as carrying it around during the feeding period.

ACCESSORY HEARTS. Pulsatory organs consisting of ampullae with valves, sometimes present near the bases of antennae, wings or legs.

ACEPHALOUS. A term applied only to larvae. Apparently without a head or having a head that is much reduced and not clearly separated from the thorax, as for instance in the larva of the house fly.

ACEROUS. Without antennae. Only Protura are entirely acerous.

ACHERONTIA. Genus of the Death's Head Hawk-moth (*Acherontia atropos*), a large Southern European moth occasionally found in Britain. The colour is black and brown with a skull-like marking on the back of the thorax. The larvae feed chiefly on potato leaves.

ACID GLAND. The principal poison gland of a bee, secreting a complex mixture of histamine-liberating enzymes and proteins of low molecular weight collectively known as *apitoxin*.

ACONE EYE. A compound eye in which crystalline cones are absent or poorly developed, as for instance in the Crane-fly.

ACORN MOTH. A moth whose larva feeds on acorns; several genera are found in America and elsewhere, *e.g. Valentinia*.

ACORN WEEVIL. *Balaninus*, a small long-snouted weevil that feeds chiefly on acorns.

ACRAEIN. A protective or distasteful secretion of certain butterflies.

ACREA MOTH. *Estigmene acraea*, the common North American Salt-marsh moth, whitish with dark spots.

ACRIDOIDEA. Short-horned grasshoppers and locusts: one of the four superfamilies of Orthoptera. Hemimetabolous straight-winged insects with biting mouth-parts and having the head bent at right angles to the body. The fore-

1

wings are generally horny and thickened to form tegmina; the femora of the hind-legs are lengthened for jumping.

ACROCERA. A genus of small flies whose larvae feed on spiders and their eggs.

ACROCINUS. The Harlequin Longhorn, a large South American beetle with the body up to 9 cm. long and antennae about twice this length. The thorax and wing-covers are orange with red and black markings. Its larvae live in fig trees.

ACROSTICHAL BRISTLES. Minute bristles arranged in longitudinal rows along the back of the thorax of certain flies, between the two rows of stronger dorsocentrals.

ACROTERGITE. The anterior or foremost part of a secondary tergite (see *Secondary Segment*).

ACROTROPHIC OVARIOLE. A type of ovariole found in certain beetles and plant bugs in which the food cells are only present at the tip of each ovariole and may be connected to the developing eggs by strands of protoplasm acting as nutritive cords (see *Ovary*).

ACTIAS. A genus of large moths including the Indian Moon Moth (*Actias selene*) and formerly also the North American Moon Moth, now known as *Tropaea luna*. Both are a delicate pale green with two large slender tails and with moon-like markings on the fore-wings. The antennae are golden and fern-like.

ACULEA (ACULEUS). (1) A sting.
(2) A minute spine such as that found on the wings of some butterflies and other insects.
(3) A microtrichium.

ACULEATA. A division of Hymenoptera which includes the stinging forms, bees, ants and wasps in contrast to the *Parasitica* which are parasites of other insects. Because of the many exceptions these divisions are out of favour in formal classification but remain convenient in general discussion.

ACULEATE. Bearing a sting or homologous organ.

ADALIA. A genus of ladybird beetles common in Europe and America. They include the two-spot and the seven-spot ladybirds, in both of which there are many variations of colour and pattern. The former, for instance, may be red with black spots or black with red spots.

ADECTICOUS PUPA. A pupa whose mandibles are non-articulated and often reduced and are not used for escaping from the cocoon.

ADELGINAE (ADELGIDAE). Minute parasitic plant-lice producing galls on young conifer shoots.

ADELOCERA. A genus of click beetles (Elateridae), slim, short-legged and able to jump several cm. off the ground by means of a spring-like mechanism under the thorax. Its larva is a wireworm, a pest of root crops.

ADELOGNATHA. A group of weevils having a short rostrum with temporary mandibles that are later cast off. Many live in soil, the larvae feeding on roots.

ADENOTROPHIC VIVIPARITY. A phenomenon in certain insects whereby the larvae are retained in the parent's body after hatching, develop by feeding on 'uterine' secretions, moult twice and are finally deposited in a mature state ready for pupation. Found only in the Tsetse flies (*Glossina*) and the Diptera Pupipara.

2

ADEPHAGA. One of the four suborders of beetles (Coleoptera) comprising families in which both adults and larvae are usually active and predatory. Land forms include the Ground Beetle *Carabus* and the Tiger Beetle *Cicindela*; aquatic forms include *Dytiscus* and *Gyrinus*.

ADMIRAL. Name for a number of medium or large butterflies of the family Nymphalidae found in many parts of the world. The Red Admiral *Vanessa atalanta* is black with red and white markings; the White Admiral *Ladoga camilla* is black or brown with white or cream markings.

AEDEAGUS. The copulatory organ or 'penis' of a male insect; authors vary in how many accessory structures such as parameres, they include in this term.

AEDES AEGYPTI. A tropical mosquito specially important as the principal carrier of the yellow fever and dengue viruses. Formerly known as *Stegomyia fasciata*.

AEGERIIDAE. Clearwing Moths often closely resembling wasps or hornets. Most of them fly by day and the resemblance to toxic insects is no doubt to their advantage, as birds will tend to avoid them. The larvae do much damage by boring into fruit trees.

AESHNA. A common genus of large handsome dragonflies having long brightly coloured bodies.

AESTIVATION. A period of inactivity similar to hibernation but occurring in warm seasons or times of drought.

AGAONTIDAE (AGAONIDAE). Fig-wasps: minute Hymenoptera living on fig trees and helping to pollinate them.

AGONODERUS. A genus of carabids or ground beetles differing from most of this group in being vegetarian. They feed chiefly on seeds.

AGRICULTURAL ANT (HARVESTER ANT). A general name for a number of species of herbivorous ants that build large mounds of loose soil or sand and clear the surrounding ground of all vegetation.

AGRIONIDAE. A family of damselflies (Odonata–Zygoptera) often brilliant green or blue in colour.

AGRIOTES. A genus of click beetles (Elateridae) whose larva, the common wireworm, is a very destructive agricultural pest of root crops.

AGROMYZIDAE. Leaf-miners: minute flies (Diptera) whose small white larvae burrow into the leaves and young shoots of a wide range of plants.

AGROTIDAE. An alternative name for Noctuidae or Owlet moths: small or medium sized, drably coloured, night-flying moths whose larvae, known as cutworms, do much damage to roots and young shoots. The group includes, among others, the Yellow Underwing moth and the Cabbage moth.

AGRYPNIA. A genus of European caddis fly whose larva uses a hollowed twig as a case.

AILANTHUS SILK MOTH. *Philosamia,* a silk moth whose larva feeds on the Tree of Heaven (*Ailanthus*). It is a native of Asia where it is bred for silk production, but has been introduced into parts of the United States.

AIR SACS. Thin-walled dilatations of the tracheae which by their elasticity increase the efficiency of respiration, particularly in fast-flying insects.

AKINESIS. A motionless state of an insect resembling sleep, particularly after loss of, or damage to, sensory organs such as antennae.

3

ALAE CORDIS. Wing-like bands of fibrous tissue suspending the heart from the pericardium in insects and other arthropods.

ALAPTUS. *Alaptus magnanimus*, a chalcid parasite on book-lice, said to be the smallest of all insects, about 0.2 mm. long.

ALAR, ALARY. Wing-like; or appertaining to wings.

ALARY (ALIFORM) MUSCLES. A series of triangular wing-like muscles inserted on to the membrane that separates the perivisceral from the pericardial cavity of an insect. Contraction of these causes blood to flow into the pericardial cavity and thence through small openings or *ostia* into the long dorsal tubular heart.

ALATE. Possessing wings.

ALAUS. A genus of large Click beetles (Elateridae) with predatory larvae; found in many parts of the world.

ALDER-FLY. *Sialis* and other members of the family Sialidae, primitive insects of the order Neuroptera (suborder Megaloptera). The predatory aquatic larvae are characterised by seven or eight pairs of conspicuous abdominal appendages fringed with gill filaments; the adults, usually of a brownish colour, have four membranous wings, are weak-flying and only live for a few days.

ALDER WOODWASP. Closely related to the Giant Woodwasp *Urocerus* but only about 2 cm. long, black with red and white markings and having a needle-like ovipositor with which it lays eggs under the bark of alder and willow trees. The larvae then tunnel into the wood (see *Xiphydriidae*).

ALEURODIDAE (ALEYRODIDAE). Whiteflies; minute plant-bugs of the order Homoptera, having the body covered with white waxy powder; the nymphs are scale-like and sessile. The group includes the greenhouse whitefly *Trialeurodes vaporariorum*, the well-known pest of tomatoes and cucumbers.

ALIENICOLAE. Viviparous wingless female aphids that reproduce parthenogenetically in enormous numbers on herbaceous plants throughout the spring and summer; eventually they give rise to winged forms that fly to another plant in the autumn and reproduce by a normal sexual process.

ALIFORM. Wing-like.

ALIMENTARY CANAL. The digestive tract which, in insects, is very variable but usually consists of the following parts:—
    (1) The mouth parts *viz.* labium, mandibles, maxillae and labrum.
    (2) The pharynx and salivary glands.
    (3) The oesophagus.
    (4) The crop, a thin-walled dilatation or food reservoir.
    (5) The gizzard or *proventriculus*, a strong chitinous muscular 'stomach' sometimes having internal teeth.
    (6) The mid-gut or *mesenteron* where most digestion and absorption take place. It may contain a *peritrophic membrane*, a thin transparent tube extending backwards into the hind-gut, possibly as a protection for the delicate epithelial cells.
    (7) The hind-gut or 'rectum' into which lead a large number of *Malpighian tubules* – the principal excretory organs.

ALIMENTARY CASTRATION. Sterility of the worker and soldier castes of some social insects, brought about by a deficiency in their diet.

ALITRUNK. The two wing-bearing segments of an insect's thorax, *i.e.* usually the second and third segments. In some Hymenoptera the first segment (prothorax) is also involved in wing-attachments.

ALKALINE GLAND. Also called *Dufour's gland*: one of the glands connected with the sting of a bee, producing an oily alkaline secretion whose function is obscure, but may be lubricatory.

ALLIGATOR BUG. An alternative name for the American Lantern fly *Fulgora lanternaria*, given on account of the peculiar prolongation of the head.

ALLOMETRIC (HETEROGONIC) GROWTH. The disproportionate growth of different parts of the body compared with that of the organism as a whole. In male stag beetles, for example, as the beetle grows larger the mandibles become relatively very much bigger in proportion to the whole body. Other organs may become relatively smaller.

ALLOSEMATIC RESEMBLANCE. Batesian mimicry: the resemblance of a harmless animal to a poisonous or distasteful one, giving protection to the former, since predators will tend to avoid both; *e.g.* the close resemblance of a clearwing moth to a wasp. (See *Aposematic*.)

ALUCITIDAE. A family of Plume moths: insects whose wings are deeply cleft and fringed, giving the appearance of a bunch of feathers (see also *Orneodidae* and *Pterophoridae*).

ALULA. A part of an insect's wing forming a small separate lobe close to the base of the hind margin (*cf. Squama*).

ALURNUS. A genus of South American leaf-beetles (Chrysomelidae) including some of the largest and brightest of this group, with contrasting colours of red, yellow and black.

AMATIDAE (SYNTOMIDAE). A family of tropical moths, small, day-flying and brightly coloured; some species resemble wasps.

AMAZON ANT. *Polyergus*, a slave-making ant that rears other species to care for its own eggs and young.

AMBROSIA BEETLE. *Xyleborus* and related genera of the family Scolytidae: a type of beetle that bores into wood and takes in fungi which it cultivates as food for the larvae.

AMBUSH BUGS. Phymatidae: predatory insects belonging to the order Hemiptera, having grotesque spiny bodies; they live hidden among flowers and leaves where they capture other insects.

AMETABOLA. Primitive wingless insects that do not undergo metamorphosis: springtails and bristle-tails. The group comprises the four orders Diplura, Thysanura, Collembola and Protura. Authorities differ as to which of these should properly be regarded as not being true insects.

AMETAMORPHIC. See *Ametabola*.

AMMOCHAETA. A stiff type of bristle occurring in bunches on the heads of ants; used for cleaning the legs etc.

AMMOPHILA. A genus of sand wasp that feeds its young on caterpillars.

AMPHIPNEUSTIC. Having only two pairs of functional spiracles, one anterior and the other posterior, as for instance in the larva of the house fly.

AMPHITOKY. Production of both males and females parthenogenetically.

AMPHIZOIDAE. A very small family of fresh-water beetles living in cold mountain streams and feeding on drowned insects. Found in North America and Tibet.

ANABRUS. Genus of the Mormon Cricket *Anabrus simplex*, a large dark brown or black, wingless bush-cricket of the family Tettigoniidae; a pest of farm crops in the western U.S.

ANAL PAPILLAE. Thin-walled outgrowths in the anal region of some aquatic insects, *e.g.* mosquito larvae. They may possibly have a respiratory function but they appear to act chiefly as organs for the absorption of chloride and other ions from the water.

ANAL VEINS. The most posterior veins of an insect's wing.

ANAMORPHOSIS. The formation of extra abdominal segments on an insect after it has hatched from the egg, as for instance in the primitive group Protura.

ANASA. A genus of American Squashbugs (Coreidae): plant-bugs of the order Hemiptera, black or dark brown speckled with red. They are common pests of melon, gourd, pumpkin, marrow etc. *Anasa tristis* is the common Squashbug.

ANAX. A genus of large dragonflies of variable colour, having rounded wings on the males. They include European and American species; the Giant Green Darner, *Anax walsinghami*, of California with a 12 cm. wing-span is one of the largest of all dragonflies.

ANDRENIDAE. Mining bees: a family of solitary bees similar in appearance to the honey bee, but living underground. The females dig deep burrows sometimes as much as 60 cm. below the surface where they lay their eggs and deposit balls of pollen and honey for the developing larvae.

ANDROCONIA. Modified wing-scales and connected scent glands of some male butterflies, producing a sexually attractive secretion.

ANECDYSIS. A long passive period between two moults of an insect or other arthropod during which there appears to be no preparation for the next moult.

ANELLUS. A chitinous ring supporting parts of the male genitalia in some insects.

ANEMOTAXIS. A tendency of some insects to fly into a current of air.

ANEPIMERON. The upper part of the epimeron or posterior sclerite of the subcoxa at the base of an insect's leg.

ANEPISTERNUM. The upper part of the episternum or anterior sclerite of the subcoxa at the base of an insect's leg (*cf. Anepimeron*).

ANER. A male insect: a term used more especially in relation to ants.

ANGLE SHADES MOTH. *Phlogophora meticulosa.* A common British moth, light brown with darker brown triangular markings on the fore-wings. When at rest it resembles a shrivelled leaf. The larva, which can be green or brown, feeds on nettles, groundsel, chickweed etc.

ANGLE WING. American common name for butterflies of the genus *Polygonia* having the margins of the wings irregularly notched and angled, and including the British and European Comma Butterfly, *Polygonia C-album*.

ANGOUMOIS GRAIN MOTH. *Sitotroga cerealella*, belonging to a widely distributed genus of moths whose larvae are pests feeding on the kernels of cereals.

ANISANDRUS. A minute Ambrosia beetle that tunnels into the wood and

6

bark of many fruit and forest trees. *Anisandrus dispar*, a British species, is a pest of apple and plum trees.

ANISOLABIS. A genus of large, dark brown earwigs inhabiting marine beaches just above high water mark.

ANISOMORPHA. A genus of large wingless stick-insects (Phasmidae) common in North America.

ANISOPTERA. One of the two suborders of dragonflies (Odonata), stoutly built insects that fold their wings horizontally when at rest and whose hind-wings are broader than the fore-wings. The group includes most of the common large brightly coloured dragonflies but not the damselflies (see *Odonata*).

ANISOZYGOPTERA. Large fossil dragonflies of the Mesozoic era showing features intermediate between damselflies and true dragonflies.

ANOBIIDAE. A family of small wood-boring beetles including the 'woodworm' (*Anobium*) and the Death-watch Beetle (*Xestobium*). The adults are usually brown and are distinguished by the fact that the pronotum covers the head like a monk's cowl.

ANOMIS. A genus of noctuid moths able to pierce the surface of fruit by means of strong spines on the tip of the proboscis; mostly tropical.

ANOMMA. A genus of driver ants in which individuals of the 'soldier' caste are many times larger than other members of the colony and have very large powerful jaws.

ANOPHELES. The chief genus of anopheline mosquitoes, differing from the culicine mosquitoes chiefly in the following features:

    (1) The abdomen is not covered with overlapping scales but only fine hairs.

    (2) The mouth-parts of the female appear like a three-pronged fork owing to the fact that the palps are as long as the proboscis.

    (3) The larvae have no respiratory siphon but breathe by resting horizontally on the surface of the water.

ANOPHELES MACULIPENNIS. The best known and most widely distributed of the malaria mosquitoes, characterised by the appearance of spots on the wings due to concentration of scales in the region of the cross-veins.

ANOPHELINI. See *Anopheles*.

ANOPLIUS. A genus of Spider Wasps: solitary wasps that capture and para-lyse spiders as food for the developing larvae.

ANOPLURA (SIPHUNCULATA) Sucking Lice: an order of wingless blood-sucking insects mostly parasites of mammals (see *Louse*).

ANOSIA. An alternative name for the genus *Danaus*, the American Monarch Butterfly.

ANT. An insect of the superfamily Formicoidea with a single family, Formici-dae. Hymenoptera with elbowed antennae and with a very narrow abdominal constriction or 'waist' sometimes known as the *petiole*. There are no solitary ants; they invariably live in highly organized colonies containing many types or castes. The queen is the only ant capable of laying eggs; mating takes place during a nuptial flight in which several colonies take part together. The females then cast off their wings and start colonies in the ground. The majority of ants in a colony are workers or incomplete females without wings and with large heads. In some species, however, there are several other castes each with its own distinctive features. The social activities of ants include such varied occupations as storing food, tending and 'milking' aphids, cultivating fungi, enslaving other ants, defending the colony etc. Some types of 'soldier ants' use their extra large jaws for defence; others shoot out formic acid from glands at the hind-end of the body.

ANT BEETLE. *Thanasimus formicarius* and related species of the family Cleridae, resembling an ant in shape and general appearance. Both adults and larvae prey upon bark beetles of coniferous trees.

ANT-COW. A name sometimes given to aphids whose sugary secretion, known as honeydew, is much favoured by ants. In some cases these insects are kept and tended in the ants' nest and may be stimulated to exude their honeydew by being gently stroked with the ant's antennae.

ANTECOSTA. A transverse chitinous ridge to which longitudinal muscles are attached on the inside of each cuticular plate (tergum or sternum) in most insects.

ANTENNAE. Elongated sensory appendages on the heads of insects and other arthropods; very varied in structure, often segmented and mobile and usually bearing olfactory and tactile receptors.

ANTENNA COMB. A row of bristles forming a comb-like structure at the proximal end of the anterior tarsus in bees; used for removing pollen etc. from the antennae.

ANTHICIDAE. A family of small beetles having a very narrow head and thorax.

ANTHIDIUM. A genus of Mason Bees, leaf-cutting bees that construct nests of mud lined with plant material.

ANTHOGENESIS. The production of males and females parthenogenetically, as in certain plant-lice.

ANTHOMYIIDAE. Root-maggot flies or flower flies: small insects related to the house fly whose larvae are generally pests of root crops.

ANTHONOMUS. The cotton-boll weevil, an important pest of the cotton plant; the larvae feed on the bolls or seed pods causing wide-spread destruction.

ANTHOPHILOUS. Attracted by flowers; feeding on flowers.

ANTHOPHORIDAE. A family of large honey-bees usually solitary and nesting in sand or clay banks.

ANTHRENUS. A genus of carpet beetles: small round beetles of the family Dermestidae, about 3 mm. long, mottled with red, yellow and black. They are found in most parts of the world and are a pest in houses where the small hairy larvae feed on woollen clothing, carpets etc.

ANTLIA. (1) The tubular proboscis of a butterfly or moth.
(2) A dilated part of the post-pharynx in some Diptera. The oesophageal pump.

ANTLIATA. An old name for sucking insects, especially Lepidoptera and Diptera.

ANT-LION. The larva of a winged insect of the family Myrmeleontidae in the order Neuroptera. Wingless, with large jaws and very voracious, it digs a pit in loose sand and lies with its jaws exposed as it waits for ants and other passing insects. It devours a large number of these and when fully grown pupates and eventually becomes a four-winged insect resembling a damselfly.

ANT-NEST BEETLE. The name of a number of small beetles that live in ants' nests and whose larvae resemble ants sufficiently to be accepted by them as members of the colony. Some of these share the food of the ants or may act as scavengers, but in many cases the larval and the adult beetles thrive by feeding on the ant larvae. A typical member of the group is the reddish brown beetle *Lomechusa strumosa* which lives in the nest of the red ant *Formica sanguinea*.

ANTS' EGGS. The pupae of ants, commonly and erroneously called eggs when they are used for feeding fish etc.

ANT-WASP. A wasp of the family Mutillidae in which the wingless females resemble ants. Many species are bright red, banded with black or white and are covered with fine hairs.

ANURIDA. A genus of Collembola (springtails) including one of the few marine insects *Anurida maritima,* found round the coasts of Europe sometimes in large numbers forming grey masses on beaches regularly submerged by the tide.

AONIDIELLA. A genus of scale-insects parasitic on citrus fruits, *e.g.* the Californian red scale *Aonidiella aurantii.*

APANTELES. A genus of small ichneumon flies of the family Braconidae whose larvae parasitize and destroy the caterpillars and chrysalids of moths and butterflies. The yellow silky cocoons of these insects are often to be seen immediately after pupation which takes place on emerging from the dead caterpillar of the cabbage white butterfly.

APHANIPTERA (SIPHONAPTERA). Fleas; wingless blood-sucking insects parasitic on mammals and birds, having a laterally compressed body and enlarged hind-legs for jumping. The larvae are without legs and have biting mouth-parts; they do not suck blood but feed on organic debris in the nest or sleeping place of the host. Pupae are enclosed in silken cocoons. There are more than 1,000 species of fleas, each specific to one or two hosts for breeding purposes, though they will bite almost any warm-blooded animal that is available.

APHELINIDAE. Sun-flies: minute chalcid flies parasitic in the bodies of aphids. They have been introduced successfully into New Zealand and elsewhere in order to parasitize and control the woolly aphis of apple trees.

APHELOCHEIRUS. A genus of water bugs (Hemiptera) of the family Naucoridae, having many millions of minute hydrofuge hairs which enable them to hold a thin film of air over the surface of the body.

APHIS (APHID). One of a number of species of plant-lice which are extremely prolific and do much damage by sucking the sap of leaves and by exuding a sticky or waxy secretion from the abdomen. They belong to the order Homoptera and usually have a very complex life-history. Wingless parthenogenetic females breed viviparously in very large numbers throughout the summer, but in the autumn winged insects are produced and these fly to another host plant where they reproduce sexually and lay eggs in the normal way. Winter is usually passed in the egg stage.

The following terms are sometimes used in connection with the life-history:
Fundatrix. The first, usually wingless, female of a season.
Fundatrigeniae. Parthenogenetic female offspring of the fundatrix.
Alienicolae. Parthenogenetic, viviparous females, many generations mostly on the secondary host; both winged and wingless forms.
Migrantes. Migratory winged females produced parthenogenetically.

Sexuparae. Winged females which produce sexual males and females.
Sexuales. Normal sexual males and females.

Common species of aphid include the greenfly of roses (*Siphocoryne rosarum*), the blackfly of beans (*Aphis fabae*) and the woolly aphis of apple trees *etc.* (*Eriosoma lanigerum*).

APHIDOIDEA, APHIDIDAE, APHIDES. See *Aphis* above.

APHIS LION, APHIS WOLF. The predatory larva of a lacewing fly (*Chrysopa, Hemerobius* etc.) that feeds on aphids and other small insects.

APHODIINAE. A group of small black, brown or reddish beetles whose larvae develop in the faeces of grazing animals etc.

APHYTIS. A genus of minute Hymenoptera that parasitize the scale insects of citrus fruits and are used to control them.

APIARY. A group of beehives or other containers for keeping and breeding bees.

APIDAE. Bees: aculeate Hymenoptera, many with social habits and specialization of types. In the case of the common hive-bee *Apis mellifera,* the males or drones are produced from unfertilized eggs by parthenogenesis whereas workers and queen develop from fertilized eggs. A normal hive contains one queen, a few hundred drones and many thousands of workers. The queen is the only complete female capable of laying eggs; the workers are incomplete females. Apidae also include Bumble Bees and Carpenter Bees.

Bees differ from wasps in the following ways: (1) They build brood cells and honey cells of wax instead of wood-pulp; (2) They feed entirely on pollen and nectar whereas wasps are partly carnivorous.

APIS MELLIFERA. The honey bee, also called *Apis mellifica.* The specific name *mellifera* was apparently used before *mellifica* and is therefore the correct name although the latter is commonly used. See *Apidae* and *Apoidea.*

APITOXIN. The poison of bees' stings consisting chiefly of histamine-producing enzymes and proteins of low molecular weight.

APOCRITA. Bees, wasps, ants and ichneumon flies: insects of the order Hymenoptera with a deep constriction between the thorax and abdomen. The larvae are grub-like, without legs (*cf. Symphytra*).

APODEME. A chitinous ingrowth of the exoskeleton to which muscles are attached; such ingrowths serve as tendons in insects, crustaceans and other arthropods.

APODOUS, APODAL. Without jointed legs, *e.g.* referring to an insect larva.

APOIDEA. A group of Hymenoptera including all the social and solitary bees but excluding the wasps which belong to the Vespoidea. The social bees include the hive-bee *Apis mellifera* of which there are numerous subspecies and strains, as well as a great many wild species, many of which are stingless. The solitary bees include Carpenter bees, Leaf-cutters, Mining bees etc. Bees, like most Hymenoptera, have two pairs of membranous wings which become hooked together in flight.

APOLLO. A name for several European and American butterflies of the genus *Parnassius.* They are medium to large, generally white with black and red or yellow markings. The largest, the true Apollo *Parnassius apollo* is found in mountainous regions from Spain to Central Asia; it has black spots on the fore-wings and two red circles on each hind-wing.

APOPHYSIS. A projection from the exoskeleton (body-wall), either internally or externally, a term applied in various special senses by different authors (see *Apodeme* and *Phragma*).

APOSEMATIC. Having a warning coloration, either indicating that an animal is dangerous, *e.g.* a wasp, or in the case of harmless insects giving some degree of protection by mimicking the colours of a more dangerous predator.

APPLE CAPSID. *Plesiocoris rugicollis*: a plant-bug of the order Heteroptera, *i.e.* having wings that are leathery at the base and membranous at the tip. Like all plant-bugs it has piercing mouth-parts which puncture the skins of leaves or fruit and cause blisters by the injection of saliva. This insect particularly attacks willows but has also become a serious pest of apples, currants and gooseberries. The family, formerly called Capsidae, or capsids, are now known as Miridae.

APPOSITION EYES. Compound eyes that form a mosaic image, *i.e.* an erect image composed of a large number of dots or points or light. This is the case with most diurnal insects in which each of the crystalline cones of the eye is surrounded by a sheath of pigment. This prevents the light from passing from one cone to another and allows only a small point of light to impinge on the retina from each cone (see *Compound eyes*).

APTERA. A name formerly used for all wingless insects, but now best avoided, since winglessness occurs both primitively and secondarily in a wide range of different orders.

APTEROUS. Without wings.

APTERYGOTA. Insects that are primitively wingless, undergo no metamorphosis and show many similarities to the crustaceans from which they have probably descended. The group comprises four orders, *viz.* Diplura, Protura, Thysanura and Collembola. These include springtails, bristle-tails and silverfish but not fleas, bugs and lice which are secondarily wingless as a result of their parasitic habit.

AQUATIC CATERPILLARS. Larvae of some moths of the family Pyralidae, *e.g. Nymphula nymphaeata*, the Water Lily Moth. The eggs are laid on water plants; the newly hatched caterpillars burrow into the plant and remain there breathing dissolved oxygen either through the skin (in *Nymphula nymphaeota*), or by means of tracheal gills (in *Nymphula stratiotata*). After the first moult the insect cuts a piece out of the leaf and makes a home by fastening this to the underside of another leaf. It may spend the winter in this state, eventually pupating there. The adult moth is able to emerge through the water.

ARADIDAE. Flatbugs: a world-wide group of wingless insects belonging to the order Hemiptera. The flattened body and dark brown colour give them a superficial resemblance to the bedbug, but they are to be found under the loose bark of dead trees where they probably feed on fungi. They give off an unpleasant odour which perhaps protects them from predators.

ARASCHNIA. A genus of nymphalid butterflies that shows seasonal dimorphism, a pale form in the spring and a dark form in late summer. Includes the Map Butterfly of Central Europe (*Araschnia levana*).

ARCHIDICTYON (ARCHEDICTYON). An irregular network of small veins like those of a leaf in the wings of the Palaeodictyoptera, primitive fossil insects of the Carboniferous period. Most present-day insects show considerable simplification of wing venation by reduction of the number of cross-veins. Mayflies and dragonflies, however, closely resemble the primitive type.

11

ARCHOSTEMMATA. A suborder of beetles (Coleoptera) including some present-day species and fossils back to Mesozoic times. They have affinities with the Adephaga (*q.v.*). The larvae inhabit timber where they undergo a complex life cycle. All present-day species are included in the two families Cupedidae and Micromalthidae.

ARCTIIDAE. Tiger moths and related species: large brightly coloured moths, the common species of which have dark brown patches on their whitish fore-wings and on their red, orange or pink underwings. The Garden Tiger (*Arctia caja*) is the largest and commonest British species but there are many others in various parts of the world. Caterpillars are hairy and known as 'woolly bears'.

ARCULUS. An arc-shaped vein forming a cross-connection between other veins in the wings of certain insects, *e.g.* that connecting the radial and median veins in dragonflies.

AREOCERUS. A genus of small brown weevils that feed on coffee beans and to some extent on cotton and dried fruits. Originally Indian, they have become established as pests in most of the warmer parts of the world.

ARGUS. A name for a number of small butterflies of the family Lycaenidae, generally having the upper surface brown or blue and the under surface whitish grey or pale yellow with black and orange spots.

ARGYNNIS. A genus of handsome nymphalid butterflies including the Silver-washed Fritillary (*Argynnis paphia*) of Europe and Northern Asia as well as the large American species *Argynnis diana* whose female is the only blue fritillary in the world.

ARILUS. A genus of large American Assassin Bugs (Reduviidae): predatory insects that feed on other insects and have a poisonous bite which they some-times inflict on humans. *Arilus cristatus*, the largest species, is also called the Wheel Bug. It is about 4 cm. long, grey or brown in colour and has a crest resembling a cog-wheel on the back of the thorax.

ARISTA. A bristle-like appendage on the antennae of Diptera, formed from the numerous segments of the flagellum (*cf. Style*).

ARISTATE. Having aristae on the antennae.

ARIXENIINA. Ectoparasitic earwigs: a suborder of Dermaptera having eyes, mandibles and forceps greatly reduced. They are found in the breast-pouches of certain bats.

ARMY ANTS. Also called Driver Ants or Legionary Ants. Carnivorous ants of tropical countries that live in temporary nests and migrate in long files like an army.

ARMY WORM. An alternative name for the cutworm, a term used to denote the larvae of various noctuid moths; common pests of agriculture (see *Leucania*, and *Lyphagma*).

AROLIUM. A median pad between the claws of an insect's foot.

AROMIA. The Musk Beetle: one of the Cerambycidae or 'longhorns' possess-ing scent glands on the hind coxae. These secrete a musk-like ester of salicylic acid. The larvae are stem-borers of willow trees.

ARRHENOTOKY. Production of males from unfertilized eggs, *e.g.* drone bees.

ARTHROPLEONA. A suborder of Collembola or springtails (primitively wingless insects) having a distinctly jointed body. This distinguishes them from the other suborder, the Symphypleona, in which most of the segments are fused together. Both groups have a powerful springing organ or furcula at the hind-end.

ARTHROPODA. A large phylum of invertebrates including crustaceans, arachnids, insects, millipedes and centipedes. Of these classes the insects form by far the greatest number, probably at least a million distinct species. All groups of arthropods have a segmented body, a thick exoskeleton that is moulted from time to time, and a number of jointed appendages modified in various ways to form legs, jaws, antennae, cerci etc. The nervous system consists of a double ventral cord, two ganglia in each segment and a collar round the pharynx. A primitive brain is formed by fusion of some of the ganglia in the head segments.

ASCALAPHIDAE. Owl-flies: a family of Neuroptera bearing a superficial resemblance to dragonflies.

ASCHIZA. A group of cyclorrhaphous Diptera which lack the ptilinum in front of the head. The principal families are Syrphidae (Hover-flies) and Phoridae.

ASH BARK BEETLE. *Hylesinus fraxini* and related species: wood-boring beetles that do much damage to ash trees by tunnelling into the bark. The main galleries have two horizontal arms with an entrance and a pairing chamber in the centre. Short larval galleries ending in pupal chambers run at right angles to the main tunnels and end in the sapwood. The beetles probably also introduce spores of canker fungi into the tree.

ASILIDAE. Robber Flies: Diptera with piercing mouth-parts and with bristly legs ending in powerful claws; the compound eyes are prominent and extremely effective for hunting prey on the wing. They will attack most other insects, piercing them in the back of the head or thorax and sucking out the body fluids. They vary in shape from elongate to short and bee-like, and in size from 3 to 40 mm.

ASPARAGUS BEETLE. A name for a number of small beetles whose larvae feed on asparagus shoots.

ASPIDIOTUS. The San José Scale Insect: one of the most serious pests of American fruit and forest trees. A member of the Coccidae, it is a small circular insect whose scale-like appearance is due to a number of cast-off skins glued together. It was probably introduced into California from Asia during the last century.

ASSASSIN BUG. A predatory insect of the family Reduviidae in the order Hemiptera: Adults fly by night and prey upon other insects which they pierce with their proboscis. They sometimes inhabit houses and will destroy the Bedbug *Cimex lectularius*. They can make a shrill sound by rubbing the proboscis against the prosternum of the thorax. The nymphs may camouflage themselves by covering their bodies with dust or particles of rubbish.

ASTHENOBIOSIS. A theoretical explanation of the phenomenon of diapause or arrested growth of an insect. It is supposed that there is an accumulation of waste products in the tissues and that these hinder normal development in much the same way as they may cause muscular fatigue. During a resting stage these substances gradually disappear because excretion continues while normal metabolism slows down.

ATLAS BEETLE. *Chalcosoma atlas:* a giant beetle of tropical Asia, up to 10 cm. long, having two long curved 'horns' extending forwards from the front of the thorax.

ATLAS MOTH. *Attacus atlas:* a giant saturniid moth of tropical Asia having a wing-span of about 25 cm. A similar and equally large species *Attacus edwardsi* is found in Australia.

ATROPIDAE. A family that includes most of the commoner book-lice (Psocoptera): minute soft-bodied insects either wingless or with vestigial wings and with biting mouth-parts. They feed on rotting organic matter including the dried paste or mould in old books.

ATROPOS. One of the commonest genera of book-lice (see *Atropidae*).

ATTA. A genus of American ants that cut and collect fragments of leaves, mix them with excreta and saliva and take them into underground galleries. They then use them as a medium for cultivating specific fungi on which they feed.

ATTAGENUS. The Common Hide Beetle or Black Carpet Beetle, a serious household pest. The adult is a dull black oval-shaped insect about 12 mm. long. The larva, which feeds on woollen clothes, carpets etc. is a red-brown hairy grub.

AUCHENORRHYNCHA. Cicadas, frog-hoppers, leaf-hoppers etc.; a group of Homoptera or plant-bugs having four transparent wings, short antennae and mouth-parts plainly arising from the head (*cf. Sternorrhyncha*).

AUCHMEROMYIA. A genus of African flies whose larvae, known as floor maggots, live on the ground and suck the blood of those sleeping on the floor.

AUTOMERIS. The Io Moth or Bull's Eye Moth: a large brightly coloured North American moth of the saturniid or giant silk-moth group. The fore-wings of the male are yellow; those of the female lavender. In both sexes there is a blue spot in the centre of the hind-wing. The caterpillar, bright green with a red and white band along the side, is covered with poisonous bristles. It damages cotton and fruit trees.

B

BACK SWIMMER. *Notonecta* and related genera of carnivorous water bugs of the group Heteroptera. They are sometimes called Water Boatmen although this name is also used for the herbivorous *Corixa* and its allies which are not back swimmers. Both *Notonecta* and *Corixa* swim by means of the flattened hairy hind-legs that move in unison like oars.

BACON BEETLE. *Dermestes lardarius:* a small beetle having elongated elytra with parallel sides, black with a broad band of yellowish brown. Both larvae and adults are pests of bacon, hides and fatty substances generally.

BAETIS. A genus of small American mayflies (Ephemeroptera) whose larvae live in fast streams and cling to stones.

BAGOUS. A large genus of aquatic weevils that feed on vegetation.

BAGWORMS. Psychidae: a family of moths, mostly tropical and subtropical, in which the caterpillars construct bags of silk, leaves, twigs etc. around them-selves. These bags hang from trees and may be quite large, differing according to species and sex. In most cases the female moths are wingless and stay in the bags throughout their entire lives, eventually laying their eggs in them and dying.

BALANCERS.   Halteres: the reduced hind-wings of Diptera, shaped like short drumsticks. During flight these balancers vibrate in a constant plane so that any change of attitude by the fly causes an activation of tension receptors at their bases and a reflex correction by the muscles controlling the wings. It has been shown in some species that if the halteres are removed the insect soon loses its balance and falls to the ground.

BALANINUS.   The Acorn Weevil (Nut Weevil): a widely distributed genus of long-legged, brown or grey beetles having a very long slender curved snout. This is used for tunnelling into acorns, hazel nuts etc. into which the eggs are laid. The larvae develop inside the nut and eventually eat their way out.

BALANOBIUS.   A genus of small weevils that infest bean-galls on willow trees and probably live as hyperparasites destroying the eggs or larvae of the Bean-gall Sawfly.

BANDED AGRION.   *Agrion splendens.* A European species of damselfly (Zygoptera) in which the wings of the male are traversed by a broad, brilliant metallic blue band that fades to brown after death; the females have clear colourless wings (see *Agrionidae*).

BANDED CRANE-FLY.   *Pachyrhina maculata,* a European species of small crane-fly having a yellow abdomen marked with a row of black bands.

BANDED PINE WEEVIL.   *Pissodes notatus:* a species of small reddish brown weevils with bands of yellow scales on the wing covers. They do much damage to pine trees by boring holes and laying their eggs in the bark. The larvae then make long winding tunnels and pupating chambers between the bark and the wood.

BANDED PURPLE.   *Basilarchia arthemis,* also known as the American White Admiral: a North American butterfly having a broad white band on blue-black wings.

BANDED SPIDER-HUNTING WASP.   *Pompilus viaticus:* a medium sized solitary wasp having the head and thorax black and the abdomen bright orange or red with two dark bands and a black tip. These wasps rarely fly far but run over the ground hunting for spiders which they paralyse by their sting and drag underground as food for the larvae.

BAR EYE.   A name given to one of the mutations of *Drosophila* in which the number of optical units in the compound eye is greatly reduced.

BARK BEETLES.   Scolytidae: a family of small beetles closely related to the weevils but without the pointed snout of the latter. They do considerable damage to trees by tunnelling between the bark and the wood, making complicated passages resembling hieroglyphics. In many cases the species of beetle can be identified by the tunnelling pattern.

BARK BUG.   A small flatbug of the order Heteroptera, living under bark and feeding on fungi etc. *Aneurus* is a common European genus.

BARK LOUSE.   A name for any of a large number of Psocidae living on or under bark and feeding on lichens, fungi etc. Closely related to book-lice, they are small soft-bodied winged or wingless insects with biting mouth-parts and with long thin jointed antennae.

15

BASICONIC RECEPTOR. An olfactory or other sense organ of an insect, consisting of a small projecting cone whose base is connected to a nerve fibre.

BASILARCHIA. A genus of North American nymphalid butterflies variously coloured with purple, brown and black. They include the Banded Purple (*Basilarchia arthemis*) and the Viceroy (*Basilarchia archippus* or *Limenitis archippus*) whose colouring mimics that of the Monarch Butterfly *Danaus*. This appears to be a case of protective resemblance, since the latter is distasteful to birds.

BASILONA. *Basilona imperialis,* the Imperial Moth of North America: a large yellow moth marked with pink and purple.

BASISTERNUM. The principal part of the sternum or ventral cuticular plate on each segment of an insect's body.

BASKETWORM. An alternative name for a bagworm (*q.v.*).

BAT FLY. A name for a number of insects of the families Nycteribiidae and Streblidae, which live in the fur of bats and suck their blood.

BATESIAN MIMICRY. The resemblance of a harmless animal to a poisonous or dangerous one giving protection to the former, since predators will tend to avoid both. The clearwing moth resembling a bee is a well-known example.

BAT PARASITES. See *Bat Fly,* also *Arixeniina, Nycteribiidae, Polyctenidae* and *Streblidae.*

BAT 'TICK'. A common misnomer for bat flies of the orders Nycteribiidae and Streblidae.

BEAKED CYCHRUS. *Cychrus rostratus:* a medium sized black ground beetle related to the carabids, having a long narrow head that gives the appearance of a beak.

BEAN APHIS. *Aphis fabae:* the black aphis that infests beans and many other plants. Like all aphids it goes through a complex life cycle producing large numbers of wingless parthenogenetic females during the summer and winged sexual individuals in the autumn (see *Aphis*).

BEAN-GALL SAWFLY. *Pontania proxima:* a small sawfly that lays its eggs in the leaf buds of willow; the larvae then hatch out and develop inside the leaves causing red or pink swellings. These are often infested by hyperparasites, namely the tiny black weevil *Balanobius* and the ichneumon fly *Angitia* that prey on the sawfly.

BEAN WEEVIL. A name for a number of small beetles of the family Lariidae (Bruchidae); common pests of leguminous plants.

BEDBUG. *Cimex lectularius* and related species: parasitic insects of the order Hemiptera living intermittently on their hosts and sucking blood from time to time. They have a flattened body with no wings, a tough skin and a suctorial proboscis. They appear to have followed man to every part of the world.

BEDEGUAR GALL. An alternative name for the 'Robin's Pincushion', a red and green hairy or bristly gall occurring on wild rose bushes and produced by the larva of the cynipid gall-wasp *Diplolepis rosae.*

BEE. See *Apidae* and *Apoidea.*

BEE BREAD. A mixture of pollen and nectar stored by bees and used as food for the developing larvae.

BEE, CARPENTER. Large, mainly black bees of the family Xylocopidae. They tunnel and nest in dry wood, mostly in tropical countries.

16

BEE CHAFER. *Trichius fasciatus:* a medium-sized herbivorous chafer beetle having yellowish hair on the head and thorax and having the elytra coloured dull yellow with three black bands.

BEE-FLY. *Bombylius* and related genera: two-winged flies of the group Brachycera having a superficial resemblance to bees; feeding on nectar and helping in pollination. The larvae are parasitic in other insects.

BEE, GIANT. *Apis dorsata:* the largest of the honey bees, about 2 cm. long, occurring throughout South-east Asia; builds a single honeycomb up to 2 metres long attached to a tree, a building or a rock.

BEE HAWK-MOTH. *Hemaris:* a genus of moths having transparent wings and closely resembling bumble bees. They fly by day, often accompanying bees and taking nectar from the same flowers. This appears to be a case of Batesian mimicry.

BEE, LEAF-CUTTING. *Megachile* and related genera: bees that build their nests from neatly cut oval or round pieces of leaves or flower petals. The female bee holds the leaf with her legs while she cuts with her mandibles. These pieces are then made into a row of neat thimble-shaped cells each containing an egg and a supply of pollen and honey for the developing larva.

BEE LOUSE. *Braula coeca:* a minute wingless insect infesting beehives and the bodies of honey bees. Although it resembles a louse it is in fact a member of the Diptera in which the absence of wings is a secondary feature connected with its way of life. These insects are so small that many may be carried on the body of a single bee causing it considerable irritation. The larvae live in the hive in large numbers, burrowing into the honeycomb and feeding on the pollen and honey.

BEE MILK. An old name for *Royal Jelly*, a predigested food substance on which the larvae of bees must be fed in order to develop into queen bees. It is produced from the pharyngeal glands of the worker bees and contains a high proportion of proteins.

BEE, MINING. A type of solitary bee that makes its nest deep in the ground (see *Andrenidae*).

BEE MOTH. *Aphomia:* a small moth of the family Pyralidae whose larva lives in the nests of bees and wasps.

BEE STING. The sting of a bee is a modified ovipositor on the hind-end of the abdomen. It can be protruded at will but normally rests in a pocket in the seventh abdominal segment. The piercing part or stylet consists of a number of 'valves' formed from long drawn-out horny outgrowths of the eighth and ninth abdominal segments. These interlock to form a channel down which venom flows from the so-called *acid gland*. The main constituents of this venom are histamine-producing enzymes and proteins of low molecular weight. In addition to the venom gland there is an *alkaline gland* secreting an oily, non-toxic liquid which may help to clean and lubricate the sting.

BEE, STINGLESS. Meliponinae: a subfamily containing many species of bees mostly living in tropical countries. They resemble the hive bee in many ways but differ from it by reason of the fact that they are much smaller and have not the ability to sting. Like hive bees they live in colonies, collect nectar and pollen and build honeycomb, nesting usually in hollow trees, rocks etc.

BEESWAX. Wax secreted by worker bees from glands under the abdomen;

used for making honeycomb. Chemically it is a mixture of esters and paraffin hydrocarbons all of high molecular weight.

BEETBUG. A name for a number of heteropterous plant-bugs that damage and spread virus diseases in beet, *e.g. Piesma.*

BEET FLY (MANGOLD FLY). *Pegomyia betae,* an agricultural pest that lays its eggs on the undersides of the leaves of mangolds and beet. The larvae tunnel in the leaves.

BEETLES. Coleoptera: an order of insects comprising about a quarter of a million species, the largest order in the whole animal kingdom. The fore-wings are thickened to form *elytra* or covers which protect the membranous hind-wings. The mouth-parts are of the biting type. In other respects these insects are very variable. Some are large, others minute; some carnivorous, others herbivorous; some terrestrial, others aquatic.

They are holometabolous, *i.e.* they undergo complete metamorphosis. The larvae are very variable: some are predatory insects of the *campodeiform* type with long legs and antennae; others such as the wireworm are entirely herbivorous and have the legs and antennae reduced. The larvae of chafer beetles are of the *scarabaeoid* type with a large soft inflated abdomen.

BELOSTOMATIDAE. A group of tropical water bugs (Hemiptera) including the giant North American *Belostoma grandis,* 10–12 cm. long. In this species the female deposits her eggs on the back of the male and the latter carries them around until they are hatched.

BEMBICIDAE. Sand Wasps: a widespread family of large wasps that burrow in sandy places.

BENA. A genus of moths of the family Cymbicidae including the Green Silver Lines, *Bena fagana,* a handsome moth whose fore-wings are light green with three silver-white cross-lines; the hind-wings are white or yellowish. The principal food plants of the larvae are oak, beech, birch and hazel.

BENACUS. A genus of Giant Water Bugs of the tropics and subtropics, *e.g. Benacus griseus* of the Southern United States (see also *Belostomatidae*).

BERLESE'S ORGAN. A glandular organ in the female bedbug *Cimex lectularius.* It is in the base of the sac that receives sperm cells from the male during copulation and probably secretes a substance that helps to activate them.

BIBIONIDAE. St. Mark's Flies and Fever Flies: a family belonging to the group Nematocera or 'long-horned' Diptera having a black or brown body about 12 mm. long and spiny legs that are prominent in flight. The large compound eyes sometimes meet on the top of the head and are peculiar in having facets of two distinct sizes. The larvae of bibionids are greyish white maggots that live in the soil and are serious plant pests; they often congregate in tangled masses.

BIG-HEADED FLIES. Pipunculidae: small two-winged flies with spherical heads and enormous eyes; found chiefly in northern Europe and Asia.

BINUCLEATE EGGS. Eggs containing two nuclei which may have different gene contents and may be fertilized by two different spermatozoa. Such a phenomenon is known to occur in a number of insects and accounts for the existence of *gynandromorphs* – insects having some male and some female features.

BIOLOGICAL CONTROL. The reduction or control of a pest by introducing a suitable predator into its habitat, *e.g.* the control of the greenhouse whitefly *Trialeurodes* by the minute chalcid wasp *Encarsia.*

18

BIOLUMINESCENCE. The production of a cold light by certain insects, fish and other organisms. Little is known of the process but it is believed to involve the oxidation of a substance *luciferin* with the help of a specific enzyme known as *luciferase*. A number of insects, principally beetles and their larvae, show this phenomenon. The best known are *Lampyris* (the glow-worm), *Luciola* (the Mediterranean firefly) and *Pyrophorus* (the West Indian Cucujo beetle). The latter is the most brilliant of all known luminescent animals.

BIORHIZA. The Oak-apple Gall-wasp, a small black hymenopterous insect of the group Cynipoidea that lays its eggs in the roots and shoots of oak trees. The presence of the eggs sets up an irritation and causes rapid growth of the plant tissues, providing food for the developing insect which eventually eats its way out.

BIOTIC POTENTIAL. An estimate of the maximum rate of increase of any species of animal if left to itself and isolated from its natural enemies, disease or other inhibiting factors. Normally this potential reproductive rate is very great (many millions per year in the case of insects for instance), but in the struggle for existence a balance is maintained and the population of any species remains roughly constant. Sometimes, however, conditions such as an extra long warm summer may enable certain insects to produce an additional generation in the same season. This results in a 'population explosion' or plague of some particular insect. Usually, however, predators that feed on these insects will increase in proportion and the balance is soon restored.

BIRCH BEETLE. *Deporaus betulae* (*Rhynchites betulae*): a small black beetle that attacks birch trees, cuts the leaves and rolls them into tight funnels within which the eggs are laid.

BIRCH SAWFLY. *Cimbex femorata* and related species. Large sawflies, resembling bees in general colour and appearance, whose larvae feed on birch and other deciduous trees; serious pests in Europe and North America but not common in Britain.

BIRD LICE. Mallophaga: external parasites living among the feathers of birds and in some cases in the fur of mammals. They are small, flattened, wingless insects with biting mouth-parts. Unlike the sucking lice they do not usually pierce the skin but bite off particles of feathers, hair etc. *Menopon pallidum* (*gallinae*), the common chicken louse is one of the best known.

BIRDWING BUTTERFLIES. See *Ornithoptera*.

BISHOP'S MITRE OR CORN BUG. *Aelia acuminata:* a brown pentatomid or shieldbug that feeds on grass.

BITING HOUSE-FLY OR STABLE FLY. *Stomoxys calcitrans.* A two-winged fly resembling the house-fly but with a stiff, piercing proboscis with which it sucks blood and may transmit anthrax, tetanus etc. It breeds in dung with a high fibrous content, *e.g.* farmyard manure, and has spread with stock to most parts of the world.

BITING LICE. See *Bird Lice* (Mallophaga).

BITING MIDGES. Minute two-winged flies of the family Ceratopogonidae, often less than 3 mm. in length, having piercing mouth-parts similar to those of mosquitoes. *Culicoides* is one of the best known examples and is the only British one that sucks human blood. As in the case of mosquitoes, its larvae and pupae live in shallow pools of fresh water or very wet farmyard litter.

BITTACOMORPHA. A genus of crane-flies of the family Ptychopteridae having an aquatic larva with a very long tail-like breathing tube.

BLACKFLY. A name for many small insects but commonly applied,
(a) to the Bean Aphis (*Aphis fabae*).
(b) to true flies of the family Simuliidae.

BLACK SCALE. *Saissetia:* a scale insect of the family Coccidae, a pest of fruit and ornamental trees in California and elsewhere.

BLAPS. The Churchyard Beetle: a dull black European beetle inhabiting damp caves, cellars etc. They are slow moving and flightless, as the wing cases are more or less fastened together. The larvae feed on decaying vegetable matter. The adult protects itself by emitting a strong-smelling irritant fluid.

BLASTOPHAGA. A genus of minute chalcid wasps that pollinate figs.

BLASTOTHRIX. A small green chalcid wasp parasitic on scale insects, common in Europe and introduced successfully into Canada in 1928 as a means of controlling the scale insects on forest trees.

BLATTA ORIENTALIS. The common Oriental and European cockroach, a dark brown species about 25 mm. long; now a pest all over the world. It differs from the American cockroach *Periplaneta* in the reduced wings. Those of the female *Blatta* are vestigial and those of the male are shorter than the abdomen (see *Blattoidea*).

BLATTARIA, BLATTODIA, BLATTIDAE. Cockroaches: a family of insects in the order Dictyoptera (formerly classed as Orthoptera) having dark brown, oval, flattened bodies with long legs and long antennae. The head is almost hidden under a large, shield-like pronotum. Mouth-parts are of the biting type and the insects, which are omnivorous, are regarded as vermin in most parts of the world.

BLATTELLA GERMANICA. The German Cockroach or Croton Bug, a pale brown species about 12 mm. long; a common pest in most parts of the world.

BLATTOIDEA. A name formerly used to comprise the two families Blattidae (Cockroaches) and Mantidae (Praying Mantids), both of which are now classed as Dictyoptera.

BLEDIUS. A genus of staphylinid (short-winged) beetles that burrow vertically into the ground and appear to be guided accurately by a sense of gravity.

BLEPHAROCERIDAE. Mountain Midges: a world-wide family of mosquito-like midges whose larvae and pupae live in fast running streams, tightly attached to rocks by means of six ventral suckers. The adults are characterized by the many creases in the wing-membrane, produced by elaborate folding within the pupa. (Compare *Deuterophlebiidae*.)

BLEPHAROTES. A genus of Robber Flies (Asilidae) from Australia, black with a very broad abdomen having tufts of black and white hairs.

BLISSUS. A genus of North American Chinchbugs, minute Hemiptera that feed on maize, wheat and other cereals.

BLISTER BEETLES. Meloidae: short-winged beetles that exude an evil smelling slimy oil in self-defence. Their blood contains the drug *cantharidin*, formerly much used medicinally for raising blisters. The adult beetles are herbivorous but the larvae are parasites on bees. The first-stage larva is minute and specially active in finding a host; it is known as a *triungulin*.

BLOOD. The blood of insects is more properly called *haemolymph* since it combines some of the functions of blood and lymph. Its main functions, however, are nutritional and excretory, not the transport of oxygen which is distributed by the tracheal system. It is a nearly colourless liquid containing several kinds of white corpuscles. The circulatory system is an open one; that is to say the blood fills all the body cavities or *haemocoels* bathing every organ. The only true blood vessels are the dorsal tubular heart with a number of compartments, its anterior extension the aorta and sometimes a pair of antennary arteries. That part of the haemocoel surrounding the heart is known as the pericardial cavity. Blood from here enters the heart through valvular openings or *ostia,* whence it is pumped forwards along the aorta and antennary arteries and ultimately re-enters the main body cavity.

BLOOD CIRCULATION. See *Blood.*

BLOOD GILLS. Tubular outgrowths from the bodies of some aquatic insects particularly the larvae of gnats (*e.g.* Chironomidae) and of some endoparasitic insects. They contain blood and were formerly thought to be respiratory organs but it has been shown recently, using Protozoa as biological indicators, that respiration of these insects takes place over the whole surface of the body. It is now believed that blood gills are chiefly concerned with the absorption of water and salts.

BLOOD RED ANT. *Formica sanguinea:* a species very similar to the Wood Ant but redder in colour. Its habits differ in several respects from those of the Wood Ant. It does not build large domed nests; it is more strictly carnivorous, feeding almost entirely on other insects; it raids the nests of smaller ants, carrying off cocoons and keeping its captives as slaves.

BLOOD-SUCKING FLIES. A number of true flies or Diptera have their mouth-parts adapted for piercing the skin and sucking blood of higher animals. The chief of these are mosquitoes and biting midges in the suborder Nematocera, Horse-flies in the suborder Brachycera and Tsetse Flies and Stable Flies in the suborder Cyclorrhapha. The last suborder has evidently evolved the blood-sucking habit independently of the others, as the structure of the mouth-parts is different. Before sucking up blood these insects inject saliva containing an anticoagulant. For this reason most of them are potential carriers of blood parasites causing such diseases as malaria, yellow fever, sleeping sickness, elephantiasis and many others.

BLOOD-SUCKING INSECTS. The blood-sucking habit, involving specialization of the mouth-parts, has evolved independently in a number of orders of insects. The chief of these are Hemiptera (bugs), Diptera (two-winged flies), Siphunculata (lice) and Siphonaptera (fleas). These have the mouth-parts adapted in various ways to form piercing stylets and a suctorial proboscis. As they go from one host to another and inject saliva before feeding, they are all potential carriers of disease (see also under *Blood-sucking Flies*).

BLOOD WORM. The worm-like aquatic larva of a chironomid fly (a non-biting midge belonging to the group Nematocera). The larva is bright red due to the presence of haemoglobin, a rarity in insects.

BLOODY-NOSED BEETLE. *Timarcha tenebricosa:* a large, black, flightless leaf-beetle of the family Chrysomelidae. The thorax and wing-cases are rounded, the latter being firmly fused together; the head is small and tucked beneath the thorax. The popular name is given from the fact that the beetle ejects a red fluid from its mouth when alarmed.

BLOTCH MINE. A dark patch on a leaf caused by a minute insect larva 'mining' or burrowing between the upper and lower epidermis. Various insects do this, including the larvae of small moths such as the Lilac Leaf-miner

(*Gracilaria syringella*) and of Diptera such as the Celery-fly (*Acidia heraclei*) Blotch Mines are only one of various patterns produced by leaf-mining insects (see *Leaf-miners*).

BLOWFLY (BLUEBOTTLE). A fly of the family Calliphoridae, especially *Calliphora vomitoria*, a common member of the order Diptera, bearing a superficial resemblance to the house fly but larger. The body is dark blue with black hairs and the eyes are reddish brown. Blowfly larvae feed on carrion, dead animals, meat or cheese, and the adult females are a nuisance when they buzz about in houses searching for a suitable medium on which to lay their eggs. The larvae are legless maggots that appear to be headless, the head being minute and invaginated into the thorax. Pupation takes place within a barrel-shaped puparium formed from hardened larval skin; emergence is by breaking through the top. As in the case of the house fly, both adult and larva feed either by sucking up liquid or by discharging saliva over solid food so that part of it is liquefied by enzyme action.

BLUE BUTTERFLIES. Members of the family Lycaenidae which also include coppers and hairstreaks. They are small swift-flying butterflies including the Common Blue (*Polyommatus icarus*), Small Blue (*Cupido minimus*), Large Blue (*Maculinea arion*), Chalk-hill Blue (*Lysandra coridon*) and a number of others. In some species the male is blue and the female brown. The larvae, shaped like woodlice, secrete a sweet liquid much liked by ants.

BODY LOUSE. *Pediculus humanus:* a wingless blood-sucking parasite belonging to the order Siphunculata (Anoplura), having a flattened body, piercing mouth-parts and short legs with large claws. Within the same species there are two distinct races, the Head Louse (*Pediculus humanus capitis*) and the Body Louse (*Pediculus humanus corporis*). These can interbreed under suitable conditions. The eggs, known as nits, are firmly cemented to the hair of the host. Lice are important as carriers of typhus and other diseases.

BOG GRASSHOPPER. *Stethophyma grossum:* a large short-horned grasshopper of the group Acrididae having the upper surface dark green with a longitudinal yellow stripe on each elytron. The under surface of the body is yellowish green. The hind-legs are banded with black and have many stout black spines.

BOLL WEEVIL. *Anthonomus:* a small weevil whose larvae feed on the bolls or seed pods of the cotton plant and cause wide-spread damage.

BOLL WORM. The larva of a noctuid moth *Heliothis armigera* which feeds on cotton bolls and other seeds.

BOMBARDIER BEETLE. *Brachinus crepitans:* a small carabid beetle, red with black elytra. When disturbed it discharges a few drops of acrid, volatile liquid from the abdomen with a minute explosion.

BOMBIDAE. Humble bees: bees with large hairy bodies usually black or brown with yellow, orange or white markings; living in less well organized colonies than those of the hive bees. Nests are often made in holes in the ground or in trees and sometimes in the disused nests of field mice. They consist of cells made from wax like those of the hive bee but dark brown and less regular. Most of the members of a colony die off in the winter, leaving only the fertilized queens to hibernate and found new colonies the following year.

BOMBUS. See *Bombidae*.

BOMBYCIDAE. A family of Lepidoptera that includes the silk-moth *Bombyx mori*. The larva or silk worm secretes the thread for its cocoon from modified salivary glands through a median spinneret near the mouth. One cocoon may contain 300 metres of silk. Adult females of these moths are incapable of flight and the males are attracted to them by scent.

BOMBYLIIDAE. Bee-flies: two-winged flies of the suborder Brachycera. The genus *Bombylius* has a superficial resemblance to a bee, feeds on nectar and helps pollination. The larvae are parasitic on other insects.

BOMBYLIOMYIA. A North American genus of tachinid fly, large with a greenish yellow thorax and a reddish yellow abdomen and with stiff black bristles all over the body. Like all tachinids it lays its eggs in or on other arthropods whose bodies provide food for the future larvae.

BOMBYLIUS. The chief genus of Bee-flies: large hairy insects resembling humble bees. This resemblance, a case of Batesian mimicry, no doubt gives them some degree of protection. The female *Bombylius* lays its eggs close to the nests of mining bees and the larvae feed on the bee larvae (see also *Bombyliidae*).

BOMBYX MORI. The Chinese Silk-worm Moth, cultivated in most countries but no longer found wild. The adult moth is creamy white and unable to fly on account of its heavy body and small wings. The larvae or silk-worms, when cultivated commercially, are fed on mulberry leaves. They prefer these but will on occasions eat other plants. There may be six generations a year. The larvae feed and grow for about six weeks and then spin cocoons from which the adults emerge after two weeks. The silk, said to be 300 metres from each cocoon, is unwound after killing the pupae in hot water (see also *Bombycidae*).

BOOK-LOUSE. *Liposcelis divinatorius* and related genera of Psocoptera: small soft-bodied insects with long thread-like antennae and with reduced wings. They feed on the dried paste of old books but other genera, closely related to book-lice, are found out-of-doors feeding on leaves etc.

BORDERED WHITE BEAUTY MOTH. *Bupalus piniaria:* a common British day-flying moth found in pine woods on whose foliage the larvae feed. The wings have a thin border of white but their background colour varies according to race and locality. In the south of England it is yellow or orange, but in the north there is a distinct race in which the male is white and brown and the female yellow and brown. The caterpillars are thin and green and are well camouflaged among the pine needles.

BOREUS. A genus of snow-flies: small black, almost wingless insects of the order Mecoptera (scorpion-flies), living in forests, feeding on dead vegetation and in winter hopping about in the snow.

BORKHAUSENIA. A genus of Brown House-moth that damages clothes, carpets etc.

BOROCERA. The Bibindandy, a type of silk-moth found in Madagascar. It is related to the Lackey Moth and belongs to the family Lasiocampidae whose larvae, because of their silk-spinning capability, are known as tent caterpillars.

BOT FLY. A name for a number of large hairy flies (cyclorrhaphous Diptera) whose larvae are parasitic in mammals, living either in the flesh or in internal cavities such as head-sinuses, throat or intestine. The term includes members of the families Oestridae, Gasterophilidae and Calliphoridae.

BOUTON. A small swelling or lobe at the tip of a bee's tongue; also called the *flabellum* or the *labellum*.

BRACHINUS. See *Bombardier Beetle*.

BRACHYCENTRUS SUBNUBILIS. The Grannom, a species of European caddis fly (Trichoptera) whose wings are grey and covered with thick hair. The larvae or caddis worms live in flowing water, anchoring their cases to weeds. These cases are very distinctive, being four-sided and made from flat slate-like stones.

BRACHYCERA. A term properly applied to all Diptera other than Nematocera, but more usually referring to Brachycera–Orthorrhapha, two-winged flies such as the Robber Flies and Horse Flies: a suborder having the antennae shorter than the thorax and often with a terminal bristle. The larvae are legless maggots with a tiny incomplete head which may be partly retracted into the thorax. The pupae are exarate, *i.e.* with free appendages.

BRACHYCEROUS. Having short antennae (see *Brachycera*).

BRACHYGASTRA. A genus of Honey-pot Ant, so-called because some of the workers fill their stomachs with the sugary honeydew secreted by aphids. The abdomen becomes enormously inflated and these ants remain in the nest as living food-stores on which the other ants can draw.

BRACHYPTEROUS. Having short underdeveloped wings and in consequence, generally incapable of flight. This phenomenon is widespread among all orders of insects, often in one sex only and particularly among parasitic insects and those which live on islands, mountain tops or in caves. Curtailment of the process of flight directly affects the distribution of the species.

BRACHYSTOLA. The Lubber Grasshopper, a large, heavy short-winged genus from North America.

BRACHYTRYPES. A genus of large crickets from West Africa, able to produce a loud penetrating noise like a crying baby. This is done by rubbing together the thickened modified tegmina.

BRACONIDAE (BRACONIDS). A family of small parasitic Hymenoptera related to the Ichneumon Flies. Eggs are laid on or in the body of some other insect such as a caterpillar and hatch out into small parasitic maggots which destroy the body of the victim before pupating. (See also *Apanteles*.)

BRAIN. The 'brain' of an insect, more correctly a group of *supra-oesophageal ganglia*, is situated on the dorsal side of the collar of nerve fibres that surrounds the oesophagus. It is formed by a fusion of three pairs of segmental ganglia. The first pair, known as the *protocerebrum*, are greatly enlarged laterally to form the optic lobes from which nerves go to the eyes. The second pair, the *deutocerebrum*, innervates the antennae. The third pair or *tritocerebrum* are poorly developed. The whole structure forms a compact mass varying in complexity in different groups of insects. Nerves from the brain go to the principal sense organs of the head and others pass round the nerve-collar which connects the brain with the rest of the central nervous system – a chain of ganglia running along the ventral part of the insect's body.

BRAULIDAE. See *Bee Louse*.

BREATHING. The breathing of insects is normally through a series of tiny holes or spiracles along the sides of the thorax and abdomen. There may be ten pairs of these but often the number is reduced. They lead into a complex system of *tracheae* and *tracheoles*. The former are tubes of varying diameter strengthened with a spiral thickening of chitin; the latter are fine, branching tubes penetrating the tissues. The segmentally arranged tracheae are usually all connected to one another by two or more longitudinal tubes. In many fast-flying insects, which require a large amount of oxygen, some of the tracheae

24

are dilated to form air-sacs filling most of the abdomen. Some aquatic insects, particularly larvae and pupae, may have tracheal openings at one end only, as in mosquito larvae; others may breathe through the thin skin, either over the whole surface or through special thin-walled extensions known as *tracheal gills* (*e.g.* mayfly nymphs). Many larger aquatic insects such as water beetles have a normal system of spiracles and tracheae but take down bubbles of air, either trapped in the body-hairs or stored under the elytra, enabling them to stay submerged for a considerable time.

BRENTHIDAE. A family of tropical and subtropical weevils that live in colonies usually under the loose bark of dead trees. The female has a very long slender snout used for boring holes into which the eggs are deposited. The male has a short thick head with a pair of large jaws. Among the males in a single colony there may be a number of castes varying considerably in size and colour and in the shape of the beak.

BREPHIDIUM. A genus that includes some of the smallest of the lycaenid butterflies (coppers and blues). *Brephidium exilis*, the North American Pygmy Butterfly, has a wing-span of about 12 mm. It is brown with white fringes and a white spot on the front wings. Frequently it is sold mounted in a brooch or locket.

BRIGHT LINE MOTH (TOMATO MOTH). *Lacanobia oleracea*: a common British moth having the fore-wings dark brown with a white line and a yellow spot near the edge; the hind-wings are paler with dark edges. The larvae are pests of the tomato plant but also feed on stinging nettles, bindweed and many other plants.

BRIMSTONE BUTTERFLY. *Gonepteryx rhamni*: a large, fairly common European butterfly of woodlands and gardens; a member of the family Pieridae. The male is a bright sulphur-yellow with a small reddish spot in the centre of each wing; the female is nearly white. They hibernate in the adult stage and in Britain are among the first to appear in the spring. The larvae, which feed on buckthorn, are green and well camouflaged.

BRIMSTONE MOTH. *Opisthograptis luteolata*. A common European geometrid moth, pale yellow with irregular brown markings on the edges of the fore-wings. The caterpillars (loopers) are dark brown, stick-like and feed on hawthorn and buckthorn.

BRINDLED BEAUTY. *Lycia hirtaria*: a common British and European geometrid moth of a mottled brown colour well blending with the bark of trees on which it rests. The stick-like larvae feed on elm, willow, lime and most common fruit trees.

BRINDLED GREEN. *Dryobotodes eremita*: a noctuid moth, common in oak woods of Britain and Europe; olive green and variegated with black and brown. The larvae feed on oak leaves and pupate in the soil.

BRISTLE-TAIL. Any member of the orders Diplura and Thysanura: small primitive wingless insects (Apterygota) with long antennae, long cerci and, in the case of Thysanura, a median tail-filament. The mouth-parts are of the biting type and resemble those of the cockroach. Their usual habitat is among stones and dead leaves. Among the Thysanura are *Lepisma*, the silverfish which can be a minor household pest, and *Petrobius*, the Bronze Fish which occurs on the seashore above high tide mark. (See *Bronze Fish*, *Firebrat* and *Lepismidae*.)

BROCHYMENA. A genus of sap-sucking pentatomid or shieldbugs, brown or dark grey, living on the rough bark of trees which they closely resemble.

25

BRONZE FISH. *Petrobius maritimus*: a primitive wingless insect of the order Thysanura (bristle-tails), closely resembling a silverfish but of a metallic brown colour and living on rocky shores among brown seaweeds where it is well camouflaged.

BROWN ARGUS. *Aricia agestis*: a small European butterfly related to the blues (Lycaenidae), common in chalky districts. The upper surface of both wings is dark brown with white and black margins and with an orange band next to the white. The underside is similar to that of the blue butterflies, grey and orange with numerous white-edged black spots. The caterpillars feed on leaves of rock-rose.

BROWN BUTTERFLIES. Members of the family Satyridae, nearly all of a brownish colour with hairy bodies. They are mostly woodland species and the larvae feed on grass. Common British species include the Meadow Brown, Hedge Brown, Speckled Wood and Wall Brown. An exception to the brown colour but belonging to the same family is the Marbled White butterfly *Melanargia galathea*.

BROWN LACEWING. *Kimminsia* and related genera: predatory insects of the order Neuroptera and the family Hemerobiidae, smaller and more hairy than the better known green lacewing fly. They are common in woodlands where eggs are laid on leaves and the larvae, which have sharp jaws, feed on large numbers of aphids before pupating in a silky cocoon.

BROWN LOCUST. *Locustana pardalina*: a common migratory locust from the Karoo area of South Africa.

BROWN SCALE. A name for a number of scale insects of the family Coccidae including the European Brown Scale (*Eulecanium corni* or *Parthenolecanium corni*), the American Brown Scale (*Eulecanium coryli*) and many others. They are highly specialized and somewhat degenerate insects of the order Homoptera in which the wingless female attaches herself to the bark of a tree and remains there until she dies after laying her eggs. The 'scales' on the surface of the tree are formed of several cast-off skins which have shrunk and remain stuck together by a glutinous secretion covering the insects.

BROWN-TAIL MOTH. *Euproctis chrysorrhoea* (also called *Nygmia phaeorrhoea*). A small white tussock moth with the tip of the abdomen brown; a close relative of the Yellow-tail Moth whose hairy caterpillars are common on hawthorn trees in Europe. The Brown-tail is less common but at one time became a serious pest of ornamental and fruit trees in North America. It was effectively brought under control by the introduction of a predatory carabid beetle, *Calosoma sycophanta*, along with the parasites *Compsilura concinnata* (Tachinidae) and *Apanteles lacteicolor* (Braconidae).

BRUCHUS. A genus of leaf-beetles that attack leguminous plants. *Bruchus rufimanus*, common in bean fields; *Bruchus pisorum*, a pest of dried peas.

BRUSH-FOOTED BUTTERFLIES. Nymphalidae, also called four-footed butterflies; the largest family of butterflies characterized by having the first pair of legs reduced. They include many of the commonest butterflies, fritillaries, tortoiseshells, peacocks etc.

BUFFALO GNATS. Members of the family Simuliidae: small, black, two-winged, blood-sucking flies with a hump-backed appearance and with broad wings. The spindle-shaped larvae live in running water and have an anal pad with setae for clinging to rocks etc. *Simulium equinum* is a common pest of horses and cattle; *Eusimulium damnosum* is an African species that transmits the parasitic nematode *Onchocera* to man.

BUFF ERMINE MOTH. *Spilosoma lutea*: a common British moth, stout, medium sized, buff-coloured with black dots on the wings and .down the centre of the abdomen. The hairy larvae feed on docks and other small plants of meadow and waste land.

BUFF-TIP MOTH. *Phalera bucephala*: a large European moth having the fore-wings of a grey-brown colour with a large oval buff or cream coloured patch at the tip. When at rest the wings are folded in such a way that the insect exactly resembles a small piece of broken twig; a case of camouflage by disruptive coloration. The caterpillars are bright yellow and black and may feed in large numbers on leaves of elm, lime, oak and other trees.

BUG. A term often loosely used for a number of insects but which should strictly be used only for members of the order Hemiptera, a large order including both winged and wingless species. The most characteristic feature is the very long proboscis adapted for piercing and sucking. It is formed from mandibles and maxillae in the form of long stylets lying in a trough-like labium; palps are reduced or absent. The mouth-parts are directed downwards when feeding but may be folded right back under the thorax when at rest. The majority of bugs belong to the suborder Heteroptera; most are plant-suckers but some prey on other insects and a few, such as the bedbug, suck blood. The absence of wings from the latter is a secondary loss connected with the parasitic way of life. Included among bugs are Shieldbugs, Capsids, Pondskaters, Water Boatmen, Water Scorpions and Assassin Bugs.

BULB FLY. *Merodon* and related genera: members of the order Diptera and the family Syrphidae or hover-flies, differing from the majority of this group by reason of the fact that the larvae are herbivorous. They live in bulbs such as those of the daffodil and do considerable damage.

BULL-DOG ANT. *Ponera* and related genera of primitive, carnivorous tropical ants living in small subterranean colonies.

BUMBLE BEES. See *Bombidae*.

BUPALUS. See *Bordered White Beauty Moth*.

BUPRESTIDAE. Metallic green, blue or red beetles whose legless larvae bore beneath the bark of trees and can be recognized by their greatly widened prothorax. The metallic sheen of the elytra in the adult beetle is caused by particles embedded in a viscous pigmented secretion from dermal glands.

BURNET COMPANION. *Ectypa glyphica*: a brown, medium sized moth, common in Britain and often seen flying with Burnet moths.

BURNET MOTH. One of several day-flying moths, black with bright red spots. These act as warning coloration since the insect is distasteful to predators. The caterpillars are green and black and feed on clover, vetch or other small leguminous plants. Pupae are in yellow silky cocoons attached to the stems of grass. Five-spot Burnet, *Zygaena trifolii*; Six-spot Burnet, *Zygaena filipendulae*.

BURNISHED BRASS MOTH. *Plusia chrysitis*: a large, fairly common British moth of a greyish brown colour with two broad golden bands on each fore-wing. The larvae feed on stinging nettles.

BURREL FLY. An alternative name for blood-sucking horse-flies and gadflies (Tabanidae).

BURROWING BEES. See *Andrenidae*.

27

BURSA COPULATRIX. A pocket formed from an infolding of the body-wall around the genital aperture of female insects etc. adapted for receiving the intromittent organ of the male.

BURYING BEETLES (SEXTON BEETLES). Necrophoridae: brightly coloured beetles that bury the corpses of small animals by excavating beneath them till they sink below the soil. The eggs are then laid in the decaying corpse which provides food for the larvae.

BUSH-CRICKET. *Tettigonia* and related genera of Orthoptera, also called longhorned grasshoppers: elongated insects distinguished from other grasshoppers and locusts by their predatory habits, by their very long thin antennae and by their usually elongated, curved ovipositor. The chief British representative is the Great Green Grasshopper *Tettigonia viridissima*.

BUTTERFLIES. Lepidoptera characterized by having clubbed antennae. The old system of classification divided the Lepidoptera into two groups: *Rhopalocera* or butterflies and *Heterocera* or moths. This system is still often used for convenience, since it has the advantage of dividing these insects into two obvious groups easily recognized by the amateur entomologist. It must be emphasized, however, that it is unsatisfactory and no longer used in *formal* classification because it ignores many fundamental features and does not take account of certain insects that appear to be intermediate between butterflies and moths. A more modern system is sometimes used which is based on wing-venation. This divides the Lepidoptera into *Homoneura* and *Heteroneura*, the former having an almost identical arrangement of veins in the two pairs of wings; the latter having the hind-wings markedly different from the fore-wings. An even more recent system, now widely used, is based on the structure of the genital organs. This divides the Lepidoptera into *Monotrysia* and *Ditrysia*. With certain exceptions the Ditrysia correspond to the Heteroneura and include all the butterflies and most of the larger moths. Monotrysia, on the other hand, correspond roughly to the Homoneura and include some of the tiny moths formerly known as Microlepidoptera and a few of the larger ones, the best known of which is *Hepialus*, the Ghost Swift Moth.

Butterflies are generally day-flying and are usually more brightly coloured than moths. The largest and most brilliant butterflies are to be found in South America and other tropical countries. The elaborate coloured patterns of the wings are due partly to the pigments in the thousands of minute scales that cover the wings, but in addition to this there is frequently a shining blue-green iridescence due to 'optical interference' caused by multiple transparent plates in the substance of each scale. Such colours are known as 'structural colours' as distinct from pigments. The largest known butterfly is the New Guinea Birdwing *Troides alexandrae*, the female of which has a wing-span of 30 cm. The smallest is the Dwarf Blue *Brephidium barberae* of South Africa with a span of about 12 mm.

The families of butterflies are based largely on size, colour and habits: Satyridae (Browns), Lycaenidae (Blues and Coppers), Pieridae (Whites and Yellows), Nymphalidae (Fritillaries and Aristocrats), Papilionidae (Swallowtails), Hesperiidae (Skippers).

BYRRHUS. The Pill Beetle, *Byrrhus pilula*: a small round beetle, dark brown or black, specially notable for its alarm reaction. When disturbed it withdraws its head into the thorax, folds its legs and tucks them beneath the body so that its appearance is that of a rabbit pellet. Living among grass, as it does, this gives it very effective protection.

C

CABBAGE WHITE BUTTERFLY. *Pieris brassicae*, also called the Large White: one of the commonest butterflies with world-wide distribution. The wings are white or yellowish with a black patch on the tip of the fore-wing and on the front margin of the hind-wing; the female has in addition two black spots on each fore-wing. The family Pieridae, to which this butterfly belongs, is characterized by having all its six legs fully formed and functional with four tiny claws on each foot. The caterpillars, green and yellow with black spots are voracious pests of cabbages and other cruciferous plants.

CABBAGE GALL-WEEVIL. *Ceuthorrhynchus pleurostigma*: a small weevil that lays its eggs on the roots of cabbage, turnip and other Cruciferae. The young larvae feed on the roots and cause the formation of large round galls about the size of marbles.

CABBAGE MAGGOT. The larva of a two-winged fly, a destructive pest that attacks the stems and roots of cabbages, radishes, cauliflowers etc. See Cabbage Root-Fly.

CABBAGE MOTH. *Mamestra brassicae*: a common noctuid moth, greyish brown with white or cream markings, whose caterpillars are common pests of cabbages and other vegetables.

CABBAGE ROOT-FLY. *Eroischia brassicae*: a two-winged fly whose larva is a common pest on the roots of cabbages and other Cruciferae.

CABBAGE SNOW FLY. See *Cabbage Whitefly*.

CABBAGE WHITEFLY. *Aleurodes brassicae*: a small plant-bug of the group Homoptera having the body and wings covered with white powdery wax. Eggs are laid on cabbage leaves to which they are stuck by a thin stalk or thread. The larvae are flattened and at first remain hidden beneath a covering of wax. Like their relatives the aphids, they suck the sap of the plant and exude a sticky secretion of honeydew.

CACAO MOTH. *Ephestia elutella*: a small moth of the family Pyralidae whose larvae are serious pests of stored cocoa beans, tobacco and other products.

CACTOBLASTIS. See *Cactus Moth*.

CACTUS MOTH. *Cactoblastis cactorum*: a small moth whose larvae feed on cacti; successfully introduced into Australia from Argentina as a means of controlling the prickly pear.

CADDIS FLY. A name for any member of the order Trichoptera: moth-like insects whose wings are covered with fine hairs and whose mouth-parts are so reduced that little food can be taken. The aquatic larvae live in tubular cases formed of particles of wood, leaf, sand, small shells etc. woven together with silk. A pair of hooks on the hind-end enables the larva to cling to the tube and drag it around when walking. A species can usually be identified by the type of tube and the material of which it is constructed.

CADDIS WORM. The aquatic larva of a caddis fly (*q.v.*).

CALATHUS. A wide-spread genus of herbivorous ground beetles (Carabidae);

the European species *Calathus melanocephalus* has the head and elytra black and the thorax, antennae and legs brown.

CALIROA. A common genus of sawfly (Hymenoptera) of the family Tenthredinidae whose larvae are pests of pear, cherry and other fruit trees. They resemble black slugs and the species *Caliroa limacina* is called the Pear and Cherry Slugworm.

CALLIDIUM. A long-horned wood-boring beetle of a metallic purple or violet colour, medium sized, with a broad flattened body and a small head. The larvae do considerable damage to the timber of larch, spruce, pine and other conifers.

CALLIDRYAS. A genus of large sulphur butterflies from Central and South America; 12 cm. or more across, pale yellow with conspicuous red spots on the wings. They are strong flyers and probably migrate long distances.

CALLIPHORIDAE. Blowflies or Bluebottles: a family of Diptera somewhat resembling the common house fly but larger, bluer and more bristly. The legless larvae pupate in a dark coloured, barrel-shaped capsule or puparium. Most of these flies breed in carrion but some attack sheep and other animals, the maggots boring into the living flesh (see also *Blowfly*).

CALLITROGA. A genus of Calliphoridae (blowflies) whose larvae, known as *screw-worms*, infest open wounds on animals or man in the New World. (See *Cochliomyia* and *cf. Chrysomya*.)

CALLOPHRYS. *Callophrys rubi*, the Green Hairstreak: a European and Asiatic butterfly related to the Blues and Coppers (Lycaenidae). The wings have the undersides bright green with hair-like marks and the upper sides dull brown. The larvae feed mostly on leguminous plants.

CALLOSAMIA. *Callosamia promethea*, the Promethea Moth: a saturniid moth of North America having a wing-span of about 10 cm. The male is dark maroon, almost black; the female is light reddish brown. The caterpillar, blue-green with red and black projecting knobs, when ready to pupate, wraps itself in a large leaf which is folded over, held together and fastened with silk to a twig.

CALLOW (TENERAL). An insect newly emerged from the pupa, having a soft body not fully coloured. The term may be used generally but is particularly applied to worker ants.

CALOPTERYX. An alternative name for the damselfly *Agrion* (*q.v.*).

CALOSOMA. A genus of Caterpillar Hunters: large carabid beetles that prey on caterpillars and are therefore very useful in protecting trees from damage by canker worms and other moth-larvae. Some European species have been successfully introduced into America for this purpose.

CALOTERMES. A genus of termites (Isoptera) that live in wood and feed on it. Since they themselves cannot digest wood, this function is performed by large numbers of symbiotic protozoa in the insect's intestine.

CALYPTER. The thoracic squama, a secondary lobe on the wing of a house fly, blowfly or similar member of the Diptera, often large enough to cover the haltere on the same side.

CALYPTRATA (CALYPTERAE). A group of cyclorrhaphous Diptera in which the wings have secondary lobes covering the halteres (see *Calypter*).

CAMBERWELL BEAUTY. *Nymphalis antiopa*, known in North America as the *Mourning Cloak*: a large handsome butterfly found in many parts of the Holarctic region and occasionally in Britain as a migrant. The wings are dark chocolate or purple-brown with broad pale yellow margins and a row of blue spots filling the inner line of the margin. The larvae feed on willows, poplars, elm and birch.

CAMNULA. A genus of clear-winged grasshoppers of North America, sometimes migratory.

CAMPANIFORM RECEPTORS. Sense organs of insects in the form of bell-like projections from the skin with a nerve-cell beneath each. They are believed to monitor stresses in the cuticle, and hence to act as proprioceptors, giving the insect information about its own attitude.

CAMPODEA. See *Campodeidae*.

CAMPODEIDAE. Small wingless insects belonging to the Diplura or bristle-tails. They are without eyes, have little body pigment and have a tail-fork formed from a pair of long abdominal cerci. They have three pairs of thoracic legs and numerous simple appendages on the abdominal segments.

CAMPODEIFORM LARVAE. Oligopod larvae: the common form of larvae among beetles and Neuroptera. They are usually predatory; have well developed sense organs and legs but no abdominal appendages other than cerci. The name is given on account of their superficial resemblance to the primitive insect *Campodea*.

CAMPONOTUS. Carpenter Ants: a genus of large black ants that bore into dead wood doing considerable damage. They may nest in the timber of buildings or in the heart-wood of a tree. *Camponotus herculeanus* is the European Giant Ant, the female of which may be up to 18 mm. long.

CANKER WORM. A name for the larvae of several species of geometrid (looper) moths that defoliate trees. The wingless female moths climb the tree trunk and lay their eggs on the leaves on which the larvae feed.

CANTHARIDAE. Soldier and Sailor Beetles and related species: brightly coloured carnivorous beetles that feed upon other insects and in some cases on slugs and snails. The larvae bite and inject saliva into a snail causing it to become paralysed. This prevents it from retreating into its shell. It is ultimately digested and consumed by the beetle larvae which then pupate inside the shells of their victims.

CANTHARIDIN. A drug extracted from the Blister Beetle or Spanish Fly, *Lytta vesicatoria*, and others of the family Meloidae.

CAPITOPHORUS. A genus of aphids which cause galls or red blister-like patches on the leaves of rose and fruit trees: *Capitophorus ribis* on red currants and black currants; *Capitophorus rosarum* on rose trees.

CAPSIDAE. Capsid Bugs: slender green or brown plant-bugs of the group Heteroptera; pests of apple, willow and other trees (see *Miridae*).

CARABIDAE. Ground Beetles: a large and varied family of carnivorous beetles, usually black but often having a bronze tinge or a violet iridescence. They have a narrow head, long thin antennae and long legs. In some species the elytra are fused together making flight impossible. The larvae, which are predatory, are of the usual campodeiform or long-legged type.

CARABOIDEA. A superfamily of carnivorous beetles which are nearly all predators, both in the adult and the larval stage. They include the Carabidae or ground beetles, the Cicindelidae or Tiger Beetles and some aquatic forms such as the Great Brown Water Beetle (*Dytiscus*) and the *Whirligig Beetle* (*Gyrinus*).

CARADRINIDAE. Noctuid or Owlet Moths, a family of fairly large, nocturnal, usually drably coloured moths including the Cabbage Moth (*Mamestra brassicae*), Turnip Moth (*Agrotis segetum*) and Yellow Underwing (*Noctua pronuba*) etc.

CARADRINOIDEA. A superfamily of moths including the Tiger Moths (Arctiidae), Noctuids (Caradrinidae), Red Underwings (Plusiidae) and Tussocks (Lymantriidae).

CARDER BEE. A name given to a number of small species of Bombidae including some of the genus *Bombus* and the genus *Anthidium*. The females of the latter have the habit of stripping the hair from moss and other plants, rolling it into a ball and carrying it away to line the nest.

CARDINAL BEETLE (SCARLET FIRE BEETLE). *Pyrochroa* and related genera; long, flat, bright red carnivorous beetles having toothed or comb-like antennae; they are often found under the bark of trees.

CARDO. Any hinge-like part of an organ but particularly the basal segment of an insect's maxilla by which it articulates with the head.

CARPENTER ANT. See *Camponotus*.

CARPENTER BEE. A name for a number of species of solitary bees that burrow into wood to make their nests. Most of these are tropical and belong to the widely distributed family Xylocopidae. Some of the Apidae also, such as the British species *Ceratina cyanea*, have similar habits.

CARPENTER MOTH. An alternative name for the Goat Moths (Cossidae) whose larvae do extensive damage to deciduous trees by burrowing into the wood.

CARPET BEETLE. A group of small, dark coloured beetles of the family Dermestidae whose larvae can be serious household pests feeding on woollen carpets, clothing etc.

CARPET MOTH. A general name sometimes used to denote geometrid moths of the subfamily Larentiinae often having elaborately patterned wings which they spread out flat and opened when at rest. The caterpillars, which are loopers, usually rest in an arched position (see also *Geometridae*).

CARPOCAPSA. The Codling Moth *Carpocapsa pomonella* (also called *Cydia* or *Ernarmonia pomonella*): a small grey-brown moth whose larvae are serious pests of apples and pears in most parts of the world. Eggs are laid on the leaves and the newly hatched larvae bore into the young fruit where they feed on the cores and eventually emerge to spin cocoons.

CARRION BEETLES. Silphidae or Necrophoridae: Burying Beetles. Brightly coloured insects that feed on flesh and in some cases bury the corpses of small animals by excavating beneath them till they sink below the soil. The eggs are then laid in the decaying carcase which provides food for the larvae.

CARRION FLY. A general name for flesh-eating Diptera, *e.g.* the Blowfly *Calliphora vomitoria*, the Flesh-fly *Sarcophaga* and many others.

CASE-MAKING CLOTHES MOTH. *Tinaea pellionella* and related species: small moths of the family Tinaeidae whose larvae make and live in portable silk cases; they feed on cloth, fur or feathers.

CASSIDINAE. Tortoise Beetles: round or oval, flattened beetles of the family Chrysomelidae, having the edges of the thorax and wing covers expanded to cover the legs and head so that the insect resembles a small tortoise walking about on a leaf. Many of them are golden and iridescent.

CASTES. Morphologically and functionally distinct types within a colony of social insects. Such castes are particularly well developed in Hymenoptera (bees, ants and wasps) and in Isoptera (termites). Among bees the three chief castes are the Queen (fertile female), Workers (sterile females) and Drones (fertile males). Among ants and termites there are often many more types varying considerably in size, form and function: *viz.* sterile and fertile members of both sexes, winged and wingless forms and 'soldier' types with large head and jaws. Such variations may be brought about by genetic factors, by variations in the nutrition of the larval forms or by a combination of both.

CATABOMBA. A common genus of large Hover-flies (Syrphidae), black or dark brown with lunate (half-moon shaped) pale markings in pairs on the abdomen. The larvae, which are flattened and maggot-like, feed in large numbers on aphids.

CATACLYSTA. The Small China-mark Moth: one of the microlepidopterous family Pyraustidae having whitish wings with dark brown borders and a central spot on each wing. The dark coloured larvae are aquatic and live in a floating case made of duckweed leaves.

CATERPILLAR. A *polypod* or *eruciform* larva: a soft-bodied larva having, in addition to the six true legs on the thorax, a number of prolegs or false legs on the abdomen. Such larvae occur in butterflies and moths (Lepidoptera) and in sawflies (Hymenoptera – Symphyta). The larvae of the latter, sometimes not regarded as true caterpillars, differ from those of butterflies and moths in having a larger number of prolegs and in the absence of rings of tiny hooks on these. The number of prolegs on the caterpillar of a butterfly or moth may be up to five pairs but in the large group known as loopers (Geometridae), only the hind pair is present. Almost without exception caterpillars are herbivorous with powerful sideways-moving jaws. Because of their voraciousness many are agricultural and horticultural pests. They are often very specific in their feeding habits so that the distribution of a butterfly or moth depends upon the distribution of its food plant.

CATERPILLAR HUNTER. A name for a large number of carabid beetles that feed on caterpillars and in some cases have been used to control pests of agriculture and forestry (see *Calosoma*).

CATOCALA. The Red Underwing Moth: a large handsome moth having the fore-wings mottled grey and the hind-wings bright red with broad black bands across the centre and along the margins.

CAT'S EAR BEETLE. *Cryptocephalus hypochaeridis*: a golden-green beetle with black legs and long antennae. The body and wings are oval shaped and the tiny head is bent down and almost hidden by the thorax. It is commonly found on Cat's Ear (*Hypochaeris*) and other composite flowers.

CATTLE WARBLE FLY. *Hypoderma bovis* and related species: two-winged flies of the family Oestridae whose larvae are parasitic in cattle and other large animals. Eggs are laid on the hairs of the host and the larvae eat their way in through the skin. They burrow through the tissues and finally emerge through holes in the skin of the back before pupating. Apart from seriously affecting the health of the host, they render the skin useless as leather.

CAUDAL GILLS. Respiratory organs in the form of thin-walled lamellae or outgrowths from the hind-end of the abdomen in some aquatic insects such as the nymphs of damselflies (Zygoptera).

CECIDOMYIIDAE. Gall-midges or gall-gnats: minute two-winged insects, seldom exceeding 3 mm. in length, belonging to the suborder Nematocera and having long thin antennae, long narrow wings and very long legs. The larvae are yellow or brown, without legs and are the cause of galls on willow, oak, beech and many other trees.

CELERY FLY. *Philophylla heraclei* or *Acidia heraclei*: a small fly belonging to the group Cyclorrhapha, having brown mottled wings and bright green eyes. The larva, a short barrel-shaped, leaf-mining maggot, is a pest of celery, parsnips and other Umbelliferae.

CELITHERMIS. A genus of small American dragonflies usually having brown spots on the wings.

CELLAR BEETLE. See *Blaps*.

CENTROLECITHAL EGG. An egg having the yolk concentrated in the centre; characteristic of insects and other arthropods.

CENTROTUS. A genus of tree-hoppers or Membracidae: minute jumping plant-bugs of the group Homoptera, found mostly in the tropics and characterized by a large hood-like extension of the prothorax over the head. British species include the Horned Tree-hopper (*Centrotus cornutus*) with horn-like projections on the thorax, and the much smaller Greenweed Tree-hopper (*Centrotus genistae*), usually found on the leguminous plant Dyer's Greenweed (*Genista tinctoria*).

CEPHIDAE. Stem Sawflies: a small family of symphytous Hymenoptera whose larvae tunnel into the stems of grasses and other plants. *Cephus pygmaeus*, the Wheat Stem Sawfly of Europe, appeared in North America in 1887 and is a serious pest there.

CERAMBYCIDAE. Longicorn or long-horned beetles: a large and world-wide family of beetles having very long antennae. Their larvae, which are yellowish grubs with hard brown heads and rudimentary legs, do immense damage to timber by excavating winding tunnels in which they pupate. They may live for four or five years in the larval state. Some tropical species are brightly coloured and up to 8 cm. in length.

CERATOCAMPIDAE. See *Citheroniidae*.

CERATOMEGILLA. A genus of North American ladybirds (Coccinellidae), flat-bodied, red with black spots; they feed on immense numbers of aphids particularly in maize crops.

CERATOPHYLLUS. A genus of fleas parasitic on birds and mammals. They include the European Rat-flea (*Ceratophyllus fasciatus*), the Rock-dove Flea (*Ceratophyllus columbae*), which is one of the largest British species, and the House-sparrow Flea (*Ceratophyllus fringillae*), the smallest.

CERATOPHYUS. *Ceratophyus typhoeus* or *Typhaeus typhoeus*: a large round dung beetle or scarab (Scarabeidae) that inhabits sandy places frequented by rabbits. The females dig deep tunnels into which the males push pellets of sheep's or rabbit's dung on which the larvae feed. This pushing is performed by means of three horns projecting forwards from the thorax of the male: a characteristic of this genus.

CERATOPOGONIDAE. Biting midges: minute blood-sucking two-winged flies closely allied to the gnats and belonging to the group Nematocera. Their size is rarely more than 1.5 mm. The larvae, like those of gnats and mosquitoes, live in stagnant water or in damp soil. *Culicoides* is a common and widely distributed genus.

CERATOTHECA. The part of an insect's pupal skin that encloses the antennae.

CERCERIS. A genus of solitary digger wasps having a narrow black and yellow striped abdomen. They burrow in sandy soil to make their nests. Here they store large numbers of weevils or other insects which they have stung as food for the larvae. The adults, however, are wholly vegetarian.

CERCI. A pair of filamentous appendages at the posterior tip of the abdomen on many insects and other arthropods. Sometimes they are very long, giving the appearance of a forked tail, as in the mayfly. Their existence in the most primitive living insects as well as in other arthropods implies that they are ancestral structures.

CERCOPIDAE. Frog-hoppers: plant-bugs of the group Homoptera whose name is suggested by the broad head, frog-like appearance and jumping power. The nymphs of many species produce and live in a frothy secretion of 'cuckoo-spit' formed by blowing air into a fluid produced by glands near the anus. This gives them protection from desiccation and from predators. *Philaenus spumarius* is the commonest British species.

CERCOPOD. An alternative name for a cercus, a filamentous appendage on the hind-part of the abdomen of an insect; or a foot-like appendage on the last abdominal segment.

CERESA. The Buffalo Tree-hopper, a small jumping plant-bug of the family Membracidae whose body has a triangular appearance due to an enlargement and backward projection of the prothorax; a pest of apple trees on which it lays its eggs.

CERURA. The Puss Moth (*Cerura vinula*): a large moth of the family Notodontidae having a fat white hairy body with small black spots; the larva or caterpillar is green with black markings and a long pair of erect cerci like a forked tail. When at rest it resembles a curled poplar leaf but when attacked it takes on a grotesque appearance, rearing its head and displaying a bright red or orange mark on the front of the thorax, at the same time waving its long red tail filaments.

CETONIA. The Rose Chafer or Goldsmith Beetle: a large round beetle of a shiny metallic green colour with a golden sheen. The adults feed principally on rose petals and fallen fruit. The larvae are fat, whitish insects with very short legs. They wriggle about upside down, feeding chiefly on dead leaves.

CEUTHOPHILUS. A genus of wingless crickets inhabiting caves in North America.

CEUTHORHYNCHUS. See *Cabbage Gall-weevil*.

CHAETOSEMA. Also called *Jordan's Organ*: a cluster of sensory bristles on the heads of some adult Lepidoptera; believed to replace the ocelli.

CHAETOTAXY. A term originally used for the pattern produced by certain strong bristles on the thorax of flies; now used more generally to designate the identification and classification of insects by the structure and arrangement of the principal bristles or chaetae on its body. Sometimes, as for instance in some mosquito larvae, this may be the only method of distinguishing between two related species.

CHAFERS. Melolonthinae: large vegetarian beetles of the family Scarabaeidae, closely related to the dung beetles. They include the Cockchafer (*Melolontha*), the Rose Chafer (*Cetonia*) and many others. They hide among leaves during the day and fly, sometimes in large numbers, in the evening. The larvae, with whitish bodies and short legs, are very destructive to young trees and shrubs.

CHALASTOGASTRA. A term no longer in common use, but formerly an alternative name for Symphyta: sawflies, woodwasps etc.

CHALCIDOIDEA. A very large superfamily of minute Hymenoptera, nearly all of which are parasitic. Some attack the larvae of other parasites, in which case they are said to be *hyperparasites*; a few species form galls and some develop within seeds. A special peculiarity is the phenomenon of *polyembryony* by which one egg may give rise to fifty or more separate embryos by a complex process of budding. The term 'chalcids' is commonly used for any members of this superfamily and is not restricted to the small family Chalcididae.

CHALCID SEED-FLY. A name for a number of small chalcids of the family Torymidae: minute insects that lay their eggs in seeds, particularly those of conifers. Most are parasites of gall-making insects, but some feed on the seeds themselves. The maggot-like larvae spend the whole summer inside the seed where they eventually pupate and emerge as adults through a tiny hole. A species of economic importance as a pest to forestry is the small yellow Douglas Fir Seed-fly *Megastigmus spermotrophus*.

CHALCOLEPIDIUS. A genus of very large, brightly coloured elaterid beetles from South and Central America and the southern United States.

CHALCOPHORA. A genus of large ornamental beetles of North America, up to 4 cm. long, having a shiny metallic appearance, a central groove in the head and thorax and a number of impressed spots on the wing covers. They belong to the family Buprestidae whose larvae are wood-borers. Other related species are brightly coloured and used for jewellery and other decorative purposes.

CHALCOSOMA. The Atlas Beetle: a Rhinoceros' Beetle of tropical Asia, up to 10 cm. long, having three long curved 'horns' extending forwards from the front of the thorax and a fourth on the head.

CHALK HILL BLUE. *Lysandra coridon*: a small European butterfly of the family Lycaenidae. The male has pale blue wings with dark borders and black-dotted white fringes; the female has dark brown wings powdered with blue at the bases. The underside in both male and female is pale brown or grey with numerous white-edged black spots and a row of black-centred orange spots along the margins. The food plant of the larvae is the horse-shoe vetch *Hippocrepis comosa*, a typical plant of chalk and limestone hills.

CHALYBION. An iridescent, steel-blue wasp of North America that builds its nest of clay under the eaves of houses.

CHAMELEON FLY. *Stratiomys chamaeleon*: a two-winged fly of the group Brachycera, related to the gadflies, commonly found on umbelliferous plants. The abdomen is flattened, much broader than the thorax and is banded with black and yellow like that of a wasp. The larva like that of the mosquito, is aquatic and breathes through a tail-siphon which breaks the surface while the head hangs down. The pupa retains its larval skin which surrounds it loosely and acts as a float.

CHAOBORUS. Also called *Corethra*, the Phantom Gnat: an insect closely related to the mosquitoes with which it was formerly classed, but differing from them in being unable to suck blood. The transparent aquatic larva has a pair of air sacs acting as hydrostatic organs at each end. The shining appearance of these in the almost invisible body gives the insect its name. The larvae are predatory and often feed on mosquito larvae.

CHARIESTERUS. A genus of North American squashbugs of the family Coreidae: pentatomid bugs that feed on melons, pumpkins etc. *Chariesterus antennator* is a small, light brown species with a leaf-like expansion on each antenna.

CHEESE SKIPPER. The larva of the Cheese-fly *Piophila casei*, one of the acalyptrate cyclorrhaphous Diptera: a pest of stored cheese and other protein foods. The larva is of the maggot type but is able to jump a considerable distance by flexing its body, grasping its tail with its mouth-hooks and suddenly releasing it.

CHEIMATOBIA. The Winter Moth, also called *Operophtera*, an important pest and defoliator of fruit trees and some forest trees. It belongs to the family Geometridae. The male has greyish-brown wings with dark wavy lines; the female is wingless. The latter climbs the trunk of a tree and lays her eggs in crevices of the bark; small green looper caterpillars emerge, feed on the leaves and drop on to the ground where they pupate in the soil.

CHEQUERED FLESH-FLY. *Sarcophaga carnaria*: one of the cyclorrhaphous Diptera related to the blowfly, having the abdomen chequered with black and grey and the thorax striped in the same colours. The larvae hatch from the eggs before leaving the parent's body and are then dropped, sometimes from a height of several inches, on to meat, carrion or dung which form their food. A single fly may drop 2,000 larvae in batches of about a dozen at a time.

CHEQUERED SKIPPER. *Carterocephalus palaemon*: a small European butterfly belonging to the primitive moth-like family Hesperiidae; brown with yellowish patches and dots. It is found locally in the south midlands of Britain.

CHERMESIDAE. Also called Adelgidae: parasitic plant-lice of minute size producing galls at the bases of young conifer shoots. Many are less than 1 mm. in size.

CHIGOE. *Tunga*, a genus of fleas originally from South America. The male feeds normally as an external blood-sucking parasite: the female burrows into the flesh on the feet of animals and man, living there and laying its eggs. The best-known species *Tunga penetrans* is often found causing sores under the toe-nails of bare-footed natives of tropical countries. Commonly called 'Jiggers' or 'Jigger-fleas' (see *Jigger*).

CHIMNEY SWEEP. *Odezia atrata*: a small day-flying, geometrid moth with wings and body completely black.

CHINA MARK MOTH. *Nymphula*: a genus of small moths of the family Pyralidae, named from the markings on the wings. The larvae are aquatic and burrow into the leaves of water lilies.

CHINCHBUGS. Small plant-bugs of the order Heteroptera: serious pests of corn, wheat and other cereals. *Blissus* (American), *Ischnodemus* (European). See also *Lygaeidae*.

CHIONASPIS. Willow and poplar scale-insects: minute members of the family Coccidae (Homoptera) forming small white scales on the bark of willow, poplar etc. These are formed from the cast-off skins of the wingless females and remain as a protection for the eggs after the insect has died.

CHIONEA. A genus of snow-gnats of North America: minute insects related to crane-flies but having the wings reduced or absent; they are found at altitudes up to 3,700 m. (12,000 ft.).

CHIRONOMIDAE. Small two-winged gnats whose aquatic larvae may be red, green, blue, yellow or colourless. The small red larvae of *Chironomus plumosus* are known as bloodworms from the fact that they are among the very few insects whose blood contains haemoglobin. This is thought to be an adaptation to life in poorly aerated water.

CHIRPING. Stridulation: the production of sound by an insect, generally by rubbing one part against another. In short-horned grasshoppers (Acrididae) the sound is produced by drawing the toothed hind femur rapidly over the thickened edge of the fore-wing. In long-horned grasshoppers and crickets the two fore-wings are rubbed together, a rough part of one against a ridge on the other. In cicadas, which are said to be the loudest of insects, there is a pair of vibratory drums or 'tymbals' at the base of the abdomen. In these the 'drum-skin' is rapidly drawn in and released by a minute muscle on its inner side. In most of these insects stridulation is restricted to the males and has either a sexual or a territorial significance.

CHITIN. A horny protective substance forming the chief part of the cuticle of an insect or other arthropod; an amino-polysaccharide or a polymer of acetylglucosamine with the empirical formula $(C_8H_{13}O_5N)_n$. It is insoluble in water, alcohol, ether and other solvents and is resistant to acids and alkalis.

CHLOEON. *Chloeon dipterum*: a species of small mayfly (Ephemeroptera) notable for two remarkable features:
(1) The hind-wings, which are reduced in all mayflies, are entirely absent in this species.
(2) The compound eyes of the male are of two kinds, *viz.* an upper section with large facets for general vision and a lower section with small facets adapted for more acute and closer vision.

CHLORION. *Chlorion ichneumonea*: a large North American wasp with a reddish abdomen, golden hair on its thorax and amber-coloured wings.

CHLOROCHROA. A genus of North American pentatomid bugs (stink-bugs), green with yellow margins. When attacked they discharge an obnoxious secretion from two scent-glands on the underside of the thorax.

CHLOROPERLA. *Chloroperla torrentium*, a greenish yellow stonefly, sometimes known as the Small Yellow Sally: a member of the order Plecoptera about 1 cm. long, having green-tinted wings and black eyes. The aquatic nymph differs from those of most stoneflies in that it has no gill-filaments but breathes through its skin throughout its larval life. It lives in fast running mountain streams.

CHLOROPIDAE. Minute two-winged flies (Diptera) whose larvae mostly bore into the stems of grasses and cereals. They include the Frit-fly of oats and the Gout-fly of barley. Some chloropid larvae are predaceous, *e.g.* those of *Thaumatomyia notata* (see *Chloropisca*).

CHLOROPISCA. An alternative name for the genus *Thaumatomyia*: small black and yellow cluster-flies, some species of which form swarms with many thousands of individuals of both sexes and settle in houses in the autumn.

38

Sometimes they may congregate on the same part of a ceiling or wall in several successive years.

CHLOROPS. A large wide-spread genus of Chloropidae; pests of wheat and other cereals (see *Chloropidae*).

CHOCOLATE-TIP MOTH. A name for several moths of the genus *Clostera* having chocolate-coloured tips to the fore-wings. When resting they fold their wings in such a way as to resemble a short broken twig.

CHORDOTONAL RECEPTORS. Sense organs of insects probably detecting changes of tension in muscles and possibly enabling the insect to balance itself while flying. Each consists of a thin fibre attached to the cuticle, passing through a rod called a *scolopale* to a sense-cell beneath the surface. A special example is Johnston's Organ in the antennae (see *Johnston's Organ*).

CHORION. The 'shell' of an insect's egg. This may be composed of a hard impenetrable layer of scleroprotein called the *endochorion* covered by a thin surface layer or *exochorion*. Often, however, the layers are more numerous than this. The whole structure may be sculptured or ornamented into elaborate patterns. Since the chorion is secreted by the ovary before fertilization, it is necessary for it to have one or more openings through which a sperm cell can penetrate. These form the *micropyle* at one end of the egg.

CHORIONIN. A name given to the scleroprotein forming the chief part of the 'shell' of an insect's egg (see *Chorion*).

CHORTHIPPUS. *Chorthippus parallelus*: the Meadow Grasshopper, a small, very common and variable European species whose colour may be any shade of brown or purple with a white or cream stripe down the back and with a green head and elytra. The latter are very short in the male and vestigial in the female. The wings in both sexes are likewise reduced to mere stumps. A similar species *Chorthippus brunneus* has pale transverse stripes on the abdomen and has full-length wings and elytra.

CHRYSALIS. The third stage in the development of a butterfly or moth: a pupa of the *obtect* type, *i.e.* one in which the wings, antennae, mouth-parts and legs are glued down to the body but are partially visible beneath the thick cuticle which may or may not be covered by a silken cocoon. The chrysalis appears to be in an inactive state and does not feed, but in fact during this apparent resting stage there is considerable internal physiological activity involving the breaking down of larval organs and their replacement by those of the adult insect. When these changes are complete the cuticle of the chrysalis is loosened by the breaking down of its inner layer to form a fluid. Finally it splits along the mid-dorsal line of the thorax and the adult insect emerges.

CHRYSIDIDAE. Ruby-tail Wasps or Cuckoo-wasps: a family of wasps having bright, shining green or red bodies. They lay their eggs in the burrows of other solitary wasps, bees or sawflies and their larvae feed on those of the other species or, exceptionally, on caterpillars which the other wasp has stored as food.

CHRYSIS. See *Chrysididae*.

CHRYSOBOTHRIS. The Flat-headed Apple Tree Borer: a genus of North American beetles of the family Buprestidae whose larvae bore beneath the bark of many fruit and forest trees. The adult is brown with roughened wing covers that well match the bark upon which they settle.

CHRYSOCHROA. A genus of brilliantly coloured buprestid beetles of South-east Asia.

CHRYSOMELIDAE. Leaf-beetles: small brightly coloured beetles such as the well known Colorado Potato Beetle *Leptinotarsa decemlineata*, the Flea-beetles (*e.g.* the Turnip Flea-beetle, *Phyllotreta nemorum*) and the Asparagus Beetle, *Crioceris asparagi*. The larvae are soft, fleshy, with short legs and usually brightly coloured. Many do extensive damage by eating leaves of trees or farm and garden crops. They pupate in the soil.

CHRYSOMYA. A genus of two-winged flies whose larva is known as the 'Old World Screw-worm'. The New World Screw-worms belong to a different genus *Callitroga* (*q.v.*). The adult bears a superficial resemblance to the blowfly but frequently lays its eggs in open wounds or in the noses of animals. The larvae then burrow through the tissues and may reach the sinuses of the head, causing death.

CHRYSOPA. The chief genus of Green Lacewing Flies (see *Chrysopidae*).

CHRYSOPHANUS. A genus of lycaenid butterflies including the North American Copper, *Chrysophanus hypophlaeus*: a small species having red fore-wings spotted with black, and black hind-wings margined with red. The larvae are bright green and feed on sorrel.

CHRYSOPIDAE. Green Lacewing Flies: insects of the order Neuroptera having pale green bodies, iridescent wings and prominent reddish golden eyes. The small white eggs are laid on long stalks affixed to leaf surfaces. Larvae are carnivorous and usually feed on plant-lice. Often these larvae camouflage themselves by carrying small plant fragments and the empty skins of their victims.

CHRYSOPS. The Deer-fly: a genus of blood-sucking Diptera belonging to the family Tabanidae, closely related to horse flies and gadflies but smaller and often having a yellowish abdomen with black markings and banded wings. They live in woodlands and will attack almost any mammals including humans.

CHRYSOTOXUM. A common genus of hover-fly (Syrphidae) having four straight transverse yellow lines interrupted by a black central longitudinal line on the abdomen. The larvae are maggot-like and feed on aphids.

CHURCHYARD BEETLE. See *Blaps*.

CIBARIUM. A food pocket on the head of certain insects, in front of the mouth, between the clypeus and the hypopharynx.

CICADA. See *Cicadidae*.

CICADA KILLER. *Sphecius speciosus*: the largest of the solitary wasps of North America, having a black and yellow body and shining amber-coloured wings. After burrowing in the ground the female catches a cicada larva, para-lyses it with its sting and deposits it in the burrow. It then lays its eggs on the still living victim which provides food for the newly hatched larvae.

CICADELLIDAE. Formerly called Jassidae. Leaf-hoppers: homopterous plant-sucking insects closely related to frog-hoppers and to aphids. They have small elongated bodies and can jump and fly with great speed. They probably spread many virus and fungus diseases among plants.

CICADETTA. A genus of small cicadas, the most northern and the only British representative of the family. They live on bracken, piercing the young shoots and sucking the sap. The larvae live in the soil, burrowing into roots (see *Cicadidae*).

CICADIDAE. Cicadas: homopterous plant-bugs of warm regions having four membranous wings and long piercing mouth-parts. The males, which live only for a few days, can make a very loud rattling noise with drum-like membranes on the sides of the body; the females are silent. They lay their eggs in small holes which they bore into twigs. The larvae fall to the ground and live, sometimes for many years, in the soil.

CICINDELIDAE. Tiger-beetles: active predatory insects having large jaws with which they hunt their prey at great speed in sandy places. The larva is a sluggish animal living in a vertical burrow with its head out ready to seize any passing insect.

CIMBICIDAE. A family of large sawflies with caterpillar-like larvae that feed on the leaves of elm, willow, poplar, hawthorn etc., a serious pest of trees in Europe and North America.

CIMEX. *Cimex lectularius*: the Bedbug (*see Cimicidae*).

CIMICIDAE. Bedbugs: parasitic insects of the order Hemiptera living intermittently on their hosts and sucking blood from time to time. They have a flattened body with no wings, a tough skin and a suctorial proboscis (see *Bug*).

CINNABAR MOTH. *Callimorpha jacobaeae*: a European moth, bright scarlet and black, belonging to the group Caradrinoidea, closely related to the tiger moths. The caterpillar, striped in black and yellow, feeds on ragwort and groundsel. It has been introduced into New Zealand in an attempt to control these weeds.

CINNAMON SEDGE. *Limnephilus lunatus*: a species of caddis-flies (Trichoptera) whose larvae make a case from pieces of twig laid lengthways. The adult has hairy wings with transparent moon-shaped patches on the fore-wings.

CIONUS. A genus of weevil that attacks figwort (*Scrophularia*). When disturbed it withdraws its beak or rostrum and its limbs beneath the body so that it is almost impossible for it to be seen. The larva eats all the soft tissue of the figwort leaf, leaving only the skeleton of ribs and veins. When fully grown it pupates forming a cocoon which shows a remarkable resemblance to the seed capsules of the plant on which it is found.

CIRCULATORY SYSTEM. See *Blood*.

CIRCUMOESOPHAGEAL COMMISSURES. The two halves of the nerve collar surrounding the oesophagus and linking the ventral nerve-cord with the dorsal cerebral ganglia in insects and other arthropods as well as in earthworms and a number of other invertebrates.

CIRCUMPHARYNGEAL COMMISSURES. See *Circumoesophageal Commissures*.

CITHAERIAS. A genus of glass-winged butterflies: large insects with transparent, almost scale-less wings from the tropical forests of South America.

CITHERONIIDAE (CERATOCAMPIDAE). Imperial or Regal Moths: large moths of North America related to the Moon Moth and the Atlas Moth but differing from these chiefly in not producing silk cocoons; the caterpillars burrow into the ground to pupate. The caterpillar of *Citheronia regalis*, the Royal Walnut Moth, is known as the Horned Devil. It is about 12 cm. long, greenish with black and white spots and with six long red and black horns that curve back and are displayed when the insect is disturbed.

CITRUS MEALYBUG. *Pseudococcus citri*: a small plant-bug of the group

Homoptera having an oval flat body with a white, waxy coating resembling flour. Eggs are laid on citrus and other plants in a mass of sticky or waxy threads. Like all plant-bugs it has a long proboscis with which it sucks the juice of the plant.

CLADIUS. The Poplar Sawfly: a member of the Hymenoptera that burrows into the leaves of various species of poplar and lays its eggs beneath the surface. The resulting caterpillars are orange and black and feed gregariously in large numbers on the leaves. Other species occur on roses and are sometimes mis-called 'slugs'.

CLADOGNATHUS. The Giraffe Stag Beetle: a large brown and black beetle of South-east Asia, the male having slender mandibles as long as the body and sharply toothed on the inside.

CLASPERS. Any pair of processes on the hind-end of the abdomen of a male insect serving to grasp other structures during mating. The term is applied to different organs by different authors and in different orders; *e.g.* the 'claspers' of male dragonflies grip the neck of the female, but in Diptera they grip the female abdomen.

CLAVICORNIA. A large heterogeneous group of beetles comprising 22 families all of which usually have club-shaped antennae.

CLAWS. Most insects have two horny claws derived from the last segment of the tarsus. Generally there is a median pad or *arolium* between them, but structures vary greatly in different orders (see *Tarsus*). Some of the more primitive insects such as Protura and Collembola, a few higher insects such as some of the Hippoboscidae, and the larvae of a few others have only one claw. In most cases the claws can be flexed by muscles that run up in the leg and are attached to the inside of the exoskeleton.

CLEARWINGS. Sesiidae: a family of moths having transparent wings so that they resemble bees and wasps; a case of Batesian Mimicry.

CLEG. A common name for blood-sucking flies of the family Tabanidae belonging to the genus *Haematopota*, particularly *Haematopota pluvialis*.

CLEISTOGASTRA. See *Clistogastra*.

CLEPTOBIOSIS. A form of symbiosis in which one species of ant lives in or near the colony of another species and steals food from them.

CLERIDAE. Ant-beetles: brightly coloured predatory beetles commonly found feeding on the smaller bark-beetles that infest pine trees. The common British ant-beetle, *Clerus formicarius*, is black and red with white bands on the wing-cases. Its larva is scarlet with a dark head. Some members of the family such at *Necrobia rufipes* and other species are predacious on other larvae, but may cause damage among stored products.

CLICK BEETLE. Any member of the family Elateridae: long, slim, short-legged beetles having the habit of springing into the air with a clicking sound when placed on their backs. The larvae are well known as wireworms, agricultural pests living in the soil and attacking roots.

CLICK-MECHANISM. A device similar to that of a tumbler-switch, causing the wings to move abruptly from the raised to the lowered position and *vice versa* (see *Flight*).

CLIFDEN NONPAREIL. *Catocala fraxini*: a large European moth occasionally found in Britain, related to the Red Underwing but with blue-grey on the hind-wings.

CLISTOGASTRA. An alternative name for Apocrita, *i.e.* Hymenoptera with a deep constriction between the thorax and abdomen. They include ants, bees and wasps.

CLOTHES MOTH. *Tineola* and related genera of Microlepidoptera: small dull coloured moths having long narrow wings with long fringes. The small white caterpillars feed on wool, fur, feathers etc.

CLOUDED BRINDLE MOTH. *Apamea crenata*: a creamy white moth with brown markings whose larvae feed on grasses. In some districts a black variety is spreading (industrial melanism).

CLOUDED YELLOW. *Colias croceus*: a European butterfly, occasionally visiting Britain as a migrant. The wings are deep orange yellow, broadly edged with black and with a black spot in the centre of each fore-wing; the hind-wings have a wide, deep orange central spot. The caterpillars feed on clover, vetch and other leguminous plants. *Colias hyale*, the Pale Clouded Yellow and *Colias australis*, the 'New' or Berger's Clouded Yellow also migrate to Britain occasionally. *Colias philodice*, the closely related Clouded Sulphur Butterfly of North America is a pest of leguminous plants.

CLUSTER FLY. *Pollenia rudis*: a species of two-winged fly related to the blowfly but smaller, grey with curly yellow hairs and distinguished by closing the wings together like scissors instead of holding them apart. It hibernates in large numbers clustered together in crevices of old buildings, thatched roofs etc. The larvae are parasitic in earthworms.

CLYPEUS. A cuticular plate on the front of an insect's head immediately anterior to the *frons* and above the *labrum*.

CLYTRA. *Clytra quadripunctata*: a small beetle somewhat resembling a ladybird in size and shape, having orange yellow wing-cases with two black spots on each. Probably this resemblance is a case of Müllerian mimicry (*q.v.*). Eggs are laid in the nests of ants on which the larvae feed.

CLYTUS. The Wasp-beetle: one of the Cerambycidae or longhorns with a long body and elytra striped in black and yellow like a wasp. The larvae tunnel into oak and beech trees.

CNIDOCAMPA. A Japanese moth whose slug-like caterpillar hibernates in a hard cocoon and is able to withstand temperatures down to −15°C. for many weeks without any ill effects.

COARCTATE PUPA. A type of pupa found in many Diptera, *e.g.* the house fly in which the last larval skin forms a hard barrel-shaped case or *puparium*. When the adult fly emerges, the puparium splits and the top is pushed away by means of an eversible head-sac known as the ptilinum. The pupa itself is not essentially different from any other, but is merely protected by the puparium which can be regarded as being analogous to a cocoon.

COCCINELLIDAE. Ladybirds: small brightly coloured hemispherical beetles with well defined spots and other markings on the wing-cases. The larvae are of the *campodeiform* type (*q.v.*) but differ from those of ground beetles in having the appendages and sensory organs much reduced. They feed voraciously on aphids and other small insects and have been used effectively for controlling these pests.

COCCOIDEA. Mealy bugs and scale-insects: highly specialized and somewhat degenerate insects of the group Homoptera. In this superfamily, which is divided into 15 or 16 families, the males are generally normal active insects but

43

the females are inactive and sometimes scarcely recognizable as insects. Females of mealy bugs are covered with a fine waxy secretion; those of scale insects appear like small white or brown scales on the bark of trees. The 'scale' is formed of several cast-off skins which have shrunk and remain stuck together by a glutinous secretion. Many species are very injurious to trees; others have commercial value yielding such products as cochineal and shellac.

COCHINEAL. A red dye extracted from the bodies of the minute scale-insect *Dactylopius coccus*, a native of Mexico and Central America, but introduced into many other countries. The insects are brushed from the cactus plants on which they feed and it is estimated that about 70,000 are needed to produce a pound ($\frac{1}{2}$ kg.) of the colouring matter. (See *Coccoidea*).

COCHLIDIIDAE. Also called Limacodidae, Heterogeneidae or Eucleidae: a family of moths whose larvae, known as slug caterpillars, are practically legless; the true legs and the prolegs are reduced to mere rudiments and the caterpillars appear to slide about like slugs. Many of them are armed with spines and hairs that are said to secrete an irritant poison.

COCHLIDION. *Cochlidion avellana*, the Festoon Moth: a British and European species of Cochlidiidae (*q.v.*). A small brown moth whose larva is slug-like with reduced legs and head. During its early life it has numerous spines which later become reduced to warts on the skin. At the front end is a special flattened spinneret that produces a ribbon of silk used to help locomotion (see *Cochlidiidae*).

COCHLIOMYIA (CALLITROGA). The Screw-worm fly of Central America and the southern United States: a genus of Calliphoridae (blowflies) whose larvae infest open wounds as well as the nose, ears, navel and other apertures in animals and man.

COCKCHAFER. *Melolontha* and related genera of large chafer beetles also called May Bugs: herbivorous beetles with light brown elytra, fan-like antennae and a grey or blackish body with wedge-shaped white markings along the sides of the abdomen. The larvae, with fat whitish bodies and short legs, live for several years in the soil and are most destructive to crops.

COCKROACH. *Blatta* and related genera: large brown insects having a flattened body with head bent at right angles to it and with horny brown elytra covering a pair of membranous wings. Although they show a superficial resemblance to beetles, they are in the order Dictyoptera (formerly included with Orthoptera). These insects are hemimetabolous, *i.e.* the young closely resemble their parents and become adult without passing through a pupal stage. Cockroaches have typical biting mouth-parts consisting of *labrum*, *mandibles*, *maxillae* and *labium*; they are omnivorous and are pests in most parts of the world. The commonest species are: *Blatta orientalis*, the Asiatic and European cockroach; *Blattella germanica*, the small German cockroach and *Periplaneta americana*, the much larger American cockroach.

COCOA MOTH. See *Cacao Moth*.

COCONUT MOTH. *Levuana iridescens*: a moth whose caterpillars are most destructive to the leaves of coconut palms and can completely strip a tree in a short time. In 1925 it became a serious threat to the coconut industry in Fiji but was effectively controlled by the introduction of a parasitic Tachinid fly.

COCOON. A protective covering for the egg or more usually for the pupa of an insect. Cocoons are most often constructed of silk secreted by the larva and mixed with particles of soil, wood etc. The silk comes from modified salivary glands and issues from a median spinneret near the mouth. Saliva may be used instead of silk, and a special type of cocoon is constructed from the last larval skin (see *Coarctate Pupa*).

CODLING MOTH. *Ernarmonia pomonella* or *Carpocapsa pomonella*: a small grey or brown moth whose caterpillars are most destructive to apples and pears in most parts of the world. Eggs are laid on the leaves and the newly hatched caterpillars bore into young fruits where they feed on the cores and eventually emerge to spin cocoons.

COELIOXYS. A genus of cuckoo-bees closely related to the leaf-cutter bees and belonging to the family Megachilidae. The queen cuckoo-bee lays her eggs in the nests of another species and her larvae are reared by the workers of the latter.

COELOCONIC RECEPTORS. Olfactory or other sense-organs of an insect, more advanced than basiconic receptors and differing from them in having the terminal process of the sense-cell sunk in a small pit (see *Basiconic Receptor*).

COENAGRION. A genus of Damselflies (Odonata–Zygoptera) having a black thorax with blue at the sides and a pale blue abdomen with black markings. The wings, which are petiolate or narrow at the base, are completely transparent with no black or brown pigment. The aquatic nymphs are slender and short-legged with the tail-gills forming a triple fork.

COENONYMPHA. *Coenonympha pamphilus*, the Small Heath Butterfly and *Coenonympha tullia*, the Large Heath of Britain and Europe belong to the family Satyridae and have light tawny wings with dark edges and a small black eye-spot on the underside of each fore-wing. Butterflies of this family have only four functional legs, the anterior pair being rudimentary. The caterpillars feed on various kinds of grasses.

COLEOPHORIDAE. Case-bearers: small brownish or grey moths with marginal fringes on the wings. The caterpillars, which are pests of larch and other trees, construct portable cigar-shaped cases of silk and leaf particles.

COLEOPTERA. Beetles: an order of insects comprising about a quarter of a million species, the largest order in the whole animal kingdom. They are characterized by having the fore-wings thickened to form elytra or covers which protect the membranous hind-wings. The mouth-parts are of the biting type.

Beetles are *holometabolous*, *i.e.* they undergo complete metamorphosis. The larvae are very variable: some are predatory insects of the *campodeiform* type with long legs and antennae; others such as the wireworm are entirely herbivorous and have the legs and antennae reduced. The larvae of Chafer beetles are of the *scarabaeoid* type with a large soft inflated abdomen. Most of the herbivorous and omnivorous beetles (Polyphaga) are pests of agriculture or forestry; they include weevils, root and leaf feeders and wood-borers. The other large group, the Adephaga, include carnivorous water beetles such as *Dytiscus*, tiger beetles such as *Cicindela* and carnivorous ground beetles such as *Carabus*, Ladybirds, although they feed on aphids, are related to the herbivorous groups.

COLIAS. See *Clouded Yellow*.

COLLEMBOLA. Springtails: very small primitive wingless insects, often regarded as not being true insects. They have biting mouth-parts, short antennae and legs without tarsi. The abdomen has six segments which are sometimes fused together. On the fourth segment is a *furcula* or springing organ which. when not in use, is held beneath the abdomen by a 'catch' or *retinaculum*, When this is released the furcula springs back, propelling the insect through the air (see also *Ametabola* and *Apterygota*).

COLLETES. Gum Bees: small blackish or dark brown bees that burrow into sandy soil forming tunnels lined with a parchment-like substance secreted as a glue by the female bees. Some of this secretion forms transverse partitions dividing the tunnel into a line of cells in which eggs are laid and pollen and honey stored. *Colletes* and *Prosopis* are distinguished by their short, blunt tongue compared with the elongate *glossae* of most bees.

COLONICI. Insects that live in colonies. This term may be used for bees etc. but is applied more particularly to the first generation of wingless female aphids that form large colonies on fruit and rose trees etc.

COLORADO BEETLE. *Leptinotarsa decemlineata:* a leaf-beetle of the family Chrysomelidae resembling a ladybird in shape but having conspicuous black and yellow longitudinal stripes on the wing-cases. The larvae are orange-red with black spots. The beetle originated in North America but has been found in Europe many times since about 1875. It is a serious pest of potato crops in those countries where it has become established.

COLUMBICULA. A minute ectoparasitic louse of the order Mallophaga commonly found among the feathers of pigeons.

COLYMBETES. A genus of large European water beetles common in ditches, ponds and streams. The only British species is *Colymbetes fuscus*. The thorax is yellowish brown with a dark stripe down the middle; the elytra and abdomen are dark brown and the legs reddish.

COMMA BUTTERFLY. *Polygonia C-album:* a European butterfly of the family Nymphalidae, related to the Red Admiral, the Peacock and the Tortoiseshells. The wings are a deep reddish orange with black spots and a black border deeply notched and ragged. A white C-shaped mark on the underside of the hind-wing gives it its name.

COMMISSURE. Any link between two structures, whether it is a connecting structure or a line of division. Generally used in the plural to denote the two halves of the nerve-collar that surrounds the pharynx and connects the 'brain' to the ventral nerve-cord in insects and other arthropods.

COMMUNALISM. The association of insects of various castes in a colony (*e.g.* of bees).

COMPOUND EYES. Eyes of insects and crustaceans consisting of numerous visual units or *ommatidia*. The number of these ranges from many thousands in dragonflies and beetles to less than a dozen in some ants and a single facet in some parasitic flies (Nycteribiidae). When crowded together the facets are hexagonal, but are circular when there are only a few. Each ommatidium consists of a cuticular lens beneath which is a crystalline cone and a retinula or group of light-sensitive cells. The whole eye is convex or hemispherical with the apices of the cones converging towards the optic nerve in the centre. A black pigment normally surrounds each cone and it is thought that an insect perceives a 'mosaic image', *i.e.* one made up of a large number of dots. In some cases, however, the layer of pigment surrounding each cone is capable of being retracted and the image, although brighter, will be blurred owing to its being formed by overlapping points of light. This is the case with many nocturnal insects. Recent work has drawn attention to several successive images at intervals along the length of the ommatidium, but it is not yet known whether insects can perceive these or make use of them.

COMPSILURA. A genus of tachinid fly whose larvae parasitize and destroy caterpillars of a number of moths and butterflies. The species *Compsilura concinnata* was successfully introduced into the United States to control the Gipsy Moth which had become a serious pest of fruit trees.

COMSTOCK-NEEDHAM SYSTEM. The most widely used system of nomenclature for the veins of the wing, intended by its authors to be applicable to insects of all Orders, and to be a 'natural' system related to the mode of formation of the principal veins from tracheae. It is least successful in Hymenoptera (see *Venation*).

CONCAVE AND CONVEX VEINS. The wing-membrane is stiffened, and made more effective, by a series of longitudinal pleats radiating from the base, and, in principle, the major veins run either along a ridge (convex vein) or a trough (concave vein). This arrangement is adhered to most closely in fossil insects and in their most primitive living descendants, notably the mayflies (Ephemeroptera). In most living insects, evolution of a more specialized wing has modified the venation and blurred the relationship of the veins to the remaining pleats in the membrane.

CONE NOSE. A name given in the United States to a number of Reduviid bugs having the base of the proboscis cone-shaped. Some prey on other insects; others are blood-suckers of man and domestic animals. Many can transmit trypanosomes and other protozoan parasites.

CONGLOBATE GLAND. A median gland of unknown function opening into the ejaculatory duct of the male reproductive system in certain insects.

CONIOPTERYGIDAE. Mealy-wings: small insects of the order Neuroptera, having very simple wing-venation and having the body covered by a powdery exudation from epidermal glands. The hind-wings may be greatly reduced. The larvae infest trees and prey upon minute insects, mites etc.

CONOPIDAE. Two-winged insects (Diptera) having a remarkable protective resemblance to wasps and bees and sometimes starting life as parasites on them.

CONOTRACHELUS. The Plum Weevil, *Conotrachelus crataegi* and related species in the family Curculionidae. Serious pests of fruit trees, particularly in North America. The larvae feed on apples, plums, cherries, peaches etc.

CONTARINIA. The Pear Midge: a small two-winged fly whose larvae are pests of pears. They enter the developing fruit by way of the flower and cause swellings around the core of the fruit, causing it to blacken and fall. They have spread from Europe to the United States and elsewhere.

CONVOLVULUS HAWK-MOTH. *Herse convolvuli:* a large hawk-moth found sometimes in Britain as a migrant from the Mediterranean. Its range includes Europe, Asia, Africa and Australia. The wings are mottled greyish and the abdomen is banded with red, black and white. The wing-span is about 12 cm. and the exceptionally long proboscis is also about 12 cm. enabling the moth to suck nectar from deep tubular flowers such as those of the tobacco plant while hovering in flight. The larvae feed on various species of convolvulus.

COOTIE. A name used in the United States for the body-louse *Pediculus humanus* and the head-louse *Pediculus capitis*.

COPIDOSOMA. A genus of Encyrtidae (Hymenoptera: Chalcidoidea) whose larvae are parasites in caterpillars. It is a well known example of the phenomenon of *polyembryony;* a single egg laid in the body of the host may give rise to as many as a thousand embryos which eat and destroy it from the inside. It therefore acts as an effective control of some moths that are pests of forest trees or agricultural crops.

COPPER BUTTERFLIES. A widely distributed group of butterflies of the family Lycaenidae closely related to the Blues. The general colouring of the wings is a bright copper, spotted and margined with dark brown. The larvae of many species feed on docks and sorrel (*Rumex*). The Small Copper *Lycaena phlaeae* is common in Britain; the Large Copper *Lycaena dispar* has been extinct for a hundred years in this country but has been re-introduced into the Fens from Holland.

COPRIS. A large dung beetle of the family Scarabaeidae, shiny black, about 20 mm. long with wide thorax having lobe-like projections on the fore margins. The head is shovel-shaped with a curved horn, longer in the male than in the female. The insect is found chiefly among cattle dung in sandy soil; it has, however, become rather rare in Britain. It is a relative of the sacred scarab of Ancient Egypt (*Scarabaeus sacer*).

COPTOCYCLA. A genus of leaf-beetles of the family Chrysomelidae, closely related to the well known Colorado Beetle, notable for the ability to change colour from golden yellow to green, blue or violet. This is brought about by absorption and loss of water causing the thin plates in the skin to swell and shrink and thus alter the colour produced by 'optical interference'.

COPULATORY BURSA. See *Bursa copulatrix*.

CORBICULA. A pollen basket formed from long curved hairs on the hind-leg of a bee.

CORDULEGASTER. *Cordulegaster boltoni:* the Golden-ringed Dragonfly, one of the largest European species about 75 mm. long. The thorax has black and yellow markings; the compound eyes are green and are so large that they meet at the top of the head; the abdomen is black with yellow bands.

CORDULIA. *Cordulia aenea;* the Emerald Green Dragonfly: a European species about 50 mm. long, brilliant green all over the body and head including the eyes, but with yellow at the bases of the wings. The general appearance is not unlike the much commoner *Aeshna,* but the aquatic nymph of *Cordulia* differs in being shorter and having legs longer than the body.

COREIDAE. A family of plant-bugs of the order Hemiptera, known in America as Squashbugs, these being pests of melons, pumpkins etc. They resemble the Shieldbugs (Pentatomidae) and, like them, emit a nauseating smell. They differ from them in having smaller wings and a larger abdomen; many species are brightly coloured.

CORETHRA. An alternative name for *Chaoborus* (*q.v.*).

CORIXIDAE. Water bugs also known as 'Lesser Water Boatmen' belonging to the order Hemiptera and the suborder Heteroptera. Unlike the true Water Boatmen or 'Backswimmer' (*Notonecta*), the Corixidae swim in the normal way with their backs uppermost. Both insects, however, swim by means of the enlarged hind-legs. The Corixidae are plentiful among pondweeds and carry an air supply down in a hollow of the back covered by the wings. Most are herbivorous.

CORNEAGEN LAYER. Transparent epidermal cells beneath the cuticular lenses in the compound eyes of insects and crustaceans. The lenses are shed with the rest of the cuticle at each moult and are renewed by means of these corneagen cells.

CORNICLES. Two short dorsal tubes near the hind-end of the abdomen in aphids and other plant-lice. Contrary to popular belief they do not secrete the sticky *honeydew* which is much sought after by ants; this is an excess of sugars excreted from the anus. The cornicles produce the protective wax which is conspicuous in the Woolly Aphis.

CORPORA ALLATA. A pair of small ductless glands behind the brain in insects and their larvae. It is believed that they secrete a substance known as the *juvenile hormone* which maintains the insect in the larval state at each moult. When this hormone ceases to be produced metamorphosis takes place.

CORRODENTIA. An alternative name for Psocoptera or book-lice: small soft-bodied insects with long thread-like antennae. They may be winged or wingless and have biting mouth-parts. They feed on the dried paste of old books. Many related species are found among vegetation or on the bark of trees. Some are pests of cereals.

CORYDALIS. A large North American predatory insect, also called the Dobson Fly, having a wing-span of about 15 cm. and with large horn-like mandibles. It belongs to the group Megaloptera, sometimes regarded as a suborder of Neuroptera: holometabolous insects closely related to lacewing flies, having two pairs of primitively veined membranous wings, a soft body, long antennae and biting mouth-parts. The larvae are aquatic.

CORYMBITES. A large genus of click beetles (Elateridae) usually with wing-cases of a shining metallic green or bronze appearance due to optical interference. The larvae (wireworms) are often agricultural pests (see *Click Beetle*).

CORYNETES. A genus of predatory beetles living in the tunnels of bark beetles and preying upon them. They belong to the family Cleridae (*q.v.*). *Corynetes caeruleus* has the head, thorax and elytra bright blue and the legs a darker blue. It is sometimes found in the rotting timber of old houses.

COSCINOSCERA. The Hercules Moth of Australia and New Guinea, believed to be the largest moth in the world, having a wing-span of about 25 cm.

COSSIDAE (COSSOIDEA). Goat Moths: some of the largest species of European moths having a wing expanse of up to 9 cm. Related species occur in North America in temperate deciduous forests. The caterpillars do considerable damage to oak, willow, poplar and other trees. Eggs are laid at the base of the tree and in crevices in the bark and the caterpillars bore irregular tunnels between the bark and the wood. Later they enter the wood and make wide winding passages. A larva may live for several years in this way and eventually pupate in the soil. The name 'goat moth' is given on account of the strong and unpleasant odour given off by the caterpillars.

COSTAL MARGIN. The anterior margin of an insect's wing.

COSTAL VEIN (COSTA). The first vein of an insect's wing, running along the anterior margin, and either terminating completely leaving the rest of the wing margin unsupported, or merging into a narrower vein which continues either partially or completely around the hind margin. N.B. In some systems of nomenclature the 'first' vein of the wing is the first strong longitudinal, R_1 in the Comstock – Needham system.

COTINUS. The Fig-eater or Green Line Beetle: a metallic green and brownish beetle about 2.5 cm. long; the adult feeds on fleshy fruits and the larvae on roots, stems and leaves.

COTTON BOLL WEEVIL. *Anthonomus grandis:* a small North American weevil whose larvae feed on the bolls or seed pods of the cotton plant and cause wide-spread damage.

COTTON STAINER. *Dysdercus:* a genus of herbivorous plant-bugs (Hemiptera) belonging to the family Pyrrhocoridae, also called firebugs. They infest cotton plants in many parts of the world, piercing the bolls and thereby introducing a fungus which stains the fibres.

COTTONY CUSHION SCALE. *Icerya purchasi:* a small scale-insect originally from Australia but introduced into North America and other countries, a pest of citrus trees. It feeds in large numbers on these trees and secretes cotton-like fibres (see *Coccoidea, Cryptochaetum, Rodolia* and *Hermaphrodite*).

COTTONY SCALE. *Pulvinaria innumerabilis:* a common scale-insect that attacks maple, elm, vines and other plants. The insects are sometimes present in very large numbers and cover the tree with their sticky secretion of honeydew. This then forms the food for a rapidly growing black cottony fungus that covers and protects the insects and their eggs.

COW-KILLER. *Dasymutilla occidentalis:* a large wasp of the family Mutillidae, sometimes called 'velvet ants'. They are brightly coloured in red, banded with black and white. The females, which have a powerful sting, are wingless and covered with dense velvety hair.

COXA. The first segment of the leg of an insect where it articulates with the thorax. It is the functional outer, or distal part of the *coxopodite,* a basal segment of the limb in all arthropods.

COXAL GLAND. An excretory gland opening at the base of the leg in some insects.

COXAL PLATE. A plate-like extension of the hind-legs of some water beetles.

COXITE, COXOPODITE. These are more generalized terms than *Coxa.* They are used mainly when discussing various classes of Arthropoda and comparing them with one another. They refer to a region at the base of a limb, where it articulates with the segment from which it arises (see *Coxa*).

CRAB LOUSE. *Phthirus pubis,* the Pubic Louse: a blood-sucking louse of the order Anoplura that infests the pubic hairs and the armpits of humans. It is not known to be a carrier of any disease.

CRABRO. A genus of wasps of the family Crabronidae (*q.v.*).

CRABRONIDAE. A family of wasps that nest in wood and catch and store adult insects as food for their larvae. Flies are their principal prey, but some species of *Crabro* may capture insects of other Orders.

CRAMBIDAE. Grass Moths: small silvery or brownish moths that fold their wings tightly round the body as they lie head-up among the grasses which are the food of their larvae. The group includes the Sugar-cane Borer *Diatraea saccharalis.*

CRANE-FLY. Any member of the family Tipulidae (Diptera–Nematocera); the larger ones in Britain are called Daddy-long-legs. They are slender insects with long, fragile legs, a tapering body and two long membranous wings. They are larger than gnats and mosquitoes, sometimes very much larger, and have

50

shorter, non-piercing mouth-parts. When at rest the wings are stretched out and lying flat. The legless larvae are a dark brown colour and have a tough skin which gives them the name of *leatherjacket*. Most of them are soil-dwellers and do considerable damage to the roots of grass and young plants in general. Some common species can be abundant in grassland in late summer, and come into porches and to lights.

CREMASTER. A hooked appendage on the posterior tip of a chrysalis. It may be used to hang it up or to attach it to the inside of a cocoon, or to help in liberating the pupa from the soil or other surroundings just before emergence

CREOPHILUS. A staphylinid beetle, *i.e.* one with very short wing-cases, resembling the Devil's Coach-horse (*Ocypus olens*) but smaller, with the head and thorax black and the elytra clothed with short pale grey hairs. It is a carrion feeder and is commonly found in the decaying carcases of animals.

CRIBELLUM. A sieve-like plate opening near the upper surface of the mandibles and forming part of the spinneret in some insects; similar to those of spiders, but the latter are on the hind-end of the abdomen.

CRICKET. Any member of the family Gryllidae of the order Orthoptera, closely related to the long-horned grasshoppers but distinguished from them by their brown colour and by the long, unsegmented anal cerci. Like the grasshoppers they have long black legs for jumping. The chirping or 'singing' of male crickets is brought about by rubbing the bases of the fore-wings together.

CRIMSON AND GOLD MOTH. *Pyrausta purpuralis:* a small European moth of mountainous regions, having crimson wings with curved stripes and markings in gold. The larvae spin leaves of Wild Thyme together and feed inside them.

CRIOCEPHALUS. A large rusty brown beetle whose larvae bore into pine trees. Although classed with the Cerambycidae or longhorns, its antennae are shorter than the body.

CRIOCERIS. One of the Asparagus Beetles: small insects whose larvae feed on asparagus shoots; a member of the family Chrysomelidae.

CRIORRHINA. A genus of hover-flies (Syrphidae) having the general appearance of a golden-yellow, hairy humble bee.

CROCALLIS. The Scalloped Oak Moth: a common European moth having the wings of a buff yellow crossed with dark lines and brown markings in such a way that when they are folded there is a continuous disruptive pattern giving effective camouflage to the insect.

CROCHETS. Any small hook-like organs, particularly those on the prolegs of caterpillars.

CROP. An enlarged and modified part of the oesophagus where food may be kept for a time before passing on to the gizzard or stomach. It may be a simple dilatation, as in the cockroach, or a lateral diverticulum joined to the oesophagus by a narrow tube, as in the blowfly and in most butterflies and moths.

CROSS-VEINS. Transverse veins linking the principal longitudinal veins in an insect's wing and giving it greater strength. In mayflies and dragonflies they are numerous and variable but in the more specialized insects they tend to become few and located in fixed positions, so that they may be used as a basis for identification of the genus and occasionally even the species (see *Venation*).

CROTON BUG. An alternative name for the small European cockroach

Blattella germanica, also called the Shiner: a small brown insect about 12 mm. in length, related to the larger cockroaches and belonging to the order Dictyoptera.

CRY-BABY CRICKET. *Brachytrypes megacephalus:* a West African cricket that produces a loud and penetrating sound by rubbing the thickened anterior wings (tegmina) together. A row of teeth on the left wing scrapes against a thickened ridge on the right wing and the sound so produced is further amplified by a circular vibratory membrane known as the 'mirror' close to the ridge on the right wing.

CRYPTOCERATA. Insects of the order Hemiptera and the suborder Heteroptera having very small inconspicuous antennae. They include many aquatic bugs such as the well known water-boatmen *Notonecta* and *Corixa*.

CRYPTOCERCUS. A genus of North American wingless cockroaches found in rotting wood and under the bark of dead trees. They cannot themselves produce enzymes for digesting wood but this is carried out by means of symbiotic protozoa in the intestine.

CRYPTOCHAETUM ICERYAE. A fly of the family Cernidae, the larva of which parasitizes the Cottony Cushion Scale, *Icerya purchasi* (*q.v.*).

CRYPTOCOCCUS. A minute insect, related to the scale-insects (Coccidae), that attacks beech trees. The legless females, less than 1 mm. in length, attach themselves to thin parts or crevices of the bark, into which they insert their stylet-like proboscis. They produce a white woolly substance that may cover a whole tree and eventually cause it to die (see *Coccoidea*).

CRYPTOPHAGIDAE. A widely distributed family of scavenger beetles that feed on fungi and decaying organic matter. They are sometimes found in ants', bees' and wasps' nests.

CRYPTORHYNCHUS. A genus of long-snouted weevils that tunnel into the wood of poplar, willow etc. They are about 1 cm. long, black with yellowish white scales on the elytra. When not in use the snout is tucked under the thorax. The males are able to produce a sound by stridulation.

CRYSTALLINE CONE. A transparent cone acting as an additional lens between the cuticular lens and the retinal cells in each ommatidium or visual unit of an insect's eye. (See *Compound Eye.*)

CTENOCEPHALIDAE. A common and widely distributed family of fleas that includes the Dog Flea *Ctenocephalus canis* and the Cat Flea *Ctenocephalus felis*.

CUBITAL VEIN (CUBITUS). One of the principal longitudinal veins of an insect's wing. Named from the anterior these are: *costal, subcostal, radial, median, cubital* and *anal*, according to the Comstock – Needham System. In other systems the cubitus is not necessarily the same vein.

CUCKOO BEES. See *Homeless Bees*.

CUCKOO SPIT. A frothy secretion produced by the nymphs of frog-hoppers (see *Cercopidae*).

CUCKOO WASP. See *Chrysididae*.

CUCUJO BEETLES. *Pyrophorus* or Fire-beetles: large insects of the family Elateridae from Central and South America having two luminous organs on the hind part of the thorax (see also *Light-producing Organs*).

CULICIDAE. A family of two-winged insects comprising most of the common gnats and mosquitoes. They have long piercing mouth-parts and long antennae with numerous whorls of bristles, especially obvious in the males. Scales similar to those of butterflies are situated along the wing-margins and veins. In the subfamily Culicinae the abdomen is also scaly, a distinction from the Anophelinae or malaria-carrying group whose abdomen is smooth. The larvae and pupae are aquatic, the former breathing through a pair of tubes opening at the hind-end with a siphon in Culicinae; the latter by two 'trumpets' on the thorax.

CULICOIDES. A genus of minute biting midges (see *Ceratopogonidae*).

CULTELLUS. The sharp knife-like proboscis of some blood-sucking flies, or one of its blade-like lancets.

CURCULIONIDAE. Weevils: a family of beetles belonging to the suborder Rhynchophora of which there are about 60,000 species. The head is prolonged into a snout which may be used for boring into grain or other parts of plants where the eggs are laid, or perhaps to reach a deeper layer of the food material.

CURRANT CLEARWING. A small European moth with transparent wings, the fore-wings having brown margins and a black transverse bar. The head and thorax are black and the abdomen has narrow yellow bands on a black background. The larvae feed on the pith of currant and gooseberry bushes.

CURRANT GALLS. Red berry-like galls formed on the young leaves or catkins of oak trees by the gall-wasp *Neuroterus lenticularis*. The summer generation of this species produces quite a different gall on the under surface of oak leaves in October.

CURRANT HOVER-FLY. *Syrphus ribesii*, a common black and yellow hover-fly that frequents currant bushes, feeding on pollen and nectar. The larvae live on the leaves and feed on aphids.

CURRANT MOTH. *Abraxas grossulariata*, also known as the Magpie Moth (see *Abraxas*).

CURSORIA. A name formerly used for cockroaches and mantids which were regarded as the running members of the order Orthoptera, as distinct from the jumping members or Saltatoria (grasshoppers etc.). These names are, however, no longer generally used and the Cursoria, now known as Dictyoptera, are regarded as a separate order.

CUTEREBRA. A genus of large hairy bot flies whose larvae are parasitic under the skin of rodents (see *Bot Fly*).

CUTICLE. A horny, non-cellular covering layer secreted by the epidermis of an animal. In insects it usually consists of the following three layers:
(1) The *Epicuticle*, a thin outer waterproof layer of *sclerotin* often with minute hairs or *microtrichia*.
(2) The *Exocuticle*, a thicker middle layer composed of proteins and chitin together with melanin which colours the insect black or brown.
(3) The *Endocuticle*, a thick, flexible, laminated layer of protein and chitin. When the insect is about to moult the endocuticle becomes liquefied by the action of enzymes secreted by epidermal *moulting glands*. The effect of this is to detach and loosen the two outer layers of the cuticle which are then cast off.

CUTWORM. A general name given to the grey or greenish caterpillars of Owlet Moths (Noctuidae). Many are agricultural pests on account of the habit of biting through the stems of young plants close to the soil.

CYCHRUS. A genus of large, rough, black beetles having a long narrow head and thorax allowing it to be inserted into the shell of a snail, on the soft body of which it feeds.

CYCLORRHAPHA. One of the three suborders of Diptera, strictly Brachycera – Cyclorrhapha, *i.e.* with short antennae and emerging from the pupa by a circular slit. The larvae are without head or legs and the pupae are co-arctate, *i.e.* contained in a barrel-shaped puparium formed from the last larval skin. The common House Fly is an example.

CYDIA. See *Codling Moth.*

CYDNIDAE. Burrowing Bugs or Negro Bugs: a family of Heteroptera resembling small shieldbugs. They are black, hemispherical insects, often with a large shield or scutellum covering the thorax and extending back over the abdomen. Like all plant-bugs they have piercing mouth-parts which can be bent back under the thorax when not in use.

CYLLENE. A North American genus of wood-boring longicorn beetles (Cerambycidae), black with transverse yellow bands; a pest of the Honey Locust Tree (*Robinia*).

CYMBIDAE. A family of moths including the Green Silver Lines, *Bena fagana* (see *Bena*).

CYNIPOIDEA (CYNIPIDAE). Gall-wásps: narrow-waisted or apocritous Hymenoptera having straight antennae and a laterally compressed body. The majority produce galls on oak or other trees and the formation of these is thought to be due to the production of some type of auxin either by the insect or by the injured tissues of the plant.

CYNOMYIA. The Bright Bluebottle: a flesh-fly similar to the blowfly but smaller and of a much brighter metallic blue colour.

CYTORHINUS. A tropical plant-bug that feeds on the eggs of the Sugar-cane Leaf-hopper.

D

DACTYLOPIIDAE. Cochineal insects: minute scale-insects (Coccoidea) from which the red dye cochineal is extracted. They live and feed on cactus plants and, although originally from Mexico, have been introduced into many other countries. The body of the insect is crimson but is usually covered with a white woolly secretion (see *Cochineal*).

DACUS. A genus of tropical fruit fly of the family Trypetidae: a serious pest whose larvae feed on fruits and flowers, particularly of the family Compositae.

DADDY-LONG-LEGS. See *Crane-fly.*

DAGGER MOTH. *Apatele* or *Acronycta*: a genus of medium sized noctuid moths having grey wings with black dagger-shaped markings. The two species *Apatele psi*, the Grey Dagger and *Apatele tridens*, the Dark Dagger are sometimes very difficult to distinguish but the larvae of the former are brightly coloured white, red and black; those of the latter much less bright.

DALOPIUS. *Dalopius marginatus*, the Bordered Skipjack, a common woodland click beetle having yellow-brown wing-cases with dark stripes (see *Elateridae*).

DAMSEL BUGS. Small predatory bugs (Hemiptera) belonging to the family Nabidae (Nabiidae) and closely related to the Assassin Bugs (*q.v.*). Both adults and young feed on aphids and other small insects. The larvae of some species resemble black ants and are sometimes found in their nests.

DAMSELFLY. A general name for dragonflies of the group Zygoptera, usually smaller and more delicate than the 'true dragonflies' (Anisoptera). Usually blue or green, with narrow-based wings which are held vertically when at rest. The aquatic nymphs have legs as long as the body and have three elongated caudal gills at the hind-end of the abdomen.

DANAIDAE. Milkweed or Monarch Butterflies and related species: a widespread family of large migratory butterflies of America, South-east Asia, Pacific Islands and Australia. The general colour is orange-brown with thick black lines outlining the veins. Many migrate long distances; the American Monarch Butterfly *Danaus plexippus*, for instance, flies from the Canadian border to the Gulf of Mexico. At times many thousands of these may be seen resting in trees. It has even been known to fly the Atlantic and is occasionally found in Britain and Western Europe (see *Milkweed Butterfly*).

DANCE FLIES. *Hilara* and other genera of the family Empididae: minute flies that move up and down in large swarms and mate while in flight. The name 'Dance Fly' is often applied to the entire family, though the bigger species do not 'dance'. The larvae of most species are believed to be predatory, and live in damp soil, leaf-mould, decaying wood; occasionally in water.

DANCE OF BEES. A behaviour pattern of bees which has long been known but which has recently been observed in detail and interpreted by Von Frisch as a 'language' by which in-coming worker bees are able to communicate information regarding direction and distance of food supplies. There are two types of movement known respectively as a 'round dance' (performed when food is close) and a 'wagtail dance' (when food is further away). In the latter case the movement resembles a figure of eight in which the two loops are separated by a straight run. The orientation of this and its frequency are said to give other bees the required information. The dancing of the bees has been studied in great detail but it is known also that some moths, blowflies and beetles perform similar activities.

DARK ARCHES MOTH. *Apamea monoglypha*: a medium sized European noctuid moth usually of a greenish grey colour with paler zig-zag lines. A black (melanic) variety, however, is becoming increasingly common. The larva, a large grey-green caterpillar feeds on grass.

DARKLING BEETLES. Tenebrionidae, also called False Ground Beetles. These insects are usually black, sluggish, nocturnal and mostly vegetarian with short or vestigial wings. The best known species is *Tenebrio molitor* whose larvae are mealworms, pests of flour and other food products. These are bred in large numbers as food for zoo animals and birds.

DARNING NEEDLE (DARNER). Names used in America for some of the larger species of dragonflies. *Anax junius*, the common Green Darner; *Anax walsinghami*, the Giant Darner of California with a wing-span of 12 cm.

DARTER. Any large dragonfly of the family Libellulidae: fat-bodied, broad-winged dragonflies that dart out on brief flights with great speed.

DASYCHIRA. *Dasychira pudibunda*, the Pale Tussock Moth: a medium sized, pale grey noctuid moth of the family Lymantriidae. The larvae are brightly coloured yellow, white and black and are thickly coated with hairs that secrete an irritant substance. They feed on a variety of trees and spin strong silky cocoons among the leaves.

DASYLLIS. A genus of North American Robber Flies (Asilidae) having a rounded hairy body coloured black and gold so that it resembles one of the bumble bees (see *Asilidae*).

DASYMUTILLA. The largest of the 'velvet ants': brightly coloured wasp-like insects of the family Mutillidae. (See *Cow-killer*.)

DASYNEURA. A genus of midges (Cecidomyidae) whose larvae feed on leaves and in some cases produce galls. The Pear Leaf-curling Midge, *Dasyneura pyri*, is sometimes a pest of pear trees.

DASYPODA. A genus of mining bees of the family Melittidae, buff coloured with black abdomen banded with whitish hairs and having very large pollen baskets on the hind-legs. The females burrow into the soil and deposit balls of pollen and honey in which they lay their eggs.

DAYFLY. An alternative name for the mayfly (Ephemeroptera) given on account of the short duration of the adult life.

DEALATION. Loss of wings by ants or other insects. In the case of ants, mating takes place during flight after which the fertilized queen descends and rubs or pulls her wings off. The loss of these appears to stimulate in her an instinct to go below ground and to start laying her eggs.

DEATH FEIGNING. Many insects apparently feign death if disturbed. Stick insects, many beetles, caterpillars and other insects, for instance, immediately become motionless if touched. Some drop from a twig or leaf and lie completely stiff on the ground. Stick insects draw their legs in close to the body and their stillness makes them even more stick-like, giving them a high degree of camouflage by protective resemblance to the plant to which they are attached. In many cases the stimulus for such an action appears to be the loss of contact between the feet and the surface of the substrate.

DEATH'S HEAD MOTH. See *Acherontia*.

DEATH-WATCH BEETLE. *Xestobium rufovillosum*: a small brown wood-boring beetle of the family Anobiidae distinguished by the fact that the pronotum extends forwards and covers the head like a monk's cowl. They do considerable damage by tunnelling into old timber. At mating time they call to each other by tapping on the wood with their heads.

DEBIS. The Pearly Eye: a satyrid butterfly of North America, light brown with three black eye-spots on each fore-wing and five on each hind-wing.

DEBRIS BUG. A predatory bug of the order Heteroptera, family Cimicidae, allied to the bedbug, found among dead leaves, rotting wood etc. *e.g. Xylocoris galactinus*.

DECTICOUS PUPA. An exarate pupa (*i.e.* one with free limbs and other appendages) having powerful mandibles which help the insect to escape from its cell or cocoon.

DEER FLY. See *Chrysops*.

DEFENSIVE SECRETIONS. Many insects produce caustic, irritant or evil-smelling fluids which they discharge as a means of defence. These may be applied by means of a sting which is a modified ovipositor, as in bees and wasps; be irritant secretions from hairs, as in many caterpillars; discharges of formic acid from some ants; blistering chemicals such as *cantharidin* from the beetle *Lytta vesicatoria*; butyric acid from carabid beetles; salicylaldehyde from some leaf-beetles; a poisonous vapour from the Bombardier Beetle and many others.

DEFOLIATORS. Insects that completely strip trees and other plants of their leaves. This may be brought about by large numbers of insects feeding on the leaves, as in the case of the larvae of the Cinnabar Moth, the Gooseberry Sawfly or the Colorado Beetle; or by spreading virus and fungus diseases which cause the leaves to curl up and eventually die, as is the case sometimes when attacked by plant-lice and plant-bugs or beetles.

DEILEPHILA. The Elephant Hawk-moth (*Deilephila elpenor*) and the Small Elephant Hawk-moth (*Deilephila porcellus*) of Britain and the Sphinx Moth and related species of North America. The two British species are medium sized, handsome moths coloured crimson and green. The caterpillars are brownish green with head tapering and resembling an elephant's trunk; they feed chiefly on willow herbs and related plants.

DEILINIA. The White Wave Moth: a geometrid having white wings traversed by a narrow grey wavy line. The larvae feed on alder, birch and sallow.

DEINOCERITES. A genus of mosquitoes that breed in the burrows of marine crabs in Florida and other Southern States.

DEIONE. The Gulf Fritillary: a large nymphalid butterfly of North America, copper coloured with black markings on the upper surface and silvery markings on the underside. The larvae feed on the Passion Plant.

DELIA BRASSICAE. The Onion Fly: a small two-winged fly of the family Anthomyidae. It lays its eggs on young leaves and shoots of onions and the larvae move down to enter and feed on the bulbs.

DELIAS. A genus of large, brightly coloured pierid butterflies found in many parts of the world, particularly in the tropics and subtropics, *e.g. Delias aganippe* of Australia with a wing-span of 70 mm. In some species the larvae are gregarious and feed on mistletoe.

DEMETRIAS. A small light brown European ground beetle (carabid) often found on nettles.

DEMOISELLE. See Damselfly.

DENDROCTONUS. A genus of bark beetles that attack pine, spruce and other conifers in the forests of North America.

DEPORAUS. A genus of leaf-rollers: weevils of the family Attelabiidae that cut and roll leaves in which they lay their eggs. *Deporaus betulae*: the Birch Leaf-roller.

DERMAL GLANDS. Modified epidermal cells or groups of cells on the outer surface of the body that secrete wax, scent, silk, irritant poisons etc. May also be applied to the hypodermal glands that secrete moulting fluid containing enzymes which liquefy the endocuticle prior to moulting.

DERMAPTERA. Earwigs: hemimetabolous insects in which the fore-wings are reduced to small thickened elytra and the membranous hind-wings are roughly semicircular in shape. There is a pair of large forceps at the hind-end of the abdomen. They have biting mouth-parts and are omnivorous; a few wingless species are ectoparasites, particularly on bats in tropical countries. The common European earwig, *Forficula auricularia*, has spread almost all over the world.

DERMATOBIA. The human Bot Fly: a large hairy two-winged fly of the family Cuterebridae, found chiefly in Central America. It is famous for laying its eggs on ticks, mosquitoes or other flies and when these come in contact with man the bot fly larvae are transferred to the latter. They hatch from the warmth of the host's body, bore through the skin and establish themselves in the muscles where they feed and develop. Eggs are also laid on leaves, where they lie until a warm-blooded animal brushes against them.

DERMATOPHILUS. A sedentary flea. See *Chigoe* and *Jigger*.

DERMESTES. The principal genus of Dermestidae (*q.v.*). *Dermestes lardarius*, the Bacon Beetle; *Dermestes maculatus*, the Leather Beetle.

DERMESTIDAE. Skin Beetles: small destructive beetles that feed, both as larvae and adults, on fur, wool, hides and food products such as bacon. The adults are usually dark brown and oval shaped; the larvae are hairy. They can be serious pests in the home or in museums and warehouses. The Hudson's Bay Fur Company at one time offered a reward of £200,000 for an effective means of destroying these beetles.

DESERT LOCUST. *Schistocerca gregaria*: a locust of the dry grasslands of Africa and Asia; related species of the American continent include *Schistocerca paranensis* of South America and *Schistocerca americana* of North America which is non-migratory. *Schistocerca gregaria* arrives in the Punjab district of India during the summer monsoon and breeds there. Then in the autumn it migrates through Iran and Arabia to the Middle East where it meets with others from the African continent. Together they spread through Egypt, Syria, Palestine and Soviet Asia. The migrations of the Desert Locust have lately been shown to follow the movements of low-pressure systems, which provide the rain necessary for the survival of the egg-pods in the soil.

DESMERGATE. An ant intermediate between a soldier and a worker.

DEUTERONOMOS. A genus of European geometrid moths including the Canary-shouldered Thorn Moth, *Deuteronomos alniaria*, a bright yellow moth that closely resembles a shrivelled leaf when the wings are folded; the larvae feed on oak, birch, elder etc.

DEUTEROPHLEBIIDAE. Mountain Midges of Asia, Japan and North America: small two-winged flies, the adults with large, much-folded wings and without mouth-parts. The aquatic larvae live in fast streams. (*cf. Blephaloceridae.*)

DEUTOCEREBRUM. Also called the *Deuterocerebrum* or the *Mesocerebrum*: the middle portion including the antennary lobes in the brain of an insect or other arthropod.

DEVIL'S COACH-HORSE. *Ocypus olens*: a large European beetle of the family Staphylinidae, having very short wing-cases but with long wings that fold underneath. The body is dull black, narrow, pointed at the hind-end and about 3 cm. long. The jaws are large and powerful. When disturbed the beetle adopts a defensive attitude with jaws wide open and the abdomen elevated. It then discharges a strong-smelling liquid from glands at the hind-end.

DEVIL'S DARNING NEEDLE. A name used in America for some of the larger species of dragonflies, *e.g. Anax walsinghami*, the Giant Darner of California with a wing-span of 12 cm.

DEXIOSOMA. A long-legged tachinid fly that lives among bracken; the larva is a parasite in the larvae of cockchafers.

DIABROTICA. Cucumber beetles: a genus of Chrysomelidae or leaf-beetles that feed on cucumber, marrow etc. Adults attack leaves; larvae the roots. They transmit the disease known as 'cucumber wilt'.

DIACRISIA. *Diacrisia virginica*: the Virginian Tiger Moth and related species in Europe. Large moths of the family Arctiidae, having white wings with a few black spots and a yellow abdomen. The caterpillars are hairy and feed on a variety of garden plants.

DIAMPHIDIA. A beetle from which arrow poison is extracted by the bushmen of the Kalahari Desert.

DIAPAUSE. A slowing down of metabolism and delay of development of insects etc. often connected with seasonal changes of atmospheric conditions but sometimes apparently due to an inborn rhythm. It may take the form of normal hibernation, but in some cases the diapause lasts for several years. This is probably due to the fact that the insect fails to produce the normal hormones necessary for continued growth or development. A prolonged diapause may, however, be ended by some sudden shock such as invasion by a parasite.

DIAPHEROMERA. A genus of stick-insects (Phasmidae) that feed chiefly on oak leaves and are widely distributed in North America. Related species in the tropics may attain a length of 25–30 cm.

DIARSIA. *Diarsia brunnea*: the Purple Clay Moth, a noctuid with the fore-wings purplish and the hind-wings grey. The larvae feed on birch, sallow, brambles and many other woodland plants; they pupate below ground.

DIARTHRONOMYIA. The Chrysanthemum Gall-fly: a minute two-winged insect of the family Cecidomyiidae that produces galls on the buds and leaves of chrysanthemums and related flowers.

DIASPIDIDAE. A family of scale-insects that attack many shrubs and trees, sucking the sap and secreting a waxy scale. They include the San José Scale (*Quadraspidiotus perniciosus*), a pest of fruit trees in California and elsewhere.

DIATARAXIA. A genus of noctuid moths, dark brown with a zig-zag white line near the edges of the fore-wings. They lay their eggs on tomato and a number of other plants on which the larvae feed.

DICERCA. A large buprestid beetle of North America, about 25 mm. long, of a shining golden colour with flecks of darker brown. The larvae bore into wood and the adults can often be seen on dead branches of beech, maple etc.

DICRANURA. *Dicranura vinula*: an alternative name for *Cerura vinula*, the Puss Moth (see *Cerura*).

DICTYOPTERA. An order of insects comprising the cockroaches and the mantids. These were formerly included with the grasshoppers and locusts in the order Orthoptera, but there are many points of difference, the chief being the shorter back legs of the Dictyoptera and their inability to jump. For this reason they were previously known as Orthoptera–Cursoria. (See *Blattaria, Blattoidea* and *Mantidae*.)

59

DICYPHUS. *Dicyphus epilobii*: a plant-bug of the order Hemiptera that feeds particularly on the Great Hairy Willow Herb (*Epilobium hirsutum*). The insect has long legs, transparent wings and a pale green body with the eyes and the bases of the antennae red.

DIGGER WASP. A name for a number of wasps that burrow into the ground to make their nests. Most of them belong to the family Sphecidae and are coloured either all black or black with yellow, red and white markings. Generally they catch other insects by stinging and paralysing them; their victims are then taken down into the nests and kept alive as food for the developing larvae.

DILOPHUS FEBRILIS. The Fever Fly: a large black, hairy two-winged fly of the family Bibionidae, very similar to St. Mark's Fly, *Bibio marci* (see *Bibionidae*). The Fever Fly is non-biting and quite unconnected with any human disease, in spite of its name.

DINERGATE. A soldier-ant: a particular caste having the head and jaws greatly enlarged (see *Ant*).

DINGY SKIPPER. *Erynnis tages*: a small European butterfly of the family Hesperiidae, grey-brown with transverse rows of darker patches on the wings and small white spots round the margins. When at rest the wings are laid flat like those of a moth. The larva feeds on Birdsfoot Trefoil (*Lotus corniculatus*).

DINOCRAS. A genus of stoneflies (Plecoptera): primitive hemimetabolous insects having much in common with mayflies, having four large membranous wings, long antennae and two long slender cerci. *Dinocras (Perla) cephalotes* is one of the two largest British stoneflies with a wing-span of about 5 cm.

DIOCTRIA. A genus of Robber Flies of the family Asilidae: two-winged flies with piercing mouth-parts and with long bristly legs. They are common in meadows and hedgerows of Britain where they prey upon ichneumon flies which they somewhat resemble. There are six British species.

DIOPSIDAE. A group of tropical flies having the eyes on the tips of long stalks. They are distinguished from a few stalk-eyed flies of other families by having the antennae, as well as the eyes, out on the stalks.

DIPLOLEPIS. The Robin's Pin-cushion Gall-wasp: a small insect of the group Cynipoidea in the order Hymenoptera. A parasite on rose bushes producing swellings or galls covered with long, branched, reddish hairs.

DIPLOPTERA. A genus of cockroaches in which some of the tracheae have become modified to form glands producing a repellent scent.

DIPLOSIS. *Diplosis (Contarinia) tritici*: the Wheat Midge, a small two-winged gall-fly that has spread from Europe to other countries wherever wheat is grown.

DIPLURA. Bristle-tails: small, white, primitively wingless insects living in the soil. They have a forked tail formed from two long thin cerci and have biting jaws lying in sockets from which they are protruded when feeding.

Diplura come nearest to the probable ancestral type of insect and form a link between insects and millipedes. *Campodea*, one of the Diplura, gives its name to the *campodeiform larva*, an active running form with three pairs of thoracic legs.

DIPRION. A large species of sawfly resembling a bee whose pale green caterpillar-like larvae feed on pine needles. European species were accidentally introduced into North America and became serious pests of forestry.

DIPTERA. Two-winged flies: a large and varied order of holometabolous insects with a single pair of membranous wings and a reduced hind pair modified to form *halteres* or balancers. The mouth-parts are always adapted for sucking, and are often lengthened into a proboscis for piercing and for sucking blood. The larvae are legless and the pupae exarate or co-arctate. There are about 85,000 species of Diptera, many of which transmit diseases to animals and humans either by blood-sucking or by carrying the germs on their bodies.

Diptera are divided into three suborders, *viz.*

(1) *Nematocera*, with filamentous antennae. All the various midges, gnats, mosquitoes, crane-flies etc.

(2) *Brachycera* (properly Brachycera–Orthorrhapha). About fourteen families of such flies as gad-flies (horse-flies), Robber Flies and Bee-flies.

(3) *Cyclorrhapha* (properly Brachycera–Cyclorrhapha). Hover-flies, fruit-flies, blowflies and flies resembling the House Fly.

DIRECTION FINDING. Most insects have a very good sense of direction and are able to find their way either by keeping a constant angle to the sun or to the polarized light of the sky (*e.g.* ants). Bees have much the same ability and also appear to be able to 'memorize' the landmarks of their neighbourhood. The returning bees can communicate information about the distance and direction of food supplies to other bees of the colony by means of their 'dance'. Some insects are guided chiefly by the scent from others. Certain male butterflies, for instance, can fly several miles to the female, using this means. (See *Light-compass Reaction* and *Dance of the Bees*.)

DISEASE, TRANSMISSION OF. Many insects can spread diseases to humans and other animals and to plants. In some cases bacteria, viruses, protozoa, fungal spores etc. may be carried on the feet of an insect or by its mouth-parts. In this way house flies and blowflies can spread diarrhoea and dysentery. In other cases blood-sucking insects can transmit infection by means of the saliva which they discharge into the skin of their victim. Lice can spread typhus; fleas from rats transmit bubonic plague; fleas on rabbits spread myxomatosis; mosquitoes spread malaria, yellow fever, elephantiasis, encephalitis etc.; tsetse flies spread sleeping sickness. In the case of malaria and certain other diseases the organism responsible must spend a certain time in the body of the mosquito where it undergoes some stages of its complex life-cycle. In such cases the carrier is very specific. Certain species of mosquito spread one disease; different species spread another.

Diseases of trees and other plants are usually caused by fungi or viruses and these may be spread by such insects as bark-beetles, aphids, leaf-hoppers and many others.

DISMORPHIA. A genus of pierid butterflies common in Brazil. The wings are narrow and pale yellow, marked with chocolate-brown in the form of thick margins and thick transverse bands and lines following the veins. The abdomen is also dark brown.

DISSOSTEIRA. The Carolina 'locust': a large, long-winged grasshopper common in the southern United States; not a true locust.

DIURNAL RHYTHM. Many insects show a daily rhythm of activity which is apparently in some cases due to a periodic build up of certain hormones. An insect appears to have a sense of time but this is not necessarily the case.

A stimulus may be provided by changes of light, temperature etc. Examples of rhythmic activity are: the glowing of fireflies, some of which will light up every 24 hours, even when kept all the time in the dark; the change of colour of stick insects, light in the daytime and dark at night; the rhythmic timing of the chirping of crickets etc. and the general periodic variations of activity of diurnal and nocturnal insects.

DIVERSICORNIA. An ill-defined group of beetles which include about forty families belonging to the suborder Polyphaga. Beetles of diverse types, which could not easily be put into any more definite classification, were placed in this group for convenience. They included Coccinellidae (ladybirds), Dermestidae (larder beetles) and Elateridae (click beetles). Modern classifications do not recognize this group.

DIVING BEETLE. See *Dytiscidae.*

DIXIDAE. Two-winged insects (Diptera) which resemble mosquitoes but have a smaller proboscis, long slender antennae and have no scales on the wings. Their larvae inhabit shady pools and could be mistaken for those of *Anopheles.*

DIXIPPUS. Also called *Carausius:* a common genus of wingless stick insects (Phasmida) from India and other parts of Asia. *Dixippus morosus* or *Carausius morosus* is frequently bred and used in laboratory experiments, reproduction being parthenogenetic. It feeds principally on the leaves of privet and related plants.

DIZYGOMYZA. A genus of cambium-borers: minute two-winged flies of the family Agromyzidae whose small white larvae bore into willow wood.

DOBSON FLY. See *Corydalis.*

DOG-DAY HARVEST FLY. A name given in the United States to a number of species of large cicadas that appear as adults in late summer and autumn, having started life in the ground two years previously.

DOG-FACE BUTTERFLY. *Colias caesonia:* a pierid butterfly from the Southern States of North America having yellow and black wings; the pattern of the colours on the fore-wings is said to resemble a side view of a dog's head.

DOG, ORANGE. The Orange Dog is a colloquial name in the United States for the caterpillar of the Giant Swallowtail Butterfly, *Papilio thoas,* which feeds on the leaves of citrus trees.

DOLICHONABIS LIMBATUS. The Marsh Damsel Bug: a predatory insect of the order Hemiptera, family Nabidae, that feeds on aphids and other small insects; commonly found in damp meadows.

DOLICHOPODIDAE. Long-legged Flies: a world-wide family of minute predacious two-winged flies that prey upon smaller insects. They are slender, usually black or greenish insects with long legs and with a habit of standing with the head and thorax raised. The larvae are either aquatic or dwell in wet mud or rotting vegetation.

DOLICHOVESPULA. A genus of wasps of the family Vespidae: *Dolichovespula maculata,* the White-faced Hornet, is a large black and white species of North America that builds its paper-like nest·in lilac and fruit trees. Similar species are to be found in Europe.

DOLYCORIS. The Sloe Bug: a large green shieldbug that lives and feeds on sloes, plums and related *Prunus* trees.

DONACIINAE. Reed Beetles: long narrow beetles with long antennae, having the body and wing-cases usually of a metallic green colour and with their undersides covered with dense silky hairs that repel water. They live among water plants, flying from one to another; their aquatic larvae breathe by embedding the tail spiracles into the stems of reeds.

DOODLE BUG. An American name for the Ant-lion (*q.v.*).

DOR BEETLE. A name given to a number of large, black or shining blue dung-beetles of the family Scarabaeidae, particularly *Geotrupes stercorarius*, a robust beetle that flies with a droning sound. These beetles burrow into the ground and take down a ball of dung in which they lay their eggs.

DORCUS. The Lesser Stag Beetle: a medium sized, elongated black beetle of the family Lucanidae, having large jaws; a nocturnal insect found in rotting wood, particularly beech, ash and elm on which the larvae feed.

DORITIS. A medium sized papilionid butterfly found in the mountains of Turkey and the Balkans; pale yellow with mauve body and mauve-bordered wings.

DORMANCY. See *Diapause*.

DORYLINAE. Tropical Driver Ants that build no nests, march through the jungle in a long line foraging on either side and, when not marching, bivouac in large numbers. They will swarm through native villages cleaning them up completely, feeding on all kinds of spiders, cockroaches etc. and will completely devour the bodies of dead animals. They can kill small mammals if these are not able to escape.

DOT MOTH. *Melanchra persicariae*: a European noctuid moth having the fore-wings dark grey or black with a conspicuous white spot on each; the hind-wings are a lighter grey. The larvae feed on Persicaria and a number of other plants.

DOTTED BORDER MOTH. *Erannis marginaria*: a geometrid moth having greenish-grey wings with a broad brown transverse band and a row of brown dots along the edges of all four wings of the male. The wings of the female are small and functionless. The caterpillar, a looper or geometer, resembles a short green twig.

DOUBLE DART MOTH. *Noctua augur*: a common noctuid moth having the fore-wings greyish-brown, marked with two dark brown or black wavy transverse lines and a dark ring-like mark between them. The hind-wings are a lighter grey and unmarked. The larvae feed on sloes and hawthorn.

DOWNY EMERALD DRAGONFLY. *Cordulia aenea*: a medium sized dragonfly of the group Anisoptera having the body, head and eyes of a brilliant green; yellow-green patches at the bases of the wings and dense yellow hair on the thorax.

DRAGONFLY. Any member of the order Odonata: large hemimetabolous insects with long brightly coloured bodies and two pairs of membranous wings with numerous cross-veins. The jaws are large and powerful for seizing small insects in flight; the eyes are very well developed but the antennae are small. The aquatic nymph or larva is predatory and is characterized by an elongated, and extensible, prehensile labium forming the so-called *mask*.

Dragonflies are closely related to the *Protodonata* which are found as Palaeozoic fossils and sometimes attained great size with a wing expanse exceeding 60 cm. Present day dragonflies are divided into two suborders, *viz.* Anisoptera or true dragonflies and Zygoptera or damselflies (see *Anisoptera* and *Zygoptera*).

DRAGONFLY, EMPEROR. *Anax imperator*: one of the largest European dragonflies with a wing-span of about 10 cm., having a greenish yellow body with a median black stripe down the back, a bluish thorax and bright blue eyes.

DREPANIDAE. Hook-tips: a family of moths in which the tips of the fore-wings are turned back to make a blunt hook. The caterpillars are without claspers and are hump-backed with warts and swellings on the skin. They rest with the head and tail directed upwards.

DRILUS. A genus of thin elongated beetles related to the Cantharidae (Soldier Beetles). The males have a normal beetle structure but the females are wingless and worm-like. They feed on snails and then pupate in the empty shell.

DRINKER MOTH. *Philudoria potatoria*: a medium sized moth of the Eggar group (Lasiocampidae) having a fat reddish brown body with wings of the same colour and two silvery white marks on the fore-wings; the antennae are large and comb-like and the tongue is poorly developed. The large, brown, hairy caterpillars are to be found on grasses and reeds; they have a habit of drinking the dew.

DRIVER ANT. See *Dorylinae*.

DRONES. Male bees that develop by parthenogenesis, *i.e.* from unfertilized eggs. They are somewhat larger than workers and have a broader head and large eyes. Their life is short, as they either die soon after mating or are killed by the others at the beginning of winter.

DRONE FLY. *Eristalis* and related genera of hover-flies (Syrphidae): two-winged flies closely resembling bees not only in their appearance but also in their habit of feeding on pollen and nectar. White eggs are laid on the edges of ponds and these hatch into larvae known as *rat-tailed maggots*. They are legless and can swim freely or may rest on the bottom, breathing through the 'tail'. Although the maggot is less than 2 cm. long, the 'tail' containing two tracheae may, when extended, be as much as 15 cm.

DROSOPHILIDAE. A family of small two-winged fruit-flies that feed on fruit juices, vinegar, beer, wines etc. They are to be found breeding prolifically in decaying fruit. *Drosophila melanogaster* is the well known fruit-fly used extensively for genetic experiments for which it is most suitable on account of its short life-cycle, large chromosomes and great number of easily recognizable hereditary variations, as well as its readiness to breed indefinitely in jars in the laboratory.

DRYOBOTODES. *Dryobotodes eremita*, the Brindled Green: a medium sized, European noctuid moth having greenish wings with black and brown markings. The grey-green caterpillars feed on oak leaves.

DRYOCOETES. A genus of small brown wood-boring beetles that tunnel beneath the bark, usually in dying or felled trees. *Dryocoetes villosus* is found in oak and sweet chestnut; *Dryocoetes autographus* in spruce and other conifers.

DRYOPIDAE. A family of small water beetles about 5 mm. long covered with hydrofuge hairs; they live most of the time in water, feeding on micro-algae, but may fly out at night.

DUFOUR'S GLAND. See *Alkaline Gland*.

DUKE OF BURGUNDY FRITILLARY. *Hamearis lucina*: a European butterfly of the family Riodinidae, not closely related to the other fritillaries. It is small and dark brown with three rows of yellowish spots across each fore-wing. The caterpillar is short and fat, resembling a wood-louse and feeds on primrose and cowslip leaves.

DULOSIS. Slavery among ants: the brown ant, for instance, living in the same nest and working for the red.

DUMBLE DOR. *Geotrupes stercorarius* (see *Dor Beetle*).

DUN. The sub-imago of a mayfly (Ephemeroptera): a stage immediately following the last moult of the aquatic nymph, but preceding the final adult stage. It is winged and resembles the adult in size and shape. It is, however, of a dull brown colour. It casts its skin off almost immediately and reveals the brightly coloured, shining adult which, being unable to feed, lives only for a few hours or a day.

DUN-BAR MOTH. *Cosmia trapezina*: a small, light brown noctuid moth with green caterpillars which are notorious for their cannibalistic habits. Although they feed on the foliage of many trees, they will if hungry readily attack and eat each other.

DUNG BEETLE. A name for a number of beetles whose larvae feed on dung. Some species lay their eggs in animal dung; others take balls of it down into underground burrows (see also *Dor Beetle*).

DUNG FLY. *Scatophaga stercoraria*: a yellowish two-winged fly of the group Cyclorrhapha with very hairy males, often found frequenting dung heaps in large numbers. Here the eggs are laid and the larvae feed. They afterwards pupate in the soil. The adults suck nectar but will also kill and suck the juices from other insects.

DUOMITUS LEUCONOTUS. The Beehole Borer: a moth of the family Cossidae (goat-moths) whose larva bores holes in teak and other hard woods, particularly in India.

DYAR'S RULE. An empirical law based on the observation that the head capsule and certain other parts of caterpillars grow in geometric progression, increasing in size by a constant ratio at each moult. Thus if the logarithm of the size of the head is plotted against the number of the instar, the resulting graph will be a straight line. Although not always accurate, this rule has sometimes been of use in deducing facts about the life history of an insect in cases where other information is lacking, especially indicating when one instar has been overlooked.

DYNASTIDAE. A family of very large beetles some of which are armed with large 'horns' or protuberances extending forwards from the thorax. *Dynastes hercules*: the Hercules Beetle of Central and South America may be up to 15 cm. long. The male has a large 'horn' curving forwards and downwards and another curving upwards to meet it. *Dynastes tityus*, the Unicorn Beetle of North America is about half this size and is greenish grey, spotted with brown. It has a single large thoracic horn and two smaller ones.

DYNATOSOMA. A genus of fungus gnats of the family Mycetophilidae: small insects with thread-like antennae and a hump-backed thorax. The larvae of some species, small white maggots, feed on bracket-fungi growing on trees.

DYSDERCUS. See *Cotton Stainer*.

DYSSTROMA. The Marbled Carpet Moth: a small moth of the group Geometridae whose wings are marbled in patterns of white, green and black. The caterpillars, which are loopers, are green and stick-like and feed on hawthorn, birch and a number of other plants.

DYTISCIDAE. Large water-beetles: a family of aquatic carnivorous beetles, most of them with a large oval body and powerful back legs which are flattened and fringed with bristles for swimming. When submerged they carry a store of air beneath the wing-covers. The male is distinguished by the broadened front tarsi which form cup-like suckers for gripping the female when mating. *Dytiscus marginalis*, the Great Diving Beetle, about 35 mm. long, is the best known European member of the family.

E

EARED LEAF-HOPPER. *Ledra aurita*: the largest of the British leaf-hoppers (Cicadellidae), greyish green, about 15 mm. long, having a flattened body with two ear-like projections from the thorax. It is to be found actively leaping on lichen-covered oak trees.

EARIAS. *Earias clorana*, the Cream-bordered Green Pea Moth: a small noctuid moth having white hind-wings and pea-green fore-wings with cream coloured front borders. The larvae feed on the leaves of osiers and willows. Other species of *Earias* are to be found in Africa, Asia and Australasia where they are pests of the cotton plant.

EARLY BROWN. *Protonemoura meyeri*: a common European stonefly (Plecoptera) found near water in the early spring.

EARLY GREY MOTH. *Xylocampa areola*: a small dark grey European noctuid moth with whitish patterns on the fore-wings; the larvae feed on honeysuckle (*Lonicera*).

EARLY HUMBLE-BEE. *Bombus pratorum*: a relatively small species of humble-bee, black with a red tail, a greyish yellow band on the thorax and a thin band of the same colour on the abdomen. The nest is usually below ground. In Britain this bee is the earliest to appear in the spring.

EARLY MOTH. *Theria rupicapraria*: a small brown European geometrid moth to be found in winter or early spring on hawthorn and other hedgerow shrubs. The females have reduced wings.

EARLY SHOOT-BORER. *Chilotraca infuscatella*: a moth of the family Pyralidae whose larva attacks young shoots and seedlings of sugar cane in India.

EARLY THORN. *Selenia bilunaria*: a European geometrid moth with brown stick-like larvae that feed on blackthorn, hawthorn and other shrubs. The adults have yellow-and buff-coloured wings, ragged or serrated at the edges. In Britain there are two broods a year, the later summer ones being smaller and paler than those of the spring; there is also a melanic variety.

EAR MOTH. *Hydraecia nictitans*: a medium sized European moth with reddish brown fore-wings having a prominent pale ear-shaped spot; the hind-wings are pale grey. The caterpillars feed on the roots of grass.

EAROPHILA. *Earophila badiata*, the Shoulder-stripe Moth: a medium sized, reddish brown geometrid moth having a prominent dark curved line near the base of each fore-wing; the larvae feed on the leaves of wild roses.

EARWIG. Any member of the order Dermaptera, the best-known being *Forficula auricularia* which has spread from Europe to most parts of the world. They are hemimetabolous insects in which the fore-wings are reduced to small thickened elytra and the membranous hind-wings are roughly semi-circular. There is a large forceps at the hind-end of the abdomen. They have biting mouth-parts and are generally omnivorous scavengers but will occasion-ally attack other insects; a few wingless forms are ectoparasites.

EBURIA. A genus of wood-boring beetles that attack ash, hickory, locust and other North American trees. They are remarkable for the long life of the larvae; that of *Eburia quadrigeminata* has been known to remain alive in dry wood for forty years.

ECDYONURUS. A genus of large mayflies (Ephemeroptera) whose larvae are found in fast running streams. They are well adapted to this habitat by having flattened bodies and long legs with large claws which enable them to cling to rocks etc.

ECDYSIAL FLUID. Moulting fluid: a liquid secreted by glands in the epider-mis of an insect, having the function of dissolving away the endocuticle by enzyme action. In this way the exocuticle and the epicuticle, which together form the hard outer part of the exoskeleton, are loosened prior to being shed when the insect moults.

ECDYSIS. A periodic shedding of the hard outer cuticle or exoskeleton of an insect. Generally this takes place a definite number of times during the larval stage and, in holometabolous insects, once more when the adult emerges from the pupa. This enables the insect to grow rapidly after each moult before the new cuticle hardens. The stages between each moult and the next are known as *instars*.

The process of ecdysis is initiated by a hormone apparently secreted by the *thoracic glands* which lie behind the brain and close to the oesophagus. The action of this hormone, or possibly of several hormones, is to stimulate the secretion of moulting fluid from glands in the epidermis. This fluid dissolves away the endocuticle, loosening the harder exocuticle and epicuticle which together form the outer layer of the exoskeleton. The insect then contracts its abdominal muscles, increases the blood pressure in the thorax and causes the cuticle to split in the weakest part, usually the mid-dorsal line. The insect emerges leaving the cast-off skin or *exuviae* behind. After a period of growth a new cuticle is formed.

ECDYSON. A name given to the principal moulting hormone of insects (see *Ecdysis*).

ECHIDNOPHAGA. The Stick-tight Flea: a pest of poultry in tropical and subtropical countries; also sometimes found on other birds and mammals. Generally it attaches itself to the bare parts of the skin of a bird, *i.e.* the comb and wattles and around the anus and eyes. The females bury their heads in the skin causing ulcerated swellings in which the eggs are laid and hatch. The larvae fall to the ground and infect other birds.

ECHINOMYIA GROSSA. The Hedgehog Fly: a two-winged fly of the family Tachinidae having roughly the size and appearance of a bumble bee with bristly hairs. Its larvae are parasites in the caterpillars of larger moths such as the Oak Eggar.

ECHINOPHTHIRIUS (ECHINOPHTHIRUS). A blood-sucking louse of the order Anoplura, parasitic on seals.

ECITON. A genus of tropical Driver Ants that live in temporary nests and migrate in long lines like an army. They are carnivorous and predatory and among them are large numbers of the 'soldier' caste with greatly enlarged mouth-parts. One of the best known species is the Peruvian Driver Ant, *Eciton rapax*, light yellowish brown and about 15 mm. long. Armies of at least 100,000 of these will march together attacking every living thing in their path.

ECLOSION. The emergence of an insect from the pupa or from the cocoon or puparium. In the case of a simple pupa, the cuticle is loosened by softening of the endocuticle (see *Ecdysis*); it then splits at the weakest part and the insect wriggles out. If the pupa is surrounded by a silken cocoon the insect may gnaw its way out or may use spines to split the silk or in some cases may secrete a liquid which dissolves the silk. In the case of the house fly and similar insects in which the pupa is surrounded by a capsule or puparium made from the cast-off skin of the last larval stage, the insect uses a *ptilinum* or bladder-like swelling on the head for pushing open one end.

ECTADENIA. Accessory glands arising from the ectoderm of the male's ejaculatory duct in some insects and other invertebrates.

ECTOBIUS. A genus of small European woodland cockroaches varying in colour from grey to brown, 10–12 mm. long, some with short or vestigial wings. Dusky Cockroach, *Ectobius lapponicus*; Tawny Cockroach, *Ectobius pallidus*; Lesser Cockroach, *Ectobius panzeri*.

ECTOGNATHOUS. Having the mouth-parts projecting outwards and well developed (*cf. Entognathous*). A distinction particularly important in studying relationships between insects and other arthropods. Among Apterygote insects, Thysanura are ectognathous whereas Diplura, Protura and Collembola are entognathous.

ECTOPARASITES. Parasites that live on the outside of their hosts or near the outside, as for instance in the mouth or rectum. They include sucking lice (Anoplura), fleas (Siphonaptera), louse-flies (Hippoboscidae) and bedbugs (Hemiptera). All these have specially adapted mouth-parts for piercing the skin of the host in order to suck blood; their saliva contains an anticoagulant. Other ectoparasites include such insects as the biting lice (Mallophaga) which do not suck blood but feed on hair, feathers etc., and many others. Nearly all ectoparasites live on their own particular host-species and will not generally survive for long on any other.

ECTROPIS. See *Engrailed Moth*.

ECTYPA. See *Burnet Companion*.

EGG. The eggs of insects are very variable. Essentially they consist of a nucleus and a mass of yolk, the latter being within the meshes of the central protoplasm a state known as *centrolecithal*. This is surrounded by a thin *vitelline membrane*, and outside this a relatively thick outer shell or *chorion* secreted by the ovarian follicle, sometimes with a wax layer in between. Small holes or micropyles permit a sperm cell to enter. The eggs of most flies have only a simple micropyle at one end, but locusts and grasshoppers may have 30–40. The size of insects' eggs ranges from 0.15 mm. in some midges to 3 mm. in the larger moths. The most obvious variations are in the shape, colour and structure of the chorion which may have a most complicated structure revealed by the electron microscope. The egg may be spherical, elliptical, conical or cylindrical; smooth, ridged or spiny; sometimes surrounded by a glue-like substance for attachment to leaves; sometimes having silken threads or filaments as in the lacewing flies; sometimes fastened together to form a floating raft as in some mosquitoes. The number of eggs is in some cases very large; a queen termite, for instance, may lay a million during her life.

EGGAR MOTHS. Lasiocampidae: a family of medium or large, reddish brown moths having a stoutly built body and prominent comb-like antennae, but with the tongue reduced or absent. The caterpillars are brown and hairy. The best known British members of this family are the Oak Eggar, *Lasiocampus quercus*; the Drinker, *Philudoria potatoria* and the Lappet, *Gastropacha quercifolia*.

EGG BURSTER. A set of hard spines or ridges on the head of an embryo insect, used for breaking open the egg-shell when hatching. The Colorado Beetle larva, for instance, has three pairs of spines; the embryo flea has a knife-like projection.

EIGHT-SPOTTED PACHYTA. *Pachyta cerambyciformes*: a long-bodied beetle, broad in front and narrow behind, dingy yellow with eight black spots, and covered with fine grey hairs; common on umbelliferous flowers.

ELAPHRAS. A genus of small greenish black ground-beetles (Carabidae), fast running, common on the muddy edges of ponds and streams.

ELASMOSTETHUS. A genus of Birch Shieldbugs: medium sized greenish grey pentatomid bugs; plant-sucking insects of the group Heteroptera having a green triangular dorsal shield or scutellum formed from the enlarged tergum of the mesothorax.

   The female lays her eggs on the undersides of birch leaves and protects them with her body after the young have hatched. This she continues to do for some time, an example of maternal care unusual in insects.

ELASMUCHA. *Elasmucha grisea*, sometimes called *Elasmostethus griseus*, the Grey Shieldbug (see *Elasmostethus*).

ELATER. A name sometimes used for any beetle belonging to the family Elateridae (Click Beetles), but strictly applicable only to the genus, typical of the family Elateridae.

ELATERIDAE. Click Beetles: a family named on account of their habit of springing into the air with a clicking sound when placed on their backs. The larvae are well known as wireworms, agricultural pests living in the soil and attacking roots.

ELATERIFORM LARVA. A larva resembling a wireworm or mealworm, cylindrical with a tough skin, short legs and biting mouth-parts. They are found in the Elateridae (Click Beetles), Tenebrionidae and several other families.

ELATOBIA. An alternative name for *Tineola*, the common genus of clothes moths.

ELENCHUS. A minute insect of the order Strepsiptera, living as a parasite in some species of cicadas.

ELEODES. A genus of large black nocturnal beetles of North America, belonging to the family Tenebrionidae. They are herbivorous and may be very destructive to crops. When disturbed they feign death by standing motionless with head down.

ELEPHANT BEETLE. A name given to a number of very large beetles of the family Dynastidae from the tropics of Central and South America. They have a trunk-like 'horn' projecting forwards from the thorax and two smaller 'horns' resembling tusks. The largest is *Megasoma*, up to 10 cm. long with a wing-span of 20 cm.

ELEPHANT BUG. A colloquial American name for a weevil.

ELEPHANT HAWK-MOTH. See *Deilephila*.

ELEPHANT LOUSE. *Haematomyzus elephantis*, a single species of Mallophaga (biting lice), found on both Indian and African elephants. The head is prolonged into a rostrum with mandibles at its apex. This one species constitutes the suborder Rhynchophthirina.

ELEPHANTOLOEMUS INDICUS. A warble fly that attacks the Indian Elephant and is a serious pest among domesticated herds in India, Burma, Malaysia etc. Like the warble flies of cattle it lays its eggs on vulnerable parts of the skin; the larvae eat their way in, perforate the tissues and eventually emerge forming ulcerous swellings and perforations.

ELM BARK BEETLE. *Scolytus destructor*, the Large Elm Bark Beetle, *Scolytus multistriatus*, the Small Elm Bark Beetle and others of the family Scolytidae; weevils adapted for burrowing in wood. The typical snout of the weevil is short or absent; the head is bent under the thorax and the legs are short and thin. They are very destructive to elm and other trees, tunnelling beneath the bark and making longitudinal galleries with numerous lateral branches in which the larvae live. More serious than the physical damage caused by the tunnels is the destructive effect of *Ceratocystis ulmi*, a fungus introduced by the beetle (Dutch Elm Disease).

ELM BORER. A name for a number of beetles that bore into elm trees, particularly those of the Cerambycidae (*q.v.*) and Scolytidae (see *Elm Bark Beetle*).

ELM COCKSCOMB GALL FLY. *Colopha ulmicola*: a small plant-bug of the group Homoptera that attacks elm leaves, first feeding on the upper surface, later causing the leaf to fold inwards and produce a pocket in which the insect feeds.

ELM GALL BUG. *Anthocoris gallarum-ulmi*: a plant-bug of the group Heteroptera that lives in the curled leaf infected by the aphis *Eriosoma*.

ELM LEAF BEETLE. *Galerucella xanthomelaena*: a small yellowish beetle of the family Chrysomelidae that feeds on elm leaves both as a larva and as an adult insect. It may completely defoliate a tree. Originally European it has spread to America and elsewhere. Related species attack willow and other trees.

ELM LEAF MINER. *Agromyza aristata*: a minute cambium borer, one of the Diptera whose small white larvae burrow into the leaves and young shoots of elm and other trees.

ELM SAWFLY. *Kaliofenusa ulmi*: a minute leaf-mining sawfly, originally European, which has now spread to America and elsewhere and does considerable damage to elm trees. Sometimes twenty or thirty larvae mine into a single leaf and their tunnels merge to form a single large cavity occupying nearly all the interior of the leaf.

ELM SCALE. *Eriococcus spurius*: a scale-insect of the family Kermidae in the order Homoptera, hemispherical and covered with cottony wax; a common pest of elm trees in Europe and America (see *Coccidae*).

ELMIDAE. A family of small water beetles, 3–4 mm. long that do not normally swim but crawl about on pondweeds, feeding on these and on plant debris. The body is covered by numerous bent hydrofuge hairs that enable the insect to take air down for breathing.

ELOPHILA. A genus of moths whose aquatic caterpillars, supplied with numerous blood gills, live in submerged silken 'tents' attached to rocks or on the bottom of a stream.

ELYMNIAS. *Elymnias hypermnestra*: a butterfly of the family Satyridae, found in Africa, Asia and Australia, whose larvae feed on palm leaves. It is specially notable for the great number of variations of colour and pattern and for its mimicry of other butterflies.

ELYTRA. Thickened horny fore-wings of beetles etc., covering and protecting the membranous hind-wings. In a few species of beetle, whose flying wings are reduced or absent, the elytra are cemented together down the middle line.

EMATURGA. *Ematurga atomaria*, the Common Heath Moth: a small European geometrid moth, grey-brown with a number of curved bands of dark brown; the males are larger and darker than the females and have feathery antennae. The small twig-like caterpillars feed chiefly on heather and leguminous plants of heaths and moors.

EMBIIDINA. See *Embioptera*.

EMBIOPTERA. A small and rather uncommon order of hemimetabolous insects with soft, elongated, flattened bodies; the males have two pairs of wings but the females are wingless. They are social insects living in silken tunnels beneath stones or under bark. The silk is produced from glands in the front legs of both sexes, nymphs as well as adults.

EMBOLIUM. The costal region of the *hemelytron* or horny basal half of the wing in certain Heteroptera (plant-bugs).

EMERALD MOTH. A name for two geometrid moths, *viz.* the Large Emerald Moth *Geometra papilionacea* and the Light Emerald, *Campaea margaritata*. The former is bright green and is to be found chiefly on birch, hazel and beech; the latter is paler and is found on a variety of trees. The caterpillars are greenish brown and stick-like, but those of the Large Emerald become much greener as they become older.

EMESA. Spider bugs: a genus of predatory bugs with long thread-like legs; they belong to the family Ploiariidae.

EMPEROR DRAGONFLY. *Anax imperator*: the largest of the British dragonflies with a wing-span of about 10 cm. The colour is blue-green with a black stripe down the centre of the abdomen; the head and eyes are bright blue (see also *Anax*).

EMPEROR MOTH. *Saturnia pavonia*: a large hawk-moth, the only British member of the family Saturniidae which includes the Atlas Moth and other large silk-moths of tropical countries. The Emperor Moth is pale purplish grey with a very conspicuous dark circular eyespot surrounded by white on each wing. The caterpillar is bright green with rings of black; it feeds chiefly on

71

heather and pupates within a brown silky cocoon. This moth is sometimes called the Lesser Emperor Moth to distinguish it from the Greater or Viennese Emperor Moth *Saturnia pyri* which has similar markings but is about twice as large.

EMPICORIS. A predatory Assassin Bug of the order Hemiptera, family Reduviidae, elongated and resembling a gnat. The middle and hind-legs are long and thin but the front legs are shorter, strong and prehensile and are used for seizing flying insects. It inhabits European forests but is also sometimes found in houses and stables where it is a useful pest-controller.

EMPIDIDAE. Empid flies: small carnivorous two-winged flies, some of which have interesting mating habits. The male kills a small insect, wraps it up in silk thread and presents it to the female. While she is unravelling it and feeding on it, copulation takes place. The significance of this is not understood and there have been various fanciful and speculative explanations.

EMPOASCA. A genus of leaf-hoppers of the family Cicadellidae, about 4 mm. long, very common on a great many plants which they damage by their toxic saliva causing 'leaf-burn'. *Empoasca flavescenes* causes yellow-brown marks on vine leaves; it also attacks forest and fruit trees. *Empoasca fabae* attacks beans, potatoes, apples etc. *Empoasca alfalfae* on lucerne (alfalfa).

EMPODIUM. A median bristle between the two claws on the feet of Diptera.

EMPUSA. *Empusa fasciata*: a Praying Mantis from Southern Europe, about 7 cm. long (see *Mantidae*).

EMUS, HAIRY. *Emus hirtus*: a European beetle of the family Staphylinidae (*i.e.* with very short elytra), having a black body with golden hairs on the head, thorax and part of the abdomen and having a grey band of fine hairs on each elytron; found on or near farmyard dung.

ENALLAGMA. *Enallagma cyathigerum*: the common blue damselfly. The male is entirely bright blue; the female grey-green and black with a spine below the eighth abdominal segment. They lay their eggs in plant stems under water. The nymphs are slender and of variable colour (see *Damselfly*).

ENCARSIA. *Encarsia formosa*: a minute parasitic Chalcid wasp used to control the Tomato Whitefly *Trialeurodes vaporariorum*.

ENCHIRINAE. A group of large beetles from South-east Asia in which the males have the front legs remarkably long and thick with a number of projecting spines making movement extremely clumsy. They feed on the fermenting juices of palm trees. *Propomacrus jansoni*, a member of this family from China is about 60 mm. long.

ENCOPTOLOPHUS. *Encoptolophus sordidus*: the Clouded Locust of the eastern United States, a common insect in those parts. When in flight the males make a loud crackling sound said to be like burning stubble.

ENCYRTIDAE. A family of minute parasitic wasps that lay their eggs in the bodies of many other insects.

ENDALUS. A genus of aquatic weevils that feed on pondweeds.

ENDERLEINELLUS. A genus of blood-sucking lice (Anoplura) that parasitize squirrels.

ENDOCHORION. The inner layer of the chorion or shell of an insect's egg.

ENDOCUTICLE. The flexible inner layer of the cuticle of an insect or other arthropod, composed of chitin and proteins. During moulting this layer is digested away by enzymes from special epidermal glands. It thus leaves the outer layers of cuticle loose and ready to be cast off (see *Ecdysis*).

ENDOMYCHIDAE. A family of beetles of which the Ladybird Mimic, *Endomychus coccineus* is typical: small beetles, orange or red with black spots but differing from ladybirds in having long, thin, unclubbed antennae.

ENDOPARASITES. Insects that parasitize animals are usually *ectoparasites* or external parasites such as fleas, lice and bugs. There are, however, a number of insects whose larvae live as *endoparasites* or internal parasites. Usually they leave the host before pupation and the adult is non-parasitic. In such cases a new host is infected either by the eggs being laid under its skin; by larvae entering through the skin and penetrating the tissues, or by the host swallowing the eggs or larvae. Endoparasites of humans and other vertebrates are usually larvae of Diptera such as the warble fly or bot fly; infestation by these is known as *myiasis*. Parasites that live in the bodies of other insects are usually the larvae of small Hymenoptera such as chalcid wasps and ichneumon flies and some diptera, mainly Tachinidae. These can sometimes be used as a means of controlling pests of agriculture or horticulture. Many of them are *hyperparasites*, *i.e.* they live in the bodies of other parasitic insects (see also *Bot Fly* and *Chalcidoidea*).

ENDOPLEURITES. Y-shaped ingrowths of cuticle from the sides of the thorax, forming part of the internal or endophragmal skeleton of arthropods. In the wing-bearing segments of insects, these form the pleural ridge which supports the wing above and articulates with the coxa of the leg below.

ENDOPTERYGOTA. Insects in which the wings are developed internally until the final moult (*cf. Exopterygota*). They are also called *Holometabola*, a name indicating that there is always complete metamorphosis involving a pupal stage. Nine orders are included in this group (see *Holometabola*).

ENDOSTERNITES. Apodemes or ingrowths from the ventral cuticular plates of an insect or other arthropod. They form part of the endophragmal skeleton to which important muscles are attached.

ENDROMIS (ENDROMIDIDAE). *Endromis versicolora*: the Kentish Glory, a large forest-dwelling moth of the group Bombycoidea, now rare in Britain but ranging across Europe as far as Siberia. The male is rust-brown with a black and white pattern on the fore-wings; the female is paler. While the latter spend most of their time immobile on tree trunks, the males may fly long distances by day in large numbers seeking the females by their scent. The caterpillars, which are green with oblique white stripes, feed on birch, hazel, beech and lime.

ENDROSIS. *Endrosis sarcitrella*: the White-shouldered House Moth, a small grey-brown moth with the head and the front of the thorax white; a night-flying insect whose larvae are scavengers feeding on all kinds of animal and vegetable refuse as well as on clothes etc.

ENEMA. *Enema pan*, the Brazilian Rhinoceros Beetle: a large beetle about 5 cm. long, dark brown and shiny, belonging to the family Dynastidae. The males are characterized by a very long 'horn' (about 2 cm. long) projecting upwards from the front of the thorax.

ENGRAILED MOTH. *Ectropis biundulata*: a medium sized geometrid moth, common in Britain and Europe, having pale grey wings with a complicated pattern of brown. The larvae feed on oak and other trees and the adults rest by day on the bark where they are well camouflaged.

ENGRAVER BEETLE. See *Bark Beetle*.

ENNOMINAE. A subfamily of geometrid moths whose larvae generally resemble sticks or twigs. They include the Magpie, Emerald, Swallowtail, Brimstone and a large number of other well known moths; in some, such as the Early Moth *Theria* and the Umber Moth *Erannis*, the females are wingless.

ENNOMOS. *Ennomos autumnaria*: the Large Thorn Moth whose stick-like caterpillars feed on hawthorn and are remarkably well camouflaged (see *Ennominae*).

ENOICYLA. A genus of small caddis flies (Trichoptera) differing from most others in having wingless females and terrestrial larvae. The latter live in damp moss or grass and make tubular cases of sand grains etc.

ENOPLOCERUS. *Enoplocerus armillatus*: a longhorn beetle from Peru about 12 cm. long, brown with sharp red thorn-like projections on the sides of the thoracic shield.

ENSIFERA. Long-horned grasshoppers, crickets and mole-crickets: a suborder of Orthoptera having very long antennae (see *Gryllidae*, *Gryllotalpidae* and *Tettigoniidae*).

ENTEROMYIASIS. Infection of the intestines by the larvae of flies (see *Bot Fly* and *Warble Fly*).

ENTIMUS. *Entimus imperialis*: a large green weevil from Brazil, about 3 cm. long. The genus also includes other related species known as Diamond Beetles, notable for showing a brilliant variety of iridescent colours due to optical interference.

ENTOGNATHOUS. Having the mouth-parts in pockets from which they can be protruded when feeding (*cf. Ectognathous*).

ENTOMOBRYA. A genus of springtails (Collembola) that feed chiefly on fungi.

ENTOMOPHAGOUS. A term used to denote any animals that feed chiefly on insects; insectivorous.

ENTOMOPHILY. Pollination of flowers by insects.

EOSENTOMON. The only genus in the primitive order Protura that possesses a tracheal system (see *Protura*).

EPHEMERA. The largest and best known of the European mayflies from which the order Ephemeroptera takes its name. *Ephemera danica*, the 'Green Drake' and *Ephemera vulgata*, a similar large species (see *Ephemeroptera*).

EPHEMEROPTERA (EPHEMERIDA, EPHEMEROIDEA). Mayflies: a primitive order of insects having four membranous wings of which the front pair is considerably larger than the hind-pair. The veins of the wings are in the form of a simple network like that of the dragonfly. The eyes are large and the antennae short; at the hind-end are three long tail filaments. The larvae or nymphs are aquatic and herbivorous; they may live for several years in a pond or stream before metamorphosis. There is no pupa, but the first winged stage, known as the *sub-imago* or 'dun', resembles the adult in size and shape. It is, however, of a dull brown colour. This casts its skin off almost immediately and reveals the brightly coloured shining adult or 'spinner' which, being unable to feed, lives only for a few hours or a day.

EPHESTIA. A genus of small moths (Microlepidoptera) whose larvae are common pests of food products. They include the Mediterranean Flour Moth

Ephestia kuhniella, the Fig Moth *Ephestia cautella* which attacks dried fruit in Australia and California and cocoa beans in West Africa, the Tobacco Moth *Ephestia elutella* and many others.

EPHIALTES. A genus of large black and brown Ichneumon flies, up to 3 cm. long. *Ephialtes imperator*, a Central European species, develops as a larva in the body of the Capricorn Beetle *Ergates*.

EPHIPPIGER. The Saddle-backed Grasshopper: an insect of southern and central Europe, one of the long-horned grasshoppers (Tettigoniidae), with very short wings and with the upper side of the thorax arched into a saddle-shape.

EPHORON. A genus of mayflies (Ephemeroptera) whose nymphs burrow into the mud at the bottom of ponds and streams.

EPHYDRIDAE. Shore-flies: a family of predatory Diptera living near salt marshes or brackish ponds in Europe, Asia and North America. They capture small gnats and mosquitoes by means of bristles or spines on the front legs. The larvae of some species are purely aquatic, feeding on sewage or carrion; others may burrow into the leaves of pondweeds or into the stems of meadow grass. The larvae of the Koo-tsabe Fly *Ephydra hians*, which are able to live in the heavily salt water of Mono Lake, California, are much favoured as food by the native Indians.

Another unusual species in the same family is the Petroleum Fly *Psilopa petrolei* whose larvae live in pools of crude petroleum, catching insects trapped there.

EPIA. The Viper's Bugloss Moth: a medium sized moth found on the high plateaux and dry warm plains of southern Europe and western Asia; olive green with a complex pattern of brown. The caterpillars feed on *Silene* and *Gypsophila*.

EPIAESHNA. *Epiaeshna heros*, a species of large brown dragonflies with smoky wings, found in the eastern United States; one of the largest species in these parts. It frequently enters houses.

EPICAUTA. *Epicauta vittata*, the Striped Blister Beetle, a pest of the family Meloidae remarkable for having several distinctly different types of larva. The first instar is a long-legged and active *triungulin*; the second is flattened with short legs and resembles a wireworm; the third is fat and white resembling the larva of the cockchafer; the last instar is coarctate like the pupa of a house fly.

EPICOMETES. A beetle of central and southern Europe and Asia Minor, related to the Rose Chafers (Cetoniinae). It is completely covered with bristly hairs, yellow on the head, grey on the elytra and white under the abdomen. The larvae feed on rotting vegetation but the adults are often found on dandelion flowers.

EPICRANIAL PLATES (EPICRANIUM). Two cuticular plates covering the dorsal surface of an insect's head.

EPICRANIAL SUTURE. A line of weakness on the head, above the antennae, and shaped like an inverted 'Y'. Not a true suture, and without reference to segmentation. It is often miscalled the 'frontal suture' (*q.v.*).

EPICUTICLE. The outer layer of the cuticle of an insect or other arthropod; it is usually very thin and is made of *sclerotin* which is impervious to water.

75

EPILACHNA. A genus of ladybirds (Coccinellidae) differing from most others in being plant-feeders and sometimes serious pests. They include the Mexican Bean Beetle *Epilachna varivestis*, the American Squash Beetle *Epilachna borealis* and a number of others that feed on potatoes, tomatoes etc. in Africa, India and Australia.

EPIMERON. The posterior part of the subcoxa of an insect (see also *Episternum*).

EPINOTIA. A small moth whose larva feeds on the needles of pine and spruce, fastening a number of these together with silk to form a tube within which it lives and feeds.

EPIOPTICON. The middle section of the optic lobe of an insect's brain, also called the external medullary mass (see *Periopticon* and *Opticon*).

EPIPHARYNX. The membranous roof of the mouth of an insect, provided with taste receptors and sometimes elongated to form part of the proboscis, being associated with the labrum.

EPIPLEURITE. A small lateral cuticular plate sometimes present on the thorax of an insect, when a pleurite is divided horizontally into two parts.

EPIPLEURON. The turned-down outer edge of the elytron of a beetle.

EPIPROCT. A small plate above the anus of an insect, formed from the reduced terga of the 10th and 11th segments.

EPIPYROPIDAE. A family of small Australian moths whose larvae are parasitic in plant-bugs.

EPIRRHOE. A genus of Carpet Moths (Larentiinae), geometrids that rest with the wings spread out and whose larvae rest in a hooped position. *Epirrhoe alternata*, the Common Carpet Moth, has a pattern of alternate light and dark brown on the fore-wings with two paler transverse lines. The larvae feed on Bedstraw (*Galium*).

EPISEMA. *Episema caeruleocephala*, the Figure-of-eight Moth or Blue-head; a noctuid moth of Europe and Asia, grey-brown with a white or cream mark shaped like a figure 8 on each fore-wing. The caterpillar, which is bluish with black, orange and yellow spots, feeds on the leaves of hawthorn, sloe, apple and other trees and shrubs of the family Rosaceae. It pupates in a cocoon woven of silk with pieces of leaf.

EPISIMUS. *Episimus argutanus*: the Witch-hazel Leaf-folder of North America, a moth of the family Tortricidae whose caterpillars roll leaves into small cones within which they live and feed.

EPISITE. A predator: an organism that attacks and feeds on another.

EPISTEME. A large noctuid moth from the warmer parts of China, dark. brown with yellow, orange and blue markings and a wing-span of about 7 cm

EPISTERNUM. The anterior part of the subcoxa of an insect, the posterior being called the *epimeron*. The two are separated from each other by the *pleural suture*.

EPITRIX. A genus of flea-beetles, pests of potatoes and other crops in North America, the West Indies and Australia.

EPOCHRA. *Epochra canadensis*: the Currant Fruit-fly of North America, a minute two-winged fly of the family Trupaneidae whose larvae are fruit-borers and leaf-miners.

ERANNIS. A genus of geometrid moths whose females are wingless and whose larvae are pests of agriculture and forestry. They include the Mottled Umber Moth *Erannis defoliaria*, the Spring Usher *Erannis leucophaearia* and the Dotted Border Moth *Erannis marginaria*. The larvae of all these attack oak, birch, elm etc.

ERASMIA. A genus of large Burnet Moths of the tropics: *Erasmia sanguiflua* of India and Burma, for example, has wings of purple, brown and blue, spotted with black and white. Its wing-span is about 10 cm.

EREBIA. A genus of Brown Butterflies (Satyridae) including species from the Alps, Himalayas, Andes and other mountainous regions. The principal European species are *Erebia epiphron*, the Mountain Ringlet and *Erebia aethiops*, the Scotch Argus. Both are dark brown; the former has a number of dark spots surrounded by pale rings on both wings; the latter has a patch of orange with three white-centred black rings on each fore-wing. The larvae of both feed on grass.

EREBUS. A genus that includes the world's largest moth *Erebus agrippina* with a wing-span of 28 cm. It ranges from the lowlands of Brazil to the mountains of Ecuador up to 3,000 metres (10,000 ft.). A smaller species, the Black Witch, *Erebus odora*, migrates between the Gulf of Mexico and the United States.

ERETMOCERUS SERIUS. A parasitic hymenopteran from Cuba that has been successfully used to control the Oriental Whitefly *Aleuracanthus*, a pest of citrus, coffee and other crops in India, Malaysia, Central America and East Africa.

ERGATANER. A male ant resembling a worker, because it has lost its wings.

ERGATE. A worker ant.

ERGATES. *Ergates faber*: the Carpenter Longhorn, the largest of the Central European longhorn beetles (Cerambycidae), dark brown and about 55 mm. long; an inhabitant of old pine trees.

ERGATOGYNE. A female ant without wings and looking like a worker.

ERGATANDROMORPH. An ant which combines some of the characteristics of both male and worker.

ERIBOEA. *Eriboea eudamippus formosanus*: a large butterfly of Taiwan (Formosa), yellow and brown with a wing-span of 7 cm. It sucks the juices from carrion, dung or other refuse.

ERICERUS PE-LA. A scale insect, one of the Coccidae, that produces a useful waxy substance known as 'China Wax'.

ERIOCAMPA. The Cherry Sawfly, a pest of cherry and pear trees; its larvae resemble small black slugs.

ERIOCERA. A genus of crane-flies having an aquatic larva, an unusual feature in this family, the Tipulidae.

ERIOCRANIIDAE. A family of small primitive moths of the group Micropterygidae which have biting mouth-parts in the larval and the adult stages and have deep fringes on the edges of the wings. They are found in Europe, Asia and North America. *Eriocrania spermanella*, a European species, is golden-yellow with blue veins and yellowish grey fringes; the caterpillars burrow into birch leaves.

ERIOGASTER LANESTRIS. The Small Eggar Moth, one of the Lasiocampidae, having a thick hairy body and chocolate brown wings with light spots. The caterpillars live in silken webs on many deciduous trees (see *Eggar Moths*).

ERIOISCHIA. *Erioischia brassicae*, the Cabbage Root-fly, a major pest of cabbages and similar plants of the order Cruciferae that has spread from Europe to North America and other parts. It is a small two-winged fly of the family Anthomyidae. The adults lay their eggs on the soil near cabbage plants and the larvae burrow into the roots and stems.

ERIOSOMA (ERIOSOMATIDAE). *Eriosoma lanigerum*, the Woolly Aphis: a small plant-louse, generally yellow or brown, originally from North America but now found in many parts of the world. It attacks apple trees, sucking the sap and producing a white woolly secretion, a mass of which may conceal many of these insects. A warm climate favours the reproduction of this species but in more temperate climates they reproduce chiefly by parthenogenesis. They may spend the winter in cracks in the bark but in adverse conditions they migrate down to the roots and produce nodules resembling galls.

ERIOTHRIX. A genus of tachinid flies whose larvae are parasites of the Tiger Moth caterpillar (*Arctia*) and of various Noctuidae.

ERISTALIS. See *Drone-fly*.

ERMINE MOTH. *Spilosoma lubricipeda* the White Ermine and *Spilosoma lutea* the Buff Ermine: two moths of the family Arctiidae, the former white with black spots; the latter buff with black spots. Both have dark brown hairy caterpillars that feed on dock, dandelion etc.

ERNARMONIA. See *Codling Moth*.

ERNOBIUS. A small wood-boring beetle of the family Anobiidae, about 6 cm. long, dark brown with yellowish hairs; found under the bark of dead or dying conifers.

ERONIA. A pierid butterfly of South Africa, white with a broad black margin; found chiefly near the edges of forests.

EROTYLIDAE. Brightly coloured, usually red and black, hemispherical beetles some of which are up to about 25 mm. in length but many smaller. They belong to the Clavicornia, a group characterized by club-shaped antennae. They are found in the warmer parts of America and are commonly known as Pleasing Fungus Beetles. Most of them feed on fungi in rotting wood but a few are pests of vegetable crops.

ERUCIFORM LARVA. A polypod or caterpillar type of larva having a fleshy body, a thin skin and prolegs or cushion-feet on the abdomen.

ERYCIDES. A skipper butterfly (Hesperiidae) of Brazil having a wing-span of about 7 cm., *i.e.* much larger than the European skippers; coloured black with blue and white markings.

ERYCINIDAE (RIODINIDAE). A family of butterflies found chiefly in Central and South America, the nearest relative in Europe being the Duke of Burgundy Fritillary (*Hamearis lucina*). Most of the South American species, from Peru, Brazil and Ecuador, are small and brilliantly coloured. The largest, *Helicopis acis*, is about 5 cm. across, yellow, brown and black with about six 'tails' on each hind-wing and with silvery spots on the underside.

ERYNNIS. *Erynnis tages*, the Dingy Skipper, a small dark brownish, moth-like butterfly of the family Hesperiidae. The larvae are green and feed on Bird's-foot Trefoil (*Lotus corniculatus*), making a 'tent' of leaves bound together with silk.

ERYTHRODIPLAX. A dragonfly of Central America that changes its colour from pale yellow to dark brown or black as it becomes older.

ERYTHRONEURA. The Grape Leaf-hopper: a small yellow, red and brown plant-bug of the family Cicadellidae; a serious pest of vines.

ESCUTCHEON. An alternative name for the scutellum, particularly of beetles; a shield-like covering over the thorax.

ESTIGMENE. The Salt-marsh Moth of North America, a whitish moth with dark spots, whose caterpillar can be a serious pest of many vegetables.

ESTIVATION. See *Aestivation*.

EUCALYPTUS WEEVIL. *Gonipterus scutellatus*: an Australian weevil that has spread to other countries but has to some extent been controlled by introducing a minute hymenopteran parasite. Both larvae and adults feed on the leaves of the eucalyptus plant.

EUCEPHALOUS. A term applied to insect larvae that have a definite head as distinct from the *hemicephalous* and *acephalous* types in which it is much reduced or absent.

EUCERA. *Eucera longicornis*, the long-horned bee: a large hairy bee in which the males have antennae as long as the body; it nests in the ground and is sometimes the host of the Cuckoo Bee *Nomada*.

EUCHLOE. *Euchloe cardamines* or *Anthocharis cardamines*: the Orange-tip Butterfly, a European species of the family Pieridae whose larvae feed on the pods of cruciferous plants. The male has bright orange patches on the tips of the fore-wings and has a dappled green pattern on the underside of the otherwise white hind-wings; the female is similar but without the orange patches.

EUCHROMA. *Euchroma gigantea* or *Euchroma goliath*, the Goliath Beetle of Central America and the West Indies. A wood-boring beetle, the largest of the family Buprestidae, about 7 cm. long, variable in colour but generally an iridescent purple, red and green. The wing-covers have for centuries been used by the natives for making ornaments.

EUCLEIDAE. Also called Limacodidae or Cochlidiidae: Slug-moths, a family of moths whose caterpillars have reduced feet and move about on wet leaves with a sliding motion like a slug. Some have their bodies covered with poisonous spines or hairs; others have leaf-like projections along the sides of the body. Included in this family are the Saddleback Moth *Sibine* and the Green Slug Moth *Euclea*.

EUCLIDIMERA. The Mother Shipton Moth: a small day-flying Owlet Moth having a wing pattern of dark and light brown said to resemble the head of an old woman. The larvae feed on clover and pupate in silk cocoons attached to grass.

EUCONE EYE. The normal type of compound eye of an insect containing true crystalline cones (see *Compound Eyes*).

EUCORETHRA. See *Chaoborus*.

EUDAMUS. *Eudamus proteus*: the Long-tailed Skipper, a hesperiid butterfly of North America; dark brown with white markings and with long 'tails' on the hind-wings. The caterpillar is a leaf-roller that feeds on leguminous plants.

EUDIA. *Eudia pavonia* or *Saturnia pavonia*, the Lesser Emperor Moth (see *Emperor Moth*).

EUDIOPTIS. The Melon Stem-borer, a small moth of the family Pyralidae whose larvae feed on the stems of melons etc. attacking them near or below the ground.

EUGASTER. A genus of North African desert crickets, about 4 cm. long, shiny black with bright red swellings on the thorax; they hide in crevices during the day and come out in the evening to feed on desert plants. They can protect themselves by squirting out a poisonous liquid from the sides of the body.

EUGEREON. The Bug-nosed Dragonfly: a fossil insect of the Permian Period; one of the oldest dragonflies differing from present-day species in having suctorial mouth-parts. It had a wing-span of about 16 cm.

EUGLOSSA. A genus of bees from tropical South America having a tongue or proboscis considerably longer than the whole body. They feed on deep-seated nectar and are instrumental in pollinating certain orchids.

EULECANIUM. A North American genus of scale-insects of the family Coccidae including *Eulecanium tulipiferae* which attacks tulip trees and magnolias and *Eulecanium nigrofasciatum*, the Terrapin Scale, a pest of peach trees. These scale-insects are attacked and can be controlled by certain parasitic wasps of the family Encyrtidae.

EUMENIDAE. Potter Wasps and Mason Wasps: a family of solitary wasps that build flask-shaped nests made from clay, small pebbles etc. glued together with saliva. The nests of *Eumenes coarctata* are like small pots attached to stems of heather. Here the wasps lay their eggs and store caterpillars that have been stung and paralysed to form a reserve of food for newly hatched larvae.

EUMENIS. *Eumenis semele*, the Grayling Butterfly also called *Hipparchia semele*: a medium sized, dark brown European butterfly of the family Satyridae, having two black spots on patches of cream colour on each fore-wing. The larvae feed on grasses and pupate in underground cocoons.

EUMERUS. The Narcissus Fly: a genus of hover-flies (Syrphidae) whose larvae feed on the bulbs of daffodils, narcissus, onions etc.

EUMOLPUS. *Eumolpus candens*: one of the largest of the leaf-beetles (Chrysomelidae) from Brazil; green, hemispherical and about 2 cm. long.

EUPATORUS. *Eupatorus gracilicornis*: the Rhinoceros Beetle from Vietnam, about 65 mm. long, black with brown wing-covers, having a large upwardly-directed 'horn' on the head and four smaller horns on the shield of the thorax.

EUPECILIA. *Eupecilia australasiae*, the Australian Rose-beetle: a chafer of the family Scarabaeidae, about 2 cm. long with glossy, brown and yellow wing-covers having an elaborate ceramic-style pattern. They feed on young leaves and flowers of roses etc.

EUPETHECIA. An alternative spelling for *Eupithecia* (*q.v.*).

EUPHOLUS. A genus of large weevils from New Guinea, about 25 mm. long, having long legs, a long bent proboscis and a large black thorn-like outgrowth from each wing-cover.

EUPHORIA. *Euphoria fulgida*, a beetle that attacks peach leaves in California etc. It has a sharp spine on the outer edge of each front tibia and uses these to cut into the glands at the bases of the peach leaves so that it can suck the sticky sap.

EUPHYDRYAS. The Marsh Fritillary of Europe, *Euphydryas aurinia*, and the related Chequerspot Butterfly of North America, *Euphydryas chalcedona*.

Both species have an elaborate pattern of brown, yellow and orange spots suggesting a chequerboard. The food plant of the Marsh Fritillary larvae is the Devil's Bit Scabious, *Scabiosa pratensis*, on which they live gregariously in a silken web. The American species is sometimes a pest of cultivated plants.

EUPHYIA. The Yellow Shell Moth: a small European Carpet Moth of the group Larentiinae that folds its wings out flat when at rest. The caterpillar is a bright green geometrid (looper) that feeds on grass, dock, chickweed etc.

EUPITHECIA. Pug Moths: a genus of Geometridae; small moths whose wings are generally mottled with brown, green or grey and white and are spread out flat when resting. The caterpillars, which are loopers, feed on a number of flowers, fruits and seed-pods and pupate underground in cocoons woven from silk and soil particles. Sometimes the caterpillars take on the colour of the food-plant by absorbing the anthocyanin pigments of flowers or fruits.

EUPLAGIA. *Euplagia quadripunctata*: the Jersey Tiger Moth, a species found chiefly in Central and Southern Europe and Western Asia. The markings resemble those of the common Tiger Moth but the fore-wings are dark brown and yellow; the hind-wings ginger coloured with black spots.

EUPLOEA. Crow Butterflies: a genus of tropical butterflies of the family Danaidae from India, South-east Asia, New Guinea, Australia etc. Some of them have a wing-span of up to 11 cm. The commonest colours are blues, mauve or brown with white patches but many have a shiny texture like a mirror, enabling them to reflect the background colours, so making them almost invisible. The males commonly have scented wing-scales or *androconia* enabling them to attract the females prior to mating.

EUPROCTIS. A genus of Tussock Moths (Lymantriidae) including *Euproctis similis*, the Gold-tail and *Euproctis chrysorrhoea*, the Brown-tail. Both are white with a black dot on each fore-wing. The former has a yellow tip on the abdomen; the latter a brown tip. The caterpillars are black, red and white with irritant hairs. They pupate in yellow silky cocoons. The Gold-tail is common in Britain. The Brown-tail is rarer but has been a pest of forest trees in North America.

EUPSALIS. A genus of wood-boring weevils of the family Brentidae. *Eupsalis minuta* is a small North American species, brown with yellow markings on the wing-covers. The females are about 1 cm. long; the males have several different forms varying in size and in the shape of the beak.

EUPSILIA. *Eupsilia transversa*, the Satellite Moth: a small European noctuid moth having brown fore-wings with a pale spot on each and light brown hind-wings. The caterpillars feed on leaves of oak, elm and beach but will sometimes eat other caterpillars.

EUREMA. Grass Yellows: a genus of pierid butterflies found in many of the warmer parts of the world. *Eurema hecabe*, a small yellow species with black edged wings, is found over most of Asia; *Eurema nicippe*, slightly larger, orange with brown edges, is also common in Asia and in the southern United States.

EUROSTA. A small two-winged fly of the family Trupaneidae whose larvae produce spherical galls on the stems of Golden Rod, *Solidago canadensis*.

EURRHYPARA. *Eurrhypara hortulata*, the Small Magpie Moth, a member of the family Pyralidae. The pattern of the wings is white, spotted with black and yellow having a superficial resemblance to the Magpie Moth *Abraxas grossulariata*, although of a different family. The larvae feed on stinging nettles.

EURYACANTHA. *Euryacantha horrida*: a large spiny stick-insect from New Guinea about 13 cm. long.

EURYGAMY. Being unable to mate in a confined space: a phenomenon characteristic of many gnats and mosquitoes.

EURYGASTER. The Sun Pest: a minute plant-bug of the family Scutelleridae that feeds in large numbers on grain crops in south-west Asia. It migrates to the mountains in hot weather and invades the valleys in the spring.

EURYOPHTHALMUS. *Euryophthalmus succinctus*: a species of firebug (Pyrrhocoridae) of North America, brownish black with brilliant red markings above and with bright blue hairs covering the underside. It is found on orange and other fruit trees where it possibly feeds on the fungi that infest these trees.

EURYTOMIDAE. A family of minute gall-making chalcid wasps whose larvae are known as straw-worms. *Eurytoma felis* attacks citrus trees in Australia; *Bruchophagus gibbus*, a member of the same family, is a major pest of leguminous plants in Australia, New Zealand and North America.

EUSCHESIS. *Euschesis comes*, the Lesser Yellow Underwing and *Euschesis orbona*, the Luna Yellow Underwing: two noctuid moths smaller but otherwise very similar to the Large Yellow Underwing *Noctua pronuba*. All these have mottled brownish fore-wings and yellow or orange hind-wings with a broad band of black or dark brown round the edge. The larvae of all these feed on grasses and a great variety of other plants.

EUSCHISTUS. A genus of small predatory pentatomid bugs (Heteroptera) that attack pests of many fruit and vegetable crops and are thus a means of controlling the latter.

EUSTHENIIDAE. Stoneflies (Plecoptera) of Australia and New Zealand, having nymphs of a very primitive type with lateral gills on the abdominal segments. They may live for several years and pass through as many as thirty instars before the adult fly is formed.

EUTERMES. A typical genus of tropical termites (Isoptera). *Eutermes parvulus*, a small species from West Africa, is one of the *nasutiform* termites, *i.e.* the colonies include 'soldiers' of the nasute type with large, hard heads ending in a syringe-like snout from which a sticky fluid can be ejected.

EUTHISANOTIA. A noctuid moth that resembles a fungus when at rest; creamy with purple markings and tufts of hairs on the thorax.

EUTHOCHTHA. A North American genus of large predatory squashbugs (Coreidae) having a slender body and large hind-legs with a row of spines on each tibia.

EUZOPHORA. A genus of small moths of the family Pyralidae (Microlepidoptera) whose larvae are cambium-borers.

EVACANTHUS. A genus of small leaf-hoppers of the family Cicadellidae; *Evacanthus interruptus*, a pest of hop fields in Britain.

EVERGESTIS. *Evergestis forficalis*, the Garden Pebble Moth: a small light brown moth of the family Pyralidae whose green caterpillars are pests of cabbages etc. Eggs are laid under the leaves and the larvae eat out the centres of the vegetables; afterwards they pupate underground in silken cocoons.

EVETRIA. A genus of moths whose caterpillars are pests of pine forests in Europe and have been introduced into America and elsewhere. They include *Evetria buoliana*, the Pine Shoot Moth; *Evetria turionana*, the Pine Bud Moth and *Evetria resinella*, the Pine Resin Moth.

EXARATE. A type of insect pupa in which the legs and other appendages are free and clearly visible and the abdomen is movable. In some cases such a pupa is capable of limited locomotion.

EXARTEMA. A genus of moths whose caterpillars are leaf-rollers and leaf-tiers. *Exartema inornatanum* and *Exartema connectum* make nests in the rolled leaves of dogwood in which they feed. *Exartema ferriferanum*, the Hydrangea Leaf-tier, uses its silken threads to bind together the leaves that enclose the flower bud. This forms a pouch or sac in which the caterpillar nests and feeds on the developing hydrangea flower.

EXCRETION. The principal excretory organs of insects are the Malpighian tubules which absorb nitrogenous products from the blood or haemolymph and discharge them into the rectum or hind-gut. Some water is re-absorbed during its passage down these tubes, so that most of the waste substance finally discharged consists of uric acid. Since this is only very slightly soluble it is excreted in the form of crystals with a minimum loss of water. Another form of excretion is carried out by the fat-body which occupies a large part of the space around and between other organs. Certain cells known as *nephrocytes* in this tissue can absorb urates and other waste products which are then stored to be eliminated later when the insect pupates. Some pigments appear to be a form of 'storage excretion'.

EXOCHORION. The thick outer layer of the shell or chorion of an insect's egg, variously shaped and sculptured and having a small hole or micropyle at one end through which fertilization takes place (see *Egg*).

EXOCONE EYE. A compound eye in which the cones are not true crystalline cones but are formed by invagination of the cornea. Such eyes occur in lampyrid beetles.

EXOCUTICLE. The middle cuticular layer of an insect or other arthropod, outside the endocuticle and beneath the epicuticle. It is usually very thick and is composed of chitin and proteins impregnated with sclerotin and sometimes melanin.

EXOPTERYGOTA (HEMIMETABOLA). Insects in which there is no pupal stage and in which metamorphosis involves very little change at each instar. The young, which are known as nymphs, are generally similar to the adult but are smaller and have external wing-buds at an early stage. The group includes cockroaches, earwigs and all kinds of bugs and lice, as well as such insects as dragonflies and mayflies. The two latter have aquatic nymphs differing more markedly from the adults than do the nymphs of other orders.

EXOSKELETON. The thick cuticle of an insect, crustacean or other arthropod, usually made of chitin impregnated with calcium compounds making it very hard; it is, however, thinner and more flexible at the joints. Ingrowths from the exoskeleton known as *apodemes* serve as points of attachment for muscles. Since the presence of a hard exoskeleton hinders growth, the animal must of necessity cast it off from time to time and can only grow between the loss of one cuticle and the formation of the new one. Moulting is known as *ecdysis* (*q.v.*), though this is sometimes restricted to the actual shedding of cuticle.

EXTATOSOMA. *Extatosoma tiaratum*: a large leaf-insect (phasmid) from New Guinea, about 12 cm. long resembling a cluster of thorny twigs and leaves.

EXUDATIONS. Secretions or modified excretory products from epidermal glands including such substances as oil (from oil beetles), wax (from bees), silk (from caterpillars), nutrient or sugary secretions (from termites and aphids), scents to attract other insects (from butterflies), unpleasant scents and irritant fluids for self-defence (from earwigs, stink-bugs, bedbugs, caterpillars etc.). Some of these substances exude through pores in the cuticle; others are discharged from special openings or tubes; *e.g.* wax in greenfly and whitefly.

EXUVIAE. A plural noun (never used in the singular) signifying the remains of the cast-off skin of an insect (see *Ecdysis*). Sometimes they remain to form the scale of a scale-insect (see *Coccidae*) or the puparium in the case of Diptera such as the house fly.

EXUVIAL FLUID. Moulting fluid (see *Ecdysis*).

EYE. See *Compound Eye* and *Ocellus*.

EYED ELATER. *Alaus oculatus*: a large species of Click Beetle (Elateridae) from North America, about 4 cm. long, black flecked with white scales and having on the thorax two deep black eye-spots encircled with white. The larvae feed on decaying wood.

EYED HAWK-MOTH. *Smerinthus ocellata*: a large brown and grey moth of the family Sphingidae having two conspicuous blue eye-spots on the pinkish underwings. They normally rest with these hidden but display them if disturbed. The caterpillars are pale green with oblique lines of white and darker green and with a large horn characteristic of hawk-moths at the hind-end. They feed on sallow, willow and apple leaves.

EYED LADYBIRD. *Anatis ocellata*: the largest of the British ladybirds (Coccinellidae), about 6 mm. long, having elytra red with eight black spots each ringed with yellow. The thorax is black with the sides yellow and with a black spot resembling an eye on each side.

EYELESS CAVE BEETLE. *Horlogion speokoites*: a ground beetle of the family Carabidae having long legs and antennae but with degenerate functionless eyes; found in caves in Virginia.

F

FACETS OF EYE. The facets of an insect's eye are formed from the cuticular lenses covering the crystalline cones. The number varies considerably: worker ants usually have under a dozen; the house fly has about 4,000 and some dragonflies 20,000 or more. Parasitic insects and those living in caves often have very few facets, or even a single one. When few, the facets are circular, but become hexagonal when tightly packed together.

FAIRY FLIES. Chalcid wasps of the family Mymaridae whose larvae are parasites in the eggs of other insects. They include some of the world's smallest insects with a wing-span of less than 1 mm.

FALL CANKERWORM. The larva of a small North American geometrid moth *Alsophila pomataria*, a pest of fruit and forest trees. As in the case of the March Moth and the Winter Moth, wingless females crawl up the trunks of trees and lay their eggs in young shoots. The caterpillars feed on leaves, flower buds and young fruits; they pupate in the soil.

FALL WEBWORM. *Hyphantria cunea*: a North American arctiid moth whose caterpillars attack many forest and fruit trees. They are gregarious and live in silken nests which they make to enclose the leaves on which they feed.

FALLING REFLEX. A reflex action by which a falling insect will, in a short distance, right itself so that it will either land on its feet or adopt a suitable position for flying. Legs and antennae are spread out so that the effect of air currents on these gives the insect the appropriate stimulus to adjust its position.

FALSE KATYDID. *Microcentrum retinerve*: the Angular-winged Grasshopper of North America, a green species with long antennae, belonging to the family Tettigoniidae.

FALSE LEGS. Prolegs or pseudopods: fleshy pad-like outgrowths from the abdomen. Caterpillars of butterflies and moths usually have five pairs; those of sawflies seven pairs. Prolegs are used for gripping whereas true jointed legs, which are on the thorax, are used for walking. In the case of butterflies and moths the prolegs bear rows of tiny hooks; those of sawfles are without these. Many larvae of flies (Diptera) have false abdominal legs, either on the ventral surface only, and used for walking on a surface, or in rings all round the body, and used for pushing through narrow spaces (*e.g.* maggots).

FANNIA. *Fannia canicularis*. The Lesser House Fly and related species: two-winged flies very similar in appearance to the house fly but somewhat smaller. They breed in dung and other refuse but do not generally spread disease. The larvae and pupae are covered with bristles and spines. They have occasionally been found living in the human intestine and causing *myiasis*. The males often hover for long periods.

FAT BODY. A mass of fatty tissue filling most of the body cavity of an insect. The food stored in this tissue includes fats, proteins and glycogen which form a reserve for hibernation or pupation. (See also *Excretion*.)

FEATHERED GOTHIC MOTH. *Tholera popularis*: a medium sized European noctuid moth with a pattern of dark and light brown on the wings, the veins showing up whitish against a brown background. The antennae of the male are feather-like. The caterpillars are dark brown and feed on various grasses.

FEATHERED THORN. *Himera pennaria*: a medium sized European woodland moth with wings of tawny orange, the fore-wings being crossed by two dark transverse lines. Near the tip of each fore-wing is a round white spot. The hind-wings are paler.

FECIFORK. A 'dung-fork': a flattened fork-like appendage, also called an 'anal comb', attached to the hind-end of the abdomen on the larvae of certain beetles and moths. It can be elevated and is used for shovelling up dung which is then deposited on the back of the larva to serve as camouflage and for protection from the sun.

FECUNDITY OF INSECTS. The average number of eggs laid by an insect is from 100–200 but in some particular cases, especially the social insects, there may be many more than this. A queen bee may lay 2,000 eggs a day; a queen termite 60 eggs a minute with a total of several millions. Likewise partheno-genetic female aphids may produce many millions of offspring during a season in which perhaps twelve generations may develop. Although such large numbers are produced, most insects have many enemies and on the whole the number destroyed or eaten by other insects nearly balances the number produced.

The population of a particular species will therefore tend to remain constant unless some abnormal factor upsets the balance (see *Biotic Potential*).

FEELERS. See *Antennae* and *Palps*.

FEET. The foot of an insect is formed from the *pretarsus*, *i.e.* the terminal segment of the tarsus. In primitive insects such as the Protura it bears a single claw, but in most higher insects there are paired retractile claws. Sometimes these bear teeth or are branched giving the appearance of four claws (as for instance in some mosquitoes and some flies living in fur or feathers, *e.g.* Hippoboscidae). Between the claws there is usually a median pad or *arolium* and sometimes two lateral pads or *pulvilli*. A median bristle or *empodium* may also be present. The arolia and the pulvilli bear fine hairs and may secrete a small amount of fluid, making an airtight junction between the foot and the surface on which the insect is walking.

FEMALE REPRODUCTIVE SYSTEM. The principal parts of the female reproductive system of an insect are the two ovaries, sometimes of great size and complexity; these lead into oviducts which join to form a median duct or 'vagina' opening in the 9th. abdominal segment. Leading into the vagina there is usually a pair of accessory glands or *colleterial* glands. These may secrete a sticky substance with which the eggs are attached to a surface; in some cases, such as the cockroach, they secrete a horny capsule or *ootheca* in which the eggs are laid. In most cases there is a sac or *spermatheca* leading dorsally from the median oviduct or vagina. This receives seminal fluid from the male, stores it, and releases it over the eggs just before they are laid.

FEMUR (Pl. FEMORA). The first long segment of an insect's leg, between the trochanter and the tibia.

FENISECA. A genus of butterflies of the family Lycaenidae whose larvae prey on the Woolly Aphis and whose pupae resemble the spiral shell of a mollusc.

FENUSINAE. Birch Leaf-miners: a group of minute sawflies whose larvae eat away the insides of birch leaves, several larvae usually living together and sometimes hollowing out the entire contents of a leaf. *Fenusa pumila* is a European species now commonly found in North America.

FERTONIA. A genus of solitary wasps that store ants as food for the larvae.

FESTOON MOTH. See *Cochlidion*.

FEVER FLY. *Dilophus febrilis*: a large black, hairy, two-winged fly of the family Bibionidae, very similar to St. Mark's Fly *Bibio marci*. The males have very large spreading compound eyes with facets of two sizes. This may relate to the fact that they perform aerial courtship dances above the females which remain passively on the ground.

FIDIA. *Fidia viticida*, the Grape Rootworm: a small beetle of the family Chrysomelidae whose larvae bore into the roots of vines.

FIDONIA. *Fidonia plumistraria*: the Clover Heath Moth, a species common in Central and Southern Europe and North Africa. The wing-span is about 4 cm. and the wings are golden yellow with an elaborate pattern of dark brown spots. The antennae are large and comb-like. The larvae feed on clover but the adult lacks a proboscis and is unable to feed.

FIELD CRICKET. A name for a number of crickets (Gryllidae) that live in burrows and feed on grass. *Gryllus campestris*, the European Field Cricket is black with a band of yellow across the base of the elytra. The hind-wings are shorter than those of the House Cricket and are covered by the leathery fore-wings. Another species, *Acheta servillei*, damages pastures in Australia and New Zealand; *Acheta assimilis* is found in North and South America.

FIELD CUCKOO BEE. *Psithyrus campestris*, a large hairy bee, black with yellow on the fore and hind margins of the thorax and with yellow hairs fringing the extremity of the abdomen. Like other cuckoo bees it does not store pollen and honey for its young, but lays its eggs in the nest of another species, *e.g.* the Carder Bee, whose workers will feed the larvae of the intruder.

FIELD DIGGER WASP. *Mellinus arvensis*: a small, long-waisted, black and yellow wasp that burrows into sandy soil, making a nest with several cells in each of which she lays an egg and deposits a few small flies as food for the developing larvae.

FIELD GRASSHOPPER. A name for a number of grasshoppers but especially for *Chorthippus brunneus*, one of the commonest European species. It varies in colour but is generally brown, has long wings and is hairy underneath (see also *Chorthippus*).

FIELD GROUND BEETLE. *Carabus arvensis* and related species: medium sized, carnivorous beetles with long legs and long thin antennae. The wing-cases are rounded and black with a greenish sheen and with several longitudinal ridges and rows of granules. The larvae are of the campodeiform type (*q.v.*) and are predatory.

FIELD SANDWASP. *Sphex campestris*: a common digger wasp of the family Sphecidae, small with a long narrow waist; head and thorax black; abdomen orange with a black tip. It burrows into sandy soil and stocks its nest with insects that have been stung and paralysed as food for the developing larvae.

FIERY COPPER. *Heodes virgauriae*: a butterfly of the family Lycaenidae found in Central Europe. The wings of the male are a bright iridescent copper colour edged with black. The female is less brilliant and is spotted with black. The larvae feed on docks (*Rumex*).

FIG CHALCID. *Blastophaga psenes*: a minute parasitic hymenopteran of the family Agaontidae that produces galls in fig plants and is essential for the pollination of the Smyrna Fig. This cultivated variety produces only female flowers and no fruit can be produced without receiving pollen from the wild, inedible fig or *caprifig*. The two plants are therefore grown together and the chalcid, looking for somewhere to lay its eggs, carries pollen from the caprifig to the Smyrna Fig. Blastophaga has been introduced into California and other fruit-growing countries for this purpose.

FIG INSECT. See *Fig Chalcid*.

FIG MOTH. *Ephestia cautella*, a small moth, almost world-wide, whose larvae are pests of dried fruit, particularly in Australia and California and also of cocoa beans in West Africa.

FIG WASP. See *Fig Chalcid*.

FIGWORT WEEVIL. See *Cionus*.

FIGITIDAE. A family of gall-wasps that parasitize aphids, scale-insects and flies.

FIGURE-OF-EIGHT MOTH. See *Episema*.

FILIFORM. Thread-like, as for instance of antennae.

FIRE ANT. *Solenopsis*: a genus of ants that occur in tropical South and Central

America and the southern United States. They are a serious pest on account of their highly irritant poisonous bite.

FIREBRAT. *Thermobia domestica*: a member of the Thysanura or bristle-tails, similar to the Silverfish (*Lepisma*); primitive wingless insects with antennae nearly twice as long as the body and with long tail-filaments in the form of a triple fork. They have biting mouth-parts and are commonly found in warm kitchens and bakehouses where they may be a pest.

FIRE BUG. A general name for plant-bugs of the family Pyrrhocoridae, most of which are tropical. They include the Cotton Stainer *Dysdercus* which stains cotton fibres bright red by introducing fungi when it pierces the bolls. A British species, *Pyrrhocoris apterus*, is a small, rather uncommon black and red insect that feeds on plant juices and is not a pest. The fiery colours of most of these insects are probably a warning coloration, as they are distasteful to predators.

FIREFLY. A name given to many luminiscent insects but particularly to beetles of the family Lampyridae. These bear luminous organs on the 6th and 7th abdominal segments. Here a specialized fatty tissue is permeated by tracheae and a substance called *luciferin* is oxidized with the help of an enzyme, *luciferase*. This produces a cold light or chemo-luminescence. In some cases both sexes are luminous; in others the females only. The European glow-worm is the wingless female of one of these beetles, *Lampyris noctiluca*.

FISHING FLY. A name given both to Mayflies (Ephemeroptera) and Alderflies (Megaloptera).

FISH KILLER. A name given in the United States to giant water bugs of the genera *Lethocerus*, *Benacus* and *Belostoma*. Some of these insects, especially those in the tropics, attain a length of 8–9 cm. They grip small fish, frogs etc. with their front legs and kill them with their strong piercing proboscis.

FISH MOTH. *Lepisma saccharina*: the Silverfish (See *Bristle-tail* and cf. *Firebrat*.)

FIVE-SPOT BURNET. *Zygaena trifolii* (see *Burnet Moth*).

FLABELLIFERINAE. Crested Crane-flies from the forests of Europe and Western Asia: Tipulidae with thicker legs than those of the common crane-fly, varying in colour from black to yellow and red. The males have large antennae resembling feathers or combs.

FLABELLUM. A spoon-like lobe at the tip of the proboscis of a bee.

FLAME CARPET MOTH. *Coremia designata*: a geometrid moth of the subfamily Larentiinae; small moths which rest with their wings spread out and whose larvae rest in a hooped position. The wings of this species are pale grey, the fore-wings having a thick purple-brown band edged with black; the hindwings have a dark central dot and several wavy lines.

FLAME SHOULDER MOTH. *Ochropleura plecta*: a small noctuid moth with white hind-wings and with the fore-wings purplish brown and having a conspicuous white line near the base and along a part of the front edge. The caterpillars are greenish grey and feed on bedstraw (*Galium*).

FLANNEL MOTH. *Lagoa crispata* and related species belonging to the family Megalopygidae. The wings are covered with a loose coat of soft scales giving a flannel-like texture. The caterpillars are covered with poisonous hairs.

FLASH COLOURING. Colouring on a part of the body that is normally concealed but which flashes into view the moment an insect is disturbed.

The brilliant red or orange hind-wings of some moths and grasshoppers, for instance, are normally concealed by the upper wings and when the insect is at rest it is well camouflaged. As soon as it moves, however, the bright colour becomes visible and may serve to frighten away potential enemies. The sudden appearance of the eye-spots on the hind-wings of the Eyed Hawk-moth is another example.

FLAT ARADUS. *Aradus depressus*, a common European species of flatbugs: gregarious Heteroptera with flattened body, living under the bark of trees and feeding on fungi.

FLAT BODIED LIBELLULA. *Libellula depressa*: a European member of the Libellulidae or Darter Dragonflies. The wings are broad with brown patches at their bases; the head and thorax are brown; the broad, flattened abdomen of the male is bright blue with yellow spots along the side edges. In the female the blue of the abdomen is replaced by brown.

FLATBUGS. Members of the family Aradidae: plant-bugs of the group Heteroptera having the body very much flattened as an adaptation for living under the bark of trees. They are gregarious and feed on microscopic fungi.

FLATFLY. Any member of the family Hippoboscidae: Diptera, some of which are wingless, having a flattened body and living as blood-sucking parasites on mammals or birds. *Melophagus*, the Sheep Ked is an example; another is the flightless *Crataerina pallida*, a parasite of the Swift.

FLAT-HEADED APPLE TREE BORER. See *Chrysobothris*.

FLEA. See *Aphaniptera*.

FLEA-BEETLES. A group of small jumping beetles of the family Chrysomelidae and the subfamily Halticinae, characterized by having thickened femora on the hind-legs. The larvae generally feed on the roots of plants and the adults attack young shoots and leaves. The Potato Flea-beetle *Psylliodes affinis*, a common pest in many countries, will also attack related plants such as the tomato. The Turnip Flea-beetle *Phyllotreta nemorum* infests any crops of the cabbage family (Cruciferae). There are also a number of species that feed on forest trees.

FLESH FLY. *Sarcophaga* and related genera: viviparous two-winged flies related to the blowflies. They deposit their larvae in carrion or other decaying animal matter and these maggot-like larvae produce a large amount of digestive fluid which breaks down and liquefies the flesh in which they live. They are prevented from drowning in it by being able to close the specially recessed spiracles at the hind-end.

FLESH FLY, CHEQUERED. *Sarcophaga carnaria*: a species with the thorax striped grey and black and the abdomen chequered in the same colours (see *Flesh Fly*).

FLIGHT. The movement of an insect's wings during flight is brought about by two sets of muscles. Within the thorax there are vertical muscles and longitudinal muscles. The former pull the roof of the thorax down and force the wings up; the latter arch the thorax and force the wings down. These muscles work automatically in turn by means of a special type of muscle-fibre (see *Click-mechanism*). In addition to these there are other muscles attached to the wing bases, giving a turning movement to the wings at each up and down stroke. These are under direct nervous control and enable the insect to move in any direction.

In Diptera only the first pair of wings is functional, the second pair being reduced and acting as balancers. In beetles and cockroaches, locusts etc. the second pair is functional and the first pair form the wing-cases or elytra. In bees and in some moths the fore and hind-wings interlock and act as one pair during flight.

The rate of wing movement varies from about ten per second in a butterfly to several hundred per second in bees and even more in mosquitoes and midges. The frequency determines the note of an insect's 'hum' when flying.

FLIGHTLESS INSECTS. Most insects have two pairs of functional wings but there are three categories of flightless insects, *viz.*

(1) Primitive insects such as springtails and bristle-tails that have never evolved to the stage of having wings. These are collectively known as Apterygota and comprise the four orders Diplura, Thysanura, Protura and Collembola.

(2) Insects such as ants and termites in which there are winged and wingless castes in the colony, or wingless generations as in aphids.

(3) Insects that are secondarily flightless, *i.e.* they have evolved from winged insects but their mode of life has made the presence of wings a disadvantage. In some cases they may possess vestigial wing-structures. Included in this category are parasitic insects such as fleas, lice, certain bugs and flies, and also a few beetles in which the wing-cases are fused together and the underlying wings are reduced and functionless.

FLOUR BEETLE. *Tribolium* and related genera: beetles of the family Tenebrionidae whose larvae are a world-wide pest of flour and other cereal products. The species *Tribolium confusum* has been used experimentally for the study of population dynamics. (See also *Meal Beetle* and *Mealworm*.)

FLOUR MOTH. *Ephestia kuhniella*: the Mediterranean Flour Moth, a small dark grey moth whose larvae are pests of flour and other cereal products (see *Ephestia*).

FLOUR WORM. A name used for many insect larvae that infest flour.

FLOWER BEE. A name for a number of bees, other than hive bees, that are useful for pollinating flowers, particularly *Halictus*, *Sphecodes* and *Anthophora*.

FLOWER BUGS. A name for a number of bugs but particularly the Anthocoridae; predatory bugs of the group Hemiptera that live on or in flowers and prey upon mites, aphids and other pests.

FLOWER FLIES. A name sometimes given to Hover-flies (Syrphidae) and also to members of the family Anthomyidae such as the Cabbage Root-fly and the Wheat Bulb Fly.

FLOWER POTTER BEES. Anthophoridae: a family of large hairy bees that burrow into the ground and make nests of cells like small clay pots which they fill with honey and pollen before laying an egg in each and closing them.

FLUSHWORM. The larva of the moth *Cydia leucostoma*, a pest of tea plants in India.

FLUTED SCALE. An alternative name for the Cottony Cushion Scale (*q.v.*).

FLY. A general name for many insects but more strictly for two-winged flies or Diptera.

FLYBUG. *Reduvius personatus*, an Assassin bug with long, brown, oval body, long legs and antennae, a small head and a curved rostrum. It flies at night and preys on other insects (see *Assassin Bug*).

FLYING HAIRS. A name sometimes used for certain very long hairs, of which there are usually six, on the wing-cases of carabid beetles.

FOOT LOUSE. *Linognathus pedalis*, a louse that infests the feet of sheep in Australia, New Zealand and other countries. Other species of *Linognathus* infest other domestic mammals.

FOOTMAN MOTH. A group of moths so-called because they wrap their wings tightly round the body when at rest, suggesting a footman's livery. They belong to the subfamily Lithosiinae and are related to the Tiger Moths. Their antennae are long and thin; their tongues well developed; their front tibiae have a leaf-like appendage and their hind tibiae bear spurs. The caterpillars are very hairy and are to be found on the bark of trees where they feed chiefly on algae and lichens.

FOOT-SPINNER. See *Embioptera*.

FORAGING ANTS. A name for a number of genera of tropical ants that have no permanent nests but march in large numbers in search of food. Generally they travel in dense columns foraging on either side and driving out or killing all animal life. They drag or carry the queen, the eggs, larvae and pupae as they go. Species of the genera *Dorylus*, *Eciton* and *Anomma* occur in most tropical countries. (See also *Driver Ants, Army Ants, Legionary Ants, Dorylinae* and *Eciton*.)

FORCEPS. Pincers or claspers at the hind-end of the abdomen of certain insects, either for copulation or for defence, *e.g.* earwigs (Dermaptera).

FORCIPOMYIA. A genus of minute biting midges of the family Ceratopogonidae that suck blood from caterpillars as well as adult insects, often attaching themselves to the wing-veins. Some species will also attack frogs. The larvae live in manure or decomposing vegetation.

FORCIPULAE. See *Forceps*.

FORE-GUT. The anterior part of the alimentary canal; that part which is lined by ectoderm, *viz.* the buccal cavity, pharynx, oesophagus, crop and gizzard (see *Alimentary Canal*).

FOREST BLOWFLY. Also called the Toad Greenbottle, *Lucilia silvarum*; a flesh-fly of the family Calliphoridae that lays its eggs on the eye-rims and nostrils of frogs and toads. The developing larvae feed on these parts, consuming the entire eyes and only killing the toad when they reach its brain. They then pupate in the ground under the dead body of their victim.

FOREST BUG. *Pentatoma rufipes*: a medium sized, greenish grey shieldbug found on oak, alder and other trees. It feeds on caterpillars but will also eat leaves and fruits of cherry etc.

FOREST FLY. *Hippobosca equina*: a European and Asiatic blood-sucking fly that attacks horses, particularly on the thin skin round the anus, and will also occasionally attack cattle, dogs and humans. It is a little larger than a house fly, but much flatter and more leathery and is flecked with brown and yellow. It is viviparous and the larvae are dropped on decaying humus.

FORESTER MOTH. A name given to a number of moths; in Britain to three species of *Procris*: small, bright green, day-flying moths whose larvae feed on sorrel. In America the genus *Alypia* is also called a Forester Moth. It is velvety black with white and yellow spots; the caterpillars feed on grape vines and Virginia Creeper.

FORE-WINGS. The first pair of wings of an insect, growing from the middle segment of the thorax. In Diptera these two are the functional wings, the second pair being reduced to form balancers or *halteres*. In beetles and cockroaches the fore-wings are thickened and horny and are known as *elytra*; in grasshoppers and locusts they are called *tegmina*. In such insects they form covers to protect the more delicate membranous hind-wings.

FORFICULA. See *Earwig*.

FORMICA. The typical genus of ants: *Formica rufa*, the Wood Ant, the largest British species, makes large dome-like nests of leaves, grass, pine-needles etc.; *Formica sanguinea*, the Blood-red Ant, makes slaves of other species; *Formica fusca* and *Formica lemani* are two common species of dark brown ant. (See *Ant*.)

FORMICOIDEA, FORMICIDAE. See *Ant*.

FOSSIL INSECTS. Fossil insects have been found as impressions in limestone and as preserved specimens in amber, resin etc. Although a few have been recorded from the Silurian and Devonian Periods these are doubtful and the earliest fossils that can with certainty be called insects occur in the Carboniferous Period. Many of the present-day orders can, however, be recognized as early as this and there were about ten additional orders that have since become extinct. The more specialized orders, as might be expected, did not make their appearance until relatively late in geological time. The earliest fossils of Diptera and Hymenoptera are found in rocks of the Jurassic Period and the first Lepidoptera in the Tertiary Era. By the time the Oligocene Period was reached, about 30 million years ago, there were a great many insects that hardly differed at all from their present-day counterparts; about 10,000 of these have been described. Since wings are far more often preserved than the rest of the body, the bulk of the evidence provided by fossils relates to wing-venation. The earliest known winged insects were the Palaeodictyoptera whose primitive wing-venation closely resembled that of dragonflies and mayflies. Some of these attained a great size. A dragonfly from the coal shale of Commentry in Central France had a wing-span of about 75 cm. and many from other parts of the world were more than 30 cm. across.

Although the fossil record is far from complete and although we know little or nothing about the conditions under which various insects became fossilized, nevertheless it appears that some orders have passed their peak of dominance. Cockroaches, for instance, according to the fossil evidence, constituted 34% of the insects of Permian times, but are now less than 1% of living insects. Beetles on the other hand are apparently on the upward trend, having risen from 1% in Permian times to 41% of all known insects at the present day. They are now the largest order in the whole animal kingdom. These figures should, however, be treated with caution since it is possible that the known fossils may be unrepresentative samples of past faunas.

FOSSORIAL WASPS. See *Digger Wasp*.

FOUR-BANDED LONGHORN. *Strangalia quadrifasciata*, a medium sized beetle of the family Cerambycidae with long antennae and elongated elytra of a brownish yellow colour, banded with black. The larvae feed on the rotting wood of old tree stumps.

FOUR-DOTTED FOOTMAN MOTH. *Cybosia mesomella*, a medium sized moth with creamy white fore-wings having yellow margins and with two dark dots on each wing; the hind-wings are grey with pale yellow fringes (see *Footman Moth*).

FOUR-FOOTED BUTTERFLIES. Nymphalidae and Satyridae, two families of butterflies in which the first pair of legs is reduced and functionless. The Nymphalidae include the Fritillaries and Aristocrats (Red Admiral, Painted Lady, Tortoiseshell, Peacock, Purple Emperor etc.) as well as many large and colourful species from tropical countries. The Satyridae are the Browns that occur in most parts of the world.

FOUR-SPOTTED CLYTHRA. See *Clythra.*

FOUR-SPOTTED FOOTMAN MOTH. *Oeonestis quadra,* a large yellow moth of the subfamily Lithosiinae with two black spots on each fore-wing. Like all the moths of this group it wraps its wings tightly round the body when at rest (see *Footman Moth*).

FOUR-SPOTTED IPS. *Ips quadripunctata:* a small destructive bark beetle common on pine trees; black with two bright red spots on each wing-case.

FOUR-SPOTTED LIBELLULA. *Libellula quadrimaculata:* one of the Darter Dragonflies (Libellulidae) having a stout but tapering brown body with yellow spots along the sides. Each of the four wings has two black spots near its front edge and the hind-wings each have a dark brown triangular patch at the base.

FOUR-SPOTTED SILPHA. *Silpha quadripunctata:* a predatory beetle of the family Silphidae, dull yellow with a large central black patch on the thorax and two black spots on each wing-case. It is found in oak woods where it feeds on caterpillars.

FOX-COLOURED SAWFLY. *Neodiprion sertifer,* a small European sawfly that attacks Scots Pine and other conifers sometimes causing serious defoliation. It has spread to North America but has to some extent been controlled by the introduction of a virus disease.

FOX MOTH. *Macrothylacia rubi,* a medium sized, light brown moth of the Eggar family (Lasiocampidae). The female is greyer than the male; both have two pale oblique lines crossing the fore-wings. The dark brown, hairy caterpillars feed on heather, bilberries, brambles etc. and pupate in brown hairy cocoons (see *Eggar Moths*).

FRANKLINIELLA. A minute fringe-winged insect related to the thrips; a pest of bulb flowers in temperate regions (see *Thysanoptera*).

FREE PUPA. See *Exarate.*

FRENATAE. A group of Lepidoptera comprising the majority of moths; those whose wings have a *frenulum, i.e.* one or more strong bristles on the hind-wing which interlock with the fore-wings during flight. (See also *Lepidoptera, Moth, Heterocera, Heteroneura.*)

FRENULUM. See *Frenatae.*

FREQUENCY OF WING-BEAT. Generally large insects such as butterflies move their wings slowly and tiny insects such as gnats and midges very rapidly. The latter make use of a special type of muscle which contracts suddenly when it is suddenly stretched and relaxes equally quickly when released. The frequency of wing movement can be determined by comparing the 'hum' with the corresponding sound of a tuning fork or other musical instrument in which the frequency of each note is known. The following are the estimated wing-frequencies per second of some common insects: Butterflies 10, larger moths 50–70, bees and house flies 200, mosquitoes 600, small midges 1,000 or more (see also *Flight*).

FRINGE-WINGED FLY. See *Thysanoptera*.

FRIT FLY. *Oscinella* and other members of the family Chloropidae: minute black two-winged flies whose larvae bore into the stems of cereal crops.

FRITILLARIES. A group of butterflies of the family Nymphalidae, usually brown or orange with black markings in a chequerboard type of pattern and with silver spots on the undersides of the wings. The group includes nine British species, many North American and a number of large, brightly coloured tropical butterflies.

FROG-HOPPER. *Philaenus spumarius* and related species of plant-bugs (see *Cercopidae*).

FRONS. The frontal cuticular plate of the head of an insect, bounded dorsally by the *epicranium* and laterally by the *genae*. In descriptions, often used loosely for the space between the ocelli and the antennae.

FRONTAL GANGLION. A median ganglion in the head of an insect just in front of the brain and connected to the ventricular ganglion on the hind part of the oesophagus. It forms part of the visceral or sympathetic system.

FRONTAL GLAND. A gland in the front of the head from which poison is discharged from certain insects, *e.g.* termites.

FRONTAL PORE. The pore of the frontal gland of a termite or other insect (see *Frontal Gland*).

FRONTAL SAC. The *Ptilinum*, a sac or vesicle on the head of a fly by which the insect pushes open the puparium as it emerges. Afterwards the sac is withdrawn into the head leaving a U-shaped line, the *ptilinal suture*, enclosing a crescentic structure, the *lunule*.

FRONTAL SUTURE. A term used ambiguously and therefore best avoided. It is sometimes applied to the *ptilinal fissure*, the scar left when the ptilinum is withdrawn in adult Cyclorrhapha (Diptera); in other insects it is often used to denote the epicranial suture (*q.v.*).

FRONTO-CLYPEUS. A cuticular plate formed by fusion of the *frons* and the *clypeus* on the heads of some insects.

FROSTED ORANGE MOTH. *Ochria ochracea*: a medium sized European moth having the fore-wings bright yellow with reddish brown spots and two transverse bands of brown. The hind-wings are buff coloured with a grey spot.

FROTH GLANDS. Glands of the Frog-hopper that produce 'cuckoo-spit' (see *Cercopidae*).

FRUIT AND VINEGAR FLIES. See *Drosophilidae*.

FRUIT BORERS. A name for a number of insects that lay their eggs in fruits or whose larvae bore into fruits. They belong to many different orders and include fruit-flies, sawflies, weevils and other beetles, codling moths etc.

FRUIT-FLY. A name given to two distinct families of Diptera, *viz*. Trypetidae and Drosophilidae. The first is a group of about 1,500 species of small, often brightly coloured flies that attack flowers and fruits of various kinds, sometimes producing galls. They include well known pests such as the Celery Fly, Cherry Fly and Hawthorn Fruit-fly of Europe, the Melon Fly and the Olive Fly of warmer countries etc. The second group, the Drosophilidae are the Fruit and Vinegar Flies that do no harm but are extremely prolific. They include the well known *Drosophila melanogaster* which is bred extensively in laboratories for genetic experiments (see *Drosophilidae*).

FRUIT GALL FLIES. Trypetidae. See *Fruit-fly*.

FULGORA. *Fulgora lanternaria*, the largest of the Lantern-flies from tropical South America (see *Fulgoridae*).

FULGORIDAE. Lantern-flies: large brilliantly coloured tropical plant-bugs of the group Homoptera. They may be up to 7 cm. long with a wing-span of 9 cm. The head is curiously elongated and rounded, for which reason they are sometimes called Alligator Bugs. It was formerly thought that the head was luminous but there is little definite evidence for this.

FUMARIA. A genus of Bagworm Moths, some species of which live in the steppes and forested plains of Europe. The caterpillars feed on grasses.

FUNDATRIGENIAE. Wingless parthenogenetic female aphids that later give rise to winged sexual forms (see *Aphis*).

FUNDATRIX. The first wingless female aphis of a season, later giving rise to numerous parthenogenetic females and eventually to winged sexual forms (see *Aphis*).

FUNGUS ANTS. Ants that cultivate fungi as food (see *Atta* and *Fungus Cultivation*).

FUNGUS BORERS. A name for a number of insects whose larvae bore into fungi. They include some Diptera, Coleoptera, Lepidoptera and Hymenoptera.

FUNGUS CULTIVATION. Both ants and termites apparently cultivate fungi as food. The genus *Atta*, the Leaf-cutting Ant or Parasol Ant of South America, is particularly noteworthy. Workers carry pieces of leaves etc. into the nest, chew them and mix them with saliva. This forms a medium for the growth of certain specific fungi which have apparently evolved in association with the ants. A queen founding a new colony will take a pellet of this fungus into the new nest.

In the case of termites, leaves are taken in and fungi that grow on these are used as food, but this is probably a random and perhaps accidental activity.

FUNGUS GNATS. Small flies of the family Mycetophilidae whose larvae, like tiny white maggots with black heads, bore into mushrooms and other fungi.

FURCA (FURCULA). (1) Any fork-like structure; used of various parts of the body of an insect, *e.g.* caudal furca, labellar furca etc.

(2) The term *furcula* is also used with particular reference to the forked tails of Collembola (springtails). In these insects the furcula is normally bent forwards and retained beneath the abdomen by a 'catch' or *retinaculum* known as the *hamula*. When the catch is released the furcula springs back propelling the insect forwards.

FURNITURE BEETLE. A name for a number of small beetles of the family Anobiidae whose larvae bore into wood. They include the common brown furniture beetle or 'woodworm' *Anobium punctatum* and the larger Death-watch Beetle *Xestobium rufovillosum* (see *Anobiidae* and *Death-watch Beetle*).

G

GADFLY. A name given to a number of blood-sucking flies but particularly the Tabanidae which attack cattle, horses and other animals. The European gadfly *Tabanus bovinus* is about 25 mm. long, coloured black and yellowish brown; other common species are about half this length. The female sucks the blood of horses and cattle, attacking them in vulnerable parts and causing sores. Some species are carriers of Trypanosomes and other parasites. The larvae, which are predatory, live mainly in wet situations, in mud or under shallow water. They move to a drier place to pupate.

GAEAD. A term suggested to denote the young of Ametabola, *i.e.* those insects that undergo no metamorphosis. Since the young are practically identical with the adults in form and habits, the names *larva* and *nymph*, used for the young of other insects, are inappropriate.

GALEA. A hood-like outer lobe on the maxilla of an insect.

GALEATUS. A genus of lacebugs of the family Tingidae: minute plant-bugs, less than 5 mm. long with transparent lace-like upper wings.

GALERUCINAE. A subfamily of leaf-beetles of the family Chrysomelidae with soft oval bodies and sometimes with very enlarged abdomens. Some are pests of woodland trees; others are semi-aquatic and feed on lily pads or other floating plants. Of the woodland species *Galerucella xanthomelaena* feeds on elm leaves and *Galerucella lineola* attacks willows.

GALL. An abnormal growth of plant tissues caused by various organisms which irritate the plant and possibly lead to the production of some type of growth hormone. The principal gall-causing insects or *gallicolae* belong to four different orders: (1) Gall-wasps and some sawflies belonging to the Hymenoptera; (2) Gall-midges belonging to the order Diptera; (3) Certain Aphids, coccids and their allies among the Hemiptera; (4) The larvae of certain moths (Lepidoptera). Galls are also sometimes formed by mites, eel-worms and fungi. Galls in general may be classed as open or closed. The former, produced by aphids, coccids etc. are formed by the insect feeding from the outside, causing the leaf to fold over and make a pocket in which it continues to feed. Closed galls, on the other hand, are those in which a larva lives and develops completely within the gall, only emerging as an adult insect. Galls of this type are generally produced by the larvae of beetles, wasps, moths or flies. Eggs may be deposited beneath the skin of the host plant, or the larva may bore into the tissues. In any case the gall completely surrounds the larva and grows as it grows. Finally the adult insect eats its way out. Oak-apples and oak marble-galls are of this type.

GALLERIIDAE. Honeycomb Moths and related species: a family of small brown or grey moths whose larvae infest beehives. The larva of *Galleria mellonella* is known as the wax-worm and is a well known pest of beehives, where it feeds on pollen and wax and causes considerable loss of honey. Some species also attack wasps' nests and others are scavengers feeding on dead animal or vegetable matter.

GALL-FLY. A name given to some members of the family Trypetidae: a group of about 1,500 species of small, often brightly coloured two-winged flies whose larvae feed upon various flowers and fruits, sometimes forming galls.

GALL-GNAT. See *Cecidomyidae*.

GALLICOLAE. A name given to any insects that produce and live in galls, but more particularly to the gall-dwelling stages of certain plant-lice such as the Adelgidae.

GALL-LOUSE. A name for a number of minute plant-lice (Homoptera) that produce galls. They include the Woolly Aphis of apple trees and other aphids that attack elms and poplars; closely related to the aphids are the Adelgidae which produce galls on young shoots of spruce and other conifers.

GALL-MAKING MAPLE BORER. *Xylothrechus aceris*, a small long-horned beetle of the family Cerambycidae whose larvae bore into the wood of maples and related trees and produce galls.

GALL-MIDGE. See *Cecidomyidae*.

GALL NUTS. A name given to any galls of the hard, round, woody type (see *Gall*).

GALL-SAWFLY. A number of sawflies (Hymenoptera–Symphyta) can produce galls by boring into plants and inserting their eggs. One of the best known is the Bean-gall Sawfly, *Pontania proxima*, which produces red, pink or orange bean-like swellings on willow leaves.

GALL-WASP. A name for a large group of small wasp-like insects of the family Cynipidae whose larvae produce a variety of galls on many different plants. These include oak-apples, robin's pincushion, silk button and blister galls etc. (see *Cynipoidea*).

GALL-WEEVIL. *Ceuthorhynchus* and related genera: small weevils whose larvae produce rounded galls on the roots of many plants. *Ceuthorhynchus pleurostigma*, the Turnip and Cabbage Gall-weevil is a well known example.

GARDEN BLACK ANT. *Acanthomyops (Lasius) niger*, also known as the Small Black Ant: one of the commonest species in Britain and elsewhere, having workers of two kinds; the larger about 6 mm. and the smaller about 3 mm. This species may nest in the earth, in old tree stumps, beneath paving stones or in the walls of houses. It may invade dwellings in large numbers but is not a serious pest.

GARDEN CHAFER. *Phyllopertha horticola*, a beetle of the family Scarabaeidae similar in colouring to the cockchafer *Melolontha* but very much smaller. The wing-cases are light brown and the rest of the body greenish black. The fat, soft-bodied larvae feed on various plants and are found in woods and gardens.

GARDEN FLEA. *Papirius*, a common genus of Collembola or Springtails: a pest of young vegetables in some countries.

GARDEN PEBBLE MOTH. *Evergestis forficalis*: a small brown and white moth of the family Pyralidae having prominent snout-like palps, narrow whitish fore-wings and fringed hind-wings marked with oblique brown lines. Eggs are laid under the leaves of cabbages etc. on which the green caterpillars feed. They hibernate underground in silk cocoons.

GARDEN SWIFT MOTH. *Hepialus lupulina*: a medium sized, light brown moth with white markings on the wings of the male. Like other members of

97

the family Hepialidae it is in many ways a primitive moth; there is no proboscis; the palps are poorly developed; the fore and hind-wings have similar venation and the interlocking of the wings during flight is not brought about by a *frenulum* or bristle, as in most moths, but by a *jugum*, a projecting lobe on the fore-wing which lies on top of the hind-wing during flight, but is capable of being tucked under the hind-wing when at rest. The caterpillars are whitish with a brown head; they live underground and feed on the roots of grass and other plants, or in wood.

GARDEN TIGER MOTH. *Arctia caja*: one of the largest and commonest of the Tiger Moths of Europe and Asia. It has a scarlet body; the fore-wings are prominently marked in a mosaic of chocolate and cream; the hind-wings are scarlet with dark brown spots. The caterpillars, known as Woolly Bears, are large, brown and hairy; they feed on stinging nettles, dandelion, dock etc.

GARDEN WEBWORM. *Loxostege similalis*, a small pyralid moth whose caterpillars are gregarious and live in webs of silk which they spin over the leaves of maize, cotton, lucerne etc. They are common pests in North America.

GASTEROPHILIDAE (GASTROPHILIDAE). See *Bot Fly*.

GASTEROPHILUS (GASTROPHILUS). The principal genus of Horse Bot Flies. *Gasterophilus intestinalis* is a large hairy fly with colouring much like that of a bee. It lays its eggs on the hairs or the legs of horses and these are licked off and swallowed. The larvae, sometimes in large numbers, attach themselves to the stomach wall by means of hooks. Here they develop, are cast out with the faeces and pupate in the soil. A closely related species *Gasterophilus haemorrhoidalis* lays its eggs on the lips or in the nose of horses. Its life history is much the same as that of *Gasterophilus intestinalis*.

GASTRODES. *Gastrodes grossipes*: a plant-bug of the order Hemiptera, family Lygaeidae, living in the cones of pine, spruce and other conifers.

GASTROPACHA. *Gastropacha quercifolia*, the Lappet Moth: one of the larger members of the family of Eggar Moths (Lasiocampidae) having reddish brown wings and body; the fore-wings, which are serrated along their outer edge, have three dark zig-zag lines running obliquely across them. When resting the moth resembles a bunch of dead leaves. The caterpillars are large, grey-brown and hairy and have fleshy 'lappets' on each side of the body. They feed on blackthorn, hawthorn, fruit trees etc.

GASTROPHYSA. *Gastrophysa viridula*, the Dock Leaf Beetle, a small oval beetle with wing-cases of a shining metallic green colour; one of the Chrysomelidae. *Gastrophysa polygoni* is a smaller species with red thorax and legs. Both feed on the leaves of dock, knotgrass and other plants of the family Polygonaceae.

GASTROTHECA. The part of an insect's pupal case covering the abdomen.

GATEKEEPER. An alternative name for the Hedge Brown or Small Meadow Brown Butterfly *Maniola tithonus*: a common European butterfly of the family Satyridae having wings of bright orange-red with broad margins of dark brown and with a small black eye-spot on each fore-wing. The pale whitish grey caterpillars feed on grass.

GELASTOCORIDAE. Toad Bugs: small hemipteran bugs with broad rough bodies and prominent eyes giving an appearance of small toads. They hop along in search of prey and are to be found on the muddy shores of lakes and streams, principally in North America.

GELECHIIDAE. Palp Moths: a large family of small moths with prominent palps and with fringed hind-wings. The larvae feed in various ways. Some make galls; others tie the terminal buds and leaves of plants into silk-bound nests within which they feed. The best known pest species in this family are the Angoumois Grain Moth (*Sitotroga cerealella*) and the Pink Boll-worm of cotton (*Platyedra gossypiella*). *Gelechia nundinella* is a pest of potato plants.

GELIS. A genus of small parasitic or hyperparasitic ichneumon flies whose wingless, ant-like females lay their eggs in the bodies of other insects; some species, for instance, are parasites within the body of the Braconid *Apanteles* which itself is a parasite of caterpillars. Another species *Gelis melanocephala* lays its eggs inside the eggs of spiders within a cocoon.

GENAE. The lateral cuticular plates of an insect's head, below and behind the eyes: the 'cheeks'.

GENICULATE. A term used to describe any organ that is bent in the middle like a knee or elbow, as for instance the antennae of an ant.

GENITALIA. The genitalia or genital organs of an insect are very variable but are usually made up of the following parts:

(1) *External Organs: male.* These are on the ninth abdominal segment and consist of (a) a pair of claspers or *gonopods* for grasping the female when mating; (b) a pair of processes called parameres; (c) the penis or intromittent organ from which the *gonopore* opens.

(2) *Internal Organs: male.* (a) Two testes each made up of a number of sacs or follicles; (b) a *vas deferens* or genital duct leading from each testis, the two meeting in the middle to form a single ejaculatory duct running through the penis; (c) a number of seminal vesicles or storage vessels for holding seminal fluid; (d) a number of accessory glands.

(3) *External Organs: female.* Many insects have a conspicuous ovipositor consisting of three pairs of long narrow 'valves' or outgrowths from the 8th and 9th abdominal segments. These may interlock or may be permanently united to form a tubular egg-laying device. In some cases, for instance in worker bees and wasps, the ovipositor is modified to form a sting.

(4) *Internal Organs: female.* These consist of (a) two ovaries each made up of a number of branches or *ovarioles* in which the eggs develop; (b) two oviducts meeting in the middle to form a main duct leading to the vagina; (c) several accessory glands secreting a glue-like substance for sticking the eggs on to leaves etc.; (d) a *spermatheca* or sac for receiving and storing the seminal fluid and releasing it as the eggs are laid.

Although the above scheme is generally true, there are many variations and specialized adaptations.

GEOFFROY'S TUBIC MOTH. *Alabonia geoffrella*: a small woodland moth of the family Oecophoridae having a wing-pattern of light and dark brown with patches of creamy yellow on the fore-wings. There are broad fringes of hairs on the hind-wings and on the ends of the fore-wings. The caterpillars feed on rotting wood.

GEOMETRIDAE. A very large world-wide family of moths, sometimes regarded as several families but all characterized by having 'looper' caterpillars, otherwise known as geometers or 'earth-measurers'; in America they are called 'inchworms'. They move by a looping action owing to the absence of abdominal feet or prolegs except at the hind-end. Progress is made by holding on with the thoracic legs and then drawing up the hind-part by arching the body. The abdominal feet or claspers at the hind-end then grip the support and the whole body moves forwards. Some caterpillars of this group are very stick-like, especially when they stand up on the claspers and stiffen the body.

GEOPINUS. A North American ground beetle of the family Carabidae, well adapted to a wide range of temperature. It lives in underground burrows in sandy soil and makes a small mound above the entrance to its nest.

GEOTAXIS. A tendency to move or crawl towards or into the earth (positive geotaxis) or away from the earth (negative geotaxis). The larvae of some insects, for instance, go upwards towards food and go downwards or underground as soon as they have fed.

GEOTRUPES. A genus of large, black or shining blue dung beetles or Dor Beetles (Scarabaeidae) that burrow into the ground and take down balls of dung as food for the developing larvae: *Geotrupes stercorarius*, the Common Dor Beetle; *Geotrupes sylvaticus*, the Wood Dor Beetle; *Geotrupes vernalis*, the Spring Dor Beetle etc. (see *Dor Beetle*).

GERMAN COCKROACH. *Blattella germanica*, also called the Croton Bug, a pale brown species of cockroach about 12 mm. long; a common pest in most parts of the world.

GERMAN WASP. *Vespula germanica*: a common species of wasp very similar to *Vespula vulgaris* but with the black bands on the abdomen wider and more pronounced.

GERMARIUM. That part of an ovary or testis that contains the primary germinal cells, *oogonia* and *spermatogonia* respectively. The ovary of an insect usually consists of a number of branches or ovarioles, each containing a germarium and a *vitellarium*, the latter producing the yolk. A testis consists of a number of tubules or follicles with a germarium near the apex of each.

GERRIDAE. Pondskaters; elongated water-bugs of the group Heteroptera that glide with a fast jerky movement on the surface of ponds. They feed on any living or dead insects that fall into the water, grasping these with their front legs; the middle and hind-legs are used for locomotion. The under part of the body is covered with fine hydrofuge hairs that trap a cushion of air under the insect, preventing it from sinking and enabling it to move rapidly. *Gerris lacustris*, about 10 mm. long and *Gerris paludum*, slightly larger, are the two commonest species.

GHOST LARVA. The aquatic larva of the Phantom Midge (see *Chaoborus*).

GHOST MOTH. *Hepialus humuli*: a medium sized moth of the family Hepialidae, a primitive group with small antennae, no proboscis and no frenulum on the hind-wings. The fore-wings of the males are white with brown borders; the body and hind-wings are brown and in the case of the female both wings are brown. The name 'Ghost Moth' is given from the fact that the males with their prominent white fore-wings fly with a gentle swaying movement in large numbers at dusk giving a ghostly appearance.

The larva, white with a brown head, lives underground and feeds on a variety of roots. (See *Hepialidae*.)

GIANT CHROMOSOMES. Exceptionally large, many-threaded chromosomes sometimes up to 0.2 mm. in length, found in the salivary glands of *Drosophila* and some other Diptera. They arise from the pairing of homologous chromosomes which then repeatedly split lengthwise without the newly-formed chromatids separating. The fact that the fruit-fly Drosophila contains only four pairs of these easily seen chromosomes and the fact that many clearly visible features are capable of undergoing mutation are the chief reasons why this insect has been used so extensively for experimental work on genetics.

GIANT COCCID. *Margarodes* and related genera of large scale-insects that live underground enclosed in shining waxy secretions known as 'ground pearls'. In parts of South America these are worn by natives as ornaments.

GIANT LACEWING. *Osmylus fulvicephalus*: one of the largest of the European Neuroptera having a slender, dark grey or brown body and two pairs of large lace-like wings with a span of about 5 cm. It is to be found near streams, the larvae living among wet moss and feeding on other insects.

GIANT ORANGE TIP. *Hebomoia* and related Asiatic genera of large pierid butterflies. *Hebomoia glaucippe*, white with orange-pink wing-tips bordered with black has a wing-span of about 12 cm. *Hebomoia vossi* of Indonesia is slightly smaller and has bright yellow wings with similar orange tips.

GIANT SILKWORM MOTHS. Saturniidae: a family which includes some of the world's largest and most brightly coloured moths whose larvae spin silken cocoons, many of which are used commercially. They include *Samia cecropia*, the largest North American moth; *Philosamia cynthia*, the Cynthia Moth of China, Japan and Indonesia; the Atlas, Hercules and Luna Moths and many others, mostly from South-east Asia. Attempts have been made to introduce some of these into the United States but without much success.

GIANT SKIPPER. *Rhopalocampta benjamini*: a medium sized butterfly of the family Hesperiidae, subfamily Megathyminae, having greenish black wings with the veins specially strengthened in the male. It is in many ways moth-like and sometimes flies by night; found all over India and South-east Asia.

GIANT WATER BUG. See *Belostomatidae*.

GIANT WOODWASP. *Sirex gigas* or *Urocerus gigas*, also called the Horntail: a very large member of the sawfly family (Hymenoptera–Symphyta) resembling a hornet but without the narrow waist. The head and thorax are black and the abdomen yellow. The female has a broad black band across the middle of the abdomen, but the most noteworthy feature is the extremely large needle-like ovipositor, often mistaken for a sting. This is about 2 cm. long and the whole insect may be up to 5 cm. The ovipositor is used for boring deeply into pine and other soft woods. Here the eggs are laid and the larvae may take up to three years to mature. For this reason they sometimes emerge long after the timber has been cut and perhaps used for building or other purposes.

GILLS. The so-called gills of aquatic insects are thin-walled outgrowths of the abdomen in the form of lamellae or filaments. In mayfly nymphs (Ephemeroptera) there are paired lateral gills on nearly all the abdominal segments; in the nymphs of Damselflies (Zygoptera) there are three elongated caudal gills; in Dragonflies (Anisoptera) the nymph has rows of gills projecting into the rectum. In all these cases the gills are liberally supplied with tracheae and are therefore known as *tracheal gills*. In some other aquatic insects such as mosquito larvae there are gill-like structures known as *blood-gills* but it is now considered that these are primarily for the absorption of dissolved salts and that respiration takes place over most of the body surface.

GILPINIA. *Gilpinia hercyniae*, the Spruce Sawfly: a European species that has been accidentally introduced into North America and elsewhere but has been kept in check by a virus disease. The larvae feed on the needles of spruce and other conifers.

GIPSY MOTH. *Lymantria dispar*: a Tussock moth introduced accidentally from Europe into North America where it has become a serious pest of forestry, but has now been largely controlled by the introduction of suitable parasites. The moth has been extinct in Britain for over 100 years.

GIRDLED BURROWING BEE. *Andrena cingulata*: a medium sized mining bee, black with grey hairs on the thorax and with a broad reddish yellow band across the middle of the abdomen; a good pollinator of fruit trees and one whose sting is too weak to penetrate human skin.

GIRDLED COLLETES. *Colletes succincta*: a mining bee resembling a small hive bee in shape and colouring; the head and thorax are densely covered with brown hair; the abdomen has rings of short white hairs with shining black spaces between them. They nest in burrows in sandy soil or in the crumbling mortar of old masonry.

GIZZARD. Also called the *proventriculus*: a part of the alimentary canal immediately behind the crop, varying greatly in different insects but having as its main function the sifting of food before digestion and absorption can take place in the mid-gut. It is poorly developed in sucking insects but in those that chew solid food it is usually enlarged and horny and is sometimes equipped with powerful circular muscles and radial teeth with which the harder particles of food can be crushed.

GLANVILLE FRITILLARY. *Melitaea cinxia*, a European butterfly rare in Britain except in the Isle of Wight, having wings of pale golden brown streaked and spotted with black and edged with white. The undersides of the hind-wings are cream coloured, dotted with black and with two transverse bands of golden brown. The larvae, which are dark brown and hairy, feed gregariously in silken bags on plantain.

GLASSHOUSE THRIPS. *Heliothrips haemorrhoidalis*, a minute insect of the order Thysanoptera having narrow wings fringed with fine hairs. The larvae are pests of apple and other trees, feeding on the leaves and leaving characteristic stains of brown excrement.

GLASS-WINGED BUTTERFLIES. See *Haetera*.

GLISCHROCHILUS. A genus of predatory beetles of the family Nitulidae having flattened bodies and living under the bark of trees. They feed, both as adults and as larvae, upon the eggs and larvae of bark beetles. They are therefore beneficial to the forester. *Glischrochilus quadripustulatus*, about 5 mm. long, is black with four red spots on the wing-covers.

GLOSSAE. A pair of tongue-like lobes in the middle of the labium of an insect (see also *Paraglossae*).

GLOSSINIDAE. Tsetse flies: a family of viviparous, biting flies similar in general appearance to the house fly but a little larger and of a brownish colour. They are found in Central Africa and are notorious as transmitters of trypanosomes, the blood parasites that cause sleeping sickness and other diseases. *Glossina palpalis* is the carrier of *Trypanosoma gambiense*, the cause of Gambian sleeping sickness in man, and *Trypanosoma vivax* causing the disease *surra* in horses and cattle; *Glossina morsitans* carries Rhodesian sleeping sickness in man and *nagana* in horses, cattle, pigs and goats.

GLOSSOSOMA. A genus of caddis flies (Trichoptera) whose aquatic larvae build short, almost round cases of small stones etc.

GLOW-WORM. The wingless worm-like female of the beetle *Lampyris noctiluca* and a number of other species of the family Lampyridae, bearing phosphorescent organs on the sides of the abdomen, used apparently to attract the males. The exact nature of the chemical action which produces the light is not known but it is generally believed that a substance named *luciferin* is oxidized with the help of an enzyme known as *luciferase*. The energy so produced generates a continuous spectrum of visible light with very little heat. It depends upon a plentiful supply of oxygen and is under the control of the nervous system. The phenomenon should therefore strictly be called chemoluminescence rather than phosphorescence. In many species the winged males are also luminescent (see *Firefly*).

GLOW-WORM, NEW ZEALAND. The luminous larva of a Fungus Gnat *Bolitophila (Arachnocampa) luminosa*, an insect resembling a crane-fly that lives in vast numbers in certain caves. It makes sticky, branching webs with numerous hanging threads used for trapping other insects which are apparently attracted by the light and blunder into the threads, which are not luminous, and therefore remain invisible.

GLYPTA. *Glypta rufiscutellaris*, a small parasitic ichneumon fly that has been used to control the Oriental Fruit Moth, *Grapholitha molesta* and other pests of fruit trees. It is indigenous to North America but has been introduced to many other countries. The parasites lay their eggs in the bodies of the fruit-moth caterpillars; the ichneumon larvae eat away the caterpillars from the inside and eventually emerge. (See *Grapholitha*.)

GLYPTOCOMBUS. A genus of bug having the anterior legs widened and flattened for burrowing.

GNAT. A name used somewhat loosely for many different two-winged insects of the suborder Nematocera in which the males fly in dancing swarms. They include the less virulent mosquitoes such as *Culex pipiens*; the Winter Gnats (Trichoceridae), Fungus Gnats (Mycetophilidae), Phantom Gnats (Chaoborinae) etc.

GNATHOCERUS. *Gnathocerus cornutus*, the Broad-horned Flour Beetle: a small reddish brown beetle, a pest of flour mills and food stores in most parts of the world. The male is about 4 mm. long and has two curious horn-like projections from the vertex of the head.

GNOMA. *Gnoma bisduvali*: a longhorn beetle about 3 cm. long, having a constricted 'neck' and very long antennae. These are about twice the length of the body and are curled backwards and downwards.

GNORIMOSCHEMA. *Gnorimoschema operculella* and related species: Potato Tuber Moths. Small moths of the family Gelechiidae having narrow wings fringed with long hairs. The larvae, known as 'tuberworms', are pests in many parts of the world, feeding on the leaves of potato, tobacco etc. and tunnelling into potato tubers.

GNORIMUS. A genus of Chafer Beetles (Scarabaeidae) similar to the Rose Chafer but smaller and of a golden green colour.

GOAT MOTH. See *Cossidae*.

GOERA. A genus of caddis flies (Trichoptera) having the wings covered with thick hair. The larvae live in running water and make tubular cases of small stones weighted at the sides with extra large ones.

GOLD BEETLE (GOLD BUG). A name used loosely in America for any of a large number of beetles whose wing-cases are of a golden colour. The name possibly originated from Edgar Allan Poe's story 'The Gold Bug'.

GOLD-EYE FLY. *Chrysops caecutiens* or any other species of *Chrysops*: blood-sucking tabanid flies related to the horse flies and having brilliant golden-green eyes.

GOLD FRINGE MOTH. *Hypsopygia costalis*: a small moth of the family Pyralidae, reddish brown with yellow markings and yellow fringes on the wings. It frequents hay-stacks and thatched buildings on which the larvae feed.

GOLD-TAIL (YELLOW-TAIL). *Euproctis similis*: one of the tussock moths (Lymantriidae) having white wings and body with a bright yellow tip on the abdomen. The caterpillars are red, black and white and are covered with irritant hairs. They feed chiefly on hawthorn leaves and pupate in silken cocoons.

GOLDEN APPLE BEETLE. *Chrysomela fastuosa*: a small leaf-eating beetle about 6 mm. long, the size and shape of a ladybird, having golden-green elytra with a dark blue stripe along the inner edge of each; common on many wayside plants, particularly on nettles.

GOLDEN CRYPTOCEPHALUS. *Cryptocephalus aureolus*: a pale, golden-green beetle with elongated oval body and small head tucked under the thorax; commonly found on composite flowers.

GOLDEN-EYE. An alternative name for the Green Lacewing Fly (see *Chrysopidae*).

GOLDEN OAK SCALE. *Asterolecanium variolosum*, a scale-insect of the family Coccidae, a common pest of oak trees that has spread to many parts of the world. It was at one time a major forestry problem in New Zealand but was successfully controlled by introducing a parasitic encyrtid wasp *Habrolepis dalmani* from North America. (See *Coccidae*.)

GOLDEN PLUSIA MOTH. *Polychrisia moneta*, a European noctuid moth, light brown with white markings on the wings and with prominent tufts of scales on the thorax. It has recently spread to the British Isles and is to be found in parks and gardens where the larvae feed on delphinium and aconite.

GOLDEN ROD GALL. (1) A small spherical gall produced on Golden Rod (*Solidago*) by the larvae of the two-winged fly *Eurosta solidaginis*.

(2) A gall produced on the stems of Golden Rod by moths of the genus *Gnorimoschema*, some of which also attack the roots of asters.

GOLDEN ROD NOMAD BEE. *Nomada solidaginis*: a small hairless bee resembling a wasp with bright yellow and black stripes on the abdomen; commonly found on Golden Rod (*Solidago*). The female lays her eggs in the underground nests of *Andrena* and other mining bees. The newly hatched *Nomada* larvae feed on the pollen and nectar stored by the host as well as on its eggs and larvae.

GOLDEN SWIFT MOTH. *Hepialus hecta*: a golden brown moth, the male having three oblique white lines on the fore-wings. Like all the Hepialidae it has short antennae and no proboscis. The larvae feed on bracken.

GOLDSMITH BEETLE. See *Cetonia*.

GOLIATH BEETLE. *Goliathus meleagris* and related species of large African beetles of the family Cetoniidae. They are among the bulkiest insects in the world and may have a length of up to 10 cm. The body is covered with fine sensitive hairs and the wing-cases are marked with pearly grey and black. The males have a prominent rostrum with two horn-like projections. Other species include *Goliathus atlas*, *Goliathus regius* and *Goliathus giganteus*. The latter, the largest, is over 11 cm. long and has dark reddish brown wing-cases. Most of these beetles are rarely seen as they fly through the African forests at a great height and do not often land on the ground. The larvae develop in the rotting wood of palm and other trees.

GOLOFA. *Golofa pizarro*, the Mexican Rhinoceros Beetle: a large brown beetle about 5 cm. long with a prominent 'horn' on the head of the male. This horn curves forwards in an arch and ends in a triangular tip with yellowish hairs on its underside. *Golofa porteri*, a species from Colombia, is nearly twice as large and has two rows of sharp teeth along one side of the horn (see *Dynastidae*).

GOMPHOCERIPPUS. *Gomphocerippus rufus*, the Rufus Grasshopper: a medium sized European grasshopper found chiefly on chalk and limestone hills. The body may be various shades of red or brown and the club-shaped antennae end in distinctive white swellings.

GOMPHUS. A genus of large dragonflies sometimes classed with the Aeshnidae but more usually in a separate family, Gomphidae. They are slow-flying and the females keep away from the water except when pairing. This takes place in trees and the eggs are dropped into running streams. The nymphs are thick-set with small wing-cases and with a short flat mask (labium).

GONAPOPHYSES. An imprecise term used to denote various abdominal appendages involved in copulation and oviposition.

GONEPTERYX. *Gonepteryx rhamni*, the Brimstone Butterfly: a member of the family Pieridae found all over Europe and Asia as far as Japan. The males are a brilliant sulphur yellow and the females are greenish white. Both sexes have a small reddish spot near the centre of each wing. The larvae feed on Buckthorn (*Rhamnus*). In Britain these butterflies hibernate in the adult stage and are among the first to appear in the spring.

GONGYLUS. *Gongylus gongyloides*, the Rose Mantid of India: a predatory insect remarkable for its protective resemblance to a flower. The long slender green thorax resembles a plant stalk or petiole with leaf-like expansions on the hind-legs and with a rose-pink colour underneath the body.

GONIA. A genus of tachinid flies that parasitize caterpillars of Turnip Moths. They lay large numbers of eggs in plants such as turnips, lettuce or carrots where the young tachinid larvae will search out their victims.

GONIODES. A genus of bird-lice of the order Mallophaga. *Goniodes pavonis*, the Peacock Louse, is about 3 mm. long and has a broad head with a horn-like projection on each side.

GONIOPS. A genus of horse flies (Tabanidae) containing the single species *Goniops chrysocoma*. They lay their eggs on leaves over water and then use their claws to attach themselves to the leaf where they protect the eggs until they hatch.

GONIPTERUS. *Gonipterus scutellatus*, the Eucalyptus Weevil of Australia: a small beetle whose larvae and adults feed on Eucalyptus leaves. It has spread to many countries but has been satisfactorily controlled by the introduction of a parasitic chalcid wasp.

GONODONTIS. *Gonodontis bidentata*, the Scalloped Hazel Moth: a geometrid moth whose wings are patterned with light and dark brown. There is also a melanic (black) variety found in industrial regions. The caterpillar is brown and stick-like and feeds on oak, birch, hazel, hawthorn and many other trees.

GONOPOD (GONOPODIUM). Alternative names for claspers: paired copulatory appendages on the 9th. abdominal segment of a male insect; used for grasping the female when mating.

GONOPORE. The opening of the gonoduct (oviduct or vas deferens). The term is used for small genital apertures such as are found in insects, earthworms etc.

GOOSEBERRY SAWFLY. *Nematus ribesii,* a medium sized sawfly with black head, black and yellow thorax and, in the female, a yellow abdomen. The larvae are frequent pests of currants and gooseberries, sometimes completely defoliating them. Eggs are laid in slits in the leaves and the green larvae that emerge are extremely voracious. Originally a European species, it has spread to North America and other countries.

GORSE WEEVIL. *Apion ulicis,* a minute brown weevil that feeds on the seeds of gorse (*Ulex*). The adult weevil bores a tiny hole in the gorse pod and lays its eggs inside. About a dozen larvae are produced in each pod. In due course these develop into adult beetles which are shot out when the ripe pod splits to scatter its seeds.

GORTYNA. *Gortyna immarus,* the Hop Borer: a medium sized noctuid moth whose whitish spotted caterpillars bore into the stems of hops. *Gortyna micacea,* the Rosy Rustic Moth, is a related species of a rosy brown colour whose larvae feed on the stems and roots of potatoes, tomatoes etc.

GORYTES. *Gorytes mystaceus*: a solitary wasp, large, narrow-waisted and black with very narrow yellow stripes. It feeds on frog-hopper larvae, dragging them from their protective cuckoo-spit and stocking its nest with them.

GOTHIC MOTH. *Naenia typica*: a common noctuid moth whose wings are brown and criss-crossed with white lines in a complicated pattern resembling a spider's web. The larvae feed gregariously on a great variety of plants and pupate underground.

GOUT FLY. *Chlorops pumilionis*: a small two-winged fly related to the fruit-flies, whose larvae burrow into the stems of barley and other cereals causing swelling and distortion which may prevent the ears from developing. Pupation is within the stem.

GRACILARIA. *Gracilaria syringella,* the Lilac Leaf-miner and related species: minute moths whose larvae burrow inside the leaves of lilac, privet etc., several together hollowing out the leaf and causing a shrivelled brown blotch. When these caterpillars become too big for the space within the leaf they emerge and roll the leaf into a funnel-shaped shelter in which they continue to feed.

GRAIN BEETLE. *Oryzaephilus surinamensis,* the Saw-toothed Grain Beetle and related species: minute beetles about 3 mm. long that live within grains of rice, wheat and other cereals and dried fruits. They have spread to many parts of the world and can be a serious pest. Some species are not strong enough to bore into mature grain but will enter after the skin has been pierced by weevils.

GRAIN MOTH. *Sitotroga* and related genera of minute moths whose larvae feed on grain. *Sitotroga cerealella,* a European species has spread to North America and is now a major pest of wheat, maize and other cereal crops.

GRAIN WEEVIL (GRANARY WEEVIL). *Sitophilus* and related genera of minute weevils; world-wide pests that bore into grains of wheat, maize, rice etc. The larvae feed and pupate within the grain and the adults finally eat their way out. *Sitophilus granarius* attacks wheat and maize; *Sitophilus oryza* prefers warmer climates and attacks rice.

GRANNOM. A fishermen's name for *Brachycentrus subnubilis*, the Green-tailed Caddis Fly: a common European species with smoky grey wings. The female is larger than the male and is frequently seen with a bright green cluster of eggs beneath the abdomen. The larval case is usually attached to vegetation.

GRAELLSIA. *Graellsia isabellae*, a large silk-moth from the mountains of Spain and Southern France. It has a wing-span of about 8 cm. and the hind-wings are extended into tails, particularly long in the male. The wings are bluish green with translucent brownish red veins. Each wing has a large translucent eye-spot with rings of blue, yellow and red. The caterpillars feed on conifers.

GRAPE BERRY MOTH. *Polychrosis viteana*: a small moth whose larva feeds on vines and pupates in a rolled-up leaf.

GRAPE CANE GALL MAKER. *Ampeloglypter sesostris*, a small weevil that burrows into vine stems and produces galls.

GRAPE LEAF FOLDER. *Desmia funeralis*, a medium sized moth having dark brown wings edged with white and with two white spots on each. The cater-pillar is a pest of grape vines in North America and elsewhere. It folds the leaves over, binding them with silk and feeds from the inside until the leaf is reduced to a skeleton.

GRAPE LEAF-HOPPER. *Erythroneura comes*: a small yellow, red and brown plant-bug of the family Cicadellidae; a serious pest of vines, which passes the winter as an adult, and feeds on other plants in the spring until vine leaves are available.

GRAPE PHYLLOXERA. *Phylloxera vitifoliae* or *Viteus vitifoliae*: a minute plant-bug of the order Homoptera resembling an aphid and undergoing a very similar life-cycle involving sexual and asexual individuals. At certain stages it makes galls on the stems and roots of vines. It is a serious pest in almost all countries where grapes are grown.

GRAPE ROOTWORM. *Fidia viticida*, a small beetle of the family Chrysome-lidae whose larvae bore into the roots of grape vines in eastern North America.

GRAPHOCEPHALA. *Graphocephala coccinea*, the Rhododendron Leaf-hopper: a small plant-bug of the family Cicadellidae, recently introduced into Britain from America. It feeds on the leaves of Rhododendron and spreads a fungus disease which causes the flower buds to turn brown and die.

GRAPHOLITHA. A genus of moths whose larvae are pests of fruits and seeds. *Grapholitha molesta*, the Oriental Fruit Moth, particularly attacks peaches and has spread to North America and elsewhere. The larvae bore into the stems and into the fruits causing considerable damage. *Grapholitha saltitans* is the cause of the movements of the Mexican Jumping Bean (*Sebastiana*). The larva eats away the inside of the seed and when conditions are warm throws itself from side to side within the hollow seed causing it to jump. Eventually it pupates, hibernates in the seed and emerges as an adult moth. (See also *Glypta*.)

GRAPHOPTERUS. *Graphopterus serrator*, the Masked Ground Beetle: a member of the family Carabidae living on the edges of the North African deserts; the wing-cases have a striking black and white pattern resembling a mask.

GRAPHOSOMA. *Graphosoma italicum*, the Striped Bug of Central and Southern Europe: a black and red pentatomid bug with a large scutellum extending back over the abdomen; commonly found on umbelliferous flowers.

GRAPTA. A genus of butterflies also called *Polygonia* or Angle Wings, having the margins of the wings irregularly notched and angled. *Grapta interrogationis*, the largest, has two silver markings resembling question marks on the undersides of the hind-wings; *Grapta comma* (*Polygonia C-album*) is a smaller species with marks resembling commas (see also *Comma Butterfly*).

GRAPTODERES. A genus of water beetles of the family Dytiscidae; one of the commonest in Central Europe, about 20 mm. long, brown with two dark bands across the thorax and with long, thickly fringed hind-legs.

GRASS GRUB. The larva of a chafer beetle *Costelytra zealandia*, a pest of pastures and cereals in New Zealand. The larva is similar to that of the European cockchafer, having a fat whitish body and short legs. It lives for several years in the soil feeding on roots. It has, however, to some extent been controlled in New Zealand by the introduction of a specific bacterial disease.

GRASSHOPPER. Any of the jumping members (formerly called Saltatoria) of the order Orthoptera: straight-winged hemimetabolous insects with biting mouth-parts and usually having the head bent at right angles to the body. The fore-wings are thickened to form horny *tegmina* which cover the membranous hind-wings; a few species are wingless and all go through a wingless stage in early life. A feature generally associated with grasshoppers is their power of stridulation, a noise made either by rubbing the hind femur against the tegmen or by rubbing the two tegmina together. Most grasshoppers belong to the short-horned group or Acrididae which have very short antennae. These also include locusts but the term grasshopper is usually only used for the non-migratory species. The other group, the long-horned grasshoppers or Tettigoniidae, sometimes called Katydids, have antennae as long as or longer than the body. These include the Great Green Grasshopper *Tettigonia viridissima* of Europe, Asia and North Africa and the Mormon Cricket *Anabrus simplex* a wingless species which is a pest in the western United States.

GRASS MOTH. A name for a number of small pyralid moths of the group Crambinae, sometimes called Crambid Moths. They have narrow fore-wings, broad fringed hind-wings and prominent palps. The larvae make silken tents among the grass on which they feed. *Crambus* and *Agriphila* are two common genera.

GRASS SAWFLY. *Pachynematus*: a genus of small sawflies that lay their eggs on blades of wheat and other cereals on which the larvae feed; pests in North America and elsewhere.

GRASS YELLOW BUTTERFLY. See *Eurema*.

GRAYLING BUTTERFLY. *Eumenis semele* (see *Eumenis*).

GREAT BLACK AND YELLOW DRAGONFLY. *Cordulegaster boltonii*, also called the Golden-ringed Dragonfly: a large species of Hawker Dragonfly (Anisoptera) about 7–8 cm. long, having very large green eyes, broad wings, a black and yellow thorax and a black abdomen ringed with narrow yellow bands.

GREAT BLACK ICHNEUMON. *Rhyssa persuasoria*, the largest of the British ichneumon flies, mostly black but with pale yellow margins on the abdominal segments. The body is about 30 mm. long and the filamentous ovipositor twice this length. It uses this to bore deeply into soft pinewood in order to lay its eggs on the larvae of the Giant Woodwasp *Urocerus gigas*, on which the ichneumon larvae feed.

GREAT DIVING BEETLE. *Dytiscus marginalis*, the largest British species of carnivorous water beetle, although a larger species *Dytiscus latissimus* is found in Central Europe. Both have dark brown, flattened oval bodies with yellow margins on the elytra (see *Dytiscidae*).

GREAT GREEN GRASSHOPPER. *Tettigonia viridissima*, a brilliant green long-horned grasshopper common all over Europe, North Africa and parts of Asia; a predatory insect of hedges, thickets and reed-beds (see *Grasshopper*).

GREAT HORNTAIL. See *Giant Woodwasp*.

GREAT HORSE FLY. *Tabanus sudeticus*: the largest of the European gadflies, blood-sucking flies that attack horses, cattle and other animals; a stoutly built insect about 24 mm. long with grey thorax, greyish brown striped abdomen and a wing-span of about 50 mm. (see *Gadfly*).

GREAT PURPLE HAIRSTREAK. *Quercusia quercus* (sometimes called *Thecla quercus*): a European and British butterfly of the family Lycaenidae having blackish purple iridescent wings and a short 'tail' on each hind-wing. The undersides are grey with black and white transverse lines and a black-centred orange spot on each hind-wing. The larvae feed on oak leaves and pupate in the ground.

GREAT SILVER WATER BEETLE. *Hydrophilus piceus*: the largest British water beetle about 40 mm. long, having an oval black body with reddish antennae. It is slow moving and herbivorous but the larvae are predators. Eggs are laid in silk cases attached to plants.

GREEN AND BLACK LEAF-HOPPER. *Evacanthus interruptus*, a small jumping plant-bug about 6 mm. long, black with yellow stripes, commonly found on oak trees. It was formerly a pest of hop-fields.

GREEN APPLE APHIS. *Aphis pomi* or *Aphis mali*: an aphid that passes its entire life-cycle on apple trees; a pest in almost every part of the world where apples are grown (see *Aphis*).

GREEN ARCHES MOTH. *Anaplectoides prasina*, a noctuid moth having olive green or grey wings marked with black zig-zag lines and a paler greenish band across the fore-wings. The larvae feed at night on hawthorn, birch and other trees.

GREENBOTTLE. A name for a number of bright green flesh flies of the sub-family Calliphorinae, closely allied to the blowflies. *Lucilia caesar* lays its eggs in carrion on which the larvae feed; *Lucilia sericata* and *Lucilia cuprina* may also lay them on sores of sheep etc. the larvae living in open wounds and sucking blood; *Lucilia bufonivora* attacks the eyes and nostrils of frogs and toads.

GREEN CARPET MOTH. *Colostygia pectinaria*: a common geometrid moth having fore-wings of pale green with patches of darker green and brown; the body and hind-wings are greyish. The larva, a grey-brown looper caterpillar, feeds on bedstraw (*Galium*).

GREEN DRAKE. *Ephemera danica*, the largest and best known of the European mayflies (see *Ephemeroptera*).

GREENFLY. A general name for a number of species of green Aphis (see *Aphis*).

GREEN GRASSHOPPER. *Tettigonia viridissima* (see *Great Green Grass hopper*),

GREEN HAIRSTREAK. *Callophrys rubi*: a European and Asiatic butterfly of the family Lycaenidae having brownish wings whose undersides are bright green with thin white hair-like marks. The caterpillars feed on a number of plants, particularly leguminous; they are also occasionally cannibals.

GREEN-HEAD. A name given to several species of *Tabanus*, especially North American, on account of their large, greenish, iridescent eyes (see *Gadfly*).

GREEN JUNE BEETLE. *Cotinis nitida*, also called the Fig-eater: a large metallic green beetle common in the Eastern States of North America, whose larvae live in the soil and feed chiefly on leaf mould, but also damage plants either directly or by loosening the soil round their roots. The Adults feed on figs and other soft fruits.

GREENHOUSE LEAF-TYER (CELERY LEAF-TYER). *Phlyctaenia rubigalis*: a moth of the family Pyralidae whose larvae attack celery and other plants, drawing the leaves and flower buds together and tying them with silk.

GREENHOUSE THRIPS. See *Glasshouse Thrips*.

GREENHOUSE WHITEFLY. *Trialeurodes vaporariorum*, a minute homopteran plant-bug of the family Aleurodidae, having the body covered with fine white waxy powder; a well known pest of tomatoes and other plants. It can be controlled by the introduction of the parasitic chalcid wasp *Encarsia formosa*.

GREEN LACEWING FLY. See *Chrysopidae*.

GREEN LESTES. *Lestes sponsa*, a small metallic blue or green damselfly common among the vegetation of stagnant ponds and ditches of Britain. The female lays her eggs in the stems of plants below the water surface. The nymphs are slim, greenish brown and have three prominent caudal gills at the hind-end of the abdomen (see *Damselfly*).

GREEN LONGHORN MOTH. *Adela viridella*: a small moth of the family Incurvariidae having greenish brown wings bordered with black. Both sexes have very long antennae but those of the male are more than twice the length of the body. They are to be found in oak woods, the males dancing in swarms round the trees. The larvae are leaf-miners attacking oak, birch and other trees. When the leaves drop to the ground the larvae make portable cases of the fragments of dead leaf and feed on these from the inside.

GREEN OAK MOTH. *Tortrix viridana*, also called the Green Oak-roller: a small green moth whose caterpillars are a major defoliator of oak woods. The moth is about 12 mm. long with pale green fore-wings and greyish hind-wings, both wings having a narrow white fringe round the edges. The larvae are green with a black head; they feed on oak leaves, particularly the pedunculate variety, rolling the leaves up and feeding from the inside.

GREEN SILVER LINES. See *Bena*.

GREEN SOLDIER BUG (GREEN STINKBUG). *Acrosternum*: a genus of green pentatomid bugs of North America and elsewhere. Some species are predatory, attacking pests of fruit and vegetable crops; others, *e.g. Acrosternum hilare*, suck the juices of fruits such as peaches, as well as alfalfa, Lima beans and cotton, causing extensive damage.

GREEN SPRUCE APHIS. *Neomyzaphis abietina* also called *Rhopalosiphum abietinum*: a minute green aphis with red eyes, that sucks the juices from young shoots of spruce. The Sitka Spruce, *Picea sitchensis*, is particularly vulnerable but the Norway Spruce and other varieties may also be attacked.

GREEN STONEFLY. See *Chloroperla*.

GREENTAIL. The Green-tailed Caddis Fly *Brachycentrus subnubilis* (see *Grannom*).

GREEN VEINED WHITE. *Pieris napi*: a butterfly closely related to and very similar to the Large White or Cabbage Butterfly *Pieris brassicae*. It differs from it in having a concentration of black scales along the veins on the undersides of the wings. The caterpillars, like those of the Large White, feed on the leaves of cabbages and other cruciferous plants.

GREENWOOD CENTROTUS. See *Centrotus*.

GREGARIA (GREGARIOUS PHASE). A name given to the stage in the life of a locust when millions of them swarm together and migrate. This may only occur after several generations of the solitary phase during which they behave like ordinary grasshoppers. Eventually, however, perhaps due to overcrowding, there comes a change in their appearance and habits. In the solitary phase they are light green, grey or brown; in the gregarious phase boldly patterned in yellow and black. Finally they become excited as they crowd together and eventually fly off in a huge swarm to find new feeding or breeding grounds (see also *Desert Locust*).

GREY BACK. A name sometimes given to the Body Louse or Clothes Louse *Pediculus vestimenti*. Many entomologists, however, regard it as merely a variety or subspecies of the Head Louse *Pediculus capitis*. The name *Pediculus humanus* was used by Linnaeus for both.

GREY DAGGER. See *Dagger Moth*.

GREY HORSE FLY. *Tabanus bromius*, a medium sized blood-sucking fly of the family Tabanidae; a pest of horses.and cattle similar in appearance but much smaller than *Tabanus sudeticus*, the Great Horse Fly (*q.v.*) (See *Gadfly*.)

GREY SHOULDER KNOT. *Grapholitha ornithopus*, a medium sized European moth having pale brownish grey wings with a dark streak at the base of each and with a dotted black line along the front edge of the fore-wing; closely related to the Mexican moth *Grapholitha saltitans* whose larvae live in 'jumping beans' (see *Grapholitha*).

GREY SUGAR CANE MEALY-BUG. *Pseudococcus boninsis*: a small plant-bug of the family Coccidae whose wingless females attach themselves to plant stems, sucking the juices and secreting a white waxy substance. They are pests of sugar cane in Queensland, the West Indies and elsewhere.

GRIPOSIA. The *Merveille du Jour* (*Griposia aprilina*), a European noctuid moth whose greenish mottled wings make a perfect camouflage on the lichen-covered trees on which it rests; the larvae, which are dark brown mottled with green, feed on oak leaves.

GRIZZLED SKIPPER. *Pyrgus malvae*, a small butterfly of the family Hesperiidae having blackish brown wings mottled with cream and with creamy white chequered margins. The greyish larvae feed on wild strawberry leaves, bramble, mallow etc. folding the leaves and binding them together with silk to form a sac within which they feed.

GROMPHADORRHINA. *Gromphadorrhina portentosa*: a giant cockroach of Madagascar, dark brown, about 8–9 cm. long and without wings. When disturbed it emits a snake-like hiss.

GROOVED ACILIUS (SULCATED DIVING BEETLE). *Acilius sulcatus*: a greyish brown water beetle with oval, flattened body about 15 mm. long. The abdomen is black, spotted with yellow along the sides. The elytra of the female have four broad longitudinal furrows or grooves. The larvae are shrimp-like and feed on small aquatic animals.

GROUND BEETLE. See *Carabidae*.

GROUND BUG. A name for a number of small or medium sized plant-bugs (Hemiptera) of the family Lygaeidae. They are elongated, usually dark brown with small head and broad abdomen. The Nettle Bug *Heterogaster urticae* is common on stinging nettles; the Pine Cone Bug *Gastrodes grossipes* lives inside old cones of Spruce, Scots Pine etc. on which it feeds.

GROUND HOPPER. *Tetrix* and related members of the family Tetrigidae, also called Grouse-locusts. They belong to the order Orthoptera and resemble small grasshoppers. They differ from them, however, in having very short front wings partly or completely covered by a large pronotal shield that extends backwards over the body. Most of them live in the tropics and some species have bizarre shapes. They may be flattened resembling a leaf or may have a number of points or thorn-like projections on the body. The colour is usually brown. European species include the Common Ground Hopper (*Tetrix undulata*), the Slender Ground Hopper (*Tetrix subulata*) and the Two-pointed Grouse-locust (*Tetrix bipunctata*). The latter is found in most parts of central and southern Europe, in Asia as far as China and as far north as Siberia.

GROUND IVY GALL-WASP. *Aulax glechomae*, a small chalcid wasp that attacks the stems and leaves of Ground Ivy (*Glechoma hederacea*) causing red or purple galls about the size of peas. These were at one time used as food in France and are said to have an agreeable taste and a sweet odour.

GROUND-NUT APHID. *Aphis craccivora*, a common pest in Africa; a carrier of the virus that causes Ground-nut Mosaic Disease.

GROUND PEARL. See *Giant Coccid*.

GROUSE LOCUST. See *Ground Hopper*.

GRUB. A general name for an *apodous* or legless larva having a tiny head and few sense organs. The body is fleshy and rounded with little difference between the two ends. The larvae of bees and some beetles are of this type. They should be distinguished from the more pointed legless larvae or maggots of the house fly.

GRYLLIDAE. Crickets: members of the order Orthoptera resembling long-horned grasshoppers but distinguished from them by their brown colour, by the long unsegmented anal cerci and by their less predominantly vegetarian habits. *Gryllus domesticus* is the common European House Cricket whose chirping can be heard in bakehouses and other warm places. *Gryllus campestris* is the closely related Field Cricket and *Gryllus assimilis* is the Black Cricket of North America. All these are small, but *Bradyporus dasypus* is a much larger species of Southern Europe and Western Asia, measuring 8 cm. in length.

GRYLLOBLATTODEA. The most primitive of all orthopterous insects, forming a separate order which combines the features of cockroaches and crickets. The few known species are wingless and occur in the mountains of North America, Japan and Russia. The earliest, *Grylloblatta campodeiformis*, was discovered in Canada as recently as 1914.

GRYLLOTALPIDAE. Mole-crickets: insects of the order Orthoptera having large flattened fore-legs modified for burrowing. They spend most of their lives underground feeding chiefly on worms, beetles and other insects but also sometimes gnawing at roots. At night they may fly clumsily with their transparent wings fluttering rapidly and their heavy body hanging vertically. *Gryllotalpa vulgaris* is found all over Europe, North Africa and Western Asia; *Gryllotalpa borealis* is a common North American species.

GRYLLUS. The principal genus of crickets (see *Gryllidae*).

GULA. A median ventral cuticular plate on the head of an insect, situated between the genae and separating the labium from the 'occipital' foramen through which the nerves, oesophagus etc. pass into the thorax.

GULF FRITILLARY. *Deione vanillae*: a bright orange-red butterfly common in Texas and other southern states of North America. It has a wing-span of about 7 cm., has a pattern of black lines and dots on the upper surface of the wings and silvery dots on the underside. The larvae feed on the Passion Plant.

GYMNOCERATA. Insects of the group Hemiptera–Heteroptera comprising most of the terrestrial forms of bug. They are distinguished from the aquatic forms (Cryptocerata) by their conspicuous antennae. Notable among the Gymnocerata are the bedbugs (Cimicidae) and the plant-eating shieldbugs (Pentatomidae).

GYNANDROMORPH. A sexual mosaic, with some areas of the body showing male structures and others female. In some butterflies, for instance, the wings on one side show the female pattern and those on the other the male. This is brought about by a variation in chromosome content of cells in different parts of the body, these having arisen from a binucleate gamete in the parent insect. (Compare *Hermaphrodite* and *Intersex*.)

GYRETES. A common genus of Whirligig Beetles (Gyrinidae) from North America.

GYRINIDAE. Whirligig Beetles: aquatic beetles characterized by a rapid gyratory movement. The middle and hind-legs are flattened and oar-like with a fringe of long stiff bristles. A peculiar feature of these beetles is that the compound eyes have two definite regions with large and small facets respectively. One theory is that the upper portion serves for vision in air and the lower portion for vision under water.

H

HABROBRACON (MICROBRACON). A long-legged braconid wasp whose larvae are parasites in the caterpillars of the Flour Moth *Ephestia*. The wasp uses its sense of smell to search out its victim. It then stings and paralyses it, lays its eggs on it and the larvae of the braconid eat away the body of the host.

HABROCYTUS. A genus of Chalcid wasps, parasitic on ichneumon flies.

HABROSYNE. *Habrosyne pyritoides*, the Buff Arches Moth: a small night-flying moth of the family Thyatiridae having buff coloured hind-wings and having the fore-wings marked with brownish buff and dark grey, crossed by two white lines. The dark brown caterpillars feed on bramble leaves.

HADENA. *Hadena rivularis*, the Campion Moth: a small dark brown noctuid moth having a zig-zag pattern of thin white lines on the fore-wings. The larvae feed on Bladder Campion *Silene vulgaris* and related species.

HADENOECUS. *Hadenoecus subterraneus*: a species of long-horned cave-cricket found only in the celebrated Mammoth Cave of Kentucky, U.S.A.

HAEMAGOGUS. A genus of small mosquitoes from the jungles of Central and South America; transmitters of the yellow fever virus.

HAEMATOBIA. *Haematobia irritans*, previously called *Lyperosia irritans*: the Horn Fly, also known as the Texas Fly, a blood-sucking two-winged fly similar in appearance to the house fly but much smaller (5 mm. long). A pest that infests cattle on the parts around the bases of the horns. Originally European it reached America about 1887.

HAEMATOMYZUS. *Haematomyzus elephantis*: a parasitic louse of the order Mallophaga, a pest of Indian elephants. It is about 3 mm. long, red in colour, relatively long-legged, and has a long proboscis capable of piercing the elephant's skin (see also *Elephant Louse*).

HAEMATOPINUS. A genus of blood-sucking lice of the order Siphunculata: small, flattened, wingless insects with sharp claws and piercing mouth-parts. *Haematopinus suis* is the Hog Louse, possibly a vector of swine fever; *Haematopinus asini* infests horses; *Haematopinus tuberculatus* and *Haematopinus eurysternus* are parasites of cattle, buffaloes and related animals.

HAEMATOPOTA. *Haematopota pluvialis* and related species: Clegs. Greyish-brown blood-sucking flies of the family Tabanidae; pests of humans and domestic animals; closely related to Gadflies but differing in the way they hold their speckled wings together like a roof. They are very numerous in Old World tropics, but rare in the New World.

HAEMATOSIPHON. *Haematosiphon inodorus*, the Adobe Bug: a large flattened bug of the family Cimicidae, closely related to the bedbug but having a long rostrum; a pest of poultry in Central America, Mexico and the Southern States.

HAEMOCOEL. A blood-filled cavity or sinus surrounding most of the organs in insects and other arthropods as well as in a number of other invertebrates. Blood from the dorsal tubular heart is pumped forwards; it does not go into capillaries but goes directly into the haemocoel, so that every organ is bathed in it. Finally it reaches the pericardial sinus from which it re-enters the heart through small openings called *ostia*.

HAEMOCOELOUS VIVIPARITY. A phenomenon that occurs in certain insects which have no oviducts, *e.g.* in Strepsiptera, and in some larval Cecidomyiidae which develop parthenogenetically. Eggs escape into the haemocoel, develop into larvae and finally escape through secondary openings in the body wall.

HAEMOCYTES. A general name for blood corpuscles; those of insects are colourless and are of various kinds, the more important being:
Prohaemocytes (= *Proleucocytes*) – young cells.
Plasmatocytes (= *Phagocytes*) – amoeboid cells that digest bacteria etc.
Granular Haemocytes (also phagocytic).
Oenocytoids – rounded acidophil cells whose function is obscure.

Cystocytes – specialized granular haemocytes.
Sphaerule Cells – containing large round inclusions.
Adipohaemocytes – containing fat globules.

HAEMOGLOBIN. The red pigment of vertebrate blood, found very rarely in insects; the best known species containing this substance are the small red 'bloodworms', aquatic larvae of Chironomid gnats.

HAEMOLYMPH. The colourless blood of insects, filling all the body cavities and combining the functions of blood and lymph (see also *Haemocoel* and *Blood*).

HAEMONIA. A genus of aquatic leaf-beetles of the family Chrysomelidae that feed on floating leaves of water lilies etc. They are able to breathe under water by taking down an air bubble trapped by the layer of fine hydrofuge hairs on the body.

HAEMORRHAGIA. A name formerly used for the genus *Hemaris*: Bee Hawk-moths (*q.v.*).

HAETERA. A genus of Glass-winged Butterflies from the forests of Peru and other parts of South America; large slow-flying butterflies with transparent wings.

HAGENIUS. A genus of North American dragonflies whose aquatic nymphs have a short, fat, almost circular abdomen.

HAIR. Insects' hairs originate from the epidermis and cuticle and may be any of the following types:
  (1) *Microtrichia*: minute non-movable hairs formed from the cuticle.
  (2) *Spines*: similar but thicker and stronger.
  (3) *Macrotrichia*: single or branched hairs, sometimes called *setae*; these are hollow, longer than microtrichia, and arise from a pit or socket. They may be fine or thickened.
  (4) *Glandular hairs* such as those of some caterpillars that secrete an irritant fluid.
  (5) *Sensory setae* acting as tactile, auditory, or sometimes chemical receptors with nerve cells leading from their bases.
  (6) *Scales* such as those of butterflies and some other insects, *e.g.* mosquitoes. They are flattened and coloured but otherwise essentially similar to setae in their structure.

HAIRFLY. An alternative name for flies of the family Bibionidae (*q.v.*) including St. Mark's Fly (*Bibio marci*), the Fever Fly (*Dilophus febrilis*) and the Garden Hairfly (*Bibio hortularius*) of Central Europe and North Africa.

HAIRSTREAKS. A group of butterflies characterized by a thin white streak on the undersides of the wings and short 'tails' extending back from the hind-wings. They belong to the family Lycaenidae and are related to the Coppers and the Blues. There are five British species, the commonest being the Purple Hairstreak (*Thecla quercus* or *Quercusia quercus*) and the Green Hairstreak (*Callophyrs rubi*). Others live in many parts of the world, *e.g.* the Colorado Hairstreak (*Thecla crysalus*) and the North American Purple Hairstreak (*Thecla halestis*). Although the caterpillars are predominantly vegetarian, they will sometimes eat other insects.

HAIRY ATHOUS. *Athous hirtus*, a Click Beetle of the family Elateridae having a shiny black body with fine grey hairs. The wing-cases are very long and slightly grooved and pitted (see *Click Beetle*).

HAIRY DRAGONFLY. *Brachytron pratense*, a medium sized dragonfly having the thorax dark brown, marked with pale green and yellow and covered with fine velvety hairs. The male has blue eyes and a black and blue abdomen; the female has brown eyes and a black and yellow abdomen.

HAIRY EMUS. *Emus hirtus*, a beetle of the family Staphylinidae (Rove Beetles) having a long narrow body and short wing-cases. The head, thorax and abdomen are black with fine golden hairs; the elytra have a broad band of grey hairs. The beetle is to be found in horse or cattle dung (see *Staphylinidae*).

HAIRY FLOWER BEES. Anthophoridae: a family of stout, usually solitary, mining bees that make nests underground like small clay pots. They have very long tongues enabling them to obtain deep seated nectar from tubular types of flowers. Both sexes are very hairy; the males have brushes of very long black hairs on the middle pair of legs; the females have orange hairs on the hind-legs.

HAIRY FLOWER WASPS. Scoliidae: a family of black and yellow hairy wasps whose larvae are ectoparasites on the grubs of certain beetles.

HAIRY SANDWASP. *Sphex hirsuta,* a mining wasp of the family Sphecidae having the thorax and legs black and very hairy. The front of the abdomen is in the form of a long thin stalk and the hind-part has a broad orange-red band.

HALESUS. A North American genus of caddis flies (Trichoptera) whose larvae construct wide straight tubes of small stones etc.

HALF-INSECTS. A name sometimes used for the Protura, the most primitive group of insects, minute, colourless and without eyes or antennae.

HALICTIDAE. A large family of mining bees: medium sized, short tongued social insects that burrow deeply into the ground making communal nests with numerous cells and interconnected passages. They resemble honey bees but are generally smaller. *Halictus xanthopus*, the largest British species is, however, considerably larger with two white lines across the abdomen and with bright golden legs.

HALIPLIDAE. Crawling Water Beetles: a family of small brown or yellowish beetles that crawl about on submerged vegetation in shallow water. Their legs, unlike those of most water beetles, are not adapted for swimming.

HALOBATES. A genus of wingless water skaters (Gerridae) that live on the surface of the sea, often far from land; *Halobates micaris* off the coast of Florida and *Halobates sericeus* off the coast of California and Mexico.

HALTERES. Balancers: the reduced hind-wings of Diptera, shaped like short drumsticks. They vibrate and act as gyroscopic stabilizers. It has been shown in some species that if they are removed the insect soon loses its balance and falls to the ground.

HALTICINAE. Flea-beetles: minute jumping beetles of the family Chrysomelidae having long thick hind-legs. They are common pests of many farm and garden crops, the larvae feeding on the roots and the adults on leaves and shoots (see *Flea-beetles* and *Phyllotreta*).

HAMADRYAS. *Hamadryas antiopa*: an alternative name for *Nymphalis antiopa*, the Camberwell Beauty Butterfly, known in North America as the Mourning Cloak (see *Camberwell Beauty*).

HAMAMELISTES. *Hamamelistes spinosus,* the Spiny Witch-hazel Gall Aphid: a plant-louse that causes leaves to fold and produce open-type galls on the North American Witch-hazel *Hamamelis virginea* and on birch trees.

HAMEARIS. See *Duke of Burgundy Fritillary.*

HAMITERMES (AMITERMES, OMITERMES). A genus of termites from Australia, Africa etc., whose large mound-like nests are nearly always constructed with their long axes in a north-south direction. For this reason they are sometimes known as 'Magnetic Termites'.

HAMMERHEAD BEETLES. A group of small wood-boring beetles of the family Buprestidae whose larvae have very small heads but have the segment behind the head greatly enlarged. For this reason they are sometimes known as Flat-headed Borers or Hammerheads. Many of them are pests of economic importance in the forests of North America.

HAMMOCK MOTH. *Perophora sanguinolenta*: a South American moth whose larvae construct hammock-like tubes of silk interwoven with particles of faeces; within these they live and grow, feeding on adjacent foliage.

HAMULA. A hook-like structure also called the *retinaculum* which, together with the furcula, enables insects of the order Collembola (springtails) to leap forwards into the air. The hamula is formed from a pair of appendages on the ventral side of the abdomen. Before leaping, the caudal furcula is bent forwards and locked to the hamula. When this 'catch' is released the furcula springs back propelling the insect violently forwards.

HAMULUS. Any hook-like process but particularly the small hooks on the anterior of a bee's hind-wing by which it interlocks with the front wing when the bee is in flight.

HANDSOME PHILONTHUS. *Philonthus decorus,* one of the Rove Beetles or Staphylinidae having a narrow elongated body with short wing-cases, black with a coppery bronze sheen; an active beetle that hunts small insects in dung, carrion etc.

HANGING FLY. A name given to several species of Scorpion-flies (Mecoptera) that hang from vegetation by their fore-legs and use the other legs for seizing small insects flying past.

HAPLOEMBIA. A genus of Embioptera (foot-spinners) from Southern Europe; social insects about 1 cm. long, living in silken tunnels beneath stones or under bark.

HARDBACK BEETLE. An alternative name for *Tenebrio,* the mealworm beetle whose larvae, pests of flour mills and grain stores, are commonly bred as food for small animals and birds.

HARLEQUIN BUG. *Murgantia histrionica,* a red and black pentatomid bug; a serious pest of cabbages and other vegetables in North America.

HARMOLITA. A genus of chalcid wasps whose larvae tunnel into the stems of wheat and are pests in North America. *Harmolita grandis* the Wheat Straw-worm, *Harmolita tritici* the Jointworm and several other species.

HARPAGO. A claspette: one of a pair of small claspers on the hind-end of the abdomen of certain insects, *e.g.* mosquitoes. They do not form the principal tail forceps but are smaller and nearer to the median line. The term is sometimes used for other clasping organs including the *harpes* of male Lepidoptera.

HARPALINAE. A group of herbivorous ground beetles (Carabidae), occasional pests of forest trees. *Harpalus affinis* is a common British species of a metallic green or bronze colour with reddish antennae and legs. It is nocturnal and burrows under roots or stones.

HARPES. Claspers formed from modified stylets at the hind-end of the abdomen of male butterflies and moths etc. (See also *Harpago*.)

HARTIGIA. A genus of stem-sawflies of the family Cephidae; about 12 mm. long with a long, narrow neck and a relatively large head. The larvae bore into plant stems.

HARVESTER ANT. *Messor* and other related genera: herbivorous ants that build large mounds of soil and sand and clear the surrounding ground of all vegetation; also called Agricultural Ants.

HARVESTER TERMITE. *Hodotermes* and related genera of African and Asian termites that gather grass in large amounts and take it down into their subterranean nests.

HARVEST FLY. An alternative name for a cicada (see *Cicadidae*).

HATCHING SPINE. A spine or series of spines on the head of an embryo insect, used for breaking open the egg-shell when hatching; also called an egg-burster.

HAUSTELLATE INSECTS. Insects whose mouth-parts are adapted for sucking.

HAUSTELLUM. This term is sometimes used in general for any suctorial mouth-parts of an insect but is often used in a more restricted sense to denote the large distal portion of the proboscis of a blowfly or similar insect, bearing at its extremity two large oral lobes or *labella* containing numerous tubes or *pseudotracheae* through which food is sucked.

HAWKER. A general name sometimes used for the large fast-flying dragonflies of the group Anisoptera.

HAWK-MOTHS. Sphingidae: a family of large, stoutly-built fast-flying moths whose fore-wings are much larger than the hind ones. The proboscis is sometimes extremely long and the antennae end in hooks. The larvae have ten prolegs and usually bear a horn or spine at the hind-end. The Death's Head Hawk-moth, *Acherontia atropos*, is the largest British member of this family, sometimes having a wing-span of over 13 cm. but there are larger species in many tropical parts of the world; an Australian species, for instance, with a wing-span of 23 cm. Most hawk-moths pupate underground, sometimes in cocoons; the pupae are usually dark brown (see also *Humming-bird Hawk-moth*).

HAWTHORN FRUIT-FLY. *Phagocarpus permundus*, a small two-winged fly of the family Trypetidae whose larvae feed on hawthorn berries.

HAWTHORN GALL-MIDGE. *Perrisia crataegi*, a small insect of the family Cecidomyiidae whose reddish larvae cause the formation of rosette galls on the ends of hawthorn shoots. The terminal leaves become deformed and covered with small reddish outgrowths which provide food and camouflage for the developing larvae.

HAWTHORN SAWFLY. *Trichiosoma tibiale*, a large black, hairy, bee-like insect whose green 'caterpillars' feed on hawthorn leaves and pupate in yellowish parchment-like cocoons attached to the twigs.

HAWTHORN SUCKER. *Psylla peregrina*, a minute, bright green, jumping plant-louse that sucks the sap of hawthorn leaves and, like its close relative the aphis, exudes a sticky secretion of honeydew.

HAY MOTH. An alternative name for the Pale Mottled Willow Moth *Caradrina clavipalpis*, a noctuid moth having greyish brown fore-wings with a few small dark spots along the front edge, and having almost transparent white hind-wings. The larvae feed on chickweed, grasses, plantain etc. and may be a pest in haystacks.

HEAD. The head of an insect is formed from six embryonic segments fused together and contained in a cuticular capsule strengthened by an endoskeleton or *tentorium* formed from ingrowths of the cuticle. This forms points of attachment for muscles as well as supporting the brain and the oesophagus. Externally the head generally bears two compound eyes and sometimes several simple eyes or *ocelli*, two antennae and the mouth-parts consisting of the *labrum, mandibles, maxillae* and *labium*. In insects such as the cockroach and the locust, the head is bent at right angles to the body so that the mouth-parts are ventral. This arrangement is known as *hypognathous*; others such as beetles are of the *prognathous* type with the mouth-parts in front. The back of the head is perforated by the *occipital foramen* through which the nerves and the oesophagus pass into the thorax. (See also *Head Capsule*).

HEAD CAPSULE. The cuticular covering of the head of an insect, consisting of a number of plates or sclerites fused together or sometimes showing lines of suture but showing little if any of the original embryonic segmentation. The principal parts of a generalized head capsule are:
  (1) The dorsal plate or *epicranium.*
  (2) The frontal plate or *frons.*
  (3) The *clypeus* to which the *labrum* or upper lip is attached.
  (4) The lateral plates or *genae.*
  (5) A median ventral plate or *gula.*
The head capsule may be incompletely sclerotized and partly or wholly retracted into the thorax, especially in larval insects.

HEAD LOUSE. *Pediculus humanus capitis*, a small, wingless, blood-sucking insect of the group Siphunculata; a potential carrier of typhus and other diseases. This and the Body Louse (*q.v.*) are generally considered to be biological races of one species, *Pediculus humanus.*

HEARING ORGANS. Some insects possess well developed auditory organs and it has been shown in a few cases that these are sensitive to frequency modulation, although it is doubtful whether this is generally the case. There may be a built-in sensitivity to one particular frequency, which excites reflex behaviour. These organs are formed from modified mechano-receptors or chordotonal receptors grouped together and attached to a vibratory cuticular membrane or 'tympanum'. They may be on many different parts of the body but are most often on the sides of the abdomen or the thorax (*e.g.* in many moths) or on the legs (grasshoppers and cicadas). Some insects can also perceive sounds by means of their antennae.

HEART. The heart of an insect is a dorsal tubular vessel with a muscular wall and with a series of lateral openings or *ostia* by which blood enters. In some insects it is divided into compartments roughly corresponding to the segments of the body, but more often it is a continuous straight vessel. By the contractions of the heart, blood is pumped forwards into the 'aorta' and thence to the haemocoels or cavities of the body, there being no other true arteries, veins or capillaries, By means of this sluggish 'open circulation' the blood eventually finds its way to the *pericardial sinus* from which it again enters the heart through the ostia.

HEART AND CLUB. *Agrotis corticea*, a noctuid moth very similar to the Heart and Dart Moth (*Agrotis exclamationis*) but with a dark club-shaped mark replacing the 'dart' on the fore-wings.

HEART AND DART MOTH. *Agrotis exclamationis*: a greyish brown noctuid moth with two conspicuous black marks on each fore-wing; one shaped roughly like a heart and the other a narrow streak or 'dart'. The greyish caterpillars feed on turnips and other vegetables and pupate underground.

HEATH BUTTERFLIES. A name for two common European butterflies of the family Satyridae: *Coenonympha tullia*, the Large Heath and *Coenonympha pamphilis*, the Small Heath, both of which inhabit mountainous moors, bogs and heathland. Both are tawny brown with a number of eye-spots in the form of small white rings with dark centres. The larvae of both are lined longitudinally with pale and dark green. They feed on sedges and grasses.

HEATH FRITILLARY. *Melitaea athalia*: a small European butterfly of the family Nymphalidae having on both wings a chequerboard type of pattern of dark brown and orange-yellow. The caterpillars are blackish with brown and grey spikes all over the body; they feed on plantain (*Plantago*) and Cow-wheat (*Melampyrum*).

HEATH MOTHS. A name for two common European geometrid moths. *Ematurga atomaria*, the Common Heath Moth is light brown with dark brown wavy transverse lines on both wings and brown dots round the margins; the male, the darker of the two, has very large feathery antennae. The larvae are grey-brown and stick-like and feed on heather and leguminous plants. *Chiasmia clathrata*, the Latticed Heath Moth has a much more marked lattice-like pattern of dark brown lines on a cream background. Its larvae feed chiefly on clovers and trefoils.

HEATH RUSTIC MOTH. *Agrotis agathina*: a European noctuid moth closely related to the Heart and Dart Moth (*Agrotis exclamationis*); greyish brown with a row of dark arrow-head shaped spots along the margin. The fore-wings have a whitish central spot on a background of a black patch; the hind-wings have a dark central spot.

HEATHER WEEVIL. *Strophosomus lateralis*, a small, shiny black weevil about 5 mm. long, having pinkish or silvery scales along the sides of the body and having reddish antennae. It normally feeds on heather but may attack Corsican Pine and other conifers.

HEBOMOIA. See *Giant Orange Tip*.

HEBREW CHARACTER MOTH. *Orthosia gothica*, a common European noctuid moth of a grey-brown colour with a very distinctive black mark on each fore-wing, said to resemble certain letters of the Hebrew alphabet. The adult moths are frequently found on Sallow catkins; the larvae feed on a variety of trees and shrubs.

HEBRIDAE. Velvet Water-bugs: a family of small hemipteran bugs whose bodies are covered with fine hydrofuge hairs enabling them to take down bubbles of air. They are found in shallow water at the edges of ponds and slow streams.

HEDGE DAGGER MOTH. An alternative name for the Grey Dagger Moth, *Apatele psi* (see *Dagger Moth*).

HEDGEHOG OAK GALL. A hard, brown, oval, prickly gall produced on the leaves of certain species of oak by the summer generation of the cynipid *Acraspis erinacei*; the sexual generation, produced in the spring, makes small reddish galls on the tips of the buds.

HEDYCHRUM. *Hedychrum nobile*, the Gold Wasp of Central Europe having a shining gold abdomen, green and red thorax and a green head.

HELAEUS. A genus of Australian 'pie-dish beetles', with concave flanges round the elytra and prothorax, the latter extending to meet in front of the head.

HELICOMYIA. *Helicomyia saliciperda*, the Willow Gall-midge: a minute two-winged insect of the family Cecidomyiidae which may infest willow trees in large numbers producing galls in the form of dark spots all over the bark.

HELICONIIDAE. A family of large, brightly coloured butterflies of Central and South America. They have long slender wings and the numerous species are very varied in their colouring. *Heliconius leopardus* of Bolivia is dark brown with black borders and patches; *Heliconius amaryllis* of Brazil and Peru is black with a broad red band across each fore-wing and a pale yellow band across each hind-wing; *Heliconius doris*, common all over tropical South America, has blue hind-wings and black and yellow fore-wings. Most of these species have many colour variations, mimicking other species and thus giving themselves a high degree of protection. They are also protected by their pungent and distasteful odour which is most noticeable when they congregate in large numbers on trees and bushes at night.

HELICOPIS. A genus of South American butterflies of the family Erycinidae, small, brightly coloured and having a number of 'tails' on the hind-wings (see *Erycinidae*).

HELICOPSYCHE. A North American genus of caddis flies (Trichoptera) whose aquatic larvae make spiral cases of sand grains.

HELIOCOPRIS. *Heliocopris gigas*, a large Central African dung beetle, the male having a large horn-like projection on the thorax and two smaller horns on the head.

HELIOTHIS. A genus of noctuid moths whose larvae are serious pests affecting a great many crops in various parts of the world: *Heliothis obsoleta*, the Corn Ear-worm attacks American maize; *Heliothis armigera*, the Old World Boll-worm, is a pest of cotton, citrus fruits and tobacco in Southern Europe, Africa, Asia and Australia; *Heliothis virescens*, the Tobacco Bud-worm is a pest in the Southern United States; it also attacks cotton plants in Peru.

HELIOTHRIPS. See *Glasshouse Thrips*.

HELIOTROPISM. A term sometimes used to denote the attraction of insects to the sun; a misuse of the word which more strictly signifies a turning or orientation to the sun (positive) or away from it (negative). A special case of *phototropism*.

HELLGRAMMITE. A colloquial name used in North America for the predatory aquatic larva of the Dobson-fly (see *Corydalis*).

121

HELODIDAE. A family of small terrestrial beetles whose bodies are soft and covered with numerous fine hairs; the larvae are generally aquatic.

HELOPELTIS. A plant-bug of the family Capsidae; a pest of tea, cacao and cotton in tropical countries: *Heliopeltis theivora*, the Tea Mosquito Bug of India.

HELOPHILUS. The Sun-fly *Helophilus pendulus* and related species of hover-flies (Syrphidae), black with longitudinal yellow stripes on the thorax and transverse yellow bands on the abdomen. The larva is aquatic with a very long respiratory tube, for which reason it is known as a rat-tailed maggot. It belongs to the subfamily Eristalinae. (See also *Drone-flies*.)

HELOPHORUS. *Helophorus aquaticus* and related species of small water beetles of the family Hydrophilidae, having a metallic sheen of yellowish brown with darker spots on the elytra. The hind-legs are flattened and fringed with hairs to form paddles for swimming. They inhabit slow streams and the edges of ponds.

HELOPS. *Helops caeruleus*, the Blue Helops: a handsome beetle of the family Tenebrionidae, about 20 mm. long and of a greenish-blue or purple colour; an inhabitant of rotting wood. The larvae are yellowish and worm-like with two sharp upwardly curved spines at the hind-end.

HEMARIS. See *Bee Hawk-moth*.

HEMELYTRON (HEMIELYTRON). An insect's wing in which the basal half is hardened and the remainder membranous. Such wings are found in plant-bugs of the order Hemiptera–Heteroptera, *e.g.* the shieldbugs.

HEMEROBIIDAE. Brown lacewing-flies: predatory insects of the order Neuroptera, smaller and more hairy than the closely related green lacewing-flies. They are to be found on the bark of pines and other conifers.

HEMEROCAMPA. The White Marked Tussock Moth: a genus of Lyman-triidae found over most of the United States. The caterpillars are yellow and black striped, with a red head and prominent tufts or tussocks of white and black hairs. They feed on, and sometimes completely defoliate deciduous trees.

HEMICEPHALOUS. A term used to denote insect larvae in which the head is incomplete posteriorly and is partly embedded in the prothorax (*cf. Acephalous*).

HEMIELYTRON. See *Hemelytron*.

HEMIKYPHA. *Hemikypha punctata*, a giant Tree-hopper from Brazil: the largest of the Membracidae about 2 cm. long, reddish brown with yellow spots and having the thoracic shield extended into two large horns.

HEMILEUCINI. A subfamily of moths of the family Saturniidae including the North American Bull's Eye Moth *Automeris io*, yellow with two large black circles or 'bull's eyes' on the hind-wings and the European Nail-mark Moth *Aglia tau*, reddish brown with a white 'nail' on each hind-wing. Both have a wing-span of up to 8 cm.

HEMIMERINA. A suborder of Dermaptera, with only one family, Hemi-meridae: wingless earwigs ectoparasitic on the Pouched Rat *Cricetomys* of tropical Africa.

HEMIMETABOLA. Also called Exopterygota: insects in which there is no pupal stage and in which metamorphosis involves very little change at each instar. The young, known as nymphs, are generally similar to the adult, but are smaller and have external wing-buds at an early stage. Sixteen orders are comprised in the group; they include cockroaches, earwigs and all kinds of bugs and lice, as well as such insects as dragonflies and mayflies. The two latter have aquatic nymphs differing more markedly from the adults than do the nymphs of other orders.

HEMIPNEUSTIC. A term used to denote insects in which one or more pairs of spiracles are non-functional.

HEMIPTEROID INSECTS. A group name suggested in a system of classification proposed by Wardle (1936) to include Hemiptera, Psocoptera, Anoplura and Thysanoptera.

HEMIPTERA (RHYNCHOTA). A large order of insects including bedbugs, cicadas, aphids and many kinds of plant-bugs. The mouth-parts are adapted for piercing and sucking, with mandibles and maxillae in the form of long stylets lying in a trough-like labium; palps are reduced or absent. For convenience this large order of 40,000 species is divided into two suborders named respectively *Homoptera* and *Heteroptera*. The former have fore-wings of uniform consistency, either leathery or membranous; the latter have them half membranous and half thickened. There are also many wingless forms.

HEMITELES. A genus of small ichneumon flies living as hyperparasites in the bodies of the larger ichneumon *Apanteles glomeratus* which is itself a parasite of various caterpillars.

HEMOCOEL. See *Haemocoel*.

HEMOLYMPH. See *Haemolymph*.

HEN LOUSE (SHAFT LOUSE). *Menopon gallinae*, a common member of the Mallophaga or Biting Lice, frequently found as an ectoparasite on poultry where it feeds chiefly on fragments of skin and feathers (see *Louse*).

HENBANE BUG. *Rhopalus hyoscyami*: a red and black plant-bug about 8 mm. long, of the family Coreidae, resembling a shieldbug but with shorter wings; feeds chiefly on Henbane *Hyoscyamus niger*. Some authorities place this bug in a separate family, Rhopalidae.

HEPIALIDAE. Swift Moths or Ghost Swift Moths: a family of primitive moths with elongated wings which interlock by means of a *jugum* or process arising from the base of the fore-wing. The caterpillars frequently damage young trees by tunnelling into the pith of the roots or young stems; some species, however, feed on the roots of herbaceous plants such as carrots, sorrel, meadowsweet etc. The adult moths have no proboscis and are unable to feed (see also *Ghost Moth*).

HEPTAGENIA. A group of mayflies (Ephemeroptera) whose aquatic nymphs have flattened bodies enabling them to cling to the undersurfaces of stones in fast-flowing streams.

HERALD MOTH. *Scoliopteryx libatrix*: a medium sized noctuid moth with deeply indented wings; greyish with a broad patch of reddish orange across the fore-wing. They fly in the autumn and hibernate in the adult stage; when at rest they resemble a shrivelled autumn leaf. The larvae feed chiefly on willows and poplars.

HERCULES BEETLE. *Dynastes hercules*, a large beetle about 15 cm. long from Central and South America and the West Indies; black with greenish elytra. The male has an enormous 'horn' curving forwards and downwards and another curving upwards to meet it (see *Dynastidae*).

HERMAPHRODITE. Bisexual: having the ability to function both as a male and as a female, either simultaneously or in succession. This condition is very rare among insects; the best known example is the Californian Fluted Scale Insect or Cottony Cushion Scale *Icerya purchasi*. These insects, members of the family Coccidae, are self-fertilizing. True males are rare and true females unknown, the apparent females being functional hermaphrodites.

HERMETIA. A genus of brightly coloured Soldier Flies (Stratiomyidae). One species, *Hermetia illucens*, was originally American but has now spread throughout the world. Its larvae live in a variety of decaying materials, and are sometimes accidentally swallowed by eating over-ripe fruit.

HERSE. *Herse convolvuli*, the Convolvulus Hawk-moth: a large European moth with a wing-span of about 11 cm. The wings are grey with fine black streaks; the head and thorax are also grey and the abdomen has stripes of black and pinkish across the sides. The most characteristic feature is the extremely long proboscis which can be extended to about 12 cm. enabling the moth, while hovering, to suck nectar from deep tubular flowers such as tobacco. The caterpillars, which feed on convolvulus, are green with a brown or purple stripe on each segment and an orange or pink horn at the hind-end. The moth is found chiefly in Southern Europe, North Africa and Western Asia; it is an occasional migrant to Britain.

HESPERIIDAE. Skippers: a cosmopolitan family of butterflies represented in Europe by a few small, usually brown and rather insignificant species. In South America, however, there are many larger, often brightly coloured representatives of this family. They are characterized by being rather moth-like with wide, hairy bodies and wide heads; they fly rather jerkily (hence the name Skipper) and when at rest often have the wings flat or half open like those of a moth.

HESPEROLEON. A genus of Neuroptera, four-winged insects resembling damselflies, whose wingless voracious larvae are known as ant-lions (see *Ant-lion*).

HESSIAN FLY. *Phytophaga destructor* or *Mayetiola destructor:* a small gall-midge of the family Cecidomyiidae whose maggot-like larvae are pests of wheat, barley and other cereals. They penetrate the leaves, move down the stem and suck the sap from the base of the plant. Originally European, they have become serious pests in North America, New Zealand and other wheat-growing countries.

HESTIA. A genus of large butterflies from the Philippines, Malaysia and Taiwan (Formosa). They are pale yellow, about 12 cm. across and have a network of black lines and spots following the veins. The wing-area is very large so that they fly gracefully and hover stiffly like a kite.

HETAERIAS. A genus of small flat beetles of the family Histeridae that live in ants' nests and act as scavengers.

HETERARTHRUS (=PHYLLOTOMA). *Heterarthrus aceris* and related species: small sawflies whose larvae live inside the leaves of sycamore etc. between the upper and lower epidermis. They mine out the inside of the leaf and when fully grown, cut out a circle from the upper epidermis. They remain attached to this in a hammock of silk. The disc, hammock and insect fall to the ground where the latter hibernates and pupates. Sometimes by its wriggling

124

movement the insect makes the little disc of leaf jump till it finds a suitable resting place.

HETEROCAMPA. *Heterocampa guttivitta*, a moth of the family Notodontidae (Prominents) whose larvae, which feed on oak leaves, show a remarkable change of form from one instar to another. The young larvae of the first instar have a row of 'horns' all along the body, the first pair being much larger than the others and branched like antlers. They lose these in later instars.

HETEROCERA. Moths: a name referring to their varied antennae and used in the old method of classification which divided all Lepidoptera into butterflies and moths. The name is no longer used and the order is more rationally classified according to the wing-venation and other characteristics.

HETERODACTYLA. A group-name sometimes used in the classification of Diptera to denote those Brachycera (short-horned flies) whose feet each have two lobes with a hair or bristle in between, in contrast to the Homeodactyla (*q.v.*) which have a pad-like *empodium* in the centre of the foot. They include the Bombylidae (Bee-flies) and the Asilidae (Robber Flies).

HETEROGASTER. *Heterogaster urticae*, the Nettle Groundbug: a small elongated plant-bug of the order Heteroptera (family Lygaeidae) having a narrow black body and grey elytra. They are common on nettles.

HETEROGENEIDAE. See *Cochlidiidae* and *Cochlidion*.

HETEROGONY (HETEROGONIC GROWTH). See *Allometric growth*.

HETEROMERA. A name used in some systems of classifying beetles: a group having the first and middle tarsi composed of five segments and the hind tarsi of four segments.

HETEROMETABOLA. Insects which do not undergo a complete metamorphosis: an alternative name for Hemimetabola or Exopterygota. In some systems of classification, however, the two orders Odonata and Ephemeroptera are not included in this group (see section on Classification).

HETERONEURA. Lepidoptera in which the veins of the fore-wings are differently arranged from those of the hind-wings. The group comprises all the butterflies and the majority of moths with the exception of the Micropterygidae and the Hepialidae (*cf. Homoneura*).

HETERONOTUS. A genus of Brazilian tree-hoppers (Membracidae), light and dark brown, about 10 mm. long and having a complicated and bizarre horn-like growth from the thorax.

HETERONYMPHA. A genus of satyrid butterflies found only in Australia. *Heteronympha merops* is found in woods and mountains. It has a wing-span of about 7 cm. and is orange-yellow with a broad brown margin broken by yellow patches.

HETEROPTERA. A suborder of bugs (Hemiptera) having the fore-wings in the form of a hemelytron, *i.e.* having the proximal half of the wing horny and the distal half membranous. Included in this group are most plant-bugs, water boatman, water scorpions and the common bedbug. The latter is placed in the Heteroptera on account of the general similarity of its body and mouth-parts to those of the rest of the group. The absence of wings is considered to be a degenerate or secondary feature which has arisen in connection with its parasitic habits.

HEXAGENIA. A genus of mayflies whose nymphs burrow in the mud at the bottom of ponds.

125

HEXAPODA. An alternative name for insects, so-called on account of the six legs.

HEXARTHRUS. A genus of large stag beetles (Lucanidae) about 8 cm. long from South-east Asia and Indonesia.

HIBERNATING AGGREGATION. A phenomenon of insect life by which sometimes many thousands of insects congregate together before hibernating in a suitably sheltered place. This gives them a greater degree of protection from extreme winter conditions.

HIBERNATION. A slowing down of metabolism in winter when an insect goes into a state of dormancy or arrested development; a specialized form of diapause in regions where there is a well defined cold season. Although the lowering of temperature is generally the immediate cause of dormancy, in many insects there appears to be an innate rhythm connected with an increase and decrease in the secretion of certain hormones. In some cases a shortage of food is the stimulus and hibernation may commence some time before the onset of cold weather. In other cases a shortening of the period of daylight may give the required stimulus.

Hibernation occurs most often in the pupal stage but there are many cases in which it takes place in the larval or in the adult stage. The mosquito *Anopheles claviger* is an example of the former; the Small Tortoiseshell Butterfly *Aglais urticae* is a case of the latter. Most insects instinctively find a suitable sheltered place for hibernation. Many go underground; some go under stones or logs; others enter domestic buildings. Some such as the Ladybird beetle *Hippodamia convergens* assemble in very large numbers and return to a particular place year after year.

HICKORY BORER. A name for several species of beetles whose larvae burrow into the wood and cambium of the North American hickory tree.

HICKORY HORNED DEVIL. The caterpillar of the North American Royal Walnut Moth *Citheronia regalis*, about 12 cm. long, greenish with black and white spots and with six long red and black horns that curve back and are displayed when the insect is disturbed.

HIDE BEETLE. *Dermestes* and related genera of beetles whose larvae damage skins and furs (see *Dermestidae*).

HIGH BROWN FRITILLARY. *Argynnis adippe* or *Argynnis cydippe*, a European woodland butterfly of the family Nymphalidae, slightly paler than most of the fritillaries but similar in having the characteristic chequerboard pattern of light brown and black and the silvery spots on the undersides of the wings. The larvae feed on violets and pupate in a tent of leaves bound with silk.

HILARA. A common genus of Empid Flies, small black carnivorous Diptera able to secrete silk threads from the swollen lower parts of the fore-legs. The males have the interesting habit of wrapping up a dead insect in silk and presenting it to the female before mating. While she is unravelling it and feeding on it, she is too contented and busy to devour the male, as she might otherwise do, and he is enabled to fertilize her safely.

HIMACERUS. *Himacerus mirmecoides* also called *Aptus mirmecoides*, the Ant Damsel Bug: a light brown, elongated bug of the group Heteroptera having short wings, a piercing proboscis and strong front legs for grasping its prey. They hunt aphids and other insects at night. The young nymphs resemble ants and sometimes live with them.

HIND-WINGS. The hind-wings of an insect, when present, are on the third thoracic segment. They may be similar to, or different from the fore-wings which are on the second segment. In most insects both pairs of wings are functional for flying but in Coleoptera, Orthoptera and Dictyoptera the delicate membranous hind-wings only are used; when at rest they are folded and protected by the thicker fore-wings or elytra. In male Strepsiptera (stylopids) the fore-wings are club-like and ineffectual in flight. In Diptera and male Coccids, on the other hand, the fore-wings are used for flying and the hind-wings are reduced to form small balancers or *halteres* (*q.v.*).

HIPOCRITA. *Hipocrita jacobaeae*: an alternative name for *Callimorpha jacobaeae* (see *Cinnabar Moth*).

HIPPARCHIA. The generic name for Grayling Butterflies, sometimes called *Eumenis*: brown butterflies of the family Satyridae. There are many species, most of which have patches of white or yellow and one or more ringlet eye-spots on the wings. The larvae generally feed on coarse grasses.

HIPPISUS. *Hippisus apiculatus*, the Coral-winged Locust of North America, a species found on dry pastures and hillsides; brown with the bases of the wings a bright coral pink.

HIPPOBOSCIDAE. Cyclorrhaphous Diptera always living as blood-sucking parasites on mammals or birds. A peculiarity of the group is their mode of birth, which they share with the Tsetse Fly *Glossina*. Eggs are not laid but the young larvae develop to an advanced state inside the body of the parent, and pupate almost immediately after release. The best known species, the Forest Fly (*Hippobosca equina*) attacks horses, cattle, dogs and sometimes humans; the bird parasite *Ornithomyia* attacks rooks, starlings etc. The Sheep Ked *Melophagus ovinus*, although belonging to the same family, is exceptional in being wingless. In temperate countries Hippoboscidae over-winter as pupae.

HIPPODAMIA. A genus of Ladybird beetles (Coccinellidae) common in North America. *Hippodamia convergens* is noted for the fact that many thousands of individuals assemble together to hibernate.

HIPPOTION. A genus of hawk-moths (Sphingidae) whose larvae are pests of sweet potatoes and of grape vines in Australia and of cotton in Central Africa.

HIPPURIPHILA. A genus of minute brown leaf-beetles of the family Chrysomelidae whose larvae are leaf-miners of sorrel and dock (*Rumex*).

HISPELLA. *Hispella atra*, the Hedgehog Beetle: a small blue-black beetle of Central Europe having sharp spines all over the thoracic shield and the elytra; the larva is a leaf-miner.

HISPINAE. Hedgehog Beetles: a group of beetles, mostly tropical, having a spiny thorax and wing-covers (see *Hispella*).

HISTERIDAE. Hister Beetles: a family of small, flattened, clavicorn beetles with elytra not quite covering the abdomen. They are predators or scavengers beneath bark, in the burrows of wood-boring insects, in the nests of ants or termites, in dung or carrion. A feature of most of the family is their ability to feign death when disturbed, drawing in their legs till they resemble small black seeds.

HISTORIS. A genus of large Central American nymphalid butterflies. *Historis orion*, ranging from Mexico to Argentina, has a wing-span of about 11 cm. and is dark brown with a yellow patch and a white spot on each fore-wing.

The underside resembles a dry brown leaf. This butterfly is commonly found sucking fruit juices or drinking from puddles.

HIVE BEE. See *Apidae*.

HODOTERMES. A genus of Harvester Termites of Africa and Asia, so-called because they gather grass in large quantities to line their subterranean nests.

HOFMANNOPHILA. *Hofmannophila pseudospretella*, also called *Borkhausenia pseudospretella*: The Brown House Moth, a common moth of Europe and Western Asia, brown with black markings, whose whitish caterpillars often infest houses, feeding on refuse of various kinds.

HOG LOUSE. *Haematopinus suis*, a small, flattened, wingless blood-sucking insect of the order Siphunculata; a common parasite of pigs and possibly a potential carrier of swine fever or other diseases.

HOLLY BLUE BUTTERFLY. *Celastrina argiolus*, a woodland butterfly of the family Lycaenidae occurring across Europe and Asia as far as Japan. The wings are lilac blue above and paler blue with a few black spots beneath. The larvae feed on holly leaves in the spring and summer but a second brood in the autumn feed on ivy.

HOLLY LEAF-MINER. *Phytomyza ilicis*, a small black fly of the family Agromyzidae whose larvae bore into holly leaves causing yellowish brown blotches. They pupate within the leaf.

HOLOCEPHALOUS. A term used to denote insect larvae in which the head is fully developed (*cf. Hemicephalous* and *Acephalous*).

HOLOMETABOLA. Also called Endopterygota: insects which pass through a complete metamorphosis in which the larva is very different from the adult and does not become more like the adult, but transforms suddenly by means of a pupal stage. Nine orders are included in this group, *viz.* Neuroptera (Lacewings etc.), Mecoptera (Scorpion Flies), Trichoptera (Caddis Flies), Lepidoptera (Butterflies and Moths), Coleoptera (Beetles), Strepsiptera (Stylops), Hymenoptera (Bees, Wasps and Ants), Diptera (Two winged Flies) and Siphonaptera (Fleas).

HOLOPNEUSTIC. A term used to describe insects which have the maximum number of functional spiracles. In present-day adult insects this is generally ten pairs; eight on the abdomen and two on the thorax. There are, however, a few primitive insects of the order Diplura which have more than this. *Japyx*, for instance, has eleven pairs, four of them on the thorax.

HOMELESS BEES. Nomadidae or Cuckoo Bees: a family of bees usually resembling wasps with a yellow and black striped abdomen; they have no pollen baskets on the legs and do not make or store honey. Eggs are laid in the underground nests of mining bees. The larvae eat the food stored by the host and later they may also eat the eggs and larvae of the latter.

HOMEODACTYLA. A name given in some systems of classification to those Brachycera (short-horned flies) which have feet with three equal lobes, the central pad or *empodium* being similar to those on each side (*pulvilli*). They include Horse Flies and Gadflies (Tabanidae), Snipe Flies (Rhagionidae), Soldier Flies (Stratiomyidae) and Acroceridae (Cyrtidae), small bulbous flies with small heads (no common name).

HOMODYNAMIC INSECTS. Insects in which there is no hibernation, diapause or other interruption to their regular development.

HOMONEURA. A name formerly used to denote moths having almost identical venation in the two pairs of wings. According to this system the group included the small biting moths Micropterygidae and the much larger, but somewhat primitive moths such as *Hepialus* and related genera. In more recent systems of classification, however, which take into account many features besides wing-venation, the Micropterygidae are placed in a separate order Zeugloptera. *Hepialus*, *Eriocrania* and a few others are placed in the group Monotrysia, a suborder of Lepidoptera.

HOMOEOSIS (HOMOOSIS). The replacement of a damaged appendage by a different one. If, for instance, the antenna is removed from the Stick Insect *Dixippus*, the regeneration that follows may not produce another antenna but sometimes gives rise to an extra leg in place of it.

HOMOPTERA. A suborder of Hemiptera or Bugs, distinguished from the Heteroptera by having the fore-wings of uniform consistency. All the common plant-lice, aphids, frog-hoppers, cicadas etc. are included in this group.

HONEY-BEE. See *Apidae*.

HONEYCOMB. Wax cells made by the honey-bee for storing honey and as brood-cells. They are made from wax secreted by four pairs of glands situated in the membrane below the 3rd, 4th, 5th and 6th abdominal segments. This wax is produced as small white scales which the bee manipulates with its feet and mandibles to make regular hexagonal prisms of uniform size. The geometrically perfect shape ensures the most economical use of the wax, because every wall forms part of two cells; moreover this shape packs the maximum number of cells into a given area.

HONEYCOMB MOTH (WAX MOTH). *Galleria mellonella*, a greyish brown moth of the family Pyralidae; one of the larger members of the Microlepidoptera. The larva, known as the waxworm, is a pest of beehives in many parts of the world,

HONEYDEW. A sugary waste substance produced by aphids and other plant-lice. These insects feed almost continuously on the juices of plants and take in far more sugar and water than they need. The excess is passed out through the anus. It is much sought after by ants.

HONEY MOTH. *Achroia grisella*, a small member of the family Pyralidae; one of the Microlepidoptera having greyish brown fore-wings and white hind-wings; similar in habits to the Honeycomb Moth *Galleria*. The larvae live and pupate in old or neglected beehives, feeding on the wax and on dead insects.

HONEY-POT ANT. A name for several species of ants in which certain members of the colony, known as 'repletes', are able to engorge themselves with large amounts of honey till the abdomen is distended to many times its normal size. In this state they remain hanging from the roof of the nest as living food stores or 'honey-pots' from which the other ants can benefit in times of shortage. *Myrmecocystus horti-deorum* of Central and South America and the Southern United States is one of the best known examples. Others occur in Australia and many tropical and subtropical parts of the world.

HONEY STOMACH. The crop of a honey bee in which nectar is mixed with enzymes from the salivary glands and converted to honey before being disgorged.

HONEY STOPPER. A valve at the posterior end of a bee's crop, specialized for preventing the passage of nectar into the stomach (see *Honey Stomach*).

HOOK-TIP MOTHS. Drepanidae: a family of moths in which the tips of the fore-wings are turned back to make a blunt hook. The caterpillars are without claspers and are hump-backed with warts and swellings on the skin. They rest with the head and tail directed upwards. *Drepana falcatoria*, the Pebble Hook-tip is a well known British member of the family; the larvae feed on birch leaves.

HOP BORER. See *Gortyna*.

HOP FLEA-BEETLE. *Psylliodes attenuata*, a small jumping beetle of the family Chrysomelidae (see *Flea-beetles*).

HOPLOCAMPA. *Hoplocampa testudinea* and related species: Apple sawflies, members of the family Tenthredinidae whose larvae feed in developing fruits of apple, cherry, pear and other members of the rose family; the eggs are laid in the ovaries before the fruit is formed.

HOPPERS. (1) Leaf-hoppers (Cicadellidae), Tree-hoppers (Membracidae) and Frog-hoppers (Cercopidae): small plant-bugs of the group Homoptera, closely related to the Aphids, very varied but all having powerful hind-legs for jumping. (2) Nymphs of locusts which 'march' in bands.

HORISTONOTUS. *Horistonotus uhlerii*, a species of Click Beetle (Elateridae) whose larvae, known as Sand Wireworms, are commonly found as root-pests of maize and cotton in North America.

HORLOGION. A genus of eyeless cave-beetles of the family Carabidae having long antennae, long legs and six long tactile hairs on the elytra; found in caves in North America.

HORMAPHIS. *Hormaphis hamamelidae*, the Witch-hazel Gall-maker: a plant-bug of the group Homoptera whose larvae produce cone shaped galls in the American Witch-hazel *Hamamelis virginea*. The insects enter the leaves from the lower surface and cause the upper surface to thicken and develop into hollow cones in which a subsequent generation of insects is produced.

HORMONE, JUVENILE. See *Neotenin*.

HORNED TREE-HOPPER. See *Centrotus*.

HORNET. *Vespa crabro,* the largest of the social wasps, similar in general appearance to the common wasp but up to 35 mm. in length. It nests in old trees, is a voracious predator and also sucks fruit juices. This species is common throughout Europe and has spread to America and elsewhere. *Dolichovespula*, the White-faced Hornet is another genus from Europe and North America; large, black and white, it makes a nest of chewed wood fibre in papery form.

HORNET CLEARWING MOTH. *Sesia apiformis* or *Trochilium apiformis*: a moth of the family Sesiidae that mimics a hornet. Its wings are almost transparent with narrow brown margins; the body is smooth and the abdomen is banded with yellow and dark brown. The whitish caterpillars can be pests of forestry, burrowing between the bark and the wood of poplars and aspens.

HORNET-FLY. *Asilus crabroniformis*: the largest of the British Robber Flies (Asilidae) about 25 mm. long. The head is brown with yellow markings; the thorax brown and hairy; the abdomen black at the base and the tip, the rest being bright yellow. It has large bulging eyes and a beak-like proboscis with which it pierces its prey after seizing it with the front legs. It will attack quite large insects such as bees, wasps, dragonflies, beetles etc. It lives mainly in meadowland; its larvae in cow-dung.

HORNET MOTH. See *Hornet Clearwing Moth*.

HORN FLY. See *Haematobia*.

HORNTAIL. *Sirex gigas* or *Urocerus gigas*, the Woodwasp or Giant Sawfly (see *Giant Woodwasp*).

HORSE ANT. An alternative name sometimes used for the Wood Ant *Formica rufa* (see *Ant* and *Formica*).

HORSE BOT FLY. See *Gasterophilus*.

HORSE FLIES. An alternative name for Gadflies or Tabanidae: a family of large two-winged insects, the females of which suck blood by means of mouth-parts combining the piercing method of the mosquito and the filter-feeding method of the blowfly (see *Gadfly*).

HORSE STINGER. An old and erroneous name for the dragonfly.

HOT-BED BUG. *Xylocoris galactinus*, a predatory bug of the group Heteroptera inhabiting manure heaps; a close relative of the bedbug.

HOTTENTOT BUG. *Eurygaster maurus*: a European shieldbug of the family Scutelleridae having a greatly enlarged greyish-brown scutellum with a pale line down the middle; commonly found in cornfields.

HOUSE CRICKET. *Gryllus domesticus* (see Gyrllidae).

HOUSE FLY. *Musca domestica* and related tropical species: two-winged flies of the suborder Cyclorrhapha whose larvae are without head or legs and whose pupae are *co-arctate, i.e.* contained in a barrel-shaped puparium. The mouth-parts of a fly are highly specialized and the method of feeding is to regurgitate saliva or gastric juice over the food; this partly digests and softens it so that it can then be sucked up. Eggs are laid in dung or in any decaying animal or vegetable matter on which the larvae feed. Owing to their feeding and breeding habits flies are potential carriers of a great number of diseases.

HOUSE MOTH. A name sometimes given to various species of Clothes Moths: Microlepidoptera of the family Oecophoridae. *Borkhausenia pseudospretella*, the Brown House Moth; *Endrosis sarcitrella*, the White-shouldered House Moth.

HOVER-FLIES. Syrphidae: a large family of two-winged insects, many of which hover over flowers and shrubs and are sometimes mistaken for wasps when in flight on account of the pattern of yellow bands on the abdomen. The small legless larvae of certain species feed on aphids and are to be found among them on rose bushes or fruit trees. The larvae of some species live in dung or in water; others are scavengers in the nests of ants, wasps etc. While most hover-flies are beneficial, a few are economic pests.

HUMAN BOT FLY. *Dermatobia hominis* (see *Dermatobia*).

HUMAN DISEASES TRANSMITTED BY INSECTS. Many viruses, bacteria and other parasites are carried on the bodies, feet or mouth-parts of a great variety of insects, but the prinicpal carriers of specific diseases are insects that suck blood. In many cases a parasitic organism, virus, bacterium, protozoon, nematode, tapeworm, etc. spends part of its life cycle in the body of an insect and is transmitted to humans or other animals when the insect pierces the skin and discharges saliva before commencing to suck blood. Mosquitoes can carry malaria, yellow fever, dengue and elephantiasis; typhus is carried by lice; bubonic plague by fleas; sleeping sickness by tsetse flies. It is possible that many other diseases, especially those caused by viruses, may be carried by insects.

HUMAN LOUSE. See *Body Louse*.

HUMBLE BEE. Also called Bumble Bee; social bees of the family Bombidae, larger and more hairy than the hive bee and living in smaller colonies which have a very limited life, ceasing to produce workers after they have once produced queens. In temperate countries the colonies die out each winter, only fertilized queens surviving. (See *Bombidae*).

HUMERAL CROSS-VEIN. A cross-vein joining two longitudinal veins of an insect's wing in a position nearest to the wing-base and to the anterior edge of the wing, *e.g.* in the wing of a mosquito.

HUMMING-BIRD HAWK-MOTH, *Macroglossum stellatarum,* a hawk-moth of the family Sphingidae found in Central and Southern Europe and as a migrant to the British Isles. The fore-wings are brownish-grey and the hind-wings orange; both are orange underneath. The body is grey with a wide tuft of hairs at the hind-end. The proboscis or 'tongue' is as long as the whole insect and can reach for nectar in deep tubular flowers while the insect hovers with wings beating rapidly after the manner of a humming-bird. The light green larvae feed on Lady's Bedstraw (*Galium*) and related plants.

HUMP-BACKED FLY. *Megaselia* and related flies of the family Phoridae: tiny black flies with broad wings and a humped thorax; the larvae feed on decaying animal and vegetable matter.

HYALOPHORA. *Hyalophora cecropia,* the Robin Moth or Giant Silk-moth of North America, brown, white and brick-red with a wing-span of 13 cm. The large light green caterpillars feed on leaves of deciduous trees including many fruit trees.

HYALOPTERUS. *Hyalopterus pruni,* the Plum Greenfly or Mealy Plum Aphid: a common species of aphid, light green with two pale stripes running lengthwise and with red eyes; the body is covered with powdery wax. It infests plums, sloes, apricots and others of the genus *Prunus*.

HYBERNIA. *Hybernia defoliaria* or *Erannis defoliaria,* the Mottled Umber Moth: a small geometrid moth whose females are wingless and whose larvae are pests of many fruit and forest trees. The fore-wings of the male are white or brownish with a broad zig-zag transverse brown band. The caterpillars are brown and stick-like (see *Erannis*).

HYDRANGEA LEAF-TYER. See *Exartema*.

HYDRELLIA. A genus of shore-flies: predatory Diptera whose larvae are leaf-miners in aquatic plants (see *Ephydridae*).

HYDRIOMENIDAE. A family of moths sometimes regarded as a subfamily of Geometridae: *Hydriomena furcata,* the July High-flyer of Britain and Europe is greenish grey with several brown transverse lines on the fore-wings; its brown and grey striped larvae feed on willow, poplar, hazel etc.

HYDROBIUS. A common and widely distributed genus of water beetles of the family Hydrophilidae, vegetarian but with carnivorous larvae. The Common Hydrobe or Red-legged Water Beetle *Hydrobius fuscipes* is a medium sized, brown, oval insect found in stagnant water all over Britain and elsewhere. It deposits its egg cases below the water surface and attaches them to submerged stems or leaves by means of a ribbon of silk.

HYDROCAMPA. *Hydrocampa nymphaeata* or *Nymphula nymphaeata,* the Brown China Mark Moth: a small moth of the family Pyralidae having elaborate brown and white patterns on the wings, suggesting a design on porcelain.

The eggs are laid underneath leaves of aquatic plants and the larvae make a floating case of these on which they live and feed.

HYDROCYRIUS. A tropical genus of Giant Water Bugs: Heteroptera of the family Belostomatidae having the fore-legs enlarged to form a pair of pincers with which they capture their prey. They swim with the enlarged hairy hind-legs and the males carry the developing eggs on their backs.

HYDROFUGE (HYDROPHOBE). Having a waxy surface that repels water and is not wetted, *e.g.* the cuticle and cuticular hairs of most insects. This property enables many aquatic insects to breathe under water by taking down a bubble of air trapped by the hairs under their bodies (see *Plastron*).

HYDROMETRIDAE. Water Measurers: a family of water bugs closely related to the pondskaters. Agile predatory insects that move rapidly on the surface of water owing to the fact that their skin is unwetted and they do not break the surface-tension film of the water. This is due to the fact that the cuticle is of a waxy chitinous substance and is covered with fine hairs which form an insulating layer between the insect and the water. They belong to the order Hemiptera and the suborder Heteroptera.

HYDROMYZA. *Hydromyza confluens*, a brownish, hairy, predatory fly of the family Scatophagidae whose larvae live in the submerged stems of water lilies etc.

HYDRONOMUS. *Hydronomus alismatis*, the Water Plantain Weevil: a small greyish black weevil whose larvae mine in the leaves of Water Plantain (*Alisma plantago-aquatica*).

HYDROPHILIDAE. A family of scavenging water beetles, some small and some very large. Although the adults are generally vegetarian, the larvae are often carnivorous. Many of these beetles are large and black with a silvery appearance due to the air trapped by the hydrofuge hairs under the body. Air is also carried under the wings. *Hydrophilus piceus* or *Hydrous piceus*, 45 mm. or more in length, is the largest member of the family.

HYDROPHOBE HAIRS. See *Hydrofuge*.

HYDROPSYCHE. A genus of small caddis flies (Trichoptera) whose larvae live in running water and do not build cases; they catch their prey in silken webs which they spin among stones and debris.

HYDROPYLE. A specialized region of the shell of an insect's egg through which water can enter.

HYDROSCAPHIDAE. A family of small, oval, aquatic beetles inhabiting running water in North America and southern Europe.

HYDROTAEA. *Hydrotaea irritans*, the Sweat Fly: a common member of the family Muscidae, closely related to the House Fly. It swarms in large numbers in woodlands and feeds on the sweat of people and animals. Eggs are laid in dung on which the larvae feed.

HYDROUS. A genus of water beetles of the family Hydrophilidae. *Hydrous piceus*, the largest member of the family is about 45 mm. long, black with a greenish sheen; the adult feeds on water plants but the larvae are predatory (see *Hydrophilidae*).

HYGROBIA. *Hygrobia hermanni*, the Screech Beetle: a water beetle of ponds and ditches; medium sized, oval and brown with long legs. It feeds on insect larvae, worms etc. The larvae live on the bottoms of ponds and feed on the small fresh-water worm *Tubifex*. The adult beetles if disturbed produce a loud squeak by rubbing the tip of the abdomen against the undersides of the wing-cases. Other members of the genus are widely scattered in Europe, Asia and Australia.

HYLASTES. A genus of small bark-beetles whose larvae bore into stems and roots of conifers. *Hylastes ater*, the Black Pine Beetle, is a forestry pest in Europe, Australia, New Zealand, South Africa etc.

HYLASTINUS. *Hylastinus obscurus*, the Clover Root Borer: a beetle of the family Scolytidae whose larvae tunnel into the woody tap-roots of some species of clover, gorse and other leguminous plants.

HYLECOETUS. A genus of elongated beetles, bright orange or light brown, belonging to the family Lymexylidae, having soft wing-cases; the males are characterized by their large comb-like maxillary palps. The larvae tunnel into oak, birch, pine etc. producing horizontal galleries between the bark and the wood.

HYLEMYIA. A genus of root-maggot flies of the family Anthomyidae, some of which have been reclassified and are now in the genera *Delia* and *Erioischia*. They are small insects whose larvae are pests of agriculture, burrowing into roots, stems and seeds. *Hylemyia brassicae (Erioischia brassicae)* is the Cabbage Root Fly. Others attack onions, beans, maize etc.

HYLESININAE. Ash-bark beetles, a subfamily of the Scolytidae whose larvae burrow galleries beneath the bark and in the new wood of ash trees. There are several species most of which are black or grey and less than 5 mm. long. *Hylesinus* (or *Leperesinus*) *fraxini*, the Common Ash Bark Beetle; *Hylesinus crenatus*, the Large Ash Bark Beetle; *Hylesinus oleiperda*, the Lesser Ash Bark Beetle.

HYLOBIUS. *Hylobius abietis*, the Large Pine Weevil or Great Brown Weevil: one of the largest of the European weevils about 15 mm. long, light brown with a covering of fine yellowish hairs. The adults gnaw the bark and eat the buds of young conifers; the yellowish white larvae bore into the cambium of young stems and roots.

HYLOICUS. *Hyloicus pinastri*, the Pine Hawk-moth: a large European moth with a wing-span of about 8 cm.; the abdomen is striped black and white; the wings are greyish brown; the fore-wings have a dark band along the inner edge and three black dashes near the centre. The caterpillars feed on pine needles. Although it is a rare visitor to Britain it is not uncommon in the pine forests of Europe.

HYLOPHILA. An alternative name for the genus *Bena*, the Green Silver Lines Moth (see *Bena*).

HYLOTOMA. A genus of sawflies including the Rose Sawfly *Hylotoma rosae* (also called *Arge ochropus*): a small insect, black with a bright yellow abdomen and with the front margin of the fore-wings very dark. The antennae are short. Eggs are laid on rose leaves on which the greenish larvae feed.

HYLOTRUPES. *Hylotrupes bajulus*, the House Longhorn, a beetle of the family Cerambycidae, 15–20 mm. long, brownish grey with two pale shiny spots on the thorax. The larvae tunnel into dry timber, particularly of conifers. They may do considerable damage in new buildings.

HYLURGOPS. A genus of small brown beetles about 4 mm. long with a broad thorax; pests of forestry, tunnelling into pine, spruce, larch etc.

HYLURGUS. *Hylurgus ligniperda*, the Pine Bast Beetle: a dark brown beetle about 6 mm. long, a forest pest whose larvae tunnel into stems and roots of pines.

HYMENOPTERA. Bees, wasps, ants, sawflies etc., insects having two pairs of membranous wings which can be linked together by small hooks when flying. The mouth-parts are of various types; in the case of the bee they are very much lengthened to form a proboscis through which nectar is sucked. The ovipositor may be adapted for sawing, piercing or stinging. The order is divided into two suborders: *Apocrita* with a narrow waist and *Symphyta* without. Social insects such as certain species of bees, ants and wasps, although better known than the solitary species, nevertheless form only a small minority of Hymenoptera.

HYPANDRIUM. The ventral part of the *andrium* or male external genitalia: a plate formed from the ninth abdominal sternum. It may bear two short stylets, as for instance in the cockroach. This and its complementary term *epandrium* are more often used by taxonomists than by morphologists.

HYPENA. *Hypena proboscidalis* and related species of Snout Moths: noctuids having long palps projecting forwards in front of the head like a snout. The larvae feed on stinging nettles.

HYPERA. *Hypera punctata*, the Clover Leaf Weevil: a large European species of a greenish brown colour with longitudinal black stripes on the elytra. The green larva feeds on the leaves of clover and other leguminous plants. *Hypera postica*, the Alfalfa or Lucerne Weevil is a pest in North America, introduced from Europe.

HYPERECHIA. A genus of African Robber Flies (Asilidae) that show a remarkable resemblance to carpenter bees of the genus *Xylocopa* on which they feed. Different species of *Hyperechia* resemble corresponding species of *Xylocopa* so that the former can live among the latter, not only catching and killing them but also laying their eggs in the nests of their victims where the larvae of the Robber Fly can feed on the larvae of the bees.

HYPERMETABOLA. Insects having several distinct and different forms of larva (see *Hypermetamorphosis*).

HYPERMETAMORPHOSIS. Development in which the larva passes through several successive instars each different in form and habits from the previous one. Some Blister Beetles (Meloidae), for instance pass through at least four larval stages including *triungulins, caraboids, scarabaeoids* and *co-arctate* larvae.

HYPERPARASITE. A parasite that lives on or in another parasite, *e.g.* the minute Ichneumon Fly *Hemiteles* which is parasitic in the larger Ichneumon *Apanteles,* the latter itself being a parasite in caterpillars.

HYPHANTRIA. *Hyphantria cunea*, the Weaver Tiger Moth: a North American arctiid, whitish with black spots, whose caterpillars, known as Fall Webworms, weave large loose nests of silk sometimes enveloping whole branches of a tree They are serious pests of fruit and forest trees and have spread to the warmer parts of Europe.

HYPHORAIA. *Hyphoraia aulica,* also known as *Arctia aulica*, the Brown Tiger Moth: a member of the family Arctiidae similar in general appearance to the other Tiger Moths but of a browner colour. The fore-wings are brown and yellow; the hind-wings yellowish orange with black spots. The hairy caterpillars feed on a variety of grasses and small plants, particularly dande-

135

lions. They are found in mountainous country in Central and Southern Europe and Western Asia.

HYPOCEPHALUS. *Hypocephalus armatus,* the Brazilian Longhorn: a large beetle of the family Cerambycidae having a greatly enlarged thoracic shield extending forwards to cover the head and backwards to cover the abdomen.

HYPODERMA. *Hypoderma bovis,* the Cattle Warble Fly: a large yellowish brown fly of the family Oestridae; a serious parasite of cattle and other domestic animals. Eggs are laid on the hairs of the host; the newly hatched larvae may bore through the skin and into the tissues; others may be licked off and reach the gullet where they rest for a time. Whichever way they enter, they penetrate the tissues and eventually make their way to the back of the animal. Here they emerge leaving small holes in the skin, impairing its value as leather in addition to undermining the health of the animal.

HYPOGLOTTIS. A sclerite or cuticular element sometimes present between the mentum and the labium of an insect, i.e. at the base of the 'tongue' (*e.g.* in some Coleoptera).

HYPOLIMNAS. *Hypolimnas misippus,* a brightly coloured nymphalid butter-fly of South-east Asia, Australia, Africa and South America, notable for its sexual dimorphism and for its mimicry of other butterflies. The male is dark brown with mirror-like patches of violet-blue sheen on the wings. The female is rust brown with patterns of white which are very variable and mimic the appearance of another butterfly *Danaus chrysippus.* Since the latter is unpalatable to predators, this mimicry gives a considerable degree of protection to *Hypolimnas*: a case of Batesian Mimicry.

HYPONOMEUTIDAE. A family of moths whose larvae are very destructive to trees. They include the Larch Shoot-borer, the Ash-bud Moth and the Ermine moths.

HYPOPHARYNX. A chitinous sclerite arising from the floor of the mouth of an insect. Normally it bears the salivary apertures; in blood-sucking insects like mosquitoes it is enormously elongated and forms part of the proboscis down which saliva flows. In robber-flies (Asilidae) and some others, the hypopharynx becomes the principal piercing organ.

HYPOPNEUSTIC. Also called *Oligopneustic*: having a reduced number of functional spiracles, as for instance in the Coccidae and the Thysanoptera.

HYPOPYGIUM. The terminal segments of the abdomen of an insect, often modified for copulation; a term chiefly applied to male Diptera.

HYPSAUCHENIA. *Hypsauchenia hardwigii,* the Indian Tree-hopper from Sikkim: a fantastically shaped member of the family Membracidae having a long horn-like process extending upwards from the thorax, curving backwards and ending in two banner-like outgrowths.

HYPSOPYGIA. See *Gold Fringe Moth.*

HYSTRICHOPSYLLA. *Hystrichopsylla gigas,* the Wood Rat Flea of North America: one of the world's largest fleas about 5 mm. long; often found in the nests of *Neotoma,* the Wood Rat or Pack Rat of Florida and California. *Hystrichopsylla talpae,* the European Mole Flea, is about the same size (4 mm. in the male and 6 mm. in the female).

136

I

IALMENUS. *Ialmenus evagoras*, a hairstreak butterfly common throughout most of Australia: a member of the family Lycaenidae, pale green with a wide brown border and narrow brown wavy 'tails' on the hind-wings. The gregarious larvae feed on Acacia leaves.

IAPYGIDAE. An alternative spelling of Japygidae (*q.v.*).

IBALIINAE. Wasps of the group Cynipoidea, including some of the largest of this group; parasites of the woodwasp *Urocerus*. *Ibalia leucospoides*, the only European species, is about 10 mm. long, black and brown with the abdomen laterally compressed like a knife-edge. The long ovipositor is normally coiled up underneath within a sheath. The wasp uses its long sensitive antennae to search out the tunnels of the woodwasp. It then extends its saw-like ovipositor and lays its eggs in the body of the host.

IBIDOECUS. *Ibidoecus plataleae*, a rather large louse of the order Mallophaga: a parasite of the European Spoonbill *Platalea leucorodia*.

IBIS FLY. *Atherix ibis*, a two-winged fly of the group Brachycera resembling a stoutly built crane-fly with a black and yellow banded abdomen. Both adult and larva are carnivorous. The Ibis Fly is closely related to the Snipe Flies, often called 'Down-lookers', of the family Rhagionidae. It differs from them, however, in having an aquatic larva, and is also remarkable for forming clusters of ovipositing females hanging from leaves over water, like a small swarm of bees.

ICERYA. See *Cottony Cushion Scale*.

ICHNEUMONOIDEA. A large superfamily of parasitic wasps comprising the Ichneumon Flies and the Braconids: Hymenoptera with a narrow waist and a large, sharp, piercing ovipositor with which they lay their eggs in the bodies of other insects. The developing larvae live for some time in the body of the victim, eventually killing it and emerging to pupate in a silky cocoon. The largest European species is *Rhyssa persuasoria*, black and brown, about 25 mm. long with an ovipositor twice this length; it is a parasite of the wood-wasp *Urocerus gigas*. Many ichneumons and braconids are beneficial to man because they parasitize and help to control specific pests of agriculture and forestry.

IDIOGASTRA. A name sometimes given to the Orussoidea, a small group of parasitic Hymenoptera intermediate between the Apocrita and the Symphyta.

ILYBIUS. A genus of small, oval water beetles, black with a bronze sheen; the underside brown; the antennae and legs reddish. *Ilybius ater* and *Ilybius obscurus* are two common European species.

ILYOCORIS. *Ilyocoris cimicoides*, the Saucer Bug: a European water bug of the group Heteroptera which, although it has wings, does not fly. Oval, light brown and about 15 mm. long, it is commonly found in muddy ponds or slow flowing streams where it swims actively in search of small crustaceans and other organisms on which it feeds.

IMAGINAL DISCS (IMAGINAL BUDS). Clusters of cells which undergo rapid division to form the rudiments of future organs during the metamorphosis of an insect.

IMAGO. The adult form of an insect after metamorphosis.

IMPERIAL MOTH. *Basilona imperialis*, sometimes called the Yellow Emperor: a large North American moth, yellowish with spots and bands of pink and purple. The caterpillars are hairy, brown and green, with four short 'horns' on the thorax. They are voracious feeders on a large variety of trees and shrubs.

INCHWORM. A colloquial American name for any of the caterpillars of the Geometridae (earth-measurers).

INCURVARIIDAE. A family of small moths, often metallic and then called 'bright moths'. Their caterpillars bite circular pieces out of leaves and use two of these as shields between which they hide, or make portable cases of them.

INDIAN MEAL MOTH. *Plodia interpunctella*, a small moth of the family Pyralidae having brown and yellow fore-wings and white hind-wings. The larvae are pests of grain, seeds, fruit, nuts etc.; they may live for up to two years feeding on these, spinning webs and leaving droppings. They have spread to nearly all parts of the world and were first observed in Britain about 1840.

INDIRECT METAMORPHOSIS. Complete metamorphosis in which there are four stages: egg, larva, pupa and adult (see *Holometabola*).

INDUSTRIAL MELANISM. The existence of black varieties of moths or other insects in industrial regions. The best known example is the Peppered Moth *Biston betularia*. The exact cause of this mutation is obscure but, once the new variety is established, it tends to increase in smoke-blackened regions where its dark colour helps to camouflage it. In some industrial parts of Britain the black varieties of Peppered Moth have almost entirely replaced the normal members of the species.

INQUILINE. An animal living in the home of another and sharing its food; among insects there are many cases of a species inhabiting the galls made by a different species. The small gall-wasp *Periclistus brandtii*, for instance, lives in the 'Robin's Pincushion' made by the larger gall-wasp *Rhodites* (*Diplolepis*) *rosae*. Other cases include larvae of Cecidomyidae living in leaf-mines made by other insects, and, best known of all inquilines, many species living as 'guests' in the nests of ants and termites.

INSECTA. A class of the phylum Arthropoda comprising nearly all those that breathe by spiracles and tracheae and have the body divided into a distinct head, thorax and abdomen, the former bearing antennae and usually compound eyes. Certain primitively wingless groups – *Collembola, Protura* and *Diplura* – which used to be regarded as orders of insects, are currently treated as distinct classes of Arthropoda, which, together with Insecta, form the superclass Hexapoda. In all these the thorax consists of three segments with three pairs of legs; the abdomen is segmented and without legs. The mouth-parts are complex and variously adapted for different modes of feeding. Most insects have two pairs of wings on the thorax; some have secondarily lost one or both pairs. In addition to the above features insects have the general characteristics of all arthropods, *viz.* a thick cuticle or exoskeleton, a ventral nervous system with segmental ganglia and a dorsal tubular heart connected to an open blood system. Most insects undergo some form of metamorphosis during development. Those in which there is a pupal stage are known as *Holometabola;* those without are *Hemimetabola.* Insects form the largest known group of animals consisting of nearly a million species (see also *Arthropoda*).

INSECT LARVAE. A larva may be defined as a free-living, immature stage differing in structure and habits from the adult. The larvae of insects are very variable but may be roughly classified into the following types:

(1) *Protopod Larvae.* Primitive parasitic larvae with barely incipient limb-buds and with no segmentation of the abdomen. They are found in some parasitic Hymenoptera.

(2) *Polypod or Eruciform Larvae.* Typical caterpillars with six legs on the thorax and a number of 'cushion feet' or prolegs on the abdomen. Typical of Lepidoptera and sawflies.

(3) *Oligopod or Campodeiform Larvae.* These are usually predatory and therefore have efficient sense organs and long legs but no 'cushion feet'; they are common among beetles.

(4) *Apodous* or *legless larvae.* The body is segmented and has a minute head with few sense organs and no legs or limbs of any kind. The absence of these is probably a secondary feature arising from the fact that they are either fed by other members of the colony, as in bees, or the eggs are laid in suitable food such as meat or dung, as in house flies etc.

INSECTORUBIN. A brown pigment, usually incorporated with melanin, in the epidermis and cuticle of insects, formerly considered to be a mixture of a group of pigments called *ommochromes.*

INSECTOVERDIN. A green pigment present in the bodies of some insects; usually a mixture of the blue-green waste substance *biliverdin* with yellow carotinoid substance derived from the food.

INSTAR. Properly the form assumed by an insect during the *stadium* or 'stage' between two moults. Thus 'second instar larva' means what the larva looks like during the second larval stage or stadium. Often, however, the word 'instar' is used to mean the same as 'stadium', *i.e.* the interval rather than the form. The number of larval instars varies from three to about thirty.

INTEGUMENT. See *Cuticle* and *Exoskeleton.*

INTERCALARY VEINS. See *Cross-veins.*

INTERCASTES. Types that are intermediate between the recognized castes, especially in social insects such as bees, ants and termites. Such variations may be due to variations in diet or to invasion by parasites. Either of these factors may have an effect on the relative dominance of certain genes or may cause arrested allometric development (see *Castes* and *Allometric Growth*).

INTERNAL PARASITES. See *Endoparasites.*

INTERSEX. An individual which shows both male and female features due to an upsetting of the balance between the sex-producing factors associated with the sex chromosomes. A 'strong' female crossed with a 'weak' male, for instance, may produce some male offspring with female characteristics. The best known example of this is the Gipsy Moth *Lymantria.* (Compare *Gynandromorph.*)

INTESTINAL MYIASIS. Disease of man or other vertebrates caused by the larvae of certain Diptera living as internal parasites in the intestines.

IO MOTH. See *Automeris.*

IPHICLIDES. *Iphiclides podalirius,* the Scarce Swallowtail or Sail Butterfly of Central and Southern Europe, North Africa and the temperate parts of Asia as far as China; pale greenish yellow with oblique transverse bands of black on both wings, with blue crescents bordering the hind-wings and with long narrow black 'tails'. It frequents lilac blossoms but the large greenish yellow caterpillars feed principally on blackthorn and mountain ash.

IPHIS. *Iphis madagascariensis,* one of the largest of the Click Beetles (Elateridae), about 4 cm. long, glossy black and covered with short white hairs.

IPINAE. Bark Beetles and Ambrosia Beetles: a subfamily of the Scolytidae characterized by having the head concealed by the lengthened prothorax. They are very serious pests of forest trees in which they make numerous branching tunnels between the wood and the bark; in doing this they spread fungal diseases such as Dutch Elm Disease. The Ambrosia Beetles apparently cultivate fungi on the walls of the tunnels in order to provide food for the larvae.

IPS. The principal genus of bark beetles of the group Ipinae (*q.v.*) including some of the most harmful pests of woodland trees. Both larvae and adults burrow between the bark and the wood, making extensive branching tunnels and infecting the trees with fungal and virus diseases. Pines and other conifers are affected.

IRIDESCENCE. The production of brilliant colours by optical interference, as for instance in the bodies of dragonflies, the wings of some butterflies and the elytra of some beetles. The effect is caused by the presence in the cuticle of numerous thin transparent lamellae separated by material with a different refractive index.

IRIDOMYRMEX. *Iridomyrmex humilis,* the Argentine Ant: a small brown ant about 2.5 mm. long that has become established as a household pest in the warmer parts of North America, South Africa, Australia and many other countries. It bites freely and is omnivorous. In Britain it is sometimes found in artificially heated buildings but will not survive the winter climate out of doors.

IRIS BORER. *Macronoctua onusta,* a small moth whose larva bores into the roots and rhizomes of Iris.

IRIS CELLS. Pigmented cells surrounding each ommatidium or optical unit of a compound eye. In bright light they spread round each crystalline cone, isolating it from its neighbours so that vision is *mosaic*; in dim light they may retract so that the light entering each ommatidium merges with that of its neighbours causing continuous but rather ill-defined vision (see *Compound Eyes*).

IRIS TAPETUM. A network of fine tracheae surrounding the ommatidia or optical units in some compound eyes. They are particularly well developed in nocturnal insects such as the Noctuid moths and serve to reflect light, so giving the sensitive retinal cells an increased stimulation (see *Compound Eyes*).

ISABELLA TIGER MOTH. *Isia isabella,* a North American moth of the family Arctiidae, yellow with a few tiny brown spots and a red abdomen. The caterpillar, reddish brown in the middle and black at each end, is one of the woolliest of 'woolly bears'.

ISCHNOCERA. A group of biting lice (Mallophaga) including the two families Philopteridae (head-lice of fowls) and Trichodectidae (parasites of mammals). The latter include *Damalina ovis,* the Sheep Louse and *Damalina bovis,* the Red Louse of cattle.

ISCHNODEMUS. A genus of plant-bugs (Hemiptera) including the European Chinchbug (*Ischnodemus sabuleti*) commonly found in reedy swamps. The body is light brown, about 5 mm. long with greenish wings that are often reduced or incomplete. Related species in other countries are often serious pests of wheat, maize and other cereals.

ISCHNURA. A common and widely distributed genus of damselflies (Zygoptera). *Ischnura elegans*, a British species, has green eyes, a black thorax striped with pale green and a dark blue abdomen with a pale blue band near the tip. The females are polychromatic, *i.e.* exist in several colour-forms.

ISIA. See *Isabella Tiger Moth*.

ISLE OF WIGHT DISEASE. A common disease of honey bees caused by the minute parasitic mite *Acarapis woodi* which infests and blocks their tracheal tubes.

ISONYCHIA. A genus of mayflies (Ephemeroptera) of which the nymphs have the fore-legs fringed with long hairs.

ISOPERLA. A genus of green stone-flies (Plecoptera) in which the aquatic nymphs breathe through the skin and do not develop gills.

ISOPNEUSTIC. A term used to denote a primitive arrangement of the spiracles, two thoracic and eight abdominal pairs, all situated in the intersegmental membranes. Most present-day insects have some degree of specialization or reduction of spiracles as well as migration on to one of the adjacent segments. The isopneustic arrangement persists only in some embryos.

ISOPTERA. Termites or 'White Ants': social insects living mostly in the tropics, which do much damage to woodwork and other materials. They live in large communities in huge nests tunnelled in wood or built of earth and wood cemented together. Sometimes these are as high as 6 metres (20 ft.) Although these insects bear no relation to ants they resemble them in having numerous castes: queen, workers, soldiers etc. The queens sometimes grow up to 10 cm. or more in length.

ISOTOMA. *Isotoma viridis,* the Green Glacier Springtail and related species: small members of the order Collembola, a few millimetres in length and coloured green, yellow, blue or violet. They feed on rotting vegetation and are active even in very cold conditions. They can sometimes be seen in very large numbers on the snow in early spring.

ITAME. *Itame wauaria,* the V-moth: a small greyish geometrid moth with a black V-shaped mark on each fore-wing, The yellowish grey caterpillars are pests of currants and gooseberries.

ITHOMIIDAE. A family of butterflies from tropical America having a very long slender body and yellow or orange transparent wings with thick black venation.

ITONIDIDAE. Gall-midges: an alternative name for the family Cecidomyidae (*q.v.*). Now disused because the old paper in which it appeared (Meigen, 1800) has been ruled invalid.

ITUNA. *Ituna phenarete*: a common butterfly of Peru belonging to the family Ithomiidae, having a long, thin, light brown body and whitish transparent wings with thick dark brown venation and borders.

ITYCORSIA. *Itycorsia zappei,* a web-spinning sawfly that infests pine trees in North America.

IXIAS. *Ixias pyrene*, a common Asiatic butterfly of the family Pieridae, resembling the Clouded Yellow but smaller. The fore-wings are orange and the hind-wings yellow, both with a broad dark brown margin. There are many regional variations.

J

JAMIDES. A common genus of small Asiatic butterflies of the family Lycaenidae, bright blue with broad black margins round the fore-wings and a border of black spots round the hind-wings.

JANUS. A genus of stem sawflies of the family Cephidae. *Janus integer*, the Currant Stem-girdler, lays her eggs in the stems of currants and related plants as well as poplar and willow trees; she then moves a little way up the stem and rings it with her ovipositor causing the tip of the plant to wilt. The developing larvae move down the plant, feeding on the pith. *Janus femoratus* is a similar species that attacks young oak twigs; other species are pests of cereals.

JAPANESE BEETLE. *Popillia japonica* and related species of the family Scarabaeidae common all over Eastern Asia. First introduced accidentally into the United States about 1916, it has now become a major pest of grasses and cereals all over the North-eastern States and is spreading to the Middle West. The larvae live in the soil feeding on roots; the adults attack leaves, flowers and fruits.

JAPYGIDAE. A family of Diplura or Bristle-tails: small wingless insects having a forked tail formed from two long thin cerci and having biting mouth-parts lying in pockets from which they are protruded when feeding. *Japyx* and related genera are relatively large and darkly pigmented; they live in the soil and are predators. Like all the Diplura they are primitive and may perhaps be considered as an evolutionary link between insects and millipedes.

JASSIDAE. An alternative name for Cicadellidae or leaf-hoppers, a family of agile plant-bugs which infest trees and leap from leaf to leaf with great speed (see *Cicadellidae*).

JAWS. A typical insect has two pairs of horizontally moving jaws, namely the *mandibles* or upper pair and the *maxillae* or lower pair; the latter bear a pair of palps or short feelers. Both these may show many modifications according to the feeding habits of the insect. In biting insects such as the cockroach and in many beetles the mandibles are stout, thickly sclerotized and toothed. The maxillae have two movable lobes, an inner *lacinia* and an outer sheath-like *galea*. In fiercely predatory insects such as the Dytiscidae the mandibles may be very sharp and sickle-like and may have openings at their tips through which the juices of their victims are sucked. In dragonflies the mandibles, maxillae and labium all bear teeth. In insects such as butterflies, which feed by sucking, the mandibles are reduced or absent but the galeae of the maxillae are extended to form a tubular proboscis. In Hemiptera both mandibles and maxillae are extended to form long, piercing stylets; when not in use these are bent back under the head and thorax. In female mosquitoes and related

Diptera the arrangement is somewhat similar but the stylets are very thin, sharp and sometimes toothed for piercing the skin of their victims. No male Diptera use the mandibles to obtain blood but both sexes of Tsetse Flies, Stable Flies and Pupipara use the stiffened labium as a piercing organ.

JEWEL WASPS. A name given to several families of brightly coloured wasps: Pteromalidae, minute metallic coloured parasites of other wasps; Chrysididae, brilliant blue, green or red Cuckoo Wasps which lay their eggs in the nests of other wasps or bees.

JIGGER. Also called the Chigger or Chigoe: *Tunga penetrans* or *Dermatophilus penetrans*, a flea of tropical South America and Africa that burrows into the skin of the feet and under the toe-nails (see *Chigoe*).

JOHNSTON'S ORGAN. A collection of chordotonal receptors near the base of the antenna of an insect. Their function is probably to enable the insect to perceive movements of its antennae and thus to become aware of air-vibrations, either as sound or as air currents.

JOINTWORM. The larva of the chalcid wasp *Harmolita tritici* which tunnels into stems of wheat and is a pest in North America.

JUGATAE. See *Homoneura* and *Jugum*.

JUGUM. A small lobe at the base of the fore-wing which catches under the anterior edge of the hind-wing and so locks the wings together during flight; present in moths of the group Homoneura and in Caddis Flies (Trichoptera).

JULY HIGHFLYER. See *Hydriomenidae*.

JUMPING. Insects may use jumping as their principal means of locomotion or they may use it only for sudden escape movements when disturbed. In the former case the hind-legs, especially the femora and tibiae, are usually specially strong and lengthened, as for instance in grasshoppers, fleas, flea-beetles, leaf-hoppers etc. They may be extremely powerful; a flea has been known to jump about 30 cm. or about 100 times its own length. When jumping is only occasionally resorted to there are several methods of doing this without using the legs. Springtails (Collembola), for instance, have a *furcula* extending forwards beneath the abdomen and held in place by a 'catch' or *retinaculum*. When the latter is released the furcula springs back throwing the insect into the air. Click beetles (Elateridae) on the other hand jump by the sudden movement of a projection beneath the thorax. Many larvae (*e.g.* Cheese-skippers, larvae of the fly *Piophila*) bend the body, grip the posterior end with the mouth-hooks, and suddenly release it.

JUMPING BEANS. A phenomenon caused by the larvae of the Mexican moth *Laspeyresia saltitans* or *Grapholitha saltitans* which lives and develops in the seeds of the plant *Sebastiana*. The seed is thin-walled and when the inside has been eaten away the jerking movements of the larva cause the bean to 'jump' (see *Grapholitha*).

JUMPING PLANT-LICE. Minute plant-lice of the family Psyllidae having transparent wings, long antennae and long legs. Like the Aphids they suck plant juices and exude a sticky secretion of honeydew or in some cases a wax-like substance. The group includes *Psylla mali,* the Apple-sucker (yellowish green), *Psylla pyri,* the Pear-sucker (dark red) and *Psylla peregrina,* the Haw-thorn-sucker (bright green).

JUNE BUG (JUNE BEETLE). Names sometimes given to various species of Chafers of the family Scarabaeidae, *e.g. Phyllopertha horticola* (see *Chafers* and *Cockchafer*).

JUNE CHAFER. See *June Bug.*

JUNIPER BUG. *Pitedia juniperina,* a shieldbug having the head, scutellum and elytra bright green with small black spots; an insect of chalk hills.

JUNONIA. A genus of butterflies closely related to the Peacock (*Inachis*) and resembling it in having large conspicuous eye-spots. The Buck-eye *Junonia coenia* of the southern United States is brownish with three large blue spots on each fore-wing and two on each hind-wing; its larvae feed on plantain and antirrhinum. *Junonia almana* is a related species of India, Malaysia, China and Japan; its larvae feed on *Acanthus.*

JUVENILE HORMONE. See *Neotenin.*

K

KAKOTHRIPS. *Kakothrips robustus,* the Pea Thrips: a small insect of the order Thysanoptera, about 2 mm. long and having a dark body with brown, deeply fringed wings; a serious European pest of peas and beans from which they suck the sap, causing stunted growth, silvery leaves and distorted pods.

KALIOFENUSA. *Kaliofenusa ulmi* (also called *Fenusa ulmi* and *Kaliosphinga ulmi*), a minute sawfly whose larvae are leaf-miners in elms. Sometimes a large number of these occupy a single leaf, their tunnels coalescing to form a large cavity. They are serious pests in Europe and have spread to North America and other countries.

KALLIMA. A genus of butterflies whose wings when folded show a remarkable protective resemblance to a dead leaf with markings in various shades of reddish brown and green. *Kallima inachis,* the Indian Leaf Butterfly and *Kallima philarchus* from Ceylon are well known examples.

KALOTERMES. An alternative spelling of *Calotermes,* a genus of termites that do much damage by boring into wood. *Kalotermes flavicollis* is the European Yellow-necked Termite; others are found in North America and elsewhere (see *Calotermes*).

KANGAROO BEETLE. *Sagra papuana* of the Melanesian Islands, a large, deep blue leaf-beetle of the family Chrysomelidae, having the hind femora greatly lengthened and thickened. Other species live in tropical America and elsewhere.

KANISKA. A genus of butterflies of the family Nymphalidae, closely related to the vanessids, the Red Admiral and the Painted Lady. *Kaniska canace,* dark brown with broad blue bands across each wing, is common in all parts of Asia.

KATEPIMERON. The lower part of the epimeron of an insect in those cases in which it is divided by a transverse suture (see also *Epimeron* and *Anepimeron*).

KATEPISTERNUM. The lower part of the episternum or anterior sclerite of the subcoxa at the base of an insect's leg (see *Episternum*).

KATYDIDS. A colloquial name used in the United States for a number of the larger and more noisy nocturnal long-horned grasshoppers (Tettigoniidae): green, brown or pinkish insects with very long filamentous antennae. *Amblycorypha oblongifolia* is the largest American species.

KED. *Melophagus ovinus*, the Sheep Ked: a wingless, blood-sucking fly of the family Hippoboscidae that spends its whole life on the body of a sheep. The larvae, which are produced viviparously, attach themselves to the wool by a sticky secretion. They then pupate and the emerging adults continue to suck blood (see *Hippoboscidae*).

KEELED ORTHETRUM. *Orthetrum coerulescens*, a small or medium sized European dragonfly found over marshes or still water. The female has brown eyes, a yellowish brown striped thorax and a pale brown abdomen; the male has the brown parts replaced by pale blue.

KELP FLY. A general name for two-winged flies of the family Coelopidae whose larvae live in and feed on rotting seaweed on the shore above high-tide mark. They are flattened, bristly flies which can take off from water.

KENTISH GLORY. See *Endromis*.

KERMIDAE (ERIOCOCCIDAE). A family of scale-insects, also called Chermesidae and sometimes classed with the Coccidae. They are found on oaks, elms and other trees. Some, such as the Elm Scale *Gossyparia spuria*, are pests of forestry; others such as *Lecanium ilia* produce a useful crimson dye similar to cochineal. This insect feeds on oak trees in the Mediterranean region and the dye has been known since ancient times.

KILLER SHORE-FLY. *Ochthera mantis*, a two-winged predatory fly of the family Ephydridae. The larva is aquatic and lives in salt marshes or brackish water. The adult catches small gnats or other insects in flight by means of spiny bristles on its legs (see *Ephydridae*).

KIMMINSIA. See *Brown Lacewing*.

KINETOPAUSE. An arrestation of activity without necessarily an arrestation of development. It is therefore not the same as a diapause but may accompany it. Rest, sleep and death-feigning are examples. Many insects show long periods of motionless inactivity interrupted occasionally by bursts of energy.

KISSING BUG. A colloquial name used in the United States for *Reduvius personatus,* a predatory insect that enters houses and hunts for bedbugs and other insects. Some related species also suck human blood (see *Reduviidae*).

KITTEN MOTHS. A group of small Prominent Moths of the genus *Harpyia*, also called *Cerura*; greyish with black spots. *Cerura bifida* the Poplar Kitten Moth and *Cerura furcula* the Sallow Kitten Moth are common European examples. Like the Puss Moth *Cerura vinula*, they have curious shaped larvae with two long thin tail filaments.

KLINOKINESIS. An 'avoiding action' manifested by some insects that normally fly in a straight line when the environment is favourable but perform rapid turning movements as soon as there is any unfavourable stimulus. The turning appears to be a random movement and takes place when the stimulus is an undirected one such as a change in temperature or humidity.

KLINOTAXIS. A movement of an insect in a definite direction in relation to a stimulus, *e.g.* towards or away from light.

KNAPWEED CARDER BEE. *Bombus sylvarum*, one of the smaller species of bumble bee, about 15 mm, long. commonly found on Black Knapweed

Centaurea nigra. It has a black head, black thorax with yellowish grey borders and a yellowish abdomen with two black bands and a white tail. The shallow nest is made just beneath the surface of the ground.

KNEE. The joint between the femur and the tibia of an insect, named by analogy with the knee of a vertebrate.

KNOB-HORNS. Also called Club-horns; a group of sawflies whose antennae end in a knob or swelling, *e.g.* the Birch-leaf Sawfly *Climbex.*

KNOT-GRASS BEETLE. *Gastrophysa polygoni,* a small oval leaf-beetle of the family Chrysomelidae having shining green elytra with the thorax, antennae, legs and tip of the abdomen red. It feeds on Knot-grass *Polygonum aviculae* and related plants.

KNOT-GRASS MOTH. *Acronycta rumicis,* a small noctuid moth whose larvae feed on Knot-grass, Dock and other members of the family Polygonaceae. The fore-wings are mottled with light and dark drey; the hind-wings are pale brownish grey.

KNOT-HORNS. A name sometimes given to moths of the family Pyralidae on account of the swelling which they have at the bases of the antennae.

KOENIGINIRMUS. A genus of bird-lice of the order Mallophaga that infest sea birds and are sometimes found in dry seaweed. *Koeniginirmus normifer* and *Koeniginirmus punctatus* are both white with patterns of dark brown on the head, thorax and abddomen. They infest different species of gulls.

KOO-TSABE FLY. *Ephydra hians,* a predatory fly found in large numbers near the shores of lakes in California and Nevada. The pupae are collected by the native Indians as food (see *Ephydridae*).

KYNURENINE. An oxidation product of the amino-acid tryptophane that gives rise to some of the red and brown pigments in insects.

L

LABELLUM. One of a pair of oral lobes or pads present at the distal end of the proboscis in Diptera. They may be little developed, as in the mosquito, but in the blowfly and similar insects they are greatly enlarged and partly covered by a membrane containing a series of channels or *pseudotracheae* up which liquid is sucked.

LABIA. *Labia minor,* the Lesser Earwig: a widely distributed species found near dung heaps or rotting vegetation or among nettles. It is yellowish brown, about 8 mm. long and, unlike the Common Earwig *Forficula,* it flies at night and is attracted to light.

LABIAL HOOKS. Hooks or spines on the labial palps of the nymphs of dragon-flies (Odonata). In these insects the whole labium forms an enlarged prehensile organ known as the *mask* which is capable of being shot out rapidly to catch tadpoles or other creatures.

LABIAL KIDNEYS. Excretory glands in the head with tubules opening near the base of the labium; present in some Springtails and Bristle-tails (Collembola and Thysanura).

LABIAL PALPS. A pair of segmented sensory organs or feelers borne on the labium of an insect.

LABIDURA. A genus of earwigs (Dermaptera) including the Giant or Tawny Earwig *Labidura riparia*, sometimes known as the Shore Earwig, a pale brown species about 35 mm. long found on wet sand under seaweed.

LABIUM. The lower lip of an insect formed by the union of a pair of appendages homologous with the second maxillae of a crustacean. It consists of the fixed *mentum* and the movable *prementum* to which are attached laterally the two labial palps and distally the *ligula*. The latter, in a generalized insect such as the cockroach, consists of a pair of inner lobes or *glossae* and outer lobes or *paraglossae*. In some specialized mouth-parts such as those of the bee the ligula may be lengthened to form a tubular proboscis.

LABRUM. The upper lip of an insect or crustacean.

LAC INSECT. *Laccifer lacca,* sometimes called *Carteria lacca* or *Tachardia lacca*: a scale insect similar to the coccids and cochineal insects, found in India and South-east Asia. The females crowd together on the stems of banyan, fig and other trees and secrete a resinous substance from which lac or shellac is obtained. Entire twigs or branches may be covered to a depth of several millimetres and in India about four million pounds are obtained annually.

LACCIFERIDAE. A family of Scale Insects including the Lac Insect *Laccifer lacca* which secretes a resinous substance from which shellac is obtained (see *Lac Insect*).

LACEBUGS. Small plant-bugs of the family Tingidae having a lace-like network of veins on the fore-wings and a lace-like embossed pattern on the head and prothorax; commonly found on gorse, thistles etc.

LACEWING BUTTERFLY. *Cethosia,* a genus of large, brightly coloured, nymphalid butterflies from North Australia and Indonesia, so named on account of the intricate lace-like pattern on the undersides of the wings.

LACEWING FLIES. A group of predatory Neuroptera having a narrow brown or green body and large gauze-like wings; both adults and larvae prey on aphids (see *Chrysopidae, Brown Lacewing* and *Giant Lacewing*).

LACHESILLA. *Lachesilla pedicularia,* a minute winged insect of the order Psocoptera related to the book-lice; an occasional pest of stored food.

LACHNAEA. A genus of leaf-beetles of the family Chrysomelidae: *Lachnaea sexpunctata* is a common species found in oak woods of Southern Europe. It is about 10 mm. long, light brown with three prominant black spots on each elytron.

LACHNUS. A genus of greenish grey aphids found on the needles and bark of pine, larch, spruce and other conifers.

LACINIA. The inner spiny lobe of the maxilla of an insect, sheathed by the outer hood-like lobe or *galea*.

LACKEY MOTH. *Malacosoma neustria,* a medium sized, light brown moth of the family Lasiocampidae, closely related to the Eggar Moths and, like them, having a stoutly built body, prominent comb-like antennae and reduced mouth-parts. The caterpillars are hairy, have brown, black and blue-grey longitudinal lines and live in communal webs; they feed on leaves of black-thorn, hawthorn, hazel and other trees.

LACON. *Lacon variabilis,* a Click beetle of the family Elateridae whose larvae (wireworms) are pests of sugar cane in Queensland and elsewhere.

LADYBIRD. See *Coccinellidae.*

LADYBIRD MIMIC. See *Endomychidae.*

LAGOA. See *Flannel Moth.*

LAMELLICORNIA. Leaf-horn Beetles: a group characterized by having the last few segments of the antennae expanded into movable leaflets or lamellae. They include Chafers (Scarabaeidae) and Stag Beetles (Lucanidae), and are currently called the Superfamily Scarabaeoidea

LAMIA. *Lamia textor,* the Weaver Beetle: a longhorn beetle of the family Cerambycidae, about 25 mm. long, dull black with thick legs and thickened bases of the antennae; common in Central Europe but rare in Britain. It is found on willows, poplars etc. where its larvae live and feed on the roots for two years. The name is given on account of its supposed habit of weaving small twigs together to make a nest.

LAMMERT'S CYCLE. A daily cycle of temperature changes observed in beehives during winter. The temperature falls to a minimum of 13°C. This stimulates the bees to greater muscular activity and the temperature rises rapidly to about 25°C. At this temperature the bees cease their activity and the temperature again falls gradually to 13°C. In an average hive about 20 gms. of sugar are consumed during this cycle.

LAMPIDES. *Lampides boeticus,* the Long-tailed Blue Butterfly: a small, pale blue butterfly of the family Lycaenidae having thin black 'tails' on the hind-wings. It breeds in Asia and migrates across Europe where it is common in gardens. The larvae feed on leguminous plants.

LAMPRA. *Lampra fimbriata,* the Broad-bordered Yellow Underwing: a medium sized noctuid moth with light brown or greyish fore-wings and bright orange hind-wings with very broad black borders. The larvae feed on birch, hazel, hawthorn and other trees.

LAMPRONATA. *Lampronata setosa,* a large Ichneumon Fly, dark brown with orange or reddish legs. The body is about 18 mm. long but the very long antennae and ovipositor make the total length more than twice this. The larvae are parasites on the caterpillars of Goat Moths which live in tunnels in ash, elm, poplar and other trees. The long sharp ovipositor of the ichneumon is used to bore through the wood in its search for its victims.

LAMPRONIA. *Lampronia rubiella,* the Raspberry Moth: a small moth, one of the Microlepidoptera, dark brown with yellow spots on the fore-wings. The larvae are pests of raspberries and loganberries where they live in the flowers and fruit and pupate in the stem.

LAMPYRIDAE. A family of predatory beetles including glow-worms and fireflies as well as many non-luminous species. They have an elongated soft body and leathery wing-cases and are allied to the Soldier Beetles (Canthari-dae). In many species, as for instance the European Glow-worm *Lampyris noctiluca,* the females are wingless (see also *Firefly* and *Glow-worm*).

LANGURIA. *Languria mozardi,* the Clover Stem Borer: a beetle of the family Erotylidae (Languriidae) most of which feed on fungi but this species is exceptional in that it bores into the roots and stems of clover, lucerne etc. (see *Erotylidae*).

LANTERN FLY. See *Fulgoridae*.

LAOTHOE. *Laothoe populi*, the Poplar Hawk-moth: a large European moth of the family Sphingidae having serrated wings coloured in various shades of brown and grey with a rust-red patch on each hind-wing. The general appearance is that of a dried leaf. The caterpillars are bright green with oblique yellow lines along the sides and a yellow horn at the hind-end. They feed on poplar, willow etc.

LAPARA. *Lapara bombycoides*, Harris's Sphinx Moth, a pest of pine trees; a small moth whose larvae have green and yellow longitudinal stripes exactly matching a bunch of pine needles in which they hang in a vertical position.

LAPHRIA. A genus of Robber Flies (Asilidae) including many large black or grey and yellow hairy flies, savage predators that use their bristly front legs for catching other insects in flight and their piercing proboscis for sucking their victims dry. They frequent deciduous forests and open woodland and are found in many parts of the world (see *Asilidae*).

LAPHRIINI. A tribe of robber flies (Asilidae) closely resembling bees (see *Laphria*).

LAPHYGMA. A genus of noctuid moths whose larvae, known as Army Worms, are pests of grassland, cereals and some leguminous crops in many parts of the world. *Laphygma frugiperda* is a North American species; *Laphygma exempta* and *Laphygma exigua* are South African.

LAPLAND FRITILLARY. *Euphydryas iduna*, one of the northernmost butterflies living well within the Arctic Circle; similar in appearance to the Marsh Fritillary *Euphydryas aurinia* but with a more pronounced chequerboard pattern of pale yellow and orange. The larvae feed on bilberry, cranberry and other mountain plants.

LAPP COCKROACH (DUSKY COCKROACH). *Ectobius lapponicus*, a small brown European woodland cockroach about 10–12 mm. long. The male has long elytra covering the abdomen; the female has much shorter elytra and vestigial wings.

LAPPET MOTH. See *Gastropacha*.

LARCH LEAF MINER. *Coleophora laricella*, a small grey moth of the family Tineidae with a wing-span of about 10 mm. The caterpillar is about 5 mm. long, reddish brown with a black head; it feeds on young larch needles and uses the remains of these to construct a portable case in which it lives with the head projecting. It hibernates and pupates within this case.

LARCH SAWFLY. *Pristiphora erichsonii* (*Lygaeonematus erichsonii* or *Nematus erichsonii*), a pest and defoliator of larch trees, originally European but introduced into North America. The adult is black with a central band of orange on the abdomen; the larvae are greyish with a black head; they pupate in the ground.

LARCH SHOOT BORER. *Argyresthia atmoriella*, a small moth of the family Tineidae having greyish wings fringed on the hind-margins. The caterpillars are greenish with a black head; they bore into larch shoots, feeding on the soft tissues just beneath the surface.

LARCH TORTRICID. *Steganoptycha diniana*, a small grey-brown moth of the family Tortricidae whose caterpillars bind larch needles together into bunches within which they feed.

LARDER BEETLE. *Dermestes lardarius* (see *Bacon Beetle*).

LARENTIINAE. Carpet Moths, a subfamily of the Hydriomenidae: geometrid moths which rest with their wings spread out exposing the hind-wings and whose looper caterpillars rest in an arched position. *Larentia clavaria*, the Mallow Moth is typical.

LARGE BLUE BUTTERFLY. *Maculinea arion*, a butterfly of the family Lycaenidae ranging throughout Europe and Asia as far as Siberia and China. The upper surfaces of the wings are bright blue with white fringes; the undersides are greenish grey with numerous black spots. The butterfly is of special interest on account of its relationships with the ant *Myrmica scabrinodis*. The caterpillars feed on Wild Thyme (*Thymus serpyllum*), but after the third moult they leave the plant and are taken by the ants into their nests. They are tended by the ants and exude a sweet fluid much liked by the latter. The ants do not apparently object to the fact that the caterpillars eat some of their larvae. Finally pupation takes place while still in the ants' nest and the butterflies eventually make their way through the galleries and out into the open.

LARGE COPPER. *Lycaena dispar*. See *Copper Butterflies*.

LARGE ELM BARK BEETLE. *Scolytus destructor*. See *Elm Bark Beetle*.

LARGE EMERALD. *Geometra papilionaria*, the largest of the European Emerald Moths with a wing-span of about 5 cm., bright green with wavy white lines on both wings. The caterpillars, which are typical geometrids or loopers, feed on birch, hazel and beech; they gradually change from brown to green, matching their surroundings at all stages of development.

LARGE SKIPPER. *Ochlodes venata*, a common butterfly of Europe and northern Asia belonging to the family Hesperiidae. The wings are tawny brown with darker margins. The caterpillars are green and construct tube-like shelters in blades of grass. They feed, hibernate and pupate in these (see *Hesperiidae*).

LARGE TABBY MOTH. *Aglossa pinguinalis*, a medium sized moth of the family Pyralidae having the fore-wings patterned with light and dark brown and the hind-wings paler. As in all the Pyralidae the fore-wings are narrow and the hind-wings fringed. It has prominent palps but a reduced proboscis. It can be a pest in barns and warehouses where the larvae live in silken tubes among hay, cereals and other foodstuffs.

LARGE THORN MOTH. See *Ennomos* and *Ennominae*.

LARGE TORTOISESHELL. *Nymphalis polychloros*, a typical nymphalid butterfly of western and southern Europe but rather rare in Britain; a rich orange brown with black patches and spots on the fore-wings, black slightly serrated margins on both wings and small blue crescents along the margins of the hind-wings; the legs and palps are covered with black hairs. The dark brown caterpillars live on elms and other trees, feeding communally under a silken shelter which they make along a branch.

LARGE WHITE. See *Cabbage White Butterfly*.

LARRIDAE. A family of solitary hunting wasps that burrow into the ground and stock their nests with other insects that have been stung and paralysed to provide food for the developing larvae. Many of these wasps are very specific with regard to their victims. *Larra anthema*, for example, stocks its nest with mole-crickets. Others prefer cutworms, cicadas or ants.

LARVA. See *Insect larvae.*

LARVAEVORIDAE (TACHINIDAE). Bristly flies similar to the Blowfly whose larvae are parasites in caterpillars. The largest British species is *Echinomyia grossa* which lays its eggs in the larvae of Eggar Moths.

LARVARIUM. A nest or shelter made by insect larvae, sometimes a silken hammock or tube but often made from pieces of leaf, pine-needles, soil particles etc. woven together.

LARVIPAROUS. Giving birth to larvae instead of eggs, as for instance the Forest Fly *Hippobosca*, the Sheep Ked *Melophagus* or the Tsetse Fly *Glossina*.

LASIOCAMPIDAE. Eggars, Lackey Moths and related species having heavy, hairy bodies, short legs, feathery antennae and rudimentary mouth-parts. The hairy caterpillars, some of which are destructive pests, live gregariously in silken 'tents'. The Syrian Silkworm *Pachypasa otus* is a species whose silk was used in the Middle East long before the Chinese silkworm was introduced. Most of the European species are brown and medium sized but there are many much larger related species in tropical Africa, Asia and South America (see also *Eggar Moths, Drinker Moth* and *Gastropacha*).

LASIODERMA. A genus of anobiid beetles whose small hairy larvae are pests of tobacco and other stored products (see *Anobiidae*).

LASIOPTERA. *Lasioptera rubi*, the Raspberry Stem Gall-midge: a minute insect of the family Cecidomyidae whose larvae infest raspberry and blackberry bushes causing spherical galls on the stems.

LASIOPTICUS. A genus of hover-flies, yellowish white and black, whose long, greyish green, legless larvae feed on plant-lice.

LASIUS. A common genus of small ants found in many parts of the world: *Lasius niger*, the Garden Black Ant of Europe, is known as the Cornfield Ant in North America; *Lasius flavus*, the Yellow Meadow Ant and *Lasius fulginosus*, a shiny black species, are also common. All these species are well known for their habit of tending and 'milking' aphids.

LASPEYRESIA. *Laspeyresia saltitans*, an alternative name for *Grapholitha saltitans*, the Mexican Jumping Bean Moth (see *Jumping Beans*).

LATERNARIA. *Laternaria laternaria*, the largest of the Lantern-flies from tropical South America; also known as the Alligator Bug (see *Fulgoridae*).

LAWN BEE. *Andrena armata*, a mining bee that makes communal nests in lawns, throwing up little piles of soil. It resembles a honey bee but is larger and covered with chestnut brown hairs.

LEAF-BEETLES. Chrysomelidae: a very large family of beetles, generally small, oval and sometimes brightly coloured or with a metallic sheen. Antennae and legs are usually short and the head is often sunk into the thorax. Both adults and larvae are voracious feeders on plants and are often pests of agriculture. The group includes the Colorado Beetle *Leptinotarsa decemlineata*, the Bloody-nosed Beetle *Timarcha tenebricosa*, the Tortoise Beetles (Cassidinae) and many others.

LEAF-BUG. A name given to many insects that feed on or suck the juices from leaves. More strictly the name is applied to the family Miridae or Capsidae, often called Capsid Bugs. These are elongated green or brown members of the order Heteroptera. They include the Apple Capsid *Plesiocoris*, the Potato Capsid *Calocoris* and many others (see *Apple Capsid*).

LEAF BUTTERFLY. A name given to many tropical butterflies which, when at rest with the wings folded, resemble leaves. The best known is the Indian *Kallima;* others include the Asiatic genus *Doleschallia*, the South American *Zaretes* and many others (see *Kallima*).

LEAF CRUMPLERS. Moths whose larvae live in twisted conical silken tubes, usually covered and mixed with pellets of faeces. Sometimes these tubes are quite large and wide open at one end. Leaves are drawn in and tied together in crumpled masses on which the insects feed. *Mineola*, the Apple Leaf Crumpler and various species of *Acrobasis* are examples.

LEAF-CUTTING ANTS. Tropical ants, particularly the genus *Atta* of South America also known as the Parasol Ant. These insects cut pieces of leaf, carry them above the head like a parasol and take them down into their underground nests. Here they smother them with saliva and faeces and use them as a medium on which to cultivate fungi as food for the colony. Some of their nests are as much as 10 metres across and the ants are so numerous that they will strip a large tree in a single night (see *Atta* and *Fungus Cultivation*).

LEAF-CUTTING BEE. *Megachile* and related genera: a group of bees resembling small bumble bees that cut pieces of leaves with which to line their nests. These nests, which are usually tubular, may be in holes in the ground, under stones, in wood or inside the pith of brambles etc. Tubes of rolled leaves are constructed and these are partitioned off by circular pieces of leaf to make a line of cells in which eggs are laid and pollen and nectar deposited. The British species *Megachile centuncularis* is well known for cutting pieces out of rose leaves.

LEAF-FOLDERS. Also called Leaf-sewers: insects that fold over the edges of leaves, fasten them together with silk and make a nest inside. Most leaf-folders are the larvae of moths such as members of the families Tortricidae and Pyralidae but a few midges of the family Cecidomyidae also behave in this way.

LEAF-FOOTED BUGS. Plant-bugs of the family Coreidae, mostly living in the tropics, having leaf-like dilatations on the hind-legs.

LEAF-HOPPERS. Cicadellidae or Jassidae: homopterous plant-sucking insects closely related to the Frog-hoppers and Aphids. They have small elongated bodies and can jump and fly with great speed. They probably spread many virus and fungus diseases among plants.

LEAF-INSECTS. Insects of the group Phasmida, related to stick-insects but having the body greatly flattened to resemble a leaf. One of the best known examples is *Phyllium siccifolium* from Ceylon. The hind-wings are atrophied and the wing-cases are expanded giving a perfect appearance of a dead leaf. The legs also have flattened leaf-like outgrowths. These insects are common in tropical forests and their camouflage is most effective when they keep perfectly still.

LEAF-MINERS. Insects whose larvae, generally minute, tunnel in between the upper and lower surfaces of a leaf often hollowing it out completely and destroying it. Many types of insects do this, *viz.* Coleoptera, Lepidoptera, Diptera and Hymenoptera. Some move progressively forwards to produce *linear* or *serpentine* mines; others feed around a centre and produce *blotch* mines.

LEAF ROLLERS. Insects whose larvae make nests of rolled leaves held together with silk. They include a large number of moths, particularly of the family Tortricidae, a few beetles and sawflies and the unique leaf-rolling grasshopper *Camptonotus* of Carolina.

LEAF TIERS. Insects that make nests from a number of leaves or sometimes pine needles held together by silken threads. Most leaf tiers are the larvae of moths, *e.g.* the Poplar Leaf Tier *Melalopha inclusa* and the Pine Tube Moth *Argyrotaenia pinatubana*.

LEAF WEBBER. A name given to moths whose larvae use silken threads to bind together a large number of leaves making a nest in which they live gregariously, *e.g. Cacoecia cerasivorana* which makes a nest in cherry leaves.

LEATHER BEETLE. *Dermestes maculatus*, a small beetle that damages hides, fur and other animal products (see *Dermestidae*).

LEATHERJACKETS. The thick-skinned, brown, legless larvae of crane-flies living in the soil and doing extensive damage to the roots of grass and other crops (see *Crane-fly*).

LECANIIDAE. Hemispherical scale insects related to the Coccidae: plant-bugs in which the wingless females attach themselves to a plant and remain protected by a scale-like covering formed from cast-off skin. In *Lecanium hemicryphum* the scales are dark brown globular structures prominent on young twigs of spruce; another species *Lecanium corni* is a pest of fruit trees in Europe and North America. *Lecanium ilia* produces a useful crimson dye. (See also *Coccidae*).

LEDRA. *Ledra aurita*, the Eared Leaf-hopper: a small jumping plant-bug of the family Cicadellidae living on oak trees and matching them with its mottled green colour. Two small ear-like projections on the head give it its name.

LEG. When applied to insects, this term only refers to articulated organs, and does not include various *prolegs* or *pseudopods* which may be developed, especially on the abdomen. The true legs are always on the thorax and an insect normally has three pairs. Each leg consists of the following segments:
  (1) The *coxa*, a short segment by which the leg is joined to the thorax.
  (2) The *trochanter*, another short segment, giving greater flexibility at the articulation.
  (3) The *femur*, long, thick and strong, especially in jumping insects such as the grasshopper and in many predatory insects.
  (4) The *tibia*, usually long and thin, often armed with strong spines.
  (5) The *tarsus* consisting of up to five subsegments or *tarsomeres* usually called 'segments'.
  (6) The *pretarsus* or 'foot' usually bearing a pair of claws and other structures.
  There are many modifications of the typical leg. The bee's pollen basket, for instance, is borne on the tibia and the pollen-brush on the first tarsal segment. Water Boatmen and Water Beetles have fringes of long hairs, usually on the hind-legs, which serve as 'oars'; grasshoppers have greatly enlarged femora for jumping and these often bear a row of bristles for the production of sound by rubbing them against the thickened wing-cases; predatory insects such as the Mantis and the Water Scorpion have the front legs modified for grasping their prey by a jack-knife movement; others such as the mole-cricket have them flattened and spade-like for burrowing; ectoparasites such as lice have short legs with a single large claw by which they cling to their host. There are numerous other variations.

LEGIONARY ANTS. Also known as Army Ants and Driver Ants: carnivorous insects that live in temporary nests and migrate in long lines like an army, sometimes as many as 100,000 marching together (see *Eciton*).

LEIOPUS. *Leiopus nebulosus*, a small long-horned beetle of the family Cerambycidae, about 8 mm. long with antennae twice this length. The body is brownish grey with a band of yellow across the middle of the elytra. It is commonly found on oak, elm and other broad-leafed trees.

LEISTUS. A common genus of small, shiny blue ground-beetles of the family Carabidae; active predators.

LEMA. *Lema* (*Cyanella*) *lichensis*, the Blue Corn Beetle and related species: small, dark blue beetles with a metallic sheen on the wing-cases. They belong to the family of Leaf-beetles (Chrysomelidae) and live, sometimes in vast numbers, among grass and cereal crops where they do extensive damage. They pupate in capsules attached to the grasses.

LEMNAPHILA. *Lemnaphilia scotlandae*, a Shore-fly of the family Ephydridae living near the brackish water of some sea-lochs of Scotland. The larvae bore into aquatic plants; the adults hunt small gnats and midges (see *Ephydridae*).

LENGTH OF LIFE. The length of life of insects ranges from a few hours to many years, usually depending on the availability of food and the degree of activity of the insect. Often the greater part of their lives is spent in the larval stage, as for instance in some cicadas which take many years to develop. The aquatic nymph of the mayfly lives for two years or more but the adult, which cannot feed, dies after a few hours. The same is true of some butterflies and moths. A very active life may cause an insect to 'wear itself out'; a worker bee, for instance, lives on an average for about six weeks but a queen bee lives for four or five years. A queen ant may live for 15 years and some inactive scale-insects have been known to live for at least 17 years.

LEOPARD MOTH. *Zeuzera pyrina*, a large moth of the family Cossidae related to the goat moths; greyish white with black spots. The adults are without functional tongues but the larvae are very destructive, boring into the wood of oak, ash and other trees and taking two or three years to mature (see *Cossidae*).

LEPIDOPSYCHE. One of the Bagworm Moths (Psychidae) whose larvae live in tubes similar to those of caddis worms, made from pieces of dead leaf etc. woven together with silk. *Lepidopsyche unicolor* is common in forests of Europe and Asia (see *Bagworms*).

LEPIDOPTERA. Butterflies and moths: a large order of insects with over 140,000 species characterized by having pigmented scales all over the wings and body. The mouth-parts are in the form of a long coiled tubular proboscis through which nectar can be sucked. The larvae or caterpillars are usually herbivorous and are of the *polypod* (*eruciform*) type, *i.e.* they have prolegs or cushion feet on the abdomen in addition to the three pairs of true legs on the thorax. Pupae are of the *obtect* type and are sometimes contained in silky cocoons.

In systematic classification the old division into butterflies and moths, based on differences in the antennae, has been superseded by other systems based on the venation of the wings, the wing-coupling apparatus and the genitalia. One view is that the butterflies comprise two superfamilies, Papilionoidea and Hesperioidea among many superfamilies of moths.

LEPIDOSAPHES. A genus of scale-insects of the family Coccidae. *Lepido-*

saphes ulmi, the Mussel-scale, is so named because the scales resemble tiny mussel shells. It is a pest of many trees, particularly apples and pears, and has spread from eastern Asia to most parts of the world. Another species *Lepidosaphes beckii,* known as the Purple Scale, is a pest of citrus trees (see *Coccidae*).

LEPIDOSCELES. A genus of small parasitic wasps whose females ride on the backs of grasshoppers and lay their eggs in those of the grasshoppers.

LEPIDOTE. Covered with small scales, as for instance the wings of a butterfly.

LEPISMACHILIS. *Lepismachilis notata,* a species of bristle-tails of the order Thysanura inhabiting mountains and hills in the warmer parts of Central Europe. It is closely related to the common Silverfish *Lepisma saccharina* but differs from it in having a multicoloured pattern of scales on the back.

LEPISMATIDAE. Silverfish: a family of primitive insects of the order Thysanura or bristle-tails having a scaly body without wings, long antennae, biting mouth-parts and a triple tail-fork formed from two long cerci and a median filament. *Lepisma saccharina* is a very common and world-wide species inhabiting houses and feeding on starch in old books, wallpaper, clothing etc. (see *Thysanura*).

LEPTIDEA. *Leptidea sinapis,* the Wood White Butterfly and related species ranging through Europe and Asia as far as Japan: small members of the family Pieridae, white or pale yellowish with a grey-green patch near the tip of each fore-wing. The caterpillars are green and feed on vetches, trefoils and other leguminous plants where they are well camouflaged.

LEPTINOPTERUS. A genus of small brown stag beetles (Lucanidae) from Brazil.

LEPTINOTARSA. See *Colorado Beetle.*

LEPTOCERUS. A common genus of Caddis Flies (Trichoptera) having very long antennae and thickly haired wings; they sometimes fly in large swarms by day. The larvae make long conical cases.

LEPTOCIRCUS. *Leptocircus curius,* a small Swallowtail Butterfly from China having black wings with two large transparent 'windows' in the fore-wings and two very long 'tails' on the hind-wings. The wing-span is only about 3 cm.

LEPTOCONOPS. A genus of minute biting midges of the family Ceratopogonidae having aquatic larvae and pupae; especially common in the lake regions of California and Nevada.

LEPTOCORISA. A genus of plant-bugs belonging to the small family Corisidae (formerly grouped with Coreidae or Squashbugs. They feed in large numbers on grasses and low shrubs or seedlings. *Leptocorisa trivittatis,* the Box Elder Bug of North America, attacks elders and maples; other species are pests of rice-fields in China.

LEPTODIRUS. *Leptodirus hohenwarti*: a blind, long-legged beetle of the family Anisotomidae, formerly included in Silphidae, living in caves of southern Europe and feeding on organic remains such as the droppings of bats.

LEPTOGASTER. A genus of Robber Flies (Asilidae) occurring all over the world, from Northern Europe to Australia; characterized by its thin, elongated body and legs, and by the absence of any pulvilli or pads beneath the tarsal claws. It lives among grass and clings by curling its hind tarsus round a stem.

LEPTOGLOSSUS. *Leptoglossus phyllopus*, the Leaf-footed Bug: a North American plant-bug of the family Coreidae having large leaf-like expansions of the hind tibiae. The body and wings resemble an elongated, brown shieldbug with a transverse white line across the middle of the front wings.

LEPTOHYLEMYIA. *Leptohylemyia coarctata*, the Wheat Bulb Fly: a small black fly resembling a house fly and belonging to the closely related family Anthomyiidae. The maggot-like larva bore into the new shoots of wheat, barley, rye and other cereals. Originally from Europe, it has spread to many parts of the world.

LEPTOPHYES. *Leptophyes punctatissima*, the Speckled Bush-cricket: a medium sized, bright green insect of the family Tettigoniidae having long legs and very long antennae. The wings of the female are vestigial and those of the male reduced; a common European insect of woods and thickets.

LEPTOPTERNA. *Leptopterna dolabrata*, the Meadow Plant-bug: an insect of the family Miridae, also known as Capsid Bugs; elongated, brown with yellowish wings and very long antennae. Both adults and larvae live in moist places and feed on grasses of all kinds.

LEPTOTHORAX. A genus of small reddish yellow ants having a hairy head and thorax but a shiny hairless abdomen. *Leptothorax acervorum*, a common European species nests under bark or stones. Other species live near rivers and in times of flood carry the larvae and pupae up the stems of plants to which they cling while waiting for the water to subside. *Leptothorax emersoni*, a North American species, lives in the nests of another species *Myrmica brevinodis* and shares its food.

LESSER BLACK WATER BEETLE. *Hydrobius caraboides*, a member of the family Hydrophilidae: a glossy black, slow-moving, oval water beetle about 18 mm. long, common in ponds and ditches of Europe. The adult is vegetarian but the larva is a voracious predator.

LESSER COCKROACH. *Ectobius panzeri*, a small, pale greyish brown cockroach about 6 mm. long, common in European woodlands; only the males can fly as the females have both wings and elytra greatly reduced (see *Blattaria* and *Blattoidea*).

LESSER EARWIG. *Labia minor* (see *Labia*).

LESSER HORNTAIL. *Sirex noctilio*, a blue-black woodwasp similar in shape to the Large Horntail *Urocerus gigas* (sometimes known as *Sirex gigas*) but only about 18 mm. long; a member of the Symphyta or sawfly family, Hymenoptera without a narrow waist between the thorax and abdomen. The ovipositor is relatively short and is used for laying eggs in soft woods such as pine or larch.

LESSER MARSH GRASSHOPPER. *Chorthippus albomarginatus*, a small brown or green grasshopper, common in Europe, distinguished from other species by the white margin along the front of the fore-wings of the female. It is most commonly found in marshes and sand dunes near the sea, but also occurs in inland water meadows, swamps and heaths.

LESSER WATER BOATMAN. See *Corixidae*.

LESSER WATER SCORPION (SAUCER BUG). *Ilyocoris cimicoides*, a predatory water bug of the group Heterocera, brown, oval, flattened and about 12 mm. long. The hind-legs are fringed for swimming; the front pair are hinged and sharp for grasping their prey. Unlike the Greater Water Scorpion *Nepa*, it does not have a long breathing siphon at the hind-end.

LESSER YELLOW UNDERWING. *Euschesis comes,* sometimes included with the Large Yellow Underwing in the genus *Noctua* (see *Euschesis*).

LESTES. See *Green Lestes.*

LETHOCERUS. A genus of Giant Water-bugs of the family Belostomatidae, sometimes reaching a length of 10–12 cm. They are predatory insects with elongated bodies, fringed hind-legs for swimming and sharp, flexible front legs for grasping their prey. They will capture other insects, small frogs, tadpoles etc. They fly by night and are attracted to light. *Lethocerus americanus* is a well known species but most of the larger members of the family live in the tropics (see also *Belostomatidae*).

LETHRUS. *Lethrus apterus,* the Grape-cutter: a scarabaeid beetle, round, black and shiny with large sharp jaws, differing from the majority of these dung-beetles in that it feeds on grapes and other fruit.

LEUCANIA. A genus of small, brownish, noctuid moths whose larvae generally feed on grasses, rushes etc. There are several common European species known as Wainscot Moths. The American *Leucania unipunctata,* a pest of cereals, has spread to many countries. Its green, brown and yellow caterpillars are known as Army Worms and these may infest wheat fields in very large numbers.

LEUCODONTA. *Leucodonta bicoloria,* the White Prominent: a European moth of the family Notodontidae, white with black and orange zig-zag markings on the fore-wings. The caterpillars feed on birch leaves.

LEUCOMA. *Leucoma salicis,* the White Satin Moth: a medium sized white moth of the Tussock family (Lymantriidae) whose caterpillars are black with red, yellow and white markings. These are sometimes found in very large numbers on poplar trees from which they may completely strip the foliage.

LEUCOPTERIN. A white pigment in the scales of the Cabbage and other Pierid butterflies; a derivative of uric acid.

LEUCORHAMPHA. *Leucorhampha ornatus,* a Hawk-moth from Brazil whose caterpillars exactly match the twigs on which they are found but which, when alarmed, inflate the front of the body, exhibit a warning coloration and sway with a snake-like movement.

LEUCOTRICHIA. A genus of caddis flies (Trichoptera) whose larvae make a flat, ovoid, transparent case.

LEUCTRA. *Leuctra fusca,* the Needle-fly: a common stonefly of rivers and streams, having dark brown wings which can be folded tightly round the body giving a needle-like appearance.

LEVUANA. *Levuana iridescens,* the Coconut Moth: a member of the family Zygaenidae whose caterpillars feed on the leaves of coconut palms. At one time they threatened ruin to the copra industry of Fiji but were effectively controlled by introducing a parasitic Tachinid fly from Malaya.

LIBELLULIDAE. A widely distributed family of large, fat-bodied, broad-winged dragonflies also known as Darters on account of their rapid speed of flight. The body is often brightly coloured and the wings usually have one or more black spots near the anterior edge and a brown or black triangular patch near the base (see *Dragonfly*).

LIBYTHEIDAE. A family of butterflies having long palps giving the appearance of a beak. Although there are not many species, the family is widely distributed. *Libythea celtis* of Southern Europe, Asia and North Africa is

157

brown with large orange marks on all the wings and two white spots on each fore-wing; *Libythea geoffroyi* of Northern Australia and New Guinea has mauve or lilac coloured fore-wings with a broad brown margin and hind-wings half brown and half mauve.

LIFE HISTORY. The life history of an insect is made up of a series of *instars* and a series of moults or *ecdyses* between each instar and the next. The word *instar* strictly means the *form* assumed by an insect during any particular stage or *stadium*. Many reputable authors, however use 'instar' as synonymous with stadium. In the more primitive insects known as Ametabola or Apterygota there is very little change in food or habits from one stage to the next. This group includes the wingless Springtails and Bristle-tails, some of which are not now regarded as true insects. In the group known as Hemimetabola or Ex-opterygota the main difference between the juvenile or *nymph* and the adult is that the former is without wings. In the earlier instars rudiments of wings may be visible and after each moult they become larger until in the adult stage they are fully formed. This group includes such insects as cockroaches, locusts and earwigs. Dragonflies and mayflies, although the adult is very different from the nymph, are also included in this group because they have no pupal stage. The third group of insects is known as the Holometabola or Endopterygota. In these there is complete metamorphosis. After the last larval moult a pupa or chrysalis is produced. This is an apparent resting stage in which, however, numerous complicated internal changes take place. These involve the breaking down of larval organs and tissues and the growth of adult organs so that when the fully grown insect or *imago* emerges it is very different in habits and appearance from the larva. This group includes butter-flies and moths, beetles, flies, bees, ants, wasps and many others (see also *Ametabola, Hemimetabola, Holometabola* and *Metamorphosis*).

LIGHT ARCHES. *Apamea lithoxylaea*, a medium sized noctuid moth having yellowish-white wings with grey streaks and a row of tiny dark dots near the edges. The larvae feed on grasses.

LIGHT-COMPASS REACTION (SUN-COMPASS REACTION). Ants and other insects are able to move in a straight line by keeping the sun in a definite position on the retina of the eye. If they are kept in the dark for a few hours and then released, they are said to start off in a direction which makes an angle with the original route equal to that through which the sun has moved in the meantime.

LIGHT EMERALD. *Metrocampa margaritaria* or *Campaea margaritaria*, a moth of the geometrid family Selidosemidae having a white body and pale emerald green wings. The fore-wings have two transverse dark green and white lines; the hind-wings have one similar line. The stick-like caterpillars feed on oak, birch, beech and many other trees.

LIGHT-PRODUCING ORGANS. The light produced by luminous insects such as the glow-worm and the firefly is not strictly phosphorescence but *chemo-luminescence,* a process of oxidation of the substance *luciferin* in the presence of the enzyme *luciferase*. This is a chemical change under the control of the nervous system. Some of the chemical energy is converted into light which is limited to a narrow band of the spectrum and involves very little production of heat. During the change a considerable amount of oxygen is used up and so the luminous organs of insects are well supplied with res-piratory tracheae. The colour and brightness of the light and the position and number of light-organs varies considerably from insect to insect. *Pyro-*

phorus gives a greenish light; *Photinus* gives orange; *Photuris* gives yellow and the South American 'Railroad Worm' *Phrixothrix* has red and green lights. Some insects emit a steady light which can, however, be 'switched off'; others such as the Mediterranean firefly *Luciola* emit flashes at regular intervals. In some insects the eggs and larvae glow; in others only the adults. In some the males are the chief light producers; in others the females. The luminous organs may be distributed over the whole body or may be concentrated in particular areas such as on the head or the tip of the abdomen (see also *Glow-worm* and *Firefly*).

LIGHTNING BEETLE (LIGHTNING BUG). Alternative names for the Firefly (*q.v.*).

LIGULA. The distal part of the labium of an insect consisting typically of a pair of inner lobes or *glossae* and a pair of outer lobes or *paraglossae*. In some insects the latter are reduced or absent and in bees the glossae are greatly lengthened to form a tubular proboscis.

LILAC BORER. *Podosesia syringae*, a small clearwing moth of the family Aegeriidae whose larvae bore into the stems of lilac (*Syringa*).

LILAC LEAF-MINER. See *Gracilaria*.

LIMACIFORM LARVAE. Legless slug-like larvae, as for instance those of some sawflies and moths.

LIMACODIDAE. Also called Heterogeneidae and Cochlidiidae: a family of moths whose caterpillars are legless and slug-like (see *Cochlidiidae* and *Cochlidion*).

LIME HAWK-MOTH. *Mimas tiliae*, a common Hawk-moth of the family Sphingidae having pinkish brown wings with patches of dark green and with the edges of the fore-wings irregularly notched or scalloped. The caterpillars are bright green with oblique lines of yellow and a prominent 'horn' at the hind-end. They feed on leaves of lime and elm.

LIMENITIS. *Limenitis camilla*, the White Admiral butterfly: a member of the family Nymphalidae ranging across Europe and Asia as far as Japan. The wings are brown with a broad white band across each; the undersides are orange-brown with white bands and small black spots. The caterpillars feed on honeysuckle (*Lonicera*). Other European species include the Large Poplar Admiral, *Limenitis populi,* and the smaller Southern White Admiral *Limenitis reducta.* There are also several North American species, the best known of which is the Viceroy, *Limenitis archippus* or *Basilarchia archippus* which is a perfect mimic of the Monarch or Milkweed Butterfly *Danaus plexippus.*

LIMNAS. A genus of African and Asiatic butterflies of the family Danaidae. *Limnas chrysippus* is pale brown with black borders and a number of white spots. It is found in Africa, Asia and Australia. *Limnas alcippus* of tropical Africa and Asia is probably a regional variation of *chrysippus* with paler hind-wings. There are many such variations throughout Africa and Asia and in most cases these are mimicked by various forms of another butterfly, *Hypolimnas misippus* of the family Nymphalidae.

LIMNEPHILUS. A common genus of caddis flies (Trichoptera) having hairy wings, with transparent patches on the fore-wings. The larvae of some species build conical tubes of small twigs placed lengthways; others make them of small snail shells; others again use small pieces of water plants.

LIMNOBATES. An alternative name for *Hydrometra,* a common genus of water bugs that walk on the surface of ponds (see *Hydrometridae*).

LIMNOBIIDAE. A family of long-legged wingless crane-flies from the snows of the Carpathians.

LIMNOPHORA. A genus of small flies of the family Anthomyidae having carnivorous aquatic larvae. The adults of some species regularly hibernate in houses in large numbers, sometimes returning to the same place year after year.

LIMOSINA. A large genus of small flies of the family Sphaeroceridae (Borboridae). They are associated with decaying materials including dung, and may travel on the backs of dung beetles sharing their food.

LIMOTHRIPS. *Limothrips cerealium*, the Grain Thrips: a migratory insect of the order Thysanoptera, about 2 mm. long with a narrow dark brown body and fringed wings. The larvae are serious pests of cereals.

LINED CLICK BEETLE. *Agriotes lineatus*, a common species of Click Beetle (Elateridae) having long narrow elytra, brown lined with black. The larvae or wireworms live in grassland for four or five years and are very destructive to roots (see *Elateridae*).

LINGUA. Any tongue or tongue-like organ: a name sometimes used loosely and incorrectly for any elongated proboscis such as that of a bee or butterfly.

LINOGNATHUS. A common genus of blood-sucking lice (Anoplura) having a narrow head and mouth-parts; frequent parasites on domestic animals. *Linognathus pedalis*, the foot-louse and *Linognathus ovillus*, the Blue Louse are both commonly found on sheep in Australia, New Zealand, South Africa and North and South America. *Linognathus vituli* is the Long-nosed Cattle Louse and *Linognathus setosus* is found on dogs everywhere.

LIOCORIS. *Liocoris tripustulatus*, a plant-bug of the family Miridae (Capsid Bugs) commonly found on nettles which are its food during all stages of development. The adult is about 3 mm. long, yellowish green with dark brown markings which vary according to the age of the insect. The antennae are nearly as long as the body.

LIOGRYLLUS. *Liogryllus campestris*, an alternative name for *Gryllus campestris*, the European Field Cricket: a flightless insect about 20 mm. long, black with a yellow band across the wing-covers. It feeds on grass etc. and lives in holes or under stones (see *Field Cricket* and *Gryllidae*).

LIPARA. *Lipara lucens* and related species: Reed Gall-flies of the family Chloropidae, sometimes known as Frit-flies. They live among grasses and cereals where the larvae make long cigar-shaped galls on the stems.

LIPARIDAE. An alternative name for Lymantriidae or Tussock Moths. *Liparis monacha*, the Nun Moth is a pest of conifers in Europe and of oak trees in North America.

LIPEURUS. A genus of bird-lice of the order Mallophaga having long, narrow, light brown bodies with a semicircular projection or 'rostrum' on the head. They are parasites on pheasants and other fowls.

LIPHLOEUS. A genus of small grey-brown weevils common in Central Europe where they feed on small herbaceous plants and grasses.

LIPHYRA. *Liphyra brassolis*, a lycaenid butterfly of Australia, red-brown with bands of dark brown and yellow on the fore-wings and dark brown patches on the hind-wings. The larvae live in the nests of ants of the genus *Oecophylla*, feeding on the ant larvae and pupae. They are protected against the ants by a hard integument, within which they pupate. The newly emergent adult is protected by being covered with loose white scales which come off and stick to any attacking ants.

LIPOPTENA. *Lipoptena cervi*, the Deer Ked: a small grey-brown blood-sucking fly of the family Hippoboscidae. Living in forests it is at first winged and flies freely in search of a victim. It will suck the blood of humans or other animals but after settling on a deer or other ruminant it loses its wings and spends the rest of its life among the hairs of its victim (see *Hippoboscidae*).

LIPOSCELIS. See *Book-louse*.

LISSORHOPTRUS. *Lissorhoptrus simplex*, the Rice Weevil: a semi-aquatic insect whose larvae feed on the roots, and adults on the leaves of rice and other water plants in Guyana.

LISTRONOTUS. A genus of aquatic weevils that feed on water plants.

LITHINA. *Lithina chlorosata*, the Brown Silver-line: a common European geometrid moth whose larvae feed on bracken.

LITHOCOLLETIS (= PHYLLONORYCTER). A large genus of small moths whose larvae are leaf-miners. They attack many plants and different species work in different ways. Usually they feed first on the sap and later on the parenchyma cells, making extensive flat cavities either just beneath the upper epidermis or just above the lower epidermis. They line this with silk and eventually pupate within it.

LITHOSIINAE. Footman Moths: a group of Arctiidae related to the Tiger Moths but differing from them by reason of their habit of wrapping the wings tightly round the body when at rest. *Lithosia lurideola*, the Common Footman is grey with a yellow band along the front edges of the forewings and with yellowish hind-wings (see *Footman Moth*).

LITTLE EMERALD MOTH. *Iodis lactearia*, a small European geometrid moth with a wing-span of about 25 mm., having very pale green wings crossed by two white lines.

LITTLE STAG BEETLE. See *Dorcus*.

LITOMASTIX. A minute chalcid wasp that lays its eggs inside those of the Silver Y Moth (*Plusia gamma*). Fertilized eggs produce females and unfertilized eggs males: both kinds may be laid in a single moth's egg and will go on developing after the caterpillar has hatched out. Chalcids are notable for the phenomenon of *polyembryony*, each egg producing a number of embryos. In this way several hundreds or even thousands of parasites may develop within the body of a single caterpillar.

LIVIA. *Livia juncorum*, the Rush Sucker: one of the Jumping Plant-lice of the family Psyllidae; a small insect with transparent wings, long legs and long antennae. It lays its eggs in rushes and the developing nymphs produce tassel-like galls (see *Jumping Plant-lice*).

LIVID COCKROACH. *Ectobius lividus*, a small woodland cockroach about 10 mm. long, pale yellowish brown with elytra and wings as long as the abdomen in both sexes (see also *Blattaria* and *Blattoidea*).

LIVID FROG-HOPPER. *Philaenus lividus*, a yellowish green frog-hopper similar in appearance to the more common *Philaenus spumarius*, the Cuckoo-spit Insect. *Philaenus lividus*, however, is only found on grasses (see *Cercopidae*).

LIXUS. *Lixus concavus*, the Rhubarb Weevil: a small insect that bores into the stalks of rhubarb, dock and other plants of the genus *Rumex*.

LOBSTER MOTH. *Stauropus fagi,* a large member of the family of Prominent Moths (Notodontidae), greyish brown, spotted and hairy, resembling the Puss Moth but darker coloured. The fantastic shape of the brown caterpillar suggests a lobster; the first two pairs of legs are long and jointed; the body has angular and conspicuous segmentation; the hind-end is swollen with two tail filaments. When alarmed the caterpillar raises its legs and its tail in a warning attitude. It feeds chiefly on birch, beech and oak leaves.

LOCUSTIDAE. Locusts. Migratory members of the orthopteran family Acrididae or Short-horned grasshoppers: hemimetabolous insects with biting mouth-parts, with the head bent at right angles to the body and with very short antennae. The fore-wings are thickened to form horny tegmina which cover the folded membranous hind-wings; the hind femora are greatly enlarged for jumping. Locusts differ from grasshoppers in being gregarious, migratory and extremely voracious. This is, however, only a phase in their life. They may live for many years in a *solitary* or non-migratory phase but at times they become greatly overcrowded and then enter the *gregarious* phase. The colour changes from green to reddish brown; they become greatly excited, collect together in vast numbers and then start to fly in a swarm of many millions, often travelling hundreds of miles. When they settle they strip the land of every living plant, converting a fertile area into a desert. *Locusta migratoria* is the best known Old World Locust of Africa, Asia and Southern Europe. *Schistocerca gregaria,* the Desert Locust migrates between Africa and Asia. *Locustana pardalina* is the Brown Locust from South Africa. Other species exist in many parts of the world (see also *Desert Locust*).

LOCUSTANA. *Locustana pardalina,* the Brown Locust, a common migratory species from the Karoo area of South Africa.

LOEPA. *Loepa katinka,* a large and beautiful species of Emperor Moth from India and Southern China, about 8 cm, across with wings of pink and violet with dark brown markings and a large brown eye-spot on each wing.

LOMASPILIS. *Lomaspilis marginata,* the Clouded Border Moth: a small geometrid moth, pale green or nearly white with a wide dark brown crenated border. The small green stick-like larvae feed on leaves of willow etc.

LOMECHUSA. A genus of staphylinid beetles that live in ants' nests and, although they eat the eggs and larvae of their hosts, are tolerated and tended by the ants on account of the sweet liquid which they secrete.

LONCHODIDAE. A family of stick insects including the well known *Dixippus* or *Carausius,* a wingless genus that breeds parthenogenetically and is much used in laboratory experiments.

LONG-HORNED BEETLES. See *Longicornia* and *Cerambycidae.*

LONG-HORNED GRASSHOPPERS. Bush-crickets: members of the family Tettigoniidae, a sub-group of Orthoptera differing from true grasshoppers and locusts by having very long antennae and differing from crickets by the absence of long cerci. They are generally carnivorous and many are predatory. The males can produce a loud 'song' or stridulation by rubbing a rough part of one fore-wing against a thickened part of the other. The group includes the Great Green Grasshopper of Europe, *Tettigonia viridissima* and the Mormon Cricket of North America, *Anabrus simplex* as well as many others known in the United States as Katydids (see *Grasshopper*).

LONG-HORNED GREEN BUG. *Megaloceraea recticornis,* a pale green plant-bug of the order Heteroptera, about 10 mm. long, having a narrow, soft, oval body, long legs and elytra and very long antennae. It feeds on small herbacious plants in grassy places.

LONGICORNIA. Long-horned Beetles also called Cerambycidae: a large and world-wide family of beetles having very long antennae; most of them are pests of timber (see *Cerambycidae*).

LONG-LEGGED FLIES. Dolichopodidae, a family of small, predatory, long-legged flies of a bluish or greenish colour. The head and thorax are large and are raised to give a characteristic appearance when the insect is at rest. The larvae live in wet sand or mud.

LONG-TAILED BUTTERFLY. See *Lampides*.

LONG-TAILED SKIPPER. See *Eudamus*.

LOOPERS. Caterpillars of Geometrid Moths or Geometers, a name signifying 'earth-measurer'; known in the United States as 'inch-worms'. They move by a looping action owing to the absence of abdominal feet or prolegs except at the hind-end. Progress is made by holding on with the thoracic legs and then drawing up the hind-part by arching the body. The abdominal feet or claspers at the hind-end then grip the support and the whole body moves forwards. Some caterpillars of this group are very stick-like, especially when they stand up on the claspers and stiffen the body.

LOPHOPTERYX. *Lophopteryx capucina* also called *Ptilodon capucina*, the Coxcomb Prominent Moth: a very common European moth of the family Notodontidae having reddish brown fore-wings crossed by a dark zig-zag line, and pale buff-coloured hind-wings. As in all the Prominent Moths there is a tooth-like tuft of scales projecting backwards from the centre of the fore-wing and overlapping the hind-wing. The larvae feed on oak, beech, birch and many other trees.

LORICERA. *Loricera pilicornis*, a small predatory ground-beetle of the family Carabidae, about 6 mm. long, shiny blue-black with long hairs on its antennae.

LORUM. The submentum: a sclerite or cuticular plate of the head, having a variety of forms and functions in different orders of insects. In bees, for instance, it is a V-shaped plate supporting the elongated proboscis.

LOUSE. A name for a number of wingless ectoparasitic insects chiefly belonging to the two groups Anoplura and Mallophaga. These are sometimes classed as separate orders and sometimes as suborders of the order Phthiraptera. Anoplura or Sucking Lice are mostly parasites of mammals. The body is flattened and the legs have strong claws for clinging to the host. Antennae, eyes and cerci are reduced or absent. The loss of these and of the wings is considered to be a secondary feature connected with the parasitic habit. The human Body Louse *Pediculus humanus*, a carrier of typhus and other diseases, is included in this group. Mallophaga or Biting Lice are chiefly parasitic on birds but some species live on mammals. Unlike the sucking lice they do not pierce the skin but use their mouth-parts to bite off small particles of feathers, hair etc. The common Hen Louse *Menopon gallinae* is a well known example.

LOUSE FLY. An alternative name for blood-sucking flies of the family Hippoboscidae (*q.v.*).

LOUSY WATCHMAN. A name sometimes used for the Dor Beetle *Geotrupes stercorarius* on account of its being infested with mites (see *Dor Beetle*).

LOXOCERA. A genus of two-winged flies of which the female of some species has a long ovipositor resembling that of an ichneumon fly. It lays its eggs in roots, stems and leaves. *Loxocera albiseta,* a European species, has a yellow head and scutellum and very long antennae.

LOXOSTEGE. A genus of moths of the family Pyralidae whose larvae, known as webworms, live in tubular nests of silk and feed on roots. Many are agricultural pests. *Loxostege sticticalis,* also known as *Margaritia sticticalis,* is a British and American species that feeds on beet; *Loxostege similalis* attacks cotton, maize and alfalfa in North America. *Loxostege affinitalis* of Australia and *Loxostege frustralis* of South Africa are similar in their habits.

LUBBER GRASSHOPPER. *Romalea microptera, Brachystola magna* and other related species from the Southern United States: clumsy, short-winged, flightless grasshoppers up to about 7 cm. long.

LUCANIDAE. Stag Beetles: large wood-boring beetles belonging to the Lamellicornia, all of which have the distal parts of the antennae enlarged and flattened. The common stag beetle *Lucanus cervus,* in which the male is distinguished by its very large antler-like mandibles, is one of the largest European species.

LUCERNE FLEA. *Sminthurus viridis,* a small, green, globular insect of the order Collembola or Springtails; very common in grasslands, particularly in Australia where it has become a pest. Its eggs can withstand desiccation for periods of a year or more and then rapidly swell up and hatch when the rain comes.

LUCIFERASE. An oxidizing enzyme which, acting on the protein *luciferin,* causes luminosity in glow-worms and similar insects (see *Firefly, Glow-worm* and *Light-producing Organs*).

LUCIFERIN. See *Luciferase.*

LUCILIA. See *Greenbottle.*

LUCIOLA. The European or Mediterranean Firefly, a beetle of the family Lampyridae (see *Firefly* and *Glow-worm*).

LULWORTH SKIPPER. *Thymelicus acteon,* a small butterfly of Europe, North Africa and Asia Minor; rare in Britain and confined to the southwest. It belongs to the family Hesperiidae and resembles the Small Skipper and the Essex Skipper but is darker in colour. The wings are dull brown above and uniformly orange below. The female has a conspicuous orange-yellow semicircular mark on the upper surface of each fore-wing. In both sexes the palps are white below with orange hair in front. The larvae, green with longitudinal yellow stripes, feed on grasses in damp places.

LUMINESCENCE. See *Light-producing Organs, Firefly* and *Glow-worms.*

LUNA MOTH. An alternative name for Moon Moths of the genus *Actias* (*Tropaea*). The North American Luna Moth, *Actias luna,* with a wing-span of about 15 cm. is common in the valleys of the Mississippi and Ohio. The Asiatic Luna Moth *Actias selene,* often called the Indian Moon Moth, is found in India, Ceylon, China and Japan. Both are a delicate pale green with two large slender 'tails' on the hind-wings and with moon-like markings on the fore-wings. The antennae are golden and fern-like.

LUNAR HORNET MOTH. *Sphecia bembeciformis,* a Clearwing Moth of the family Sesiidae, closely resembling a hornet. The wings are transparent; the abdomen is yellow with two brown bands; the head and thorax are brown with a distinct yellow collar between them. The larvae are whitish caterpillars that bore into the trunks of willows and poplars.

LUNAR UNDERWING MOTH. *Omphaloscelis lunosa*, a small noctuid moth, light brown with a pattern of dark brown or black dots and patches. The caterpillar is also brown and is commonly found feeding on grasses.

LUNULE. Any moon-shaped structure but particularly the frontal lunule of many Diptera: a crescent shaped scar between the eyes and above the bases of the antennae.

LUPERINA. *Luperina testacea*, the Flounced Rustic Moth: a small greenish brown noctuid moth with whitish hind-wings; very common among grasses on which the larvae feed. The latter are sometimes a pest of wheat and other cereals.

LURKER. *Tibicina haematodes*, a species of Cicada common in Central and Southern Europe. It has a wing-span of about 7 cm. The body is black and the wings have brilliant red veins. The larvae live in the soil for about four years feeding on roots (see *Cicadidae*).

LUTESTRINGS. A name sometimes given to moths of the family Polyplocidae: fat, hairy noctuid moths with no waist between thorax and abdomen, with a well-developed proboscis and usually with patterned fore-wings and plain whitish hind-wings. Both wings are held roof-wise over the body when at rest. There are leaf-like appendages on the front legs and spurs on the hind-legs. The caterpillars feed on brambles, raspberries and a number of forest trees, fastening the leaves together with silk to make a shelter.

LYCAENIDAE. A world-wide family of small butterflies comprising the Coppers, Blues and Hairstreaks. The upper surfaces of the wings, particularly of the males, are usually bright blue, green or copper coloured. The undersides are usually paler and are decorated with a pattern of dots, circles or lines by which the species can be identified. The caterpillars are generally slug-like and some are predatory (see *Blue Butterflies, Copper Butterflies* and *Hairstreaks*).

LYCIA. *Lycia hirtaria*, the Brindled Beauty Moth: a medium sized European geometrid moth, dark brown with paler brown transverse lines on both wings, having a fat, hairy, brown body and feather-like antennae. The caterpillars are stick-like and feed on lime, willow and other trees.

LYCOPHOTIA. *Lycophotia varia*, the Lover's Knot Moth: a small noctuid moth with wings elaborately patterned in deep red with white lines. The larvae feed on heather.

LYCOREA. A genus of South American butterflies of the family Danaidae, related to the better known Monarch or Milkweed Butterfly (*Danaus plexippus*). *Lycorea halia* from Brazil is coloured yellow and orange with wide black bands and margins. It mimics another butterfly, *Heliconius*; both are poisonous and unpalatable and therefore both are to some extent protected by their similarity which is a case of Müllerian Mimicry (see *Danaidae*).

LYCTIDAE. Powder-post Beetles: small wood-boring beetles which reduce oak and other woods to a fine powder. They differ from the common furniture beetle in having the body flattened dorso-ventrally and in not having the head covered by the pronotum. *Lyctus fuscus* and *Lyctus brunneus* are two common species.

LYGAEIDAE. Ground Bugs and Chinchbugs: small, elongated, soft-bodied plant-bugs of the order Heteroptera, often brightly coloured. Some kinds are short-winged and flightless; others have long wings. In many species both kinds are to be found. The common North American Chinchbug *Blissus leucopterus*, a black, white and red species, is a great pest of cereal crops. The European chinchbug *Ischnodemus sabuleti* is found in very large numbers on grasses and reeds.

LYGAEONEMATUS. See *Larch Sawfly*.

LYGOCORIS. A common genus of capsid bugs of the family Miridae: medium sized, oval-shaped plant-bugs of the order Heteroptera. The Common Green Capsid *Lygocoris pabulinus* is a European species that feeds on currants, gooseberries etc. *Lygocoris vosseleri* is a Central African species feeding on cotton plants; *Lygocoris lineolaris*, the Tarnished Plant-bug of North America, attacks cotton, fruit trees, alfalfa and many other crops.

LYGRIS. *Lygris mellinata* and related species known as Spinach Moths. There are several common European species all having the fore-wings orange or reddish brown, crossed with wavy bands of brown and yellow; the hind-wings are paler yellow without transverse bands; both fore- and hind-wings have brown dotted fringes. The larvae are green and are of the looper type (geometrid). They feed on the leaves of currants, cranberries, whortleberries and other fruits.

LYGUS. A genus of capsid bugs (Miridae): pests of agriculture, fruit trees and forest trees. *Lygus rugulipennis*, the European Tarnished Plant Bug attacks many field and garden crops; *Lygus pratensis* is a similar species from North America.

LYMANTRIIDAE. Tussock Moths, a family whose caterpillars, often brightly coloured, are characterized by having a number of conspicuous tufts or tussocks of hair which exude an irritant poison when handled. Many of these are destructive defoliators of trees (see *Gipsy Moth*).

LYMEXYLIDAE. A family of wood-boring beetles having elongated bodies, soft wing-cases and serrated antennae. The males have large comb-like maxillary palps. The larvae bore horizontal galleries in oak, birch and other trees.

LYNCHIA. A genus of blood-sucking flies of the family Hippoboscidae, common parasites of birds. Some species formerly included in this genus have now been renamed and are included in the genera *Icosta* and *Pseudolynchia, e.g.* the Pigeon Fly *Pseudolynchia canariensis*.

LYOCHROMES. Yellow and red pigments of insects; flavine derivatives possibly originating from the anthocyanin pigments of plants.

LYONETIIDAE. Long-horned Leaf-miners: a family of minute moths, sometimes brightly coloured, with deeply fringed wings and very long antennae. The larvae bore tunnels in leaves of deciduous trees. *Lyonetia speculella* bores into apple leaves; *Lyonetia clerkella* attacks birch trees.

LYPEROSIA. A genus of blood-sucking flies closely related to the house fly; they include *Lyperosia irritans*, the Horn Fly of cattle and *Lyperosia exigua,* the Buffalo Fly which also attacks humans (see also *Haematobia*).

LYPHAGMA. A genus of South African moths whose caterpillars are Army Worms. These, like locusts, may show two phases in which they differ in appearance and habits. When living in small numbers they are greenish grey and relatively inactive; this is known as the *solitary phase*. When overcrowded they enter a *gregarious phase* in which they become much darker in colour and migrate in large numbers.

LYROPTERYX. *Lyropteryx apollonia*, a small butterfly of tropical South American forests, belonging to the family Erycinidae. The upper surface is brown with a pattern of brilliant green and yellow rays; the underside is spotted in pink (see *Erycinidae*).

LYSANDRA. See *Chalk Hill Blue*.

LYSIPHLEBUS. *Lysiphlebus testaceipes*, a minute Braconid wasp, parasitic in aphids. The female wasp lays her eggs in the body of the aphis; the larva of the parasite eats away the body of the host and pupates within the dried skin.

LYSOLECITHIN. One of the substances in the venom of bees and wasps: a very toxic substance which breaks down the cells of its victim and sets free histamine.

LYTTA. *Lytta vesicatoria*, the Blister Beetle or Spanish Fly: a brilliant golden-green beetle of the family Meloidae living in Central and Southern Europe; the chief source of the drug *cantharidin*.

M

MACHAERITES. A genus of cave beetles that are without functional eyes when living deep in a cave but those living near the entrance may have normal eyes.

MACHILIDAE. A primitive group of Thysanura or Bristle-tails having a scaly body, a pair of long abdominal cerci, a medium tail filament and stylets on nearly all the abdominal segments. They are commonly found under stones.

MACHIMUS. A woodland genus of Robber Fly of the family Asilidae: medium sized, grey-brown, having long narrow wings, prominent eyes, strong legs for grasping other insects in flight and a well developed piercing proboscis for sucking the juices of their victims.

MACRANER. An unusually large male ant (see *Ant* and *Castes*).

MACREMPHYTUS. *Macremphytus varianus*, the Dogwood Sawfly: a small insect that lays its eggs in a pattern of lines just beneath the surface of dogwood leaves (*Cornus sanguinea*). The emergent larvae feed on the leaves and cluster together for mutual protection.

MACRERGATE. An unusually large worker ant (see *Ant* and *Castes*).

MACROCENTRUS. A genus of parasitic Braconids that lay their eggs in the bodies of caterpillars. Some species are used as a means of controlling fruit-moths, leaf-rollers and other pests of fruit trees (see *Braconidae*).

MACRODACTYLUS. A common genus of Rose Chafers: large, oval shaped scarabaeid beetles with a metallic green sheen, short antennae and biting

167

mouth-parts. The larvae feed on roots and the adults attack leaves of roses and other shrubs (see *Chafers*).

MACRODONTIA. A genus of large longhorn beetles (Cerambycidae) from the tropical forests of South America. The males have very long saw-toothed mandibles. *Macrodontia cervicornis* and *Macrodontia dejeani*, both about 9 cm. long, are among the world's largest insects. Both have a pattern of brown on the wing-cases resembling the bark of the trees on which they live.

MACROGLOSSUM. See *Humming-bird Hawk-moth*.

MACRO. ΞPIDOPTERA ('MACROS'). The larger butterflies and moths: a name formerly used in the classification of Lepidoptera but now obsolete although occasionally used for convenience, especially in contrast to Micro-lepidoptera (*q.v.*).

MACRONOCTUA. *Macronoctua onusta,* the Iris Borer: a small moth whose larvae bore into the roots and rhizomes of Iris.

MACROPTEROUS. Large-winged: a term used with particular reference to the various castes of insects such as ants and termites (*cf. Micropterous*).

MACROSILA. *Macrosila cruentis,* the Brazilian Sphinx Moth and related species of hawk-moths from Madagascar and other tropical countries, having an extremely long proboscis, sometimes more than 23 cm., with which they can obtain deep-seated nectar from large tubular flowers.

MICROSIPHUM. A common genus of aphids: *Macrosiphum rosae* attacks rose trees; *Macrosiphum pisum* is found on peas and other leguminous plants. Both can carry the virus of mosaic and other diseases.

MACROSTELES. A genus of leaf-hoppers common in many parts of the world; carriers of virus diseases (see *Cicadellidae*).

MACROTERMES. A genus of tropical termites that build very large nests or *termitaria* above ground. These are made of earth and sand cemented together with saliva. They contain numerous galleries and ventilation shafts and may be up to 3 m. (10 ft.) high. It is estimated that a nest may contain more than two million workers.

MACROTHYLACIA. See *Fox Moth*.

MACROTRICHIA. Large hairs or *setae* consisting of extended epidermal cells surrounded by cuticle. They may be of various types including the following:

(1) Simple or branching hairs covering most of the body; including also the larger hairs on wings (*cf. Microtrichia*).

(2) Sensory setae with nervous connections which respond to touch, taste, smell etc.

(3) Setae which exude irritant secretions, as on certain caterpillars.

(4) Pigmented scales such as those on butterflies' wings and on the bodies of mosquitoes.

MACROVELIIDAE. A small family of plant-bugs (Hemiptera) living on vegetation and debris near the edges of ponds or streams.

MACULINEA. See *Large Blue Butterfly*.

MAGGOT. A small legless larva with a pointed head-end and a truncated rear, *e.g.* those of house flies, bluebottles and similar Diptera (see *Insect Larvae*).

MAGICICADA. *Magicicada septendecim,* the Seventeen-year Cicada of North

America: a species whose nymphs spend up to seventeen years living underground and feeding on roots. They then emerge in their penultimate instar as wingless individuals; they climb the nearest tree, cast their skins and become winged adults which live only for a short time after mating and laying their eggs in holes pierced in trees or shrubs.

MAGPIE MOTH. See *Abraxas.*

MAIDEN'S BLUSH MOTH. *Cosymbia punctaria,* a small geometrid moth common in European woodlands; yellowish pink with two rows of fine black dots and a band of dark brown running transversely across both wings. The tips of the fore-wings are distinctly pointed. The stick-like caterpillars are loopers that feed on oak leaves.

MALACHIUS. *Malachius bipustulatus,* the Red-tipped Flower-beetle: a medium sized, elongated, soft-bodied beetle with metallic green elytra tipped with red; a close relation of the Soldier and Sailor Beetles (Cantharidae). Larvae and adults are predatory, hunting their prey in decaying wood.

MALACOCORIS. *Malacocoris chlorizans,* sometimes known as the Delicate Apple Capsid (in contrast to the common Apple Capsid *Plesiocoris rugicollis*). A pale green, elongated plant-bug of the family Miridae, found throughout Britain on the leaves of apple, hazel, elm and many other trees where both adults and larvae feed on mites as well as on the host plant.

MALACODERMATA. Soft-bodied beetles: a name used in some systems of classification to include Lampyridae (glow-worms), Cantharidae (Soldier Beetles), Lymexylidae (wood-borers), Elateridae (Click Beetles) amd some others.

MALACOSOMA. A genus of moths belonging to the family Lasiocampidae, having heavy, hairy bodies, short legs, feathery antennae and rudimentary mouth-parts. The hairy caterpillars are destructive pests living gregariously in silken 'tents'. They include the European Lackey Moth *Malacosoma neustria* and the two American species *Malacosoma americana* and *Malacosoma disstria* whose larvae are known as 'Tent Caterpillars' (see *Lackey Moth* and *Lasiocampidae*).

MALARIA MOSQUITO. See *Anopheles, Anopheles maculipennis* and *Mosquito.*

MALAXATION. Softening by chewing with the mandibles, as for instance by a wasp.

MALE REPRODUCTIVE SYSTEM. See *Genitalia.*

MALLOPHAGA. Biting Lice: ectoparasites of birds and mammals sometimes regarded as a distinct order of insects and sometimes included as a suborder of the Phthiraptera. Unlike the sucking lice they rarely pierce the skin but use their mouth-parts to bite off small particles of feathers etc. (but see *Ricinidae*).

MALLOW MOTH. *Larentia clavaria,* a fairly large species of Carpet Moth with wide transverse bands of light and dark brown. The bright green caterpillars are stick-like and feed on hollyhock, mallow and other Malvaceae (see *Larentiinae*).

MALAGASY SILK MOTH. *Argema mittrei,* one of the largest moths in the world with a wing-span of about 20 cm. and with 'tails' on the hind-wings of the male about three times as long as the body; those on the female are slightly shorter. The colour is bright yellow with reddish brown markings and multicoloured eye-spots.

MALPIGHIAN GLANDS. Glands lining the Malpighian tubules of an insect, normally functioning as excretory organs but in the larvae of some Coleoptera and Neuroptera they are able to spin silk threads (see *Malpighian Tubules*).

MALPIGHIAN TUBULES. The chief excretory organs of insects and most other terrestrial Arthropods: narrow glandular tubes, sometimes branched and in large numbers, opening into the alimentary canal near the commencement of the hind-gut. Waste products from the insect's blood are excreted by the glandular lining of these tubes and pass into the rectum where they mix with the faeces.

MAMESTRA. See *Cabbage Moth*.

MANDIBLE. See *Jaws*.

MANDIBULATA. (1) A name given to all those arthropods that have maxillae, mandibles and antennae, *i.e.* Insects, Crustacea, Millipedes and Centipedes, but not spiders and other Arachnida which are classed as *Chelicerata*.

(2) Insects with biting mouth-parts as distinct from those with a sucking or *haustellate* proboscis.

MANGOLD FLY. Also called the Beet Fly, *Pegomyia betae* or *Pegomyia hyoscyami*, var. *betae*. A two-winged fly of the family Anthomyiidae, a common agricultural pest. It lays its eggs on young leaves and shoots and the larvae move down the stem to feed on the bulbs and roots.

MANIOLA. *Maniola jurtina* or *Epinephele jurtina*, the Meadow Brown Butterfly: a very common member of the family Satyridae found in Europe, Asia and North Africa. The wings are dark brown; the fore-wings partly golden brown, each with a single white-centred black spot. The caterpillars are bright green and feed on grasses.

MANNA SCALE-INSECT. *Coccus manniparus* or *Trabutina mannipara*, a scale-insect of the family Coccidae living and feeding on shrubs of tamarisk (*Tamarix mannifera*) in Asia Minor, Arabia and other parts of the Middle East. It produces a secretion containing a large proportion of sugar which dries and accumulates in thick layers on the bushes. This is said to be the Manna of the Bible and is still collected and eaten by the Arabs of the Sinai mountains.

MANSONIA. A genus of culicine mosquitoes also known as *Taeniorhynchus*: carriers of Rift Valley Fever and various diseases of sheep, cattle and goats in Africa. A British species *Taeniorhynchus richiardii* is apparently harmless. The aquatic larvae differ from those of most mosquitoes in having a specialized respiratory siphon which is able to pierce and attach itself to submerged vegetation from which the insect can extract oxygen.

MANTICHORA. *Mantichora herculanea*, the Night Hunter, the largest of the Tiger Beetles (Cicindelidae): a dark brown, carnivorous beetle about 7 cm. long with a wide abdomen and elytra, a narrow thorax and very large, toothed jaws. It is found in the African savannah.

MANTIDAE. Praying Mantids: predatory insects of the order Dictyoptera, suborder Mantodea, formerly classed with the Orthoptera. Medium or large insects with an elongated thorax and a flexible head with biting mouth-parts. The fore-legs are specially adapted for catching their prey; apart from being greatly enlarged they can be folded back like a jack-knife and the edges are sharply toothed. The wings are normally folded back close against the sides of the body; usually only the males can fly. The name 'Praying Mantis' is given on account of their habit of extending the fore-legs forwards in the attitude of prayer when waiting to catch insects on which they feed. The European species *Mantis religiosa* and the Asiatic species *Paratenodera sinensis* have both been introduced into North America and are common in the Southern States. Many other species are found in tropical countries.

MANTISPIDAE. Praying Lacewing Flies: a family of predatory insects having a superficial resemblance to mantids but belonging to the order Neuroptera and having large transparent wings. Like the Praying Mantis they have the fore-legs enlarged and able to be bent back in a jack-knife position for grasping their prey. The Styrian Praying Lacewing *Mantispa styriaca* of Southern Europe is a yellowish brown insect with a wing-span of about 35 mm. The larvae are parasites in the egg-cocoons of wolf-spiders.

MANTODEA. See *Mantidae.*

MANY-PLUMED MOTH. *Alucita hexadactyla*, a small brown moth whose wings are each deeply cleft to form six plume-like branches. The larvae of this European species feed on leaves and flowers of honeysuckle (*Lonicera*). Many closely related species are to be found in Asia and Africa.

MAP BUTTERFLY. *Araschnia levana*, a European and Asiatic butterfly of the family Nymphalidae having an elaborate wing-pattern of brown, yellow and white, said to suggest a map of the world with lines of latitude and longitude. Eggs are laid in strings beneath nettle leaves on which the larvae feed.

MAPLE BORER. A general name for several moths and beetles whose larvae bore into maple trees.

MAPLE CASEBEARER. *Paraclemensia ace⁻ifoliella*, a small moth of the family Incurvariidae whose larvae feed on maple leaves. A circle of leaf is cut out and attached by silken threads to another leaf, making a case within which the larva feeds. When it needs a new feeding ground it cuts through the silken threads and carries the case to be attached to another leaf.

MARBLED BEAUTY. *Cryphia perla*, a small European noctuid moth whose wings are mottled with grey and white suggesting a pattern on marble. The hairy larvae are similarly mottled and feed on lichen on stone walls.

MARBLED CARPET MOTH. *Dysstroma truncata*, a small European Carpet Moth of the subfamily Larentiinae having wings variously coloured with a marble-like pattern of white, brown and grey. The green looper caterpillars feed on hawthorn, birch and a number of other plants (see *Larentiinae*).

MARBLED CORONET MOTH. *Hadena conspersa*, a moth of the family Caradrinidae having smoky grey hind-wings and having the fore-wings variously marked with white and grey-black suggesting a marbled pattern. They are found near the sea-shore, the food-plant of the larvae being Sea Campion *Silene maritima*.

MARBLED FRITILLARY. *Brenthis daphne*, a European and Asiatic butterfly of the family Nymphalidae, orange-yellow with numerous dark brown or black spots typical of fritillaries but having part of the hind-wings marked on the undersides with a lilac and black marble-like pattern. The larvae feed on violets (see *Fritillaries*).

MARBLED MINOR. *Procus strigilis*, a small noctuid moth whose wings generally have a marble-like pattern of white, brown and black. Completely black or *melanic* forms are also not uncommon. The greenish brown larvae feed on grasses of various kinds.

171

MARBLED WHITE. *Melanargia galathea,* a handsome butterfly of the family Satyridae found in Europe and Western Asia. Although most of the family are brown, this species is exceptional in having a well-marked chequer-board type of pattern in cream and black. The larvae feed on grasses.

MARBLE GALLS. Dark brown spherical galls formed on oak trees by the larvae of the Cynipid wasp *Andricus kollari* or *Cynips kollari*; sometimes mistakenly called oak-apples (see *Cynipoidea*).

MARCH BROWN. An anglers' name for several species of mayflies of the genera *Ecdyonurus* and *Rhithrogena.*

MARCH FLY. A name sometimes given to various members of the family Bibionidae including St. Mark's Flies and Fever Flies (see *Bibionidae*). In Australia this name is applied to Horse Flies (Tabanidae).

MARCH MOTH. *Alsophila aescularia,* a small European geometrid moth whose green caterpillars feed on a large variety of deciduous trees. The adult males have brownish-grey wings crossed by two brown transverse lines; the female is wingless with a tuft of bristles on the abdomen.

MARGARODIDAE. Ground Pearls: large coccid bugs or scale-insects whose females live underground for many years enclosed in layers of shining waxy secretions much prized by the natives of Chile and Peru and worn as ornaments.

MARGARONIA. *Margaronia hyalinata,* the Melon Moth: a white and black moth of the family Pyraustidae whose larvae feed on the leaves of melon and cucumber.

MARGINED DYTISCUS. *Dytiscus marginalis,* one of the best known of the large carnivorous water beetles: a fierce predator about 35 mm. long with a brown body and elytra bordered with dull yellow (see *Dytiscidae*).

MARGINED SYROMASTUS. *Syromastus marginalis* (now renamed *Coreus marginatus*), a plant-bug of the order Heteroptera, grey-brown with a reddish abdomen expanded at the sides so that its edges are visible on each side of the elytra. It feeds on brambles and other shrubs.

MARINE BUG. *Aepophilus bonnairei,* a small sandy-coloured predatory bug of the order Heteroptera living among seaweed and in crevices of rocks between high and low tide levels.

MARSH CRANE-FLY. *Ptychoptera paludosa,* a species of crane-fly with a reddish brown body and spotted wings, about half the size of the common crane-fly; common in marches.

MARSH FLY. Any member of the family Sciomyzidae (Tetanoceridae), also called Snail-flies: small cyclorrhaphous Diptera with a big head and prominent antennae. They inhabit marshy places and also the edges of ponds or streams on chalk downland. The larvae feed on snails.

MARSH FRITILLARY. See *Euphydryas.*

MARSH HOPPER. Any of a number of small grasshoppers inhabiting marshy places, *e.g. Tetrix subulata,* also called the Slender Groundhopper; *Stethophyma grossum,* the Large Marsh Grasshopper and *Chorthippus albomarginatus,* the Lesser Marsh Grasshopper.

MARSH TREADER. An alternative name for the Water-measurer *Hydrometra* and related species (see *Hydrometridae*).

MARTIN BUG. *Oeciacus hirundinis*, a blood-sucking bug similar to the bed-bug, commonly found in the nests of house martins.

MARUINA. A genus of North American moth-flies, members of the family Psychodidae: large, gnat-like flies of the group Nematocera whose bodies and wings are densely covered with hairs. The small aquatic larvae are similar to those of gnats and mosquitoes but live in fast-flowing streams and can attach themselves to vegetation etc. by means of a ventral sucker or disc.

MARUMBA. *Marumba quercus*, the Oak Hawk-moth: a large yellowish-brown hawk-moth of central and southern Europe, the Mediterranean and Asia Minor. The caterpillars feed on leaves of the Turkey Oak *Quercus cerris*.

MASK. The enlarged prehensile labium of a dragonfly nymph (see *Labium* and *Labial Hooks*).

MASKED BEDBUG HUNTER. *Reduvius personatus*, a large Assassin Bug that sometimes flies into houses and preys an bedbugs and other insects. The larvae are often camouflaged or 'masked' by being covered with dust etc. which adheres to mucus secreted by the skin.

MASON BEES. *Osmia, Anthidium* and several other genera of the family Megachilidae: bees that make their nests of particles of wood, sand or soil cemented together with saliva and occupying cracks or holes in buildings. In appearance they resemble the honey bee but some species are considerably larger.

MASON WASPS. Eumeninae, a group of small, solitary, hunting wasps that make their nests from particles of sand, soil etc. stuck together with saliva. These may be in burrows or cracks in the soil, in crevices of wood or stone walls. They stock the cells of these nests with caterpillars and other insects that have been stung and paralysed to provide food for the larvae. *Ancistrocercus* and *Odynerus* are common genera. (See also *Potter Wasps*).

MASTIGIUM. A telescopic anal filament such as those on the caterpillars of the Puss Moth *Cerura vinula*.

MASTOTERMES. A genus containing the single species *Mastotermes darwiniensis*. Termites from Northern Australia and other tropical countries where they are pests of sugar cane and also cause serious damage to trees and structural timber.

MATING. Sexual reproduction of insects involves internal fertilization for which mating or copulation is necessary. This may take place in flight or on the ground or under water. The male and female apertures are at the hind-end of the abdomen and in many cases the male is equipped with claspers with which the female is gripped during the process. In some cases the legs and even the antennae may be modified for helping to hold on to the female. Introduction of sperm cells into the female may be facilitated by the formation of a *spermatophore*, a gelatinous case enclosing the spermatozoa. This dissolves away, releasing them in the body of the female. In most cases the eggs are not fertilized immediately but the semen goes into a pocket or *spermatheca* adjacent to the oviduct of the female. In this way a single mating may be sufficient to fertilize many subsequently produced eggs. Each egg has a small hole or *micropyle* in its shell through which sperm cells can enter. The spermatheca releases a little semen at a time immediately prior to the eggs' being laid.

Dragonflies are unique in their manner of mating. The male, by flexing the abdomen, first transfers some semen to a special receptacle beneath the second abdominal segment. He then uses his terminal claspers to grasp the female round the neck while she bends her abdomen forwards to bring the genital aperture opposite the second segment of the male. Transference of sperm takes place in this position, sometimes while flying but more usually while resting on a plant. The male may still be grasping the neck of the female while she is laying her eggs under water.

MATING FLIGHT. Many insects refuse to mate in a confined space and therefore a mating flight occurs. This is generally the flight of a large swarm of males following one or more females prior to copulation, as for instance in the case of bees and ants. The instinct of the female to fly out on this 'nuptial flight' may be stimulated by the production of particular hormones but the actual departure may be triggered off by suitable atmospheric conditions such as temperature and humidity. There is usually a great deal of excitement prior to leaving; the insects become very active and noisy and in some cases there is a sexual 'display' or colour change. Many insects fly very high before the actual copulation takes place, the males being attracted to the female by scent or sound. In the case of a queen ant, once she has been fertilized she descends to the ground and immediately rubs or pulls off her wings so that she never flies again.

Many other insects form 'mating swarms' which are not centred round a female. Usually males, but sometimes females, dance or hover over a 'marker', or in the lee of an obstruction and form a conspicuous cloud of insects which attracts solitary members of the other sex, *e.g.* swarms of midges on a summer evening.

MAXILLA. See *Jaws*.

MAXILLARY PALP. A jointed sensory appendage or feeler attached to the maxilla of an insect. The number of segments forming a palp may be up to seven and these are sometimes enlarged or specialized in various ways; they may bear many different types of sensory receptors. Often the palps are much the bigger and most obvious part of the maxillae.

MAY BEETLE. An alternative name for the Cockchafer *Melolontha* and related insects.

MAY BEETLE PARASITE. *Pelecinus* and related genera of the proctotrupoid family Pelecinidae: parasitic wasps having a very long ovipositor with which they lay their eggs on the bodies of cockchafer larvae.

MAY BUG. See *May Beetle*.

MAYFLY. See *Ephemeroptera*.

MAYETIOLA. See *Hessian Fly*.

MEADOW BROWN. See *Maniola*.

MEADOW FRITILLARY. *Mellicta parthenoides*, a fairly uncommon fritillary of Western Europe found up to 2000 metres (7000 ft.) in the Alps, Jura and Pyrenees (see *Fritillaries*).

MEADOW GRASSHOPPER. See *Chorthippus*.

MEADOWSWEET GALLS. Small red swellings often seen in large numbers on the leaves of Meadowsweet (*Filipendula ulmaria*), caused by the small orange-coloured larvae of the gall-midge *Perrisia ulmariae*.

MEAL BEETLE (MEALWORM BEETLE). *Tenebrio molitor*, a medium sized, dark brown or black beetle with elongated, grooved elytra; a pest of flour and grain on which both adults and larvae feed. The adults fly at night and are attracted to light. (see also *Mealworm*).

174

MEAL MOTH. *Pyralis farinalis*, a small pyralid moth whose larvae are common pests in flour mills, granaries etc. The wings are dark brown with a broad, wavy, transverse band of lighter brown edged with thin white lines. When disturbed they often run rather than fly. The whitish larvae, which feed on flour and other organic matter, may live for about two years protected by long silken tubes (see also *Indian Meal Moth*).

MEALWORM. The yellowish maggot-like larva of the beetle *Tenebrio molitor*, a common pest in flour mills and granaries; bred in large numbers as food for birds, mammals and reptiles, as bait for fish and for laboratory experiments (see *Meal Beetle*).

MEALY BUGS. Coccids (scale-insects) whose body is covered by a white flour-like or waxy secretion; destructive pests of many trees (see also *Coccidae*, *Dactylopiidae* and *Citrus Mealy Bug*).

MEALY-WINGS. *Coniopteryx tineiformes* and related species of small predatory Lacewings flies whose body is covered with a fine powdery wax-like secretion (see *Coniopterygidae*).

MEASURING WORM. An American name for geometrid or looper caterpillars; those that move by a repeated arching of the body due to the fact that abdonimal prolegs are only present at the hind-end (see *Geometridae*).

MECHANO-RECEPTORS. Sensory receptors which perceive sound, pressure, tension, movement etc. They may occur anywhere on an insect's body but particularly on the antennae and cerci and at the bases of the halteres of flies. (See *Campaniform Receptors, Chordotonal Receptors, Hearing Organs, Trichoid Sensillae*).

MECOMMA. *Mecomma ambulans*, a common species of capsid bug of the family Miridae found on sedges and rushes. They feed on other insects as well as on the juices of the plants where they live. The small nymphs are greenish yellow but the adults are brown and about 5 mm. long with antennae of equal length. The females have the wings reduced to about a quarter of the length of the abdomen.

MECONEMA. *Meconema thalassinum*, the Oak Bush-cricket: a member of the family Tettigoniidae or Long-horned Grasshoppers, light green, about 20 mm. long with filamentous antennae nearly twice this length. They are omnivorous and live on oak and other trees, hiding by day and becoming active at night. The males are only capable of weak stridulation but make a feeble noise by drumming on the leaves.

MECONIUM. A dark red or brown fluid excreted as a butterfly emerges from its chrysalis, and consisting of the waste products of pupal metabolism.

MECOPTERA. Scorpion-flies: a family of small or medium sized carnivorous insects living in damp places and recognizable by the large biting mouth-parts and by the upturned abdomen of the male giving it the appearance of a scorpion. The wings are narrow, membranous and usually spotted with brown or black; the antennae are long and filamentous. *Panorpa communis* with a wing-span of 30 mm. is the common European Scorpion-fly; *Panorpa nebulosa* is a North American woodland species.

MECYNORRHINA. *Mecynorrhina torquata*, a large green and grey chafer beetle from the tropical forests of Africa, similar in appearance to the Rhinoceros Beetles. The male has a short 'horn' on the head and sharp thorn-like processes on the front legs. The overall length is about 7 cm.

MEDITERRANEAN FLOUR MOTH. See *Ephestia*.

MEDITERRANEAN FRUIT-FLY. *Ceratitis capitata*, a small fly of the family Trupaneidae whose larvae are fruit and leaf-borers in tropical and subtropical countries. They have spread to many parts of the world and have become serious pests.

MEGACHILIDAE. Leaf-cutting Bees: insects which build their nests from neatly cut oval or round pieces of leaves or flower petals. The female bee holds the leaf with her legs while she cuts with her mandibles (see *Leaf-cutting Bee*).

MEGACHROMOSOMES. See *Giant Chromosomes*.

MEGALODACNE. A genus of North American Fungus Beetles (Erotylidae) of the group Clavicornia. *Megalodacne fasciata* is a common species found on old tree stumps where fungi are growing. It is about 15 mm. long, shiny black with two reddish bands across the elytra. *Megalodacne heros* is a similar but larger species. Both range throughout the eastern United States from Canada to Mexico. (See *Erotylidae*).

MEGALOPREPUS. A genus of damselflies from Central America having a wing-span of about 18 cm. and flying with a slow movement suggesting a helicopter; one of the world's largest dragonflies but not as big as some fossil species.

MEGALOPTERA. A suborder of Neuroptera having primitive wing-venation but otherwise being somewhat varied and including alder-flies, snake-flies and the giant American Dobson Fly with its 15 cm. wing-span (see *Cordydalis*).

MEGALOPYGIDAE. Flannel Moths: a family characterized by having the wings covered with a loose coating of soft scales giving a flannel-like texture. The caterpillars are covered with poisonous hairs.

MEGALORRHINA. *Megalorrhina harrisii*, a large chafer beetle from the equatorial forests of Africa, about 5 cm. long, dark green with spotted red and yellow elytra. The male has a large two-branched 'horn' on the head resembling those of rhinoceros beetles.

MEGALURA. *Megalura chiron*, a medium sized butterfly of Central and South America, Mexico and the West Indies. The upper surfaces of the wings have broad longitudinal bands of yellow and dark brown; the under surfaces are brownish grey, white and violet. The hind-wings each have a long tail. The larvae feed on the leaves of fig and mulberry trees.

MEGANEURA. A fossil dragonfly of the Carboniferous and Permian periods having a wing-span of 70 cm., the largest known insect.

MEGANOSTOMA. *Meganostoma caesonia* also called *Colias caesonia* (see *Dog-face Butterfly*).

MEGARHYSSA. *Megarhyssa lunator*, one of the largest of the Ichneumon flies with an ovipositor up to 10 cm. long. This is used for boring through wood and laying eggs in the body of the woodwasp *Tremex* in N. America.

MEGASELIA. See *Hump-backed Fly* and *Phoridae*.

MEGASOMA. *Megasoma elephas*, the Large Elephant Beetle: a Central American insect of the family Dynastidae, about 12 cm. long, black with a coating of fine yellow hairs. The male has a trunk-like 'horn' projecting forwards from the head and three smaller horns or knobs on the thoracic sheath.

MEGASTIGMUS. *Megastigmus spermatrophus*, the Douglas Fir Seed-fly:

a small chalcid of the family Torymidae that lays its eggs in the seeds of Douglas Fir and related conifers. The larva lives and pupates within the seed; the adult fly emerges through a tiny hole. Originally from North America it has spread to Europe and other parts of the world.

MEGOPIS. *Megopis scabricornis*, a European Longhorn Beetle of the family Cerambycidae, about 5 cm. long with elongated wing-cases of a dull brown colour. The larvae live and feed in old tree trunks of willow, poplar etc.

MELAMPIAS. *Melampias trimenii*, Trimen's Brown Butterfly: a small South African species similar in appearance to the Ringlet butterflies of Europe; dark brown with patches of reddish-orange and with two white spots encircled by black on each fore-wing. The larvae feed on grass.

MELANACTES. *Melanactes piceus*, a large shiny black Click Beetle (Elateridae) of North America, commonly found under loose bark.

MELANAGROMYZA. *Melanagromyza phaseoli*, a small fly of the family Trypetidae whose larvae burrow into stems and leaves; a pest of beans in warm countries.

MELANARGIA. See *Marbled White*.

MELANCHRA. *Melanchra persicariae*, the Dot Moth: a European noctuid moth whose fore-wings are nearly black with a prominent white dot on each; the hind-wings are a lighter shade of grey-brown. The larvae feed on *Persicaria* and other wild and cultivated plants.

MELANDRIA. A genus of small predatory flies characterized by having 'false mandibles', *i.e.* pincer-like extensions of the labium; one of the family of Long-legged Flies or Dolichopodidae.

MELANIC MUTATION. See *Industrial Melanism*.

MELANIN. An insoluble black pigment laid down in the cuticle of many insects as well as in the skins of a great many other animals; formed by oxidation of the amino-acid *tyrosine* in the presence of specific *melanogenic* enzymes (see also *Industrial Melanism*).

MELANISM. See *Melanin* and *Industrial Melanism*.

MELANITIS. *Melanitis leda*, a large butterfly of the family Satyridae, found in most parts of tropical Asia and in Northern Australia. The wings are light brown with two white spots encircled with black on each fore-wing. The wing-span may be up to 8 cm. and there is a short 'tail' on each hind-wing. The larvae feed on grasses.

MELANOPLUS. A genus of North American short-horned grasshoppers: pests of crops and grassland. *Melanoplus femur-rubrum*, the Red-legged Grasshopper; *Melanoplus spretus*, the Rocky Mountain Grasshopper and several others. Most of these are 'voiceless', *i.e.* their powers of stridulation are poorly developed.

MELANOPHTHALMA. A genus of minute brown scavenger beetles that feed on the faeces of caterpillars.

MELANOSTOMA. A genus of small Hover-flies (Syrphidae) having a narrow black and yellow abdomen. They live in damp places among grasses from which the adults take pollen; the larvae feed on aphids and other small insects.

MELANOXANTHERIUM. *Melanoxantherium salicis* (= *Pterocomma salicis*), a fairly large species of aphid commonly found on willows and poplars; brown with bright orange legs, antennae and cornicles.

177

MELANTHIA. *Melanthia procellata*, the Chalk Carpet Moth: a geometrid moth of the subfamily Larentiinae living in chalk or limestone regions. The wings are mottled with white and dark brown; the caterpillars feed on Traveller's Joy (*Clematis vitalba*).

MELASOMA. *Melasoma populi*, the Poplar Leaf-beetle: a member of the family Chrysomelidae, about 12 mm. long, oval shaped with a small head, a shiny dark green thoracic shield and reddish brown elytra. The larvae feed gregariously on poplar leaves, reducing them to skeletons.

MELECTA. A genus of large greyish-black Cuckoo Bees that lay their eggs in the nests of the Flower Bee *Anthophora*.

MELIERIA. A genus of medium sized gall-flies of the family Otitidae, having a striped body and a sharp ovipositor with which they lay their eggs in vegetation of damp marshy places.

MELINDA. A genus of Tachinid flies whose larvae are parasites of snails.

MELIPONIDAE. Stingless bees: a family of small honey bees, rarely more than 6 mm. long, living in colonies in nests made of wax mixed with faeces, resin, plant debris etc., mostly in the tropics.

MELITAEA. A world-wide genus of Fritillary Butterflies chiefly of temperate grasslands in Europe, Asia and North America. European species include the Glanville Fritillary *Melitaea cinxia*. The Desert Fritillary *Melitaea deserticola* is found in the Atlas Mountains and in oases of the Sahara.

MELITTIA. *Melittia cucurbitae*, the Squash Vine Borer: a clearwing moth of the family Aegeriidae having metallic green fore-wings, transparent hind-wings, a red abdomen and red hind-legs which are greatly thickened and fringed with black. The larvae feed on the leaves of melons, marrows etc.

MELITTIN. A poisonous protein like substance present in the venom of bees.

MELLICTA. A genus of nymphalid butterflies including the Heath Fritillary *Mellicta athalia* which is common in temporate regions all over Europe and Asia as far as Japan (see *Fritillaries*).

MELLINUS. A genus of hunting wasps of the family Sphecidae that make their nests underground in sandy places and stock them with flies that have been stung and paralysed. *Mellinus arvensis*, the Field Digger Wasp, is a common European species with a yellow and black striped abdomen and a dark head and thorax with whitish spots.

MELOIDAE. Oil and Blister Beetles: elongated, greenish or black beetles often short-winged and flightless. They exude an oily, irritant secretion which is the chief source of the drug *cantharidin* (*q.v.*). An almost unique feature of this family is their mode of development involving three or four different kinds of larvae, some of which are parasitic on bees (see *Hypermetamorphosis*).

MELOLONTHIDAE. See *Chafers* and *Cockchafer*.

MELON MOTH. *Margaronia hyalinata*, a white and black moth of the family Pyraustidae whose larvae feed on the leaves of melon and cucumber.

MELON STEM BORER. See *Eudioptis*.

MELOPHAGUS. *Melophagus ovinus*, the Sheep Ked: a wingless, blood-sucking fly of the family Hippoboscidae that spends its whole life on the body of a sheep. The larvae, which are produced viviparously, attach themselves to

178

the wool by a sticky secretion. They then pupate and the emerging adults begin to suck blood (see *Hippoboscidae*).

MEMBRACIDAE. Tree-hoppers: plant-bugs of the group Homoptera found mostly in the tropics and characterized by a large hood-like extension of the pronotum. They are generally small; many of them are protectively coloured and often have bizarre shapes.

MENACANTHUS. A genus of bird-lice of the family Menoponidae: one of the Biting Lice or Mallophaga that feed chiefly on fragments of skin and feathers. *Menacanthus stramineus,* the Large Hen Louse or Chicken Body Louse, is a serious pest of poultry and turkeys.

MENOPHRA. *Menophra abruptaria,* the Waved Umber Moth: a medium sized geometrid moth, light brown with a band of darker brown across each wing. The caterpillars are remarkably stick-like and feed on the leaves of lilac and privet. They pupate in cocoons of silk mixed with chewed pieces of wood.

MENOPON. One of the commonest genera of bird-lice of the order Mallophaga: small wingless insects with flattened body, short legs with large claws, reduced antennae and biting mouth-parts with which they feed on fragments of skin and feathers (see *Louse*).

MENOTAXIS. Movement in a direction that makes a constant angle with a source of light, as for instance in the case of some ants (see *Light-compass Reaction*), or so as to keep a constant visual pattern.

MENTUM. Part of the base of the labium of an insect between the *submentum* and the *prementum*.

MERODON. A genus of Narcissus Flies: hover-flies (Syrphidae) whose larvae feed on bulbs of daffodil and narcissus.

MEROISTIC OVARIOLE. An ovariole or egg-tube containing food-cells or *trophocytes* for nourishing the developing oocytes. In some insects these food-cells are contained in all the ovarian follicles, a state known as *polytrophic*; this is the case in Dermaptera, Phthiraptera and the majority of Holometabola. In others they are only at the apex of the ovarioles (*acrotrophic or telotrophic*). Siphonaptera and Heteroptera belong to the latter group. (See *Ovary* and *Ovariole*.)

MEROMYZA. A genus of Frit-flies (Chloropidae) whose larvae bore into the stems of grasses and cereals. *Meromyza americana,* the Wheat-stem Maggot of North America is an example.

MERVEILLE DU JOUR MOTH. See *Griposia*.

MESADENIA. Accessory glands arising from the mesodermal lining of the seminal vesicles of certain insects; evaginations of the *vasa deferentia*.

MESEMBRINA. *Mesembrina meridiana,* a large, shiny black dung-fly with yellowish wing-bases. The males are commonly found resting on tree trunks or palings and the females on dung heaps where they lay their eggs. These are very large (up to 5 mm. long), are laid singly and hatch out immediately after being laid.

MESENTERON. The mid-gut: that part of the alimentary canal which is lined by endodermal tissue and in which most of the digestion and absorption of food normally take place, although in some insects a certain amount of predigestion takes place earlier (see *Alimentary Canal*).

179

MESOCEREBRUM. Also called the *Deutocerebrum*: the middle part of the brain of an insect, including the antennary lobes.

MESOLEIUS. *Mesoleius tenthredinidis*, an Ichneumon Fly about 10 mm. long, black with red legs, whose larvae are parasites in the larvae of the Larch Sawfly *Pristiphora erichsonii*.

MESOLEUCA. *Mesoleuca albicillata*, the Beautiful Carpet Moth: a geometrid moth of the subfamily Larentinae having cream coloured wings with dark brown patches near the bases and tips of the fore-wings. The caterpillars are bright green with reddish dorsal markings; they feed on leaves of bramble, raspberry etc.

MESOMPHALIA. A genus of tropical Tortoise Beetles (Cassidinae) from Brazil. *Mesomphalia gibbosa*, black and grey; *Mesomphalia aenea*, black and yellow (see *Cassidiane*).

MESONOTUM. The notum or dorsal cuticular plate covering the middle segment of an insect's thorax.

MESOSCUTELLUM. A scutellum or shield-like plate covering the hind-part of the mesothorax of an insect.

MESOSCUTUM. The middle and largest of three sclerites which typically form the mesonotum or cuticular covering of the middle segment of an insect's thorax.

MESOSTERNUM. The sternum or ventral plate under the mesothorax or middle segment of an insect's thorax.

MESOTHORAX. The middle segment of the thorax of an insect

MESOVELIIDAE. Water-treaders: a family of long-legged, carnivorous water-bugs (Heteroptera) living on the surface of ponds and among floating vegetation.

MESSOR. See *Harvester Ant*.

METABOLA. All those insects that undergo metamorphosis (see *Hemimetabola* and *Holometabola*).

METACEREBRUM. Also called the *Tritocerebrum*: the hind-part of the brain of an insect, consisting of the fused ganglia of the embryonic third somite.

METALLIC COLOURS. See *Iridescence*.

METAMORPHA. *Metamorpha dido-wernickei*, a large butterfly of tropical South America belonging to the family Heliconiidae, having bright blue-green and black translucent wings. The caterpillars feed on the Passion Flower.

METAMORPHOSIS. The change from a larval stage to an adult or *imago* which may be totally different in appearance and habits. In some primitive insects such as springtails and bristle-tails (Ametabola) there is practically no difference between larva and adult; in others, such as the cockroach or the earwig there are only slight changes at each moult, the main difference being gradual increase in size of the wing-buds. Such insects are known as Hemimetabola. In the more highly developed insects such as bees, butterflies, flies, beetles etc. (Holometabola), there is a pupal stage in which, although the insect is apparently inactive, rapid and complete changes are taking place involving the breaking down of larval organs by enzymes and phagocytes and the rapid growth of adult organs from existing growth-centres. The change from a caterpillar to a butterfly and its subsequent emergence from the chrysalis is perhaps the most spectacular example of such metamorphosis. The emergence of a dragonfly from the skin of the aquatic nymph, perhaps an equally spectacular change, is an example of metamorphosis without a pupa. (See also *Life History, Holometabola, Hemimetabola, Chrysalis* and *Ecdysis*.)

METANOTUM. The notum or dorsal cuticular covering of the third thoracic segment of an insect (see *Thorax*).

METAPLEURON. The lateral cuticular plate of the metathorax, the hind-segment of an insect's thorax.

METAPNEUSTIC. A term used to describe insects which have spiracles only at the posterior end of the abdomen, as for instance in the mosquito larva.

METASCUTELLUM. The scutellum or dorsal cuticular shield covering the hind-part of the metathorax or third segment of an insect's thorax (see also *Metascutum*).

METASCUTUM. The largest part of the dorsal cuticular shield covering the metathorax or third segment of an insect's thorax. In most insects each segment is covered by a single plate or *notum* but in some cases this is made up of three parts, *viz.* a *prescutum, scutum* and *scutellum*

METASTERNUM. The sternum or ventral plate below the metathorax or hind thoracic segment of an insect.

METATARSAL SPINNERS. Insects such as the Embioptera which have numerous silk glands opening on the enlarged metatarsus (basitarsus) or first tarsal segment of each front leg. Both sexes and all ages of insects of this order have such glands with which they make communal underground silk-lined nests (see *Embioptera*). Similar glands occur in males of the genus *Hilara* (Diptera of the family Empididae).

METATARSUS. A term often used for the first segment of the tarsus of an insect, but the analogy with the metatarsal bones of the human foot is a false one because they *follow* the tarsus instead of coming first. Better terms are *basitarsus* or first tarsomere, or even first tarsal 'segment'.

METATHETELY. Delay in the appearance of adult characters as a result of too much juvenile hormone, which may be due to an upsetting of the balance between the hormones from the *corpus allatum* and from the *thoracic gland*. This may result in the production of an insect intermediate in form between a pupa and an adult or between a nymph and an adult. Such an effect may be induced artificially or may take place in nature in the case of certain hybrids or by the presence of parasites. (Cf. *Prothetely*).

METATHORAX. The hind-segment of the thorax of an insect.

METECDYSIS. The period after a moult, in insects or other arthropods, when the new cuticle is still soft.

METEORUS. A genus of small Braconid flies that lay their eggs in the bodies of caterpillars and in some cases can be used as a means of controlling cutworms or other pests.

METHOCA. *Methoca ichneumonides*, a primitive wasp whose red and black female is wingless and ant-like and lays its eggs in the larvae of Tiger-beetles.

METOECUS. *Metoecus paradoxus*, the Wasp Fan-beetle: a member of the family Rhipiphoridae about 15 mm. long, having fan-shaped antennae and black or yellow-brown wing-cases that are normally half open exposing the wings. The larvae live in underground wasps' nests and feed on the wasp larvae.

METOPINA. *Metopina pachycondylae*, a small North American fly of the family Phoridae whose larva clings to young ants by means of a sucker and takes food from their mouths.

METOPIUS. *Metopius croceicornis*, a European ichneumon fly about 18 mm. long, having a pattern of black and yellow rings and red-brown antennae. It lays its eggs in the larvae of various butterflies.

METOPODONTUS. *Metopodontus bison*, a large stag-beetle from New Guinea about 6 cm. long, dark brown with a broad yellow border along the sides of the thorax and elytra. As with all members of the family Lucanidae, the males have greatly enlarged antler-like jaws.

METRIOPTERA. A genus of Bush Crickets or Long-horned Grasshoppers (Tettigoniidae), usually brown or green with short wings and very long antennae; common on heaths and moorland bogs.

METYLOPHORUS. *Metylophorus nebulosus*, one of the largest of the European Psocoptera: an insect related to the book-louse having a thick-set brown body, four transparent wings with a span of about 12 mm. and very long antennae; it is commonly found on conifers and fruit trees.

MEXICAN BEAN BEETLE. See *Epilachna*.

MEXICAN JUMPING BEAN MOTH. See *Jumping Beans*.

MIASTOR. A genus of minute gnats of the family Cecidomyidae whose larvae live in decaying wood and feed on moulds. They are notable as being the first insects in which the phenomenon of *paedogenesis* was observed. An immature larva may give birth parthenogenetically to 20–30 daughter larvae which eat their way out of the body of the parent. This process may be repeated for many generations, pupae and adults being only rarely produced.

MICRANER. An abnormally small male ant (see *Castes*).

MICRERGATE. A dwarf worker ant (see *Castes*).

MICROBRACON. See *Habrobracon*.

MICROCENTRUM. *Microcentrum retinerve*, the Angular-winged or False Katydid of North America: a bright green long-horned grasshopper of the family Tettigoniidae.

MICRODON. A genus of Hover-flies (Syrphidae) whose short, slug-like larvae live as scavengers in ants' nests.

MICROGASTER. An alternative name for the small Braconid fly *Apanteles* whose larvae are parasites in the caterpillars of the Cabbage White and other butterflies. (See *Apanteles*).

MICROLEPIDOPTERA ('MICROS'). The smallest moths including the primitive Micropterygidae only a few millimetres in length. Butterflies and moths were formerly classified according to size as *Macrolepidoptera* and *Microlepidoptera*, but this division is an artificial one and is no longer used in formal classification. It has been replaced by a more natural system based on the type of wing-venation and other characters.

MICROMALTHUS. A genus of beetles whose immature larvae exhibit the phenomenon of *paedogenesis*. (Cf. *Miastor*.)

MICROPHOTUS. *Microphotus angustus,* the Pink Glow-worm from the grasslands of the Western United States (see *Glow-worm, Firefly* and *Light-producing organs*).

MICROPTEROUS. Having small or vestigial wings: a term often used with particular reference to the various castes of insects such as ants and termites. More extreme than *brachypterous.*

MICROPTERYGIDAE. A family of moths seldom more than a few milli-metres across and of world-wide distribution. They belong to the Homoneura, a suborder in which the venation is almost identical in the two pairs of wings. In many other ways they are primitive, feeding chiefly on pollen by means of biting mouth-parts not elongated into the normal proboscis. Some authorities do not regard them as true moths and place them in a separate order Zeug-loptera.

MICROPYLE. A small pore in the shell of an insect's egg through which spermatozoa can enter; this is necessitated by the fact that the shell is secreted before fertilization.

MICROTERMES. A genus of small termites that do considerable damage to the roots of young cotton plants in North Africa and other places.

MICROTHORAX. A thin neck-like prothorax of some insects, *e.g.* dragon-flies.

MICROTRICHIA. Minute cuticular hairs such as those on the wings of some insects, which at low magnifications may produce an impression of cloudiness or colour.

MIDGE. A name given to many small gnat-like insects including Biting or Blood-sucking Midges (Ceratopogonidae), Gall-midges (Cecidomyidae) and the smaller members of the family Chironomidae or non-biting gnats whose aquatic larvae are known as bloodworms.

MIDGUT. The mesenteron: that part of the alimentary canal which is lined by endodermal tissue and in which most of the digestion and absorption of food normally take place (see *Alimentary Canal*).

MIGRATION. Many insects migrate in large numbers and travel very long distances in search of food or of more favourable climatic conditions. Some insects have summer and winter breeding grounds often many miles apart. Migration may take place on the ground, as with the Army Ants, or in the air as is the case with locusts and numerous species of butterflies and moths. The Desert Locust *Schistocerca* migrates annually between the Middle East and Northern India; the Milkweed Butterfly *Danaus plexippus* has summer breeding grounds in the Northern United States and winter breeding grounds in Mexico and Central America; at times it flies the Atlantic and is found in Western Europe and Britain. There are numerous other examples of insect migration including bees, beetles, dragonflies, aphids and many more.

Among locusts there are often two phases of their life, a solitary, non-migratory phase and a gregarious migratory phase. They may remain for several years in the former state but when they become overcrowded they also become greatly excited, change their habits and sometimes their appear-ance and then millions of them take to the air together (see *Desert Locust, Locustidae* and *Milkweed Butterfly*).

MILKWEED BUG. A name for several black and yellow plant-bugs that feed on the North American Milkweed (*Asclepias*).

MILKWEED BUTTERFLY. *Danaus plexippus*, also called the Monarch Butterfly: a large butterfly of the family Danaidae having a wing-span of 10 cm. or more; light brown with black-lined veins and black wing-borders containing a number of white spots. The fore-legs are reduced and functionless; the skin is tough so that they can survive attack or damage. Additional protection is given by the presence of poisonous glands whose secretion is distasteful to birds. These butterflies are noted for their long-distance migrations. There is a North American race whose breeding grounds extend from Canada to Mexico, and a southern race found all over South America. Milkweed Butterflies are also occasionally found in many of the Pacific islands, Australia and New Zealand, the Azores and Canary Islands, Western Europe and Britain. They are apparently still absent from Africa and most of Asia. The caterpillars are brightly striped in yellow, white and brown; their food-plant in America is the milkweed *Asclepias curassavica* but in some countries they have adapted themselves to other plants. The chrysalis is bright green and is to be found hanging upside down from the food-plant.

MILLER MOTH. (1) *Acronycta leporina*, a medium sized European heathland moth having the fore-wings grey, dotted with black and the hind-wings white.

(2) A name given (particularly in North America) to a number of noctuid moths whose wings are covered with fine white scales which come off easily and resemble flour.

MILL MOTH. The Mediterranean Flour Moth *Ephestia kuhniella*, a small dark grey moth whose larvae are pests of flour and other cereal products.

MIMAS. See *Lime Hawk-moth*.

MIMESA. *Mimesa equestris*, the Mimic Wasp: a hunting wasp of the family Sphecidae, having a long narrow waist like that of an ant. The base of the abdomen is red and the rest of the body black. It nests in sandy places in large communities but not as a social group. Each wasp stocks the cells of its nest with aphids and other small insects as food for the developing larvae.

MIMICRY. The resemblance of one species to another, in most cases giving some degree of protection. This generally takes the form of similarity in appearance but sometimes also in behaviour. A number of insects and some spiders resemble ants and live with them in their nests; the clearwing moths and the hover-flies resemble bees and wasps; some leaf-eating beetles resemble the predatory ladybird; the colour and pattern of some harmless butterflies closely resemble those of different and often poisonous species. There are innumerable other examples among insects (see also *Batesian Mimicry* and *Müllerian Mimicry*).

MIMIC WASP. See *Mimesa*.

MINEOLA. *Mineola indigenella*, the Apple Leaf-crumpler: a moth of the family Pyralidae whose larvae make tubes of silk mixed with black particles of faeces. These tubes are attached to the bark of a tree and are open at one end. The larvae live in them and use the open end for feeding on adjacent leaves. They later pupate and hibernate within the tube. Larvae of *Mineola vaccinii* are destructive to cranberries in Canada.

MINING BEES. Solitary bees that burrow in the earth to make their nests. Although a number may nest together they do not form a true social colony, as each leads an independent life (see *Andrenidae* and *Halictidae*).

MINOTAUR BEETLE. *Typhaeus typhoeus*, a large European dung beetle closely related to the Dor Beetle (*Geotrupes*), blue-black and shiny with two prominent horns on the head of the male. They live under dung heaps and roll balls of dung as food in which they lay their eggs.

MINT TORTOISE BEETLE. *Cassida equestris,* a small, oval leaf-beetle of the family Chrysomelidae, flattened with the edges of the thorax and elytra expanded to cover the legs and head so that the insect resembles a small tortoise walking about on a leaf. The head, thorax and wing-covers are green and the legs yellowish brown. They feed on several species of mint.

MIRIDAE. Also known as Capsid Bugs or Capsidae, a large family of small plant-bugs of the group Heteroptera, usually elongated and brown or greenish. A few are predators but the majority are vegetarian and include such major plant pests as the Apple Capsid *Plesiocoris rugicollis*.

MOCK WEEVILS. Pythidae, a family of small, elongated, bluish-black beetles resembling weevils but without such an obvious snout. *Pytho depressus,* a European species is found under the bark of conifers.

MOLANNIDAE. A family of Caddis Flies (Trichoptera) with long antennae and very hairy wings and palps. The larvae use grains of sand to make tubular cases which are wide and flattened on the under side.

MOLE CRICKET. See *Gryllotalpidae*.

MOLORCHUS. A genus of long-horned beetles (Cerambycidae). *Molorchus minor,* the larvae of which tunnel under the bark of Spruce and other conifers, is about 8 mm. long, black with short, reddish wing-covers each having a conspicuous oblique white line. The antennae of the male are twice as long as the body; those of the female shorter. *Molorchus umbellatarum* has its larvae in deciduous trees.

MONALOCORIS. *Monalocoris filicis,* the Bracken Bug: a green, oval shaped plant-bug of the group Heteroptera found on the under side of bracken and other ferns where it feeds on the sporangia.

MONARCH BUTTERFLY. See *Milkweed Butterfly*.

MONARTHROPALPUS. A genus of gall-midges of the family Cecidomyidae whose larvae combine the habits of leaf-mining and gall making. They eat away the cells between the upper and lower surfaces of a leaf but at the same time stimulate the growth of cells so that the leaf becomes thicker. *Monarthropalpus buxi* is a pest of Boxwood trees (*Buxus*), particularly in North America.

MONK MOTHS. A group of noctuid moths of the genus *Cucullia*, also called Shark Moths, generally of a greyish brown colour with a tuft of long hairs on the thorax projecting forwards and resembling a monk's cowl. The caterpillars of several species are bright yellow with a large number of conspicuous black spots. They are very specific in their feeding habits. *Cucullia umbratica* feeds on dandelions and other Compositae; *Cucullia scrophulariae* on Figwort (*Scrophularia*); *Cucullia campanulae* on Campanula etc.

MONOBIA. A genus of Carpenter Wasps (Eumeninae) which builds its nest in the burrows of other insects. *Monobia quadridens* is a large, long-winged North American species that stings and paralyses cutworms and leaves them in its nest as food for developing larvae.

MONOCHAMUS. The Pine Sawyer, a genus of longhorn beetles whose larvae bore into the wood of conifers. *Monochamus scutellatus*, the White-spotted Pine Sawyer, is a common pest of forestry in North America. When resting on the bark of a tree it is perfectly camouflaged.

MONOHAMMUS. A genus of Pine Sawyers: longhorn beetles whose larvae bore into pine wood and are a serious pest of forestry both in Europe and North America. They may live for many years in the larval state and cases have been recorded of adults emerging from furniture or the beams of buildings more than 20 years after the trees have been cut down.

MONOMORIUM. *Monomorium pharaonis,* Pharaoh's Ant: a tiny yellow species about 2 mm. long that has spread nearly all over the world and nests in immense numbers in centrally heated buildings, bakehouses or other warm places.

MONOPHAGOUS. Feeding on one particular type of food or parasitic only on one specific host.

MONOTHALAMOUS GALLS. Galls with a single cavity containing a single insect larva, *e.g.* the Oak Marble Gall.

MONOTRYSIA. An alternative name for Homoneura, *i.e.* moths having almost identical venation in the two pairs of wings and having reduced mouthparts (see *Homoneura*).

MONTEREY PINE ENGRAVER. *Ips radiatae,* a beetle of the family Scolytidae that tunnels under the bark of the Monterey and other pine trees, particularly in California, making a large number of radiating galleries (see *Ips* and *Ipinae*).

MOON MOTH. See *Luna Moth.*

MORDELLIDAE. Bristle-beetles or Tumbling Flower-beetles: a large family of small beetles having a boat-shaped, silky body with the abdomen extended to a point at the hind-end. When disturbed they leap quickly away. Most species are tropical but *Mordella aculeata* is a European species about 5 mm. long.

MORDELLISTENA. *Mordellistena unicolor,* a small beetle of the family Mordellidae which live in the galls made by the fly *Eurosta*.

MORIMUS. *Morimus funereus,* the Weeping Longhorn: a Central European beetle of the family Cerambycidae, about 4 cm. long with very long antennae. The elytra are grey, each having two conspicuous black spots. The larvae feed on decaying beech wood.

MORMO. *Mormo maura,* the Old Lady Moth: a large noctuid with an elaborate wing-pattern in two shades of dark brown. The larvae feed on docks and other herbaceous plants. The adults are often found resting in houses by day.

MORMOLYCE. *Mormolyce phyllodes,* the Ghost Walker: a large ground-beetle from Indonesia, about 6 cm. long, having long filamentous antennae, a very narrow head and thorax and a very wide abdomen with leaf-like lateral extensions.

MORMON CRICKET. *Anabrus simplex,* a large, brown or black wingless bush-cricket of the family Tettigoniidae, about 5 cm. long: a pest of crops in the Western United States.

MORPHIDAE. A family of tropical butterflies from Central and South America including some of the world's largest and most beautiful species. Some of those in Brazil are up to 20 cm. across and are of a brilliant iridescent blue. These include *Morpho menelaus* and *Morpho rhetenor* which are much used for making ornamental objects; others are brown with silver, green, red or orange patterns. *Morpho hecuba,* the largest of the family, is one of these; others again such as *Morpho catenarius* are whitish and translucent.

MORPHOIDAE. See *Morphidae.*

MOSAIC VISION. See *Compound Eyes.*

MOSQUITO. A name for two-winged blood-sucking flies of the group Nematocera and the family Culicidae. They have long legs; thin branched antennae which are larger and more bushy in the male; a long suctorial proboscis with piercing stylets; small scales similar to those of butterflies and moths along the veins of the wings and in most cases also all over the body. The elongated legless larvae are aquatic, breathing through openings or by a siphon at the hind-end. The pupae are also aquatic and are active swimmers. Within the family Culicidae are the two subfamilies Culicinae and Anophelinae. The latter, which include the Malaria Mosquito, have scales on the wings but not over the rest of the body; their larvae have no siphon or breathing tube at the hind-end and lie flat on the surface of the water. Mosquitoes are notorious as carriers of protozoan and virus diseases, the best known being *Anopheles maculipennis* (Malaria) and *Aedes aegypti* (Yellow Fever and Dengue Fever).

MOSQUITO HAWK. A colloquial American name sometimes used for a dragonfly on account of its habit of feeding on mosquitoes.

MOSS CARDER BEE. *Bombus muscorum,* a large bumble bee having a brown and yellow thorax and a deep brown abdomen banded with yellow; found in marshy places nesting among moss.

MOSS FLIES. Boreidae, a family of very small ant-like, wingless insects of the order Mecoptera. They run and jump over moss, damp earth and sometimes snow. The group includes the Snow-flea *Boreus hyemalis.*

MOSS GALL. An alternative name for the Bedeguar Gall or Robin's Pincushion, a red and green, hairy or bristly gall occurring on wild rose bushes and produced by the larva of the cynipid gall-wasp *Diplolepis rosae* (formerly called *Rhodites rosae*).

MOTHS. All Lepidoptera other than butterflies, *i.e.* those that generally fly by night; have a large body and sometimes relatively small wings; have a mechanism for hooking the wings together when flying; have antennae that are not clubbed but are usually hairy, branched or feather-like (see *Lepidoptera*).

MOTH-FLIES. Psychodidae, a family of minute flies whose body and wings are covered with hairs and scales resembling those of moths; they are usually not more than about 4 mm. long. The larvae feed on decaying vegetation and are useful in the breaking down of dead animal and plant matter. Most members of the family are harmless but one exceptional group, the sandflies, are tropical blood-sucking flies that spread the protozoan parasite *Leishmania,* the cause of the disease *Kala azar.* These are often placed in a separate family Phlebotomidae.

MOTHER-OF-PEARL MOTH. *Sylepta ruralis* or *Pleuroptya ruralis,* a pyralid moth of a pearly-grey colour patterned with wavy brown lines; one of the larger members of the Pyralidae. The larvae feed on leaves of stinging nettle which they roll up to form silk-lined nests.

MOTHER SHIPTON MOTH. See *Euclidimera.*

MOTTLED BEAUTY. *Boarmia repandata* or *Cleora repandata*, a geometrid moth of the family Selidosemidae, greyish brown mottled with darker brown and having two dark, wavy, transverse lines across the fore-wings. Melanic varieties exist and are spreading, particularly in industrial regions. The caterpillars are brown and stick-like,

MOTTLED GRASSHOPPER. *Myrmeleotettix maculatus*, a common European short-horned grasshopper of the family Acridiidae, mottled and varying in colour but predominantly brown, green and black and having clubbed antennae; common on sand dunes and chalk hills.

MOTTLED UMBER MOTH. See *Erannis*.

MOULTING. See *Ecdysis*.

MOULTING GLANDS. Epidermal glands that secrete a fluid which softens the lower layer of the cuticle prior to moulting (see *Ecdysis*).

MOULTING HORMONE. A hormone or group of hormones which stimulate the production of moulting fluid from glands in the epidermis. They are believed to be secreted by the *thoracic glands* under the infiuence of neuro-secretions from the brain.

MOUNTAIN FRITILLARY. *Boloria papaea*, a fairly small fritillary butterfly found in the mountains of northern Europe, Arctic Asia and Alaska (see *Fritillaries*).

MOUNTAIN MIDGE. A name given to a number of midges or small gnats of the family Ceratopogonidae found in mountainous regions. The name is also particularly applied to the non-biting family Deuterophlebiidae of North America and Asia: minute flies with relatively large, elaborately folded wings and with reduced mouth-parts; the aquatic larvae live in fast mountain streams.

MOURNFUL WASP. *Pemphredon lugubris*, a completely black solitary wasp of the family Sphecidae having a very narrow waist and neck. It nests in rotting wood or in holes made by beetles and other insects. These are stocked with aphids that have been stung and paralysed and are stored as food for the developing larvae.

MOURNING CLOAK. An alternative name, used chiefly in America, for the Camberwell Beauty Butterfly *Nymphalis antiopa* (see *Camberwell Beauty*).

MOUSE MOTH. *Amphipyra tragopoginis*, a small noctuid moth that is not only mouse-coloured but also runs away in a mouse-like fashion when disturbed. The caterpillars are smooth and bright green with longitudinal yellow lines; they feed on hawthorn and other trees.

MOUTH-HOOKS. Chitinous hooks with which maggots and other larvae of Diptera tear open plant or animal material on which they feed; well developed in leaf-miners. They take the place of the normal mandibles and maxillae, but it is not certain whether or not they are modified from these.

MOUTH-PARTS. The mouth-parts of an insect normally consist of the *labrum* or upper lip, the *labium* or lower lip and between these, two pairs of sideways-moving jaws, the *mandibles* and the *maxillae*. The labium and the maxillae bear sensory appendages or *palps*. In biting insects such as the cockroach the jaws are simple, strong, movable and sometimes toothed or serrated; occasionally they contain poisonous glands. In insects that suck blood or suck the juices of plants, the labium and the jaws may be extended and modified in a variety of different ways to form a suctorial proboscis or piercing stylets. (See *Jaws* and *Labium*.)

MUD DAUBER WASPS. A group of wasps of the family Sphecidae that build nests by daubing mud or clay under the eaves of houses, hollow trees or other suitable places.

MULLEIN CIONUS. *Cionus verbasci*, a small grey weevil with yellow down on the edges of the elytra; common on Mullein (*Verbascum*).

MULLEIN MOTH. *Cucullia verbasci*, a noctuid moth with long, rather narrow, grey-brown wings edged with dark brown. The larvae are conspicuously yellow with numerous spots of dark brown or black. They feed on Mullein (*Verbascum*) or on Figwort (*Scrophularia*).

MÜLLERIAN MIMICRY. A form of mimicry common among insects in which two or more harmful or distasteful species resemble each other. Each benefits from the similarity because would-be predators, tasting one, learn to avoid the other also; thus the loss from predators is shared among the species.

MURGANTIA. See Harlequin Bug.

MUSCIDAE. A family of Diptera which includes the House Fly *Musca domestica* and numerous others of a similar type belonging to the group Cyclorrhapha. All have short antennae and rather thick, bristly bodies with two wings and two halteres or balancers which are vestigial and modified hindwings. The mouth-parts are of a highly specialized kind in which the main part is a flattened, cushion-like pair of *labella* containing numerous tubes or *pseudotracheae*. Saliva is discharged over the food; enzymes partially digest it externally and the liquified food substances are then sucked up. The larvae of flies are small, legless maggots and the pupae are contained in a barrel-shaped puparium. Both adults and larvae generally feed on meat, carrion or dung. Because of the way they feed, flies are notorious carriers of diseases such as cholera, typhoid, dysentery, diarrhoea etc. In modern classifications many of the species most injurious to crops, because of their larval feeding, are segregated into the related family Anthomyiidae.

MUSEUM BEETLE. *Anthrenus museorum* and other beetles of the family Dermestidae whose larvae feed on fur, wool, hides etc.

MUSHROOM BODY. A crowd of nerve cells grouped together into a mushroom shape, their axons forming the stalk. Large numbers of such bundles are frequently present in the fore-brains of insects.

MUSHROOM-SHAPED GLAND. A cluster of glandular seminal vesicles at the junction of the two *vasa deferentia* with the ejaculatory duct of a male insect.

MUSK BEETLE. *Aromia moschata*, a European longhorn beetle of the family Cerambycidae, greenish gold with a metallic sheen. The body and elytra are elongated and the antennae are as long as the body. The larvae burrow into willow trees.

MUSLIN MOTH. *Cyonia mendica*, a small European moth of the family Arctiidae. The male is dark brown with black spots; the female white with black spots. A distinct Irish race exists in which both sexes are cream or yellowish but the males have thicker antennae. The larvae are brown and very hairy; they feed on dandelions, docks etc.

MUSSEL SCALE. *Mytilaspis pomorum* and related species of scale-insects

(Coccidae) whose scales resemble tiny mussel shells; pests of apple and other fruit trees (see *Coccidae* and *Lepidosaphes*).

MUSTARD BEETLE. *Phaedon cochleariae* also called the Watercress Beetle, a common leaf-beetle of the family Chrysomelidae; about 3 mm. long, oval shaped and having a metallic blue sheen. This and several related species feed, both as larvae and as adults, on the leaves of mustard, cress and other Cruciferae.

MUTILLIDAE. A family of parasitic wasps whose wingless females resemble ants. For this reason they are sometimes called Velvet Ants. *Mutilla europaea* is about 12 mm. long with a reddish thorax and a dark blue abdomen with pale velvety hairs; it is a parasite in the nests of bumble bees.

MYCETOCYTES. Specialized cells in the bodies of insects containing symbiotic bacteria or protozoa necessary for the life of the host. Those which break down cellulose in termites and cockroaches are an example; others are believed to be a source of necessary vitamins, particularly in some blood-sucking insects. Sometimes these cells are grouped together in a special organ called the *mycetome*.

MYCETOME. See *Mycetocytes*.

MYCETOPHAGIDAE. A family of beetles known as Hairy Fungus Beetles; many of them are brown or red with black spots and resemble ladybirds. They are to be found feeding on dead and decaying fungi.

MYCETOPHILIDAE. See *Fungus Gnats*.

MYCETOPORUS. A minute, quick-moving beetle often found on dead leaves, moss etc., a member of the family Staphylinidae or Rove Beetles characterized by very short elytra. *Mycetoporus splendidus* is about 2 mm. long and light brown in colour.

MYDAIDAE. Mydas Flies, a family of medium or very large flies found in tropical and subtropical areas all over the world. *Mydas clavatus* of the North-eastern United States is black with a bright orange band round the abdomen. The wings are smoky grey with a span of 5 cm. *Mydas luteipennis* is a yellow-winged species from Mexico and *Mydas heros,* the largest known species with a wing-span of 12 cm., is found in the forests of Brazil; the larvae live in decaying vegetation.

MYELOPHILUS. Also called *Blastophagus;* a genus of beetles of the family Scolytidae; pests of forestry. *Myelophilus piniperda,* the Pine Shoot Beetle tunnels under the bark of pine trees, usually attacking after the damage has been started by the larvae of moths.

MYIASIS. Diseases of man and other animals due to infestation by the larvae of Diptera which are not necessarily parasitic. Most cases of human myiasis are accidental infestations of the intestine through swallowing larvae in food; others are infestations of wounds and sores (see *Bot Fly* and *Gasterophilus*).

MYIATROPA. A genus of Hover-flies (Syrphidae) resembling bees and wasps. *Myiatropa florea,* a common species in gardens, has a brownish thorax and a dull yellow abdomen with three black or dark brown transverse bands and a dark median stripe. The larva is of the 'rat-tailed' type.

MYLABRIS. *Mylabris cichorii,* a Blister Beetle from India belonging to the family Meloidae: a valuable source of the drug *cantharidin* (see *Meloidae* and *Blister Beetles*).

MYMARIDAE. Fairy-flies: the smallest known insects; black and yellow Chalcid Wasps with narrow, hair-fringed wings; sometimes with a length of less than a quarter of a millimetre. The larvae are parasites in the eggs of other insects.

MYRMECOCYSTUS. See *Honey-pot Ant*.

MYRMECOPHILES. Miscellaneous insects, mites, spiders etc. which inhabit the nests of ants either as true guests, fed and tended by the ants, or as scavengers.

MYRMEDONIA. A genus of beetles of the family Staphylinidae or Rove Beetles, living in ants' nests and having a superficial resemblance to ants.

MYRMELEONIDAE (MYRMELEONTIDAE). See *Ant-lion*.

MYRMELEOTETTIX. See *Mottled Grasshopper*.

MYRMICA. A common and widely distributed genus of ants. *Myrmica ruginodis*, the common Red Ant, is a small species that nests under stones or in old tree stumps. It takes the larvae of the Large Blue Butterfly into its nest to milk them.

MYRMUS. *Myrmus miriformis*, an elongated, green or brown plant-bug of the order Hemiptera which feeds on grasses in damp heathland. The females usually have vestigial wings and are unable to fly.

MYRSIDEA. A genus of lice of the order Mallophaga that infest rooks and other common birds.

MYSCELIA. *Myscelia orsis*, a small nymphalid butterfly common in Brazil, brilliantly coloured in several shades of blue.

MYSTACIDES. *Mystacides azurea*, a small Caddis Fly about 10 mm. long, commonly known as Silverhorns. Its wings are bluish and its very long curved antennae are black and white giving a silvery appearance. The larvae build tubes of small stones or sand grains.

MYSTAX. A patch of bristles or stiff setae above the mouth in certain Diptera; often called the 'moustache'.

MYTHIMNA. An alternative name for the genus *Leucania* or Wainscot Moths: light brown or greyish noctuid moths whose larvae feed chiefly on grasses. *Mythimna (Leucania) pallens*, the Common Wainscot Moth of Central and Northern Europe; *Mythimna lithargyria*, the Clay Moth. There are also species in North America and elsewhere (see *Leucania*).

MYTILOCOCCUS. An alternative name for *Lepidosaphes*, the Mussel Scale: a scale-insect of the family Coccidae resembling a small mussel shell; a pest of apple, pear and other trees (see *Coccidae* and *Lepidosaphes*).

MYZUS. *Myzus persicae*, the Peach Aphid, a pink or green species particularly common on peach trees but also sometimes found on spinach, potato, sugar beet and other plants in many parts of the world. It spreads the virus of mosaic, leaf-roll and other diseases.

191

N

NABIDAE (NABIDIDAE). Damsel Bugs, a family of Heteroptera similar in habits to the Assassin Bugs (Reduviidae) and sometimes classed with them. Like the assassins they prey on plant-bugs, plant-lice, caterpillars and other insects, using their front legs for catching them and their sharp beak-like proboscis for piercing them. *Nabis ferus*, a widely distributed species, is an elongated, winged insect about 8 mm. long, greenish grey with long legs and long antennae. The larvae resemble ants and mix with them.

NACERDES. A genus of beetles of the family Cantharidae, related to the Soldier Beetles: elongated, soft-bodied with long thin antennae, large head and narrow parallel-sided elytra. *Nacerdes melanura*, a common European species, has a yellow head and thorax and greyish yellow, finely hairy elytra tipped with black. It is found in old timber especially near the seashore.

NAENIA. See *Gothic Moth*.

NAEOGEUS. A common North American genus of Velvet Water-bugs (Hebridae): minute bugs of the order Hemiptera, found near the edges of ponds and streams. The body is covered with fine velvety hairs (see *Hebridae*).

NAIAD. The aquatic nymph of a dragonfly, mayfly or other hemimetabolous insect.

NAIL-MARK MOTH. *Aglia tau*, a European (but not British) member of the family Saturniidae: a large brownish moth with a wing-span of up to 80 mm., having a white nail-shaped mark on each fore-wing. The male is slightly smaller and darker than the female. Melanic variations are known. The caterpillars feed chiefly on beech leaves.

NANOSELLA. *Nanosella fungi*, one of the smallest known beetles, about a quarter of a millimetre long: a tropical and subtropical species that feeds on moulds; a member of the family Ptiliidae or Trichopterygidae.

NARCISSUS FLIES. Hover-flies (Syrphidae) whose larvae feed on bulbs of daffodils and narcissus, entering them at the top and hollowing them out from the inside. *Merodon equestris*, a common species, is a large bee-like insect of this group, dark brown and hairy with a yellow and brown abdomen.

NARROW BORDERED BEE HAWK-MOTH. *Hemaris tityus* or *Hemaris scabiosae*, a day-flying moth of the family Sphingidae having a remarkable resemblance to a bee. The wings are transparent with a narrow brown border and with thin brown lines following the veins. The body is yellowish and hairy with two dark bands round the abdomen. The caterpillars, which are light green with red markings, feed on Scabious and other plants of the order Dipsaceae.

NARROW-WINGED PUG MOTH. *Eupithecia nanata*, a small geometrid moth of the group Larentiinae with an elaborate wing-pattern of cream and brown. The larvae feed on heather (see *Eupithecia*).

NASTURTIUM LEAF-MINER. *Agromyza propepusilla*, a small two-winged fly whose larvae tunnel into Nasturtium leaves.

NASUTES. Soldier-termites: specialized forms within the genus *Nasutitermes*, able to defend the colony by discharging an acrid secretion from glands situated at the end of a long snout or rostrum.

NASUTITERMES. A genus of termites whose 'soldier' caste are *nasutes*, *i.e.* they have a long pointed snout from which they can discharge a poisonous fluid; a tropical genus that builds very large nests of wood pulp and sand etc. above ground.

NATATORIAL LEGS. Legs specially adapted for swimming by having a fringe of long hairs, *e.g.* on water boatmen and water beetles.

NAUCORIDAE. Creeping Water-bugs: flattened, oval or round insects of the group Heteroptera, sometimes called Saucer Bugs, that hunt their prey among under-water vegetation. They can fly but do not often do so, preferring to stay under water breathing by means of a bubble of air trapped between the wings and the abdomen.

NAUPACTIS. *Naupactis leucoloma* or *Pantomorus leucoloma*, the White-fringed Beetle: a serious pest of cotton, maize and other crops in North America, accidentally introduced into Florida.

NEANURA. A genus of Springtails (Collembola) noted for their pale green luminescence; found in North America and elsewhere.

NEBRIA. A very common genus of ground beetles (Carabidae): elongated beetles about 10 mm. long, living under stones or loose bark. Both adults and larvae are predators. *Nebria livida* is brownish yellow; *Nebria brevicollis* is blue-black.

NECROBIA. A world-wide genus of Hide Beetles, members of the family Cleridae that feed on dried meat, carcases, skins etc. Some are also pests of copra (coconut). *Necrobia rufipes* is a typical species, about 6 mm. long with a soft leathery body and elytra. The head and thorax are reddish; the elytra blue-black.

NECRODES. A common genus of Burying Beetles (Necrophoridae). *Necrodes litoralis* is a blue-black species about 15 mm. long, often found among dead fish etc. on the seashore (see *Burying Beetles*).

NECROPHORIDAE. See *Burying Beetles*.

NECYDALIS. *Necydalis major*, the Ichneumon Longhorn Beetle, a member of the family Cerambycidae found in south-eastern Europe. A narrow, elongated insect about 35 mm. long, black with yellowish brown wing-covers and with long antennae. The larvae live in poplars and willows.

NEEDLE FLY. See *Leuctra*.

NEGRO ANT. *Formica fusca*, a common and widely distributed black, rather long-legged ant, 5–6 mm. long. It nests under stones and in old tree stumps etc. It is often taken into the nests of the red ant *Formica sanguinea* where it is made a 'slave'.

NEGRO BUG. *Thyreocoris* and related genera of the family Cydnidae: small black shieldbugs often found in large numbers on spring flowers, especially on sand dunes and chalk hills.

NEMAPOGON. *Nemapogon granellus*, a small brown and white moth of the family Tineidae whose larvae are pests in stored grain, dried fruit etc.

NEMATOCERA. A suborder of Diptera characterized by having branched, many-jointed, filamentous antennae. They are usually slim, long-legged insects and include crane-flies, mosquitoes and many kinds of gnats and midges. The larvae have well developed heads and jaws but are without true legs, though some (*e.g.* Chironomidae) have false legs on the abdomen. Many of these larvae are aquatic. Pupae are of the *orthorrhaphous* type, *i.e.* they split longitudinally along the mid-dorsal line and are not contained in a puparium like that of the house fly.

NEMATUS. See *Gooseberry Sawfly*.

NEMERITIS. A genus of ichneumon flies whose larvae are parasites in the caterpillars of the Mediterranean Flour-moth.

NEMOBIUS. A genus of Wood-crickets: small, brown, widely distributed insects commonly found in rotting wood or dead leaves. *Nemobius sylvestris*, the common European Wood-cricket, is about 10 mm. long, dark brown with short fore-wings and no hind-wings.

NEMOGNATHA. An oil-beetle of tropical America belonging to the family Meloidae but differing from most of this family in having its maxillae elongated and fused together to form a tubular proboscis through which nectar can be sucked.

NEMOPTERIDAE. Thread Lacewings Flies: a family of predatory insects of the order Neuroptera, found in the warmer parts of Europe, Asia, Africa and Australia. They differ from the normal lacewing flies in having the hind-wings drawn out into ribbon-like threads several times as long as the body. *Nemoptera sinuata*, common in the Balkans, has yellow-green wings with a brown pattern and a span of about 5 cm. Its predatory, long-necked larvae live in sandy places.

NEMOURA. A widely distributed genus of stoneflies whose nymphs live in stagnant water. *Nemoura flexuosa* is a European species about 2 cm. long, brown with long filamentous antennae. The nymph has thick legs and long thin cerci but the latter are lost in the adult.

NEOCHERITRA. *Neocheritra amrita*, a small Hairsteak Butterfly of the family Lycaenidae from South-east Asia, having bright yellow fore-wings and whitish hind-wings with dark brown spots and wavy lines and with very long flexible 'tails'. (See *Hairstreaks*).

NEODIPRION. *Neodiprion pinetum*, Abbott's Sawfly: a pest of pine trees in North America and other parts. The larvae, which are of the typical *eruciform* or caterpillar type, feed on pine needles.

NEOLAMPRIMA. *Neolamprima adolphinae*, a Stag Beetle (Lucanidae) from the forests of New Guinea, about 5 cm. long, greenish gold with a fiery red head. The male, as in other stag beetles, has large antler-like jaws.

NEOMYSIA. *Neomysia oblongoguttata*, the Streaked Ladybird: a beetle of the family Coccinellidae differing from the majority of ladybirds in having pale streaks instead of dark spots on the elytra. It is commonly found on pine trees.

NEOMYZAPHIS. *Neomyzaphis abietina* also called *Rhopalosiphon abietinum*, the Green Spruce Aphis: a very common, widely distributed genus of aphids, green with red eyes and with a wing-span of about 5 mm., a common pest of young spruce trees, often causing defoliation.

NEONYMPHA. *Neonympha eurytus*, the Wood Satyr and related species: very common butterflies of North America, members of the family Satyridae, dark brown with dark eye-spots ringed with yellow; paler brown on the underside; frequently seen in the shady parts of forests.

NEOPHASIA. A genus of South American pierid butterflies, greenish white mottled with patches of black, resembling the European Bath White, *Pontia daplidice.*

NEOPHILOPTERUS. A bird-louse about 3 mm. long, belonging to the order Mallophaga, living on the feathers of the Black Stork *Ciconia nigra* of Eastern and Northern Europe.

NEOPTERA. A name sometimes given to all the more highly developed winged insects: those that can fold the wings back over the body and whose wing-venation has a definite pattern other than a simple network. The group comprises all present-day winged insects except dragonflies and mayflies which are classed with some fossil insects as Palaeoptera.

NEOTENIN. A substance better known as the *juvenile hormone* secreted by the *corpus allatum* of larval insects. Its function appears to be to maintain the juvenile characters of the larva after each moult. At a later stage, production of this hormone ceases and metamorphosis then takes place.

NEOTERMES. A widely distributed tropical genus of termites. *Neotermes gestri* attacks the cacao plant in West Africa; *Neotermes militaris* and *Neotermes greeni* attack tea plants in India.

NEPHOTETTIX. A genus of Leaf-hoppers (Cicadellidae) that spreads virus diseases of rice in China and other places. *Nephotettix bipunctata* is a pest in the rice fields of Malaya and Ceylon.

NEPHROTOMA. *Nephrotoma maculata*, a very common European crane-fly (family Tipulidae) having clear wings and a black and yellow striped abdomen; about half the size of the common crane-fly.

NEPIDAE. Water scorpions: predatory aquatic insects of the group Heteroptera, resembling a dark brown leaf or stick crawling about on the bottom of a pond, having a long breathing tube resembling a sting at the hind-end and bent front legs like the pincers of a scorpion. They have wings but are unable to fly. The two commonest genera, both world-wide, are *Nepa* (broad and stoutly built) and *Ranatra* (long and stick-like.)

NEPTICULA. A genus of small moths of the family Tineidae whose larvae are leaf-miners in oak, beech and other trees.

NEPTIS. A genus of nymphalid butterflies closely related to the White Admiral *Limenitis camilla.* There are many species spreading over south-eastern Europe, Asia and North Africa. Nearly all are dark brown with broad white bands. *Neptis rivularis*, the Hungarian Glider and *Neptis sappho*, the Common Glider are found as far west as Austria and across Asia to Japan.

NERICE. *Nerice bidentata*, a North American moth whose bright green larva feeds on the edges of elm and other leaves. The dorsal part of the caterpillar is serrated in an irregular manner resembling the edge of an elm leaf so that when feeding it is perfectly camouflaged.

NERVE-WINGED INSECTS. See *Neuroptera.*

NERVOUS SYSTEM. The nervous system of an insect is essentially similar to those of other arthropods and of annelids. A double nerve cord runs ventrally along the body with, in the more primitive insects, a pair of ganglia corresponding to each segment. Frequently the two ganglia of a pair are joined into one and in more highly specialized insects many of these pairs may be fused together to form larger ganglia so that the original metameric arrangement is lost. Anteriorly there is a collar of nerve fibres surrounding the

195

oesophagus and connecting the ventral cord with the 'brain'. This so-called 'brain' is situated immediately above the oesophagus and is formed from fusion and enlargement of three pairs of ganglia. The first pair are enlarged to form the optic lobes and the second the antennary lobes. Owing to the high degree of development and the efficient functioning of the eyes and antennae in most insects, these lobes form the largest part of the brain. In addition to all these structure there is a somewhat primitive visceral or sympathetic nervous system consisting of a number of small ganglia innervating the various internal organs.

NERVURE. One of the 'veins' of an insect's wing: a chitinous tube usually containing a central trachea surrounded by haemolymph (see also *Venation*).

NESSAEA. A genus of nymphalid butterflies from the tropical forests of South America, characterized by having the undersides of the wings a bright leaf-green. *Nessaea obrinus* is a Brazilian species whose upper surface is brown with a broad band of bright blue on each fore-wing.

NETTED PUG MOTH. *Euphithecia venosata*: a common moth of the family Geometridae, subfamily Larentiinae, small and greenish grey with an elaborate network of thin brown lines. The caterpillars feed in the seed capsules of various species of campion (*Silene*). (See *Eupithecia*.)

NETTLE GROUND-BUG. *Heterogaster urticae*, a small greyish black plant-bug of the family Lygaeidae with a narrow, soft body about 6 mm. long; sometimes found in large numbers on stinging nettles.

NETTLE SCALE-INSECT. *Orthezia urticae*, a small plant-bug of the family Ortheziidae, closely related to the Coccidae. About 4 mm. long, the female has a black and white pattern on the back but this is completely hidden by a secretion of white wax which covers the insect for a considerable thickness and forms a pocket for the eggs at the hind-end. *Orthezia insignis* is a related species which is widely distributed as a greenhouse pest, attacking a variety of crops. (See also *Coccidae*.)

NETTLE WEEVIL. *Phyllobius urticae*, a bright, shining green weevil about 7 mm. long, having a short thick snout and elbowed antennae; commonly found on stinging nettles.

NETTLING HAIRS (URTICATING HAIRS). Irritant hairs of some caterpillars. These are hollow and have poison glands at their bases; the tip of the hair is often barbed so that, when this is broken, the poison is released.

NET-WINGED. Having membranous wings with numerous cross-veins, *e.g.* Odonata, Ephemeroptera and Neuroptera. Also applied to the 'net-winged midges', Blepharoceridae and Deuterophlebiidae.

NEUROPTERA. Lacewings, Alder-flies and Snake-flies: an order of holometabolous insects having two pairs of membranous wings and a soft body. They have biting mouth-parts and are usually predators; the antennae are well developed but there are no abdominal cerci. The larvae, which are also predators, are of the *campodeiform* or long-legged type. They may be aquatic of terrestrial. Those of the family Myrmeleontidae are 'ant-lions' (*q.v.*).

NEUROTERUS. The Oak Spangle-gall Insect, *Neuroterus quercus-baccarum* and related species: small black gall-wasps of the group Cynipoidea which lay their eggs in oak leaves. Small, flat, red galls about 1 mm. across are produced on the surface of the leaf. The larvae spend the winter in these and, after pupation, the emergent insects lay eggs in the young oak catkins producing galls of a different kind which resemble small hanging red berries (see *Cynipoidea, Gall* and *Silk-button Gall*).

NEUROTOMA. A genus of sawflies common on hawthorn and fruit trees of the rose family. *Neurotoma flaviventris* is a small insect about 8 mm. long, black with a yellow-tipped abdomen. The larva is orange with a black head.

NEVADA BLUE. *Plebicula golgus*, a small blue butterfly of the family Lycaenidae having the upper surface deep sky blue and the under surface pale grey-brown with black spots; it is found up to 3,000 m. in the Sierra Nevada of Spain.

NEVADA GRAYLING. *Pseudocharaza hippolyte*, a butterfly of the family Satyridae found high up in the Spanish Sierra Nevada and in the mountains of southern Russia and Asia Minor; pale grey-brown with broad straw-coloured bands and with two black spots on each fore-wing.

NEW ZEALAND GLOW-WORM. *Bolitophila luminosa* or *Arachnocampa luminosa*, a two-winged fly resembling a crane-fly but belonging to the family Mycetophilidae, whose larvae glow by means of luminescent organs formed from modified Malpighian tubules. They live in large numbers on the roofs of caves in New Zealand. 'Glow-worm Cave' at Waitomo is a famous tourist attraction. (See also *Light-producing Organs*).

NEZARA. A world-wide genus of Pentatomid bugs, also called *Acrosternum*, that feed on fruit and seeds. *Nezara viridula* is a pest of developing cereals, legumes, tomatoes, cotton etc. *Nezara hilare* attacks peaches.

NIGHT HUNTER. See *Mantichora*.

NIGHT VISION. In most nocturnal insects the compound eyes have a large number of optical units or ommatidia. The crystalline cones in these are often short and their inner ends are some distance from the corresponding retinal cells. In addition to this the black pigment which, in diurnal insects, surrounds each crystalline cone like a sleeve, is either absent or can be retracted at night. The effect of this is that light entering through each cone can reach retinal cells of its neighbours as well as its own. Each retinal cell therefore receives multiple stimulation and the net result, instead of being a mosaic image formed of dots, will be a continuous, bright but rather blurred image known as a *superposition* image. In many moths there is also a *tapetum* or 'mirror' formed from a large number of tracheae surrounding the retinal rods. The effect of this, besides giving a good oxygen supply to the eye, is to reflect some of the light forwards from the back of the eye so that some of it reaches the retinal cells twice. The total result of these arrangements is that nocturnal insects in general are extremely sensitive to small amounts of light but at the expense of clarity of perception (see also *Compound Eye*).

NIPTUS. *Niptus hololeucus*, the Golden Spider-beetle: a long-legged round-bodied beetle of the family Ptinidae about 12 mm. long, golden brown with a covering of fine gold hairs. The length of the legs and the large size of the abdomen give it a superficial resemblance to a spider. It was introduced into Europe from the Middle East and is sometimes a pest of flour, sugar or other stored foods.

NIT. The egg of a louse, particularly of the human louse *Pediculus humanus*, usually glued firmly to the hair of the host (see *Louse*).

NITIDULIDAE. Gloss Beetles: a family of small clavicorn beetles about 5 mm. long with an oval, flattened body. Some inhabit the tunnels made by bark-beetles; others feed on carrion, decaying fruit or decaying fungi; some feed on nectar and pollen. The larvae are predatory.

NOCTUIDAE. Noctuid Moths or Owlet Moths: a large family of medium sized, usually brownish, stoutly built moths having a well developed proboscis with which they suck nectar. The larvae, some of which are known as cutworms, do much damage to young trees and other crops by feeding on roots and young shoots which they cut off close to the ground. They are most active at night and hide under the soil during the day. The group includes such well known species as Yellow Underwings, Cabbage Moths, Heart-and-Dart, Gothic, Wainscot Moths, Marbled Beauty, Mouse Moth, Angle Shades, Green Silver Lines and many others.

NOCTURNAL GROUND BEETLES. Tenebrionidae, also called False Ground Beetles: a family of small or medium sized, elongated beetles, many of which are unable to fly owing to the fact that the wing-cases are firmly fused together. The larvae are worm-like and vegetarian. Some are pests of grain or other food stores (see *Meal Beetle* and *Mealworm*).

NODUS. (1) The narrow waist between the thorax and abdomen of an ant, wasp, ichneumon or similar member of the Hymenoptera.

(2) A notch marking the position of a prominent cross-vein near the middle of the front edge of a dragonfly's wing.

NOMADIDAE. See Homeless Bees.

NOMADACRIS. *Nomadacris septemfasciata*, the Red Locust: a migratory species that breeds in Rhodesia, Zambia and Tanzania and invades most of southern Africa.

NOMOPHILA. *Nomophila noctuella*, the Rush Veneer Moth: a medium sized, brown moth of the family Pyralidae having narrow fore-wings and fringed hind-wings. The larvae feed on clover, knotgrass and other meadow plants. Sometimes these moths migrate long distances. Specimens have been found in Britain containing radio-active substances derived from a nuclear explosion that took place in North Africa a month previously.

NONAGRIA. *Nonagria typhae*, the Bulrush Wainscot Moth: a grey-brown noctuid moth whose larvae live and pupate within the hollow stems of bulrush, reed-mace and similar plants.

NOON-FLY. *Mesembrina meridiana*, a large and handsome fly with dark brown head, shiny black body and bright orange wing-bases; a relative of the blowfly, it lays its eggs in dung on which the larvae feed.

NORSE GRAYLING. *Oeneis norna*, a satyrid butterfly of mountainous arctic and subarctic regions including Lapland, northern Asia and North America; pale yellowish-brown with darker edges and wing-bases and with a number of black spots on both wings. The larvae feed on grasses and sedges.

NORTHERN BROWN. *Erebia aethiops*, also called the Scotch Argus: a small satyrid butterfly, variable but generally dark brown with three or four white-centred black eye-spots on an orange background. It is found throughout the Alps, the mountains of Scandinavia, Asia Minor, the Urals and the Caucasus. The wing-span is 3–4 cm., the Scottish variety being slightly smaller. The larvae feed on grasses (see *Erebia*).

NORWEGIAN WASP. *Vespula norvegica*, a fairly common species of wasp similar to the Tree Wasp (*Vespula sylvestris*) but darker yellow and with thicker black bands on the abdomen. The nests are built in bushes, shrubs or hedges.

NO-SEE-UM. A colloquial name used in the United States and Canada for any of a number of small biting midges, particularly the most minute members of the family Ceratopogonidae.

NOTIOPHILUS. *Notiophilus biguttatus*, an active little ground beetle about 3 mm. long: a predator of the family Carabidae having an elongated body, large eyes and shiny metallic green wing-cases; it is common in woods and gardens.

NOTODONTIDAE. Prominents: a world-wide family of moths, many of which are characterized by having a large tuft of scales projecting backwards from the centre of the hind-edge of each fore-wing. They include the Puss Moth, the Lobster Moth and many others. The larvae are often destructive pests of common trees such as willow, poplar, oak, elm and lime. They pupate in silken cocoons containing chewed pieces of leaf or wood so that they are well camouflaged.

NOTONECTAL. Swimming on the back, as for instance the Water Boatman (see *Notonectidae*).

NOTONECTIDAE. Water Boatmen: a family of predatory bugs of the group Heteroptera which always swim on their backs using for this purpose their powerful hind-legs which are flattened and fringed with hairs. *Notonecta glauca*, a well-known and world-wide species is yellowish green and about 15 mm. long with a boat-shaped body. It hunts tadpoles, small fish, beetle larvae etc. using its powerful proboscis as a weapon which can also be very painful to humans. Although it hunts in the water, it often flies at night.

NOTOPTERA. An alternative name for the order of primitive insects also known as Grylloblattodea (*q.v.*).

NOTUM. A tergum or dorsal cuticular plate, particularly those covering each of the three thoracic segments of an insect. According to their position they are named *pronotum, mesonotum* and *metanotum*.

NOVEMBER MOTH. *Oporinia dilutata*, a common geometrid moth of the subfamily Larentiinae: medium sized with a pattern of wavy transverse bands of light and dark brown; melanic varieties are also known. The bright green caterpillars do widespread damage by feeding on leaves of oak, elm, birch etc.

NOVIUS. *Novius cardinalis*, also called *Rodolia cardinalis*: a species of bright red Australian ladybirds (Coccinellidae) which were imported into the United States and successfully used as a means of controlling scale-insects on Californian citrus trees.

NUDAURELIA. *Nudaurelia cytherea*, the Pine Tree Emperor: a large saturniid moth of South Africa. The subspecies *Nudaurelia cytherea capensis* is a pest whose larvae are defoliators of pine trees.

NUN MOTH. *Lymantria monacha* (or *Liparis monacha*) also known as the Black Arches Moth: a Tussock Moth of the family Lymantriidae, closely related to the Gipsy Moth *Lymantria dispar*. The fore-wings have a zig-zag pattern of transverse black and white lines; the hind-wings are greyish. The abdomen of the male is grey but in the female it has a reddish tip. Melanic varieties are also known. The moth is a serious pest of coniferous forests in Central Europe and of oak woods in North America.

NUPTIAL FLIGHT. See *Mating Flight*.

NURSES. Young worker bees whose chief occupation is the feeding of the larvae.

NURSE CELLS. Nutritive cells or *trophocytes* in the ovaries of insects (see *Meroistic Ovariole*).

NUT BORERS. There are many insects that bore into nuts but the best known are various species of weevils (Curculionidae). *Curculio nucum* is the common Nut Weevil that bores into hazel nuts. This insect is brown with a rounded body about 4 mm. long and with a snout of the same length. It uses this to bore deeply into the nut. A single egg is laid in the hole and the ensuing larva eats its way out. Other similar species attack acorns.

NUT WEEVIL. See *Nut Borers*.

NYCTALEMON. *Nyctalemon menoeticus*, a nocturnal moth of India and South-east Asia with a wing-span of about 13 cm., dark brown with a conspicuous white stripe running down the middle of each of the four wings parallel to the body. The hind-wings are irregularly toothed and have long, broad 'tails'. The insect belongs to the family Sematuridae.

NYCTERIBIIDAE. A family of wingless flies with long spider-like legs, living in the fur of bats and sucking their blood. Some are blind; others have eyes of either one or two facets.

NYCTERIDOPSYLLA. One of the genera of fleas associated with bats. *Nycteridopsylla pentactena*, the Yellow and Red Flea, is about 2.5 mm. long with a large abdomen, a narrow thorax and small head. On its back are five comb-like structures.

NYMPH. An insect larva which hatches out in a well developed state closely resembling the adult except for the fact that the wings and reproductive organs are undeveloped. The former appear as wing-buds at an early age and gradually increase in size with each instar. There is no pupal stage. (See *Life History, Metamorphosis* and *Hemimetabola*. Compare *Larva*.)

NYMPHALIDAE. A family of large and handsome butterflies including the Fritillaries and the Vanessids. They belong to the so-called 'four-legged' group, the front legs being greatly reduced and functionless. Most of these butterflies are brightly coloured. The Fritillaries form a natural group all very similar in the pattern of their wings; the Vanessids, sometimes known as 'aristocrats', are very variable and generally beautifully patterned. Among European species they include the Red and White Admirals, Painted Lady, Peacock, Large and Small Tortoiseshells, Camberwell Beauty, Purple Emperor and many others. North American species include the Buck-eye, the Banded Purple and the Viceroy. Asiatic species include the Indian Leaf Butterfly *Kallinia* and the Map Butterfly *Cyrestris*. South America also has many large and beautiful nymphalids and there is hardly any part of the world where the family is not represented (see also *Fritillaries*).

NYMPHULA. See *China Mark Moth*.

NYSSON. *Nysson spinosus*, a cuckoo wasp of the family Sphecidae, having a black and yellow striped abdomen and two spines above its waist. It lays its eggs in the nest of another wasp *Corytes* which is very similar in appearance.

O

OAK APPLE. A large spongy, spherical gall, greenish red and turning brown, produced by the larvae of the small black cynipoid wasp *Biorhiza pallida* (see *Gall, Gall-wasp* and *Oak Root-gall*).

OAK BARK BEETLE. *Scolytus intricatus* and related species: small weevil-like beetles usually only a few millimetres in length, with a black head and thorax and reddish brown wing-covers. Although they belong to the group Rhynchophora (Curculionoidea) they differ from true weevils (Curculionidae) in the fact that the snout is short and the head bent under the thorax. Both larvae and adults bore tunnels between the bark and the wood of oak trees.

OAK BEAUTY. *Biston strataria*, a medium sized geometrid moth having whitish-grey wings with broad, wavy, transverse bands of dark brown and black. Like its close relative the Peppered Moth (*Biston betularia*) it has black or melanic varieties. The brown stick-like larvae feed on leaves of oak, elm and birch.

OAK BUSH-CRICKET. See *Meconema*.

OAK BUTTON-GALLS. Small, flat, circular galls produced on the surface of oak leaves by the cynipoid wasp *Neuroterus quercusbaccarum* (see also *Neuroterus*).

OAK EGGAR. *Lasiocampa quercus*, a large, stoutly built, reddish brown moth with a distinctive white spot on each fore-wing; having a heavy, hairy body, feathery antennae and reduced mouth-parts. The larvae are ringed with brown and black and covered with irritant hairs; they feed on a variety of plants including oak, sallow, hawthorn, bramble etc. A northern variety, living on moors and heaths, feeds on heather and has a life-cycle of two years (see *Eggar Moths* and *Lasiocampidae*).

OAK HEDGEHOG GALL. See *Hedgehog Oak-gall*.

OAK HOOK-TIP. *Drepana binaria*, a small European moth of the family Drepanidae having the tips of the fore-wings turned back to make a blunt hook. The fore-wings are brown with two pale transverse lines and two central dots. The hind-wings are similar but paler (see *Hook-tip Moths*).

OAK MARBLE GALL. See *Marble Galls*.

OAK PINHOLE BORER. *Platypus cylindrus*, a small dark brown, shining beetle about 6 mm. long with a broad head, an elongated cylindrical thorax and straight, parallel-sided wing-covers. The larvae are yellowish white with dark brown heads. Both adults and larvae bore narrow tunnels in oak, ash and beech, leaving small heaps of wood splinters near the pinholes which they make.

OAK PRUNER. *Hypermallus villosus*, a small elongated beetle that lays its eggs beneath the bark of young oak twigs. The developing larvae then eat out the inside of the twig until it is sufficiently weakened to break off.

OAK ROLLER. See *Green Oak Moth*.

OAK ROOT-GALLS. Galls on the roots of oak trees, produced by the same gall-wasp *Biorhiza pallida* that produces oak apples. The life-cycle of the insect

201

involves alternation of generations. Females that emerge from the oak apple, after being fertilized, crawl down and lay their eggs on the young roots of the oak tree. These produce root-galls which are brown, clustered together and about the size of peas. The insects that emerge from these are all wingless, parthenogenetic females which crawl up the stem and lay their eggs in the oak buds to produce a new crop of oak apples (see *Gall, Gall-wasp* and *Oak Apple*).

OAK UGLY-NEST TORTRICID. *Cacoecia fervidana*, a small moth of the family Tortricidae which lays its eggs in a cluster on the bark of an oak tree. The gregarious larvae attack the young buds, rolling and tying the leaves together with silk threads to form an 'ugly nest' in which they pupate.

OAT FLY. An alternative name for the Frit Fly (*Oscinella frit*, family Chloropidae), a minute black fly whose larvae bore into the stems of oats and other cereals.

OBEREA. *Oberea bimaculata*, the Raspberry Cane Borer: a small beetle of the family Cerambycidae whose larvae bore downwards into raspberry canes, working their way from the top towards the roots and hollowing out the stem as they go.

OBRIMUS. *Obrimus asperrimus*, a phasmid or stick insect from Borneo having the head, thorax and legs covered with sharp thorns.

OBTECT PUPA. The type of pupa or chrysalis found in most butterflies and moths in which the wings and appendages are glued down to the body and most of the abdominal segments are immovable.

OCCIPITAL FORAMEN. An opening in the back of an insect's head through which the oesophagus, nerve cord etc. enter the thorax.

OCCIPITAL REGION (OCCIPUT). The back of the head, where it joins the thorax; in a restricted sense the area between the vertex and the neck.

OCEANIC INSECTS. Conditions in the sea are generally unfavourable to insect life. There are, however, one or two noteworthy exceptions. The best known are the two species of *Halobates*, water skaters of the family Gerridae. *Halobates micans* is found off the coast of Florida; *Halobates sericeus* off California. Both these have been found feeding on floating organic debris several hundred miles from the coast. These insects are strictly only semi-aquatic as they breathe air from the atmosphere. *Pontomyia natans*, a chironomid gnat, skates on the surface like *Halobates*; it is found in the lagoons of Samoa and other Pacific islands. Some Chironomidae of the subfamily Clunioninae penetrate below the surface, but only temporarily and by utilizing trapped pockets of air, *e.g.* among a colony of mussels.

OCELLUS. (1) A simple eye consisting of a few sensory cells and a single cuticular lens; present in some insect larvae and in many adults. The ocelli of larvae are lateral; those of adults are dorsal and have a different nerve supply.
(2) An eye-spot or eye-like pattern on the wing of a butterfly or moth.

OCHLODES. A genus of Hesperiid butterflies including the Large Skipper *Ochlodes venatus*, found throughout the temperate parts of Europe and Asia as far as China and Japan; a small, tawny brown butterfly with margins of darker brown and yellow spots. The male has an oblique black streak on the fore-wings. The larvae feed on grasses and make tube-like nests from grass blades.

OCHROPLEURA. See *Flame Shoulder Moth.*

OCHTHERA. *Ochthera mantis*, the Killer Shore-fly: a minute black fly of the family Ephydridae whose aquatic larvae feed on carrion and sewage. The adults are predators using their spiny front legs to catch small gnats and mosquitoes in flight (see *Ephydridae*).

OCYPUS. See *Devil's Coach-horse.*

ODONATA. Dragonflies: large hemimetabolous insects with long brightly coloured bodies and two pairs of membranous wings with numerous cross-veins. The jaws are large and powerful for seizing small insects in flight; the eyes are very well developed but the antennae are small. The aquatic nymph or larva is predatory and is characterized by an elongated prehensile labium forming the so-called *mask*. The order is divided into two suborders, *viz.* Zygoptera or Damselflies and Anisoptera or true dragonflies.

The Odonata are closely related to the *Protodonata* which are found as Palaeozoic fossils and sometimes attained great size with a wing expanse exceeding 60 cm.

ODONESTIS. *Odonestis potatoria*, the Drinker Moth which is sometimes also named *Philudoria potatoria* or *Cosmotriche potatoria* (see *Drinker Moth*).

ODONOPTERA. A name occasionally used synonymously with Odonata (*q.v.*).

ODONTOCERUM. A genus of caddis flies whose larvae make tubes of sand grains in the form of a curved horn wider at the front and narrowing to an apex at the hind-end.

ODONTOLABIS. *Odontolabis alces*, a stag beetle of the family Lucanidae from South-east Asia; dark brown, flattened, about 10 cm. long and 3 cm. wide: the largest known stag beetle.

ODONTOMYIA. A genus of Soldier Flies of the family Stratiomyidae commonly found on Umbelliferous plants near water. The larvae are grey, legless and aquatic with a tapering hind-end which pierces the surface of the water and contains spiracles with which they breathe.

ODONTOTERMES. A genus of termites (Isoptera) in which the soldier caste have large, heavily armoured heads and very powerful jaws; *Odontotermes obesus*, the Indian termite and *Odontotermes formosanus* from Southern China and Taiwan.

ODYNERUS. A genus of solitary Potter Wasps of the family Eumenidae that make hard, flask-shaped nests of clay in which they store paralysed caterpillars as food for the developing larvae.

OECANTHUS. A genus of tree-crickets of the family Tettigoniidae, generally green and with very long antennae. The Snowy Tree-cricket *Oecanthus niveus* of North America lays its eggs in holes cut in young twigs. The developing larvae eat away the insides of the twigs and fungi then take over, eventually causing the death of the tree.

OECOPHORIDAE. A family of small moths whose caterpillars live between two pieces of leaf which they fasten together with silk to make a portable protective shelter from which they feed.

OECOPHYLLA. A genus of ants that construct sack-like nests of leaves and silk with extraordinary skill using silk produced from the labial glands of ant-larvae. A large number of ants co-operate in this work, some holding the edges of two leaves together while others carry the larvae in their jaws and manipulate them in such a way that the silk from these binds the edges of the leaves together.

OECOPTOMA. *Oecoptoma thoracicum*, a carrion beetle of the family Silphidae having a broad, oval-shaped body with a brick-red thorax. Eggs are laid either on carrion or on putrid fungi on which both larvae and adults feed.

OEDEMERIDAE. Flower Beetles: a family of brightly coloured, elongated, soft-bodied beetles with long filamentous antennae. The adults feed on flowers and the larvae on dead wood. *Oedemera nobilis*, the Thick-legged Flower Beetle, is about 1 cm. long, bright green and shiny with narrow, parallel-sided elytra. The males have thickened hind-legs.

OEDIPODA. A genus of grasshoppers whose hind-wings are brightly coloured red, blue or yellow due to the presence of carotenoid pigments combined with various proteins. The rest of the body and the front wings or *tegmina* are usually cryptically coloured with grey or brown so that the insect is well camouflaged when at rest but exhibits the 'flash colours' of its wind-wings as soon as it flies. *Oedipoda germanica*, the red species, is found in mountains of Central Europe; *Oedipoda caerulescens*, the blue species, inhabits heaths and dry quarries or waste-land in Southern Europe, North Africa and Asia Minor.

OEMIDA. A genus of longhorn beetles of the family Cerambycidae: pests of hardwood forests and structural timbers in South and East Africa.

OENEIS. *Oeneis semidea*, the White Mountain Butterfly of North America, a small species with a wing-pattern of marbled grey and brown, found high up in isolated regions of the White Mountains and the Rocky Mountains; an example of discontinuous distribution of a cold-loving species.

OENOCYTES. Large cells present in various parts of the bodies of insects, probably producing a hormone connected with the moulting process. They are usually amber, but may be of other colours, or colourless.

OENOCYTOIDS. Rounded acidophil corpuscles of unknown function in the blood of insects.

OESOPHAGEAL GANGLIA. A pair of small ganglia behind the main parts of an insect's brain and joined to it by thin connecting nerves. They rest upon the dorsal surface of the oesophagus, are closely connected with the *corpora allata* and form part of the visceral or sympathetic system (see also *Nervous System*).

OESTRIDAE. Warble Flies and Bot Flies: Diptera that lay their eggs on the hairs, lips or nostrils of cattle, horses and other animals. The larvae may hatch out after the eggs have been swallowed or they may bore into the skin. They develop inside the body of the victim, penetrate the tissues and eventually emerge leaving tiny holes in the skin. *Hypoderma bovis*, the Cattle Warble Fly is a well known enemy to the farmer and to the leather industry. The Bot Fly of horses has a similar life-history but the mature larvae pass out with the faeces instead of through the skin. For this and other reasons warble flies and bot flies are sometimes classed in two different families. In some related species such as the Sheep Nostril Fly, *Oestrus ovis*, the female insect deposits live larvae instead of eggs (see *Bot Fly, Gasterophilus* and *Hypoderma*).

OIL BEETLE. See *Meloidae*.

OLD LADY MOTH. See *Mormo*.

OLEANDER HAWK-MOTH. *Daphnis nerii*, a handsome hawk-moth of Southern Europe, North Africa and Asia Minor; a very rare visitor to Britain. It has a wing-span of about 10 cm. and is coloured in an elaborate pattern of green and pink. The caterpillar is yellowish green with a white stripe along each side and with two blue and black spots behind the head.

OLETHREUTIDAE. A large family of small moths whose larvae are destructive pests of fruit trees, feeding on leaves, flowers and fruit. The Codling Moth *Cydia pomonella* or *Carpocapsa pomonella*, whose larvae attack apples and pears, is one of the best known. Others such as *Olethreutes nimbatana* and *Olethreutes cyanana* bore into rose buds. Many of the family are leaf-rollers, *i.e.* the larvae make nests by rolling or folding leaves and binding them together with silk threads (see *Leaf-rollers* and *Leaf-folders*).

OLFACTORY PITS. Small pits on the antennae and sometimes also on the palps of insects, containing a number of hair-like receptors and nerve connections by which the insect has a sense of smell (see *Olfactory Sense*).

OLFACTORY SENSE. Many insects have an extremely efficient sense of smell by which they are attracted to the food-plant or to a potential mate. Some moths and butterflies, for instance, will fly very great distances apparently attracted by the scent glands of the opposite sex. Chemo-receptors of various kinds are generally distributed over the antennae but are sometimes also on the palps. It has been estimated that each antenna of a drone bee may have as many as 30,000 such receptors. Sometimes, as for instance in the house fly and related flies, there are definite olfactory organs each consisting of a small pit with a number of hair-like cells connected to nerve endings. The antennae may be held out in a particular direction when the insect is flying so that these pits are exposed to the flow of air and the maximum sense of smell is achieved.

OLFERSIA. A genus of two-winged blood-sucking flies of the family Hippoboscidae, parasitic on owls and hawks. A few are very specific in their host, *e.g. Olfersia spinifera* on Frigate Birds.

OLIGONEOPTERA. A group name used in some systems of classification to denote insects with a substantial degree of reduction in the number of veins in the wings. These are the orders usually classed as Holometabola or Endopterygota.

OLIGOPHAGOUS. Having a very restricted range of food or, in the case of parasites, infesting a limited number of host species.

OLIGOPNEUSTIC. Having a reduced number of spiracles (see *Breathing*).

OLIGOPOD LARVA. A larva with well-developed thoracic legs but no abdominal prolegs. There are two types, *viz.* (a) *Campodeiform* larvae (*q.v.*) which are usually active predators, and (b) *Scarabaeiform* larvae which are grub-like with a very swollen, soft abdomen. (See *Insect Larvae, Apodous, Polypod, Campodeiform, Scarabaeiform*.)

OLIVE SKIPPER. *Pyrgus serratulae*, a small butterfly of the family Hesperiidae having an elaborate chequerboard type of wing pattern in olive green or brown and white; found in mountainous regions of central and southern Europe and western Asia. The caterpillars feed on *Potentilla* and other herbaceous members of the Rosaceae.

OMMATIDIUM. A single optical unit of the compound eye of an insect or crustacean. Each ommatidium is a cone-shaped structure consisting of a cuticular lens, a crystalline cone and *retinulae* or sensitive cells at the base. The whole eye is roughly hemispherical with all the ommatidia converging inwards towards the optic nerve (see *Compound Eyes*).

OMMOCHROME PIGMENTS. Red, brown or yellow pigments which give the characteristic eye-colours of many insects but are sometimes also found in other parts of the body: derivatives of the amino-acid *tryptophane* (see also *Insectorubin*).

OMOCESTUS. A common genus of grasshoppers: *Omocestus viridulus*, the Common Green Grasshopper is one of the best known European grassland species about 15–20 mm. long with elytra and wings as long as the abdomen. The colour varies from emerald to olive green with some brown, especially on the legs. *Omocestus rufipes*, the Woodland Grasshopper and *Omocestus ventralis*, the Red-bellied Grasshopper are less common (see *Grasshopper*).

OMPHALOSCELIS. See *Lunar Underwing Moth*.

OMUS. A genus of black, wingless Tiger Beetles of the family Cicindelidae: nocturnal predatory beetles common in North America and elsewhere.

ONCIDERES. *Oncideres cingulatus*, a small wood-boring beetle of the 'girdling' type whose larvae feed on the soft wood of pear, peach and other trees. The female girdles a twig, boring beneath the bark till she has completely encircled it and so checks its growth before laying her eggs.

ONCOMERA. A genus of Flower Beetles of the family Oedemeridae having a long narrow body, tapering wing-cases and long thread-like antennae. *Oncomera femorata* is a common nocturnal species found on ivy, willows and other trees. The male is characterized by a thickening of the femora (see *Oedemeridae*).

ONCOPELTUS. A genus of Chinchbugs, plant-sucking hemipteran bugs of the family Lygaeidae. *Oncopeltus fasciatus* is a large North American species, bright red with a black band across both wings and a black spot on the centre of the thorax. It feeds on the American milkweed, *Asclepias curassivica* and can transmit protozoan parasites from one plant to another.

ONION FLY. A name for a number of flower flies of the family Anthomyidae whose larvae are pests of onions and similar plants. *Delia antiqua*, a common species of Europe and elsewhere, lays its eggs on the young leaves of the onion plant; the newly hatched larvae then move down the stem and enter the bulb on which they feed. *Hylemyia antiqua*, the Onion Fly of North America, is the European species introduced.

ONION MAGGOT. See *Onion Fly*.

ONION THRIPS. *Thrips tabaci*, a small insect of the order Thysanoptera having fringed wings with a span of about 2 mm. The sap-sucking larvae are serious pests not only of onions and related plants but also of ragwort, yarrow and a number of other wild and garden flowers.

ONISCIFORM LARVA. A larva resembling a wood-louse, as for instance the caterpillars of the Lycaenid butterflies (Blues, Coppers and Hairstreaks).

ONOMARCHUS. *Onomarchus cretaceus*, a large long-horned grasshopper from Assam whose appearance, when the wings are folded, is like a large greenish yellow leaf. Countless numbers of these roost in trees and are perfectly camouflaged.

ONTHOPHAGUS. *Onthophagus rangifer*, a large Central African dung-beetle of the family Scarabaeidae, coppery red with two very prominent antler-like horns.

ONYCHIUM. A term applied to a variety of hook-like or pad-like structures associated with the feet of insects.

ONYCHIURUS. A genus of Collembola or springtails noted for their luminescence, a phenomenon rare in this group (see *Light-producing Organs*).

OOCYTES. The egg-cells within an ovariole (see *Ovariole*).

OOTHECA. A horny egg-case or capsule, as for instance that of the cockroach, formed by the hardening óf a sticky secretion from the colleterial glands.

OPATRUM. *Opatrum sabulosum*, the Dust Beetle: a small, flat, grey beetle about 8 mm. long belonging to the family Tenebrionidae; both adults and larvae are pests of vines.

OPEN BLOOD SYSTEM (OPEN CIRCULATION). A system characteristic of insects and other arthropods in which the blood is not contained in arteries, veins and capillaries but fills all the body cavities (see *Blood*).

OPEROPHTERA. *Operophtera brumata*, the Winter Moth: a small brown geometrid moth whose females are wingless. After emerging from the pupa at the base of a tree these wingless females crawl up the trunk of the tree, are fertilized by winged males and then lay their eggs in bark crevices or buds. The green caterpillars feed on leaves of many kinds causing extensive defoliation.

OPHION. *Ophion luteus* and related species: large Ichneumon flies about 20 mm. long that lay their eggs in the bodies of caterpillars. The body is yellow or orange and the abdomen is flattened. The ovipositor is relatively shorter than those of most ichneumons. They are attracted by light and are often found in houses.

OPHTHALMOPHORA. *Ophthalmophora claudiaria*, a large brownish Brazilian moth whose hind-wings each have a most realistic eye-spot; a black circle ringed with gold and with white markings in the centre suggesting the reflection of light from a cornea.

OPISTHOGRAPTIS. See *Brimstone Moth*.

OPORINA. See *November Moth*.

OPTIC LOBES. Lateral expansions of the protocerebrum of an insect innervating the compound eyes and ocelli; they form the largest part of an insect's brain and are situated immediately above the oesophagus (see *Brain* and *Nervous System*).

OPTICON. The inner zone, or internal medullary mass of the optic lobes (see *Periopticon* and *Epiopticon*).

ORANGE DOG. The caterpillar of the Giant Swallowtail Butterfly *Papilio thoas*, a pest of orange and other citrus trees in California, Mexico, Central and South America.

ORANGE MOTH. *Angerona prunaria*, a medium sized moth of the family Selidosemidae having all the wings deep orange speckled with grey; the females are slightly lighter in colour but otherwise similar to the males. The larvae feed on hawthorn, sloe, beech and other trees.

ORANGE TIP. *Anthocharis cardamines*, a European butterfly related to the Whites of the family Pieridae. The background colour of the wings is greenish white but the males have bright orange patches on and near the tips of the fore-wings. Both sexes have a mottled green pattern on the undersides. The caterpillars are green and, like those of the Cabbage White Butterfly, feed on leaves and seed pods of cruciferous plants.

ORANGE UNDERWING. *Archiearis parthenias*, a small geometrid moth having the front wings brown with wavy transverse bands of darker brown and white; the hind-wings are orange with patches of brown. The caterpillars are green with longitudinal stripes of lighter green or yellow; they feed on birch.

ORCHESELLA. *Orchesella flavescens*, a bright yellowish, hairy insect of the order Collembola or springtails, about 5 mm. long; a Central European species that lives and feeds on moss.

ORCHESTES. A genus of small weevils whose larvae are leaf-miners. *Orchestes fagi*, the Beech Leaf-miner, is grey-black and about 2 mm. long; the larvae tunnel between the upper and lower surfaces of beech leaves. *Orchestes (Rhynchaenus) pallicornis*, the Apple Flea-weevil, is a similar insect from the United States, a pest of apple, cherry, alder, willow, elm etc.

ORECTOCHILUS. *Orectochilus villosus*, the Hairy Whirligig Beetle: a small, brown, elongated beetle about 4 mm. long, living in running water, gyrating on the surface at night and hiding by day. Eggs are laid on water plants and larvae live on the bottom (see *Gyrinidae*).

OREOPSYCHE. *Oreopsyche plumifera*, a Bagworm Moth of the family Psychidae living in forests and mountainous regions of Central Europe. The body is black and very hairy; the wings, with a span of 15 mm. are without scales and almost transparent. The caterpillars spin bag-like homes similar to those of caddis worms (see *Bagworms*).

ORGANS OF HEARING. See *Hearing Organs*.

ORGYIA. *Orgyia antiqua*, the Vapourer Moth: a Tussock Moth of the family Lymantriidae. The male is brown with a small but prominent white triangle on each fore-wing. The female has the wings reduced to stumps and is unable to fly. She does not move far and lays her eggs on the remains of the silken cocoon from which she has emerged. The members of this family are generally very hairy, have reduced mouth-parts and the males have comb-like antennae. The caterpillars, which feed on oak, lime, hawthorn etc., are black, red and yellow with tufts of yellow hairs all along the back and extra long ones at the two ends. As in many hairy caterpillars, these secrete an irritant poison.

ORIENTAL FRUIT MOTH. See *Grapholitha*.

ORIENTAL MEADOW BROWN. *Hyponephele lupina*, a Satyrid butterfly similar in appearance to the common European Meadow Brown but much paler; the fore-wings are yellowish, edged with light brown and with a small black circular eye-spot; the hind-wings are light brown. It is found in mountainous parts from Spain to the Himalayas.

ORIENTAL SKIPPER. *Carcharodus orientalis*, a small butterfly of the family Hesperiidae with a chequerboard wing-pattern of smoky black or grey and white; found in mountainous parts of Eastern Europe and Western Asia.

ORIUS. A genus of flower bugs of the family Anthocoridae: small, flattened, predatory insects useful in controlling agricultural pests. *Orius insidiosus* of North America preys on pests of maize.

ORNATE CRANE-FLY. *Ctenophora ornata*, a common European crane-fly of the family Tipulidae, about 18 mm. long with a thick body and yellowish wings each with a brown patch near the apex.

ORNEODIDAE. Many-plume Moths: small brownish moths whose wings are divided to form six feather-like plumes; common in Africa and Asia but rare in Europe. *Orneodes grammodactyla* with a wing-span of 7 mm. is a species of Central and Southern Europe and Asia Minor; the larvae feed on Scabious. *Orneodes hexadactyla*, also called *Alucita hexadactyla*, is a more common European species whose larvae feed on honeysuckle (see *Alucitidae* and *Many-plume Moth*).

ORNITHOICA. A genus of blood-sucking flies of the family Hippoboscidae, parasites on many wild birds; *e.g. Ornithoica turdi* on thrushes and other hedgerow birds. (See *Hippoboscidae*.)

ORNITHOMYIA. A genus of blood-sucking flies of the family Hippoboscidae, parasitic on birds. As with most flies of this family, eggs are not laid but fully formed larvae are dropped, usually into the nests of the birds they infest. Host selection is by habitat rather than by bird species; thus *Ornithomyia avicularia* on woodland birds; *Ornithomyia fringillina* on hedgerow birds; *Ornithomyia chloropus* on moorland birds.

ORNITHOPTERA. Birdwings; a genus of brilliantly coloured papilionid butterflies from South-east Asia, New Guinea and Australia, including some of the largest butterflies in the world. The fore-wings are usually narrow and much longer than the hing-wings. The colours generally include bright greens, blues and yellow with borders and veins outlined in black. The males often differ markedly from the females. *Ornithoptera alexandrae* of New Guinea has a span of 25 cm.; *Ornithoptera paradisea* and *Ornithoptera goliath*, also from New Guinea, are nearly as large. *Ornithoptera priamus*, slightly smaller, is a common species of Australia with many regional variations.

OROSIUS. *Orosius argentatus*, a leaf-hopper of the family Cicadellidae that spreads the virus of Yellow Dwarf disease of tobacco in Australia and other countries.

ORTHRETUM. *Orthretum caerulescens*, a small European dragonfly having a brown and cream thorax, a blue abdomen in the male and a pale brown abdomen in the female. The fore-wings are edged with yellow.

ORTHEZIIDAE. See *Nettle Scale-insect*

ORTHOKINESIS. A simple reaction of insects by which a particular stimulus can cause them to move in a straight line but they come to rest as soon as the stimulus is removed.

ORTHOPELMA. *Orthopelma luteolator*, an Ichneumon Fly whose larva parasitizes that of the gall-wasp *Diplolepis rosae* which is itself a parasite of the wild rose and produces the gall known as the 'Robin's Pincushion'.

ORTHOPODOMYIA. A genus of woodland mosquitoes found chiefly in America and Asia. The larvae are generally to be found in water that collects in tree-holes. The only European species, *Orthopodomyia pulchripalpis*, has bands of white round the proboscis, the palps and the hind tarsi.

ORTHOPTERA. Straight-winged insects: a large order of Hemimetabola with biting mouth-parts and usually having the head bent at right angles to the body. The fore-wings are thickened to form horny tegmina which cover the folded membranous hind-wings; a few species are wingless. The order includes crickets, locusts, grasshoppers etc. Cockroaches and mantids, which were formerly classed as Orthoptera, are now placed in a separate order Dictyoptera.

ORTHORRHAPHA. Two-winged flies whose pupae split longitudinally along the mid-dorsal line. They include the *Nematocera* (with long antennae) and the *Brachycera* (with short antennae). Gnats, mosquitoes and crane-flies belong to the former group; horse flies and robber flies to the latter.

ORTHOSIA. A genus of noctuid moths which includes the Hebrew Character, the Small and Large Quaker Moths, the Clouded Drab Moth and several others. All are rather small, brownish, inconscpicuous moths whose caterpillars are green with longitudinal lines of white or yellow. They are found chiefly on willows and poplars but occasionally on oak, birch and other trees.

ORTHOSOMA. A genus of Longhorn Beetles (Cerambycidae) found in North America and elsewhere. *Orthosóma brunneum*, a shiny, light reddish brown insect, is about 4 cm. long. Its white grub-like larvae feed on logs and dead tree-stumps, chiefly oak.

ORUSSOIDEA. A small group of sawflies, also called Idiogastra, differing from others in having a slender, curved ovipositor. Their legless larvae are ectoparasites on the larvae of wood-boring beetles. The group is sometimes regarded as being intermediate between the Apocrita (bees, ants and wasps) and the Symphyta (true sawflies).

ORYCTES. *Oryctes nasicornis*, the European Rhinoceros Beetle: a member of the family Dynastidae about 5 cm. long with a prominent 'horn' on the front of the thorax. The worm-like larvae live in rotting wood and peat.

ORYSSIDAE. See *Orussoidea*.

OSCINELLA. See *Frit Fly*.

OSCINOSOMA. A genus of Frit flies: minute black two-winged flies whose larvae bore into the stems of cereals and grasses.

OSIRIS BLUE. A small blue butterfly of the family Lycaenidae found high up in the mountains of southern and eastern Europe. The larvae feed on leguminous plants.

OSMETERIUM. A gland consisting of an eversible sac or pocket in which a repellent scent or other secretion collects. Such glands are found in many caterpillars including those of the Puss Moth and the Swallowtail Butterfly. When attacked the insect causes this pocket to be suddenly everted, dispersing the scent and acting as an efficient defence mechanism.

OSMIA. A common genus of Mason Bees of the family Megachilidae. *Osmia rufa* and *Osmia bicolor* are two common European species. The former nests in cracks of old buildings; the latter in empty snail-shells (see *Mason Bees*).

OSMYLIDAE. Giant Lacewing-flies: insects belonging to the order Neuroptera and closely related to the green and brown lacewing-flies though considerably larger. They are to be found along banks of woodland streams where there is dense overhanging vegetation. The larvae live in wet moss or under stones.

OSTIA. Openings by which blood flows into the heart from the pericardial sinus in insects and other arthropods (see *Blood*).

OTHIUS. A woodland beetle of the family Staphylinidae which are characterized by having very short elytra. *Othius fulvipennis* is a small European species about 9 mm. long, black with red legs, antennae and elytra and with yellow hairs on the abdomen.

OTHREIS. *Othreis fullonia*, a noctuid moth whose fruit-piercing larvae are pests of citrus plants in West Africa.

OTIORRHYNCHUS. A genus of wingless, thick-mouthed weevils from Europe, North America and other parts. They can breed parthenogenetically and are serious pests of many trees and agricultural crops. *Otiorrhynchus clavipes*, the Coal-black Weevil, is a European species about 1 cm. long, common on trees of chalk and limestone districts; *Otiorrhynchus sulcatus* attacks strawberry plants.

OURAPTERYX. *Ourapteryx sambucaria*, the Swallow-tailed Moth: a medium sized geometrid moth of the family Selidosemidae, pale sulphur-yellow with two thin greenish brown transverse lines on the fore-wings and one on each hind-wing. Short pointed tails edged and spotted with reddish brown extend back from the hind-wings. The larvae are greenish brown and very stick-like; they feed on leaves of ivy, privet, hawthorn, oak and other trees. The yellow pigment of the adult, like that of the Brimstone Moth, is brilliantly fluorescent in ultra-violet light.

OVARIOLE. One of the separate egg-tubes or branches of the ovary. There are two main types: *panoistic* in which there are no specialized nurse-cells, and *meroistic* which have nurse-cells or *trophocytes*, distinct from the *oocytes* or egg-cells. Meroistic ovarioles again fall into two groups: *telotrophic* with the trophocytes all gathered together at one end, and *polytriophic* where each oocyte has its own nurse-cells.

OVARY. An insect normally has two ovaries or egg-producing organs leading into a common duct. Each ovary is composed of a number of separate branches or *ovarioles* in which eggs are produced. Primitive insects such as the cockroach have only 8 ovarioles in each ovary but specialized insects like the queen bee may have more than 200. In each ovariole the oocytes are produced in the *germarium* near the distal tip of the tube and as they move down they develop into eggs which may be nourished by special food-cells or *trophocytes*. The latter may be scattered throughout the ovariole (polytrophic) or concentrated at the apex (acrotrophic or telotrophic). (See also *Female Reproductive System, Genitalia* and *Ovariole*.)

OVIDUCT. In most insects each of the two ovaries has its own duct into which eggs from the ovarioles are discharged. These two ducts join to form a median oviduct which, in embryo and primitive insects, has an opening (gonopore) in the 8th abdominal segment (7th in Dermaptera). In most present-day insects this original aperture is closed and the oviduct becomes connected to a wider duct or *vagina* with an opening in the 9th abdominal segment. Accessory glands or *colleterial* glands open into the vagina, the function of these being to produce a glue-like substance which either forms a capsule to enclose the eggs or cement to attach them to leaves or other objects on which they are laid (see also *Ovary* and *Genitalia*).

OVIPOSITOR. A specialized egg-laying organ which, in most insects, is formed from outgrowths of the 8th and 9th abdominal segments. There are six of these outgrowths known as *valves* and they may be modified to form a variety of structures. In some insects they are short and compact but in others they are drawn out into a long stylet-like tube, the channel of which is generally formed from the anterior and posterior valves. This lengthening is shown in its most extreme form in the sawflies, wood-wasps and ichneumons some of which have an ovipositor longer than the whole body. Although, in a general way primitive insects have less complex ovipositors, the form of these is usually more obviously related to egg-laying habits than directly to ancestry. Thus the long-horned grasshoppers (Tettigoniidae) have a large and conspicuous ovipositor. In such an advanced order as Diptera many have little or no ovipositor, while others have highly complicated ones. In worker bees and wasps (sterile females) the ovipositor has become modified to form the sting.

OWL BUTTERFLIES. Large handsome butterflies of the genus *Caligo*: members of the family Brassolidae found in Central and South America. The upper sides are variously coloured with iridescent blues, purple and orange. The undersides are mottled with brown and white and have two enormous eye-spots on the back of the hind-wings. These give the butterfly an owl-like appearance when seen from below. The largest of the Owl Butterflies is *Caligo atreus*, about 15 cm. across. The larvae feed on banana leaves.

OWLET MOTH. See *Noctuidae*.

OX BEETLE. *Strataegus antaeus*, a large Central American beetle of the family Dynastidae, reddish brown with three large 'horns' on the front of the thorax of the male and one on the female.

OX BOT FLY. A name sometimes given to the Warble Fly *Hypoderma bovis* (see *Hypoderma*).

OX WARBLE FLY. See *Hypoderma*.

OXYBELUS. *Oxybelus uniglumis*, the Spiny Digger Wasp: a hunting wasp of the family Sphecidae having a yellow and black abdomen and a black thorax with a short but distinct neck connecting it to the head. The thorax has a spine at the back and wing-like lateral outgrowths. The nests are made in sandy places and stocked with flies as food for the larvae.

OXYCANUS. *Oxycanus cervinatus*, a New Zealand moth allied to the Swift Moths (Hepialidae). The larvae are pests of grassland and clover.

OXYCARENUS. A genus of plant-bugs of the family Lygaeidae: pests of cotton seed in Africa, India and other countries.

OXYCERA. *Oxycera pulchella* and others: small two-winged flies coloured like wasps and belonging to the family of Soldier Flies (Stratiomyidae): day-flying insects of damp places whose larvae are aquatic.

OXYPODA. *Oxypoda alternans* and related species: small, brownish Rove Beetles (Staphylinidae) found in decaying fungi.

OXYPORUS. *Oxyporus rufus*, a small European Rove Beetle of the family Staphylinidae, about 12 mm. long, black but with part of the thorax and the front of the abdomen orange. It is found among woodland fungi on which both adults and larvae feed.

OXYTELUS. A genus of very small Rove Beetles (Staphylinidae) having a flattened, shiny body with a ridged thorax. *Oxytelus laquaetus* has short orange coloured elytra; *Oxytelus tetracarinatus* is black all over. Both of these are only 2 or 3 mm. long and are found in cow dung.

OYSTER-SHELL SCALE. A name given to several members of the family Coccidae in which the wingless females are covered with a tiny shell-like scale formed from cast-off skins. The Mussel-scale *Lepidosaphes ulmi* is sometimes called an oyster-shell scale but the name is also given to another species *Quadraspidiotus ostreaeformis* (see *Lepidosaphes* and *Coccidae*).

P

PACHYNEMATUS. See *Grass Sawfly*.

PACHYPASA. *Pachypasa otus*, a moth of the family Lasiocampidae whose larvae produce silk and have been cultivated for its production in Mediterranean regions since Ancient Greek times. They feed on oak and cypress. The adult moth is grey-brown with two dark zig-zag lines on the fore-wings; it is closely related to the Eggars, Lackey, Lappet and Drinker moths.

PACHYRHINA. *Pachyrhina maculata*, the Striped Crane-fly: a common European species having a yellow and black striped abdomen. The larvae (leatherjackets) are common pests of farms and gardens.

PACHYSCHELUS. A North American genus of leaf-mining beetles of the family Buprestidae whose larvae tunnel between the upper and lower surfaces of leaves and make pupal cases from two circular pieces of leaves fastened together with silk.

PACHYTA. A genus of long-bodied, slender beetles with long antennae and yellowish brown elytra marked with black spots; common on Umbelliferous plants.

PACHYZANELLA. A genus of moths of the family Pyralidae whose larvae feed on grasses and make tubular nests of silk, soil and vegetable matter.

PAEDERUS. A genus of Rove Beetles of the family Staphylinidae having short elytra and reduced wings. *Paederus litoralis*, found under stones near the seashore, is about 6 mm. long, black with reddish yellow antennae, legs and thorax and the basal part of the abdomen. *Paederus riparius* is a similar species found on river banks.

PAEDOGENESIS. Precocious maturity: the production of offspring, usually parthenogenetically, by an immature or larval animal. Among insects the best known case is that of the gall-midge *Miastor* whose larvae may give birth to twenty or thirty daughter larvae which eat their way out of the body of the parent. This process may be repeated for many generations, pupae and adults being only rarely produced. Paedogenesis also occurs in some beetle larvae such as that of *Micromalthus*.

PAINTED BEAUTY. *Vanessa virginiensis*, a North American nymphalid butterfly smaller but otherwise very similar in appearance to the European Painted Lady *Vanessa cardui*. Both are predominantly orange with dark brown patches and white spots. The American species occasionally migrates to Western Europe and has become established in Madeira and the Canary Islands. The larvae feed on plants of the family Compositae.

PAINTED LADY. *Vanessa cardui*, a medium sized nymphalid butterfly found in most parts of the world except South America; rosy-orange with patches of dark brown and with irregular white spots near the tips of the fore-wings. The larvae feed on thistles and nettles.

PALAEODICTYOPTERA. Primitive insects of the Carboniferous period resembling dragonflies but having a pair of short wing-like appendages on most of the segments of the body. Possibly in the first place these helped the insect to glide and at a later stage two pairs became greatly enlarged to form true wings.

PALAEOPTERA. A group of insects comprising the two orders Ephemeroptera (mayflies) and Odonata (dragonflies) both of which have primitive wing venation.

PALE BRINDLED BEAUTY. *Apocheima pilosaria*, a small geometrid moth whose males have smoky brown or greenish grey wings with a pattern of transverse wavy lines and dots of darker brown. The hind-wings are paler than the fore-wings but otherwise similar; the females are wingless. The moth is common in forests all over Europe where the brown stick-like larvae feed on the leaves and wood of oak, elm, hawthorn etc.

PALE CLOUDED YELLOW. *Colias hyale*, a Pierid butterfly of Eastern and

Northern Europe and an occasional visitor to Britain. The female is greenish white and the male primrose yellow. Both have wing-borders mottled with black, widening to a double black patch at the tips of the fore-wings. In both sexes there is a black dot in the centre of each fore-wing and a bright orange dot in the centre of each hind-wing. The larvae feed on clover and other leguminous plants.

PALE EARWIG. *Forficula lesnei*, a wingless earwig smaller and paler than the Common Earwig *Forficula auricularia* but otherwise similar.

PALE MOTTLED WILLOW MOTH. *Caradrina clavipalpis*, a small noctuid moth with white hind-wings and pale brown fore-wings dotted with black. The larvae are light brown, smooth caterpillars that feed on a variety of grasses and other plants and are sometimes a pest of grain crops.

PALE OAK EGGAR. *Trichiura crataegi*, a small moth of the family Lasiocampidae having ashy grey wings with a dark central band and dark marginal dots. The hind-wings of the male are lighter than those of the female. The larvae feed on hawthorn (*Crataegus*).

PALE TUSSOCK. *Dasychira pudibunda*, a European moth of the family Lymantriidae; pale grey with wavy transverse lines and dots of darker grey. The larvae are yellow with black markings and with numerous tufts or tussocks of white hairs. There is a bright red pencil of hairs on the eleventh segment. They feed on beech, birch and oak.

PALEACRITA. *Paleacrita vernata*, the Spring Cankerworm Moth: a small brownish geometrid moth of North America whose wingless females lay their eggs on various fruit trees on which the larvae feed. They are destructive pests and an unsuccessful attempt was made to combat them by introducing the English sparrow into North America.

PALISADE SAWFLY. *Stauronematus compressicornis*, a small black sawfly about 5 mm. long whose green larvae feed on poplar leaves and construct 'palisades' of dried saliva surrounding the part of the leaf on which they are feeding.

PALM-BORER BEETLE. *Rhynchophorus palmarum*, a large tropical weevil, blackish with a conspicuous pointed snout, whose white maggot-like larvae do considerable damage to the leaves of coconut and date palms.

PALOMENA. *Palomena prasina*, the Green Stinkbug or Green Shieldbug: a plant-bug of the group Heteroptera from Europe, Asia and North Africa, having a dark greenish body, yellowish legs and bright shining green wings, thorax and thoracic shield. The colour changes to brown in the autumn and back to green in the spring. In Europe it feeds chiefly on the juices of bilberries and other fruits but in Britain it is often found in large numbers on hazel trees.

PALP. A sensitive tactile organ, usually near the mouth, on many invertebrates such as polychaetes, molluscs and arthropods. In insects they are on the labium and the maxillae but never on the mandibles. They are often multisegmented and elongate, but may be short, inflated, and equipped with obvious tactile and olfactory cells.

PALPARES. *Palpares libelluloides*, the Giant Ant-lion: an insect of the Mediterranean area having brown-flecked wings with a span of about 15 cm. The wingless larva is very voracious and digs a pit in which it lies in wait for its prey (see *Ant-lion*).

PALPICORNIA. A group of beetles including the vegetarian water beetles

Hydrophilidae, having short antennae and conspicuous, thick palps as long as or longer than the antennae (see *Hydrophilidae*).

PALPIFER (PALPIGER). A lobe bearing a palp, *e.g.* on the maxillae of insects.

PAMPHILIIDAE. A family of wood-wasps or large sawflies having a flattened body, broad wings and a large ovipositor. *Pamphilius sylvaticus*, a common European species, is black with a wing-span of about 2 cm. The larvae live on rose trees where they construct nests of rolled leaves held together with silk. Some species are mainly parthenogenetic, and males are rare.

PANAXIA. *Panaxia dominula*, the Scarlet Tiger Moth: an arctiid moth that lives in damp forests of Europe and Asia. It is slightly smaller than the Garden Tiger Moth and the fore-wings are black with a greenish sheen and yellow markings; the hind-wings are bright scarlet with black markings. The larvae feed on stinging nettles and a number of other plants.

PANCHLORA. *Panchlora cubensis*, a handsome, pale green cockroach about 3 cm. long from the West Indies.

PANGONIA. *Pangonia longirostris*, a horse fly from India having a proboscis three or four times the length of the body. It uses this to feed from deep flowers, but the female also has mandibles and is able to pierce human skin even through thick clothes. The tribe Philolichini, to which this genus belongs, have the labium elongated to a variable extent, though the piercing stylets (mandibles, maxillae and labrum) remain of the usual length.

PANOISTIC OVARIOLES. Ovarioles or egg-tubes which contain no special feeding cells but secrete a nutrient fluid for the developing eggs; they are found in the more primitive groups of insects (see *Ovary* and *Ovariole*).

PANOLIS. A genus of small, brownish noctuid moths whose larvae feed on pine needles. They are light green with longitudinal stripes of paler green or yellow and are therefore well camouflaged. They pupate in silken cocoons in crevices on the pine trunks or among moss. *Panolis piniperda* is a species that causes extensive damage to European pine forests; *Panolis flammea*, the Pine Beauty, is found on Scots Pines.

PANORPIDAE. A common family of Scorpion-flies (Mecoptera): carnivorous insects with large, biting mouth-parts and membranous wings usually spotted with black or brown. The male has the hind-end of the abdomen turned up like that of a scorpion. It is, however, quite harmless. *Panorpa communis* and *Panorpa germanica* are common European species of damp woodlands and hedgerows; *Panorpa nebulosa* and *Panorpa rufescens* are North American species (see *Mecoptera*).

PANTOGRAPHA. A genus of leaf-rollers: moths whose larvae make tubes by cutting and rolling pieces of leaves and fastening them together with silk threads. They feed from the inside of this roll and, when fully grown, make another one in which they pupate. An example is the Basswood Leaf-roller, *Pantographa limata* which feeds on the North American lime tree or basswood tree *Tilia americana*.

PANTOMORUS. The White-fringed Beetle, a pest of cotton and other crops in North America (see *Naupactis*). Other weevils, formerly placed in this genus and now removed to *Graphognathus* and *Asynonychus*, are pests in South America and Australia.

PANZER'S COCKROACH. *Ectobius panzeri*, sometimes called the Lesser Cockroach: a small European species about 6 mm. long, pale greyish brown

215

with darker dots. The males can fly but the wings and elytra of the female are vestigial. In Britain it is mainly found in coastal regions.

PAPAIPEMA. A genus of noctuid moths whose larvae are root-borers and stalk-borers. They hollow out the root or stalk and live inside the tube so formed. *Papaipema nebris nitella* is a pest of maize and other crops of North America; *Papaipema purpurifascia*, the Columbine Root-borer attacks roots and stems of many garden plants.

PAPER WASPS. Social wasps that build their nests of chewed wood pulp resembling paper. These nests are usually spherical and contain a large number of cells in which the eggs are laid. The construction of the nest is begun by the queen wasp in the spring and enlarged by subsequent generations of workers It is usually in a hole in the ground or under an old tree or similar place. The Common Wasp *Vespula vulgaris* and others of the families Vespidae and Polistidae make nests of this type.

PAPILIONIDAE. Swallowtails and similar butterflies characterized by having 'tails' on the hind-wings. The European Swallowtail *Papilio machaon* is also found in Asia and North Africa while closely related species live in North America. Others of the same family, although not always having wing-tails, include the Giant Birdwings (*Ornithoptera*) of South-east Asia, the Sword-tails of South America, Australia and Indonesia as well as many large and brightly coloured species from Africa and other tropical countries.

PAPILIONOIDEA. A superfamily containing all butterflies. Formerly classed as Rhopalocera, they are now included in the Heteroneura. They may be distinguished from moths by their clubbed antennae and by the absence of frenulum and jugum on the wings (see *Butterfly*).

PAPIRIUS. A common genus of Springtails, sometimes known as 'Garden Fleas' of the order Collembola. *Papirius fuscus* (also called *Dicyrtoma fusca*) is sometimes a pest of young vegetables.

PARACLEMENSIA. *Paraclemensia acerifoliella*, a small moth whose larvae are at first leaf-miners and at a later stage become 'case-bearers'. They cut two oval pieces out of a leaf and make a transportable protective case by fastening these together with silk. They live between these two pieces.

PARAGIOXENOS. A genus of Strepsiptera of the family Stylopidae: minute insects whose larvae and wingless females parasitize bees and other insects causing them to be 'stylopized', *i.e.* causing degeneration or modification of the sexual organs.

PARAGLOSSAE. The two outer lobes of the ligula of an insect (see *Glossae* and *Ligula*).

PARAMERES. A pair of inner processes which, together with the claspers and the penis, comprise the external genitalia of a male insect.

PARAMYSIA. *Paramysia oblongoguttata*, a species of Ladybird (Coccinellidae) of a brownish colour with irregular light yellow patches on the wing-covers; an insect of coniferous forests in Europe.

PARAMYZUS. *Paramyzus heraclei*, the Yellow Plant-louse: a common species of aphid that infests Cow Parsnip (*Heracleum*) and similar umbelliferous plants.

PARANEOPTERA. A group of insects consisting of the five orders Psocoptera (book-lice), Mallophora and Anoplura (lice), Thysanoptera (thrips) and Hemiptera (bugs). See Section on Classification.

PARANEUROPTERA. An alternative name for Odonata (dragonflies).

PARANTICA. *Parantica sita*, a large Asiatic butterfly of the family Danaidae having whitish wings bordered broadly with brown and, like the Milkweed Butterfly, having brown lines marking the positions of the principal veins.

PARAPROCTS. A pair of ventral plates below the anus in some insects: the reduced sternal lobes of the eleventh abdominal segment.

PARAPTERON. A small additional sclerite sometimes present in the mesothorax and metathorax of an insect, just below the wings.

PARARGE. A genus of Brown Butterflies (Satyridae) common in Europe, Asia and North Africa. They include the Wall Brown (*Pararge megera*) and the Speckled Wood (*Pararge aegeria*). Both are light yellowish brown dappled and lined with darker brown. The larvae of both feed on grasses.

PARASEMIA. *Parasemia plantaginis*, the Wood Tiger Moth: a small member of the family Arctiidae having a general wing-pattern similar to that of the larger tiger moths but with more dark brown on both wings and with the scarlet of the hind-wings replaced by dull orange. The hairy caterpillars feed chiefly on plantain and dandelions.

PARASITE. An organism which lives and feeds in or on another. *Ectoparasites* live on the surface of the host; *endoparasites* within its body; *facultative* parasites can live either parasitically or free; *obligate* parasites live only parasitically (see also *Ectoparasite, Endoparasite, Parasitica* and *Parasitoid*).

PARASITICA. One of the two customary divisions of the Hymenoptera-Apocrita. Aculeata are the stinging forms and Parasitica those whose larvae are parasites. They include the following four superfamilies:

(1) Ichneumonoidea or Ichneumon flies most of which lay their eggs in the bodies of caterpillars.

(2) Chalcidoidea or Chalcid flies which are generally parasites or hyperparasites of other insects but occasionally also of plants.

(3) Cynipoidea whose larvae produce galls on oak and other trees.

(4) Proctotrypoidea whose minute larvae live in the eggs of other insects.

PARASITIC BEE. See *Homeless Bees*.

PARASITOID. A term applied to those insects such as Ichneumon flies which kill their host, in contrast to true parasites such as warble flies which do not. The distinction is not always valid.

PARASOL ANTS. Leaf-cutting ants that carry pieces of leaf or flower petal held over the head and gripped in the jaws so that they appear to be carrying a parasol. These they take down into their nests and use as a basis for cultivating fungi. The best known genus is the South American *Atta* (see *Fungus Cultivation* and *Atta*).

PARATENODERA. *Paratenodera sinensis*, the Oriental Mantis of China and South-east Asia; introduced into North America and now one of the commonest species of the Southern States (see *Mantidae*).

PARATRIOZA. A genus of Jumping Plant-lice of the family Psyllidae; transmitters of potato diseases, *e.g. Paratrioza cockerelli*.

PARECTOPA. *Parectopa robinella*, a small moth whose larvae are leaf-miners making branched or digitate cavities in the leaves of the North American Locust tree *Robinia pseudacacia*.

PARENT BUG. *Elasmucha grisea*, a small grey shieldbug of the group Heterop-

217

tera, notable for the unusual fact that the parent cares for her young. She lays her eggs under a birch leaf and covers them with her body for two or three weeks until they hatch. She then leads them to the birch catkins and protects them until they can fend for themselves.

PARHARMONIA. *Parharmonia pini*, the Pitch Pine Moth whose larvae bore into the cambium of pine trees, releasing a large amount of resin in which they live and pupate.

PARNASSIUS. *Parnassius apollo*, the Apollo Butterfly from mountainous areas in the warmer parts of Europe and Asia; related species also live in North America. A member of the family Papilionidae having greyish white, translucent wings with a span of about 8 cm. The front wings have a number of black spots and the hind-wings have several red or yellow eye-spots ringed with black and with white centres. There are several regional variations. The hairy caterpillar, black with red spots, feeds on Orpine, a species of *Sedum*.

PARORNIX. *Parornix aglicella*, a minute moth of the family Gracilariidae whose larvae are first leaf-miners and then leaf-rollers, usually attacking strawberry leaves.

PARROT CARPET MOTH. *Chloroclysta siterata*, a moth of the group Larentiinae, also called the Red-green Carpet Moth: a small European woodland species of a dark greenish grey colour with dark red markings on the fore-wings. The larvae are green with a row of red spots; they feed on leaves of oak, ash, birch and other trees.

PARSNIP WEBWORM. *Depressaria pastinacella*, a small moth of the family Oecophoridae whose larvae feed on the terminal heads of umbelliferous plants such as parsnip (*Pastinaca*) and Cow Parsnip (*Heracleum*). They make nests from pieces of leaf woven together with silk threads.

PARTHENOGENESIS. Development of an unfertilized ovum into a new individual genetically identical with the parent. Such development is fairly common among insects and in many cases may be induced artificially by various chemical or physical stimuli. Aphids and other plant-lice often have a complex life-history in which wingless parthenogenetic females alternate with winged sexual individuals. In bees the males or drones are produced by parthenogenesis but the workers and queen comes from fertilized eggs. In the case of the Stick Insect *Dixippus* parthenogenesis is the normal method of reproduction, males being very rare. The same is true of Scale-insects and Mealy Bugs (Coccidae). Many other insects such as cockroaches and some moths, butterflies and flies will occasionally develop by parthenogenesis.

PARTHENOLECANIUM. A common genus of scale-insects, brown, hemispherical and about 5 mm. long; common parasites of fruit trees (see *Coccidae*).

PASSALIDAE. Sugar Beetles: a family of black or brown beetles, mostly tropical, inhabiting old timber and living a social life in which the young are tended and protected by the parents. They are about 3–4 cm. long, have a waist-like constriction behind the thorax, have grooved wing-covers and elbowed antennae expanded into three lamellae at the distal end. The best known species, an inhabitant of North America, is *Passalus cornutus* so named on account of a horn-like projection on the head. The larvae are peculiar in being able to make a stridulating noise by rubbing the reduced third pair of legs against ridged plates on the second pair.

PATAGIUM. A short lobe or wing-like outgrowth on each side of the prothorax in certain insects, *e.g.* in some noctuid moths. They were well developed in primitive fossil 'dragonflies' of the order Palaeodictyoptera.

PATANGA. *Patanga succincta*, a species of migratory locusts common in China, Malaysia, Borneo and the Philippines.

PAUROMETABOLA. A name sometimes used for those Hemimetabola in which the nymphs are terrestrial and differ little from the adults except for the absence of functional wings. They thus include grasshoppers, cockroaches earwigs and plant-bugs (Hemiptera) but not dragonflies, mayflies and stoneflies in which the nymph is aquatic and differs in form and habits from the adult (see *Hemimetabola* and *Metamorphosis*).

PAURURUS. *Paururus juvencus*, a common European woodwasp about 3 cm. long, shiny blue-black with a reddish stripe down the back of the male. They belong to the group of sawflies or Symphyta, *i.e.* Hymenoptera in which the body is straight without a waist. The ovipositor of the female is thick and straight but not as long as that of the Giant Woodwasp or Horntail *Urocerus gigas*. Eggs are laid in pine wood and the developing larvae do considerable damage to the timber.

PAUSSIDAE. A family of ground beetles that inhabit ants' nests in tropical countries. The ants feed the beetles and in return receive a sugary secretion from the latter. Beetles of this family are characterized by having very large club-like antennae which, in some species such as *Platyrhopalopsis melyi* from Burma, are enormously exaggerated, each being about twice as large as the head.

PEA GALLS. Spherical green galls about the size of peas but having a number of small green spike-like projections. They occur on rose leaves and are caused by the gall-wasp *Diplolepis nervosa* and related species.

PEA GREEN MOTH. See *Green Oak Moth*.

PEACH APHID. *Myzus persicae*, a widely distributed pink or green aphid: a pest of peach and other fruit trees.

PEACH BLOSSOM MOTH. *Thyatira batis*, a medium sized moth of the family Polyplocidae having olive-green or brownish fore-wings each with five large circular spots of pink with brownish centres; the hind-wings are grey. The caterpillars, greenish with brown triangular markings along the sides, feed on bramble leaves.

PEACH BORER. A name for a number of moths, particularly those of the family Sesiidae or Clearwings, whose larvae bore into the wood of peach trees. The commonest of these is the North American *Sanninoidea exitiosa*, a small moth having blue wings with yellow markings. The larvae feed under the bark at the base of the tree doing considerable damage.

PEACOCK BUTTERFLY. *Nymphalis io* or *Inachis io*, a handsome butterfly of the family Nymphalidae ranging from Europe across Asia to Japan. The upper surfaces of the wings are reddish brown bordered with darker brown or black and each has a large eye-spot consisting of a yellow or whitish ring with a purple centre. The black, spiny larvae feed gregariously on stinging nettles.

PEANUT BUG. An alternative name sometimes used in the United States for Lantern Flies or Alligator Bugs (see *Fulgoridae*).

PEAR MIDGE. *Diplosis pyrivora*, a small gnat-like insect whose larvae are sometimes pests of pears.

PEAR PHYLLOBIUS. A small oval-shaped beetle about 6 mm. long having elytra of a bright metallic green with scattered reddish purple scales; common on hawthorn and other shrubs.

PEAR SUCKER. *Psylla pyricola*, a minute, dark red Jumping Plant-louse of the family Psyllidae which, like the Aphids, do extensive damage by smothering leaves with a sticky secretion of 'honeydew' (see *Jumping Plant-lice*).

PEARL-BORDERED FRITILLARY. *Argynnis euphrosyne* or *Clossiana euphrosyne*, a fritillary of Europe and Northern Asia having wings with a light brown and black chequerboard pattern typical of fritillaries but differing from others in having conspicuous silvery spots round the margins of the wings. The larvae feed principally on leaves of violet and pansy.

PEBBLE HOOK-TIP MOTH. *Drepana falcatoria*, a medium sized moth of the family Drepanidae having light brown wings crossed by wavy or zig-zag dark lines. There is a greyish spot in the centre of each wing and the fore-wings have the tips turned back to form a blunt hook. The caterpillars are greyish and without claspers at the hind-end; they feed on birch leaves.

PEBBLE PROMINENT. *Notodonta ziczac*, a light brown moth of the family Notodontidae having a large oval pebble-like mark on each fore-wing. Like others of the family it has a prominent tuft of scales extending back from the centre of each fore-wing. The greenish brown larvae have a somewhat grotesque and irregular appearance; they feed on willow leaves.

PECTEN. Any comb-like structure or organ, *e.g.*
(1) A comb-like stridulating organ on some insects.
(2) A row of spines or hairs on a palp or chelicera of various arthropods, on the respiratory tube of a mosquito larva, on the antennae of some moths etc.

PECTINATE. Comb-like, as for instance the antennae of some insects (see *Pecten*).

PECTINATION. Having comb-like or pectinate antennae with exceptionally long side branches: a characteristic of some male moths that have a good sense of smell, the olfactory receptors being situated on the antennae. This is most noticeable in the case of moths in which the male is attracted from long distances by the scent-glands of the female.

PECTINOPHORA. *Pectinophora gossypiella* or *Platyedra gossypiella*, the Pink Boll-worm Moth whose larva is a common pest of cotton plants.

PEDICEL. Any short stalk or stem of an organ, *e.g.*
(1) The second segment of an antenna, especially in the elbowed antennae of ants.
(2) The petiole or narrow waist of an ant consisting of the first two abdominal segments.

PEDICIA. A genus of crane-flies (Tipulidae) whose larvae live in brooks and streams.

PEDICINUS. A genus of blood-sucking lice (Anoplura) living as ectoparasites on baboons.

PEDICULUS. A genus of blood-sucking lice (Anoplura) found on humans and chimpanzees: small wingless insects with piercing mouth-parts, large abdomen and short legs with clawed feet. The eggs, known as nits, are fastened firmly to the hairs of the host by means of a sticky secretion. *Pediculus humanus*, the Human Louse, exists in two distinct races, *viz. Pediculus humanus capitis*, the Head Louse and *Pediculus humanus humanus* (often called *corporis*), the Body

Louse. The former is only found on the head or on other hairs, whereas the latter, which is larger and darker coloured, is found on the body and clothing in contact with it. The Human Louse is a dangerous carrier of typhus, relapsing fever and other diseases.

PEGOMYIA. A genus of small flies whose larvae are leaf-miners and sometimes also bore into young stems and roots. *Pegomyia betae* is a pest of beet and mangolds in Europe and North America; *Pegomyia hyoscyami* attacks spinach and beet; *Pegomyia calyptrata* is the Dock-leaf miner.

PELECINUS. *Pelecinus polyturator*, the May Beetle Parasite: a large, shiny black, North American wasp whose larvae are parasites on the larvae of cockchafers.

PELLUCID HOVER-FLY. Also called the White-belted Hover-fly, *Volucella pellucens*, a common woodland species whose larvae live as scavengers in the nests of the common wasp *Vespula vulgaris*. The adult fly, which feeds on nectar, is about 15 mm. long and is black with a white pellucid band round the front half of the abdomen.

PELOBIUS. A genus of water beetles about 8 mm. long, oval-shaped, reddish brown with the underside and edges of the thorax black. *Pelobius tardus* (also known as *Hygrobia hermanni*) is a common European species of ponds and slow streams. It is able to make a squeaking sound by rubbing the tip of the abdomen against the undersides of the elytra, and is sometimes called the 'Squeak Beetle' (see also *Hygrobia*).

PELOCORIS. A North American genus of Creeping Water-bugs or Saucer Bugs: oval, flattened, predatory bugs that live in streams and ponds (see *Naucoridae*).

PELTOPERLA. A North American genus of stoneflies (Plecoptera) with broad, flat, fish-like nymphs.

PEMPHIGUS. A genus of aphids that produce galls in the leaf-stalks of poplar trees: *Pemphigus filaginis* on the Lombardy and Black Poplars and *Pemphigus bursarius* on White and Black Poplars.

PEMPHREDON. See *Mournful Wasp*.

PENICILLIDIA. A genus of Nycteribiidae, wingless flies that live as ectoparasites on bats. *Penicillidia dufouri* is rusty brown, about 5 mm. long with a spider-like appearance. It is to be found in winter on sleeping bats of the genus *Myotis*, *e.g.* Natterer's Bat, Bechstein's Bat and Daubenton's Bat.

PENIS. A male intromittent or copulatory organ containing the gonopore from which seminal fluid is discharged. It is formed from two elongated outgrowths of the 9th abdominal segment and is situated between the two claspers. In primitive insects such as the mayfly the paired structures can be seen but in most insects these are fused together to form a single tubular structure.

PENTAGENIA. A genus of mayflies whose nymphs or naiads burrow into the mud at the bottom of ponds.

PENTALONIA. *Pentalonia nigronervosa* and related species: aphid pests of bananas in tropical countries; carriers of a virus causing a disease known as 'bunchy top'.

PENTATOMIDAE. Shieldbugs: large and sometimes brightly coloured shield-shaped insects of the group Heteroptera, *i.e.* bugs in which the proximal half of the wing is horny and the distal half membranous. Like all plant-bugs

221

they have a long piercing proboscis that can be folded back beneath the thorax when not in use. Although generally herbivorous, some species will eat caterpillars, beetles or other insects. The distinctive features by which the Pentatomidae can be recognized are the five-segmented antennae and the very large triangular dorsal shield or scutellum formed by the tergum of the mesothorax extending back over the abdomen.

PENTHETRIA. A genus of flies of the family Bibionidae: hairy flies with long antennae and large eyes. *Penthetria funebris*, about 1 cm. long, is black with brown wings. The males, however, have very short wings and are unable to fly. The legless, maggot-like larvae live and feed on damp compost.

PEPPERED MOTH. *Biston betularia*, a large geometrid moth notable as being one of the first in which the phenomenon of Industrial Melanism was observed. The normal or non-melanic form is a mottled grey colour and perfectly matches the lichens on the tree trunks where it rests. The melanic form, sometimes known as *carbonaria*, is uniformly black and is found chiefly in industrial regions where it is less conspicuous on a smoke-blackened background. There is also an intermediate form known as *insularia* which is black speckled with white. The larvae of all these are brown and stick-like; they feed on oak, birch, elm and other trees (see *Industrial Melanism*).

PEPSIS. A genus of large, long-legged, solitary wasps known as Tarantula Hawks or Spider Wasps because they stock their underground nests with spiders which they have stung and paralysed. They belong to the family Pompilidae which includes some of the largest of the Hymenoptera. *Pepsis obliquerugosa*, the largest, is blue and has a wing-span of about 10 cm. *Pepsis formosa* is slightly smaller and is blue with red wings. Both these are found in in the Southern United States.

PEREUTE. A genus of pierid butterflies basically black in colour unlike the majority of the Pieridae which are white or yellow. *Pereute callinice* of Peru is a medium sized, black species with a broad, broken band of red across each fore-wing.

PERICALLIA. *Pericallia matronula*, the Augsburg Tiger Moth: the largest of the European Tiger Moths with a wing-span of about 85 mm., basically similar in appearance to other tiger moths with a red body and a black and yellow wing pattern.

PERICARDIAL SINUS. A part of the haemocoel or body cavity surrounding the heart in an insect or other arthropod. Blood flows from this cavity directly into the dorsal tubular heart by way of a number of *ostia* or valvular openings (see *Blood*).

PERICARDIAL CELLS. Nephrocytes in the heart region of an insect; believed to be connected with excretion as they can absorb nitrogenous waste substances from the blood, but the whole process is not understood.

PERICLISTUS. *Periclistus brandtii*, a small gall-wasp that behaves like a cuckoo-wasp, laying its eggs inside the 'Robin's Pincushion', the large red, hairy gall made on the wild rose plant by the larger gall-wasp *Diplolepis rosae*.

PERICOMA. A common North American and European genus of Moth Flies of the family Psychodidae: scaly, hairy flies with aquatic larvae.

PERILLUS. *Perillus bioculatus*, a small orange or yellow pentatomid bug that preys on the larvae of the Colorado Potato Beetle *Leptinotarsa* and takes up the carotenoid pigments from its victim.

PERIOPTICON. The outer layer of the optic lobes, nearest the eyes (see *Opticon* and *Epiopticon*).

PERIPLANETA. *Periplaneta americana*, the American cockroach: a large, light brown species about 3 cm. long whose origin is uncertain but which has now become a pest in almost all the warmer parts of the world. Unlike the European cockroach it has fully developed wings in both sexes. The Australian species *Periplaneta australasiae* is very similar.

PERIPNEUSTIC. Having lateral spiracles on all the segments of the abdomen (*cf. Amphipneustic* and *Metapneustic*).

PERISPHAERIIDAE. A family of cockroaches including the giant cockroach of Madagascar, *Gromphadorrhina portentosa*, a flightless insect about 85 mm. long that makes a snake-like hiss when disturbed.

PERITHEMIS. *Perithemis domita*, the Amber-wing: a small North American dragonfly in which the male has amber-coloured wings and the female has transparent wings with two amber spots on each.

PERITROPHIC MEMBRANE. A thin chitinous tube lining the mid-gut and enclosing the gut contents. It protects the epithelial cells from damage by the passage of food, but is permeable to enzymes and to digested foods. The peritrophic membrane is continuously produced by secretion, either at the junction with the fore-gut or over the whole epithelium of the mid-gut simultaneously. In either case the membrane is also excreted continuously as a container for the faeces.

PERIZOMA. *Perizoma affinitata*, the Rivulet Moth: a small dark brown geometrid moth with two narrow zig-zag white lines across the fore-wings. The larvae are reddish brown and feed on the seed capsules of various species of campion (*Silene* and *Lychnis*).

PERKINSIELLA. *Perkinsiella saccharicida*, a leaf-hopper of the family Delphacidae: a major pest of sugar-cane plants in South Africa, Australia, Mauritius, Fiji and other places; a carrier of the virus of *Fiji disease*. After being accidentally introduced into Hawaii it has been controlled to some extent by the introduction of a capsid bug from Fiji. The latter, *Tytthus mundulus*, feeds on the eggs of the leaf-hopper.

PERLARIA. An alternative name for Plecoptera (stoneflies).

PERLIDAE. One of the largest families of stoneflies (Plecoptera): hemimetabolous insects with four membranous wings, the hind pair being wider than the front pair and with larger anal lobes. The antennae and cerci are long and filamentous though the latter are not as long as those of the mayfly. Mayflies and stoneflies are in many ways very similar and both have aquatic larvae. *Perla bipunctata* is one of the largest European species of Perlidae with a wing-span of 4–5 cm.

PERLISTA. *Perlista placida*, one of the commonest North American stoneflies (Plecoptera) about 10 mm. long, brown with a yellow band and yellow front edges to the wings.

PERRHYBRIS. A South American genus of pierid butterflies. *Perrhybris pyrrha* is a common species from Peru and Colombia having black and white males but the females are orange, black and yellow, mimicking another genus, *Mechanitis*.

PERRISIA. A genus of gall-midges including *Perrisia ulmariae* which causes numerous small reddish swellings on the leaves of Meadowsweet (*Filipendula* *ulmaria*) and *Perrisia crataegi* which causes terminal rosette galls on shoots of hawthorn (*Crataegus*). (See *Cecidomyidae*.)

PETIOLATA. An alternative name for Apocrita: bees, ants, wasps and ichneumon flies, *i.e.* all those Hymenoptera that have a narrow waist between the thorax and abdomen. (Compare *Symphyta*.)

PETIOLE. Any narrow stalk, *e.g.* the narrow part of the abdomen forming the waist of bees, ants and wasps.

PETROBIUS. *Petrobius maritimus*, a species of Bristle-tail of the order Thysanura: a primitive wingless insect similar to the Silverfish (*Lepisma*) but having a brown, scaly body and living among seaweed and under rocks near the high tide mark.

PETROGNATHA. *Petrognatha gigas*, a large West African longhorn beetle of the family Cerambycidae, about 75 mm. long, brown and covered with velvet hairs. The male has antennae more than twice the length of the body and these can be folded back when the insect is at rest.

PETROLEUM FLY. *Psilopa petrolei*, a small fly of the family Ephydridae whose larvae live in pools of petroleum among the Californian oil wells, preying upon other insects that are trapped in the oil.

PHAEDON. See *Mustard Beetle*.

PHAGOCARPUS. A genus of fruit-flies of the family Trypetidae whose larvae feed on berries of hawthorn and related plants. Sometimes called *Anomoia*.

PHALAENIDAE. An alternative name for Noctuidae or Agrotidae often known as Owlet Moths: a large family of brownish, stoutly built moths with a well developed proboscis. The family is sometimes divided into two, *viz.* Caradrinidae and Plusiidae, or into several subfamilies (see *Noctuidae*).

PHALERA. See Buff-tip Moth.

PHALERIA. *Phaleria cadaverina*, a small oval-shaped beetle, reddish yellow with a dark brown spot on each elytron; common on seashores where it feeds on dead fish, crabs or other creatures.

PHANAEUS. A genus of brightly coloured North American dung beetles of the family Scarabaeidae, the males having a prominent 'horn' on the head. Unlike most insects they show some degree of parental care, guarding the eggs until they hatch. *Phanaeus quadridens* is a violet coloured species about 20 mm. long.

PHANEROGNATHA. A group of weevils (Curculionidae) characterized by the absence of mandibles but having conspicuous maxillae not hidden by the mentum (*cf. Adelognatha*).

PHANTOM CRANE-FLIES. Ptychopteridae, a family of large crane-flies having almost transparent aquatic larvae with a long posterior respiratory tube.

PHANTOM LARVA. The transparent aquatic larva of the gnat *Chaoborus crystallinus* (see *Phantom Midge*).

PHANTOM MIDGE (PHANTOM GNAT). *Chaoborus crystallinus*, a gnat or mosquito of the family Culicidae, a harmless non-blood-sucking species, whose predatory aquatic larva is so transparent that its internal organs are clearly visible.

PHARAOH'S ANT. See *Monomorium*.

224

PHARATE INSTAR. A stage in the development of an insect during which the cuticle has become separated from the hypodermis but has not yet been ruptured or cast off. A pharate pupa, for instance, is within but separated from the last larval cuticle; a pharate adult is within but free from the pupal integument.

PHARNACIA. *Pharnacia serratipes*, a giant tropical stick-insect of the family Phasmidae about 30 cm. long.

PHASE THEORY OF LOCUSTS. The alternation between a solitary non-migratory phase and a gregarious, migratory phase in the life of a locust (see *Locustidae*).

PHASMIDA (PHASMIDS). Stick-insects and leaf-insects: formerly classed as Orthoptera; common in tropical forests and occurring to some extent in temperate regions. Stick-insects (Family Phasmidae or Phasmatidae) are elongated thin-legged creatures whose body, stiffly stretched out on leaves or twigs and coloured to match them, becomes almost invisible. Leaf-insects (Family Phyllidae) are remarkable in having their wings, and in some cases expansions of the legs and other parts, shaped and coloured to resemble the foliage amongst which they live.

PHAUSIS. *Phausis splendidula*, the Lesser Glow-worm of Central Europe and North America: a luminous beetle of the family Lampyridae. The males are brownish-grey, winged beetles about 1 cm. long; the females are yellowish-green, wingless and worm-like. Both are luminescent.

PHEIDOLE. A genus of large tropical ants, some of which take other insects into their nests and 'milk' them, *i.e.* they suck the sweet secretions of their guests. *Pheidole punctulata* milks the Coffee Mealy Bug of Kenya; another species milks the Pine-apple Mealy Bug of Hawaii.

PHELLUS. *Phellus glaucus*, one of the world's largest Robber flies (Asilidae) from Australia: a fierce, shiny blue insect about 5 cm. long with a wing-span of 8 cm.

PHENACOCCUS. *Phenacoccus aceris*, a species of mealy bug of the family Coccidae which attacks American Maple trees and does serious damage; a light yellow insect covered with a mass of white waxy threads which it secretes.

PHENGODES. *Phengodes laticollis*, a North American firefly or luminescent beetle of the family Lampyridae, the larva of which has ten pairs of luminous spots.

PHEOSIA. *Pheosia tremula*, the Swallow Prominent Moth and *Pheosia gnoma*, the Lesser Swallow Prominent Moth: both have a brown body and wings patterned with dark brown and cream. Like all the Prominent Moths (Notodontidae) they have a tuft of scales projecting backwards from the centre of each fore-wing. The caterpillar of the former is green with a yellow line along each side; that of the latter is green and brown with white markings. Both feed on poplar, willow etc.

PHEROMONE. A chemical substance secreted by an insect by which information is given to other insects, influencing their behaviour. Such substances may be sexual attractants, as for instance those produced by female moths; they may be warning substances serving to keep away other insects; others may be used as a means of social communication and the cementing together of a colony. Ants, for instance, leave odour trails which other members of the colony will follow. Perhaps the best known pheromone is a substance produced by a queen bee. This has been chemically identified as 9-oxydecenoic acid.

The worker bees lick this substance and pass it on to each other as a means of recognizing the presence of the queen.

PHIGALIA. *Phigalia pilosaria* (also called *Apocheima pilosaria*), the Pale Brindled Beauty: a geometrid moth of which the male has dark brown fore-wings and paler hind-wings both marked with zig-zag lines and dots of darker brown. The patterns are very variable and melanic forms also exist; the females are wingless. The brown stick-like larvae feed on leaves of oak, elm and other trees.

PHILAEMATOMYIA. A genus of tropical flies of the family Muscidae, closely related to house flies but having a row of small prestomal teeth on the proboscis. These are able to pierce the skin of humans or other animals and the fly can then suck up blood after the manner of feeding of the house fly.

PHILAENUS. *Philaenus spumarius*, the common Frog-hopper whose larva produces 'cuckoo-spit' (see *Cercopidae*).

PHILANTHIDAE. A family of digging wasps that make their nests in sandy banks and stock them with honey bees that have been stung and paralysed. These bees serve as food both for the adults and for the developing larvae of the wasps. *Philanthus triangulum*, known as the Bee-wolf, is a yellow and black species about 15 mm. long.

PHILONICUS. A genus of small Robber Flies of the family Asilidae. Like many asilids it has large eyes, an elongated bristly body, bristly legs and sharp piercing mouth-parts with which it attacks other insects in flight. *Philonicus albiceps* is a very common species, about 15 mm. long, greyish brown with a black, tapering tip on the abdomen. The larvae, which live in the soil, are also predatory.

PHILONTHUS. A genus of Rove-beetles of the family Staphylinidae about 1 cm. long; active predatory insects living in dung, carrion or rotting vegetation. *Philonthus politus* is dark brown; *Philonthus flavipes* has a black shiny body with short red elytra and yellowish legs; *Philonthus aeneus* is a bluish black species with a bronze sheen.

PHILOPEDON. *Philopedon geminatus*, a small oval-shaped weevil with a short, thick snout, greyish scaly elytra, prominent eyes and short, elbowed antennae; common on sandy places near the seashore.

PHILOPHYLLA. See *Celery Fly* (*Philophylla heraclei*).

PHILOPOTAMUS. *Philopotamus montanus*, a caddis fly whose flattened, carnivorous, aquatic larvae do not make cases but spin tubular nets of silk in which they lie in wait for their prey.

PHILOPTERIDAE. A family of bird-lice (Mallophaga), particularly infesting poultry. One of the best known is the Head Louse of chickens, *Cuclotogaster heterographus*.

PHILOSAMIA. *Philosamia cynthia*, the Ailanthus Silk Moth sometimes called the Cynthia Moth: a large saturniid moth, olive-brown with a violet band across the wings and a span of about 13 cm. The cocoons have long been used to obtain silk in China, Japan and Indonesia and it has been introduced into the United States. The larvae feed on the Tree of Heaven, *Ailanthus glandulosa*.

PHILUDORIA. See *Drinker Moth*.

PHLEBOTOMUS. A genus of blood-sucking sand-flies notorious as being the carriers of the protozoan parasite *Leishmania*, the cause of the diseases Kala

Azar and Oriental Sore in Asiatic countries and of Verruga in South America. They are minute flies usually placed in the family Psychodidae, sometimes called Moth-flies on account of the scales and hairs that cover their wings and body. Because the habits of the sand-flies are so different from those of other Psychodidae, some authors separate them into the family Phlebotomidae.

PHLOGOPHORA. See *Angle Shades Moth.*

PHLYCTAENIA. *Phlyctaenia rubigallis*, the Celery Leaf-tyer: a small moth of the family Pyralidae whose larvae draw together the leaves and flower buds of celery and fasten them with silk to make a nest within which they live and feed.

PHOBOETICUS. *Phoboeticus fruhstorferi*, a tropical stick-insect of the family Phasmidae measuring up to 30 cm. in length and 15 mm. wide; the longest known insect of the present day.

PHOBOTAXIS. A reflex action by which an insect turns to avoid an adverse stimulus and by repeated trial and error eventually moves away from it.

PHOLIDOPTERA. A genus of bush-crickets or long-horned grasshoppers of the family Tettigoniidae with vestigial wings, long legs and very long antennae. *Pholidoptera griseoaptera*, the Dark Bush-cricket, is a small European species common in hedgerows; dark grey-brown, about 1 cm. long with antennae nearly three times this length.

PHOLUS. A genus of large American hawk-moths (Sphingidae); powerful flyers that can in some cases be found anywhere from Canada to southern Argentina. *Pholus labruscae*, one of the migrant species, is a large moth with a span of 11 cm. The fore-wings are green and the hind-wings black, blue and red. *Pholus tersa* and *Pholus fasciatus* are slightly smaller species found in Brazil.

PHORACANTA. A genus of longhorn beetles of the family Cerambycidae, found in South Africa, Australia and other countries. *Phoracanta semipunctata* is an Australian species that attacks the Eucalyptus plant.

PHORBIA. A genus of root-maggot flies of the family Anthomyidae whose larvae are destructive pests of agricultural and garden crops. They include *Phorbia brassicae*, the Cabbage Maggot, *Phorbia cepetorum*, a pest of onions, and *Phorbia rubivora* which attacks the tips of young raspberry and blackberry shoots. They are given other generic names in many works of economic entomology, *e.g. Phorbia cepetorum* is usually known as *Delia antiqua*.

PHORESY. A form of commensalism in which a small insect regularly uses the body of a larger one as a means of transport, perhaps to its feeding ground. Some small flies, for instance, travel on the backs of dung-beetles; a small chalcid wasp is carried on the legs of ants and the triungulin larvae of oil-beetles are carried on the bodies of bees and wasps.

PHORIDAE. Hump-backed flies: a family of small black flies with a humped thorax and distinctive wing-venation. They rarely fly but run about on flowers and foliage or on walls and windows. The larvae feed on decaying animal and vegetable matter, and the family as a whole is one of the most versatile and efficient in the Diptera.

PHORMIA. A genus of shiny blue-black blowflies with blood-sucking larvae. They belong to the family Calliphoridae and are closely related to the common bluebottle. They occur in many parts of the world including Europe and North America. *Phormia regina* is a species whose larvae feed on open sores or ulcers of farm animals as well as on carrion; *Phormia terrae-novae* is a species whose larvae are sometimes found in very large numbers in the nests of sparrows, swallows and other birds where they suck the blood of newly hatched nestlings. Both these species occur in Britain.

PHOSPHORESCENCE. See *Light-producing Organs, Firefly* and *Glow-worm.*

PHOSPHUGA. *Phosphuga atrata*, a small, shiny black carrion beetle of the family Silphidae with an oval body about 1 cm. long and with long, thin legs and antennae. Adults and late stage larvae are predacious on slugs and snails but the early larvae are vegetarian feeding chiefly on beetroot.

PHOTINUS. A North American genus of fireflies: luminescent beetles of the family Lampyridae. There are several species, all small and rather inconspicuous apart from their luminosity. The male is generally brighter than the female and each species has its own distinctive mode or duration of flashing, usually starting at dusk. *Photinus pyralis* flies near the ground, undulating and flashing with a yellow light as it ascends; *Photinus marginellus* gives a series of very rapid flashes; *Photinus consanguineus* repeatedly gives two short sharp flashes (see *Light-producing Organs*).

PHOTOGENIC ORGANS. See *Light-producing Organs.*

PHOTOPHORUS. A genus of luminous click beetles (Elateridae), related to the well-known American *Pyrophorus* but not closely to other luminous beetles which belong to the family Lampyridae. The few known species of *Photophorus* are found in South-east Asia and Indonesia; like *Pyrophorus* they have two easily seen luminous spots on the thorax.

PHOTOTAXIS. A directional movement in relation to a source of light. Moths, for instance, are positively phototactic, flying towards the light. The larvae of many insects on the other hand show negative phototaxis, moving away from light.

PHOTOTONUS. An action whereby the *tonus* of certain muscles is affected by the presence or absence of light so that an insect will take up a different attitude in the dark from that which it takes up in the light. Some flies, for instance, raise their bodies above the ground in the light and collapse limply immobile in the dark or if their eyes are covered.

PHOTURIS. A common North American genus of fireflies or luminescent beetles. *Photuris pennyslvanica*, for instance, is one of the largest and best-known species. The males live in tree-tops and flash at dusk with a pale greenish blue light; the females live in the grass and flash to attract the males. There appears to be a regular 'code' of signals. The males send out repeated bursts of about five flashes in rapid succession; the females respond with two or three flashes at a time (see also *Light-producing Organs*).

PHRAGMA. One of a series of parts of the endoskeleton of an insect or crustacean, consisting of *apodemes* or ingrowths of the integument. They are hardened and serve for the attachment of muscles and other organs. The words *phragma* and *apodeme* seem to be used interchangeably, according to the context and taste of the author.

PHRAGMATOBIA. *Phragmatobia fuliginosa*, the Ruby Tiger Moth: a small pinkish-brown moth with a red and black abdomen. It belongs to the family Arctiidae but does not resemble the other better known tiger moths. It inhabits moors and heaths where the brown hairy caterpillars feed on heather, dock, dandelions and other plants of the ground flora.

PHRYGANEIDAE. A family of caddis flies (Trichoptera) including some of the largest species. *Phryganea grandis* has a wing-span of about 6 cm. The larvae, which are omnivorous, inhabit lakes and slow-moving streams; they make tubular cases from fragments of plant material often arranged in a spiral.

PHRYXE. A genus of Tachinid flies whose larvae parasitize caterpillars of the Cabbage White and other butterflies. The fly lays its eggs on the surface of the caterpillar and the emerging tachinid larvae bore into the body of their victim, eventually killing it.

PHRYXOTHRIX. The 'Railroad Worm', a rare glow-worm of South America having a red light on its head and green lights on either side of the body.

PHTHIRAPTERA. Lice: a name sometimes used to denote a group containing the three suborders Anoplura (sucking lice), Mallophaga (biting lice) and Rhynchophthirina (elephant-lice). (See *Louse*.)

PHTHIRUS. *Phthirus pubis*, the Crab Louse and related species. Members of the order Anoplura characterized by their short, crab-like body; they infest the hairs of the pubic region and the armpits of humans (see *Louse*).

PHYLLIDAE. A family of leaf-insects (Phasmida) related to the stick-insects but resembling a leaf or a bunch of leaves; *Phyllium siccifolium*, the Dried Leaf Insect of India and Ceylon, is one of the best known. The body is flattened; the hind-wings are atrophied and the wing-covers resemble a dead, brown leaf. The legs are expanded and flattened so that they also resemble parts of dead leaves. The whole insect is perfectly camouflaged against the leaves which are its usual background.

PHYLLOCNISTIS. A genus of small moths whose larvae are shallow, linear leaf-miners. They tunnel between the upper and lower epidermis of the leaf, breaking the cells and feeding upon the sap. The air trapped in the leaf gives the mines the appearance of translucent or glistening white branching lines within the leaf, each with a dark central line caused by the deposition of frass or faeces. *Phyllocnistis populiella* attacks poplar; other species attack tulip leaves.

PHYLLODECTA. A genus of leaf-beetles of the family Chrysomelidae: small bluish or bronze beetles about 5 mm. long that attack willow and other trees. The larvae are small black insects with a spiny chitinous skin in which there are glands apparently secreting a protective fluid. This makes them fairly safe from the effects of chemical sprays. *Phyllodecta vulgatissima* and *Phyllodecta vitellinae* are two of the commonest species.

PHYLLOMORPHA. A genus of plant-bugs of the family Coreidae having a broad, flattened body covered with numerous sharp spines. They chirp or stridulate by rubbing their antennae together. *Phyllomorpha laciniata*, a European species, is light grey-brown and about 1 cm. long. The female deposits the eggs on the back of another bug of the same type where the spikes help to retain them until they hatch.

PHYLLOPERTHA. *Phyllopertha horticola*, the Garden Chafer or June Chafer: a beetle of the family Scarabaeidae similar to a cockchafer in colouring and general appearance but only about one third of the size (*i.e.* about 1 cm. long). The abdomen is pointed; the wing-cases are light reddish brown; the head, thorax and legs are greenish black and the antennae end in a fan of lamellae. The larva, like that of the cockchafer, has a fat, whitish body and short legs. It lives in the soil and is sometimes a major pest of young trees.

PHYLLOPHAGA. A genus of chafer beetles of the family Scarabaeidae, generally similar in appearance to the cockchafer. The adults feed on foliage and the larvae on roots (see *Chafers* and *Cockchafer*).

PHYLLOPORIDAE. A family of leaf-like, long-horned grasshoppers from New Guinea. *Phyllopora grandis*, the largest, is about 13 cm. long with equally long antennae. The bright green wings resemble leaves and there is also a leaf-like triangular 'hood' projecting from the thorax back over the wings. There are no stridulatory organs.

PHYLLOPTERA. A name used in the system of classification proposed by Wardle (1937) for the order usually known as Phasmida and comprising the stick-insects (Phasmidae) and leaf-insects (Phyllidae), both of which were formerly classed with Orthoptera. (Cf. *Phyloptera*.)

PHYLLOTRETA. A genus of flea-beetles: minute long-legged jumping beetles of the family Chrysomelidae. *Phyllotreta nemorum*, the Turnip Flea-beetle, is a common pest of plants of the cabbage family where the adults feed on the leaves and the minute, short-legged larvae bore into the roots (see *Flea-beetles*).

PHYLLOXERIDAE. A family of plant-lice which includes the Phylloxerinae and the Adelginae (*q.v.*).

PHYLLOXERINAE. A subfamily of plant-lice which undergo a complex life-history similar to that of the Aphis. They differ from the latter, however, in that their reproduction is never viviparous. *Phylloxera quercus* occurs on oaks and *Phylloxera vitifolii* is a serious pest of grape vines where it feeds on leaves and roots.

PHYLOPTERA. A superordinal term proposed to include all the net-veined orders, the Orthoptera and the Dermaptera (*cf. Phylloptera*).

PHYMATIDAE. Ambush bugs: predatory insects of the order Hemiptera having the front legs bent back and equipped with sharp claws after the manner of the Praying Mantis. The body is sometimes spiny and usually sculptured into a bizarre shape. *Phymata crassipes* is a species of Central and Southern Europe and parts of Asia. It is about 1 cm. long and is well camouflaged among the low plants where it remains concealed lying in wait for its victims.

PHYMATOCERA. *Phymatocera aterrima*, the Solomon's Seal Sawfly: a species whose voracious caterpillars can completely defoliate Solomon's Seal (*Polygonatum*) and related garden plants.

PHYSOCEPHALA. A European genus of Thick-headed Flies (Conopidae), having a remarkable resemblance to certain wasps. They live among flowers and lay their eggs in the bodies of bees, wasps and grasshoppers.

PHYSOPODA. An alternative name for the order Thysanoptera (Thrips).

PHYTOBIUS. *Phytobius velatus*, the Water Weevil: a beetle that lives during all its stages below the surface, usually among Water Milfoil (*Myriophyllum*).

PHYTOCORIS. A genus of small, elongated, long-legged plant-bugs of the family Miridae (Capsid bugs). *Phytocoris tiliae*, about 4 mm. long, is bright yellowish green with brown markings and is found on lime, apple, oak and ash trees. *Phytocoris tripustulatus* (sometimes called *Liocoris tripustulatus*) is a slightly larger species, orange, yellow and black; it is found on nettles and other hedgerow plants (see *Miridae*).

PHYTOLYMA. A genus of Jumping Plant-lice (Psyllidae) producing galls on African timber, causing trees to become stunted and eventually to die. *Phyto-*

lyma lata is a well known example, injurious to the Iroko Tree (*Chlorophora excelsa*), a valuable termite-resistant hardwood of tropical West Africa. (See *Jumping Plant-lice*.)

PHYTOMETRA. *Phytometra viridaria*, the Purple-barred Moth: a very small, brown noctuid moth with two crimson or purplish bands across each forewing. The caterpillars are bright green and feed on milkwort (*Polygala*).

PHYTOMYZA. A genus of leaf-miner flies of the family Agromyzidae whose larvae make tunnels between the upper and lower surfaces of leaves. There are many common species that attack wild and cultivated plants. *Phytomyza ilicis* bores into holly leaves; *Phytomyza nigricornis* attacks peaches and *Phytomyza lactuca* is the lettuce miner.

PHYTONOMUS. *Phytonomus posticus*, the Alfalfa Weevil: a beetle whose larvae feed on the leaves of alfalfa and other leguminous crops in North America.

PHYTOPHAGA. A large group or superfamily of beetles, mostly very destructive to crops and trees. They include the longhorns (Cerambycidae) and the leaf-beetles (Chrysomelidae). The well known Colorado Beetle, the pest of the potato plant, is included in the latter group.

PHYTOSAPROPHAGOUS INSECTS. A general name for insects that feed on dead or decaying plant material, *e.g.* Collembola and Thysanura, the larvae of many Diptera and numerous species of Coleoptera.

PICROMERUS. A genus of predatory shieldbugs that are useful to man as they eat caterpillars and leaf-beetles *Picromerus bidens* is a common European species about 12 mm. long, dark brown with a small red spot on the tip of the scutellum. It is commonly found among damp vegetation.

PIERELLA. A genus of South American butterflies of the family Satyridae having long, narrow fore-wings and large hind-wings with short 'tails'. *Pierella dracontis*, a common species in Brazil, has brown and green fore-wings and bluish hind-wings spotted with paler blue and white.

PIERIDAE. A world-wide family of butterflies which are characteristically white, yellow or orange. They have six functional legs with a pair of forked claws on each foot. The caterpillars are usually green or yellowish and many of them are agricultural pests, particularly of cruciferous plants. The best known member of the family is the Large White or Cabbage Butterfly, *Pieris brassicae*, which ranges across Europe, North Africa and Asia as far as the Himalayas. Other European species include the Small White, Wood White, Clouded Yellow, Orange Tip and Brimstone butterflies. There are numerous species in South America, Africa, Asia and Australia; some of those in tropical parts are quite large and, although yellow and orange predominate, some are coloured with iridescent blues and greens.

PIGEON FLY. *Pseudolynchia canariensis*, a blood-sucking fly of the family Hippoboscidae, having as its natural host various wild pigeons in warm countries It has been dispersed all over the world as a parasite of the domestic pigeon

PIGEON HORNTAIL. *Tremex columba*, a large North American sawfly with a wing-span of about 7 cm. and a body length of about 5 cm. It has a large head, a slender neck and a straight, cylindrical, purplish abdomen banded with yellow. The female has a large straight ovipositor with which she lays her eggs deep in the trunks of maple, elm and other trees. The insect belongs to the family Siricidae and is closely related to the European Woodwasp *Urocerus gigas*.

PIGEON LOUSE. *Columbicola columbae*, a small biting louse of the order Mallophaga having a pale, thin, elongated body about 2 mm. long. It is commonly found among the feathers of doves and pigeons.

PIGEON TREMEX. See *Pigeon Horntail*.

PIGMENTS. The wide variety of colours in insects is due partly to chemical pigments and partly to the effect of optical interference caused by the physical structure of the surface (see *Iridescence*). The principal pigments fall into a number of chemical categories of which the following are the most important:

(1) *Melanins*: black or brown derivatives of the amino acid *tyrosine*.

(2) *Biliverdin*: a green substance similar to the green bile pigment of humans, derived from cytochrome which is universally present and plays a part in cell respiration.

(3) *Ommochromes*: red, yellow or brown pigments in the eyes of insects and sometimes also in other parts.

(4) *Anthraquinones*: bright red substances such as cochineal obtained from scale-insects.

(5) *Carotenoids*: Yellow and red pigments obtained from plants and found, for instance, in the wing-covers of the ladybird and the Colorado Beetle.

(6) *Pterines*: white, yellow, orange and red substances in the wing-scales of butterflies.

PIGMY SAND CRICKETS (PIGMY MOLE CRICKETS). Tridactylidae, a family of small burrowing crickets that live in sand banks near water.

PIGMY SKIPPER. *Gegenes pumilio*, a small brownish butterfly of the family Hesperiidae, the male with very dark and unmarked wings; the female lighter with two pale spots on each fore-wing. They are common round the Mediterranean, Western and Central Asia and throughout Africa.

PILL BEETLE. *Byrrhus pilula*, a small, almost spherical beetle, dark brown and covered with fine golden hairs. When disturbed it withdraws its head and legs beneath the body so that it is almost indistinguishable from the dung pellet of a rabbit.

PILOPHORUS. A genus of elongated plant-bugs of the family Miridae, sometimes called Capsid bugs. *Pilophorus cinnamopterus* is brown, about 4 mm. long and lives in pine trees where it feeds on the leaves and resin as well as on aphids.

PIMPLA. *Pimpla rufata*, the Red-legged Ichneumon: a common insect that lays its eggs in the caterpillars of various moths and butterflies including the Cabbage White. It is about 12 mm. long, black with reddish brown legs and a short stout ovipositor.

PINCERS. (1) Claspers or gonopods at the hind-end of the abdomen of certain insects. They may be present in both sexes, as in earwigs, but more often they are on the males only. They may be used for attack or defence or for grasping the female when mating.

(2) Pincer-like jaws, as for instance those of most predatory insects.

PINE BEAUTY. *Panolis flammea*, a small noctuid moth whose reddish-brown markings match the bark of the Scots Pine on which it lives and whose green larvae blend with the pine needles on which they feed.

PINE BUD TORTRIX. *Evetria buoliana*, a small moth of the family Tortricidae having brick-red fore-wings with transverse silvery lines and dark grey hind-wings fringed with hairs. Eggs are laid on pine shoots and the young caterpillars eat their way into the buds where they make a nest lined with silk. They also make a canopy of silk threads covering and protecting a number of neigh-bouring buds on which they feed. Although originally European, this moth has now become a pest of forestry in the United States and Canada.

PINE HAWK-MOTH. *Sphinx pinastri*, a large hawk-moth with a wing-span of about 8 cm. whose grey, brown and black markings perfectly match the bark of the pine trees on which it lives and on which its caterpillar feeds. It is common in the forests of Central Europe and is a rare visitor to Britain.

PINE LAPPET MOTH. *Dendrolimus pini*, a large moth of the family Lasio-campidae living in dry coniferous forests of Central and Northern Europe where its caterpillars do considerable damage by feeding on pine needles. It has a wing-span of about 7 cm. and varies in colour from grey to reddish brown.

PINE LOOPER. *Bupalus piniaria*, also known as the Bordered White Moth: a medium sized European geometrid moth whose larvae feed on Scots Pine and other conifers. The wings have a thin border of white but their background colour varies according to race and locality. In the southern race it is yellow and orange but in the northern variety the male is white and brown and the female yellow and brown. The caterpillars are thin and green and are well camouflaged among the pine needles.

PINE NOCTUID. See *Panolis*.

PINE RESIN-GALL MOTH. *Evetria resinella*, a small greyish brown moth of the family Tortricidae whose orange-brown caterpillars produce resin-galls on young pine twigs. They live in these for about two years.

PINE SAWFLY. *Diprion pini*, a large sawfly resembling a bee whose pale green caterpillar-like larvae feed on pine needles; a serious pest of coniferous forests in Europe and North America.

PINE SAWYER. *Monochamus sutor*, a wood-boring longhorn beetle of the family Cerambycidae: a pest of conifers in the forests of Europe and North America. The adult is about 20 mm. long and its mottled red-brown colour perfectly matches the pine bark on which it is found. Both adults and larvae bore into new wood and also into dead or burnt timber. In some cases the larvae live for a very long time. A case was recorded in the United States of adult beetles of a related species *Monochamus confusor* emerging from furniture fifteen years after it had been made.

PINE-SHOOT BEETLE. See *Myelophilus*.

PINE TUBE MOTH. *Argyrotaenia pinatubana*, a small moth whose larvae draw together groups of pine needles and fasten them with silk to form a tube in which they live and feed.

PINE WEBWORM. *Itycorsia zappei*, a sawfly of North America whose green and black larvae make large communal nests of pine needles fastened together with silk threads.

PINE WEEVIL. See *Hylobius* and *Pissodes*.

PINE WOODWASP. *Xeris spectrum*, a woodwasp of the family Siricidae, black with two white stripes on the thorax. It is closely related to the Giant Woodwasp or Horntail *Urocerus gigas* but is only about half the size. The body is about 25 mm. long and the ovipositor of the female is about the same length.

This is used for boring into pine wood in which the eggs are laid and on which the larvae feed.

PINHOLE BORER. A name for a number of small wood-boring beetles, particularly those of the group Ipinae sometimes known as Ambrosia Beetles. These make numerous tunnels about 1 mm. in diameter into which they take spores of fungi and in doing so may spread diseases such as Dutch Elm Disease (see *Ipinae* and *Ips*).

PINK-BARRED SALLOW MOTH. *Citria lutea* or *Xanthia lutea*, a small noctuid moth, orange coloured with a broken band of pink or purple running across each fore-wing. A common European moth whose larvae feed on Sallow catkins.

PINK BOLLWORM. *Platyedra gossypiella* or *Pectinophora gossypiella*, a small moth of the group Tinaeoidea whose pink larvae feed on developing cotton seeds in North America. *Platyedra scutigera* is a similar pest of cotton in Queensland.

PINK GLOW-WORM. The larva and wingless female of the firefly *Microphotus angustus*, a beetle of the family Lampyridae common in dry grasslands of the Western United States.

PIOPHILA. *Piophila casei*, the Cheese Skipper: a small two-winged fly whose maggot-like larvae feed on cheese, meat or other fatty food substances. These larvae 'jump' when disturbed. They do this by grasping the hind-end with their mouth-hooks and then suddenly releasing it so that the body, as it straightens, is thrown forwards.

PIPE ORGAN MUD-DAUBER. *Trypoxylon albitarsus*, a solitary, black hunting wasp of the family Sphecidae which makes a nest of mud in the form of a number of tubes placed side by side and resembling organ pipes. These tubes are divided by partitions forming cells in which paralysed spiders are stored as food for the larvae.

PIPUNCULIDAE. Big-headed Flies, a family of small, predatory Diptera having spherical heads and enormous eyes.

PISSODES. A genus of Pine Weevils of Europe and North America, generally small, reddish brown with yellow scales forming bands or spots on the thorax and wing-covers. The snout is curved and tapering with the antennae inserted about half way along it. Both adults and larvae damage pine trees by burrowing between the bark and the wood. *Pissodes pini* and *Pissodes notatus* are European species; *Pissodes strobi* attacks the White Pine of North America.

PISTOL CASE-BEARER. *Coleophora malivorella*, a North American moth whose larvae feed on apple trees and make pistol-shaped nests of silk and pieces of leaf.

PITCH PINE MOTH. See *Parharmonia*.

PITHANUS. *Pithanus maerkeli*, a small brown capsid bug of the family Miridae, about 3 mm. long with antennae of the same length; omnivorous and commonly found among damp grass and rushes.

PITYOGENES. A genus of bark-beetles of the subfamily Ipinae which make extensive star-shaped galleries by tunnelling between the bark and the wood of pines and other conifers. Most species are brown or black and about 3 mm. long. *Pityogenes bidentatus* and *Pityogenes chalcographus* are two common species. They are not major pests but generally attack trees that are already weakened by frost or by fungus disease.

PITYOPHAGUS. A genus of predatory beetles of the family Nitidulidae: flattened, red, shiny beetles about 5 mm. long with whitish larvae. Both larvae and adults are predatory and are useful to the forester in keeping down the number of bark-beetles whose eggs and larvae form their principal food.

PITYOPHTHORUS. A genus of minute bark-beetles, usually less than 2 mm. long, that tunnel into the smaller branches of young conifers. They are frequently secondary pests on trees that have already been attacked by other insects or by fungi.

PLACOID RECEPTORS. Sensory organs, possibly olfactory, on the antennae of some insects. They are often called *pore-plates* and consist of a number of sensory cells beneath a very thin plate of cuticle.

PLANIPENNIA. A large suborder of Neuroptera including the brown and green lacewing flies and many other insects having two pairs of membranous wings with complex veins. The predatory larvae are terrestrial or aquatic and have piercing mouth-parts with the maxillae and mandibles interlocking to form a tube. They weave cocoons from silk produced through anal spinnerets.

PLANT-BORING CRICKET. *Cylindrodes kochi*, a unique wood-boring species of cricket from Australia having a cylindrical body with shortened legs, antennae and cerci. The legs bear sharp claws and the front pair, which are flattened, are very similar to those of the Mole-cricket *Gryllotalpa*.

PLANT-BUG. A general name for insects of the order Hemiptera and more particularly of the suborder Heteroptera. The mouth-parts of these insects are adapted for piercing and sucking with mandibles and maxillae in the form of long stylets lying in a trough-like labium; palps are reduced or absent. In most cases the proboscis can be folded back under the head and thorax when not in use. Although most members of the group are herbivorous there are a few predatory and blood-sucking species. The wings of Heteroptera are in two parts, the proximal half being horny and the distal half membranous; in a few cases, however, wings are absent. The number of species of plant-bugs is very large and includes shieldbugs, flatbugs, squashbugs, lacebugs, ground bugs, flower bugs, capsid bugs, water bugs and many others. The chief predatory species are the Assassin Bugs (Reduviidae), Water Scorpions (Nepidae) and Water Boatmen (Notonectidae). The chief blood-suckers are the wingless Bedbugs (Cimicidae). (See also *Bug, Hemiptera* and *Heteroptera*.)

PLANT-LICE. A general name for small sap-sucking insects of the order Hemiptera and the suborder Homoptera: hemimetabolous insects with piercing mouth-parts and usually with four membranous wings although many wingless forms exist. Many of them go through a complex life-cycle involving alternation between winged sexual forms and wingless parthenogenetic females. The name 'plant-lice' is often confined to the Aphids but in its broader sense may be extended to include Jumping Plant-lice (Psyllidae), Whiteflies (Aleyrodidae), Tree-hoppers (Membracidae), Leaf-hoppers (Cicadellidae), Froghoppers (Cercopidae) and a number of others (see *Hemiptera, Homoptera* and *Aphis*).

PLANTULAE. Adhesive pads on the tarsal sclerites of some insects.

PLASTRON (RESPIRATORY PLASTRON). A film or bubble of air held under the body of an aquatic insect by means of a number of curved hydrofuge hairs. Oxygen withdrawn from the plastron by respiration is replaced by diffusion from the water, and if this is enough for the needs of the insect, it need not come to the surface at all.

PLATAMBUS. *Platambus maculatus,* a small water beetle of the family Dytiscidae about 5 mm. long, oval and brown with black lines and patches on the wing-cases.

PLATEPHEMERA. *Platephemera antiqua,* a very large, extinct fossil mayfly with a wing-span of 12–15 cm.

PLATEUMARIS. *Plateumaris sericea,* a common Reed Beetle of the family Chrysomelidae, about 6 mm. long with antennae half this length and with long, narrow elytra of shiny bronze-like green, red, blue or black. It is a semi-aquatic insect and can hold a film of air under its body by means of dense, short, silky hairs that repel water (see *Plastron*). The larva is completely aquatic and obtains air by inserting its tail-spiracles into the stems of water plants.

PLATHEMIS. A genus of small dragonflies with three black spots or patches on each wing; *Plathemis trimaculatus* is a common species all over North America.

PLATYCNEMIDAE. Feather-footed or White legged Damselflies, a family of Zygoptera in which the tarsi of the hind-legs are white, flattened and hairy, resembling feathers. The nymphs have long legs and long antennae and are found in fast-running streams, *e.g. Platycnemis pennipes.*

PLATYEDRA. See *Pink Bollworm.*

PLATYGASTER. A genus of minute Hymenoptera of the group Proctotrypoidea, parasites of the Hessian Fly and other gall-midges; an example of an insect that develops by *polyembryony.*

PLATYMERIS. A genus of large Assassin Bugs (Reduviidae) equipped with a powerful salivary pump that can shoot out poisonous fluid to a distance of 30 cm. This fluid not only paralyses the insect's enemies but also starts the digestive process as it contains lipolytic and proteolytic enzymes.

PLATYPODIDAE. Pinhole-borers: minute beetles with snouts like those of weevils which bore minute holes in the bark of trees. The Oak Pinhole-borer (*Platypus cylindrus*) has in recent years become a serious timber pest in Europe; many others occur in the tropics.

PLATYPSYLLUS. *Platypsyllus castoris,* the Beaver Flea: a yellowish brown beetle of the family Leptinidae, having an extremely flattened body. It is wingless and blind and lives and breeds in the fur of the beaver.

PLATYPTERA. An obsolete name for a supposed order of insects comprising termites, book-lice and Embioptera.

PLATYPTERYX. *Platypteryx falcatoria,* an alternative name for the Hook-tip Moth *Drepana falcatoria* (see *Hook-tip Moths*).

PLATYPTILIA. *Platyptilia gonodactyla,* the Triangle Plume Moth: a member of the family Pterophoridae having narrow feather-like wings and long, spurred legs. Deep clefts divide the fore-wings into two and the hind-wings into three. The wings are patterned with light brown and white with a distinct triangle of darker brown on each fore-wing. The larvae feed on Coltsfoot (*Tussilago farfara*).

PLATYRHOPALOPSIS. *Platyrhopalopsis melyi,* a ground beetle that inhabits ants' nests in Burma; a grotesque species with flattened, club-like antennae larger than the head (see *Paussidae*).

PLATYURA. A North American genus of two-winged flies whose web-spinning larvae are luminescent and similar to the New Zealand Glow-worm *Bolitophila*. They belong to the family of fungus-eaters or Mycetophilidae, sometimes classed with the crane-flies (see *New Zealand Glow-worm*).

PLEA. *Plea atomaria*, a tiny, light brown, back-swimming water-bug about 2 mm. long, common in ponds and slow rivers where the eggs are inserted into leaves of *Elodea* and other pondweeds.

PLEASING FUNGUS BEETLES. See *Erotylidae*.

PLEBEJUS. A genus of Blue Butterflies (Lycaenidae) common throughout Europe, Asia and North Africa. They include the Silver-studded Blue *Plebejus argus*, the Zephyr Blue *Plebejus pylaon* and several others (see *Blue Butterflies* and *Lycaenidae*).

PLECOPTERA. Stoneflies: a somewhat primitive order of hemimetabolous insects having much in common with mayflies. There are four membranous wings, the hind pair having exceptionally large anal lobes. The body is soft and both the antennae and cerci are long and slender. The adult, as in the case of the mayfly, does not feed and lives only for a short time. The aquatic larvae, however, are predators.

PLEIDAE. Pigmy Back-swimmers: minute water bugs about 2 mm. long, common in ponds among dense water weeds (see *Plea*).

PLEMYRIA. *Plemyria rubiginata*, the Blue-bordered Carpet Moth: a small geometrid moth of the group Larentiinae, white with irregular patches of brown on the fore-wings which also have a broad border of bluish-brown containing a pale zig-zag line.

PLERERGATE. A worker ant with stomach enormously distended with food (see *Repletes*).

PLESIOCORIS. See *Apple Capsid*.

PLEURON. The lateral part of the cuticle in each segment of an insect or crustacean. A typical segment has four main cuticular plates, *viz.* a dorsal *tergum*, two lateral *pleura* and a ventral *sternum*. These may be further differentiated into tergites, pleurites and sternites.

PLEUROPODIA. Vestigial leg-like organs on the first abdominal segment of some insect embryos (*e.g.* those of grasshoppers and locusts), functioning as glandular organs secreting an enzyme that helps to dissolve the shell of the egg and to facilitate the hatching of the insect.

PLEUROPTYA. See *Mother-of-pearl Moth*.

PLODIA. *Plodia interpunctella*, the Indian Meal Moth: a world-wide pest of flour, cereals, nuts, dried fruit etc. (see *Indian Meal Moth*).

PLUM WEEVIL. *Conotrachelus nenuphar*, a small weevil, sometimes known as the Plum Curculio, that feeds on apples, cherries and other fruit as well as on plums. When disturbed it turns on its back and feigns death.

PLUME-MOTHS. Small moths of the family Pterophoridae characterized by having the wings deeply cleft and fringed, making them look like a bunch of feathers. The best known European species is the snow-white *Pterophorus pentadactyla* in which the front wing forms two plumes and the hind-wing three. Most of the European plume-moths are of this type but in Africa and Asia the Many-plume Moths are common in which each wing is divided into six. These, however, are rare in Europe.

PLUSIIDAE. A family of moths, sometimes classed with the noctuids but

237

differing from others in having broader fore-wings and a more slender body. They are mostly tropical moths but European species include the Silver Y (*Plusia gamma*), named from the Y- or gamma-shaped mark on the fore-wing. This breeds in southern Europe and North Africa and is a migrant to Britain.

PLUTELLA. *Plutella maculipennis*, the Diamond-back Moth: a pest of cabbages and other cruciferous plants, occasionally arriving in Britain in large numbers from Eastern Europe.

PODEON (PODEUM). A narrow stalk or petiole connecting the thorax with the abdomen in some insects.

PODEX. The pygidium or hind-part of the abdomen of an insect consisting of the last two or three segments sometimes fused together or modified for specific functions.

PODICAL PLATES. Latero-ventral plates formed by modification of the 10th abdominal segment of certain insects; they are on each side of the anus and may bear anal cerci.

PODISUS. A genus of carnivorous pentatomid bugs (also called *Troilus*), sometimes having sharp spines on the thorax. They commonly attack pests of fruit and vegetables and are therefore economically useful to man.

PODITES (PODOMERES). The limb segments of an insect or other arthropod, but only those which have independent musculature.

PODOSESIA. See *Lilac Borer*.

PODURA. *Podura aquatica*, the Water Springtail: a minute wingless insect of the order Collembola commonly found in large numbers on the surface of ponds. Owng to their small size (about 1 mm. long) and to the hydrofuge quality of their bodies these insects are not wetted and can leap about on the surface of the water. They are often carried long distances by the wind and are found in many parts of the world.

POECILASPIS. *Poecilaspis nervosa*, a Tortoise Beetle from Brazil: a black and red species about 1 cm. long, having a flattened body and broad wing-covers extending outwards to conceal the legs.

POECILOBOTHRUS. *Poecilobothrus nobilitatus*, one of the Long-legged Flies of the family Dolichopodidae: a small green, predatory fly with white tips on the wings of the male; found in large numbers on the edges of ponds and ditches where they run on the surface and make occasional short flights.

POECILOCAPSUS. *Poecilocapsus lineatus*, the Four-lined Leaf-bug of North America: a capsid bug of the family Miridae, brilliant green and red with four black longitudinal stripes; a pest of roses, dahlias and many other garden flowers.

POGONOMYRMEX. A genus of Harvester Ants: herbivorous ants that build large nests of loose soil or sand and clear the ground of vegetation all round.

POGONUS. *Pogonus chalceus*, a small, elongated beetle of an iridescent metallic purple or greenish colour, common on sea shores.

POISONS. Insects may produce poisonous substances for killing or paralysing their prey or, perhaps in weaker concentrations, merely for repelling their enemies. Poison may be discharged by way of a piercing sting which is often a modified ovipositor, as in bees and wasps; or it may be squirted, as in the case of some ants. It may be contained in the saliva injected into a wound made by a piercing proboscis prior to blood-sucking, as in bugs, fleas, mosquitoes etc. or it may enter the wound made by a bite from the large mandibles, as of certain beetles. Some insects such as arctiid caterpillars have stinging hairs; others discharge poison from special glands in their skin or by 'reflex bleeding'. In these cases mere contact may have a toxic effect on the victim.

Although there are a certain number of definite and well known poisons such as the formic acid of ants, the majority of insect poisons are extremely complicated and contain a mixture of soluble proteins and enzymes, amino acids, histamine or substances that produce it, together with various acids, alkalis, esters, blistering oils, nerve depressants, alkaloids and numerous other organic substances.

POLAR FRITILLARY. *Clossiana polaris*, a fritillary butterfly found in the extreme northern tundra of Europe, Asia and North America. The food plant of the larvae is not known but may be Mountain Avens (*Dryas octopetala*).

POLISHED APPLE BEETLE. *Chrysomela polita* or *Chrysolina polita*, a leaf-beetle of the family Chrysomelidae about 8 mm. long with rounded elytra and with a small head almost hidden by the thorax. The head and thorax are golden green and the elytra red and shiny. They are common on low herbaceous plants, particularly Labiatae.

POLISTIDAE. A widely distributed family of social wasps about 2-3 cm. long with a narrow body, black and brown or black and yellow. They build small papery nests on the sides of buildings or rocks and stock these with insects that have been stung and paralysed as food for the larvae.

POLLEN BASKET. Also called a *corbiculum*: a part of the hind-leg of a bee specially modified for carrying pollen. The tibia is flattened and bordered by long stiff hairs making a trough into which the pollen can be pushed. In leaf-cutting bees and some other solitary species the pollen basket is situated underneath the abdomen.

POLLEN BRUSH. Also called a *scopa*: a brush formed from rings of stiffened setae on the first tarsal segment of the hind-leg of a honey bee or similar species. It is used for brushing pollen off the body and into the pollen basket of the corresponding leg on the opposite side.

POLLEN COMB. (1) An alternative name for the bee's pollen brush (see above) (2) A comb-like structure in the joint between the tibia and tarsus of the first leg of a honey bee; used for cleaning pollen off the head and antennae.

POLLEN COMPRESSOR. Sometimes called the auricle on the hind-leg of a bee: a flattened plate forming the base of a concavity at the upper end of the first tarsal segment. Pollen is brushed into here and compressed by flexing the leg before being pushed into the pollen basket on the tibia.

POLLENIA. See Cluster-fly.

POLYARTHRON. A genus of longhorn beetles in which the antennae of the male are comb-like with numerous large, flattened, lateral branches on which are sensitive olfactory receptors. By means of these the male beetle can detect the presence of a female from a very long distance away, *e.g. Polyarthron komarovi*, from Asia.

POLYBIA. A genus of tropical wasps from Central and South America that make small papery nests under the leaves of palm trees.

POLYBOTHRIS. A genus of Splendour Beetles of the family Buprestidae:

large beetles from Madagascar coloured a brilliant iridescent green and red.

POLYCHRISIA. See *Golden Plusia Moth.*

POLYCTENIDAE. Bat-bugs: a family of brown, wingless bugs of the order Hemiptera living as ectoparasites on bats in tropical countries.

POLYDROSUS. *Polydrosus cervinus*, the Speckled Tree Weevil, about 5 mm. long, pale green mottled with brown; a common species in hedgerows and on nettles.

POLYEMBRYONY. The production of two or more individuals from a single egg by division of the embryo at a very early stage. This happens in many insects but is most notable among parasitic Hymenoptera, some of which produce many hundreds of embryos from one egg.

POLYERGUS. *Polyergus lucidus*, the Amazon Ant and *Polyergus rufescens* of Europe; species that make their nests in the ground and bring in the larvae and pupae of other species which they rear and enslave.

POLYGONIA. A genus of Angle-wing Butterflies: members of the family Nymphalidae having reddish brown wings mottled with black and with extremely irregular serrated edges. The undersides are dark brown and each species is characterized by a white or silvery mark whose shape gives its name to the species, *e.g. Polygonia C-album*, the Comma Butterfly and *Polygonia interrogationis*, the Question Mark etc. ´

POLYGRAPHUS. A bark-beetle of the family Scolytidae: a pest of coniferous forests in Europe and elsewhere. *Polygraphus polygraphus* is about 2 mm. long, brownish-black with yellow scales on the wing-covers. Both adults and larvae burrow beneath the bark of spruce and other conifers making numerous radiating galleries.

POLYMITARCYS. A genus of North American mayflies with burrowing nymphs that live beneath the mud at the bottom of ponds and slow-running streams.

POLYMORPHISM. The existence of several distinctly different forms within the same species. These may be simple sex differences or age differences but there are also other genetic and environmental factors which may bring about polymorphism. Bees, ants, wasps and termites have different 'castes', *e.g.* workers, drones, queens, soldiers etc. A few insects have multiple larval forms, as for instance the Blister Beetles, Meloidae. The first larval form is often very active, usually searching for a suitable host (see *Triungulin*); later instars may be relatively inactive scarabaeoid larvae. Plant-lice such as Aphids have winged sexual and wingless parthenogenetic forms. Locusts go through a solitary non-migratory phase and a gregarious migratory phase in which there is a distinct change in appearance as well as in habits. Many butterflies and other insects have regional variations of colour which may be connected with mimicry. The African *Papilio dardanus*, for instance, has forms which mimic several different butterflies living in the same region. There are numerous other examples.

POLYNEMA. *Polynema natans*, a minute chalcid wasp of the family Mymaridae or Fairy-flies, the smallest of all insects; able to swim with its wings under water and to lay its eggs in those of Water Boatmen.

POLYNEOPTERA. A group name used in some systems of classification to denote insects whose wings have a large number of veins arranged in an elaborate branching system. They include such insects as cockroaches, grasshoppers, earwigs, stoneflies etc. (see section on Classification).

POLYOMMATUS. A genus of Blue Butterflies of the family Lycaenidae common throughout Europe, Asia and North Africa. *Polyommatus icarus*, the Common Blue is found on chalk downs and grassland where the larvae feed on clover and other leguminous plants. The male is light blue with a narrow black edge and white fringes; the female is brown flushed with blue and with orange marginal spots. The undersides of both are light greyish with black and orange spots (see also *Blue Butterflies* and *Lycaenidae*).

POLYPEDILUM. A West African midge of the family Chironomidae whose aquatic larva can withstand extremes of drought and temperature for long periods. By losing most of its water it can survive in a shrunken, dried up state for several years and will withstand the temperature of liquid air (−190°C) and of boiling water. When the dried insect is immersed in fresh water it rapidly swells and starts to move and feed normally.

POLYPHAGA. The larger of the two suborders of beetles including a great diversity of families which can be distinguished from the other big suborder, the Adephaga, by the fact that the larvae are either legless or have legs with only one claw. There are also differences in the construction of the hind coxae. The antennae are of various forms and there is generally an absence of cross-veins in the hind-wings. Included in the Polyphaga are the Rove Beetles (Staphylinidae), Carrion Beetles (Silphidae), Ladybirds (Coccinellidae), Weevils (Curculionidae) and many others.

POLYPHAGOUS. Feeding on a variety of different foods or parasitizing a number of different hosts; not completely omnivorous, however, as they may still be selective.

POLYPHEMUS MOTH. *Telea polyphemus*, a giant Saturniid silk moth of North America with a wing-span of about 12 cm., yellowish pink with a transparent spot in each wing; those in the hind-wing being bordered with blue and black. The large green caterpillars feed on leaves of birch and oak. When disturbed they rear up and make a clicking sound with their jaws. They pupate in silken cocoons hanging from trees.

POLYPHYLLA. *Polyphylla fullo*, the Fuller: the largest of the European cockchafers about 4 cm. long with reddish brown wing-covers flecked with white; the males have very large, flattened, leaf-like antennae. When disturbed they make a chirping noise by rubbing the hind-wings against the abdomen, an unusual habit among beetles. These insects are to be found chiefly in pine forests of Central Europe where the larvae feed on roots of grass.

POLYPLAX. *Polyplax spinulosa*, the Spiny Rat-louse; a blood-sucking ecto-parasite of the order Anoplura infesting rats, mice and other rodents.

POLYPLOCIDAE. Lutestring Moths: a family of medium sized, fat, hairy moths with well developed tongues and short legs having leaf-like appendages on the first pair and four spurs on each hind-pair. The hind-wings are whitish and plain; the fore-wings have a delicate pattern of green and other colours. *Polyploca ridens*, the Frosted Green is a European species.

POLYPOD LARVA. Sometimes called an *Eruciform* larva: a typical caterpillar with soft body, a thin skin, six legs on the thorax and several pairs of prolegs or cushion-feet on the abdomen (see *Insect Larvae, Apodous, Oligopod*).

POLYRHACHIS. A genus of tropical ants that make sack-like nests of silk and pieces of leaves. Only the larvae can produce silk which issues from their labial glands. The adult ants hold the larvae in their jaws while other ants hold pieces of leaf. By skilful manipulation of these, the pieces of leaf are woven together to make the nest.

POLYTHALAMOUS GALL. A gall containing several developing larvae in separate compartments, *e.g.* the Hedgehog Gall on oak leaves, produced by the cynipid wasp *Acraspis erinacei*.

POLYTROPHIC. See *Polyphagous*.

POLYTROPHIC OVARIOLE. A type of egg-tube present in most insects, consisting of a successive series of chambers each of which contains trophocytes for nourishing the developing egg-cells (see *Ovary* and *Ovariole*).

POLYURA. A genus of large nymphalid butterflies from the forests of India, south-east Asia, Indonesia and Australia; powerful, high-flying insects with a wing-span of 8 cm. or more and with irregular serrations extending to form two short 'tails' on each hind-wing. *Polyura delphis* is yellowish with blue and brown markings; *Polyura pyrrhus* is pale greenish-white, edged broadly with white spots on dark brown and with an orange spot on the hind-edge of each hind-wing.

POMACE-FLIES. See *Drosophilidae*.

POMPILIDAE. Spider-wasps, a family of hunting wasps that catch spiders and store them as food for their developing larvae. They are long-legged and rarely fly long distances but run over the ground to catch their prey which they sting and paralyse. The nests may be underground or may be cup-shaped nests of mud in crevices of rocks or trees (see *Psammocharidae*).

POND AGABUS. A number of species of small carnivorous water-beetles of the family Dytiscidae, *e.g. Agabus paludosus*, about 12 mm. long, yellow strippled with dark brown; common in ponds and streams.

POND OLIVE. *Cloeon dipterum*, a species of small mayfly with an olive-green body, a double tail-fork (instead of the usual triple) and only two wings, the hind-pair being vestigial.

PONDSKATERS. Gerridae, a family of long, slender, predatory bugs of the group Heteroptera having the front legs adapted for catching their prey and the other four (which are larger) for locomotion. They rest on the surface of ponds or slow streams and make sudden rapid movements, darting in search of their prey. The body has a hydrofuge texture and is therefore not wetted by the water.

PONDWEED BUG. *Mesovelia furcata*, a small, yellowish brown water-bug of the order Hemiptera about 3 mm. long with long legs and antennae. It swims on the surface of ponds and slow streams, especially among floating leaves of pondweed where it searches for its prey.

PONERA. A genus of primitive carnivorous ants living in small underground colonies. There are two species in Britain but the majority of this and related genera of the subfamily Ponerinae are tropical. They are particularly abundant in Australia.

PONTANIA. A genus of Bean-gall Sawflies whose larvae make red or brown galls shaped like kidney beans on the leaves of willows. *Pontania vesicator*, a common species, is about 7 mm. long, black with a yellowish white abdomen.

PONTIA. A genus of pierid butterflies ranging all over Europe, Asia and North Africa. *Pontia daplidice*, the Bath White, is a rare immigrant to Britain from Europe. It resembles the Green-veined White but has a large, square, black spot in the middle of each fore-wing.

PONTOMYIA. *Pontomyia natans*, a chironomid gnat whose larvae and wingless females live completely submerged in the salt-water lagoons of Samoa (see *Oceanic Insects*).

POPILLIA *Popillia japonica*, the Japanese Beetle: a member of the family Scarabaeidae similar to a cockchafer. This species, one of several from Eastern Asia, was introduced accidentally into North America and has become a major pest of grass and cereals. The adults eat the foliage and the larvae eat the roots.

POPLAR BORER (POPLAR LONGHORN). *Saperda carcharias, Saperda populnea* and several related species of elongated longhorn beetles whose larvae tunnel between the bark and the wood of poplars and willows, in some cases producing galls on young stems. The adults are black with a coating of fine grey or yellowish hairs.

POPLAR CRIMSON UNDERWING. *Catocala elocata*, a large noctuid moth of Central and Southern Europe and Western Asia; closely related and very similar to the British Red Underwing, *Catocala nupta*. It has a wing-span of about 8 cm., the fore-wings mottled grey and brown; the hind-wings bright red with a black band and black margins. The larvae feed on poplar and willow leaves.

POPLAR GALL APHID. *Pemphigus bursarius*, an aphid that produces 'purse-galls' on the leaves and petioles of various species of poplar trees. These galls are like sacs with a narrow opening at one end from which the mature aphids emerge.

POPLAR GREY MOTH. *Apatele megacephala* or *Acronycta megacephala*, a noctuid moth with grey body and elaborately patterned grey fore-wings with wavy transverse lines and a dark-centred ring in the middle. The larvae are brown with numerous long white hairs. They pupate in silken cocoons in crevices in the bark of poplar trees.

POPLAR HAWK-MOTH. *Laothoe populi*, a common European and Asiatic hawk-moth of the family Sphingidae having serrated wings spanning about 75 mm. and varying in colour with a predominance of brown, grey and green resembling a dried leaf. The caterpillars are bright green with a horn at the hind-end and with oblique yellow lines along the sides. They feed on poplar, willow, ash and a few other trees.

POPLAR KITTEN MOTH. *Cerura bifida*, a moth closely resembling the Puss Moth (*Cerura vinula*) but having grey wings marked with black. The caterpillar, about 4 cm. long, is green with a red and violet back and with two erectile tail filaments. It feeds on poplar and aspen leaves.

POPLAR LEAF-BEETLE. *Melasoma populi* or *Chrysomela populi*, a leaf-beetle of the family Chrysomelidae, about 1 cm. long, bluish green with dark red or brown elytra. The whitish larvae, resembling those of ladybirds, feed on the soft parts of poplar leaves, reducing them to skeletons.

POPLAR LEAF TYER. *Melalopha inclusa*, a small moth whose larvae live gregariously and make nests by tying several pieces of poplar leaves together.

POPLAR LONGHORN. A name for several species of the genus *Saperda*: longhorn beetles of the family Cerambycidae whose larvae feed for several years in the trunks of poplar trees; the adults feed on the leaves. *Saperda carcharias* is light brown and about 2 cm. long; *Saperda populnea* is darker and about half this size.

POPLAR SAWFLY. *Cladius viminalis* or *Trichiocampus viminalis*, a sawfly about 8 mm. long with a black or brown head and thorax and a yellow abdo men and legs. The larvae, which are yellow with black spots, feed gregariously on the undersides of poplar leaves.

POPLAR AND WILLOW BORER. *Cryptorrhynchus lapathi*, a weevil about 1 cm. long, black with yellowish white scales on the sides of the thorax. The snout is moderately long and curved and is usually bent back and hidden below the thorax when the insect is not feeding. Both adults and larvae tunnel into poplars and willows. The males are able to stridulate.

PORPHYRASPIS. *Porphyraspis tristis*, a minute tropical South American beetle living on coconut palms; remarkable for the fact that the larva makes an elaborate, rounded nest like a miniature bird's nest constructed of inter woven threads of faecal material.

PORTHETRIA. An alternative name for *Lymantria*, the Gipsy Moth (*q.v.*).

POSTMENTUM. The proximal part of the labium of an insect, usually divided into two parts known respectively as the *mentum* and *submentum*.

POSTNOTUM. Also called the *post-scutellum*: the hindmost dorsal sclerite on either of the wing-bearing segments of an insect. A typical notum or tergum is, at any rate in its early stages, divided into three parts: *prescutum*, *scutum* and *scutellum*. The post-scutellum when present is immediately behind the scutellum and is formed by hardening of the intersegmental membrane.

POST-SCUTELLUM. See *Postnotum*.

POSTURAL HAIRS. Rows of specialized hairs or setae with sensory receptors (proprioceptors) at their bases so that a change of position of the hairs gives the insect information about its posture. They are chiefly situated at the joints, especially between the head and thorax and between the thorax and abdomen.

POTAMANTHUS. *Potamanthus luteus*, a common species of small mayfly abounding by the rivers of Central Europe. The larvae live under stones or burrow in the mud.

POTATO BEETLE. See *Colorado Beetle*.

POTATO WORM. A name colloquially used in North America for the large green and white larvae of certain hawk-moths such as *Acherontia* that feed on the leaves of the potato plant.

POTOSIA. *Potosia cuprea* or *Cetonia cuprea*, the Northern Rose Chafer: a large, rounded, shiny blue beetle whose larvae are scavengers living in the nests of wood ants.

POTTER. See *Potter Wasp*.

POTTER BEE. *Anthophora acervorum* and related species of bees, sometimes called Flower Bees, whose underground nests consist of cells in the form of little clay pots. These are filled with honey and pollen and an egg is laid in each.

POTTER WASP. *Eumenes coarctata* and related species of small black and yellow solitary wasps that make flask-shaped nests of clay. These are often attached to the stems of heather and other plants or to rocks and walls.

POWDER POST BEETLE. See *Lyctidae*.

PRAON. A genus of minute Braconid flies whose larvae are parasites in the bodies of aphids. They eat away their victims from the inside and, after crawling out, make tent-like cocoons of silk in which they pupate.

PRAYING MANTIS. See *Mantidae*.

PRAYS. *Prays curtisellus* and related species: small moths of the family Tineidae having white fore-wings and dark brown hind-wings; the caterpillars are yellowish, turning green. In the early stages they mine into ash leaves but when they become too large for this they bore into the terminal buds, doing much damage to the trees.

PRECIS. A genus of nymphalid butterflies found in many parts of the world. *Precis orithya*, blue with white and red markings, is found in Africa and right across Asia; *Precis coenia*, greyish brown with large eye-spots, is the Buck-eye from the Southern United States. *Precis octavia*, a South African species, is especially remarkable for its extreme dimorphism. A blue variety with black, red and white markings emerges in the dry season and a totally different pinkish orange variety in the wet season. These two are so different that they were at first thought to be two distinct species.

PREDATORY INSECTS. Predatory habits are to be found in many orders of insects and in all these either the mouth-parts or the legs are specially modified for catching their prey. Dragonflies, Dytiscid Beetles and Neuroptera have powerful jaws which in some cases have serrated edges. The nymph of the dragonfly has a powerful prehensile labium known as the *mask* which can be folded under the head when at rest and shot rapidly out when suitable prey presents itself. Bugs such as Pentatomids impale their prey on the sharp proboscis. The Praying Mantis has its front legs modified so that the tarsus can be folded back against the tibia like a jack-knife, the edges of both being toothed; it also has powerful jaws and a very flexible neck. Robber Flies (Asilidae) have all their legs powerful and hairy for catching small insects in flight. They hold them with their legs and then use the piercing proboscis. Some Scorpion-flies and Hunting Wasps support themselves with their front legs and catch their prey with the enlarged hind-legs. A few insects, such as the Ant-lion, dig pits in which they lie in wait with their jaws open ready to catch any passing insect.

PREHISTORIC INSECTS. See *Fossil Insects*.

PREMENTUM. The free distal part of the labium of an insect, bearing the labial palps and the ligula.

PREPONA. *Prepona demophon*, a large fritillary butterfly from tropical South America having violet wings with a large patch of sky blue on each; the wing-span is about 10 cm.

PREPUPA. The stage before the pupa in the development of a holometabolous insect. During this stage feeding usually ceases and sometimes a cocoon is produced. The prepupa may resemble the larva but is often shrunken and less pigmented. It is sometimes considered to be a pharate pupa (see *Pharate Instar*).

PRESCUTUM. The anterior of three sclerites which typically form the notum or dorsal cuticular covering over each of the three thoracic segments of an insect (see also *Scutum* and *Scutellum*).

PRESTOMAL TEETH. Small chitinous teeth round the prestomum or outer 'mouth' of a blowfly or similar insect; distinct from the *pseudotracheal teeth*, which are formed from the chitinous rings of the pseudotracheae. (See also *Prestomum* below.)

PRESTOMUM. A 'mouth' to which the food channels or *pseudotracheae* converge at the bases of the two labella or oral lobes on a blowfly, house fly or similar insect. It is not a true mouth, since this is further back at the entrance to the pharynx.

PRESTWICHIA. *Prestwichia aquatica,* a minute chalcid wasp of the family Trichogrammatidae, about 1 mm. long, having feathery wings with long fringing hairs. It can swim under water to lay its eggs in those of water-beetles and water-bugs, the larvae being parasitic in these.

PRETARSUS. The 'foot' of an insect: the last segment of the tarsus usually bearing two claws with a pad or *arolium* between them.

PRETTY CHALK CARPET MOTH. *Melanthia procellata,* a common European moth of the family Larentiinae found chiefly on chalk and limestone hills. The wing-span is about 3 cm. and the wings are elaborately patterned in brown and white. The larvae, which are brown and stick-like, feed on Traveller's Joy (*Clematis vitalba*).

PRIMITIVE INSECTS. It is generally believed that present-day insects have evolved from some form of wingless arthropod intermediate between insects and millipedes. The most primitive of existing insects and the nearest to the hypothetical ancestor are the four orders comprising the Apterygota, commonly known as Bristle-tails and Springtails, *viz.* Diplura, Thysanura, Protura and Collembola. These are all wingless insects that undergo little or no metamorphosis and have little specialization of mouth-parts or other organs. Many authorities do not regard them as true insects. The Silverfish *Lepisma* is one of the best known examples (see also *Fossil Insects*).

PRIOCNEMIS. *Priocnemis perturbator,* one of the largest of the spider-hunting wasps of the family Pompilidae: a black and red wasp that stings and paralyses spiders as food for its larvae (see *Pompilidae*).

PRIONOMERUS. A genus of weevils whose larvae are leaf-miners that tunnel into the leaves of tulips and sassafras (a form of small North American laurel).

PRIONOXYSTUS. *Prionoxystus robiniae,* a North American species of Goat Moth of the family Cossidae whose larva, known as the Carpenter Worm, does much damage by boring into timber.

PRIONUS. A genus of large longhorn beetles of the family Cerambycidae, 4–5 cm. long, brown or black with three spines on each side of the thorax and with saw-toothed antennae. The larvae feed on the stumps and roots of dead trees. *Prionus corarius,* the only British member of the family, is the largest British longhorn. *Prionus laticollis* and *Prionus californicus* are North American species, the latter being at one time much favoured as food by the native Indians.

PRIOPTERA. A genus of Tortoise Beetles from South-east Asia, brown with red spots on the thorax and elytra (see *Cassidinae*).

PRISTIPHORA. *Pristiphora erichsoni* or *Lygaeonematus erichsoni,* the Large Larch Sawfly: a member of the family Tenthredinidae with black and red body, yellow legs and a wing-span of about 25 mm., a common pest of larch trees in Europe and North America.

PRIVET HAWK-MOTH. *Sphinx ligustri,* a large European hawk-moth with the abdomen striped in black and pink; the fore-wings grey with some black, brown and pinkish patches; the hind-wings pink and black. The caterpillars, which may be 8 cm. long, are bright green with oblique reddish brown and white lines and with a prominent curved 'horn' at the hind-end. They feed on privet and lilac leaves.

PROBEZZIA. *Probezzia bicolor*, a species of Biting Midge of the family Cera-topogonidae or small blood-sucking gnats. The worm-like larvae, which are aquatic and predatory, have a tuft of 'flotation hairs' at the hind-end of the abdomen.

PROBOSCIS. The lengthened mouth-parts of an insect specially adapted for piercing, sucking or other specialized modes of feeding. The basic mouth-parts of all insects are the *labrum, maxillae, mandibles, hypopharynx* and *labium*; the proboscis may be formed by a lengthening of any or all of these. In butterflies the tubular 'tongue' is formed by the two lengthened, interlocking maxillae, the mandibles having disappeared; in bees the labium is lengthened for sucking nectar and there is a sensory pad or *flabellum* at the end of it. In plant-bugs and blood-sucking bugs the labium forms a lengthened, trough-like lower lip with the mandibles and maxillae in the form of fine piercing stylets resting in it. The whole, when not in use, is folded back under the head. In mosquitoes the arrangement is somewhat similar but the labrum, maxillae, mandibles and hypopharynx are all in the form of piercing stylets, the hypopharynx forming a channel down which saliva is discharged. In the house fly and the blowfly the proboscis is highly specialized for suction and filtration of food that has been partly digested externally by the discharge of saliva over it. The main part is the labium developed into a large pair of oral lobes or *labella* in the form of pads containing suction tubes or *pseudotracheae* which can be pressed against the surface on which the insect is feeding. In the Tsetse flies and a few others the labella have become reduced and the labium stiffened into a piercing organ. There are many other forms of proboscis (see also *Mouth-parts*).

PROCEREBRUM. A term sometimes used synonymously with protocerebrum (the fore-brain of an insect or other arthropod), but more strictly including the protocerebrum *plus* parts derived from embryonic presegmental ganglia (see *Brain* and *Protocerebrum*).

PROCESSIONARY MOTH. *Thaumetopoea processionea* or *Cnethocampa processionea*, a moth that lives in oak forests of Europe and whose caterpillars are noted for their habit of travelling along at night in procession one behind the other. During the daytime they rest gregariously in silken nests.

PROCIPHILUS. *Prociphilus tessellata*, the Maple-leaf Aphid: a plant-louse that lives gregariously in closely packed communities on the leaves of maple, alder etc. protected by white downy threads which they secrete.

PROCRIS. *Procris statices*, the Green Burnet or Forester Moth: a small, bright green moth of the family Zygaenidae found in meadows and heaths throughout Europe. The larvae feed on sorrel.

PROCTOTRUPOIDEA. Minute parasitic Hymenoptera which attack the eggs or small larvae of other insects. They differ from ichneumons, chalcids and other members of the group Parasitica in having the ovipositor in a terminal position instead of issuing further forward beneath the abdomen. Many of them are *hyperparasites* living in the bodies of other parasites such as gall-flies. Like most such insects they exhibit the phenomenon of polyembryony.

PROCULUS. *Proculus mniszechi*, a large stag-beetle from Central America, about 6 cm. long, black with brown hairs along the sides.

PROCUS. *Procus strigilis*, the Marbled Minor Moth: a small noctuid moth mottled with grey and white; a very common European species whose larvae feed on grasses.

PROECDYSIS. The period of preparation for a moult in an insect or other arthropod.

PROFENUSA. *Profenusa canadensis*, the Cherry-hawthorn Sawfly, a member of the family Tenthredinidae. The female has a reddish thorax and a black abdomen; the male has a whitish thorax and a broad white dorsal band along the abdomen. It mines the leaves of cherry and hawthorn in North America.

PROJAPYGIDAE. A primitive family of Diplura or bristle-tails closely approximating to the supposed ancestral type of insect and forming a link between insects and millepedes.

PROLEGS. Short unjointed limbs on some of the abdominal segments of caterpillars. Except for the 'loopers' (Geometridae), which have only two pairs, most caterpillars of moths and butterflies have five pairs of prolegs. Those of Micropterygidae have eight, and sawflies usually have six or seven pairs. Prolegs are used for grasping and this is often helped by numerous small hooks called *crochets*, which are not found in the larvae of sawflies.

PROMACHUS. A very large and almost world-wide genus of Robber Flies (Asilidae), which actively hunts its prey by 'patrolling' on the wing.

PROMECOTHECA. A genus of small leaf-beetles of the family Chrysomelidae: pests of coconut palms in South-east Asia, from Malaya to New Guinea.

PROMETHEA MOTH. See *Callosamia*.

PROMINENT MOTHS. Notodontidae: a world-wide family of swift, night-flying moths characterized by having a prominent tooth-like tuft of scales projecting back from the centre of each front wing. The caterpillars are often fantastically shaped and some have two long flexible tail-filaments. They include the Puss Moth *Cerura vinula*, the Lobster Moth *Stauropus fagi* and many others.

PRONOTUM. The dorsal cuticular covering of the first thoracic segment of an insect, sometimes enlarged to form a shield covering the rest of the thorax.

PRONUBA. *Pronuba yuccasella*, the Yucca Moth of North America: a small moth that pollinates the Yucca plant by collecting pollen on its specially modified proboscis, moulding it into a ball and carrying it to the stigma of another flower. At the same time it takes advantage of these visits to lay its eggs in the developing ovaries of the flower so that the larvae can feed on the seed as they form.

PRONYMPH. A newly hatched first instar nymph of a dragonfly or other hemimetabolous insect.

PROP BEETLE. *Hister fimentarius*, a small black, oval beetle about 1 cm. long, of the family Histeridae commonly found in dung or carrion. When disturbed it stiffens and feigns death.

PROPLEURON. The pleuron or lateral cuticular plate of the prothorax.

PROPNEUSTIC. A term used to denote insects whose only functional spiracles are those in the prothorax. Such a condition is rare but is found in the pupae of certain Diptera (*cf. Holopneustic* and *Metapneustic*).

PROPODEUM. The narrow posterior part of the thorax of a bee, ant or similar insect, partly surrounding the petiole or stalk of the abdomen and, together with it, forming the waist of the insect. It is considered to be the first abdominal segment, transferred to the thorax.

PROPOLIS. Bee-glue: a resinous material of vegetable origin used by bees in addition to wax for the building and repair of their nests.

PROPOMACRUS. *Propomacrus jansoni*, a large chafer beetle found on palm trees in South-east Asia; about 6 cm. long, brown and characterized by having the front legs of the male exceptionally long, thickened and curved so that movement is slow and clumsy.

PROPUPA. See *Prepupa*.

PROSERPINUS. *Proserpinus proserpina*, the Willow-herb Hawk-moth: a European species with a span of about 4 cm., the front wings olive green and the hind-wings yellow with a black border. The caterpillars feed on Willow-herb (*Epilobium*), Evening Primrose (*Oenothera*) and other plants of the family Onagraceae.

PROSOPIS. A genus of primitive bees of the family Colletidae, small, black, hairless and without pollen baskets. They may make their nests in the ground but often do so in hollow plant stems or empty galls.

PROSTEMMA. A genus of small carnivorous bugs of the family Nabiidae having a long, narrow body and very short elytra. *Prostemma guttata*, a common European species is shiny, blue-black with bright red elytra and legs.

PROTAPTERA. A suggested name for a hypothetical common ancestor of insects, millipedes and centipedes.

PROTARSUS. The tarsus of the first leg of an insect.

PROTECTIVE COLORATION. Most insects derive a certain degree of protection by their form and colour and, since the majority of insects have a predominance of brown, black, green or yellow, it is not surprising that many of them, when motionless, blend with their background and become almost invisible: grasshoppers on grass; beetles on bark; the Peppered Moth on a lichen-covered tree and its melanic variety on a smoke blackened tree; the yellow striped cinnabar caterpillar on the flowers of ragwort etc. This camouflage may be effected not only by a matching of colours but also by a disruptive pattern which disguises the insect's outline.

Many insects are protected by their shape. Imitation of form is shown in the stick-insects and leaf-insects (Phasmida), in the stick-like caterpillars of many geometrid moths and in the remarkable resemblance to a leaf shown by such insects as the Indian Leaf Butterfly *Kallima* when its wings are folded.

The resemblance of a harmless insect to a poisonous or distasteful one gives protection to the former, since predators will tend to avoid both. This is known as *Batesian Mimicry* and is shown well in some butterflies and in the clearwing moths that resemble bees and wasps. There are numerous other examples.

PROTEPHEMEROPTERA. Fossil insects of the Permian period having affinities with present-day mayflies (Ephemeroptera) and also with the primitive fossil dragonflies (Protodonata). Both are characterized by the very complete pattern of venation of the wings with numerous cross-veins forming a network or *archedictyon*.

PROTEREISMA. A fossil insect of the Lower Permian period resembling a mayfly but with the two pairs of wings alike in size and shape.

PROTHETELY. Precocious appearance of adult characters as a result of insufficient juvenile hormone (*cf. Metathetely*).

PROTHOE. *Prothoe calydonia*, a large nymphalid butterfly from the forests

PRO–PRO

of South-east Asia, having a wing-span of about 9 cm., pale green and yellow
with a broad border of chocolate brown.

PROTHORACIC GLAND. A gland in the prothorax of some insects that
secretes a moulting hormone. When the amount of this hormone reaches a
certain level it stimulates the glands in the skin to produce *moulting fluid* which
dissolves away the lower layers of the cuticle (see *Ecdysis*).

PROTHORAX. The first segment of an insect's thorax, bearing the first pair
of legs but not the wings which are on the second and third segments.

PROTOCALLIPHORA. *Protocalliphora azurea* and related species: blowflies
that lay their eggs in birds' nests so that the developing larvae can suck the
blood of the young birds.

PROTOCEREBRUM. The front part of the brain of an insect formed embry-
onically from the fused ganglia of the first somite (see also *Deutocerebrum* and
Tritocerebrum).

PROTOCOLEOPTERA. Fossil insects with thickened tegmina resembling
those of beetles; possibly they were the ancestors of both the Coleoptera and
the Strepsiptera.

PROTODONATA. Primitive dragonflies of Palaeozoic times with wing-
venation more simplified than that of present-day species. Possibly the Protodonata and the true Odonata are both derived from a common ancestor
approximating to the Palaeodictyoptera (*q.v.*).

PROTOGONIUS. *Protogonius tithoreides*, a nymphalid butterfly of Central
and South America with a wing-span of about 8 cm. The upper surfaces are
red, yellow and brown but the undersides of the wings are mottled with grey
and brown so that when the wings are folded the butterfly resembles a dead
leaf with the 'tails' of the hind-wings forming the stalk.

PROTOHYMENOPTERA. Fossil insects resembling bees and wasps, found
in the Permian and Jurassic rocks. They had two pairs of wings of equal size,
without coupling apparatus and with venation of a generalized type.

PROTOMICROPOLITUS. *Protomicropolitus connexus*, a small black or
brown Braconid fly about 2 mm. long that lays its eggs in the caterpillars of
Tussock Moths (Lymantriidae). The larvae develop and pupate within the
body of their victim. Some Tussock Moths that are agricultural pests have been
kept under control by deliberately introducing these parasites.

PROTOPARCE. A genus of North American Hawk-moths whose larvae
are pests of tobacco, potatoes and other plants of the family Solanaceae.
Protoparce sexta from the Southern States and the West Indies defoliates
tobacco and tomatoes. *Protoparce quinquemaculata*, whose larva is known as
the Tomato Hornworm, is a common pest throughout the United States.

PROTOPERLARIA. Fossil insects which were probably ancestral to present-
day stone-flies (Plecoptera) and also showed some resemblance to Orthoptera.

PROTOPOD LARVA. The most primitive type of insect larva with unsegmented abdomen and rudimentary appendages. Such larvae are usually
endoparasites and can only survive where food is abundant, making locomotion
unnecessary. They are characteristic of the Proctotrupoidea, a group of minute
parasitic Hymenoptera.

PROTOPOLYBIA. A genus of small wasps that build their paper nests on
the undersides of palm leaves.

PROTORTHOPTERA. Fossil insects of the Palaeozoic Era probably ancestral to both Orthoptera and Coleoptera.

PROTURA. Minute wingless insects, 1–2 mm. long, without eyes or antennae and with piercing mouth-parts contained in pockets from which they can be extruded when feeding. They live under bark and stones or in rotting vegetation, sometimes very deep in the ground (see also *Anamorphosis*).

PROVENTRICULUS. The gizzard or 'stomach' of insects and other arthropods, usually thick and muscular with chitinous teeth or ossicles (see *Alimentary Canal*).

PRZIBRAM'S RULE. An empirical rule observed in certain insects according to which the weight of an insect doubles during each instar and the linear dimensions are increased at each moult by the ratio 1.26 or $\sqrt[3]{2}$. This can be explained on the assumption that during each stage every cell divides once and grows to its original size.

PSAMMOCHARIDAE. A widely distributed family of Spider-wasps: long-legged, solitary wasps usually black or bluish with an orange or red band on the abdomen. They nest in burrows or crevices which they stock with stung and paralysed spiders as food for the larvae. *Psammocharus atrox* is a common North American species; *Psammocharus mirandus* and *Psammocharus ilus* are found in India. (See *Pompilidae*.)

PSELAPHIDAE. A family of small yellow or reddish beetles that inhabit ants' nests, sharing their food and in return providing a sticky secretion favoured by their hosts.

PSEPHENIDAE. Riffle Beetles, a family of small water beetles living among gravel or rocks in streams and lakes. The larvae, known as water pennies, are flattened and disc-like, and cling tightly to stones. They are found in India and America.

PSEUDAGENIA. A genus of Spider-wasps of the family Pompilidae that make thimble-shaped nests of mud in crevices or beneath stones and stock them with spiders as food for their larvae.

PSEUDAPOSEMATIC CHARACTERS. False warning colours. Batesian mimicry in which a harmless insect bears a resemblance to a poisonous or dangerous one and is thus given a degree of protection since predators will tend to avoid both.

PSEUDOCOCCIDAE. An important family of Mealy Bugs: Homoptera that suck plant juices and are destructive pests of various crops in the warmer parts of the world. The adult females are flattened, wingless insects covered with fine threads of a white waxy secretion. They reproduce very rapidly, each individual giving birth to about 300 young. *Pseudococcus njalensis* is a West African species that spreads Swollen Shoot Disease in cacao plants; *Pseudococcus kenyae* attacks coffee plants in Kenya; *Pseudococcus citri* attacks citrus plants; *Pseudococcus adonidum*, the Long-tailed Mealy Bug, is a pest of coconut and other palm trees as well as citrus, coffee and cacao; in more temperate climates it may be found on a variety of greenhouse plants (see also *Coccidae*).

PSEUDOCONE EYES. Compound eyes such as those of the house fly in which the crystalline cones are imperfectly formed and consist of a mass of liquid. In eyes of this type the cuticular lenses form the main part of the optical system (see *Compound Eyes*).

PSEUDOHALTERES. Reduced or vestigial fore-wings of Strepsiptera in the

251

form of small club-shaped processes. They resemble but are not homologous with the halteres or balancers of Diptera, the latter being reduced hind-wings (see *Strepsiptera*).

PSEUDOMYRMA. A genus of ants that make their nests inside the hollow thorns of the Acacia plant in Central and South America. They enter by boring a hole near the apex of the thorn and feed on the sugary juice inside. The presence of these ants may be beneficial to the host as they tend to drive away other more destructive insects. The hollowed thorns also provide a ready shelter.

PSEUDOPANTHERA. *Pseudopanthera macularia*, the Speckled Yellow Moth: a small geometrid moth, bright orange-yellow with numerous, rather irregular, dark brown spots. It is common in woodlands throughout Europe where the larvae feed on Wood Sage, Dead Nettle and other Labiatae.

PSEUDOPHYLLIDAE. A family of large long-horned grasshoppers (Tettigoniidae) which, when the wings are folded, resemble dry, yellowish brown leaves. When they fly, however, a pair of bright blue and red eye-spots on the hind-wings becomes visible (see *Flash Colouring*).

PSEUDOPLACENTAL VIVIPARITY. A phenomenon found in certain insects in which the egg has very little yolk and the embryo is nourished through placenta-like structures in contact with maternal tissue. It occurs in *Hemimerus*, the parasitic earwig, in some aphids and Psocoptera and in the Polyctenidae (Hemiptera).

PSEUDOPODS. See *Prolegs*.

PSEUDOPUPA. A resting stage resembling a pupa between two larval instars, as for instance in the Oil Beetles, Meloidae.

PSEUDOTERPNA. *Pseudoterpna pruinata*, the Grass Emerald Moth: a geometrid moth of a pale emerald green colour with a thin wavy transverse line of darker green across each wing. The larvae feed on gorse, broom and other leguminous plants where they are well camouflaged resembling the green seed-pods.

PSEUDOTRACHEAE. Food channels resembling tracheae in the membrane covering the labellar lobes of house flies, blowflies and similar Diptera. Each lobe has a large number of these tubes which are supported and kept open by incomplete sclerotized rings. They converge into collecting ducts which lead to the prestomum and hence to the mouth.

PSEUDOTRACHEAL TEETH. Crushing organs formed from the chitinous rings of the pseudotracheae. Contrast with *Prestomal* Teeth.

PSILIDAE. A family of small, black, two-winged flies, the larvae of some of which bore into the roots of many plants, particularly of the family Umbelliferae. The Carrot Fly, *Psila rosae*, attacks carrots, parsnips and parsley as well as wild plants such as Hemlock. The yellowish white maggots bore right into the roots and may kill the plant.

PSILOPA. *Psilopa petrolei*, a small fly whose larvae live in pools of petroleum around the oil wells of California (see *Petroleum Fly*).

PSILOTRETA. A genus of caddis flies whose larvae, like those of most caddis flies, make tubular cases from grains of sand and small stones. They pupate within the tube and, when ready to do so, they congregate in a vertical position with their heads uppermost. This arrangement facilitates a rapid emergence of the adult fly with the minimum amount of wetting.

PSITHYRUS. A genus of Cuckoo Bees that lay their eggs in the nests of Bumble Bees: *e.g. Psithyrus rupestris* which uses the nest of *Bombus lapidarius* and closely resembles its host.

PSOCOPTERA. An order of insects containing the Book-lice and related insects: small soft-bodied insects with long thread-like antennae. They may be winged or wingless and have biting mouth-parts. Some feed on the dried paste of old books. Although these are the best known, however, they are in the minority. Most of the related species are found among vegetation or on the bark of trees.

PSOPHUS. *Psophus strididulus*, the Red-winged Scraping Grasshopper from the mountainous regions of Central Europe: a member of the family Oedipodidae noted for its loud stridulation.

PSOROPHORA. A genus of blood-sucking mosquitoes with predatory larvae; found in Central and South America and noted for being carriers of the eggs of the Human Bot Fly *Dermatobia hominis* (*q.v.*).

PSYCHIDAE. See *Bagworms*.

PSYCHODIDAE. See *Moth-flies*.

PSYCHOPSIS. A genus of predatory Neuroptera in which the mandibles, which are serrated at the tips, fit into grooves in the maxillae, forming channels up which the juices of the victims are sucked. The genus is recognized by a broad double rib which strenghtens the middle of each wing.

PSYLLIDAE. See *Jumping Plant-lice*.

PSYLLIODES. *Psylliodes affinis*, the Potato Flea-beetle: a small oval beetle of the family Chrysomelidae about 2 mm. long with light brown body, long antennae, black head and black hind femora which are powerful and used for jumping. It is commonly found on leaves of potato and other plants of the family Solanaceae.

PSYLLOBORA. See *Thea*.

PTERALIA. The small sclerites at the base of an insect's wing which make up the articulation, including the humeral plate of the wing and the axillary sclerites.

PTERERGATE. An exceptional form of worker-ant having the rudiments of wings.

PTERIDINE. The basic chemical constituent of pteroic acid and of the *pterin* pigments in the wings of insects.

PTERIN PIGMENTS. White, yellow or red pigments in the bodies and wings of insects; chemically related to uric acid and possibly waste products of metabolism.

PTEROCLORUS. A synonym of the aphidoid genus *Lachnus* (*q.v.*).

PTERODONTIA. A genus of small flies of the family Acroceridae whose larvae feed on spiders and their eggs.

PTEROIC ACID. An essential substance for growth: a constituent of the vitamin *folic acid*, also important for the growth of feathers of birds and the formation of *pterin* pigments (pterines) in insects.

PTEROMALIDAE. Jewel Wasps and related species: minute chalcid wasps that lay their eggs in the bodies of caterpillars, particularly in those of the Cabbage White Butterfly. Some accompany swarms of flies hibernating in buildings.

PTERONARCYS. A genus of stoneflies (Plecoptera) including some of the largest to be found in North America. The nymphs or naiads live in running streams and climb out on to the trunks of trees before the adult insects emerge.

PTERONUS. *Pteronus ribesii* or *Nematus ribesii*, the Gooseberry Sawfly: a common member of the family Tenthredinidae having green and yellowish spotted caterpillars that feed on leaves of gooseberries and currants, sometimes completely defoliating the plant.

PTEROPHORIDAE. See *Plume-moths* and *Alucitidae*.

PTEROPHYLLA. A genus of North American Katydids or Long-horned grasshoppers. *Pterophylla camellifolia* is a common species, green and brown with short wings and very long antennae. It nests in tree-tops and is noted for its loud stridulation.

PTEROSTICHUS. Now called *Feronia*. A common and widely distributed genus of carnivorous ground beetles of the family Carabidae; medium sized, elongated beetles, shining black or greenish with longitudinal grooves on the elytra. Both larvae and adults live under stones or in vegetable refuse and emerge at night to feed.

PTEROSTIGMA. A wing-spot: a small darkly pigmented area on the foremargin of the wing of a dragonfly and of some bees, wasps, flies and other insects. Usually near or just behind the tip of vein R_1.

PTEROSTOMA. *Pterostoma palpina*, the Pale Prominent Moth: a medium sized moth of the family Notodontidae having light brown wings with a darker wavy transverse band and two rows of dark brown dots on the fore-wings. The larvae are blue-green with a yellow stripe along each side; they feed on willow, sallow and poplar.

PTEROTHECA. The part of a pupal skin that covers the developing wings of an insect.

PTEROTHORAX. The part of the thorax that bears the wings of an insect, *i.e.* the second and third thoracic segments.

PTERYGIUM. A small basal wing-lobe of certain insects. Sometimes used for other wing-like lobes on any part of the body.

PTERYGOTA. All insects that have wings or that may have lost them in the course of evolution, *i.e.* all except the four primitive wingless orders which are known as *Apterygota*. Pterygota comprise 25 out of the 29 orders of insects.

PTILIIDAE (TRICHOPTERYGIDAE). Dwarf Beetles, a world-wide family of tiny, active, scavenging beetles whose hind-wings are narrow and featherlike. They include some of the world's smallest insects less than 1 mm. long.

PTILINUM. A sac or vesicle on the head of flies of the group Schizophora by which the insect pushes open the puparium as it emerges. Afterwards the sac is withdrawn into the head leaving a U-shaped suture.

PTILINUS. A genus of small, brown, elongated, wood-boring beetles. *Ptilinus pectinicornis*, the Fan-bearing Beetle, about 4 mm. long, is common in decaying beech wood. The males have large fan-like antennae.

PTILOCERUS. A predatory bug from Indonesia having a tuft of bright red hairs beneath the abdomen close to the opening of a poison gland. Ants are apparently attracted to this, narcotized by its secretion and then pierced and sucked dry by the bug.

PTINIDAE. Spider Beetles, a family of small, brown or reddish, long-legged beetles with a rounded abdomen resembling that of a spider. They feed on decaying animal and vegetable matter.

PTYCHOMYIA. A small parasitic Tachinid Fly used as a biological control agent against the Coconut Moth of Fiji.

PTYCHOPTERIDAE. Phantom Crane-flies, a family of Diptera whose aquatic larvae have a long breathing tube at the hind-end similar to that of the Rat-tailed Maggot of the Drone-fly *Eristalis*.

PUBIC LOUSE. See *Crab Louse*.

PUG MOTHS. Small geometrid moths sometimes classed with carpet moths as Larentiinae and sometimes put in a separate family, the Hydriomenidae. There are several genera, the commonest being *Eupithecia*. Like the carpet moths they rest with their wings spread out away from the body and their larvae rest in a hooped position when not feeding inside flowers or seed-pods. The pupae, which are sometimes brightly coloured, are enclosed in cocoons made from silk and soil particles.

PULEX. One of the best known genera of fleas (Siphonaptera or Aphaniptera). The Human Flea *Pulex irritans* may sometimes live on pigs and occasionally on other large mammals.

PULICIDAE. A common family of fleas including the Human Flea *Pulex irritans*, the Dog Flea *Ctenocephalides canis*, the Indian Plague Flea of rats *Xenopsylla cheopis* and many others (see *Aphaniptera*).

PULSATILE ORGANS. Accessory pumping organs sometimes present in the blood system of an insect at the bases of the antennae and the wings (see *Blood*).

PULVILLUS. A pad or cushion underneath each claw of an insect, used as an adhesive organ by means of hairs and a sticky secretion. Chiefly developed in Diptera.

PULVINARIA. See *Cottony Scale*.

PUNKIE (PUNKY). A colloquial name for any of a wide variety of small gnats or midges, especially biting midges of the family Ceratopogonidae.

PUPA. A non-feeding and relatively inactive stage between the larva and the adult in Holometabolous insects. After the last larval moult the pupa or chrysalis is produced. Although this is an apparent resting stage, there are in fact numerous internal changes taking place. These involve the breaking down of larval organs and tissues and the growth of adult organs so that, when the fully grown insect or *imago* emerges by a splitting of the pupal skin, it is very different in habits and appearance from the larva. There are three principal types of pupa. Those with free limbs and mouth-parts and which may be capable of a certain amount of movement are known as *exarate*; that of the bee is an example. In some cases an exarate pupa is enclosed in a barrel-shaped case or *puparium* formed from the dried skin of the previous larval stage. The house fly and the blowfly are examples of this which is called a *coarctate* pupa. The pupa of a butterfly or moth, usually called a chrysalis, is of the *obtect* type, the chief feature being that it is much less mobile because the integument is thicker and the legs, wings and mouth-parts are firmly glued down to the body. In many cases it is enclosed in a silken cocoon (see also *Life History* and *Metamorphosis*).

PUPA COARCTATA. See *Coarctate Pupa*.

PUPA LIBERA. A 'free' pupa, *i.e.* one with soft integument and freely moving appendages; an *exarate* pupa.

PUPA OBTECTA. See *Obtect Pupa*.

PUPARIUM. A hard barrel-shaped case enclosing the pupa of certain Diptera such as the house fly (see *Pupa*).

PUPATION. See *Pupa*, *Life History* and *Metamorphosis*.

PUPATION HORMONES. The phenomenon of pupation appears to be controlled by the balance of several hormones. The *corpus allatum* secretes a 'juvenile hormone' known as *neotenin* and as long as this is being produced the insect will remain in a larval state after each moult. After a certain number of instars, however, the production of this hormone slows down; growth hormones take over and pupation and metamorphosis follow.

PUPIPARA. A group of blood-sucking cyclorrhaphous Diptera characterized by the fact that the young go through all their larval stages inside the body of the parent and are dropped immediately before pupation. They include the Forest Fly and the Sheep Ked (Hippoboscidae) and the Bat Parasites (Nycteribiidae and Streblidae).

PURPLE-BAR CARPET MOTH. *Mesoleuca ocellata*, a common European carpet moth, one of the Larentiinae, creamy white with brown edges and a purple-brown band across the fore-wings; the hind-wings have a central dot.

PURPLE CLAY MOTH. *Diarsia brunnea*, a noctuid moth with variable dark brown or purple fore-wings and lighter hind-wings. The larvae feed on birch, sallow, bramble etc.

PURPLE EMPEROR. *Apatura iris*, a large handsome nymphalid butterfly fairly common in oak woods of Europe but becoming increasingly rare in Britain. Its range extends eastwards across Asia to Japan. The male has an iridescent purple sheen, a brown border and a broad white band across each wing. The female is larger and browner. The underside of both sexes is light orange-brown with white markings. These butterflies usually fly high but are sometimes attracted to carrion. The larvae, which are pale green and slug-like with two horns, feed on sallow leaves.

PURPLE HAIRSTREAK. *Thecla quercus* or *Quercusia quercus*, a fairly common European butterfly of the family Lycaenidae, blackish brown with a purple iridescence on both wings of the male but only on the fore-wings of the female. The hind-wings have a very short but distinct 'tail'. The undersides of both wings are dove-grey with a black and white transverse line and there is an orange spot with a black centre on the hind-wing of the male near the anal angle. The larvae feed on oak leaves.

PURPLE TIGER MOTH. *Rhyparia purpurata*, a medium sized European moth of the family Arctiidae with a wing pattern roughly similar to that of the other tiger moths but the fore-wings are yellow with dark grey markings and the hind-wings purple with black markings.

PUSS MOTH. See *Cerura*.

PYGAERA. *Pygaera bucephala*, an alternative name for *Phalera bucephala* (see *Buff-tip Moth*).

PYGIDIAL GLANDS. Glands opening in the pygidium or posterior tip of the abdomen of certain insects. They may secrete poisonous or obnoxious substances as a protection for the insect; those of the Ground Beetle *Carabus*, for instance, secrete butyric acid.

PYGIDIUM. The hind-tip of the abdomen of an insect (see also Pygidial Glands).

PYGOPODIA. A pair of eversible foot-like organs at the hind-end of the abdomen of some insect larvae. They are used to assist locomotion in cases where true legs are reduced or absent.

PYLORIC CAECA. Also called *enteric caeca*: sac-like branches or diverticula from the mid-gut just behind the gizzard in certain insects (*e.g.* the cockroach). They provide additional surface area for secretion and absorption (see *Alimentary Canal*).

PYRACTOMENA. A genus of fireflies (beetles of the family Lampyridae) having aquatic larvae (see also *Glow-worm*, *Firefly* and *Light-producing Organs*).

PYRALIDAE. A family of small moths generally classed with the Microlepidoptera although some species are larger. They have narrow fore-wings and broad, fringed hind-wings. Many of them have well developed palps resembling those of the Snout Moths, although they are not in the same family. Pyralidae are notorious for the number of species whose larvae are pests of grain and other foods. These include the Meal Moths *Ephestia*, *Plodia* and *Pyralis*; the Sugar-cane Moth *Chilo*, the Wax-moth *Galeria* which is a pest of beehives and many others.

PYRAMEIS. *Pyrameis cardui*, the Painted Lady Butterfly sometimes called *Vanessa cardui* (see *Painted Lady*).

PYRAUSTIDAE. A family of small moths whose larvae are corn-borers feeding on stalks and crowns of cereals and other plants. They make a nest by tying the leaves together with silk and from here they extend their activities, boring into the stem and causing considerable damage. *Pyrausta nubilalis*, the European Corn-borer, has spread to North America and attacks maize, oats, barley and wheat.

PYRGUS. See *Grizzled Skipper*.

PYRILLA. The Sugar-cane Leaf-hopper of India, a genus of plant-bugs of the family Lophopidae that suck the juices of the sugar-cane.

PYROCHROA. See *Cardinal Beetle*.

PYROPHORUS. *Pyrophorus noctilucus*, the Cucujo Beetle: a large luminescent elaterid beetle from Central and South America having two light-producing organs on the hind-part of the thorax (see also *Light-producing Organs*).

PYRRHOCORIDAE. Red Bugs or Fire Bugs: a family of wingless plant-bugs, usually of a bright red colour, including the Cotton Stainers that infest cotton plants in many parts of the world and stain the fibres bright red with their excrement (see *Fire Bug* and *Cotton Stainer*).

PYRRHOSOMA. *Pyrrhosoma nymphula*, the Large Red Dragonfly: a common European species of the group Zygoptera having a slender body which is at first yellow but gradually becomes redder. The short, brown nymphs live on the bottoms of lakes and rivers.

PYTHIDAE. Mock-weevils, a family of small blue or purple beetles with flattened larvae that live under the bark of conifers.

Q

QUADRASPIDIOTUS. A genus of scale-insects of the family Coccidae: *Quadraspidiotus perniciosus*, the San José Scale-insect (see *Aspidiotus*); *Quadraspidiotus ostreaeformis*, the Oyster-shell Scale (see *Coccidae*).

QUAKER MOTH. *Orthosia stabilis*, the Common Quaker and *Orthosia cruda*, the Small Quaker: two common, inconspicuous noctuid moths of a light brown colour with darker markings. Both suck nectar from Sallow catkins and in both cases the green and yellow caterpillars feed on oak, sallow, birch and other trees.

QUEDIUS. A genus of staphylinid beetles that feed on the dung of birds on rocky islands off South America. They will survive where no plants grow. Others of the same genus live in ants' nests.

QUEEN. A fertile female. These are the only individuals capable of laying eggs in a colony of bees, wasps, ants or termites. In the latter the queen may attain a length of 10 cm. or more. In a colony of hive-bees the queen develops in a special 'queen-cell' and is produced by feeding a female larva on partly digested food known as *royal jelly*.

QUEEN ANT. The fertile female and founder of a colony of ants; a winged insect very similar in appearance to the winged males and usually larger than the wingless workers or incomplete females. When fully grown and when weather conditions are just right the queen flies out on her 'nuptial flight' followed by the males. This is the only time she flies and after being fertilized she will either return to the same nest or start a new one. Her wings are shed by being rubbed or pulled off and this loss of wings in some way evokes in her an instinct causing her to go underground, to avoid the light and to start laying eggs. A large ant colony may have many queens (see also *Ant*).

QUEEN BEE. The fertile female and founder of a colony of bees. In the honey bee *Apis mellifera* the queen is slightly longer than the workers, with a larger and more pointed abdomen but with relatively shorter wings. There is normally only one queen in a hive; after being fertilized on her 'nuptial flight' she will return to the hive and remain there unless driven out by a younger queen. She may live for four or five years during the course of which she will lay many thousands of eggs. In the Humble Bees (Bombidae) the queen hibernates and is normally the only member of a colony to survive the winter, a new colony being started each year.

QUEEN OF SPAIN FRITILLARY. *Argynnis lathonia* or *Issoria lathonia*, a fairly small nymphalid butterfly, golden brown with black spots which are smaller and fewer than those characteristic of most fritillaries. On the undersides of the hind-wings are a number of relatively large silvery spots. The butterfly migrates long distances and is found over most of Europe, North Africa and Asia as far as China. It is an occasional visitor to southern England. The larvae feed on the leaves of violets.

QUEEN SUBSTANCE. A chemical substance, identified as *9-oxydecenoic acid*, produced by the mandibular glands of queen bees. During the nuptial flight the scent of this substance probably attracts the male bees. Afterwards, during her life in the hive, the worker bees lick it and pass it on to each other as a means of recognizing the presence of the queen.

QUEEN TERMITE. Although termites (Isoptera) live in colonies and are sometimes known as 'white ants' they are in fact no relation to ants which belong to the order Hymenoptera. They do, however, resemble them in having different castes including workers, soldiers and in some cases several other winged and wingless forms all dominated by the queen. As in the case of bees and wasps, the queen is the only fertile female. After fertilization, and having lost her wings, she stays underground for the rest of her life. She hardly moves and becomes merely a vast egg-laying 'machine'. Her abdomen, becoming full of eggs, grows to many times its normal size and resembles a giant caterpillar sometimes attaining a length of 10 cm. or more.

QUEEN WASP. The fertile female or Queen Wasp is usually distinctly larger than the workers and males. In temperate climates she hibernates and is the only member of a colony to survive the winter. In the spring she starts the building of a nest, lays a few eggs in it, and the workers which subsequently emerge continue to enlarge it. This enables the queen to continue egg-laying so that throughout the summer the colony continues to grow in size and numbers (see also *Queen*).

QUERCUSIA. See *Purple Hairstreak*.

QUESTION MARK. *Polygonia interrogationis*, a nymphalid butterfly having reddish brown wings mottled with black, irregularly serrated at the edges and having short 'tails' on the hind-wings. A white or silvery question mark on the underside of each hind-wing gives the insect its name. It is common all over North America and is closely related to the European Comma Butterfly.

QUIESCENCE. A temporary slowing down of metabolism: a state of inactivity during which an insect hardly moves and may go without food for long periods. This state may be brought about by unfavourable conditions of temperature, humidity or other climatic factors; by lack of some essential vitamins or other food substances; by a failure to secrete particular hormones or by a disturbance of the balance between opposing hormones (see also *Diapause*).

QUINONES. A group of chemical substances (cyclic diketones) involved in the formation of some of the yellow and red pigments of insects and also in poisonous or repellent secretions such as those emitted by cockroaches, earwigs and beetles such as the Bombardier Beetle.

R

RABBIT BOT FLY. *Cuterebra cuniculi*, a large hairy fly of the family Cuterebridae, intermediate between the Calliphoridae and the Oestridae. The larvae are parasitic in rabbits (see *Bot Fly*).

RAILROAD WORM. *Phryxothrix*, a rare glow-worm of South America having a red light at its head and green lights on either side of the body.

RAIN FLY. An alternative name for the Cleg *Haematopota pluvialis*, a blood-sucking fly of the family Tabanidae (Horse Flies). It is slightly larger than a house fly and has a greyish brown, hairy body and blackish legs ringed with yellow; the wings are mottled with brown. The females have a sharp proboscis and suck blood of humans as well as of domestic animals. The carnivorous larvae live in damp soil.

RANATRA. A genus of elongated water scorpions: predatory bugs of the family Nepidae having the front legs modified for seizing their prey which may include other insects, tadpoles or small fish. *Ranatra linearis*, one of the best known species, is about 4 cm. long and is often called the Water Stick Insect. It lives among pondweeds and breathes through a long respiratory tube at the hind-end. The eggs are laid in the stems of various aquatic plants.

RAPE BUTTERFLY. A name given to two very similar white butterflies both of which are found all over Europe, North Africa and Asia and have been introduced to North America and other countries. *Viz. Pieris napi*, the Green-veined White and *Pieris rapae*, the Small White. The larvae of both feed on various cruciferous plants including the Swede or Rape (*Brassica napus*) and the turnip (*Brassica rapa*).

RAPHIDIIDAE. Snake-flies: predatory insects of the order Megaloptera, sometimes classed with the Neuroptera. They have four membranous wings with a complex network of veins similar to those of the Lacewing Flies and Alder-flies. The most characteristic feature is the long snake-like 'neck' formed from an elongation of the prothorax. The female has a very long ovipositor which also adds to the snake-like appearance. They live in crevices of bark and feed on aphids and other small insects. *Raphidia notata*, one of the commonest European species, is about 25 mm. long, greyish brown with large wings.

RAPTORIAL LEGS. Legs specially adapted for catching prey. These are usually the anterior pair but the others are also occasionally used for this purpose. They may be pincer-like or of the jack-knife type, the best known example of the latter being those of the Praying Mantis. Usually they have sharp claws and spines or bristles (see also *Predatory Insects*).

RASPBERRY BEETLE. *Byturus urbanus*, *Byturus tomentosus* and related species: small yellow or brownish beetles 2–3 mm. long, oval shaped and with short, club-shaped antennae. They lay their eggs in the flowers of raspberries and blackberries where the young larvae feed on the developing fruit.

RASPBERRY CANE BORER. A name for a number of small beetles of several different families. They include the following: *Oberea bimaculata*, a member of the family Cerambycidae whose larvae bore downwards into raspberry canes; *Agrilus ruficollis*, the Red-necked Raspberry Cane Borer, a member of the Buprestidae whose larvae bore upwards through the cane in a spiral and produce a gall at the top.

RASPBERRY MOTH. See *Lampronia*.

RASPBERRY ROOT BORER. *Bembecia marginata* and related species: clearwing moths of the family Aegeriidae whose larvae are serious pests of the raspberry plant, boring into the roots and pupating inside.

RAT FLEA. There are a number of species of fleas that infest rats and will sometimes migrate to man or other hosts. The most notorious of these is the Indian Plague Flea *Xenopsylla cheopis*, the carrier of Bubonic Plague, but

Nosopsyllus fasciatus is more widespread in temperate countries and also carries various diseases.

RAT-TAILED MAGGOT. The legless aquatic larva of various Syrphidae (Diptera), especially the Drone-fly *Eristalis tenax* which has a very long, telescopic 'tail' or respiratory siphon that can be extended to about 15 cm. to reach the surface of the water. It contains two tracheal tubes with their openings or spiracles at its tip surrounded by a fringe of flotation hairs. Crane-flies of the genus *Ptychoptera* have a similar larva; a case of parallel evolution.

RECEPTACULUM SEMINIS. An alternative name for the spermatheca, a sac leading off the oviduct of a female insect where seminal fluid can be received and stored so that it can be released a little at a time as eggs are laid. In this way an insect (a queen bee for instance) can mate once in her life-time and retain enough sperm cells in her body to fertilize all subsequently produced eggs.

RECEPTORS. The sensory cells or receptors of insects include *photoreceptors* such as the retinulae of simple or compound eyes; *chemoreceptors* or organs of taste and smell situated chiefly on the antennae and palps; *mechanoreceptors* which perceive touch, sound and changes of position. The latter are in the skin and may be situated anywhere on the body. Some have simple sensory 'hairs' connected to nerve cells beneath the skin; others have more elaborate structures (see *Basiconic Receptors, Campaniform Receptors, Chordotonal Receptors, Coeloconic Receptors* and *Hearing Organs*).

RECTAL GILLS. Tracheal gills or thin-walled projections well supplied with tracheae, arranged in longitudinal rows inside the rectum of an aquatic dragon-fly nymph.

RECTAL GLANDS (RECTAL PAPILLAE). Thickened bands formed from masses of glandular tissue projecting into the walls of the rectum or hind-gut of many insects. They are probably concerned largely with the re-absorption of water and chloride or other ions from the faeces, to some extent counterbalancing the excretion from the Malpighian tubules and preventing undue loss of water from the insect as a whole.

RECTAL PAPILLAE. See *Rectal Glands.*

RED ADMIRAL. *Vanessa atalanta*, a handsome nymphalid butterfly black with scarlet and white markings, found all over Europe, North Africa, Western Asia, North America and many other places to which it may have migrated or been introduced. It flies to Britain from the Mediterranean in the spring; eggs are laid on stinging nettles on which the caterpillars feed. They pupate in leafy shelters woven together with silk and a new generation of butterflies hatches out in midsummer. Some of these may fly back to the Mediterranean in the autumn.

RED ANT. A name given to many species of ant, *viz. Formica rufa* the Wood Ant; *Formica sanguinea*, the Blood-red Ant or Slave-making Ant; *Myrmica rubra*, the Small Red Ant, one of the commonest European species; *Monomorium pharaonis*, Pharaoh's Ant and many others, but particularly members of the subfamily Myrmicinae.

RED AND BLACK CAPSUS. *Capsus capillaris*, a plant-bug of the family Miridae about 1 cm. long, oval with large elytra coloured black with red tips; common on nettles.

RED AND BLACK CARRION BEETLE. *Silpha thoracica*, a scavenger of the family Silphidae commonly found on dead animals and fungi; flat-bodied, oval and about 15 mm. long having black elytra and a red thorax covered by fine yellow hairs.

RED ASSASSIN BUG. *Rhinocoris iracundus*, a predatory European bug of the family Reduviidae, about 15 mm. long, red-brown with long legs. It is commonly found on flowers where it lies in wait for its prey. Its bite can be painful to humans.

RED-BANDED LEAF-ROLLER. *Argyrotaenia velutinana*, a small moth of the family Tortricidae whose larvae feed on the leaves of peach and other fruit trees and make nests by rolling and tying the leaves with silk threads.

RED-BANDED SAND WASP. *Ammophila sabulosa*, a digger-wasp of the family Sphecidae, black with a red band round the front part of the abdomen. It nests in a hole in the ground which it stocks with caterpillars as food for its larvae. The caterpillar is often considerably larger than the wasp itself and may be dragged some distance over the ground before being deposited with an egg laid on top of it and covered with sand.

RED-BARRED SULPHUR BUTTERFLY. *Catopsilia philea*, a large pierid butterfly of South and Central America and the southern United States; bright yellow with a wing-span of 8 cm., with wide red bands on the fore-wings and wide red margins on the hind-wings. The larvae feed on the leguminous plant *Cassia*.

RED-BELLIED GRASSHOPPER. *Omocestus ventralis*, a common European short-horned grasshopper about 15 mm. long, brown with nearly black elytra and red abdomen.

RED-BELTED CLEARWING. *Sesia myopaeformis*, a small moth of the family Sesiidae having nearly transparent wings with dark borders and reddish bases. The body is bluish black with a band of red across the abdomen. The caterpillars tunnel between the bark and the wood of apple trees.

RED BUG. See *Fire Bug* and *Pyrrhocoridae*.

RED CLICK BEETLE. *Athous haemorrhoidalis*, a common European beetle of the family Elateridae about 12 mm. long, having a narrow blackish body covered with fine grey hairs. The elytra are reddish brown and the abdomen is tipped with red; common in woods and bracken.

RED CLUB-HORNED GRASSHOPPER. *Gomphocerippus rufus*, also called the Rufous Grasshopper, a small European species of a reddish brown colour with distinctive white-tipped club-like antennae resembling those of a butterfly.

RED-EYED DAMSELFLY. *Erythromma naias*, a small European damselfly (Zygoptera), generally black and green but the male has a red thorax and bright red eyes. The larvae live in still water.

RED FLOUR-BEETLE. *Tribolium castaneum*, a small reddish brown beetle of the family Tenebrionidae, about 5 mm. long; this and related species are common pests of cereals and flour all over the world.

RED-GREEN CARPET MOTH. *Chloroclysta siterata*, a small geometrid moth of the subfamily Larentiinae having dark, greyish green wings with a pattern of crimson dots and bands. The hind-wings are browner than the fore-wings and have a central black dot. The green larvae feed on leaves of oak, ash, birch and other trees.

RED-HEADED DAGGER WASP. *Scolia flavifrons*, the largest of the European Dagger Wasps (Scoliidae): fat, hairy wasps with a powerful sting. The wing-span is about 4 cm. and the body is black and yellow with red eyes. The larvae are parasites in the bodies of stag-beetle larvae.

RED-HORNED GRAMMOPTERA. *Grammoptera ruficornis*, a small, black elongated beetle with red antennae and red leg-bases. The larvae burrow into the wood of hawthorn trees.

RED-HORNED HARPALUS. *Harpalus ruficornis*, a predatory, nocturnal ground-beetle of the family Carabidae, about 12 mm. long, black with red legs and antennae.

RED-LEGGED APHODIUS. *Aphodius rufipes*, a dung beetle of the family Scarabaeidae: an elongated beetle with convex, ridged elytra, about 1 cm. long, black with some yellowish red on the legs and the hind-part of the abdomen. Eggs are laid in the dung of farm animals.

RED-LEGGED BUG. *Tropicoris rufipes* (= *Pentatoma rufipes*), an omnivorous pentatomid or shieldbug common in European woodlands; about 15 mm. long, brown with fine black spots and with the margin of the abdomen spotted yellow and black. The antennae and legs are red and the triangular thoracic shield or scutellum has an orange-red mark at the tip. Like many bugs of this family it will eat leaves, soft fruits and caterpillars or other insects.

RED-LEGGED PIMPLA. *Pimpla rufata*, a small ichneumon fly about 1 cm. long, black with reddish brown legs and with a short, thick ovipositor. It lays its eggs in the caterpillars of the Large White Butterfly where the developing larvae, after killing the caterpillar, pupate in yellow silky cocoons.

RED-LEGGED WATER BEETLE. *Hydrobius fuscipes*, sometimes called the Common Hydrobe: a small vegetarian water beetle of the family Hydrophilidae common in ponds and streams; about 8 mm. long, oval, brownish black with reddish brown legs. The elytra are marked with grooves and tiny punctures.

RED-LINE QUAKER MOTH. *Amathes lota* or *Agrochola lota*, a small noctuid moth, blackish grey with a central black dot and a dark red line near the margin of each fore-wing; the larvae feed on willow and sallow.

RED-MARKED GREEN TORTOISE BEETLE. *Cassida rubiginosa*, sometimes called the Common Tortoise Beetle of Britain and Europe; a member of the subfamily Cassidinae, one of the leaf-beetles, Chrysomelidae. The beetle is about 6 mm. long, oval and flattened with the thorax and elytra expanded to overlap the head and legs. It is a bright iridescent green with a small red triangular mark at the base of each elytron. Both adults and larvae feed on thistles.

RED-MARKED PONDSKATER. *Gerris thoracicus*, a predatory aquatic bug living on the surface of ponds and slow streams. The body is very similar to that of the Common Pondskater *Gerris lacustris*, elongated and greyish brown, but differs from it in having a yellowish red patch on the thorax (see *Gerridae*).

RED MARSH LADYBIRD. *Coccidula rufa*, a very small, oval beetle of the family Coccinellidae. Although related to the ladybirds it is only about half the size, more elongated and reddish brown all over without spots. It is found on reeds in marshy places.

RED-NECKED CANE BORER. *Agrilus ruficollis*, a North American beetle of the family Buprestidae, elongated and of a metallic greenish colour with reddish brown prothorax. The larvae bore upwards in a spiral path beneath the bark of raspberry and other canes and eventually produce galls (see *Buprestidae*).

RED-NECKED FOOTMAN MOTH. *Atolmis rubricollis*, a small dark brown moth with a bright red prothorax and an orange tipped abdomen; common in European woodlands where its hairy caterpillars feed on *Pleurococcus* and other algae on the barks of trees (see *Footman Moth*).

RED OSMIA. *Osmia rufa*, a bee of the family Megachilidae related to the leaf-cutting bees; about 12 mm. long, dark brown with reddish hairs covering the head and thorax and orange hairs on the abdomen. The legs have no pollen-baskets but pollen is carried beneath the abdomen. They nest in crevices of old walls, tree stumps, rotting fences etc.

RED POPLAR-LEAF BEETLE. See *Melasoma*.

RED-SPOTTED PURPLE BUTTERFLY. *Basilarchia astyanax*, a North American nymphalid butterfly of a dark blue colour with a black band along the margins of the fore-wings. The undersides are brown with red spots along the edges and near the bases of the wings.

RED SWORD-GRASS MOTH. *Calocampa vetusta* or *Xylena vetusta*, a noctuid moth with a wing-span of about 5 cm., pale reddish brown, darker at the wing-bases and with a dark brown kidney-shaped spot on each fore-wing. The caterpillars are large, bright green with broken lines of red and black along each side. They live in marshy places feeding on knot-grass and other low plants.

RED-TAILED CARDER BEE. *Bombus derhamellus* (= *rudevarius*), a small, hairy humble-bee, black with the tip of the abdomen bright red. It makes its nest on the surface of the ground covered with moss.

RED-TAILED CUCKOO-BEE. *Psithyrus rupestris*, a large hairy bee, black or dark brown with the tip of the abdomen of an orange-red colour. Like all the cuckoo-bees it lays its eggs in the nest of another bee and in this case it closely resembles its host, the Large Red-tailed Humble-bee *Bombus lapidarius*.

RED-TAILED HOVER-FLY. *Volucella bombylans*, a two-winged fly of the family Syrphidae, closely resembling a humble-bee, having a thick, black, hairy body tipped with orange or red. The larvae live as scavengers in the nests of humble-bees.

RED UNDERWING. *Catocala nupta*, a large noctuid moth with a wing-span of about 7 cm. The fore-wings are ash grey with a number of dark zig-zag lines; the hind-wings are bright red with central and marginal bands of black. The smooth, grey-brown larvae feed on leaves of poplar and willow.

RED-WINGED OTHIUS. *Othius fulvipennis*, a small woodland beetle of the family Staphylinidae or Rove Beetles having reddish brown legs, antennae and elytra; the rest of the body is black but the abdomen is tipped with yellowish hairs. As in all this family the elytra are much shorter than the abdomen.

RED-WINGED PROSTEMMA. *Prostemma guttula*, a small bug of the order Hemiptera having a narrow, shiny black body with bright red elytra and legs. It is common in woodlands where it feeds on small insects, using its modified fore-legs to seize them.

RED-WINGED STAPHYLINUS. *Staphylinus erythropterus*, a small rove beetle, about 1 cm. long, common in woodlands, having a black body with red legs and antennae and short red elytra. The end of the abdomen has patches of yellow hair. It belongs to the family Staphylinidae and, like others of this family, it is nocturnal and predatory. When alarmed it opens its jaws and raises its tail after the manner of a scorpion.

RED-WINGED STRIDULATING GRASSHOPPER. *Psophus strididulus*, a short-horned grasshopper from the mountains of Central Europe having bright red wings (see also *Oedipoda* and *Psophus*).

RED-WINGED WASTELAND GRASSHOPPER. See *Oedipoda*.

RED WOOD-ANT. *Formica rufa*: there are various names for this, one of the commonest of European species, *viz.* Wood Ant, Hill Ant, Horse Ant etc. It is about 6–8 mm. long, dark brown with a reddish thorax, brighter in the female. It is commonly found in coniferous and mixed woods where it builds very large domed nests, the dome consisting of a pile of pine needles and dead leaves. These may be several metres across and more than a metre high. Each nest contains a number of queens and there may be more than 100,000 workers. They are aggressive and protect themselves either by biting or by squirting out formic acid (see *Ant* and *Formica*).

REDUCED FRONT LEGS. The number of legs of an insect is normally six, *viz.* one pair on each of the three thoracic segments. There are, however, two families of butterflies in which the front pair are reduced, brush-like and useless for locomotion so that the insect appears only to have four legs. These families are the Satyridae or Browns and the Nymphalidae or Aristocrats. Both are world-wide families and the latter include some of the best known species such as the Red and White Admirals, Peacock, Tortoiseshell, Painted Lady, Purple Emperor, all the Fritillaries and many others.

Pondskaters (water-bugs of the family Gerridae) also have the fore-legs reduced, but highly efficient for catching and holding prey.

REDUVIIDAE. Assassin Bugs and related species: a world-wide family of nocturnal, predatory and blood-sucking insects of the group Heteroptera. Most of them prey on other insects which they catch with their powerful front legs and pierce with their sharp-pointed proboscis. Some will attack man and other animals giving a painful bite; a few species transmit blood-parasites such as trypanosomes and other protozoa. One of the best known European members of the group, which has also spread to America, is *Reduvius personatus*, a dark brown insect about 15 mm. long that lives in trees and invades houses. It is also known as the Fly-bug or the Masked Bug. Its nymph covers itself with dust which adheres to the sticky hairs on its body and makes an effective camouflage. It hunts small insects in dark corners and is said to be an efficient enemy of the bedbug (see *Assassin Bug* and *Masked Bedbug Hunter*).

REED BEETLES. Donaciini, a tribe of leaf-beetles of the family Chrysomelidae, 5–6 mm. long with a narrow elongated body and elytra. They are coloured black, green or red with a metallic sheen and the undersides are covered with fine hydrofuge hairs so that they do not become wet. They live and fly among water reeds and the aquatic larvae breathe by inserting their tail spiracles into submerged stems.

REED GALL-FLY. See *Lipara*.

REGAL FRITILLARY. *Argynnis idalia*, one of the large North American nymphalid butterflies, sometimes classed with the fritillaries, having red wings bordered with black. The nearest European relatives are the Silver-washed Fritillary (*Argynnis paphia*) and the Queen of Spain Fritillary (*Argynnis lathonia* or *Issoria lathonia*).

REGAL MOTH. *Citheronia regalis*, sometimes known as the Royal Walnut Moth, a large North American moth belonging to the family Citheroniidae which are similar to the Giant Silkworm Moths (Saturniidae) except that their larvae do not spin silken cocoons. The caterpillar of the Regal Moth is known as the Hickory Horned Devil; it is about 12 cm. long, greenish with black and white spots and with six red and black horns that curve back and are displayed when the insect is disturbed. They feed on the leaves of the Hickory tree *Carya alba* and the walnut *Juglans regia*.

REPLETES. A name sometimes given to the distended and honey-filled members of a colony of Honey-pot Ants (*Myrmecocystus*). They gorge themselves so that the abdomen is enormously enlarged and then hang from the roof of the nest as living stores of food for the rest of the colony (see *Honey-pot Ant*).

REPRODUCTION. See *Genitalia, Ovary, Ovariole, Oviduct* and *Female Reproductive System*.

REPRODUCTIVE CAPACITY. The number of offspring produced by most insects is very great. This is necessitated by the fact that they are generally small and have many enemies so that, although many thousands or even millions may be produced, only a small proportion of these survive to maturity. A queen bee may lay as many as 3,000 eggs a day and a termite many more than this. A wingless female Aphis, reproducing parthenogenetically, will have many millions of descendants during a season. Chalcid wasps that lay their eggs inside the eggs of other insects can increase their number even more by the phenomenon of *polyembryony*, each egg producing many embryos. These are extreme cases and the average insect produces only about 100 eggs. Even at this rate, however, if there are several generations a year the population of a particular species, increasing in geometric ratio, will be multiplied many times during a season. Prolonged favourable weather conditions may enable some insects to produce an additional generation, in which case the normal population may be increased in some seasons by a hundredfold. Fortunately for the farmer or forester, however, such an increase usually results in a corresponding increase in the number of predators so that on the whole a balance is maintained (see also *Biotic Potential*).

RESILIN. An elastic protein forming an important part of the cuticle of an insect.

RESIN GNAT. *Retinodiplosis resinicola*, a gnat of the family Cecidomyiidae whose larvae live and pupate in lumps of resin on pine trees.

RESPIRATION. Insects normally breathe through spiracles leading into *tracheae* and *tracheoles*. The latter are extremely minute tubules which penetrate deeply into every part of the body so that oxygen can diffuse directly into the cells. Except in the case of a few aquatic larvae such as those of chironomid gnats, there is no respiratory pigment corresponding to the haemoglobin of humans, and the blood of most insects plays little if any part in respiration (see also *Breathing*).

RETICULITERMES. A genus of termites that nest in damp, rotting wood. They may damage the timber of buildings and will sometimes make small covered passages over stone or brick in order to reach the wood. *Reticulitermes lucifugus* occurs in Europe as far north as Bordeaux and *Reticulitermes flavipes*, an American species, has become established in Hamburg.

RETINACULUM. (1) A hook-like structure by which the fore-wing of a moth engages with a bristle or *frenulum* on the hind-wing, thus coupling the wings together during flight.

    (2) A hook beneath the abdomen of insects of the order Collembola (spring-

tails) by which the furcula of the tail is held down beneath the insect. When released the tail propels the insect forwards into the air. (See also *Hamula*.)

(3) Other attachment structures, *e.g.* on the ovipositor of some Hymenoptera and the mandibles of some beetles.

RETINAL ROD. Sometimes called a *rhabdom*: a transparent rod surrounded by and secreted by a ring of seven or eight light-sensitive cells or *retinulae* beneath each crystalline cone in the compound eye of an insect. In each optical unit or *ommatidium*, light enters through the cuticular lens or cornea, is focused by the crystalline cone beneath this and impinges on the end of the retinal rod, passing down through it and stimulating the surrounding light-sensitive cells. A similar arrangement in a much simpler form may be present in some simple eyes or ocelli. (See *Compound Eyes*.)

RETINENE. A light-sensitive pigment in the retinal cells of insects, similar to *rhodopsin* in the human eye and derived from vitamin A.

RETINODIPLOSIS. See *Resin Gnat*.

RETINULAE. The light-sensitive cells of an insect's eye (see *Compound Eye* and *Retinal Rod*).

RHABDOM. See *Retinal Rod*.

RHABDOMERE. One of seven or eight segments making up a rhabdom or retinal rod of an insect's eye (see *Retinal Rod*).

RHABDOPHAGA. A genus of tiny, reddish brown gall-midges of the family Cecidomyidae whose minute orange-red larvae bore into the leaves and under the bark of willows and other trees, sometimes causing small, black, blister-like galls.

RHABDURA. An alternative name for Diplura (*q.v.*).

RHAGIONIDAE. Snipe-flies: a family of fairly large two-winged flies with long legs and short antennae. They make sudden darting flights probably in search of prey. The larvae are tiny white maggots living in rotting wood where they feed on other insects. One of the commonest snipe-flies is *Rhagio scolopacea* or *Leptis scolopacea* which resembles a stoutly built crane-fly about 12 mm. long with yellow and black abdomen and spotted wings. It is commonly found in woods where it stands head down on tree trunks.

RHAGIUM. A genus of longhorn beetles of the family Cerambycidae whose larvae tunnel beneath the bark of pine and other trees. There are many species in various parts of the world. *Rhagium bifasciatum*, one of the commonest European species, is about 20 mm. long with antennae nearly the same length. The body and elytra are narrow and elongated; the general colour is brownish black and each elytron has two oblique transverse yellow bands. The thorax has a short spine on each side.

RHAGOLETIS. A genus of two-winged flies of the family Trypetidae whose larvae are maggots in apples, cherries, plums etc. in many parts of the world. *Rhagoletis cerasi*, the Cherry Fly is black and yellow with speckled wings. It lays its eggs on the stalks of young cherries; the developing maggots destroy the fruit and then pupate in the soil beneath the tree. *Rhagoletis pomonella* is a similar species that attacks apples.

RHAGONYCHA. A common genus of Soldier Beetles of the family Cantharidae: elongated beetles which are brightly coloured and have long filamentous antennae. Both adults and larvae are predators. *Rhagonycha fulva*, the Black-tipped Soldier Beetle is a common species about 12 mm. long, yellowish red with black legs and antennae and black tips on the elytra. It is commonly found on umbelliferous plants.

RHAMPHOCORIXA. A genus of water boatmen that lay their eggs on the body of the fresh-water crayfish (see *Corixidae*).

RAPHIDIOPHORIDAE. Camel-crickets, primitive relatives of the crickets and grasshoppers, sometimes combined with other small families into the order Gryllacridoidea. They include the Greenhouse Camel-cricket *Tachycines asyriamorus*.

RHEOTACTIC RECEPTORS. Sensory cells, hairs or other structures that detect changes in the flow of water over the surface of a body such as that of an aquatic insect.

RHEOTAXIS. A response whereby an aquatic insect moves in a definite direction in relation to the flow of water.

RHEOTROPISM. Orientation (as distinct from locomotion) in relation to the direction of flow of water, as for instance in the case of some aquatic insect larvae (*cf. Rheotaxis*).

RHEUMAPTERA. *Rheumaptera hastata*, the Argent and Sable Moth: a carpet moth of the subfamily Larentiinae of a silvery grey colour with a pattern of black or brown dots and bars on the fore-wings. The caterpillar is of the geometrid type and is striped in light and dark brown. It feeds on birch and sallow.

RHICNOPELTELLA. *Rhicnopeltella eucalypti*, a small chalcid wasp whose larvae live in galls made by other insects in Eucalyptus trees in Australia and New Zealand. They are parasites or hyperparasites of the sawflies that make the original galls, and are therefore beneficial to the plant.

RHINA. *Rhina barbirostris*, a Brazilian weevil about 4 cm. long, black with a long, red, brush-like proboscis.

RHINASTUS. *Rhinastus sternicornis*, a Brazilian weevil 4–5 cm. long with a flattened, light brown body, a long black proboscis and a blunt, horn-like projection on the ventral side of the thorax.

RHINOCEROS BEETLES. Dynastidae, a group of large tropical or subtropical beetles in which the male has a large 'horn' on the head and sometimes two smaller horns on the front of the thorax. *Oryctes nasicornis*, the European Rhinoceros Beetle is about 5 cm. long; *Golofa pizarro* of Mexico is about the same size; *Trypoxylus dichotomus* from Japan, 7–8 cm.; *Chalcosoma atlas* from Indonesia 12 cm. There are many others and the group includes the largest known beetle the Hercules Beetle, *Dynastes hercules* of Central America which may attain a length of 18 cm.

RHINOCORIS. *Rhinocoris iracundus*, the Red Assassin Bug: a European predator of the family Reduviidae, a red-brown insect about 15–20 mm. long which can give a painful bite to humans as well as attacking most other insects (see *Reduviidae* and *Assassin Bug*).

RHIPIPHORIDAE. Fan Beetles, a family of insects characterized by having fan-shaped antennae and by having the elytra gaping apart so that the wings are normally visible. The larvae are parasitic on wasps, an unusual habit among beetles.

RHITICEPHALUS. *Rhiticephalus brevicornis*, a member of the family Brenthidae or Long Beetles from Madagascar; a weevil-like insect with a very long narrow body and head totalling about 65 mm.

RHIZOPERTHA. *Rhizopertha dominica*, the Lesser Grain-borer of India and other tropical countries: a beetle of the family Bostrychidae closely related to the Skin-beetles, Dermestidae; a pest of stored grain.

RHIZOPHAGUS. A genus of small, red-brown, predatory beetles about 5 mm. long, sometimes placed in the family Nitidulidae but often separated from them into a family Rhizophagidae. They live under the bark of trees in the tunnels made by other beetles, preying upon them and on their larvae. They are thus beneficial to the forester.

RHIZOTRAGUS. *Rhizotragus solstitialis* or *Amphimallus solstitialis*, the Summer Chafer: a beetle of the family Scarabaeidae similar in general appearance and habits to its relative the Cockchafer *Melolontha* but smaller and hairier. It flies in swarms in the summer months and, like the cockchafer, is a pest of forestry and agriculture. The larvae live in the soil and feed on roots; the adults feed voraciously on leaves of various plants.

RHODITES. A genus of cynipoid gall-wasps of which the best known is *Rhodites rosae* (now usually called *Diplolepis rosae*) whose larvae are parasites in the wild rose plant and produce the large, red, hairy galls known as *Bedeguars* or '*Robin's Pin-cushions*'.

RHODNIUS. A genus of Assassin Bugs of the family Reduviidae: blood-sucking Hemiptera of Central and South America and other tropical countries; carriers of parasitic trypanosomes than can cause *Chagas' disease*. These insects are frequently bred in laboratories and the nymphs have been much used for experiments in insect physiology.

RHODODENDRON BUG. *Stephanitis rhododendri*, a greenish brown lacebug of the family Tingidae about 5 mm. long, having relatively large wings with a lace-like network of veins. It lays its eggs in clusters on the undersides of rhododendron leaves and covers them with a secretion forming a brown scab (see *Lacebugs*).

RHOPALOCAMPTA. *Rhopalocampta benjamini*, a common nocturnal butterfly of the family Hesperiidae (Skippers) from India, China and South-east Asia, about 4 cm. across and coloured blackish, suffused with green and yellow. Like all the skippers it is to some extent moth-like and folds its wings flat over the body.

RHOPALOCERA. The name given, according to the old system of classification, to butterflies as distinct from Heterocera or moths. A modern system of nomenclature depending on the wing-venation and other features has now superseded these names (see *Butterflies* and *Lepidoptera*).

RHOPALUS. A genus of Squashbugs of the family Rhopalidae, closely related to the Coreidae: bugs of the order Hemiptera resembling shieldbugs but having a more elongated body and shorter wings. *Rhopalus subrufus* is a common woodland species with a light yellow body and greenish spotted wings. It feeds on St. John's Wort (*Hypericum*).

RHUBARB CURCULIO. *Lixus concavus*, a small weevil that bores into the stems of rhubarb, dock and other plants of the family Polygonaceae.

RHYACIONIA. Sometimes called *Evetria*: a genus of small moths whose larvae bore into young shoots and buds of pine trees (see *Evetria*).

RHYACOPHILA. A genus of caddis flies (Trichoptera) whose larvae do not make cases but live under stones in fast-running streams.

RHYNCHAENUS. A genus of weevils having thickened hind-legs enabling them to jump like flea-beetles. *Rhynchaenus saltator*, the Elm Hopper Weevil, is about 3 mm. long, light brown with darker head and legs and a dark brown patch on each elytron. The larvae are leaf-miners of elm and other trees.

RHYNCHITES. A common genus of long-snouted weevils many of which are leaf-rollers. The adult female cuts a piece of leaf and rolls it into a cone in which the eggs are laid. The larvae feed from within this. *Rhynchites betulae*, the Birch Leaf-roller and *Rhynchites populi*, the Poplar Leaf-roller are well known pests of these trees. Other species include the red and black *Rhynchites bicolor* which feeds on rose petals and seeds, and the red and bronze *Rhynchites aequatus* whose larvae feed on hawthorn berries.

RHYNCHOPHORA. A large suborder of beetles whose head is extended to form a rostrum or snout in front of the eyes; they include weevils, pinhole-borers and some bark-beetles (see also *Curculionidae*).

RHYNCHOPHORUS. *Rhynchophorus palmarum*, a large, tropical weevil whose thick, white, maggot-like larvae bore into the leaves of coconut and date palms, converting the internal tissues into a pulp, and sometimes causing serious loss of crop.

RHYNCHOPHTHIRINA. A suborder containing a single species, the Elephant Louse *Haematomyzus elephantis*: a blood-sucking louse of the order Mallophaga having the mouth-parts extended into a long, sharp snout able to pierce the skin of the elephant on which it lives.

RHYNCHOTA. A name formerly used for Hemiptera or bugs: a large order of hemimetabolous insects characterized by mouth-parts formed of long stylets for piercing and sucking. (See also *Hemiptera, Homoptera* and *Heteroptera*.)

RHYPARIA. See *Purple Tiger Moth*.

RHYSSA. *Rhyssa persuasoria*, a large Ichneumon Fly whose larvae are parasites in the larvae of the Giant Woodwasp *Urocerus gigas*. The body is black with yellowish white spots and is about 25 mm. long with an ovipositor twice this length. The latter is used for piercing wood in order to find the larva of a woodwasp in whose body the ichneumon lays its eggs. Both woodwasp and parasite have spread to forests in many parts of the world.

RIBAGA'S ORGAN. Also known as *Berlese's Organ*: a sac-like organ for receiving spermatozoa on the ventral surface of the abdomen of the female bedbug *Cimex*.

RIBAND WAVE MOTH. *Acidalia aversata* or *Sterrha aversata*, a small brownish yellow or greyish geometrid moth having two thin brown transverse lines across each wing. The caterpillars are brown and stick-like and feed on dandelion, dock, bedstraw and other meadow plants.

RIBBED PINE-BORER. *Rhagium lineatum*, a longhorn beetle of the family Cerambycidae whose larvae tunnel beneath the bark of pine trees (see *Rhagium*).

RICE WEEVIL. A name for a number of small weevils that burrow into rice and other stored grain; *Sitophilus oryza* is a well known and world-wide example.

RICINIDAE. A family of bird-lice (Mallophaga) having a narrow, elongated body about 4 mm. long and a special suctorial organ on the head by which they anchor themselves to the breast of a bird and suck its blood. *Ricinus elongatus* is a common species that infests the blackbird.

RINGED MOSQUITO. *Theobaldia annulata*, one of the largest and commonest of European and British culicine mosquitoes having conspicuous white rings round the abdomen and on the legs. The wings appear to be spotted due to clusters of scales. It commonly enters and hibernates in houses. It can give a severe bite but it is not known whether it can carry any virus or other pathogenic organism.

RINGLET BUTTERFLIES. A group of medium sized brown butterflies of the family Satyridae, mostly European and Asiatic, characterized by having several small white rings with black centres on each wing. *Aphantopus hyperantus* is very common; various species of *Erebia* are more localized.

RIODINIDAE. Sometimes called Nemeobiidae: a family of butterflies closely related to the Lycaenidae, chiefly found in Central and South America but represented in Europe by one species, the Duke of Burgundy Fritillary, *Hamearis lucina*. An unusual feature is that the fore-legs are reduced and functionless in the male but not in the female.

RIVULET MOTH. See *Perizoma*.

ROBBER ANT. An alternative name for the Slave-making Ant or Blood-red Ant *Formica sanguinea*: a European species that has the habit of raiding the nests of several species of black ants, carrying off the worker pupae and making slaves of them when they hatch out (see *Ant*).

ROBBER FLY. See *Asilidae*.

ROBIN MOTH. *Hyalophora cecropia*, a large North American silk moth of the family Saturniidae, brown, white and red with half-moon shaped eye-spots and with a wing-span of about 13 cm. The green caterpillars feed on a number of deciduous trees.

ROBIN'S PIN-CUSHION. Also called a *Bedeguar*: a large red, hairy gall commonly found on wild rose bushes, produced by parasitic larvae of the cynipoid gall-wasp *Diplolepis rosae* (sometimes called *Rhodites rosae*).

ROCK GRAYLING. *Hipparchia alcyone*, a butterfly of the family Satyridae closely related to the common Grayling *Hipparchia semele* but less brightly coloured. The wings are smoky brown with a broad white band on each and a small black ring in the corner of each fore-wing. It is found in Central and Southern Europe, North Africa and Asia Minor.

RODOLIA. *Rodolia cardinalis*, a coccinellid beetle used to control the Cottony Cushion Scale, *Icerya purchasi* (*q.v.*); introduced from Australia into other countries.

ROLLERS. See *Leaf-rollers*.

ROOT-BORERS. There are many insects that bore into the roots of plants: they include the larvae of flea-beetles and other Coleoptera, some larvae of Diptera and many larvae of moths, the most notorious of the latter being the Swift Moths, Hepialidae.

ROSALIA. A genus of longhorn beetles including the Alpine Longhorn *Rosalia alpina*; this is an elongated beetle about 4 cm. long with antennae longer than the body. The colour is a pale blue-grey with black patches on the elytra and on the antennae. It lives high up in the mountains in old tree stumps and is sufficiently rare to warrant its protection by law in some countries.

ROSE APHIDS. There are many species of aphids that attack wild and garden roses, some spending all their lives on them and others going to alternative host-plants in the winter. Some of the genera include *Siphocoryne*, *Anuraphis*, *Macrosiphum*, *Capitophorus* etc. (see *Aphis*).

271

ROSE CHAFER (ROSE BEETLE). *Cetonia aurata*, a large chafer beetle of the family Scarabaeidae having a rounded body about 20 mm. long, of a shiny metallic green colour with a golden sheen. The adults feed on the petals, leaves and fruits of roses; the larvae, which are fat whitish insects with short legs and a small brown head, live in the soil and feed on dead leaves or decaying wood. *Cetonia aurata* is a European and Asiatic beetle but there are many closely related species, some considerably larger and more brightly coloured, in tropical countries all over the world.

ROSE EMPHYTUS. *Emphytus cinctus* also called *Allantus cinctus*, a common species of sawfly whose larvae feed on rose leaves; the adult is about 6 mm. long, black with two white dots on the thorax and a white band across the abdomen; the larvae are green with white spots.

ROSE GALLS. There are many kinds of galls on rose trees. The best known are produced by cynipoid wasps of the genus *Diplolepis* (*Rhodites*). These include the Robin's Pin-cushion produced by the larvae of *Diplolepis rosae*; the Pea-gall produced by *Diplolepis eglanteriae* and the Spiny Pea-gall produced by *Diplolepis rosarium* (see *Gall* and *Robin's Pin-cushion*).

ROSE-HIP BEETLE. *Rhynchites bicolor*, a small, long-snouted, red and black weevil, about 6 mm. long, whose larvae live in rose-hips and feed on the seeds; the adults feed on rose petals.

ROSE MANTID. *Gongylus gongyloides*, a predatory mantid from India which exhibits a remarkable degree of protective coloration. The long slender thorax is green and has the appearance of a flower stalk; the middle and hind-legs have green leaf-like expansions and the under surface of the insect is rose-pink. As it rests on a rose tree lying in wait for its prey, it is not only perfectly camouflaged but its flower-like appearance probably attracts small insects into its clutches.

ROSE SAWFLY. *Arge ochropus* also called *Hylotoma rosae*, a small sawfly, black with a yellow abdomen, that lays its eggs in rose leaves and young shoots. The larvae, which are green with numerous black spots, feed voraciously in large numbers on rose leaves.

ROSE SNOUT-BORER. See *Rose-hip Beetle*.

ROSETTE GALL. A type of gall formed on the end of a growing shoot and causing the terminal leaves to become short and clustered together in a rosette, *e.g.* those on willow shoots caused by the gall-midge *Rhabdophaga* (see *Gall*).

ROSTRUM. A long projecting snout or proboscis such as that of a weevil.

ROSY APHID. *Dysaphis rosea* and related species: plant-lice of a rosy colour that infest apple trees and rose trees causing the leaves to curl up and turn brown.

ROSY RUSTIC MOTH. *Gortyna micacea*, a small noctuid moth of a rosy-brown colour whose pale buff-coloured caterpillars live and feed in the stems of potatoes, tomatoes and other plants.

ROTHSCHILDIA. A genus of large Saturniid moths of Central and South America and the Southern United States. *Rothschildia jacobeae* from Argentina and Brazil has a wing-span of about 11 cm. and is coloured brown and violet with a translucent 'window' in each wing. Another species, *Rothschildia aurota* has been cultivated in South America for the production of silk; *Rothschildia orizaba* and *Rothschildia jorulla* are found in Arizona.

ROUND-HEADED APPLE-TREE BORER. *Saperda candida* and related species: elongated longhorn beetles of the family Cerambycidae having a large head and a cylindrical body covered with fine hairs. The larvae bore into the wood of apple trees.

ROVE BEETLES. Staphylinidae: a large family of beetles, some carnivorous and some herbivorous, all characterized by the short elytra which leave the abdomen exposed. The larvae are of the campodeiform type with long legs and powerful biting mouth-parts. One of the best-known British examples is the Devil's Coach-horse *Ocypus olens*.

ROYAL JELLY (BROOD FOOD). A predigested food sustance on which the larvae of bees must be fed in order to develop into queen bees. It is produced from the pharyngeal glands of the workers and contains a high proportion of proteins. See also *Bee Milk*.

ROYAL WALNUT MOTH. See *Regal Moth*.

RUBY-TAILED WASP. *Chrysis ignita*, a solitary cockoo-wasp having a large, thick-set body of a metallic greenish colour with a shiny red abdomen; other related species are variously coloured in blue, green and red. They lay their eggs in the nests of other species of bees and wasps.

RUBY TIGER MOTH. See *Phragmatobia*.

RUBY WASPS. Bright, shiny red, blue and green wasps of the family Chrysididae (see *Ruby-tailed Wasp*).

RUFOUS GRASSHOPPER. See *Red Club-horned Grasshopper*.

RUPTOR OVI. See *Egg Burster*.

RUSH VENEER MOTH. *Nomophila noctuella*, a European pyralid moth that visits Britain as a migrant: light brown with a darker brown pattern and a wing-span of about 4 cm. which is relatively large for the Pyralidae. Like other members of the family they have narrow fore-wings, fringed hind-wings and prominent palps. The larvae, which sometimes wriggle very actively when touched, feed on clover and other plants of damp meadows.

RUSTIC MOTHS. A name for a number of reddish brown noctuid moths, viz. *Apamea secalis*, the Common Rustic Moth; *Gortyna micacea*, the Rosy Rustic Moth; *Noctua xanthographa*, the Square Spot Rustic; *Noctua rubi*, the Small Square Spot; *Agrotis agathina*, the Heath Rustic etc.

RUTELINAE. A subfamily of chafer beetles of the family Scarabaeidae, similar in general appearance to the cockchafer but usually more brightly coloured in metallic greens, blues and reds. They are herbivorous and include the Japanese Beetle *Popillia japonica* which has become a serious pest of grass and cereals in North America.

S

SACCHARICOCCUS. *Saccharicoccus sacchari* (also called *Trionymus sacchari* and *Pseudococcus sacchari*), the Pink Sugar-cane Mealy Bug: a widely distributed member of the family Coccidae, a pest of sugar plantations in many tropical countries (see *Coccidae* and *Pseudococcidae*).

SACCHIPHANTES. *Sacchiphantes abietis* (*Chermes abietis* or *Adelges abietis*), the Spruce Gall Louse: a common plant-louse of the family Adelgidae which infests spruce and other conifers forming fleshy galls at the bases of the young shoots. These galls are of the 'pineapple' type and resemble the young spruce cones; each contains a number of plant-lice in separate chambers. Originally a pest of European and Asiatic forests, it has spread to North America and other parts of the world.

SACRED SCARAB. *Scarabaeus sacer*, the emblem of ancient Egypt: a dung-beetle closely related to the chafers and giving its name to the family Scarabaeidae to which chafers and dung-beetles belong. It is a stoutly built, oval shaped beetle with a narrow constriction between the thorax and abdomen; it has bristly legs and clubbed antennae of the *lamellicorn type, i.e.* with a cluster of leaflets at the tip.

   The most distinctive habit of these and other scarab beetles is the construction of balls of dung in which the eggs are laid. Each ball (often larger than the beetle) is pushed or rolled into a hole in the ground where it is left for the eggs to hatch and to provide food for the developing larva.

SADDLEBACK MOTH. *Sibine stimulea*, a small reddish brown moth common in the eastern United States and having a poisonous caterpillar. The latter, about 25 mm. long, is green with brown at each end and with a brown 'saddle' in the middle of the dorsal side. At each end are two fleshy protuberances covered with tufts of yellow hairs containing poison. These are barbed and when broken they release an irritant substance which can be very painful.

SADDLE-BACKED GRASSHOPPER. *Ephippiger ephippiger*, a long-horned grasshopper inhabiting warm plains of central and southern Europe: about 3 cm. long, brown, with degenerate wings and with an arched 'saddle' formed from the dorsal part of the thorax. Both males and females can stridulate.

SADDLED PROMINENT MOTH. *Heterocampa guttivitta* (see *Heterocampa*).

SAGE APPLE. An aromatic gall produced on the sage plant *Salvia pomifera* by cynipoid wasps of the genus *Aulax*; eaten as a delicacy in the Middle East.

SAGRIINAE. Kangaroo Beetles: jumping leaf-beetles of the family Chrysomelidae from Indonesia, various Pacific islands and tropical America. Some are brightly coloured; others are of a metallic bluish-green. They are about 25 mm. long and are characterized by having enormously elongated hind-legs with greatly thickened femora. The best known are *Sagria buqueti* from Java and *Sagria papuana* from the Melanesian Islands.

SAHLBERGELLA. *Sahlbergella singularis*, a capsid bug of the family Miridae: a pest of the cacao plant in West Africa.

SAIL BUTTERFLY. *Iphiclides podalirius*, also called the Scarce Swallowtail:

a member of the family Papilionidae spreading across Europe, Asia and North Africa but becoming increasingly rare. Its general colouring is similar to, but paler than the common Swallowtail and the 'tails' are much longer and thinner. It is famous for its powers of gliding, hence the name 'sail' butterfly. The caterpillars feed on blackthorn, mountain ash and cultivated fruit trees.

SAILOR BEETLES. A name for a number of elongated, carnivorous beetles of the family Cantharidae varying in colour and including brown, reddish, green and grey species. *Cantharis rustica*, the Rustic Sailor; *Cantharis fusca*, the Dark Sailor; *Cantharis nigricans*, the Grey Sailor; *Cantharis pellucida*, the Wood Sailor etc. (see also *Soldier Beetle* and *Cantharidae*).

ST. JOHN'S WORT BEETLE. *Chrysomela hyperici*, a small leaf-beetle of the family Chrysomelidae, about 6 mm. long with a rounded body, small head, golden-green thorax and coppery green elytra; common on various species of St. John's Wort (*Hypericum*).

ST. MARK'S FLY. *Bibio marci*, a black, hairy, two-winged fly about 12 mm. long, having long legs, long antennae and a large head in which the compound eyes nearly meet in the middle. It is named on account of the large swarms that appear, flying with the hind-legs trailing down, on or about St. Mark's Day (April 25th).

SAISSETIA. *Saissetia oleae*, the Black-scale Insect: a member of the family Coccidae, a pest of olive and other trees. *Saissetia hemisphaerica*, a similar species that attacks the sago palm (see *Coccidae*).

SALAMIS. A genus of nymphalid butterflies from South Africa and Madagascar: large insects having the upper surface of the wings iridescent with whitish yellow, pink and green like mother-of-pearl. Most species have a number of small eye-spots with red, yellow and black rings. The wing-span is about 8 cm. and the edges are irregularly serrated with short 'tails' on both front and back. When folded the wings resemble dead leaves.

SALDIDAE. A family of small Shore-bugs: predatory insects about 5 mm. long of the order Hemiptera, found in marshes along the edges of lakes and rivers where they run over the mud hunting their prey.

SALDULA. *Saldula saltatoria*, a common species of Shore-bug, brown, oval and about 3 mm. long; found on the edges of stagnant streams and ponds (see *Saldidae*).

SALIVARY GLANDS. Most insects have a pair of salivary glands with a common duct opening on the *hypopharynx*, a median lobe on the floor of the mouth. In insects such as the cockroach which feed on a variety of solid substances, these glands are large and racemose extending back into the thorax. They produce a large amount of fluid which serves to moisten the food in the mouth. In these and other insects whose diet is chiefly vegetarian the saliva contains enzymes such as amylase and invertase which break down starch and sugars. In the house fly, the blowfly and similar insects, saliva is poured over the food enabling it to be partly digested externally so that the liquified products can be sucked up by means of the highly specialized proboscis. Insects with suctorial mouth-parts usually discharge some saliva through the tubular proboscis. In the case of plant-lice this contains enzymes that dissolve away the cell walls of the plant; in blood-sucking insects such as mosquitoes, lice and fleas, it contains an anticoagulant; in predators such as the Assassin Bugs it contains a poison that paralyses the victim. In a few insects, *e.g.* some caterpillars, the salivary glands are modified for producing silk threads.

SALIVARY GLAND CHROMOSOMES. See *Giant Chromosomes.*

SALLOW KITTEN. See *Kitten Moths.*

SALLOW MOTH. *Xanthia icteritia* or *Cirrhia icteritia*, a small noctuid moth of a lemon yellow colour with markings of light brown. The larvae, which are brown and smooth, feed on catkins and leaves of aspen and sallow; they pupate in the soil.

SALTATORIA. A name formerly used to denote those Orthoptera whose hind-legs are long and modified for jumping, *i.e.* locusts, grasshoppers and crickets, in contradistinction to *Cursoria* or running Orthoptera, which then included the cockroaches (now put in a separate order Dictyoptera).

SALTATORIAL LEGS. Legs specially adapted for jumping, usually the hind-legs, which are longer, thicker and more powerful than the others. In grasshoppers and flea-beetles the femora are enlarged; in fleas the coxae also.

SAMIA. A genus of large Silkworm Moths of the family Saturniidae including the Cecropia Moth, *Samia cecropia*. This is the largest moth in the United States, having a wing-span of 16 cm. The body is red with white stripes; the wings are banded with various shades of red and white and have a white crescent-shaped spot near the centre of each. The caterpillar is blue-green with red knobs near the front and yellow knobs at the back. *Samia gloveri* and *Samia euryalus* are similar but smaller North American species.

SAND-FLY. A name given to many small blood-sucking gnats and midges of sandy places but particularly referring to the genus *Phlebotomus*, the carrier of the parasite *Leishmania* (see *Phlebotomus*).

SAND WASP. Any of a number of Digger Wasps of the family Sphecidae that make their nests in sandy places and stock them with caterpillars or other insects that have been stung and paralysed as food for the larvae. *Ammophila sabulosa* is a common European species about 20 mm. long with a narrow body and long legs, entirely black except for an orange-red band round the abdomen.

SANGUINARY ANT. *Formica sanguinea*, sometimes called the Robber Ant or the Slave-making Ant: a European species that nests beneath logs or stones on heath and wasteland. They are notable for the habit of raiding the nests of *Formica fusca* and other black ants, carrying away the pupae and making slaves of the workers that hatch out.

SAN JOSÉ SCALE. *Quadraspidiotus perniciosus* or *Aspidiotus perniciosus*, an Asiatic scale-insect of the family Coccidae accidentally introduced into North America where it became a serious pest of fruit trees. It is now effectively controlled by insecticides and natural enemies (see *Aspidiotus*).

SANNINOIDEA. *Sanninoidea exitiosa*, the Peach Tree Borer: a clearwing moth of the family Sesiidae, subfamily Aegeriinae; a pest of fruit trees in California and other Southern States where the larvae feed under the bark at the bases of the trees.

SAPERDA. Round-headed Tree Borers: a genus of long-horned beetles of the family Cerambycidae whose larvae live, often for several years, in branches and twigs of various trees, sometimes producing galls. They include *Saperda carcharias*, the Large Poplar and Willow Borer; *Saperda populnea*, the Small Poplar Borer and *Saperda candida*, a common pest of apple trees particularly in North America.

SARBIA. *Sarbia damippe*, a Skipper Butterfly of the family Hesperiidae from the forests of Brazil: dark brown with broad yellow bands across both wings; with a bright red head and a bunch of red hairs on the tip of the abdomen.

SARCOPHAGINAE (SARCOPHAGIDAE). Flesh Flies: a subfamily or family of cyclorrhaphous Diptera closely resembling blowflies but distinguished by the grey-chequered appearance. They have larvae which feed almost exclusively on meat or other decaying flesh. Many species are viviparous (see also *Flesh Fly*).

SAROTHRUM. The pollen brush on the basitarsus of the hind-leg of a bee (see *Pollen Brush*).

SATELLITE MOTH. See *Eupsilia*.

SATURNIIDAE. Giant Silkworm Moths or Emperor Moths: a widely distributed family of large moths characterized by the silky cocoons which often hang from trees. They include some of the largest moths of the world, many of which are brightly coloured, often with large eye-spots and sometimes with transparent 'windows' in the wings. European species include the Emperor Moth *Eudia pavonia* or *Saturnia pavonia* and the greater or Viennese Emperor Moth *Saturnia pyri*. Others include the Promethea and the Polyphemus Moths of North America; the Cynthia Moth *Philosamia cynthia*, used for commercial silk production in China, Japan and Indonesia; the Indian Moon Moth *Actias selene* and the very similar American species *Actias luna*; the Giant Atlas Moth of Asia, *Attacus atlas* and its Australian relative *Attacus edwardsi*, both with a wing-span of about 25 cm. and the Hercules Moth of New Guinea, the world's largest known moth.

SATYR. Two European and Asiatic members of the family Satyridae or Brown Butterflies, much darker than the majority of the family; *Satyrus actaea*, the Black Satyr and *Satyrus ferula*, the Great Sooty Satyr. Both have the upper surfaces almost black with a few minute white dots on the fore-wings; the under surfaces are lighter brown with an orange-ringed eye-spot on each fore-wing. Related species also exist in North America.

SATYRIDAE. A world-wide family of butterflies, generally of a brown colour and often with conspicuous eye-spots which are usually black with white centres. Like the Nymphalidae they have the front legs reduced and functionless so that they appear only to have four legs. The larvae commonly feed on grasses. European species include the Meadow Brown, Grayling, Ringlet, Speckled Wood, Marbled White and many others. Similar species live in America, Asia, Australia and most other parts of the world. The Glass Butterflies of Peru and Brazil, with almost transparent wings, also belong to this family.

SATYRODES. A North American genus of satyrid butterflies: *Satyrodes canthus*, the Grass Nymph is a light brown species with eye-spots larger on the under surface than on the upper. It lives in wet meadows and swamps.

SAUBA ANT. *Atta cephalotes*, a large species of ant from the Amazon forests, commonly eaten by the natives (see also *Atta*).

SAUCER BUG. See *Ilyocoris* and *Naucoridae*.

SAWFLIES. A group of Hymenoptera consisting of several families all characterized by having no 'wasp-waist' and by having an ovipositor in the form of two small 'saws' between two lobes that act as sheaths. The saws are used for cutting into leaves or wood to make a hole in which the eggs are laid. The larvae of all sawflies and the adults of most species are plant-feeders and include some of the most important economic pests of agriculture and forestry.

The larvae resemble the caterpillars of butterflies and moths but differ from them in having more abdominal prolegs. Some feed on leaves; others live inside stems or roots; some form galls. Most sawflies are small but the group does also include the woodwasps (Siricidae) sometimes called 'Giant Sawflies'. The ovipositor of these is not saw-like but in other respects they resemble sawflies.

SAXONY WASP. *Vespa saxonica*, a yellow and black European wasp having black stripes running lengthways down its head. It builds a papery nest shaped like a balloon with a small entrance at the bottom. These nests hang from the rafters of barns, outhouses etc.

SCAEVA. Formerly called *Catabomba*. A very common genus of Hover-flies (Syrphidae), large numbers of which migrate to Britain from the Continent and lay their eggs among aphids which form the chief food of the larvae. *Scaeva pyrastri* is black with white or yellowish transverse crescents on the abdomen; *Scaeva unicolor* is black all over.

SCALE INSECTS. Members of the family Coccidae, the females of which often lose their limbs and become covered by a scale formed of cast-off skins glued together. In this state it is difficult to recognize them as insects. Many are harmful parasites of trees and shrubs; some yield useful products such as shellac and cochineal (see *Coccidae*).

SCALES. The scales of insects are modified hairs or setae, flattened and of various shapes so that they overlap one another forming a protective covering for the wings and body. Like the larger hairs or *macrotrichia* they are formed from a hollow outgrowth of cuticle containing an enlarged extension of an epidermal cell. Such scales are particularly characteristic of butterflies and moths but they are also present on the wings and bodies of mosquitoes, some beetles and a few other insects. Epidermal structures intermediate between hairs and scales are also quite common. The scales of most insects are pigmented to a varying degree with melanin so that they are coloured differing shades of brown or black. Those of butterflies may have colours due to the presence of *pterine* and other pigments. Sometimes their structure is such as to produce brilliant metallic colours due to optical interference (see *Iridescence*). A few butterflies have special scent-scales or *androconia* which secrete a substance that attracts insects of the opposite sex.

SCALLOPED HAZEL MOTH. *Gonodontis bidentata*, a medium sized geometrid moth of a light brown colour with darker brown irregular transverse lines and a dot in the centre of each fore-wing; very dark or melanic forms are also known. The edges of the wings are irregularly toothed and scalloped. The larvae, which are brown and stick-like, feed on hazel leaves.

SCALLOPED HOOK-TIP. *Drepana lacertinaria*, a moth of the family Drepanidae in which the tips of the fore-wings are bent back to form a blunt hook. The general colour is pale brown but the hind-wings are darker. The fore-wings have two dark transverse lines and both fore and hind-wings have a central dot.

SCALLOPED OAK MOTH. *Crocallis elinguaria*, a light yellowish brown geometrid moth having two darker brown transverse lines and a central dark dot on each fore-wing. Both wings have irregularly serrated or scalloped edges. The larvae are brown and stick-like; they feed on oak leaves and pupate in silken cocoons among fallen leaves.

SCALPELLUM. A piercing, needle-like stylet formed from one or more of the mouth-parts, as for instance in mosquitoes and bugs (see *Mouth-parts*).

SCANSORIAL LEGS. Legs with a single large claw which can fold against the end of the tibia and act as a climbing or grasping organ, as for instance in lice of the order Anoplura.

SCAPHIDIIDAE. Boat Beetles: small, long-legged beetles with a boat-shaped body and a pointed abdomen; they are about 5 mm. long and live in or under fungi such as *Polyporus*. *Scaphidium quadrimaculatum* is a glossy black colour with two red marks on each elytron.

SCARABAEIDAE. Scarab-beetles: large insects belonging to the group Lamellicornia whose antennae have clubs made of separate movable plates. The larvae, which live for several years and are very destructive to plants, may be recognized by the fact that the head is large and horny but the abdomen is inflated and soft with conspicuous spiracles. The group includes chafers and dung beetles (see also *Sacred Scarab*).

SCARABAEIFORM LARVA. Any larva like those of the Scarabaeidae, with a curved, fleshy abdomen, adapted to feeding in an abundance of food material and therefore not requiring great mobility.

SCARAB SPHAERIDIUM. *Sphaeridium scarabaeoides*, a small elongated beetle about 6 mm. long having narrow, shiny black elytra with a deep red spot on each and a yellow streak near the tip. They are commonly found in dung, although they belong to the mainly aquatic family Hydrophilidae.

SCARDIA. A small moth of the family Tineidae, similar to a clothes moth, whose larvae bore into the stems of fungi.

SCARITES. A genus of black or brown ground beetles having a deep constriction just behind the prothorax.

SCARLET FIRE BEETLE. *Pyrochroa coccinea*, sometimes called the Black-headed Cardinal Beetle: an elongated, flattened beetle about 18–20 mm. long having the head, antennae and legs black and the elytra bright red, and wider at the hind-end. The larva resembles a thin yellow caterpillar with two short cerci; it feeds on decaying wood.

SCARLET MOTH. See *Scarlet Tiger Moth*.

SCARLET TIGER MOTH. *Panaxia dominula* or *Callimorpha dominula*, a medium sized arctiid moth having black fore-wings with a greenish gloss and yellow or white spots; the hind-wings are scarlet with black markings and the abdomen is also scarlet with a black streak down the centre. It lives in damp forests of Europe and Asia where the hairy caterpillars feed on stinging nettles, dead nettles, blackberry leaves etc.

SCATELLA. *Scatella stagnalis*, a shore-fly of the family Ephydridae: a predatory two-winged fly that captures gnats and mosquitoes by means of bristles and spines on its front legs. The aquatic larvae of related species may live in hot springs.

SCATOPHAGIDAE. See *Dung Fly*.

SCATOPHAGOUS (COPROPHAGOUS). Feeding on dung: a characteristic of many beetles and the larvae of many flies (see also *Dung-beetle*, *Dor Beetle* and *Dung Fly*).

SCATOPSIDAE. A family of midges, small two-winged flies 2–3 mm. long whose larvae feed on dung. *Scatopse notata* is a common species.

SCAVENGER BEETLE. A name given to many beetles that feed on decaying vegetable or animal matter, but particularly to the vegetarian Water Beetles

SCA–SCH

(Hydrophilidae), the Burying Beetles (Necrophoridae) and the Carrion Beetles (Silphidae).

SCAVENGER FLY. A name used for many small flies that feed on decaying animal and vegetable matter, but particularly applied to the Spiny-legged Flies of the family Sepsidae and to the Scatopsidae (see above).

SCELIPHRON. *Sceliphron cementarius*, a Mud-daubing Wasp of North America: a solitary wasp with a long narrow waist, a black body and yellow legs. It constructs a flat nest of mud against the side of a building and stocks the cells with spiders as food for the developing larvae.

SCENOPINUS. *Scenopinus fenestralis*, the Window Fly: a small, drab, rather slow or inactive black fly often found on windows. It lays its eggs in old furniture, carpets or household rubbish where the carnivorous larvae feed on larvae of clothes moths and other insects.

SCENT GLANDS. Scented substances are secreted by many different types of glands on the bodies, wings or legs of insects. These secretions are of two principal kinds, *viz.*

(a) Repellent or unpleasant scents exuded in self-defence usually from glands on the abdomen. Examples of these are the disagreeable odours produced by stinkbugs, bedbugs, earwigs, some beetles and ants etc.

(b) Attractive substances chiefly secreted before mating and often recognizable in extremely minute amounts and at long distances by insects of the opposite sex. Examples of these are the Queen Bee Substance, the secretions from the scent scales or *androconia* of male butterflies and the secretions from the abdominal glands of some female butterflies.

SCENT SCALES. Specially modified scales known as *androconia* present in clusters on the wings, and sometimes also on the body and legs, of certain male butterflies. They produce a secretion with a strong scent that attracts butterflies of the opposite sex.

SCHISTOCERCA. See *Desert Locust* and *Locustidae*.

SCHIZASPIDIA. *Schizaspidia tenuicornis*, a minute Japanese chalcidoid wasp of the family Eucharitidae that attaches itself to the legs of ants, is carried to their nest and there attacks the larvae and pupae of the ants.

SCHIZONEURA. A genus of plant-lice similar to the Woolly Aphis. *Schizoneura lanuginosa* is about 2 mm. long, dark brown and covered with a white waxy secretion forming delicate threads. It infests elm trees where it produces large, potato-like galls at first green and later turning brown. *Schizoneura ulmi* is a similar species which causes leaf-curl on elms.

SCHIZOPHORA. A large group of cyclorrhaphous Diptera all characterized by the possession of a bladder or *ptilinum* on the head, by which the fly can push open the barrel-shaped puparium in order to emerge. Included in this group are House Flies, Blowflies, Flesh Flies, Warble Flies, Bot Flies and all the families of acalyptrate flies such as fruit-flies, seaweed-flies etc. (See *Ptilinum*.)

SCHIZURA. A genus of small moths whose larvae have a humped appearance and whose colour varies according to the plant on which they feed. *Schizura unicornis* feeds on the North American Hickory plant *Carya alba*; *Schizura concinna* is the Red-humped Apple-worm.

SCHÖNHERR'S BARYNOTUS. *Barynotus schonherri*, a weevil about 1 cm. long having a black head, thorax and legs but with pink scales covering the elytra. The snout or rostrum is short and thick and the antennae are elbowed; it may be found under stones.

SCIARIDAE. A widely distributed family of Dark-winged Fungus-gnats living in damp forests of Northern Europe, Asia and North America. The larvae feed on fungi and often migrate over the ground in very large numbers.

SCIOMYZIDAE. Formerly called Tetanoceridae: Marsh Flies and Snail Flies; small black flies whose larvae feed on snails (see *Marsh Fly*).

SCIRTOTHRIPS. *Scirtothrips citri*, the Citrus Thrips. One of several species of Thrips (Thysanoptera) that attack citrus fruits in California, South Africa, Rhodesia and other countries, causing the skins of the fruits to be scarred.

SCLERITES. Thick chitinous plates forming units separated by thinner membranes in the exoskeleton of an insect or other arthropod.

SCLEROTIN. A hard nitrogenous substance impermeable to water, found together with chitin in the cuticles of insects, crustaceans etc. It is composed of tanned proteins.

SCOLIIDAE. Dagger Wasps: a world-wide family of large, hairy wasps with a powerful sting; they are usually black with spots or patches of yellow. The larvae are parasites on the larvae of bees, beetles and other insects. The largest European species, the Red-headed Dagger Wasp *Scolia flavescens*, is about 4 cm. long. It lays its eggs on the larvae of Stag Beetles.

SCOLIOPTERYX. See *Herald Moth*.

SCOLOPALE (SCOLOPS). A sensory rod forming the apex of a chordotonal receptor on an insect. Movement or vibration of the scolopale sets up impulses in the sensory cell beneath it (see *Chordotonal Receptor*).

SCOLOPIDIUM. An alternative name for a *chordotonal receptor* (*q.v.*).

SCOLOPS. *Scolops sulcipes*, a small North American species of Lantern-fly of the family Fulgoridae; dark grey, about 1 cm. long and having a long slender extension of the front of the head. The larger South American members of this family are sometimes known as Alligator Bugs on account of the shape of this head-extension.

SCOLOPS (2). See *Scolopale*.

SCOLYTIDAE. An important family of Bark Beetles: pests that can attack and kill healthy trees by tunnelling out complex galleries beneath the bark and by spreading the spores of injurious fungi such as that which causes Dutch Elm Disease (*Ceratostomella ulmi*). They are closely related to the weevils but their snouts are short or absent; the antennae are clubbed and the head is often bent under the thorax. Most of these beetles are brown and less than 5 mm. long. Both adults and larvae make elaborate branching galleries spreading in patterns beneath the bark and in some cases deeper into the wood. The species can often be identified by the type of tunnels made (see also *Ipinae*, *Hylesininae* and *Scolytus*).

SCOLYTUS. The chief genus of bark beetles of the family Scolytidae (*q.v.*) *Scolytus scolytus*, the Large Elm Beetle; *Scolytus multistriatus*, the Small Elm Beetle; *Scolytus intricatus*, the Oak Bark Beetle; *Scolytus rugulosus*, the Shot-hole Borer; *Scolytus ratzeburgi*, the Birch Bark Beetle; *Scolytus mali*, the Fruit-tree Bark Beetle etc.

SCOPARIA. A genus of small moths of the family Pyralidae, usually light grey-brown with angular fore-wings, fringed hind-wings and prominent palps. *Scoparia ambigualis* is a common species found on moors and heaths; the larvae feed on mosses.

SCOPULA. *Scopula lactata* or *Scopula floslactata*, the Cream Wave Moth: a small European geometrid moth, cream coloured with three wavy grey lines across each fore-wing and two across each hind-wing. The larvae, which are light brown and stick-like, feed on Bedstraw, Woodruff and other small plants of the family Rubiaceae.

SCORPION FLIES. See *Mecoptera*.

SCOTCH ARGUS. See *Erebia*.

SCREECH BEETLE. See *Hygrobia*.

SCREW-WORM. The larva of the genus *Cochliomyia* (= *Callitroga*), bluish flies similar in appearance to the blowfly. Eggs are laid in open wounds or in the nostrils of man and other animals and the emerging screw-worms bore through the tissues of their victim, sometimes entering the sinuses of the head and causing death. There are two species: *Cochliomyia hominovorax* which is an obligatory parasite and may attack healthy tissues; and *Cochliomyia macellaria* which is a facultative parasite (*q.v.*). Both are found in North and South America.

SCROBES. A pair of grooves, one on each side of the snout of a weevil in which the antennae can rest when the snout is being used for boring.

SCULPTURING OF EGGS. The outer shell or *chorion* of an insect's egg is often elaborately patterned with pits, ridges or reticulations. Those of hover-flies, some leaf-mining flies and many other insects show a microscopic network of hexagonal or polygonal ridges, but the most strikingly sculptured eggs are those of butterflies and moths. The Cabbage White and other Pieridae lay yellow flask-shaped eggs with vertical ridges. Red Admirals, Purple Emperors and other nymphalids lay green, almost spherical eggs with white ribs arranged like meridians; Blues and Coppers lay round, flat eggs pitted all over and with a central hole or micropyle. There are innumerable other variations. The sculpturing is not merely decorative, but has a great deal to do with respiration and water-regulation.

SCUTELLERIDAE. One of the families of shieldbugs: brightly coloured plant-bugs with a very large dorsal shield or scutellum covering practically the whole insect and hiding the wings (see also *Pentatomidae*).

SCUTELLUM. (1) A shield-shaped plate formed from the hindmost part of the notum of an insect, behind the scutum.

(2) Loosely used for any shield-shaped plate (see also *Scutum*).

SCUTUM. (1) The middle and largest of three sclerites which typically form the dorsal cuticular covering or *notum* of each thoracic segment of an insect.

(2) Loosely used for any shield-shaped plate; the Latin words *scutum* (= a shield) and *scutellum* (= a little shield) are often interchangeable and used to signify the dorsal covering of an insect which may be formed by fusion of a number of sclerites differing in origin in different insects.

SCYPHOPHORUS. *Scyphophorus interstitialis* (sometimes called *Scyphophorus acupunctatus*), the Sisal Weevil: a pest of the Sisal plant or American Aloe (*Agave sisalana*), a tropical plant which is cultivated in many countries for making twine and rope.

SCYTHROPUS. *Scythropus mustella*, a small pine-weevil, black with yellow markings, living on conifers in the forests of Central Europe.

SEA BUG. See *Marine Bug.*

SEAM BUGS. A group of plant-bugs of the family Coreidae having the abdomen greatly expanded laterally so that it projects outside the elytra on each side. *Coreus marginatus* or *Syromastes marginatus* is a typical European species about 1 cm. long having a bright red abdomen and shiny, brownish red elytra.

SEARCHER BEETLES. A name given to a number of predatory beetles as a translation of their Latin specific names, and on account of their habit of searching out other insects beneath bark or in crevices, *e.g. Rhagium inquisitor* (a longhorn); *Necrophorus investigator* (a burying beetle) and *Calosoma inquisitor* (a ground beetle). Species of *Calosoma* were introduced from Europe into the United States as a means of controlling the Gipsy Moth.

SEASONAL DIMORPHISM. Many insects produce two or more generations a year and there is often a difference in size, shape or colour between the spring broods and the autumn broods or between those hatched in the dry season and those of the wet season. One of the best known examples is the Map Butterfly *Araschnia levana*, a European nymphalid. Those that emerge in the spring have a typical fritillary pattern of orange-brown with black spots; those that hatch in midsummer are dark brown or black with a broad white band across each wing. An even more striking example of seasonal dimorphism is the case of the African nymphalid *Precis octavia*. In the dry season it is blue with black, red and white markings; in the wet season a totally different pinkish-orange form emerges.

SEAWEED FLY. See *Kelp Fly.*

SECONDARY SEGMENT. Any apparent segmentation produced by further subdivision of the primary sclerites (see *Segmentation*).

SEDGE FLY. A name for a number of Caddis flies (Trichoptera) including the Great Red Sedge Fly *Phryganea grandis*, the Cinnamon Sedge Fly *Limnephilus lunatas*, the Medium Sedge Fly *Goera pilosa* and many others.

SEED BORERS. Many insects bore into seeds, either to feed on them or to lay their eggs in them. Some attack fresh growing seeds; others dried seeds such as stored grain. Chalcid Wasps bore holes in seeds with their long ovipositors and deposit eggs inside larvae already present within the seeds. Codling Moths such as *Laspeyresia pomonella* lay their eggs on leaves and flowers of apple trees and the newly hatched caterpillars bore into the developing seeds; weevils such as the Grain Weevil and the Bean Weevil use their snouts for boring into dried seeds.

SEED WEEVILS. See *Curculionidae, Rhynchophora, Seed Borers, Rice Weevil* and *Grain Weevil.*

SEGMENTATION (METAMERIC SEGMENTATION). Insects and other arthropods have the body divided into a number of segments with some repetition of organs in each. This segmentation is shown most completely in larvae of the caterpillar type, but is obscured in adult insects owing to the high degree of specialization and enlargement of certain organs. It remains most evident, however, in the thorax and abdomen. A hypothetical ancestral type of insect, derived from a crustacean, has twenty segments, six in the head, three in the thorax and eleven in the abdomen. In an adult insect of the present day the head shows no obvious segmentation, all the original segments having become fused to form a capsule. The thorax has three segments with a pair of legs on each; the abdomen rarely shows more than eight or nine, the

283

last few being fused together and specialized to form parts of the reproductive apparatus. The repetition of internal organs is shown most clearly in the nerve ganglia (one pair in each segment except where several are fused together), the compartments of the heart, and the tracheal system with a pair of spiracles in each segment.

SEHIRUS. *Sehirus bicolor*, the Pied Shieldbug: a common hemipteran plant-bug of European woodlands and hedgerows, about 7 mm. long, oval-shaped and black with yellow markings: one of the few insects that cares for its young and leads them to the food-plant, in this case Dead Nettle and other Labiatae (see also *Parent Bug*).

SELENIA. *Selenia bilunaria*, the Early Thorn Moth: a geometrid moth, usually light brown with three thin, dark, transverse lines across the fore-wings; darker varieties are known, however, in some industrial regions (see *Industrial Melanism*). On the brown variety the tip of each fore-wing forms a dark half-moon shaped mark bordered by a pale crescent. These give the name *bilunaria* to the species. The larvae feed on blackthorn, hawthorn etc.

SELENOTHRIPS. A genus of thrips (Thysanoptera) that feeds on the leaves and pods of the cacao plant in West Africa, the West Indies and other places; sometimes placed in other genera, either *Hercothrips* or *Heliothrips*.

SEMATURIDAE. A family of large, brightly coloured, tropical moths resembling butterflies. *Sematura lunus* of Central and South America is brown with a whitish yellow stripe running lengthways down each wing. The hind-wings have 'tails' on which are eye-spots. The wing-span is about 7 cm. Other members of the family, some even larger, live in India, China, Malaysia and the Philippines.

SENSES. The principal senses of insects are:

(1) *Sight*: detected by compound eyes and by ocelli. Most insects can perceive colours including ultra-violet which is invisible to humans. They can, to a limited extent, perceive shapes but their eyes are not capable of forming very clear and detailed pictures. Movements and distances can be detected very accurately.

(2) *Hearing*: this can be perceived by receptors on the antennae, by hairs and special receptors all over the body, and in some cases by tympanic organs usually situated on the sides of the abdomen or on the legs. Many insects can detect high frequency sounds that are inaudible to humans.

(3) *Smell and Taste*: these can be perceived by chemoreceptors chiefly on the antennae and palps but occasionally also on the legs.

(4) *Touch, vibration, movement and balance*: these are detected by sensory hairs and miscellaneous receptors on most parts of the body.

(See also *Compound Eyes, Hearing Organs, Chordotonal Receptors, Olfactory Sense* etc.)

SENSORY HAIRS. Many of the hairs or setae of insects have nerve endings close to their bases and are extremely sensitive to touch, vibration, sound etc. This is especially true of the hairs on the antennae, those of mosquitoes for example. Other types of mechanoreceptors – *chordotonal, campaniform, placoid* etc. are derived from sensory hairs and associated structures.

SEPEDON. *Sepedon sphegus*, the Snail Fly: a small black fly of the family Sciomyzidae living in marshy places where the larvae feed on snails (see *Marsh Fly*).

SEPTEMBER THORN. *Ennomos erosaria*, a common geometrid moth of the subfamily Ennominae; medium sized with yellow or buff wings and two curved oblique dark lines across the fore-wings.

SERICA. *Serica brunnea*, the Brown Chafer: a beetle of the family Scarabaeidae about 1 cm. long, smooth, hairless and reddish brown. The larva, similar to that of the cockchafer, feeds on the roots and bark of coniferous trees.

SERICIN. A water-soluble gelatinous protein forming an outer layer surrounding an inner core of *fibroin* in the silk threads of insects, spiders etc.

SERICOMYIA. *Sericomyia borealis*, a large hover-fly of the family Syrphidae resembling a wasp; the head and thorax are brown, the abdomen is striped with yellow and the legs are yellowish brown. The larva is a 'rat-tailed maggot', living in sodden peat or moorland pools rich in decomposing matter. It has a long, posterior respiratory tube.

SERICOSTOMATIDAE. A family of caddis flies (Trichoptera) having very hairy wings; the larvae are found in running water, their cases being anchored to weeds by means of silk threads produced from glands in the head. The group includes the Grannom or Green-tailed Caddis Fly (*Brachycentrus subnubilis*).

SERMYLA. *Sermyla halensis*, the Bedstraw Beetle, a small leaf-beetle of the family Chrysomelidae, oval-shaped and about 6 mm. long with shining green head and elytra, orange thorax and black and orange legs. It is found on Bedstraw and other plants of the family Rubiaceae, generally on sandy cliffs or downs near the sea.

SEROSA. A membrane covering the surface of the yolk in an egg, and later enclosing the amniotic cavity with its germ band.

SERPENT FLY. See *Raphidiidae*.

SERRICORNIA. A term formerly used for beetles with saw-like antennae including Elateridae, Buprestidae and Lampyridae.

SESAMIA. A genus of noctuid moths whose larvae bore into the stems of cereals and of sugar cane in North Africa, India and South-east Asia.

SESIIDAE. (Formerly Aegeriidae.) Clearwing Moths, a family of day-flying moths remarkable for their resemblance to bees, wasps and other insects; a case of Batesian mimicry which gives them a high degree of protection. The wings are transparent with dark borders and dark lines outlining the veins. The front wings are narrow and both wings are shaped like those of a bee. The bodies of many are black and yellow like those of wasps and hornets. The larvae are usually white and maggot-like with brown heads; they bore into plants, often living within the stems. The largest European species is the Hornet Moth *Sesia apiformis*; others include the Currant Clearwing *Aegeria tipuliformis*, the Yellow-legged Clearwing *Aegeria vespiformis*, the Red-belted Clearwing *Aegeria myopaeformis* and many others.

SESSILIVENTRES. An alternative name for Symphyta: members of the order Hymenoptera but differing from bees, ants and wasps in having no narrow constriction between the thorax and the abdomen. The group comprises the Sawflies, Woodwasps and related insects.

SETAE. See *Hair*.

SEVEN-SPOT LADYBIRD. *Coccinella septempunctata*, a very common, fairly large ladybird beetle having a black thorax and head, yellowish markings on the sides of the thorax and bright orange-red elytra with seven black spots, *i.e.* three and a half on each elytron (see also *Coccinellidae*).

SEXAVA. A genus of long-horned grasshoppers of the family Tettigoniidae that feed on the foliage of coconut palms in New Guinea and other Pacific islands. Especially *Sexava novae-guineae* and *Sexava nubila*.

SEXTON BEETLE. See *Burying Beetle*.

SEXUALES. A term used with reference to plant-lice and similar insects to denote the generation which contains male and female individuals capable of normal sexual reproduction (see *Aphis*).

SEXUPARAE. A term used with reference to plant-lice and similar insects for the generation of parthenogenetically produced females whose offspring can develop into normal males and females (see *Aphis*).

SHARD-BORNE BEETLE. An alternative name for the Dor Beetle or Dung Beetle *Geotrupes stercorarius* (see *Geotrupes*). (Named from Shakespeare: Macbeth, Act III, Scene 2.)

SHARK MOTHS. See *Monk Moths*.

SHARP-NOSED FLY. *Stomoxys calcitrans*, also called the Stable Fly or Biting House Fly: a member of the family Muscidae very similar to the house fly but with a sharp-pointed proboscis used for piercing the skin and sucking the blood of farm and domestic animals or of man. The larvae live in stable litter. The adults often come indoors and soil windows and curtains with their brown faecal spots. This fly also sometimes breeds in the litter along the shores of lakes, and bites bathers.

SHEEP BOT FLY. *Oestrus ovis*, a large, hairy, yellowish-grey two-winged fly that produces larvae viviparously and deposits them, sometimes several hundreds from one parent, in the nostrils of sheep. The blood-sucking larvae, which grow to a length of about 25 mm., penetrate the tissues and enter the head sinuses of the sheep causing great pain and often death (see also *Bot Fly* and *Oestridae*).

SHEEP KED. See *Ked*.

SHEEP LOUSE. *Trichodectes ovis*, a biting louse of the order Mallophaga parasitic on sheep and related animals. Most of the Mallophaga are bird parasites but this and a few others live on mammals; they are not bloodsuckers but use their mouth-parts to bite off small particles of hair, dried skin etc. (see *Louse* and *Mallophaga*).

SHEEP NOSTRIL FLY. See *Sheep Bot Fly*.

SHEEP TICK. See *Ked*.

SHELLAC INSECT. See *Lac Insect*.

SHIELDBUG. A name for a number of bugs, mostly plant-feeders, belonging to the Pentatomidae, Scutelleridae and a few other related families in the order Heteroptera. All are flattened, roughly shield-shaped with a dorsal thoracic shield or *scutellum* covering most of the body; some are brightly coloured. As with all the Heteroptera the wings are half membranous and half thickened; the piercing mouth-parts are normally bent back under the head when not in use. They live in most parts of the world (see *Pentatomidae* and *Scutelleridae*).

SHINER. See *Croton Bug*.

SHINING GROUND BEETLE. *Carabus nitens*, a carnivorous beetle of the family Carabidae about 20 mm. long and having a shiny red thorax and shining green elytra with red along the sides. It is found among damp mosses on moorland.

SHIP .COCKROACH. An alternative name for the American Cockroach *Periplaneta americana* (see *Periplaneta*).

SHOOT-BORERS. A name for a great variety of insects that bore into shoots of plants; they include weevils and other beetles and the larvae of moths.

SHORE-BUGS. (1) A name for a number of semi-aquatic predatory bugs of the group Heteroptera that live on mud or silt or in stagnant water around lakes, ponds or ditches and slow moving streams (see *Saldidae* and *Saldula*). (2) See *Marine Bug*.

SHORE EARWIG. *Labidura riparia*, a pale yellowish earwig sometimes as long as 30–35 mm., *i.e.* about twice as long as the Common Earwig. Another point of difference is that the forceps of the male are thin and nearly straight. It lives on the seashore, on wet sand and among seaweed.

SHORE-FLIES. See *Ephydridae*.

SHORE PAEDERUS. *Paederus litoralis*, a wingless beetle of the family Staphylinidae, about 6 mm. long, black with a yellowish red thorax, antennae, legs and the proximal half of the abdomen; the short elytra are greenish blue. It is found under stones or rubbish near the seashore.

SHORE SEXTON. *Necrodes litoralis*, a burying beetle of the family Necrophoridae: an elongated black beetle about 20 mm. long, having a small head and club-shaped antennae which are red at the tips. It is often found feeding on dead fish and other debris on the seashore.

SHORT-CIRCUIT BEETLES. Bostrichidae, a family of elongated, cylindrical beetles related to the Larder Beetles and to the Powder Post Beetles. In some species the jaws are powerful enough to bore into the insulation and lead covering of electric cables.

SHORT-HAIRED HUMBLE BEE. *Bombus subterraneus*, a species of humble bee about 16 mm. long, black with bands of yellow on the thorax and abdomen and with a yellowish white 'tail'. The hair on the body is much shorter and thinner than on most humble bees. It makes its nest underground.

SHORT-HORNED GRASSHOPPER. See *Grasshopper* and *Acrididae*.

SHORT-TAILED BLUE. *Everes argiades*, a small butterfly of the family Lycaenidae, violet-blue above and light grey, spotted with yellow and black on the underside. The hind-wings have short 'tails', a feature rare in this family of butterflies. It is found across Europe, Asia and North America.

SHORT-WINGED CONEHEAD. *Conocephalus dorsalis*, a species of bush-cricket of the family Tettigoniidae, bright green with brown elytra and brown ovipositor. The body is about 20 mm. long and the antennae twice this length. The head is roughly cone-shaped. It lives among grass in marshy places.

SHOT-HOLE BORER. See *Pinhole Borer* and *Bark Beetle*.

SHOULDER-STRIPE MOTH. See *Earophila*.

SIAGONA. A tropical ground beetle of the family Carabidae that stridulates by rubbing its anterior femora against a file on the underside of the thorax.

SIALIDAE. Alder-flies: a family of small insects of the order Neuroptera closely related to the Lacewings. The body is thin, usually black or brown and there are four large membranous wings of a smoky brown or grey colour with conspicuous black veins. The antennae and legs are long. Alder-flies are usually to be found making weak flights or resting on reeds, tree trunks etc. near water. The larvae are aquatic and carnivorous and have seven or eight pairs of hair-fringed abdominal gills. *Sialis fuliginosa* and *Sialis lutaria* are two common European species. Both are small but alder-flies of the tropics and subtropics are sometimes of great size. One of the best known of these is the Giant Alder-fly or Dobson Fly *Corydalis* of North America which is about 10 cm. long.

SIBINE. See *Saddleback Moth*.

SIGARA. A genus of aquatic bugs of the family Corixidae or Lesser Water Boatmen, notable for their habit of changing colour to match the background.

SILK. A tough material in the form of extremely fine threads secreted by various glands of insects and spiders. Chemically it consists mostly of a strong elastic protein *fibroin* covered by a layer of a more gelatinous protein *sericin*. In the silkworm (the larva of *Bombyx*) it is produced by modified salivary glands; in Embioptera and some Diptera (*e.g. Hilara*) the silk glands are on the tarsi of the front legs; in some Coleoptera the Malpighian tubules are modified to produce silk.

SILK-BUTTON GALL. Small, brown, hairy galls shaped like buttons with a central pit: produced on oak leaves by the tiny gall-wasp *Neuroterus numismalis*.

SILKEN FUNGUS BEETLES. Cryptophagidae, a widely distributed family of small beetles that feed on fungi and decaying matter in the nests of ants and wasps. They may also be found in grain and other stored products, though not usually a major pest.

SILKWORM MOTHS. The larvae of many moths produce silken cocoons but these are not all suitable for commercial silk production. The best known species, the Chinese Silkworm *Bombyx mori*, is now cultivated on a large scale in many parts of the world. Originally it was a jealously guarded secret of ancient China. The caterpillars, which feed on mulberry leaves, can each produce a continuous thread of silk up to 300 metres long. 50,000 cocoons are necessary to produce 1 kg. of silk. Other species known from ancient times are the Oak Silkworm Moths *Antherea pernyi* from China and *Antherea yamanai* from Japan. In addition to these the giant moths of the family Saturniidae produce cocoons from which silk may be obtained. In most cases, however, the process is too costly to be of commercial value. One of these, the Cynthia Moth *Philosamia cynthia*, has long been bred for silk production in China, Japan and South-east Asia. It was introduced into Europe and North America about 1860. Its native food plant is the Tree of Heaven *Ailanthus glandulosa* but although strains were produced that fed on other plants, it was found to be uneconomic. The Polyphemus Moth *Telea polyphemus* and several species of *Samia* have also been tried.

SILPHIDAE. Carrion Beetles and Burying Beetles: a family of beetles with an elongated body, short elytra and clubbed antennae. They fly well and have a good sense of smell which enables them to seek out the corpses of animals on which they feed and in which they lay their eggs. The Carrion Beetles do not bury the corpse but the true Burying Beetles or Sexton Beetles (sometimes put in a separate family Necrophoridae) bury the carcases by excavating beneath them till they sink below the soil. A number of beetles co-operate in this activity and eggs are laid in the buried corpse which provides an ample food supply for the developing larvae.

SILVER FIR ADELGES. *Adelges nuesslini*, a plant-louse of the family Adelgidae that attacks young Silver Fir trees (*Abies*). The wingless females migrate down the stem from the new shoots and rapidly increase as they produce successive generations parthenogenetically. The effect of their feeding is to alter the structure of the young wood, preventing the rise of water and causing the death of the tree from the top downwards.

SILVERFISH. See *Lepismatidae*.

SILVER-GROUND CARPET MOTH. *Xanthorhoe montanata*, a common geometrid moth of the group Larentiinae having a wing-span of about 25 mm., silvery white with a broad double band of dark brown on the fore-wings. The caterpillars, which are brown and stick-like, feed on grasses and small meadow plants.

SILVER-LINE BUTTERFLY. A name for several Lycaenid butterflies from the mountains of North Africa; light brown with black spots on the upper surface, paler or whitish underneath with a number of silver-centred spots arranged in rows.

SILVER-LINES MOTH. See *Bena*.

SILVER SPOT. A name sometimes used, more particularly in the U.S., for any of the fritillaries; butterflies having silver spots on the backs of the wings.

SILVER-SPOTTED SKIPPER. *Hesperia comma* or *Augiades comma*: a common butterfly of the family Hesperiidae ranging across Europe, North Africa, Asia and North America. A small tawny brown butterfly with dark markings and pale yellowish spots on the upper surface; the underside being greenish with a number of large silvery white spots. The larvae feed chiefly on grasses and make nests from leaves or blades of grass woven together with silk threads.

SILVER-STUDDED BLUE. See *Plebejus*.

SILVER-WASHED FRITILLARY. *Argynnis paphia*, a nymphalid butterfly, one of the largest of the fritillaries ranging across Europe, North Africa and Asia as far as Japan. The upper surface resembles other fritillaries, brown with a chequerboard type of pattern in black. The underside has, instead of the usual silvery spots, a number of broad silver bands. The larvae feed on violets.

SILVER WATER BEETLE. *Hydrous piceus* (see *Hydrous*).

SILVER Y-MOTH. *Plusia gamma* (see *Plusiidae*).

SILVERY PHYLLOBIUS. *Phyllobius argentatus*, a bright silvery green weevil about 6 mm. long with a short stout rostrum and elbowed antennae; common on flowering shrubs.

SIMPLE EYE. An ocellus: a very simple photosensitive organ consisting of a single cuticular lens, a transparent corneagen layer below it and a few sensitive cells or *retinulae* below this. Sometimes also there are a few *rhabdoms* (see *Compound Eyes*) and pigment cells which are rather indefinitely arranged. Most larvae have paired ocelli, sometimes a single pair and sometimes in clusters. Adult insects, in addition to their compound eyes, usually have three ocelli arranged in a triangle on the top of the head. They probably inform the insect of changes in the intensity of the light but their simple structure is incapable of forming any kind of clear picture.

SIMULIIDAE. Buffalo-gnats (Blackflies): small, black, blood-sucking flies with a hump-backed appearance and with broad wings. The spindle-shaped larvae live in running water and have an anal pad with setae for clinging to rocks etc. In many countries, especially in the tropics, these insects transmit parasites to animals and man but even when this is not the case their bite can be extremely painful when large clouds of them swarm round farm animals. *Simulium equinum* attacks horses and cattle behind the ears; *Simulium venustum* transmits protozoan parasites of poultry in North America; *Simulium damnosum* transmits the small nematode worm *Oncocerca volvulus* to humans in West Africa, causing painful cysts under the skin and sometimes producing blindness.

SINODENDRON.   *Sinodendron cylindricum*, a small, broad, roughly cylindrical, shiny black beetle of the family Lucanidae or Stag Beetles. The male has a curved horn on the head and for this reason the beetle has sometimes been called the Small European Rhinoceros Beetle; it should not be confused with the large Rhinoceros Beetles of the family Dynastidae.

SINOXYLON.   A wood-boring beetle of the family Bostrichidae: a pest of timber in India and Africa.

SIPHON.   A breathing tube, usually with two spiracles and two tracheae, projecting from the hind-end of an aquatic insect such as a mosquito larva. In the case of culicine mosquitoes the larva hangs from the surface of the water with its head down and its siphon piercing the surface film and enabling the insect to breathe. In some cases it is modified for piercing the tissues of water weeds and obtaining air from these. The siphon attains extreme size in the aquatic larva of the Drone-fly *Eristalis* (see *Rat-tailed Maggot*).

SIPHONA.   A genus of small black tachinid flies whose larvae are parasites in crane-flies and in certain caterpillars.

SIPHONAPTERA.   See *Aphaniptera*.

SIPHUNCULATA.   Blood-sucking lice: flattened wingless insects having a tubular proboscis which can be anchored into the skin of the host by means of a number of denticles. They are usually ectoparasites of mammals. *Pediculus*, the body-louse of humans, is a well-known example (see *Body Louse*).

SIRICIDAE.   Woodwasps, Horntails or Giant Sawflies: large insects up to nearly 50 mm. long, belonging to the symphytous Hymenoptera; four-winged insects with a cylindrical body and a very large ovipositor capable of boring into wood. Eggs are laid under the surface and the larvae penetrate deep into the tree, especially into conifers or 'soft-wood' trees. They take a long time to develop to their full size and adult insects sometimes emerge from timber long after it has been used for building or furniture making. The commonest British species, *Urocerus gigas* (formerly called *Sirex gigas*), is recognized by its black and yellow striped body and its large pin-like ovipositor.

SISYRIDAE.   Sponge-flies, a family of Neuroptera whose aquatic larvae live in association with fresh-water sponges, piercing the tissues with their mouthparts. They afterwards leave the water to hibernate and pupate in silken cocoons in cracks or crevices of bark, stones etc.

SITARIS.   A genus of oil-beetles of the family Meloidae whose larvae live in the nests of solitary bees, go through a series of distinct larval forms and are carried on the bodies of their hosts to new nests where they feed on the eggs (see *Meloidae* and *Hypermetamorphosis*).

SITODIPLOSIS.   A genus of gall-midges of the family Cecidomyidae, parasites of wheat, notable for the longevity of their larvae which have been known to lie dormant in a silken cocoon in the soil for as much as 18 years and then to pupate and emerge normally. *Sitodiplosis mosellana* is a species from British Columbia.

SITONA. A genus of weevils that attack peas and beans, the larvae feeding on the roots and the adults on the leaves. *Sitona lineata* is a species that has been accidentally introduced into North America from Europe. It was first recorded in Canada in 1936.

SITOPHILUS. See *Grain Weevil*.

SITOTROGA. *Sitotroga cerealella*, the Angoumois Grain Moth: a widely distributed pest whose larvae feed on the kernels of wheat, maize etc.

SIX-SPOT BURNET MOTH. *Zygaena filipendulae*, a medium sized, day-flying moth of the family Zygaenidae having the fore-wings greenish-black with six bright red spots on each; the hind-wings are crimson with black margins. The caterpillars, which are light green with a segmental pattern of dark green and yellow patches, feed on clover, vetch, bird's foot trefoil and other Leguminosae.

SIXTEEN-SPOT LADYBIRD. *Hylazia sexdecimguttata*, a ladybird beetle of the family Coccinellidae having pale reddish-brown elytra with sixteen paler spots on each.

SIZE OF INSECTS. Insects are limited in size by the following factors:

(1) The presence of the hard cuticle or exoskeleton which inhibits growth and has to be cast off from time to time.

(2) The nature of the respiratory and circulatory systems which would make the rapid intake and passage of oxygen into a large body difficult.

(3) The weight to be supported and the strength of the legs and wings.

(4) The fact that the muscles are *inside* the exoskeleton and cannot be made more than a limited size for a particular limb. In contrast, vertebrates can have muscles as big as necessary, limited only by the mechanical strength of the bones against which they pull.

In the Carboniferous Era some dragonflies had a wing-span of 75 cm. but present-day insects are all considerably smaller than this. The smallest known insects are the fairy-flies of the family Mymaridae with a body-length of about 0.2 mm. The insect with the largest body is probably the African Goliath Beetle *Macrodontia cervicornis* about 15 cm. long; the longest, but not the bulkiest insects are some of the tropical stick insects with a length of 35 cm. The largest known moth is the Hercules Emperor Moth *Coscinoscera hercules* with the Indian Atlas Moth *Attacus atlas* a close second. The largest butterfly is the Birdwing of New Guinea, *Triodes alexandrae* with a wing-span of 30 cm.

SKATER. See *Pondskater*.

SKELETON. See *Exoskeleton*.

SKIMMER. A name sometimes given to the larger and faster species of dragonflies, especially those of the family Libellulidae (*q.v.*).

SKIN BEETLES. See *Dermestidae*.

SKIN-WORMS. A colloquial name used by tanners for the larvae of the Skin Beetles (see *Dermestidae*).

SKIPJACK. See *Click Beetle*.

SKIPPERS. See *Hesperiidae*.

SKOTOTAXIS. A reflex response by which an insect will move towards a dark object or the darkest part of a room. Some authorities consider this to be the positive attraction to low intensity in contrast to *negative phototaxis*; a doubtful distinction.

SLAVE-MAKING ANT. Any of the species of ants that raid the nests of others, carry off the pupae and rear them to provide slave-workers for their own nest. The best known are the European Robber Ant *Formica sanguinea* and the Amazon Ant *Polyergus lucidus*.

SLEEPING SICKNESS FLIES. Tsetse flies of the genus *Glossina*, blood-sucking flies that transmit the parasite *Trypanosoma*, the cause of African Sleeping Sickness (see *Glossinidae*).

SLOE BUG. *Dolycoris baccarum*, a light brown shieldbug about 8 mm. long that feeds in all its stages on sloes, plums and similar fruit.

SLOW PELOBIUS. *Pelobius tardus* (see *Pelobius*).

SLUGWORMS. The slug-like larvae of certain sawflies, *e.g. Caliroa limacina*, a pest of pear and cherry trees.

SMALL BATH WHITE. *Pontia chloridice*, a common pierid butterfly, white with a pattern of greenish grey spots and squares; found chiefly in the high-lands of southern Europe, Asia and North America.

SMALL BLACK ANT. A name for many species but particularly for *Lasius niger*, the European Garden Ant which is also found in North America. This is the common ant that invades houses.

SMALL BLUE BUTTERFLY. *Cupido minimus*, a small European and Asiatic butterfly of the family Lycaenidae having a wing-span of about 20 mm. The male has dark brown wings powdered with blue; in the female they are dark brown without any blue. The undersides of both are greyish white with small black dots. The larvae feed on small leguminous plants.

SMALL BRISTLE-TAILED ICHNEUMON. *Lissonota sulphurifera*, a black ichneumon fly about 6 mm. long with brown legs, long antennae and an ovipositor twice the length of the body. It lays its eggs in the caterpillars of clearwing moths.

SMALL COPPER. *Lycaena phlaeas*, one of the commonest butterflies of the family Lycaenidae ranging across Europe and Asia as far as Japan; Africa as far south as Ethiopia; and the Eastern United States of North America. The fore-wings are reddish gold with eight black spots and a dark brown border; the hind-wings are dark brown with a coppery red border on which are four black spots. The greenish, slug-like larvae feed on docks and sorrel (Polygonaceae).

SMALL EGGAR MOTH. *Eriogaster lanestris*, a stout, reddish brown moth, similar to the larger Oak Eggar but only about half the size. The fore-wings have a white spot in the centre and a wavy white transverse band. It belongs to the family Lasiocampidae. The caterpillars are brown and hairy; they feed on leaves of blackthorn and hawthorn where they make communal nests of silk among the foliage (see also *Eggar Moths* and *Lasiocampidae*).

SMALL ELEPHANT HAWK-MOTH. See *Deilephila*.

SMALL HEATH. *Coenonympha pamphilus*, a small butterfly of the family Satyridae found all over Europe, North Africa and Western Asia at altitudes up to 2,000 m. Both wings are light tawny brown with a darker margin; the fore-wings have a black spot near the tip. The larvae feed on grasses.

SMALL MAGPIE MOTH. *Eurrhypara urticata* or *Eurrhypara hortulata* (see *Eurrhypara*).

SMALL PURPLE-BARRED MOTH.   See *Phytometra*.

SMALL RED DAMSELFLY.   *Ceriagrion tenellum*, a small European damselfly about 3 cm. long with black and red thorax, red abdomen and red legs; the latter feature distinguishes it from *Pyrrhosoma* which is otherwise similar but has black legs.

SMALL TORTOISESHELL BUTTERFLY.   *Aglais urticae*, a very common nymphalid butterfly found all over Europe and Asia but not in North Africa. The wings are reddish orange, paler in front, with three large black patches near the front margins of the fore-wings and three smaller black patches behind these. The edges of the wings are irregularly serrated and there is a broad black marginal band with a line of blue crescents. The butterfly may migrate considerable distances and is found up to a height of 2,000 m. In Britain it commonly hibernates indoors, particularly in outhouses or similar buildings. The larvae feed on stinging nettles.

A closely related and very similar species *Aglais milberti* is found in North America.

SMALL WHITE BUTTERFLY.   *Pieris rapae*, one of the commonest white butterflies found all over Europe, North Africa and Asia as far as Japan. It has been introduced into North America and Australia and is now common in these countries. In appearance this butterfly is remarkably like the Large White or Cabbage Butterfly *Pieris brassicae* but the three black spots and the black wing-tips are much fainter. The smooth green caterpillars feed on cabbage and other plants of the family Cruciferae (see also *Pieridae*).

SMELL.   See *Olfactory Sense*.

SMERINTHUS.   *Smerinthus ocellatus*, the Eyed Hawk-moth: a large moth of the family Sphingidae found all over Europe and Asia wherever the food plants, willow, sallow, apple and other fruit trees are growing. When at rest with the wings half open the brown and grey colour gives them the appearance of dead leaves, but when disturbed they suddenly expose the pinkish hind-wings with two large blue and black eye-spots. The caterpillars are light green with oblique lines of darker green and white and with a horn at the hind-end.

SMINTHURIDAE.   A family of springtails, small jumping insects of the order Collembola less than 1 mm. long with a fat or rounded abdomen and long legs. They feed on vegetation, are found in very large numbers all over the world and are common pests of agriculture. *Sminthurus viridis*, a green species sometimes called the 'Lucerne Flea', feeds on clover and other leguminous plants and, although found in Europe and other countries, is most prolific in Australia, New Zealand and South Africa. The eggs are laid in damp soil and can survive drought for a year or more.

SMOKY WAINSCOT MOTH.   *Leucania impura*, a common Europea noctuid moth of a pale brownish grey colour with five red or brown lines running longitudinally across the fore-wings. The larvae feed on grasses (see also *Leucania*).

SNAIL FLY.   See *Marsh Fly*.

SNAKE FLY.   See *Raphidiidae*.

SNIPE FLIES.   See *Rhagionidae*.

SNOUT BEETLES.   An alternative name for weevils: beetles having a long snout or rostrum (see *Rhynchophora* and *Curculionidae*).

SNOUT MOTHS.   A group of moths having long palps projecting in front of the head like a snout. The name is given to some noctuids and some pyralids. The European Snout Moth *Hypena proboscidalis* is one of the former, a medium sized light brown moth with the snout nearly as long as the thorax. The larvae feed on stinging nettles.

SNOW FLEAS. Boreidae: a family of small wingless insects of the order Mecoptera sometimes called moss flies. They are found in large numbers in the Tundra where they run and jump over the snow and damp earth feeding on mosses and lichens. *Boreus hyemalis* is a species found in the colder parts of Britain. The name Snow Flea is also sometimes given to *Hypogastrura socialis*, one of the springtails of the order Collembola.

SNOW FLIES. (1) Flightless crane-flies (Tipulidae) of the genus *Chionea*, which go above the snow-line in Europe and North America.

(2) A name sometimes given to Whiteflies, minute plant-bugs of the family Aleyrodidae, pests of tomatoes and other plants.

SNOW SCORPION FLY. An alternative name for the Snow Flea *Boreus hyemalis* (see *Snow Fleas*).

SNOWY TREE-CRICKET. *Oecanthus niveus*, a white tree-cricket or long-horned grasshopper of the family Tettigoniidae found in North America.

SOCIAL LIFE. Many insects live together in large communities but they are only regarded as true social insects if they fulfil the following conditions:

(1) They work together to build a common nest, sharing their food and mutually protecting one another.

(2) They show division of labour which often involves the existence of different castes: queen, workers, drones, soldiers etc.

(3) They have some means of communication which may be by sound, smell, taste or touch. In this way the presence or behaviour of some individuals will trigger off a particular behaviour pattern in others.

(4) The most important condition is *maternal care* with the mother living long enough to rear her young instead of leaving them to fend for themselves. In advanced insect societies 'maternal' care may be delegated to a worker caste.

The most highly organized of such social colonies exist among bees, wasps, ants and termites where the number of individuals in a colony may be many thousands and a very high degree of co-ordinated behaviour and division of labour is achieved.

SOGATA. A genus of leaf-hoppers, jumping plant-lice of the family Delphacidae: *Sogata distincta* is a pest of sugar cane in India; *Sogata furcifera* is sometimes a pest of rice in Malaya.

SOLDIER ANTS. Ants with large heads and powerful jaws having the primary duty of defending the colony. Some kinds can also defend themselves by shooting out formic acid from the hind-part of the body to a distance of 15 cm. or more. A similar caste of 'soldiers' exists among termites although these are no relation to true ants (see *Castes*).

SOLDIER BEETLES. See *Cantharidae*.

SOLDIER BUGS. A name given to a number of pentatomid bugs that prey upon other insects and suck their blood (see *Pentatomidae*).

SOLDIER FLIES. Stratiomyidae, a family of two-winged flies usually of bright metallic colours and having the back of the thorax armed with spines. The larvae are generally aquatic and the adults feed on marsh plants. The origin of the name 'soldier fly' is a translation of the generic name *Stratiomys* which alludes to its being armed with spines.

SOLDIER TERMITES. A sterile caste of termites specially equipped for defending the colony. Usually they have large, thickly sclerotized heads with powerful jaws; in some species there are *nasute* forms in which the head is prolonged into a sharp snout from which poison can be squirted.

SOLENOBIA. A genus of moths of the family Psychidae whose larvae or *bagworms* make silken cases covered with sand grains and particles of lichen etc.

SOLENOPSIS. A genus of predatory ants, sometimes known as Fire Ants, having a powerful and extremely painful sting. *Solenopsis geminata* and *Solenopsis saevissima* are large, pugnacious species found in Central and South America and the Southern United States; *Solenopsis molesta*, another American species, is smaller and lives in the nests of other ants, preying upon their larvae and pupae.

SOLIDAGO NOMAD BEE. *Nomada solidaginis*, a small Cuckoo Bee resembling a wasp with a hairless black and yellow banded abdomen. It lays its eggs in the nests of other bees and the ensuing larvae feed on the stored nectar and pollen as well as on the eggs and larvae of the host. The adult of thi nomad bee is often found on flowers of Golden Rod (*Solidago*).

SOLITARIA. A name given to locusts in the solitary, non-migratory phase (see *Locustidae*).

SOLITARY BEES. Bees that do not live in colonies, *e.g.* Mining Bees, Carpenter Bees, Cuckoo Bees and many others.

SOLITARY PHASE. See *Locustidae*.

SOLITARY WASPS. Wasps that do not live in colonies, *e g*. Potter and Mason Wasps and Spider-hunting Wasps.

SOLOMON'S SEAL SAWFLY. *Phymatocera aterrima*, a black sawfly whose greyish caterpillars feed on the leaves of Solomon's Seal (*Polygonatum*) often completely defoliating it.

SOOTHSAYER. A name sometimes used colloquially in America for the Praying Mantis (see *Mantidae*).

SOOTY COPPER. *Heodes tityrus*, a European and Asiatic butterfly of the family Lycaenidae similar to the other Copper Butterflies but having the upper surface much darker, sometimes nearly black.

SOOTY ORANGE TIP. *Zegris eupheme*, a pierid butterfly similar to the common Orange Tip *Anthocharis cardamines* but having the orange patch on each fore-wing reduced to a small oval area surrounded by a broad margin of black. It is found in mountainous regions of Spain, North Africa and the Middle East.

SOOTY RINGLET. *Erebia pluto*, a nearly black butterfly of the family Satyridae similar to the other ringlets but with the two white-centred rings on the fore-wings reduced to tiny white dots or sometimes completely absent. It is found high up in the Alps, Dolomites and Apennines where the larvae feed on grasses.

SORGHUM MIDGE. *Contarinia sorghicola*, a common midge in the warmer parts of North America where the larvae attack the Indian Millet plant *Sorghum vulgare* which is cultivated as fodder; also in the West Indies, Sudan and Australia.

SOUND PERCEPTION. See *Hearing Organs*.

SOUNDS OF INSECTS. Many insects produce sounds audible to humans (30–30,000 cycles per second) and many more produce sounds which are of frequencies beyond the range of human perception but perceptible to other insects. Although some insect-sounds have a regular pitch and are detected by particular hearers (*e.g.* one sex of a species by the other), insects are apparently not equipped to analyse complex sounds in the way that the human ear listens to music. Some sounds made by insects are merely incidental to their movement and apparently have no special significance. Others such as the chirping of grasshoppers are made by special sound-producing organs. Insects that do this are usually also equipped with special 'hearing' organs so that they can perceive the sounds of others and in this case there is usually a social significance such as sexual attraction. A few insects will make sudden noises if disturbed. These may serve to frighten off predators.

Wing-beat Sounds. These are produced by the rapid vibration of the wings; the faster the beat, the higher the note, *e.g.* Bees 200–400, mosquitoes 600, small midges 1,000 or more.

Stridulation. This sound is made by rubbing the hind femora against the edges of the wings or by rubbing the two tegmina together. It is characteristic of grasshoppers and crickets.

Drumming. The cicada, one of the loudest of insects, has two resonating drums with air spaces beneath them situated on the base of the abdomen.

Spiracular Sounds. A few insects can produce sounds by rapidly expelling air from the spiracles and in some cases there are leaf-like folds within the tracheae. The vibration of these helps to produce the sound. A few Diptera and Coleoptera and the larvae of some moths come in this category.

Mechanical Sounds. The clicking of the Click Beetle and the drumming of the Death-watch beetle as it taps its head against the burrow are sounds of this type. (See also *Stridulation* and *Frequency of Wing-beat*.)

SOUTHERN AESHNA. *Aeshna cyanea*, a common European dragonfly of the group Anisoptera about 7 cm. long having broad wings with the front edged golden yellow. The thorax is pale green on the male and yellow on the female; the abdomen is dark brown with stripes of the same colour as the thorax. It is a powerful flyer and is often found in woodlands far from water.

SPANGLE GALL. See *Neuroterus*.

SPANGLE-WINGED MOSQUITO. A name occasionally given to the common malaria mosquito *Anopheles maculipennis* (*q.v.*).

SPANISH CRESCENT-HORNED BEETLE. *Copris hispanus*, a large dung-beetle of the family Scarabaeidae in which the male has a prominent curved horn on the head. The insect is about 3 cm. long, black with reddish brown hairs underneath; it is common in the Mediterranean countries and the Middle East.

SPANISH FLY. *Lytta vesicatoria*, a brilliant golden-green Blister Beetle of the family Meloidae; an elongated beetle about 15 mm. long which often swarms in large numbers and strips the leaves from many kinds of trees. It is found in the warmer parts of Central and Southern Europe and is the chief source of the drug *Cantharidin* (see also *Meloidae*).

SPECKLED BUSH-CRICKET. *Leptophyes punctatissima*, a small, stoutly built cricket of the family Tettigoniidae, about 15 mm. long with antennae twice this length. The body is bright green and finely speckled with black. In both sexes elytra are absent and wings vestigial. It is common in thickets and hedgerows of Europe.

SPECKLED WOOD BUTTERFLY. *Pararge aegeria,* a common butterfly of the family Satyridae ranging from Western Europe to Central Asia. The upper surfaces of the wings are dark brown with a large number of cream coloured spots. There is a small white-centred black ring near the tip of each fore-wing and three similar rings near the edge of each hind-wing. The larvae are green and feed on various grasses. They hibernate both in the larval and in the pupal state.

SPECKLED YELLOW MOTH. *Pseudopanthera macularia,* a small day-flying moth of the family Geometridae having wings of orange-yellow speckled with purplish-brown; common in woodlands throughout Europe where the green stick-like caterpillars feed on plants of the family Labiatae.

SPECTACLE MOTH. *Unca triplasia,* a small noctuid moth of a greyish brown colour mottled and lined with darker brown and having on the front of the thorax two white rings resembling a pair of spectacles. The larvae, which are marked with light and dark green, feed on stinging nettles where they are well camouflaged.

SPEED OF INSECTS. The speed at which insects fly has been greatly exaggerated in the past as a result of a number of faulty observations. It is now believed that the upper limit of speed is about 25–30 miles per hour (40–48 km. per hour) achieved by horseflies and some of the larger dragonflies. A bee flies at about 8–15 km. per hour and most insects considerably more slowly than this. The famous Bot Fly alleged in 1926 to reach 818 m.p.h. was discredited almost at once but continued to be quoted for many years afterwards.

SPEED OF WINGS. See *Frequency of Wing-beat.*

SPERMATHECA. A sac or receptacle in a female insect in which sperm cells received from the male are stored until required for fertilizing the eggs (see *Female Reproductive System*).

SPEYERIA. A generic name given by some authorities to the Fritillary butterflies of the New World; more often, however, they are classed with others of the genus *Argynnis* (see *Fritillaries*).

SPHAERIDIUM. A common genus of small beetles of the family Hydrophilidae, shining black with varying numbers of red spots on the wing-cases: *Sphaeridium bipustulatum* with one spot near the tip of each wing-case; *Sphaeridium quadrimaculatum* with two on each.

SPHAEROCORIS. *Sphaerocoris ocellatus,* a shieldbug of the family Pentatomidae common in East Africa; yellowish brown with a number of red rings on the shield which covers the whole body and having black eyes bordered with red.

SPHAGNUM BUGS. Minute predatory bugs of the genus *Hebrus* inhabiting sphagnum moss.

SPHECIA. See *Lunar Hornet Moth.*

SPHECIDAE. A family of solitary wasps including Digger Wasps and Mud Daubers: usually large shining black, or black and orange or red insects with a long narrow waist between thorax and abdomen. Most of them make nests by burrowing into sandy soil and these are stocked with caterpillars or other insects that have been stung and paralysed as food for the developing larvae.

SPHECIFORMIA. A large group of aculeate Hymenoptera including solitary digging wasps (Sphecoidea) and bees (Apoidea) in all of which the pronotum does not extend back as far as the tegulae, near the wing-bases. (See also *Sphecoidea* below.)

SPHECIUS. *Sphecius speciosus*, the Giant Cicada-killer of North America, the largest wasp in the family Sphecidae: a shiny black and yellow insect with amber coloured wings and with long spiny legs used for digging. The nest is made in the ground; a cicada that has been stung and paralysed is placed in it and an egg laid on the living victim. The circular opening of the burrow, often as large as 20 mm. across, is then plugged with soil and the egg left to develop.

SPHECODES. A genus of small, usually hairless, cuckoo bees generally black with a reddish abdomen. They are probably degenerate and their pollen-collecting apparatus is vestigial or absent. Most species lay their eggs in the nests of other bees of the genera *Andrena* and *Halictus*.

SPHECOIDEA. A superfamily of aculeate Hymenoptera comprising several families of solitary, predaceous, digging wasps which sting and paralyse their prey before dragging it to their nests as food for the larvae. (See also *Sphecidae*.)

SPHEX. A genus of solitary wasps of the family Sphecidae some of which are diggers and some mud daubers. Most of them are shiny black with red or orange bands on the abdomen and with a long narrow waist. The adults feed on nectar but the developing larvae feed on other insects which have been stung and paralysed by the parent and deposited in the nest. The largest species, *Sphex ingens* of South America, catches locusts and other insects often larger than itself. It will even attack the large bird-catching spiders (see *Sphecidae* and *Sphecoidea*).

SPHINGIDAE. Hawk-moths: large stoutly-built moths whose fore-wings are much larger than the hind ones. The proboscis is sometimes extremely long and the antennae end in hooks. The larvae have ten prolegs and usually bear a horn or spine at the hind-end. The Death's Head Hawk-moth *Acherontia atropos*, belonging to this family, is the largest British moth, sometimes having a wing-span of over 12 cm. Other British species include the Elephant Hawk-moth, Humming-bird Hawk-moth, Poplar, Lime and Privet Hawk-moths etc. The family comprises about 1,000 species distributed all over the world. The largest species are to be found in the tropics and some Indonesian and Australian species have a wing-span of up to 20 cm.

SPHINX. A common genus of Hawk-moths including the European Privet Hawk-moth *Sphinx ligustri* and a number of American species (see *Sphingidae*)

SPHODROMANTIS. *Sphodromantis lineola*, a large West African species of Praying Mantis, pale greenish white with pink on the sides of the abdomen (see *Mantidae*).

SPICE-BUSH SWALLOWTAIL. *Papilio troilus*, a large swallowtail butterfly from the Southern States of North America, dark brown with a row of yellow spots along the edge of each fore-wing and with the posterior half of each hind-wing pale blue with marginal blue crescents outlined in brown. The Caterpillar feeds on sassafras, an aromatic shrub of the laurel family.

SPIDER BEETLES. See *Ptinidae*.

SPIDER BUGS. Slender, long-legged, predatory bugs such as *Empicoris* (*q.v.*), of the family Reduviidae.

SPIDER WASPS. Pompilidae and related families: solitary hunting wasps that stock their nests with spiders that have been stung and paralysed as food for the developing larvae (see *Pompilidae*).

SPIKED PEA GALLS. Small green galls resembling peas with spikes, formed on the leaves of roses by the larvae of the gall-wasp *Diplolepis nervosa*.

SPILONOTA. *Spilonota ocellana*, the Eye-spotted Bud-moth: a small brownish North American moth of the family Olethreutidae related to the codling moths. The larvae are pests of fruit trees, boring into buds and leaves and later forming silken nests in which they live, moult and pupate.

SPILOSOMA. See *Ermine Moth*.

SPINACH MOTH. See *Lygris*.

SPINDASIS. *Spindasis natalensis*, a common butterfly of South Africa belonging to the family Lycaenidae: a woodland and garden species of a yellowish colour streaked with brown and silvery white and with two narrow, almost filamentous 'tails' on the hind-wings. When at rest these are slowly moved up and down giving the appearance of antennae at the hind-end.

SPINNER. A name sometimes given to the brightly coloured, shining adult mayfly (see *Ephemeroptera*).

SPINNERETS. Small tubular appendages from which silk threads are exuded by spiders and by the larvae of many insects. Those of the former open at the hind-end of the abdomen but the spinneret of a caterpillar is quite different, being a median opening beneath the labium or lower lip. It comes from a pair of modified salivary glands which produce silk in the form of a fluid which hardens in contact with the air. The insect uses silk for a variety of purposes such as the formation of a rope by which the larva or pupa is suspended; the sewing together of leaves to make a nest; the construction of a sac or tent for the same purpose; the construction of a cocoon to enclose and protect the pupa etc. (see *Silk* and *Silkworm Moths*).

SPINY BEETLES. Sometimes called Hedgehog Beetles, these are leaf-beetles belonging to the Hispinae, a subfamily of the Chrysomelidae. The head, thorax and wing-covers are protected by numerous sharp spines. Most of these beetles are to be found in the tropics but there is one European species *Hispella atra*, a blue-black insect about 4 mm. long, common in the drier parts of Central Europe.

SPINY FLIES. Tachinid flies of the genus *Echinomyia* whose larvae bore into and parasitize various caterpillars. The adult insects are characterized by the large number of bristles and spines covering the legs and the rather flattened body. They are black or brown and some species have an orange or reddish abdomen. *Echinomyia grossa* is the size and shape of a honey bee; *Echinomyia fera* is slightly smaller.

SPINY GALLS. See *Hedgehog Oak Gall* and *Pea Galls*.

SPINY MASON WASP. *Odynerus spinipes*, a common wasp of dry sandy places; black with yellow or cream markings on the thorax and abdomen and with spines or bristles on the legs. They make their nests by tunnelling into a sandy bank and the cells are stocked with small caterpillars that have been stung and paralysed as food for the developing larvae.

SPINY WITCH-HAZEL GALL. See *Hamamelistes*.

SPIRACLES. See *Breathing, Respiration, Holopneustic, Metapneustic* and *Propneustic*.

SPIRACULAR SOUND ORGAN. An organ formed from a series of leaf-like folds inside the tracheae of some insects. When air is rapidly expelled from the spiracles these folds are caused to vibrate and produce a high pitched sound. Such an arrangement is not common but is believed to be present in a few Diptera and Coleoptera.

SPITTLE BUG. The larva of the frog-hopper *Philaenus spumarius*, the Cuckoo-spit insect (see *Cercopidae*).

SPLENDOUR BEETLES. Buprestidae, a family of elongated, brightly coloured beetles whose wing-cases often have a metallic sheen of blue, green, red or violet. They love sunshine and the largest, sometimes 7 cm. or more, are to be found in the tropics. South American species are much used by the natives for making ornaments. The family is closely allied to the Click Beetles (Elateridae) and their larvae are legless 'wireworms' that feed chiefly on rotting wood.

SPONDYLIS. A genus of beetles of the family Cerambycidae, sometimes called Cylinder Longhorns. They have an elongated cylindrical body and, although classed as longhorns, have relatively short antennae. They are common in coniferous forests where their larvae develop in freshly cut stumps.

SPONGE FLIES. Lacewing flies of the order Neuroptera whose aquatic larvae feed on fresh-water sponges (see *Sisyridae*).

SPONGILLA FLIES. See *Sponge Flies*.

SPOTTED ANT-LION. *Myrmeleon europaeus*, one of the largest of the European Neuroptera having brown-spotted wings with a span of 7 cm. Its voracious larva lives in a pit with its jaws exposed ready to catch ants or other passing insects (see *Ant-lion*).

SPOTTED CLUB-HORNED GRASSHOPPER. *Myrmeleotettix maculatus* (see *Mottled Grasshopper*).

SPOTTED WATER BOATMAN. *Notonecta maculata*, a back-swimming, carnivorous water-bug similar to the more common *Notonecta glauca* but having the upper surface spotted with black or dark brown.

SPRING CANKERWORM. A name sometimes given to the larvae of geometrid moths of the genus *Paleacrita*, especially *Paleacrita vernata*; pests of wild and cultivated fruit trees in North America.

SPRING DOR BEETLE. *Geotrupes vernalis*, a dung-beetle with a blue-green metallic sheen, a rounded body and a narrow waist; slightly smaller than the common Dor Beetle but similar in appearance and habits. Like the closely related scarab beetle, it pushes balls of dung into its underground nest to provide food for the developing larvae (see *Dor Beetle* and *Scarabaeidae*).

SPRINGTAILS. Collembola; very small primitively wingless insects having biting mouth-parts, short antennae and legs without tarsi. The abdomen has six segments which are sometimes fused together. On the fourth segment is a *furcula* or springing organ which, when not in use, is held beneath the abdomen by a 'catch' or *retinaculum*. When this is released the furcula springs back propelling the insect through the air (see also *Ametabola* and *Apterygota*).

SPRING USHER MOTH. *Erannis leucophaearia*. See *Erannis*.

SPRUCE BEETLE. A name for a number of bark-beetles and wood-borers that attack spruce trees; more particularly the name is applied to the genus *Dendroctonus* whose periodic outbreaks cause much damage to the coniferous forests of Canada and the United States.

SPRUCE BORER. See *Spruce Beetle*.

SPRUCE BUDWORM. *Harmologa fumiferana* and related species of tortricoid moths whose larvae bore into the buds of spruce and other conifers in the forests of North America.

SPRUCE CONE-GALL. Sometimes called a 'Pineapple Gall', a compact cone-like gall formed by the swelling of developing spruce needles at the tips of young shoots attacked by the plant-louse *Adelges abietis* (see *Spruce Gall-louse*).

SPRUCE GALL-LOUSE. *Adelges abietis*, a small plant-louse of the aphis type of which there are two distinct races. One kind, whose life-cycle is complete in one year, only attacks larch trees; the other has a two-year life-cycle alternating between spruce and larch. Both kinds produce 'pineapple galls' at the bases of young spruce shoots (see also *Aphis*).

SPURGE BUG. *Dicranocephalus*, a genus of elongated plant-bugs of the group Heteroptera that feed on spurge (*Euphorbia*).

SPURGE HAWK-MOTH. *Celerio euphorbiae*, a Central European hawk-moth with a wing-span of about 7 cm. The fore-wings are greenish white with brown patches; the hind-wings are pink and black. The caterpillar, which feeds on spurge (*Euphorbia*), is black and red with a row of yellow spots along each side.

SPURRED PHYLLOBIUS. *Phyllobius calcaratus*, also called the Light Green Tree-weevil: a shiny green beetle about 1 cm. long with a short rostrum, elbowed antennae and elongated elytra. The legs are reddish with a spur or spine on each femur.

SPURS. Thick cuticular hairs or spines on the legs of certain insects.

SQH. Initials used by some American authorities for the *Status quo Hormone*, more generally known as the *Juvenile Hormone* secreted by the *corpora allata* of certain insect larvae. Its function is apparently to inhibit premature metamorphosis.

SQUAMA. (1) One of the two small wing-lobes close to the alula in certain insects such as the house fly: alar squama and thoracic squama.
(2) Any scale-like structure.

SQUARE SPOT RUSTIC MOTH. *Amathes xanthographa*, a very common noctuid moth of a variable greyish or brownish colour with two paler spots on each fore-wing. The outer spot is roughly square and is outlined with dark brown. The larvae, which are brown with longitudinal white lines, feed chiefly on grasses.

SQUASH BEETLES. Leaf-beetles of the genus *Diabrotica* in the family Chrysomelidae. Pests of cucumber, marrow etc., the larvae feed on the roots and the adults on the leaves. Some species, particularly *Diabrotica undecimpunctata*, transmit harmful bacteria that cause leaf-wilt in cucumbers.

SQUASH BORER. See *Melittia*.

SQUASHBUGS. Coreidae, a family of elongated plant-bugs of the group Heteroptera similar in appearance to shieldbugs. The North American species *Anasa tristis* is a well known pest of squash, melon and pumpkins.

SQUASH VINE BORER. See *Melittia*.

SQUEAK BEETLE. See *Hygrobia* and *Pelobius*.

STABLE FLY. *Stomoxys calcitrans*, a two-winged blood-sucking fly similar in appearance to the house fly but with a stiff pointed proboscis. It lives in stables and lays its eggs among the litter and dung. It is found in most parts of the world and can spread anthrax and other diseases to horses, cattle and camels.

STADIUM. The interval between two moults of an insect. (Compare *Instar*.

STAG BEETLE. See *Lucanidae*.

STAGMOMANTIS. *Stagmomantis carolina*, the only species of praying mantis native to the United States although a number of others have been introduced. It is greyish brown with green feet; there is also a strain in which the females are wholly green.

STALK-EYED FLIES. Diopsidae: a group of small tropical flies having the eyes and antennae on lateral stalks.

STAPHYLINIDAE. Rove Beetles: a large family of beetles, some carnivorous and some herbivorous, all characterized by the short elytra which leave the abdomen exposed. The larvae are of the campodeiform type with long legs and powerful biting mouth-parts. One of the best-known British examples is the Devil's Coach-horse *Ocypus olens*.

STAPHYLINOIDEA. A superfamily which includes the Staphylinidae (Rove Beetles) and the Silphidae (Carrion Beetles) and their allies.

STAURONEMATUS. See *Palisade Sawfly*.

STAUROPUS. See *Lobster Moth*.

STEGANOPTYCHA. A genus of small brownish grey moths of the family Tortricidae whose larvae are very destructive to young larch shoots, binding the needles together to make a nest in which they live and feed.

STEGOBIUM. A genus of small brown beetles of the family Anobiidae, closely related to the Death-watch Beetle; both adults and larvae feed on dried animal and plant matter and are pests in museums and warehouses (see *Anobiidae*).

STEGOMYIA. A name formerly used for mosquitoes of the genus *Aedes* including the Yellow Fever Mosquito *Aedes aegypti*.

STEMMATA. An alternative name for the lateral *ocelli* or simple eyes of insect larvae such as caterpillars (see *Simple Eye*).

STEM-MOTHER. The *fundatrix* or founder of a colony of aphids or other plant-lice; the first wingless female of the season (see *Aphis*).

STEM SAWFLIES. Cephidae, a family of small sawflies with large head, long antennae and cylindrical body. They lay their eggs in the stems of wheat and other cereals where the developing larvae work their way up and down, tunnelling out and destroying the stem. A few kinds also attack young twigs of trees.

STENOBOTHRUS. A genus of short-horned grasshoppers including the European Stripe-winged Grasshopper *Stenobothrus lineatus*, green with a white line on the fore-wing. There are also related species in North America and elsewhere. Their song or stridulation is rather quiet and is performed by raising both hind-legs and rasping the femora against the outside edges of the front wings.

STENOCORUS. A genus of longhorn beetles (Cerambycidae) including the European Variable Longhorn *Stenocorus meridianus*, an elongated beetle with narrow black head and thorax and with elytra wide at the front and tapering towards the hind-end. The legs and antennae are either black or red; wing-cases vary from black to light brown. The size also is very variable, some females being several times as large as the males.

STENODEMA. A common genus of greenish brown, elongated plant-bugs of the family Miridae that feed chiefly on grasses.

STENODICTYA. A genus of large fossil insects of the Carboniferous Period belonging to the order Palaeodictyoptera. They resembled dragonflies in having two pairs of large wings with a venation of a simple net-type. In addition to these, however, there were small wing-like extensions on the prothorax and on the abdominal segments (see *Palaeodictyoptera* and *Fossil Insects*).

STENOGAMY. The ability to mate in a confined space, an ability that is rather rare among insects since most species mate while flying and this often involves the swarming of a large number of males, or at least some form of extended courtship flight.

STENOMA. A genus of small white and grey moths that resemble bird droppings when at rest on a plant.

STENOPELMATIDAE. A family of sand crickets sometimes known as Camel Crickets, usually brown or grey, wingless, with long antennae and a high, arched back. It is split into various groups, often given the status of separate families. The Greenhouse Camel Cricket (*Tachycines asynamorus*) of Britain, for example, is generally placed in the family Rhaphidiophoridae.

STENUS. A genus of small, elongated, short-winged beetles of the family Staphylinidae (Rove Beetles) having a protrusible labium and large eyes that give the head a hammer-like appearance. They are found among reeds in marshy places.

STEPHANITIS. See *Rhododendron Bug*.

STEPHANODERES. *Stephanoderes hampei*, the Coffee Berry Borer: a beetle of the family Scolytidae, originally African but now a pest in South-east Asia, Ceylon, Indonesia, South America and other coffee-growing areas.

STEREOKINESIS (= **THIGMOTAXIS**). A phenomenon by which the reflex movements and responses of an insect to light or other stimuli are inhibited by the action of tactile stimuli. When an insect is in contact with any solid body, particularly with a rough surface, it tends to remain motionless. Stimuli which would normally cause the insect to fly are apparently not strong enough to overcome the immobilizing effect induced by a sense of touch. The phenomenon is said to explain why bedbugs, cockroaches and other insects come to rest in crevices and narrow places and why large numbers of plant-lice crowd together in contact with one another.

STEREOTROPISM. See *Stereokinesis*.

STERNAL PLATES. See *Sternum*.

STERNITE. See *Sternum*.

STERNOCERA. *Sternocera boucardi*, one of the Splendour Beetles (Buprestidae) from East Africa; about 5 cm. long, black with green and yellow elytra.

STERNODES. *Sternodes caspius*, a large, black and white ground beetle of the family Tenebrionidae from the deserts of Central Asia.

STERNORRHYNCHA. Plant-bugs of the group Homoptera having a head-flexure so acute that the rostrum appears to arise from between the fore-limbs. The antennae are well developed and do not possess a terminal spine or arista. To this group belong the scale-insects (Coccidae) and the plant-lice (Aphididae). (Cf. *Auchenorrhyncha*.)

303

STERNUM. The skeletal plate on the ventral side of each segment of an insect. It may be a single plate or may be made up of several parts known as *sternites*.

STERRHIDAE. A family of moths sometimes classed with the Geometridae and including the Riband Wave Moth *Sterrha aversata*, a small yellowish brown moth with two darker brown, wavy lines crossing each wing. The brown stick-like caterpillars feed on a variety of meadow plants.

STERRHOPTERYX. A European genus of Bagworm Moths (Psychidae). The male is small with smoky grey wings; the female is wingless and lives all her life in the bag which the larva weaves from silken threads and grains of soil or plant material (see *Bagworms*).

STETHOPHYMA. *Stethophyma grossum*, the Large Marsh Grasshopper: a European species about 4 cm. long with green body, brown elytra and bright yellowish green hind-legs. It lives in marshes and fens where its stridulation takes the form of a slow rhythmic ticking sound.

STICHOPHTHALMA. A genus of large Asiatic butterflies of the family Amathusiidae having rounded wings and usually flying with a slow flapping movement at dawn or dusk. *Stichophthalma formosana* from Taiwan has a wing-span of about 10 cm. and is a light brown colour. *Stichophthalma camadeva* from Northern India is lavender blue and is even larger. Both have a prominent border pattern of dark brown or black squares, circles and crescents.

STICK INSECTS. See *Phasmida* and *Dixippus*.

STICKTIGHT FLEA. See *Echidnophaga*.

STICKWORM. A colloquial name sometimes used for the caddis worm with its stick-like case (see *Caddis Fly*).

STIGMA. (1) An alternative name for a spiracle or breathing pore of an insect. (2) Short for *Pterostigma* (*q.v.*), the conspicuous dark mark near the foreborder of the wing in many insects.

STIGMELLA. *Stigmella microtheriella*, the smallest known European moth with a wing-span of about 3 mm. (often placed in a superfamily Stigmelloidea or Nepticuloidea.)

STILETTO FLIES. Therevidae, a family of small, predatory, long-legged flies with a long narrow body and sharply pointed abdomen. They are rare and tend to favour dry habitats since the females have a circlet of spines round the ovipositor, for laying in sand or loose earth.

STILTBUG. *Neides tipularius*, an elongated, long-legged plant-bug of the family Berytinidae resembling a crane-fly.

STING. See *Poisons*.

STINGLESS BEES. Meliponinae, a subfamily of Apidae: small honey-bees rarely more than 6 mm. long, living in colonies in the ground or in old tree trunks etc. The nests are made of dark wax mixed with faeces, resin, plant material and other debris. Most species live in the tropics.

STINKBUGS. Pentatomidae or Shieldbugs usually brightly coloured and possessing two scent glands on the underside of the thorax; the nymphs have dorsal abdominal stink glands. When disturbed these insects discharge a foul smelling liquid from these glands and are thereby protected from being eaten by birds or other predators.

STINK FLIES. A name sometimes given to Lacewing Flies (Chrysopidae) on account of the disagreeable scent discharged by both adults and larvae as a means of protection.

STINK GLAND. Many insects secrete substances with a disagreeable odour. These are not necessarily poisonous but act as a deterrent to would-be predators. In some insects these substances come from hypodermal cells concentrated in pockets under the thorax or abdomen; in others the salivary glands or the accessory sex glands may be modified for this purpose. Insects notorious for their production of offensive odours include bedbugs (Cimicidae), stinkbugs (Pentatomidae), oil beetles (Meloidae), some ground beetles (Carabidae) and some caterpillars. Substances contained in the secretions include formic acid, butyric acid, hydrochloric acid, salicylic acid and salicylaldehyde, oxides of nitrogen, oils and esters.

STIRASTOMA. *Stirastoma depressum*, a longhorn beetle of the family Cerambycidae: a pest of the cocoa plant in many countries, particularly in the Caribbean.

STOMACH. See *Alimentary Canal*.

STOMOXYS. See *Stable Fly*.

STONE BEE. *Bombus lapidarius*, a large Humble Bee of the family Bombidae: a fat, hairy insect, black with a red-tipped abdomen. It lives in colonies of several hundred individuals and makes its nest in rock crevices, under stones or in mouse holes.

STONEFLIES. See *Plecoptera*.

STRACHIA. Also called *Eurydema*, a common genus of small, oval-shaped plant-bugs of the group Heteroptera. *Strachia ornata* is red with black spots; *Strachia oleracea* is greenish black with yellowish red markings. Both these species are common in hedgerows.

STRANGALIA. A common genus of longhorn beetles of the family Cerambycidae having long legs and an elongated body with tapering elytra. In many species the latter are yellowish brown with black spots, bands or other markings. *Strangalia maculata*, the Spotted Longhorn; *Strangalia quadrifasciata*, the Four-banded Longhorn; *Strangalia melanura*, the Black-tailed Longhorn etc. All these are common in hedgerows where the larvae feed on the dead wood of stumps and broken branches.

STRATAEGUS. *Strataegus antaeus*, the Ox Beetle: a large reddish brown beetle from Central and South America having three large 'horns' on the head of the male and one on the female.

STRATIOMYIDAE. See *Soldier Flies*.

STRAWBERRY LEAF-ROLLER. Any of a number of moths whose larvae feed on strawberry leaves and roll them up to form nests in which they pupate. *Ancylis* is a well known genus.

STRAWBERRY MOTH. See *Strawberry Leaf-roller*.

STRAW UNDERWING MOTH. *Thalpophila matura*, a medium sized noctuid moth having the fore-wings dark brown with two wavy yellowish lines and the hind-wings yellow with a dark border. The smooth, greenish brown caterpillars feed on grasses.

STREAK MOTH. *Chesias spartiata*, a Carpet Moth of the subfamily Larentiinae. The fore-wings are brownish grey with a pale streak running from the base to the tip. The hind-wings are paler grey. The larvae feed on broom.

STREAKED LADYBIRD. *Neomysia oblongoguttata*, a large ladybird beetle having reddish wing-cases with pale streaks instead of the usual spots; found on various fir trees.

STREAMER MOTH. *Anticlea derivata*, a small Carpet Moth of the subfamily Larentiinae, light brown with bands and patches of darker brown on the fore-wings. The larvae feed on wild roses and honeysuckle.

STREBLIDAE. A family of bat flies: blood-sucking Diptera closely related to the Nycteribiidae but, unlike them, nearly always having wings. They live in the fur of bats but are not found in cooler latitudes where the bats hibernate (see *Bat Fly*).

STREPSIPTERA. Minute insects whose larvae mainly parasitize bees and wasps. The females continue as wingless endoparasites throughout life and remain in their original host. The males, however, develop powers of flight with the hind-wings only, the fore-wings being vestigial. They fly to another host for mating but soon die. Insects which are parasitized by Strepsiptera are said to be 'stylopized' (named after one genus of Strepsiptera, *Stylops*); the result is usually a modification or degeneration of the sexual organs of the host.

STRETCH RECEPTORS. Proprioceptors or sensory receptors consisting of strands of connective tissue associated with nerve cells enabling an insect to be conscious of movements of its own body (see also *Chordotonal Receptors*).

STRIATED BORDER. The striated surface of the epithelial cells lining the mid-gut and the Malpighian tubules of insects. These are of two kinds:

(1) The *honeycomb* border made of many little rod-shaped vesicles fused together to form a palisade.

(2) The *brush* type consisting of separate filaments. There has been much controversy as to the function of these structures which change their appearance during secretory activity.

STRIDULATION. A sound emitted by insects and caused by rubbing one hard part of the body against another. In short-horned grasshoppers the sound is made by rubbing the rough inner surface of the hind femur against a projecting vein on the outside of the tegmen. In long-horned grasshoppers and in crickets the two tegmina are rubbed together. Coleoptera and Hemiptera stridulate in a variety of ways by rubbing together two parts of the body (called the 'rasp' and the 'file'). Either component may be on the head, thorax, abdomen, legs or elytra. Temperature has a great influence on the rate of stridulation which becomes accelerated as the temperature rises.

STRIGIL. (1) A comb-like structure on a bee's leg, used for cleaning the antennae.

(2) A similar structure on the fore-tibia of some Lepidoptera.

(3) A process on the dorsal surface of the abdomen in Corixidae, doubtfully associated with sound production.

STRIPED BUG. *Graphosoma italicum*, a pentatomid bug of Southern Europe about 1 cm. long with a large dorsal shield striped in red and black; common on umbelliferous plants.

STRIPED GRAYLING. *Pseudotergumia fidia*, a butterfly of the family Satyridae generally similar to the more common graylings but having the undersides variegated in brown and greyish white with a conspicuous pattern of dark zig-zag lines. It is found in Southern France, Spain and North Africa.

STRIPED HAWK-MOTH. *Celerio lineata*, a large pinkish brown hawk-moth from the Mediterranean area, having a wing-span of about 8 cm. and a wide whitish-grey stripe running from the base to the tip of each fore-wing. The larvae feed on vines and other plants.

STRIPE-WINGED GRASSHOPPER. See *Stenobothrus*.

STRONGYLOGNATHUS. *Strongylognathus testaceus*, a minute yellow ant about 2 mm. long that lives in the nests of the larger brown ant *Tetramorium caespitum*.

STROPHOSOMUS. A genus of weevils about 5 mm. long, black with reddish legs and antennae and with pinkish or silvery grey scales on the sides of the body. *Strophosomus lateralis* feeds on heather; *Strophosomus coryli* on pine, larch, oak, birch etc.

STRUCTURAL COLOURS. Brilliant iridescent colours produced, not by pigments, but by reflection, refraction, diffraction or interference of light of differing wave-lengths. Such colours are found for instance in the wings of some butterflies, the bodies of dragonflies and the elytra of beetles. The optical effect is brought about by the presence of numerous extremely thin, transparent plates either in the cuticle itself or, in the case of butterflies, in the scales that cover the wings.

STRYMON. See *Strymonidia*.

STRYMONIDIA. A genus of Hairstreak Butterflies of the family Lycaenidae including the Blue-spot Hairstreak, the Black Hairstreak and the White-letter Hairstreak. The latter (*Strymonidia W-album*) is a brown and orange butterfly characterized by having a thin white line forming a large letter W on the undersides of the hind-wings. It is found right across Europe and Asia as far as Japan; the larvae feed on lime, elm and other trees.

STYLE. A short antennal appendage of some flies (Diptera). Compare *Arista*.

STYLET. (1) Any sharp, piercing, needle-like organ such as those that form the mouth-parts of mosquitoes, bugs etc. (see *Mouth-parts*, *Jaws* and *Proboscis*).
   (2) Short unjointed abdominal appendages of some insects.

STYLOPS, STYLOPIDAE, STYLOPIZATION. See *Strepsiptera*.

STYLUS. See *Style* and *Stylet*.

SUBCOSTA. The vein of an insect's wing next to and behind the *costa* which forms the anterior edge.

SUBCOXA. A segment preceding the coxa on the legs of certain primitive insects. In the majority of insects, however, this segment has become fused with the body-wall and the second segment, the coxa, forms the functional limb-base.

SUBCUTICLE. See *Endocuticle*.

SUBIMAGO. The stage before the imago in the development of the mayfly (Ephemeroptera). It is winged and closely resembles the adult except that it has a thin dull skin covering the whole of the body and wings. When this is cast off the true brilliantly coloured imago is formed.

SUBMENTUM. The basal segment of the labium of an insect (see also *Mentum* and *Prementum*).

SUBOESOPHAGEAL GANGLION. A ganglion or pair of ganglia situated beneath the oesophagus and connecting the ventral nerve cord with the 'nerve-collar' in insects and other arthropods.

SUCKING INSECTS. Insects that suck blood, nectar, plant sap or other liquid food do this in various ways. The mouth-parts of all insects consist of the *labrum*, *mandibles*, *maxillae*, *labium* and *hypopharynx*. Any of these may be lengthened and placed in juxtaposition or interlocked to form a tube up which liquid food is sucked; others may form a second tube for the downward

307

flow of saliva while others again form piercing stylets. In butterflies and moths the long, coiled proboscis is formed from the *galeae* of the maxillae; in bees the lengthened *glossae* or central lobes of the labium are fused to form a tube ending in a spoon-like lobe or *flabellum*. In plant-lice, plant-bugs and the blood-sucking bedbug the interlocking maxillary stylets form both the food canal and the salivary canal; fleas use the *lacineae* of the maxillae. Female mosquitoes and other blood-sucking flies of the suborders Nematocera and Brachycera use mandibles and maxillae sheathed in the labium. Robber Flies use the hypopharynx and higher Diptera use a stiffened labium for blood-sucking purposes. All Diptera have *labella* or spongy lobes at the tip of the labium, but these are most highly developed with *pseudotracheae* in Cyclor-rhapha. (See also *Mouth-parts* and *Jaws*.)

SUCKING LICE. See *Louse*.

SUGAR BEETLES. See *Passalidae*.

SUGAR CANE BEETLE. *Euetheola rugiceps*, a Scarabaeoid beetle whose larvae attack roots and stems of sugar cane.

SUGAR CANE BORER. *Diatraea saccharalis*, a small silvery-brown moth of the family Crambidae whose larvae bore into the stalks of sugar cane.

SUMAC GALL. *Melaphis rhuis*, an aphid that produces irregular, smooth, fruit-like galls on the sumac tree (*Rhus cotinoides*).

SUMMER CHAFER. See *Rhizotragus*.

SUN-COMPASS REACTION. See *Light-compass Reaction*.

SUNFLY. A name for several different insects:
  e.g. (1) The Hover-fly *Helophilus* (*q.v.*).
  (2) Aphelinidae, a family of minute Hymenoptera that parasitize aphids and coccids.

SUPERDEVELOPMENT. See *Hypermetamorphosis*.

SUPERLINGUAE. Small paired lobes attached to the sides of the hypo-pharynx in certain insects.

SUPERPOSITION IMAGE. A phenomenon of some nocturnal insects in which the pigmented sheaths surrounding the optical units or ommatidia can be retracted so that the points of light which normally form a mosaic image will merge together and overlap giving a less distinct but brighter image (see *Compound Eyes*).

SUPRA-OESOPHAGEAL GANGLIA. Also named the *suprapharyngeal*, *hyperpharyngeal* or *cerebral* ganglia: a pair of nerve-centres situated on the dorsal side of the pharynx or oesophagus in insects and other arthropods and connected to the main ventral nerve cord by a 'collar' formed of two com-missures. Sometimes these ganglia are fused with others such as the optic and antennary and may be sufficiently complex to be regarded as a 'brain'.

SWALLOW PROMINENT MOTH. *Pheosia tremula*, a medium sized moth of the family Notodontidae having the wings streaked with dark and light brown and white and, like all Prominent Moths, having a tuft of scales pro-jecting back from the hind margin of each fore-wing. The larvae, green with yellow lateral stripes, feed on poplar, sallow etc.

SWALLOWTAIL BUTTERFLY. (1) The European and Asiatic Swallowtail *Papilio machaon* and related North American species, yellow and black with conspicuous 'tails' on the hind-wings.

(2) Any 'tailed' member of the family Papilionidae. These include many 'long-tailed' and 'sword-tailed' species from South America, some yellow, some black and white or black with patches of red and green. There are several African species and numerous sword-tailed species in South-east Asia and Australia. These are generally black and green or white but also include a few brilliantly iridescent species. North American swallowtails include the Black Swallowtail (*Papilio asterias*), the Spice-bush Swallowtail (*Papilio troilus*) and the very long tailed *Papilio ajax*.

SWALLOW-TAILED MOTH. See *Ourapteryx*.

SWARMING. The swarming of insects, that is the movement of a large number together, falls into four principal categories, *viz*.

(1) The swarming of a large number of males prior to mating. Midges, gnats and mosquitoes come into this group.

(2) The swarming of bees when the hive becomes overcrowded and the queen flies out followed by several thousand workers.

(3) Migratory swarms in search of new feeding and breeding grounds, as of locusts, marching ants etc.

(4) The settling together of a large number of some species of tiny flies when hibernating.

In some cases, as for instance that of locusts, there is a definite *migratory phase* involving a change in form and colour of the insects prior to swarming.

SWEAT FLY. *Hydrotaea irritans*, a small black fly of the family Muscidae similar in appearance to a house fly; a woodland species that flies in large numbers in hot weather and sips the sweat from humans, horses, cattle or other animals. The larvae live in dung.

SWIFT MOTHS. See *Hepialidae*.

SWIMMING INSECTS. Swimming can be defined as locomotion on or under water. Insects such as pondskaters, which swim on the surface, accomplish this by reason of the fact that their light weight is insufficient to penetrate the surface tension film of the water. They are also helped by their waxy cuticle and the coating of *hydrofuge* hairs which are unwetted. The 'swimming' of these insects is in fact walking on the water.

True swimming by submerged insects such as water beetles and water boatmen is accomplished by a rowing movement of the hind-legs, and in some cases by the middle pair also. These legs, used as oars, are flattened and fringed with hairs. Water Boatmen of the family Notonectidae swim on their backs; Corixid Bugs and water beetles in general swim the right way up. All these submerged insects must either take down a bubble of air or must come to the surface to breathe.

A third category of swimming insects comprises the legless larvae and pupae of gnats and mosquitoes. These swim with a rapid and jerky movement by flexing and straightening the abdomen. They have to come up to breathe through specially adapted 'siphons'.

SWORD-GRASS MOTH. *Xylena exsoleta* and related species: medium sized European noctuid moths coloured light and dark brown or reddish. The larvae are large and green with interrupted longitudinal lines of red and brown. They feed on a variety of plants.

SWORD-TAIL BUTTERFLIES. Tropical papilionid butterflies of the genus *Graphium*, usually blue-green or black and white with sharply pointed 'tails' on the hind-wings; they are found chiefly in South-east Asia and Australia (see *Swallowtail Butterfly*).

309

SYCAMORE MOTH. *Apatele aceris*, a stoutly-built noctuid moth of a mottled grey and brownish colour, common in British and European woodlands. The larvae, which feed on sycamore leaves, are hairy and brightly coloured with red spots on grey along the sides and yellow along the back.

SYMPETRUM. A genus of small or medium sized dragonflies of the group Anisoptera having narrow bodies sometimes widening towards the hind-end. They are of various colours with red and black predominating. Some species have orange or red patches at the bases of the wings. They often migrate in large swarms for long distances over land and sea.

SYMPHYPLEONA. A suborder of Collembola or springtails having a shortened body with the thoracic and some of the abdominal segments not clearly demarcated (*cf. Arthropleona*).

SYMPHYTA. Sawflies, woodwasps etc. A suborder of Hymenoptera having no narrow constriction between the thorax and the abdomen and having a large ovipositor which acts as a saw or drill for piercing plant tissues. Their larvae resemble the caterpillars of butterflies and moths but differ from them in having up to seven pairs of abdominal prolegs. (Compare *Apocrita* and *Petiolata*.)

SYNANTHEDON. *Synanthedon tipuliformis* or *Aegeria tipuliformis*, the Currant Borer or Currant Clearwing: a small moth of the family Sesiidae with transparent wings and a narrow dark brown body resembling that of a cranefly. The larvae are pests of gooseberries and currants where they live in central tunnels which they bore in the twigs. The species has spread from Europe to North America and other countries.

SYNCHRONOUS FLASHING. A phenomenon observed occasionally in the tropics, *e.g.* in Thailand, when large numbers of fireflies or other luminescent insects flash rhythmically in unison. This usually takes place at dusk (see *Light-producing Organs*).

SYNTOMIDAE. A family of small tropical moths, sometimes called Amatidae, resembling Burnet Moths with a long body and with the fore-wings much longer than the hind-wings. They are day-flying and brightly coloured, usually green, black, white and yellow. Most species live in South America but a few extend their range northwards into the United States.

SYRITTA. A genus of small hover-flies of the family Syrphidae whose 'short-tailed' larvae live in rotting vegetation and dung.

SYROMASTUS. A genus of squashbugs of the family Coreidae having a flattened body and a wide abdomen projecting beyond the elytra on either side and giving the insect roughly a rhomboid shape. *Syromastus rhombeus*, greenish grey, lives in sandy grassland; *Syromastus marginalis*, dull brown with a red abdomen, lives among brambles and shrubs.

SYRPHIDAE. See *Hover-flies* and *Drone-flies*.

T

TABANIDAE. Horse flies, gadflies and clegs: a family of fast-flying, two-winged insects, the females of most species of which suck blood by means of mouth-parts combining the piercing method of the mosquito with the filter-feeding method of the blowfly. The group includes a number of greyish brown species of the genus *Haematopota*, about 12 mm. long with speckled wings, and *Chrysops* which is about the same size and is characterized by its bright golden-green eyes and banded wings. The largest European species is *Tabanus sudeticus*, a black and brown insect with a fat body, a large head and a wing span of about 4 cm. It is a vicious pest of horses, cattle and other animals causing open sores by returning over and over again to suck blood from the same part. The larvae are predatory soil-dwellers.

TABBY MOTH. *Aglossa pinguinalis* and related species: relatively large members of the family Pyralidae having a mottled pattern of light and dark brown. They live in stables, barns etc. and when disturbed they often run rather than fly. The larvae live in silken tubes among the hay.

TABLE MOUNTAIN BEAUTY. *Aeropetes tulbaghia*, a butterfly of the family Satyridae occurring all over the mountainous parts of South Africa; coppery brown with golden-yellow patches and bands on both wings and with four bluish grey eye-spots ringed with black on each hind-wing.

TACHARDIA. See *Lac Insect*.

TACHINIDAE. A family of two-winged insects which all have parasitic larvae. The adult flies are stout bristly insects usually with grey or striped bodies. Their larvae are maggots, parasitic in other insects, spiders, woodlice or centipedes, and are important in the biological control of forest pests.

TACHYGENESIS. A shortened development involving the omission of several larval instars.

TACTILE RECEPTORS. In their simplest form an insect's organs of touch consist of simple hairs, bristles or spines with sensory cells and nerve endings at their bases. They are extremely sensitive to impulses set up by the slightest bending or movement of the base in its socket. Receptors of this sort are situated all over the body but are most numerous on the antennae and sometimes on the cerci. They may also be sensitive to low-pitched sounds which cause them to vibrate.

TACTILE SPINES. See *Tactile Receptors*.

TAENARIS. A genus of large butterflies of the family Amathusiidae from South-east Asia and Australia. They live near the edges of forests and fly clumsily at dusk. They are generally coloured with varying shades of yellowish grey and light brown with two very large, ringed eye-spots on each hind-wing.

TAENIDIUM. The spiral thickening of chitin strengthening the walls of an insect's tracheae.

TAENIOPTERYX. The Salmon Fly, a genus of Plecoptera or Stoneflies common in the western states of North America. The adults feed on foliage; the larvae are aquatic and abundant in streams and rivers. There is one British species, *Taeniopteryx nebulosa*.

TAENIORHYNCHUS. A genus of culicine mosquitoes whose larvae are characterized by having a sharp-toothed respiratory siphon able to pierce the tissues of submerged water plants or the stems of rushes etc. In this way the larvae can attach themselves below the surface and obtain air from the cavities of the plants.

TAENIOTHRIPS. A genus of thrips (Thysanoptera). *Taeniothrips inconsequens* (= *pyri*) is a common pest of pears.

TAGMA (Plural TAGMATA). A group of segments forming a unit in the body of an arthropod. In insects there are three tagmata, *viz.* the head, thorax and abdomen; in spiders there are only two.

TAGUA BORER. *Dryocoetes dactyloperda*, a weevil whose larvae bore into the nuts of the Vegetable Ivory plant (*Tagua*).

TAILED SKIPPER. *Eudamus proteus*, the Long-tailed Skipper, a butterfly of the family Hesperiidae from South and Central America and parts of North America; brownish pink with a pattern of white squares on the fore-wings and with long brownish-black 'tails' on the hind-wings.

TAMARISK MANNA SCALE. *Trabutina mannipara* or *Coccus manniparus* (see *Manna Scale Insect*).

TANNER BEETLE (TANNER LONGHORN). *Prionus corarius*, a dark brown longhorn beetle of the family Cerambycidae having saw-toothed antennae and three short spines on each side of the thorax. It is the largest British longhorn, the female being over 4 cm. long and the male slightly smaller. The larvae feed on the rotting wood of old tree stumps.

TANYPTERA. A genus of Crested Crane-flies of the subfamily Flabelliferinae in which the males have large, comb-like antennae and the females often have brightly coloured abdomens banded with red or orange. The legless larvae bore into dead wood.

TANYSPHYRUS. *Tanysphyrus lemnae*, a small weevil that lives in ponds and feeds on duckweed (*Lemna*).

TANYTARSUS. A genus of tiny, non-biting, mosquito-like insects of the family Chironomidae whose larvae live in fast running streams.

TAPESTRY MOTH. *Trichophaga tapetzella*, also called the White-tipped Clothes Moth: a member of the family Tineidae about 20 mm. across, greyish brown with broad white tips on the fore-wings and with deeply fringed hind-wings. The larvae feed on coarse cloth and make cases or tubular galleries of cloth particles woven together with silk threads.

TAPETUM. A mirror-like layer formed from numerous tracheae surrounding the retinal rods in the eyes of nocturnal moths. These reflect the light back into the retinal cells so that each receives a double stimulus and the general effect is a greater sensitivity in dim light.

TAPHROCERUS. A beetle of the family Buprestidae whose larvae are leaf-miners in sedges.

TARANTULA HAWK. *Pepsis*, a genus of very large tropical wasps of the family Pompilidae: *Pepsis femoratus* hunts tarantulas and other large spiders.

TARSAL TASTE ORGANS. Chemosensory organs on the legs of some butterflies and possibly other insects; on the Painted Lady, for instance, these tarsal organs are estimated to be about 200 times as sensitive to sugar as the human tongue.

TARSOMERES. Segments of the tarsus of an insect, usually numbering from two to five.

TARSUS. The part of an insect's leg immediately distal to the tibia, usually divided into a number of segments or tarsomeres, and bearing apical structures such as claws, pulvilli, arolium or empodium.

TASTE ORGANS. It is difficult to distinguish between the senses of taste and smell in insects as there are numerous chemosensitive receptors on many parts of the body. By analogy with humans the word 'taste' can be used for a stimulus caused by *contact* with a soluble substance which can presumably diffuse through the thin cuticle and come into contact with the nerve endings beneath the surface. Smell, in contrast, is the chemical perception of air-borne substances. Taste receptors may be of various shapes and degrees of complexity ranging from simple hairs to placoid and basiconic types. They are situated on the antennae, the palps and other mouth-parts and frequently on the feet.

TAWNY BURROWING BEE. *Andrena fulva*, a mining bee about 12 mm. long, generally black but having the thorax covered with reddish hair and the abdomen with yellow hair except at the tip; a common garden species nesting in underground burrows.

TAWNY EARWIG. See *Labidura*.

TAXIS. A movement having a definite direction in relation to a particular stimulus, *e.g.* *phototaxis* (light), *chemotaxis* (chemicals), *thigmotaxis* (touch) etc. The reaction may be positive (towards the stimulus) or negative (away from it).

TEGETICULA. An alternative name for *Pronuba*, the Yucca Moth, a highly specialized insect on which the Yucca plant depends for its pollination (see *Pronuba*).

TEGMEN. The leathery fore-wing of an insect such as the cockroach or grass-hopper.

TEGULA. A small scale-like sclerite overlapping the bases of the wings in certain insects such as Lepidoptera and Hymenoptera.

TEGUMEN. A dorsal hood-like structure covering the male genitalia of some insects: an enlargement of the ninth abdominal segment.

TEINOPALPUS. *Teinopalpus imperialis*, a large Swallowtail Butterfly from the mountains of South-east China having a wing-span of about 8 cm. and coloured dark green, violet and yellow.

TELEA. See *Polyphemus Moth*.

TELENOMUS. A genus of minute parasitic wasps that lay their eggs in the bodies of harmful plant-bugs and are sometimes used to control them.

TELOTAXIS. (1) A reaction in which an insect or other organism orientates itself and moves in a definite direction towards a source of stimulus at a distance, *e.g.* a point of light.
(2) Orientation which gives the impression of a purpose.

TELPHUSA. A genus of moths of the family Tortricidae whose larvae are leaf-rollers when young but as they become older they form larger nests by tying small leaves together. *Telphusa querciella* rolls oak leaves; *Telphusa betulella* rolls birch and *Telphusa belangerella* alder.

TELSON. A twelfth abdominal segment present in the embryos of some

313

insects and in the adults of the primitive order Protura. No other insects have more than eleven and the last two or three are usually modified, fused together or reduced so that there are usually only nine or ten visible.

TEMPERATURE RESISTANCE. Insects depend for their activity on the temperature of their surroundings. If too cold they go into a state of dormancy as the rate of metabolism slows down. Warmer conditions bring about a more rapid rate of metabolism accompanied by much activity and the necessity of more feeding. Extremes of hot or cold eventually cause death. Some insects, however, have become acclimatized to severe conditions. Aquatic larvae of gnats and other insects can live in hot springs at temperatures up to about 50°C. At the other extreme some caterpillars hibernate for several weeks at temperatures below —15°C. In conditions of drought some insects become completely desiccated and can withstand even greater extremes than these. An insect that is dried up in this way can be immersed for a short time in liquid air or boiling water and will recover when conditions return to normal.

TEMPERATURE SENSE. All insects are sensitive to changes of temperature and in general a rise of temperature causes an increased activity and a fall brings about inactivity, hibernation or diapause. The whole body is sensitive and in most insects there are no definite heat receptors. An exception to this generality is the case of blood-sucking insects. In many of these the fine hairs on the antennae are extremely sensitive to temperature changes and are used to help the insect to locate a warm-blooded animal and perhaps to locate the warmest part of its body where the skin is thin and the blood flows near the surface.

TENDIPEDIDAE. An alternative name for *Chironomidae*, and now disused.

TENEBRIONIDAE. Mealworm Beetles or False Ground Beetles: a family of dark brown, elongated, nocturnal beetles which are usually unable to fly owing to the fact that the wings are vestigial or absent and the wing-cases firmly fused together. Their larvae, like large yellow maggots, include the mealworms of bakeries and flour mills (see *Mealworm* and *Meal Beetle*).

TENEBROIDES. *Tenebroides mauritanicus*: the Cadelle, a small beetle of the family Trogositidae having a wide body and elongated elytra; a pest of flour and cereals which has spread from North Africa to many other places.

TENENT HAIRS. Clusters of minute tubular hairs that secrete an adhesive substance; present on the *pulvilli* or pads of the feet of some insects. They apparently help the insect to walk on a smooth surface.

TENERAL. Incompletely hardened; used especially of adult insects immediately after emergence from the pupa or nymph.

TENSION RECEPTORS. Sensory structures which respond to stretching or pulling of the cuticle, as for instance at the joints of insects (see also *Chordotonal Receptors*).

TEN-SPOT LADYBIRD. *Adalia decempunctata*, a small ladybird beetle of the family Coccinellidae having five spots on each elytron. The colour is very variable, the commonest being orange-yellow with black spots. There is, however, a form in which this is reversed, the spots being yellow on a black background. Another is completely black without spots. A feature common to them all is the brown underside with pale legs.

TENT CATERPILLAR. See *Malacosoma*.

TENTHREDINIDAE. A family of sawflies: small symphytous Hymenoptera

314

whose ovipositor resembles a tiny saw enabling the female to cut slits or pockets in plants where she lays her eggs. The larvae, which do considerable damage to the leaves of trees, resemble caterpillars but have more abdominal prolegs (see *Sawflies* and *Symphyta*).

TEREBRANT, TEREBRATE. Adapted for boring; having a boring organ which may be either a modified ovipositor or more rarely a modified proboscis.

TEREBRANTES. A suborder of Hymenoptera including parasitic wasps and gall-wasps having a long, sharp ovipositor. (Compare *Aculeata*.)

TEREBRANTIA. A suborder of Thysanoptera (thrips) having a sharp ovipositor with which they pierce plant tissues.

TERGITE. A constituent sclerite of a tergum (*q.v.*).

TERGUM. A dorsal cuticular plate covering each body-segment of an insect.

TERMES. A typical genus of termites; *Termes bellicosus* is one of the best known species of tropical Africa. They build erect pyramidal nests in sandy places. These may be up to 4 metres high and are elaborately constructed with numerous chambers and corridors. They may contain several million insects and the queen may grow to a length of 6 cm.

TERMITARIUM. The large elaborately built nest of a colony of termites.

TERMITE. See *Isoptera* and *Termes*.

TERMITIDAE. One of the principal families of termites including, among others, the genera *Termes* and *Nasutitermes* (see *Isoptera, Nasutes, Nasutitermes* and *Termes*).

TERMITOMIMUS. A genus of Rove Beetles (Staphylinidae), scavengers in the nests of termites.

TERMITONICUS. A genus of tiny beetles that live on the heads of termites and share their food.

TERMITOPHILES. A general name for many insects that live as inquilines in the nests of termites, scavenging or sharing the food of their hosts (see *Inquiline*).

TERMITOXENIA. A genus of two-winged flies that live in the nests of termites. They lay large eggs from which the larvae hatch and pupate almost as soon as they are laid. They are placed either in the family Phoridae or the adjacent family Termitoxeniidae.

TERRAPIN SCALE. *Eulecanium nigrofasciatum*, a scale-insect of the family Coccidae: a pest of peach and other fruit trees particularly in California (see *Coccidae*).

TESSELATED EMPIS. *Empis tesselata*, a small, day-flying, predatory fly of the family Empididae having a proboscis adapted for piercing and sucking; common on hawthorn and other plants of hedgerows (see *Empididae*).

TESSELATED SKIPPER. *Muschampia tesselium*, a small butterfly of the family Hesperiidae, dark smoky grey with a pattern of white patches and squares; the underside is a light greenish brown also with white squares. It is found in South-east Europe and Western Asia.

TESTIS. See *Genitalia*.

TETANOCERIDAE. See *Marsh Fly*.

TETHYMYIA. A genus of non-biting midges of the family Chironomidae having vestigial wings and aquatic larvae.

TETRACHA. A genus of bright green, iridescent beetles of the family Cicindelidae (Tiger Beetles); nocturnal, burrowing insects, predatory in both adult and larval stages. *Tetracha carolina* and *Tetracha virginica* are common North American species.

TETRALOBUS. *Tetralobus flabellicornis*, one of the largest of the Click Beetles (Elateridae) from South and West Africa, black with a coat of fine hairs. The females are up to 8 cm. long; the males slightly smaller. The antennae are broad and comb-like.

TETRAMORIUM. A genus of small black ants living in the ground or under stones and usually sharing their nest with several other species.

TETRAOPES. *Tetraopes tetraophthalmus*, the Milkweed Beetle: a longhorn beetle of the family Cerambycidae about 12 mm. long, bright red with three black spots on each elytron. It feeds on the North American Milkweed *Asclepias curassavica*. When disturbed it draws its legs in and feigns death.

TETRAPTEROUS. Having four wings.

TETRASTICHOUS. A world-wide genus of minute parasitic Hymenoptera that lay their eggs in those of moths, beetles or other insects. Some species are hyperparasites, the larvae being parasitic in the larvae of other parasitic insects.

TETRIGIDAE. Pygmy Locusts or Grouse-locusts, sometimes called Groundhoppers: a family of Orthoptera having an angular body sometimes bearing spines. The back legs are powerful and the front parts of the body are sometimes flattened and leaf-like. They cannot fly but can jump and swim quite well. Most of the members of this family inhabit tropical countries but there are a few European species, *viz. Tetrix bipunctata*, the Two-pointed Grouse-locust; *Tetrix undulata*, the Common Groundhopper and *Tetrix subulata*, the Slender Groundhopper.

TETRODONTOPHORA. A genus of Collembola differing from others of the order in not possessing the *furcula* or jumping organ which gives them the name of Springtails. *Tetrodontophora bielanensis* is a blue-grey insect about 1 cm. long from marshy parts of Central Europe.

TETROPIUM. *Tetropium gabrieli*, the Larch Longhorn: a small black or dark brown beetle of the family Cerambycidae, one of the commonest pests of larch trees. The adults are about 12–15 mm. long with straight, narrow, dull brown elytra having yellowish silky hairs at their bases. The antennae are shorter than those of most longhorn beetles. The larvae make branching tunnels between the bark and the wood.

TETTIGONIIDAE. Long-horned grasshoppers or Bush Crickets: long-legged jumping insects of the order Orthoptera, differing from other grasshoppers and locusts (Acridiidae) by their very long antennae and by their predatory habits. The chief British representative is the Great Green Grasshopper *Tettigonia viridissima*. The larger American species are sometimes called katydids (see *Grasshopper*).

THALASSOMYIA. A genus of semi-aquatic two-winged flies commonly found along the sea coasts of North America.

THALESSA. Also called *Megarhyssa*, a genus of giant ichneumon flies with an ovipositor up to 15 cm. long. This is used for boring through wood and laying eggs in the body of the woodwasp larva *Tremex*.

THALPOPHILA. See *Straw Underwing Moth*.

THANASIMUS. A genus of predatory beetles; small elongated insects of the family Cleridae that prey on the eggs, larvae and adults of bark beetles. *Thanasimus formicarius* is a common European species; *Thanasimus dubius* is North American.

THANATOPHILUS. A genus of carrion beetles of the family Silphidae: dark brown, oval beetles about 8 mm. long, that feed chiefly on carrion but also occasionally on putrid fungi. *Thanatophilus rugosus* and *Thanatophilus sinuatus* are two common European species.

THANATOSIS. Feigning death: going into a rigid, motionless position when disturbed. This is particularly common among beetles but also occurs in earwigs, water-bugs, water scorpions, sawfly larvae and a number of other insects.

THAUMANTIS. A genus of large, brightly coloured, iridescent butterflies of the family Amathusiidae from South-east Asia and Australasia. *Thaumantis diores* of North-east India is brown, violet and white. It flies in the evening and feeds on rotting fruit.

THAUMATOMYIA. *Thaumatomyia notata*, a well known species of cluster flies (see *Chloropisca*).

THAUMETOPOEIDAE. See *Processionary Moth*.

THEA (= PSYLLOBORA). *Thea 22-punctata*, the Twenty-two Spot Ladybird: a small beetle 3–4 mm. long of the family Coccinellidae, lemon yellow with black spots. It is to be found chiefly among nettles and grass.

THECA. Any protective covering or case, *e.g.* the chitinous covering of a pupa, the strengthening plate of a fly's proboscis etc.

THECLA. A genus of Hairstreak Butterflies of the family Lycaenidae. *Thecla betulae*, the Brown Hairstreak and *Thecla quercus*, the Purple Hairstreak are common European species. *Thecla crysalus*, the Colorado Hairstreak is a small North American species, mauve and brown with red spots on the margins of the wings. *Thecla coronata* from tropical South America is brilliant, iridescent blue on the upper side and bright green, maroon, black and white below (see *Hairstreaks*).

THECODIPLOSIS (= SITODIPLOSIS). A genus of gall-midges of the family Cecidomyidae including the Tulip Spot Gall-midge whose larvae cause minute blisters on the leaves.

THELIA. *Thelia bimaculata*, the Locust Tree-hopper: a small jumping insect of the family Membracidae. The male is dark brown with a broad yellow line on each side; the female is brown all over.

THELYTOKY. The reproduction of parthenogenetic females (see *Aphis* and *Parthenogenesis*).

THEOBALDIA. A widely distributed genus of Culicine mosquitoes chiefly of temperate climates. *Theobaldia annulata* is one of the largest European species; it has spotted wings and white-ringed legs and body. Although it commonly attacks humans it is not known to spread any disease.

THEOPHILA. *Theophila mandarina*, an Asiatic silkworm moth, grey in colour but otherwise very similar to the cultivated species which is white.

THERA. *Thera obeliscata*, the Grey Pine Carpet Moth: a small species of the subfamily Larentiinae, usually greyish brown with a broad band of darker brown or red on each fore-wing. There is also a melanic variety. The larvae feed on Scots Pine and pupate in silken cocoons.

THEREVIDAE. See *Stiletto Flies*.

THERIA. *Theria rupicapraria*, the Early Moth: a small, brown, European geometrid moth to be found in winter or early spring on hawthorn and other hedgerow plants. The females are almost wingless.

THERIOAPHIS. *Therioaphis maculata*, an aphis that attacks leguminous plants in the warmer parts of the United States, the Middle East and India: a serious agricultural pest.

THERMOBIA. See *Firebrat*.

THICK-HEADED FLIES. Conopidae, a family of Diptera resembling small bees or wasps in shape and colour and in having a narrow waist and a wide abdomen. The adults feed on plants but the larvae are parasitic in bumble bees, wasps and grasshoppers.

THICK-MOUTHED WEEVIL. See *Otiorrhynchus*.

THIGMOTAXIS. A locomotory response, sometimes an inhibition of movement, caused by the stimulus of touch. This causes many insects and other small organisms to cling to surfaces or in crevices with which they come into contact. (See also *Stereokinesis*.)

THISTLE ERMINE MOTH. *Coscinia cribraria*, a moth of the family Arctiidae having white fore-wings dotted with black and light greyish hind-wings. The larvae are usually found in the stems of thistles.

THOLERA. See *Feathered Gothic Moth*.

THORACIC GLANDS. Glands in the thorax of an insect which, when stimulated by other hormones from the brain, secrete the moulting hormone (see *Ecdysis*).

THORAX. The middle part or tagma of an insect's body, between the head and the abdomen. It consists of three segments known respectively as the *prothorax* (in front), *mesothorax* (middle) and *metathorax* (hindmost). The dorsal cuticular plates covering these are likewise known as the *pronotum*, *mesonotum* and *metanotum*.

Each thoracic segment bears a pair of legs, so that all insects have six legs. Wings are normally borne on the mesothorax and the metathorax but in the Diptera the hind pair are reduced to a pair of balancers or *halteres*, and in Orthoptera and Coleoptera the fore pair function as wing-cases.

THORN INSECT. *Centrotus cornutus*, also called the Horned Tree-hopper: a plant-bug of the family Membracidae, small and brown with a thorn-like projection on the thorax. Living on thorn bushes the shape and colour of these insects gives them a certain degree of protective resemblance.

THORN MOTHS. Selidosemidae, a family of geometrid moths having yellowish or light brown wings with thin transverse lines of darker brown and with irregularly serrated edges. The brown stick-like caterpillars feed on various trees and shrubs and pupate in silken cocoons.

THOR'S FRITILLARY. *Clossiana thore*, a nymphalid butterfly having the typical chequerboard type of pattern usual in the fritillaries, but in this case the basic colour is pale yellow. It is found in mountainous regions across Northern Europe and Asia as far as Japan. A partly melanic variety in which the pattern is largely obscured by black markings is found in some parts of the Alps and Dolomites.

THREAD LACEWING FLIES. See *Nemopteridae*.

THREAD-LEGGED BUGS. A subfamily (Emesinae) of Assassin Bugs

318

(Reduviidae) having very thin bodies and long legs giving them a mosquito-like appearance (see *Empicoris*).

THREE-HORNED DOR BEETLE. *Geotrupes typhaeus*, a black, shiny, dung beetle of the family Scarabaeidae about 18 mm. long, the male having three forward-directed 'horns' or protuberances on the front of the thorax. The female only has two such horns and they are shorter.

THREE-PRONGED BRISTLE-TAILS. Thysanura, an order of wingless insects with a scaly skin, long antennae and three very long tail-filaments. The best known are the Silverfish *Lepisma* and the Firebrat *Thermobia* (see *Lepismidae*).

THREE-SPOTTED PHYTOCORIS. *Phytocoris tripustulatus*, a small plant-bug of the family Miridae about 6 mm. long, having a yellow and black body, an orange dorsal shield and black elytra with three yellow dots on each. It is common on nettles.

THREE-STRIPED SHIELDBUG. *Cyphostethus tristriatus*, a small, bright green pentatomid bug with a tapering body, commonly found on juniper bushes.

THRIPS. A general term for any member of the order Thysanoptera, as well as being the name of the principal genus in that order. Minute insects with short antennae and four narrow wings fringed with hairs; some species, however, are wingless. Many of these insects are major pests of cereals and fruit trees which they pierce in order to suck the sap. Well known examples include the Onion Thrips (*Thrips tabaci*), the Grain Thrips (*Limothrips cerealium*), the Pea Thrips (*Kakothrips robustus*) the Plague Thrips (*Thrips imaginis*) which attacks flowers of deciduous fruit trees, and the Greenhouse Thrips (*Heliothrips haemorrhoidalis*). (See also *Thysanoptera*.)

THUNDER FLY. A common colloquial name for insects of the Thrips family (see *Thrips* and *Thysanoptera*); sometimes also applied locally to other flies, *e.g.* the Deer Fly *Chrysops* (Tabanidae).

THYATIRA. See *Peach Blossom Moth*.

THYMELICUS. A genus of Skippers, small brown butterflies of the family Hesperiidae that fly with a rapid darting movement. British species include *Thymelicus sylvestris* the Small Skipper, *Thymelicus acteon* the Lulworth Skipper and *Thymelicus lineola* the Essex Skipper (see *Hesperiidae*).

THYREOCORIDAE. Negro Bugs: a family of small black plant-bugs that gather in large numbers on spring flowers in North America; sometimes included in the family Cydnidae.

THYRIDIA. A genus of butterflies of the family Ithomiidae from tropical parts of America. They have long, narrow, almost transparent yellowish wings with wide black or dark brown borders and heavy veins. The body is long and thin like that of a dragonfly.

THYRIDOPTERYX. *Thyridopteryx ephemeraeformis*, the common North American Bagworm, a moth of the family Psychidae whose larvae weave bags of silk and pieces of vegetation. These bags hang from twigs and the developing larvae and wingless females spend all their lives in them. The male has smoky black wings, a tapering body and feathery antennae (see *Bagworms*).

THYSANIA. *Thysania agrippina*, the Brazilian Owlet Moth: probably the world's largest moth, a member of the family Noctuidae with mottled greyish brown wings having a span of about 30 cm.

THYSANOPTERA. Thrips: minute insects with short antennae and narrow fringed wings. They are classed among the Hemimetabola since they do not undergo a complete metamorphosis but there is a resting stage which may be regarded as a kind of primitive pupation. They are a major pest of cereals and fruit trees which they pierce in order to suck the sap (see also *Thrips*).

THYSANOTIS. *Thysanotis danis,* a small but beautifully coloured lycaenid butterfly from New Guinea and the tropical parts of Australia. The wings have a broad white patch in the centre, surrounded by metallic blue with a broad black border.

THYSANURA. Bristle-tails: primitive wingless insects with long antennae, long cerci and a median tail-filament. The mouth-parts are of the biting type and resemble those of the cockroach. Their usual habitat is among stones and dead leaves but the order also includes some household insects, *e.g.* *Lepisma* (the Silverfish) and *Thermobia* (the Firebrat).

THYSANURIFORM. A name sometimes used to describe *campodeiform* or *oligopod* larvae on account of their resemblance to the Bristle-tails or Thysanura. Such larvae are common among beetles, mayflies, dragonflies etc. (see *Campodeiform Larvae*).

TIBIA. The segment of an insect's leg between the femur and the tarsus; usually long and thin, straight or gently curved; often equipped with strong spines.

TIBICINA. *Tibicina haematodes,* the Lurker: a large cicada of Southern Europe having a wing-span of about 7 cm. The body is black and the wings have brilliant red veins. The larva lives underground and takes four years to develop.

TIGER BEETLES. Cicindelidae, a world-wide family of active, brightly coloured, predatory beetles having large jaws with which they hunt their prey at great speed in sandy places. The larvae also are predators usually living in vertical burrows with the head out ready to seize any passing insect.

TIGER MOTH. See *Arctiidae.*

TIGER SWALLOWTAIL. *Papilio turnus,* a large swallowtail butterfly from the southern United States. The wing-span is about 10 cm. and the hind-wings have short 'tails'. The colour is bright yellow with a pattern of chocolate brown. Melanic forms also exist.

TIMARCHA. See *Bloody-nosed Beetle.*

TIMBERMAN BEETLES. A name given to several wood-boring beetles but particularly to *Acanthocinus aedilis,* a longhorn of the family Cerambycidae. The body is light brownish grey, about 15 mm. long with the elytra tapering towards the hind-end. The antennae of the male are about four times as long as the body; those of the female twice as long. The flattened legless larvae bore tunnels under the bark of pine trees.

TIME SENSE. Insects, like most animals and plants, appear to have some sort of 'internal clock' which regulates their daily and seasonal activity. The rhythm of activity, although influenced by light, temperature etc. is not dependent on these factors alone. A nocturnal insect such as a cockroach may be kept in the dark at a uniform temperature but it will still become active between six and seven o'clock each evening. The rhythm appears to be controlled by the build up of particular hormones and in the case of the cockroach it has been suggested that these come from secretory cells in the *suboesophageal ganglia,* but other indications point to the *brain* and the *corpora allata.*

TINEA. *Tinea pellionella*, the Case-making Clothes Moth whose larvae live in portable cases of silk, from which they feed on wool, fur etc. (see *Tineidae*).

TINEIDAE. Clothes Moths and related species of Microlepidoptera: small, brownish grey moths with narrow, fringed wings, long antennae and long palps. The larvae feed on wool, fur etc. and pupate in silken cocoons. *Tinea* and *Tineola* are the common genera. There are also some members of the family to be found in gardens and woodlands; the larvae of many of these are shoot-borers and leaf-miners.

TINEOLA. *Tineola biselliella*, the Common Clothes Moth (see *Tineidae*).

TINGIDAE. See *Lacebugs*.

TINODES. *Tinodes waeneri*, a small, light brown caddis fly about 8 mm. long whose larvae do not make cases but live gregariously in mud tunnels near the edges of streams and ponds.

TIPHIIDAE. A family of small, hairy wasps whose larvae are ectoparasites on the larvae of beetles. The wasp first paralyses its victim by stinging it and then lays its eggs on the surface of the body. *Tiphia popillivora* has been used to control the Japanese Beetle *Popillia japonica*, a pest of cereals, and *Tiphia parallela* to attack Dynastid beetles injuring sugar cane in Guyana.

TIPPLING TOMMY. A colloquial name for the tropical beetle *Xyloborus perforans* on account of its habit of boring into casks of wines and spirits.

TIPULIDAE. Crane-flies or 'Daddy-long-legs': slender insects with long fragile legs, a tapering abdomen and two long wings. In the subfamily Tipulinae, most of the larvae are soil-dwellers and do considerable damage to the roots of grass and young plants in general. These larvae are of a dirty brown colour and have a tough skin which gives them the name of *leatherjacket*.

TISCHERIIDAE. A family of small fringe-winged moths whose larvae are leaf-miners. *Tischeria ekebladella* makes cross-shaped mines in the leaves of oak and sweet chestnut; *Tischeria malifoliella* makes trumpet-shaped mines in the leaves of apple trees.

TITANOPHASMA. A fossil phasmid or stick-insect from the Carboniferous Period, about 25 cm. long; one of the largest insects ever known.

TITANUS. *Titanus giganteus*, the largest known longhorn beetle of the family Cerambycidae: a reddish brown insect about 15 cm. long excluding the antennae. It is to be found in the forests of Brazil and Guyana but is becoming increasingly rare owing to the fact that the long, fat larvae are eaten and considered a great delicacy by the natives.

TOBACCO BUDWORM MOTH. *Heliothis virescens*, a noctuid moth whose larvae bore into the buds of the tobacco plant.

TOBACCO (CACAO) MOTH. *Ephestia elutella*, a small moth of the family Pyralidae, one of the Microlepidoptera having narrow front wings patterned with light and dark brown, and cream-coloured hind-wings. The larvae, which are whitish maggots with a brown head, are pests of tobacco, cocoa and stored food products in general.

TOBACCO WORM MOTH. See *Protoparce*.

TOE-BITER BUGS. A colloquial name for several of the giant water bugs of North America. Some of these are up to 10 or 12 cm. long and include the genera *Lethocerus*, *Benacus* and *Belostoma* (see *Belostomatidae*).

TOMATO HORN-WORM. The larva of the North American Hawk-moth

Protoparce quinquemaculata which feeds on leaves of tomato, potato etc. (see *Protoparce*).

TOMATO MOTH. See *Bright Line Moth.*

TOMATO WORM MOTH. See *Protoparce.*

TOMOCERUS. *Tomocerus longicornis*, a small, whitish, bristly Springtail: a wingless insect of the order Collembola, 2–3 mm. long with antennae considerably longer than the body. It is common among dead leaves and wood.

TONGUE. The word 'tongue' is often used loosely to refer to the whole proboscis of an insect, particularly when it is lengthened for sucking nectar or blood. More correctly it should refer only to the *glossae* and *paraglossae*, the two pairs of sensitive lobes on the labium (see *Mouth-parts*, *Labium* and *Ligula*).

TONOFIBRILLAE. Non-contractile tension fibrils such as those running vertically through the epidermal cells of insects and connecting the cuticle with the underlying muscles.

TONUS. The condition of a muscle which remains in a continuous state of partial contraction enabling an animal to maintain its posture; a phenomenon most noticeable when insects remain for hours or even days without moving.

TOPOCHEMICAL SENSE. The perception of scents along a path or on either side of it, enabling ants or other insects to follow a track previously used by themselves or by other insects and to return to it.

TOPOTAXIS. Any reaction by which an insect or other animal orientates itself and moves in a definite direction in relation to a stimulus.

TORMOGEN. A cell which secretes the socket of a seta or bristle on the body of an insect (see also *Macrotrichia*).

TORNUS. The anal angle of an insect's wing, a distinct notch on the hind margin, dividing it into two sections.

TORTOISE BEETLES. Cassidinae, a subfamily of leaf-beetles (Chrysomelidae) having the thorax and wing-cases flattened and widened to cover the head and the greater part of the legs like the carapace of a tortoise. European species of the genus *Cassida* are usually small and bright green. There are larger species of many colours in Brazil and South-east Asia.

TORTOISESHELL BUTTERFLY. A name for several Nymphalid butterflies having golden orange wings with a number of black patches and spots. The edges of the wings are irregularly serrated and there is a black or brown marginal band containing a row of blue or grey crescents. The Small Tortoiseshell *Aglais urticae* is found all across Europe and Asia. In Britain it frequently hibernates in sheds and outhouses. The Large Tortoiseshell *Nymphalis polychloros* is similar in appearance but a little larger. It is found in North Africa, Southern and Central Europe and Western Asia. It occurs in southern Britain but much less abundantly than the Small Tortoiseshell. There is also a North American Tortoiseshell, *Nymphalis californica*.

TORTRICIDAE. A family of small moths (Microlepidoptera) whose larvae are generally leaf-rollers and do considerable damage to trees such as oaks, pines and larches, often completely defoliating them. The Green Oak-roller Moth, *Tortrix viridana*, for instance, causes leaves of the tree to roll up, shrivel and fall. Many related species attack other trees.

TORUS. A general name for a thickened part or pedicel on which an organ is borne, *e.g.* the base of an antenna.

TORYMIDAE. See *Chalcid Seed-fly*.

TOUCH. See *Tactile Receptors*.

TOWERED GRASSHOPPER. *Acrida hungarica,* a large grasshopper from the warmer parts of Europe and Asia, about 7 cm. long with an élongated head and large, flattened antennae. Its colour varies from green to brownish red. It is found on damp grassland and is apparently harmless to agricultural crops.

TOXOTUS. *Toxotus meridianus,* the Variable Longhorn Beetle (see *Stenocorus*).

TRABUTINA. *Trabutina mannipara,* an alternative name for *Coccus manniparus* (see *Manna Scale Insect*).

TRACHEAE. The breathing tubes of an insect: branching tubes strengthened with rings of chitin and opening by spiracles situated along the sides of the body (see *Breathing*).

TRACHEAL GILLS. Respiratory organs of certain aquatic insects consisting of thin outgrowths of the body-wall containing numerous closed tracheoles into which dissolved oxygen can diffuse from the surrounding water.

TRACHEIN. A colloidal or jelly-like material forming the walls of the tracheal air-sacs in the aquatic larvae of gnats such as *Corethra*. It can apparently swell up when absorbing water and shrink on losing it. By some mechanism not fully understood, the insect can control its buoyancy by causing a swelling or shrinkage of these air bladders.

TRACHEOLES. The finer branches of an insect's tracheae (see *Breathing*).

TRANSVERSE VEINS. See *Cross-veins*.

TRAPEZONOTUS. *Trapezonotus arenarius,* a common European plant-bug about 5 mm. long, greenish-grey and oval-shaped with a dorsal shield shaped roughly like a narrow trapezium. It is found on sand dunes.

TREBLE-BAR MOTH. *Anaitis plagiata*: a carpet moth, a geometrid of the subfamily Larentiinae having the fore-wings light brown with three transverse bands of darker brown. The hind-wings are paler and unbarred. The caterpillars are brown and stick-like; they feed on St. John's Wort (*Hypericum*). There is also a Lesser Treble-bar, *Anaitis efformata,* smaller and slightly paler.

TRECHUS. *Trechus quadristriatus,* a common Ground Beetle of the family Carabidae about 3 mm. long with a narrow waist and elongated, shiny, reddish-brown elytra. It is a nocturnal predator found in sandy places.

TREE CRICKETS. A general and rather indefinite name for a number of tree-dwelling, stridulating members of the family Gryllidae, usually green or light greenish-brown and resembling long-horned grasshoppers (see *Cricket, Gryllidae* and *Tettigoniidae*).

TREE GRAYLING. *Hipparchia statilinus,* a satyrid butterfly of North Africa, Southern and Central Europe and the Middle East; similar to the common Grayling but having the eye-spots on the upper surface almost completely masked by the dark, smoky brown colour. The larvae, like those of other graylings, feed on grasses.

TREE-HOPPER. See *Membracidae*.

TREE NYMPH. A name sometimes used for the very large Danaid butterflies of South-east Asia and the neighbouring islands especially members of the genus *Hestia* which fly like kites with their large, papery wings, sometimes as much as 15 cm. across.

TREE WASP. *Vespula sylvestris* and related species: small social wasps resembling the common wasp in their colouring but making their papery nests in trees instead of in holes in the ground.

TREMEX. A Horntail or Woodwasp of the family Siricidae: a very large hymenopteran, 3–4 cm. long, having a straight body without a waist and with a stiff, straight ovipositor which it uses to bore holes in wood in order to lay eggs beneath the surface. Some species have a brown and yellow striped abdomen. They resemble the larger *Urocerus gigas* but the antennae and ovipositor are a little shorter. *Tremex fuscicornis* is a European species; *Tremex columba* is North America. The larvae make tunnels in wood and take a long time to develop so that adults occasionally emerge long after the timber has been used for building or furniture making. *Urocerus* prefers coniferous trees; *Tremex* deciduous such as maple, elm, beech etc. (see *Siricidae*).

TRIAENODES. A genus of caddis flies (Trichoptera) whose larvae make long, light cases from pieces of leaf woven into a spiral shape. These larvae differ from most caddis worms in being able to swim actively, using their hair-fringed legs.

TRIALEURODES. See *Greenhouse Whitefly*.

TRIATOMA. A genus of blood-sucking Assassin Bugs (Reduviidae) from Central and South America and the southern United States. Some species transmit the parasite *Trypanosoma cruzi*, the cause of *Chagas' Disease*.

TRIBOLIUM. A world-wide genus of flour beetles of the family Tenebrionidae. They include *Tribolium destructor*, *Tribolium confusum*, *Tribolium ferrugineum* and many others; small reddish-brown insects about 5 mm. long, destructive pests of flour and other food products.

TRIBUS. *Tribus attelabini*, a leaf-rolling weevil from Madagascar, shiny black with red wing-covers. The length is about 25 mm. but more than half this is taken up by the very long, narrow head and snout with two long antennae near the tip.

TRICHIOCAMPUS. *Trichiocampus viminalis*, the Poplar Sawfly: an insect having a black head and thorax, a pale yellow abdomen, yellow legs and long antennae. The wings have a span of about 12 mm. and the fore-wings are thickened along the front edge. Eggs are laid in poplar leaves and the developing larvae eat the leaves away from below so that in places only the transparent upper epidermis is left.

TRICHIOSOMA. A common genus of large black sawflies about the size and shape of a drone bee and covered with fine downy hairs. *Trichiosoma tibiale* has pale, greenish yellow larvae with a whitish 'bloom' on the skin. They feed on hawthorn. *Trichiosoma lucorum* is a similar species but the larvae have a dark line along the back; they feed on sallow and birch. Both species pupate in large, papery cocoons attached to twigs.

TRICHIINAE. Brush Beetles or Bee Chafers, a subfamily of Chafer Beetles (Scarabaeidae) having a coating of fine hairs on the wing-cases and long shaggy hairs on the rest of the body. *Trichius fasciatus*, the Banded Brush Beetle, has a yellowish body, dark brown legs and reddish brown elytra with three large black patches on each. It is the shape and size of a bumble bee and this resemblance may give it some degree of protection. It is common on brambles and wild roses in Scotland, but rare elsewhere in Britain.

TRICHOCERA. A genus of Winter Gnats: insects resembling small crane-flies. They could be mistaken for mosquitoes but have not the long proboscis and do not suck blood. They are often seen 'dancing' in swarms on warm winter days; they fly at other times of year, but then are less conspicuous because many more insects are about. The larvae feed on decaying leaves and pupate in the soil.

TRICHODECTIDAE. A family of Biting Lice of the order Mallophaga. Although most biting lice infest birds, this group attacks mammals, living in the fur and feeding on fragments of dried skin and hair. Some common species are: *Trichodectes canis*, the Dog Louse; *Damalina bovis*, the Red Louse of cattle and *Damalina ovis*, the Sheep Louse.

TRICHODES. *Trichodes apiarius*, the Bee-wolf: a lamellicorn beetle about 12 mm. long with reddish brown elytra having three broad black transverse bands. The larvae live in beehives and feed on the bee larvae.

TRICHOGEN. An epidermal cell which produces a cuticular hair or scale on the body or wing of an insect.

TRICHOGRAMMATIDAE. Minute fringe-winged chalcid wasps, often less than 1 mm. long, that lay their eggs in the eggs of other insects. Most species attack the eggs of butterflies and moths but some are parasites of other insects such as water beetles and water bugs. They may use their wings for swimming in order to reach the eggs of their victims. In some cases a particular species of chalcid may attack many different host-species and its offspring sometimes vary in colour or other characteristics according to the influence of hormones or other substances that it receives from the host. A number of species have been used in attempts to control various insect pests, but usually with indifferent success.

TRICHOID SENSILLAE. See *Sensory Hairs*.

TRICHOPHAGA. See *Tapestry Moth*.

TRICHOPTERA. Caddis Flies: moth-like insects whose wings are covered with hairs and whose mouth-parts are so reduced that little food can be taken. The aquatic larvae, which are usually herbivorous, mostly live in tubular cases formed of particles of wood, sand, small shells etc. A pair of hooks on the hind-end enables the larva to cling to the tube and drag it around when walking. Pupation takes place within the tube after the ends have been closed with silk.

TRICHOPTERYGIDAE. A family of beetles including some of the smallest in the world, less than a quarter of a millimetre long.

TRICHOTAPHE. A genus of small moths of the family Gelechiidae whose larvae are leaf-tiers, feeding and making nests in the young shoots of asters.

TRIDACTYLIDAE. Pygmy Sand Crickets: minute burrowing insects living in sandy banks of streams or ponds.

TRIGONA. A genus of small, tropical, stingless bees of the family Meliponidae living in colonies in dark coloured nests made of wax resin, faeces and other debris surrounded by a hard coating of clay and other materials (see *Stingless Bees*).

TRIMEN'S BROWN. *Melampias trimenii*, a common brown butterfly of the family Satyridae from the high grasslands of South Africa.

TRIOZA. *Trioza erytreae* or *Spanioza erytreae*, a jumping plant-louse of the family Psyllidae: a pest of citrus trees, to which it is confined. Found from East Africa to the Cape.

TRIPHAENA. *Triphaena pronuba* or *Noctua pronuba* or *Agrotis pronuba*: the Large Yellow Underwing, a noctuid moth with a wing-span of about 6 cm. The fore-wings are mottled grey-brown; the hind-wings are orange-yellow with a narrow black band close to the edge. The brownish caterpillars feed on dandelions and other small herbaceous plants.

TRIPHLOSOBA. A fossil insect of the Upper Carboniferous Period, placed in the order Protephemeroptera, intermediate between mayflies (Ephemeroptera) and dragonflies (Odonata).

TRIQUETRA. A Brazilian tree-hopper of the family Membracidae whose dorsal thoracic shield covers the whole body, extending to a point at the hind-end and having three horn-like projections at the front.

TRITOCEREBRUM (METACEREBRUM). The hind-part of the brain of an insect formed from the fused ganglia of the third embryonic segment (see *Brain*).

TRITOGENAPHIS. A bright red aphid from which a vermilion anthocyanin pigment can be extracted.

TRIUNGULIN. The minute, long-legged, parasitic larva characteristic of the Oil Beetles (Meloidae). The eggs of these beetles are laid on various plants and the triungulin larvae which emerge attach themselves to the bodies of visiting bees. They are carried off to the bees' nest where they feed on the eggs. For this reason, before their true nature was known, they were called Bee Lice. A similar type of triungulin larva is found in a few other insect orders, notably the Strepsiptera.

TROCHANTER. A short segment of an insect's leg between the coxa and the femur.

TROCHANTIN. (1) A small basal articular sclerite on the trochanter of an insect.
(2) Any small sclerite interposed between two others, *e.g.* on the mouth-parts.

TROCHILIUM. *Trochilium apiformis* or *Sesia apiformis*. See *Hornet Clearwing Moth*.

TROCTES. *Troctes divinatorius*, an alternative name for the common booklouse *Liposcelis divinatorius* (see *Book-louse*).

TROGIDAE. A family of beetles of the superfamily Scarabaeoidea: scavengers or carrion feeders, 18–20 mm. long and having a roughly sculptured appearance with numerous small knobs on the elytra. The head is bent down and covered by the thoracic shield.

TROGIUM. *Trogium pulsatorium*, one of the commonest book-lice of the order Psocoptera: a minute, light brown insect with reduced wings and very long antennae. It is commonly found in old books, furniture, museum specimens etc. (see *Psocoptera* and *Book-louse*).

TROGODERMA. *Trogoderma granarium*, the Khapra Beetle, a grain beetle of the family Dermestidae whose hairy larvae feed on stored cereals, particularly in tropical countries (see *Dermestidae*).

TROGONOPTERA. *Trogonoptera brookiana*, a large papilionid butterfly from the mountains and forests of South-east Asia and Indonesia. The wings are brown with a pattern in the form of a row of large green and yellow triangles. The front wings are much longer than the hind ones and have a span of about 16 cm. (see also *Troides*).

TROIDES. A genus of large Birdwing Butterflies some of which were formerly put in the genus *Ornithoptera*. They are to be found in India, South-east Asia, Indonesia and Northern Australia. Many of them have a wing-span of 12–15 cm. and are brightly coloured, usually black and green or yellow. They include *Troides paradisea* from New Guinea, *Troides victoriae-regis* from the Solomon Islands, *Troides brookiana* from Malaysia and many others (see also *Ornithoptera*).

TROILUS. (1) A genus of medium sized, brown shieldbugs (Pentatomidae).
(2) A North American swallowtail butterfly with greenish coloured wings.

TROPAEA. *Tropaea luna*, an alternative name for the North American Luna Moth or Moon Moth sometimes called *Actias luna*, a large, light green saturniid moth with moon-like markings on the fore-wings (see *Luna Moth*).

TROPHALLAXIS. The mutual exchange of food between insects of a colony, *e.g.* of bees, wasps and particularly ants; a behaviour pattern that helps to improve relationships and bind the colony together into a social unit.

TROPHAMNION. A sheath or membrane surrounding the eggs of some parasitic insects, especially those which exhibit *polyembryony* (*q.v.*). It is able to absorb food material from the tissues of the host.

TROPHOCYTES. Nurse-cells in an ovariole (see *Ovariole*).

TROPHOTHYLAX. A food pocket in the first abdominal segment of the larva, in ants of the subfamily Pseudomyrminae (see *Twig-infesting Ants*).

TROPIDIA. A genus of scavenging hover-flies (Syrphidae) whose larvae are of the 'short-tailed' type and live among damp rotting vegetation.

TROPISM. A reflex response whereby an insect turns in a particular direction in relation to a stimulus. The word is sometimes used wrongly synonymously with *taxis*, a movement in a definite direction to or from a source of stimulus (see *Taxis, Phototaxis, Rheotropism* and *Rheotaxis*).

TROPOTAXIS. A response involving the turning of an insect followed by movement in a definite direction in relation to a stimulus. It thus combines a *tropism* and a *taxis*.

TRUE LOVER'S KNOT MOTH. See *Lycophotia*.

TRUMPET MINE. A leaf-mine in which a trumpet-shaped cavity is formed with one end wider than the other. An example is that made by the larva of the moth *Tischeria malifoliella* in apple leaves.

TRYPANEIDAE (= TRYPETIDAE). A family of small flies of the group Cyclorrhapha, similar in appearance to the house fly but often brightly coloured and sometimes known as Peacock Flies on account of their habit of standing with their wings erected and gently waving them to and fro. The larvae of some are pests of soft fruits. Their activity, however, has no effect on the survival of the plant, but renders the fruit unsaleable.

TRYPODENDRON. A genus of Ambrosia Beetles: bark-beetles of the family Scolytidae, usually brown or black and 2–3 mm. long. *Trypodendron domesticum* and *Trypodendron signatum* make tunnels in deciduous trees such as oak and beech. *Trypodendron lineatum* attacks conifers (see *Ambrosia Beetles, Bark-beetles* and *Scolytidae*).

TRYPOXYLON. A mud-daubing wasp of the family Sphecidae that hunts spiders, stings and paralyses them and stocks its nest with them as food for the developing larvae.

TRYPOXYLUS. *Trypoxylus dichotomus*, the Japanese Rhinoceros Beetle: a large brown beetle of the group Dynastinae, about 7 cm. long with a large, forked, antler-like horn on its head.

TSETSE FLY. See *Glossinidae*.

TUFTED SKIPPER. *Carcharodus flocciferus*, a small Skipper Butterfly from Southern Europe belonging to the family Hesperiidae, having a marbled type of wing-pattern of dark grey-brown and white. The underside of each front wing bears a prominent tuft of dark hairs.

TUMBLE BEETLES. A colloquial American name for Dung Beetles of the genera *Copris, Phanaus* and several others (see *Scarabaeidae*).

TUNGA. *Tunga penetrans* or *Dermatophilus penetrans*, the Burrowing Flea also called the Chigger, Chigoe or Jigger (see *Chigoe*).

TURKEY GNAT. *Simulium meridionale*, a blood-sucking Black Fly of the family Simuliidae that attacks turkeys and other domestic birds and farm animals in the southern United States (see *Simuliidae*).

TURNIP FLY. The Turnip Flea-beetle *Phyllotreta* (see *Flea-beetle* and *Phyllotreta*).

TURNIP GALL-WEEVIL. See *Gall-weevil*.

TURNIP MOTH. *Agrotis segetum*, a common, medium sized noctuid moth of a mottled grey-brown colour with paler hind-wings. The caterpillars, also greyish brown, are serious pests of turnips and other root-crops.

TURNIP SAWFLY. *Athalia rosae*, a small sawfly about 6 mm. long, yellow with a black head and antennae. The larvae, like small yellow caterpillars, feed on turnips and other root-crops. As they grow they become darker until they are nearly black and are then known as Nigger-worms.

TURQUOISE BLUE BUTTERFLY. *Plebicula dorylas*, a gleaming, pale blue butterfly of the family Lycaenidae from the mountains of Southern Europe and Asia Minor; similar in general appearance to the other Blue Butterflies but paler and brighter. The underside is greyish with orange and black spots.

TURTLE BUG. *Podops inuncta*, a greyish brown plant-bug of the family Pentatomidae about 6 mm. long, having an oval body and a large dorsal shield covering much of the wings. The front of the thorax bears two small projecting knobs.

TUSSOCK MOTHS. See *Lymantriidae*.

TWELVE-PLUME MOTH. See *Many-plume Moth*.

TWENTY-TWO SPOT LADYBIRD. See *Thea*.

TWIG-INFESTING ANTS. *Pseudomyrma filiformis* and related species of ants from Central and South America having a cylindrical body with a long, slender abdomen, an elongated head and short antennae. All these features make them well adapted for wood-boring and they are to be found in large numbers in hollow twigs.

TWIN-SPOT CARPET MOTH. *Colostygia didymata*, a small, mottled, greyish brown moth of the group Larentiinae having on each fore-wing two broad double bands of lighter grey and a pair of twin black spots near the tip. The Red Twin-spot Carpet Moth, *Xanthorhoe spadicearia*, is similar with twin black spots in the same position but the general colour is more reddish brown. The larvae of both feed on small woodland and meadow plants.

TWIN-SPOT FRITILLARY. *Brenthis hecate*, a small butterfly of the family Nymphalidae having a golden-brown chequerboard type of wing-pattern similar to those of other fritillaries but having a double row of black spots near the edges of the wings on the underside. They are to be found in the highlands of Southern Europe and Central Asia.

TWO-BANDED BEETLE. *Rhagium bifasciatum* (see *Rhagium*).

TWO-COLOURED GRASSHOPPER. *Chorthippus brunneus* formerly called *Chorthippus bicolor*, the Common Field Grasshopper. One of the two commonest European short-horned grasshoppers (Acrididae), about 18 mm. long with elytra and wings as long as the abdomen. The colours are variable but consist chiefly of mottled light and dark brown with some green on the hind-parts of the elytra and with the tip of the abdomen red.

TWO-COLOURED OSMIA. *Osmia bicolor*, a medium sized solitary bee of the family Megachilidae, dark brown or black with a coating of fine orange hairs on the abdomen. They are found in chalk and limestone districts where they sometimes nest in empty snail shells.

TWO-COLOURED SEHIRUS. *Sehirus bicolor* also called the Pied Shieldbug: an oval-shaped insect about 6 mm. long, of a glossy black colour splashed with white. Eggs are laid in a shallow hole in the ground and the adult female appears to show some instinct of parental care, turning them occasionally and after they are hatched leading the young insects to labiate plants such as Dead Nettle on which they feed.

TWO-POINTED GROUSE-LOCUST. A small Groundhopper or Jumping Locust of the family Tetrigidae from the temperate parts of Europe and Asia. An angular insect about 1 cm. long with the hind-wings three or four times as long as the tegmina. Some authors refer to this insect as *Tetrix bipunctata*, but the same name has been used by British authors for *Tetrix undulata*, a short-winged species. (See *Tetrigidae*.)

TWO-POINTED SHIELDBUG. *Picromerus bidens* (see *Picromerus*).

TWO-PRONGED BRISTLE-TAIL. See *Diplura*.

TWO-SPOTTED AGABUS. *Agabus bipustulatus*, a small, brown, oval water beetle common in ponds and streams. It belongs to the family Dytiscidae and, like others of this family, both adults and larvae are carnivorous (see *Dytiscidae*).

TWO-SPOTTED GROUND BEETLE. *Badister bipustulatus*, a small, elongated beetle of the family Carabidae about 6 mm. long, reddish yellow with a black patch in the middle of each elytron; found in chalky places chiefly under stones and among rotting wood and moss at the roots of trees.

TWO-SPOTTED GRASSHOPPER. *Tetrix bupunctata* (see *Two-pointed Grouse-locust*).

TWO-SPOTTED LADYBIRD. *Adalia bipunctata*, a small species of ladybird beetle (Coccinellidae) having several colour variations. The normal variety is red with a black spot on each wing-case; there is also a black type with two or more red spots on each elytron; another occasionally found is pale yellow with a number of black spots.

TWO-SPOTTED MALACHIUS. *Malachius bipustulatus*, also called the Red-tipped Flower-beetle (see *Malachius*).

TWO-SPOT OAK SPLENDOUR BEETLE. *Agrilus biguttatus*, a European member of the family Buprestidae: an elongated beetle about 12 mm. long with elytra tapering towards the hind-end. The colour is dark green or blue with two white spots on each elytron. The legless larvae burrow in the bark of oak trees.

TWO-SPOTTED SPHAERIDIUM. *Sphaeridium bipustulatum*: a common dung beetle of the family Hydrophilidae, about 6 mm. long, shining black with a red spot at the base and another near the tip of each elytron.

TWO-SPOTTED STENUS. *Stenus biguttatus*: a Rove Beetle of the family Staphylinidae, about 6 mm. long, black with roughly punctured elytra each having a yellow spot near the inner margin. They are common on sandy banks of streams.

TWO-STRIPED MOSQUITO. *Anopheles claviger* or *Anopheles bifurcatus*: a species of mosquito common throughout North Africa, Asia Minor and most of Europe. It differs from the better known *Anopheles maculipennis* (the malaria mosquito) in having two prominent white lines along the back of the thorax and in having wings without spots.

TWO-TAILED PASHA. *Charaxes jasius*, a handsome nymphalid butterfly from North Africa and the Mediterranean coastal regions of southern Europe. The upper surfaces are dark brown with wide yellow margins; the undersides have a marble-like pattern of light brown, grey, black, white and yellow. The hind-wings are irregularly serrated and have two 'tails'. The larvae feed on the Strawberry Tree (*Arbutus unedo*).

TWO-TOOTHED BARK-BEETLE. *Pityogenes bidentatus*, a small, reddish brown bark-beetle of the family Scolytidae, about 2 mm. long, the males having a hooked spine near the hind-end of each wing-cover. The larvae burrow beneath the bark of conifers.

TWO-WINGED FLIES. See *Diptera*.

TYMBAL. The drum-like organ with which a male cicada is able to make a loud noise. There are two such organs situated at the base of the abdomen. Each consists of a tightly stretched skin with an air space beneath it. Vibration of the drum is brought about by minute but powerful muscles that cause a rapid in-and-out movement (see *Cicadidae*).

TYMPANAL ORGANS. Auditory organs on the abdomen or legs of certain insects such as grasshoppers and cicadas. In these organs there is a tympanic membrane formed from the cuticle, an underlying air-space acting as a resonator and a group of specialized receptors which can detect high-frequency vibrations.

TYPHAEUS. *Typhaeus typhoeus*, the Minotaur or Bull Beetle: a shiny, blue-black dung beetle of the family Scarabaeidae, the male being characterized by three 'horns' on the front of the thorax. These are used for rolling balls of dung (see *Scarabaeidae*).

TYPHLOCYBA. A genus of leaf-hoppers (Cicadellidae) that attack and destroy young beech and other seedlings. Though probably of European origin, various species now attack fruit trees in North America, Australia and New Zealand.

TYRIA. *Tyria jacobaeae*, an alternative name for *Callimorpha jacobaeae* (see *Cinnabar Moth*).

TYROSINE. An amino-acid important in all living organisms; in insects it is the basis for the formation of melanin in the cuticle.

U

UGLY NEST. A nest made by the larvae of certain tortricid moths, particularly those of the genus *Cacoecia*. Eggs are laid near the tip of a shoot (*e.g.* of cherry); leaves are tied together with silk threads produced by the developing larvae. As they grow larger they add more and more leaves and when these die and turn brown the nest assumes an ugly unsightly appearance.

ULTRA-VIOLET VISION. Most insects can perceive a wide range of light-frequencies including all the colours visible to the human eye as well as infra-red and ultra-violet which are just beyond the range of human vision. Their sensitiveness to ultra-violet can be shown by observing their reactions to it. It is well known, for instance, that moths are attracted by it. On the other hand ants will try to avoid it. This can be shown by using a bottle containing carbon bisulphide or some other liquid which absorbs ultra-violet light. Although it appears transparent to humans, it casts an 'ultra-violet shadow' under which ants will take shelter. A similar reaction has been observed in the case of mosquito larvae.

UMBER MOTHS. A name given to several geometrid moths of a more or less dark brown colour. The Mottled Umber, *Erannis defoliaria*, is a common pest of many trees and shrubs. The males may be dark brown all over or mottled with light and dark brown; the females are wingless. The small green larvae infest oak, elm, birch and other trees and may completely defoliate them. If disturbed they drop on silk threads and pull themselves up again when safe. The Waved Umber, *Menophra abruptaria*, is similar in appearance but the females are winged and are paler than the males. The caterpillars, which are brown and stick-like, feed particularly on lilac and privet.

UMBONIA. *Umbonia spinosa*, a tree-hopper of the family Membracidae from Central and South America: a relatively large species, green with red thorn-like spines mimicking the thorns of the plants on which it lives.

UMBRELLA ANT. More usually known as a *Parasol Ant*: a name for several species of tropical leaf-cutting ants that carry pieces of leaves over the body like a parasol. In many cases these pieces of leaves are taken underground, mixed with saliva and used as a medium for cultivating fungi. The best known genus is the South American *Atta* (see also *Fungus Cultivation*).

UNCA. See *Spectacle Moth*.

UNDERTAKER BEETLE. Any species of the genus *Necrophorus*: burying beetles of the family Necrophoridae about 12 mm. long, having orange and black banded elytra; the rest of the body, head, legs and antennae are entirely black. (See *Burying Beetles*.)

UNDERWING MOTHS. A name for a number of moths of several different families, all having cryptically coloured fore-wings and brightly coloured hind-wings. When at rest the latter are hidden but they come into view when the insect flies. Some of the best known are the Red Underwing (*Catocala nupta*), Yellow Underwing (*Noctua pronuba*) and Copper Underwing (*Amphipyra pyramidea*). (See also *Flash Colouring*.)

UNIFORM RHYNCHITES. *Rhynchites aequatus*, sometimes called the Red and Bronze Weevil: an insect about 4 mm. long with shiny reddish elytra and a very long, dark red, curved snout. It is commonly found on hawthorn (*Crataegus*).

URANIIDAE. A family of large, brightly coloured, tropical moths. *Urania leilus*, from Central and South America and the West Indies, has a wing-span of about 7 cm. with swallowtail-type hind-wings. It is iridescent blue-green, black and white; *Urania ripheus* from Madagascar is similar but with some red on the hind-wings and with three short 'tails' on each.

UROCERUS. An alternative name for the genus formerly known as *Sirex*, the woodwasp or horntail (see *Siricidae*).

UROPHORA. A genus of gall-flies of the family Trypetidae: small two-winged flies whose larvae make large round galls, at first green and soft but later becoming brown and hard. A number of larvae live in each gall. *Urophora cardui* attacks thistles, making galls resembling gooseberries on the stems (see *Gall* and *Gall-fly*).

UROPLATA. Wedge-shaped beetles: a genus of the family Chrysomelidae having delicately ridged and sculptured bodies and elytra. The tiny larvae are short-legged and flattened; they tunnel inside the leaves of grass and other plants, making large irregular mines in which they pupate.

URSALA BUTTERFLY. A North American nymphalid butterfly of the genus *Basilarchia*, pale blue, green and black.

UTERUS. A term that is strictly incorrect when applied to insects but is commonly used to denote a part analogous with the uterus of a mammal: an enlargement of the 'vagina' where the two oviducts join. In some insects such as Tsetse Flies, Sheep Keds and Forest Flies the eggs hatch here and the larvae remain in the parent's body to be deposited only when they are nearly full grown and ready to pupate.

UTETHESIA. A genus of moths of the family Arctiidae, generally brilliantly spotted with red and black. They inhabit warm countries where the caterpillars feed on rough grass and small herbaceous plants. The Crimson Speckled Moth *Utethesia pulchella* is found in Central and Southern Europe.

V

VAGINA. A median duct or chamber into which the two oviducts open; formed by a folding in of the body-wall in the ninth abdominal segment (see also *Uterus*).

VANESSIDAE. A family of handsome, brightly coloured nymphalid butterflies including the Red Admiral (*Vanessa atalanta*), Painted Lady (*Vanessa cardui*), American Painted Lady (*Vanessa virginiensis*) and the New Zealand Red Admiral (*Vanessa gonerilla*). Closely related to these are the Tortoiseshell, Peacock and Camberwell Beauty which are usually put in the genus *Nymphalis* but are sometimes classed as vanessids.

VANNUS. The anal or posterior lobe of an insect's wing: a fan-like expansion separated from the rest of the wing by a furrow.

VAPOURER MOTH. *Orgyia antiqua*, a common European Tussock Moth of the family Lymantriidae, light brown with a wing-span of about 3 cm. and with a prominent kidney-shaped white spot on each fore-wing. The female is wingless. The brown and yellow caterpillars, like those of all the Lymantriidae, have numerous tufts of bristles which secrete an irritant poison.

VARIEGATED LADYBIRD. *Adonia variegata*, a beetle of the family Coccinellidae about 6 mm. long, having a black and yellow thorax and orange elytra with from five to seven black spots.

VASCULAR SYSTEM. See *Blood* and *Heart*.

VAUCHER'S HEATH BUTTERFLY. *Coenonympha vaucheri*, a small satyrid butterfly of the high Atlas Mountains; orange with brown margins and with a large black eye-spot on each fore-wing and a row of small spots on each hind-wing.

VEDALIA. An alternative name for the ladybird beetle *Rodolia* (*q.v.*).

VEGETABLE IVORY BORER. *Dryocoetes dactyloperda*, a weevil whose larvae bore into the nuts of the Vegetable Ivory plant (*Tagua*).

VEINS. See *Wing-veins* and *Venation*.

VELIIDAE. Water-crickets, water-striders or ripple-bugs: a family of predatory bugs of the order Hemiptera, similar to pondskaters but shorter and broader with thickened hind-legs. Some species are wingless. They live on ponds and slow-flowing streams, running on the surface and occasionally diving in search of prey. *Velia currens*, *Velia caprai* and *Velia saulii* are common European species.

VELLEIUS. *Velleius dilatatus* and related species: rove beetles of the family Staphylinidae that live in the nests of wasps and hornets, feeding on the larvae.

VELOCITY. See *Speed of Insects*.

VELVET ANTS. Brightly coloured cuckoo wasps of the family Mutillidae whose wingless females resemble ants in shape, size and colour but have a coating of fine velvety hairs. They live in the nests of bumble bees, sharing their supply of food and laying their eggs in the bodies of the larvae. *Mutilla europaea* and *Mutilla marginata* are common European species; *Mutilla lilliputiana* is a dwarf American species and *Dasymutilla occidentalis* is a giant species 25–30 mm. long, also from North America.

VENA SPURIA. A false vein: a thickening resembling a vein in the wings of such insects as hover-flies (Syrphidae).

VENATION. The arrangement of the veins or nervures in an insect's wing is often an important means of identifying species. For the purpose of comparison the veins of a generalized wing are named as follows: the *costa*, a thick unbranched vein forming the anterior margin of the wing; the *subcosta*, another unbranched vein immediately below the costa; the *radius*, *media* and *cubitus* which are usually branched; the *anal* veins, short and unbranched. All these run longitudinally and may be linked by a variable number of *cross-veins* dividing the wing into 'cells'. The latter are very numerous in mayflies (Ephemeroptera), dragonflies (Odonata) and in some primitive fossil insects but the evolutionary tendency seems to have been towards a reduction in their number. (See also *Comstock-Needham System* and *Concave and Convex Veins*.)

VENOM. See *Poisons*.

VENTRAL GLANDS. Glands in the ventral part of the head of some insects (Thysanura, Ephemeroptera, Odonata, Isoptera, Dermaptera, Acrididae and Phasmida), corresponding to the thoracic and prothoracic glands of others; a source of the moulting hormone (see *Ecdysis*).

VENTRAL TUBE. A tube formed of two fused ventral appendages (sometimes called 'coxal vesicles') on the first abdominal segment in insects of the order Collembola (springtails). It is everted by blood pressure, and retracted by muscles. Its functions are not entirely certain but seem to include adhesion, especially to a water film, and sucking up water.

VENTRICULUS. The mid-gut, mesenteron or 'stomach' of an insect: the part where most digestion and absorption take place immediately behind the gizzard or *proventriculus* (see *Alimentary Canal*).

VENULES. The smaller cross-veins of an insect's wing (see *Venation*).

VERSON'S CELL (VERSONIAN CELL). A specialized apical cell at the tip of the testis in some insects.

VERSON'S GLANDS. The moulting glands of caterpillars: epidermal glands which secrete a fluid having the property of liquifying the endocuticle and thus loosening the epicuticle prior to moulting (see *Ecdydis*).

VESPA. A genus comprising the larger social wasps such as the hornet *Vespa crabro*. Formerly the smaller species such as the Common Wasp were also named *Vespa* but these are now put into a separate genus *Vespula*. Both *Vespa* and *Vespula* are black and yellow striped and both construct nests of chewed wood-pulp resembling paper (see *Wasp*).

VESPIDAE. The principal family of social wasps comprising the two genera *Vespa* and *Vespula* (see *Vespa* above).

VESPIFORMIA. A group of Hymenoptera including both ants and wasps; a larger group than the Vespidae.

VESPOIDEA. A superfamily of Hymenoptera comprising the social wasps and hornets (Vespidae) and the solitary Potter and Mason wasps (Eumenidae). Most of these are black and yellow and fold their wings longitudinally when at rest (see also *Wasp* and *Vespidae*).

VESPOPHILES. A general name for insects that live as inquilines or 'guests' in wasps' nests, *e.g.* the Rove Beetle *Velleius*.

VESPULA. *Vespula vulgaris* the Common Wasp, *Vespula germanica* the German Wasp and *Vespula sylvestris* the Tree Wasp: three very similar species all having black and yellow striped bodies. They are among the world's commonest social wasps living in large colonies in spherical papery nests in holes in the ground, hollow trees, attics, out-houses etc. (see *Wasp*).

VESTAL CUCKOO-BEE. *Psithyrus vestalis*, a species of bee that lays its eggs in the underground nest of the large bumble bee *Bombus terrestris* which it closely resembles. It kills the queen, and its own larvae are fed and tended by the workers of the host-species.

VICEROY BUTTERFLY. *Limenitis archippus* or *Basilarchia archippus*, a large North American nymphalid butterfly similar in colour and appearance to the Milkweed Butterfly *Danaus plexippus*: a case of Batesian Mimicry.

VINEGAR FLY. An alternative name for the fruit-fly *Drosophila* (see *Drosophilidae*).

VIOLET COPPER BUTTERFLY. *Lycaena helle*, a small butterfly from the mountainous parts of Northern Europe and Asia extending as far north as the North Cape and as far east as Siberia and Manchuria: the female is similar in appearance to the other copper butterflies, the upper surface being golden orange with a pattern of black dots and squares. The male has this pattern largely obscured by a suffusion of deep violet. The undersides of both are greyish-yellow with black dots and an orange border. The larvae feed on Knot Grass (*Polygonum*).

VIOLET FRITILLARY. *Clossiana dia*, a small nymphalid butterfly ranging across Central Europe and Asia as far as Western China. It has the orange and black chequerboard type of pattern characteristic of fritillaries but on the underside of the hind-wings the orange is replaced by a delicate violet shade.

VIOLET GROUND BEETLE. *Carabus violaceus*, a large flightless ground beetle of the family Carabidae about 25 mm. long, shiny black with violet borders to the oval wing-cases. Both adults and larvae are nocturnal and predatory, hiding by day under stones, logs etc.

VIOLET OIL BEETLE. *Meloe violaceus*, a large, elongated, wingless beetle about 25 mm. long, black with a bluish-violet sheen. It inhabits heaths and grassy roadsides where it lays its eggs on a variety of plants. The long-legged larvae crawl about on the flowers and take the opportunity to attach themselves to visiting bees. They are carried to the bees' nest where they live and feed on the honey stored by their host (see *Meloidae*).

VIPER'S BUGLOSS MOTH. *Dianthoecia irregularis* or *Hadena irregularis*, a moth from the dry plateaux and high ground of Central Europe and Asia: a noctuid moth with a wing-span of about 3 cm., olive green with a pattern of various shades of brown. The larvae feed on Catchfly (*Silene otites*) and Viper's Bugloss (*Echium vulgare*).

VIRGINIA CREEPER STEM-GALL WEEVIL. *Ampeloglypter ater*, a small insect of the family Curculionidae whose larvae produce galls on the stems of Virginia Creeper (*Ampelopsis hederacea*).

VISION. Insects have two kinds of eyes, *viz.* compound eyes and ocelli. Most adult insects have both kinds; larvae usually only have ocelli. Eyes, of whichever kind, contain the essential elements of lens, retina and nerve. Compound eyes contain numerous optical units or *ommatidia* each containing a cuticular lens, a crystalline cone and several retinal cells. Ocelli usually only have a cuticular lens and a few retinal cells. In both cases nerves from the retinal cells lead to the optic lobes of the brain situated immediately above the oesophagus.

Neither type of eye is well adapted to give a clear picture of distant objects. Ocelli probably do not form an image at all but merely detect changes of intensity of the light. Compound eyes can produce either a *mosaic image* composed of a large number of dots or a *superposition image* in which the dots merge to form a blurred picture. They are, however, well adapted for judging distance and for perceiving movements of objects. There is good evidence that most insects can perceive colour as well as ultra-violet and in some cases infra-red light. It is believed that many can also perceive patterns of polarization in the sky and this perhaps helps them in direction finding when flying (see also *Compound Eyes*).

VITELLARIUM. That part of the ovary of an insect that secretes yolk, *i.e.* the proximal part of each ovariole into which the oocytes are liberated from the germarium or distal region (see *Ovary* and *Ovariole*).

VITRELLAE. Cells which secrete the crystalline cone in each ommatidium or optical unit of a compound eye.

VITREOUS BODY. A name sometimes used to denote the crystalline cones in the eye of an insect (see *Compound Eye*).

VIVIPAROUS INSECTS. Some insects do not lay eggs but give birth to fully developed larvae. Since these come, however, from eggs that hatch out inside the body of the parent the term *ovoviviparous* is more strictly correct. The best known examples are some flesh flies, sheep keds, tsetse flies and the wingless parthenogenetic females of aphids.

V-MOTH. See *Itame.*

VOLUCELLA. *Volucella bombylans,* the Bumble-bee Hover-fly: a large two-winged insect of the family Syrphidae closely resembling a bumble bee in size, shape and colouring. This one species of Hover-fly exists in several colour-forms which more or less mimic several different species of *Bombus.* The resemblance is an advantage as the hover-fly lays its eggs in the nest of the bee and the developing larvae act as scavengers.

W

WAINSCOT MOTHS. A group of noctuid moths comprising several genera of the family Caradrinidae. Most of them are pale greyish brown with darker streaks. The larvae feed chiefly on grasses, reeds or rushes. *Leucania palleus,* the Common Wainscot; *Leucania impura,* the Smoky Wainscot; *Nonagria typhae,* the Bulrush Wainscot.

WALKING. When insects walk or run using their six legs the succession of movements is generally as follows:

(1) The fore- and hind-legs on the near side and the middle leg on the opposite side move forward together or nearly together while the insect is supported by a tripod formed from the other three.

(2) The fore- and hind-legs on the off side and the middle leg on the near side move forward while the first three give support. Since each leg is made up of several segments, flexure and straightening can take place at all the joints. This is carried out by means of muscles attached to ingrowths from the cuticle or exoskeleton. The tarsus, however, though divided into 2–5 tarsomeres, has only one set of muscles and therefore flexes passively, *e.g.* when gripping a stem or other support. Movement of the legs as a whole is highly efficient and, except in the case of caterpillars or other soft-bodied larvae, locomotion does not involve flexure of the body.

WALKING STICK. A colloquial name sometimes used for any of the stick insects (see *Phasmida* and *Dixippus*).

WALL BUTTERFLY (WALL BROWN). *Pararge megaera* or *Lasiommata megaera,* a common satyrid butterfly found all over Europe, North Africa and the Middle East; light golden-brown with darker borders and wing-bases, with a conspicuous small white-centred eye-spot on each fore-wing and two or three smaller rings on each hind-wing. The larvae feed on grasses.

WALL MASON WASP. *Odynerus parietum* or *Ancistrocerus parietum*, a small solitary wasp with the abdomen broadly banded with black and yellow. It makes hard cells of clay or sand stuck together with saliva and attached to cracks in walls etc. An egg is laid in each cell and before sealing it up a few small paralysed caterpillars are deposited inside as food for the developing larvae.

WARBLE FLY. See *Oestridae*.

WARNING COLORATION. Bright colours or markings on animals which are poisonous or otherwise dangerous, *e.g.* on many insects and snakes, giving them the advantage of being recognized and avoided by predators. The black and yellow stripes of the wasp are a well known example.

WART BITER. *Decticus verrucivorus*, a handsome, stoutly built, long-horned grasshopper mottled with green and brown, about 4 cm. long, having short elytra, a long abdomen and very long hind-legs. The female has a long curved ovipositor. It is found on grassy hillsides where the males can often be heard stridulating. The name 'wart biter' refers to the fact that this insect will nibble the skin of a hand, and can give a painful bite.

WASP. A name given to a large number of winged insects of the order Hymenoptera having a slender body with a narrowly constricted waist and an ovipositor modified to form a sting. They differ from bees in the fact that they do not store honey and pollen and do not secrete wax. Their mouth-parts can be used for biting or sucking and they are omnivorous. They may be social or solitary. Social wasps construct their nests in the form of a sphere of cells made from chewed wood-pulp resembling paper. Others live in holes in the ground or in trees etc. According to their habits they are classified as Digger Wasps, Hunting wasps, Mason Wasps, Sand Wasps, Spider-hunting Wasps etc. Most of them exhibit warning coloration; many have yellow and black stripes; some are black or bluish with an orange-red band round the abdomen.

WASP BEETLE. *Clytus arietis*, a small, elongated longhorn beetle of the family Cerambycidae having the body and elytra brightly marked with transverse stripes of black and yellow. This perhaps gives it some degree of protection if predators mistake it for a wasp. The adult is to be seen running actively on flowers and trees. The larvae live in rotting wood on which they feed.

WASP FAN BEETLE. *Metocecus paradoxus*, a beetle of the family Rhipiphoridae having fan-shaped antennae. The wing-covers of the female are black; those of the male are yellow and brown. The larvae develop in wasps' nests (see *Rhipiphoridae*).

WATER BEETLES. Several families of beetles lead an aquatic existence, either wholly submerged or swimming on or just below the surface. In all these the hind-legs, and sometimes the middle pair also, are flattened and fringed enabling the insect to perform a rowing movement. Some of these beetles spend all their lives in water; others fly occasionally, usually at night. When submerged they take down a supply of air either as a bubble under the wing-cases or trapped as a film by the hydrofuge hairs under the body (see *Plastron*). The larvae of water beetles are generally wholly aquatic.

The principal families of water beetles are: Carnivorous Beetles (Dytiscidae), Whirligig Beetles (Gyrinidae), and Scavengers which are chiefly vegetarian (Hydrophilidae).

WATER BETONY SHARK MOTH. *Cucullia scrophulariae* (see *Monk Moths*).

WATER BOATMAN. A name applied to several aquatic bugs that use their

337

flattened or fringed hind-legs for swimming. The true water boatman is the back-swimmer *Notonecta*, a vigorous predator that feeds on tadpoles, beetle larvae, small fish etc. Bugs of the family Corixidae, which are smaller and do not swim upside down, are sometimes known as Lesser Water Boatmen (see *Notonectidae* and *Corixidae*).

WATER BUG. A name for a large number of aquatic Hemiptera of the sub-order Heteroptera. Some swim under water; some on the surface. Some are carnivorous; some herbivorous. The principal groups include the Water Boatmen (Notonectidae and Corixidae), Water Scorpions (Nepidae), Saucer Bugs (Naucoridae), Pondskaters (Gerridae and Hydrometridae) etc.

WATER CRICKET. See *Veliidae*.

WATER ERMINE MOTH. *Spilosoma urticae*, a whitish moth of the family Arctiidae having small black spots on the wings and a golden yellow abdomen with black dots along the centre; the female has a white tail. It is found near marshes and fens where the hairy caterpillars feed on docks (*Rumex*).

WATER GNAT. *Hydrometra stagnorum* and similar species of water bugs that have long legs and walk on the surface of ponds and streams (see *Hydrometridae*).

WATER MOTH. A name sometimes loosely and colloquially used for a caddis fly (see *Trichoptera*).

WATER MEASURER. See *Hydrometridae*.

WATER RINGLET BUTTERFLY. *Erebia pronoe*, a satyrid butterfly from damp mountain slopes of Central Europe, similar to other ringlet butterflies but differing in having the undersides of the hind-wings dotted with silvery grey scales (see *Ringlet Butterflies*).

WATER SCAVENGER BEETLES. See *Hydrophilidae*.

WATER SCORPION. See *Nepidae*.

WATER SKATER. See *Pondskater*.

WATER SPRINGTAIL. See *Podura*.

WATER STICK INSECT. *Ranatra linearis*, a long, thin, predatory water bug; a form of water scorpion (see *Nepidae*).

WATER STRIDER. Another name for the pondskater (see *Gerridae*).

WATER TIGER. A colloquial name sometimes used for the fiercely carnivorous larvae of Dytiscid water beetles (see *Dytiscidae*).

WATER WEEVIL. *Lissorhapterus simplex*, a species of weevil whose aquatic larvae feed on the submerged roots of rice and other water plants. The adults feed on the leaves.

WAVE MOTHS. A name for a number of geometrid moths having grey or greenish wavy lines across the wings. *Deilinia exanthemata*, the Common Wave; *Deilinia pusaria*, the White Wave; *Sterrha aversata*, the Riband Wave etc.

WAVED UMBER. *Hemerophila abruptaria* or *Menophra abruptaria*, a geometrid moth of a light brown colour with a broad, wavy, dark brown band across each wing so that when resting on old tree trunks or fences they are well camouflaged. The caterpillars are stick-like and feed chiefly on lilac and privet (see *Umber Moths*).

WAX. Most insects secrete a mixture of wavy substances which pass out in small quantities through pore-canals in the epidermis and impregnate the epicuticle making it waterproof. In addition to this some insects secrete larger amounts of wax for special purposes. The best known of these is beeswax which is produced by glands under the abdomen. Others include China Wax from the scale-insect *Ericerus* and 'wool' from the Woolly Aphis. The function of the last two appears to be primarily to protect the insect.

Chemically these waxes consist of a mixture of various proportions of paraffins, fatty acids, alcohols of high molecular weight and esters.

WAX GLANDS. See *Wax*.

WAX INSECT. A name for a number of plant-bugs of the family Coccidae that secrete a wax-like substance. *Ericerus pe-la*, the Chinese Wax Scale-insect is bred commercially for the making of candles. At one time 3,000 tons of wax were produced annually from this source (see *Coccidae*).

WAX MOTH. *Galleria mellonella*, a moth whose larvae are common pests in beehives where they feed on the wax (see *Galleriidae*).

WAX PICK. A spur or spine on the second leg of a honey-bee, used for removing wax and pollen from the ventral part of the body.

WAXWORM. The larva of *Galleria mellonella*, a pest of beehives (see *Wax Moth*).

WEBWORM. A general name for gregarious caterpillars living in nests of silk threads. One of the best known is the North American Fall Webworm *Hyphantria cunea* whose loosely spun silk web may entirely cover the branch of a tree.

WEAVER LONGHORN BEETLE. *Lamia textor*, a Central European longhorn beetle of the family Cerambycidae, dull black and about 25 mm. long; its larvae develop in the roots of willows and poplars and are said to weave together pieces of twigs or shoots to form a nest.

WEBBING CLOTHES MOTH. *Tineola bisselliella*, one of the commonest clothes moths: a small, grey-brown moth with fringed wings and long antennae. The larvae feed on wool, fur etc. and pupate in silken cocoons (see *Tineidae*).

WEEPING LONGHORN BEETLE. *Morimus funereus*, a large beetle of the family Cerambycidae, nearly 4 cm. long, dull grey with two irregular black spots on each elytron and with antennae longer than the body. Its larvae live and develop in old stumps of beech.

WEEVILS. Curculionidae, a large family of beetles characterized by having a long snout or rostrum which is used for boring into seeds, wood etc. Many of them are major pests of grain and other stored foods (see *Curculionidae, Rhynchophora, Grain Weevil* and *Rice Weevil*).

WEISMANN'S RING. A gland surrounding the main dorsal blood-vessel just above the cerebral ganglia in insects such as the house fly and the blowfly. It is believed to secrete a hormone which induces the formation of the puparium.

WESTERN SWALLOWTAIL. *Papilio daunus*, one of the largest North American butterflies with a wing-span of about 12 cm. and having two 'tails' on each hind-wing. It is to be found chiefly in the Rocky Mountains.

WHAME FLY. A local British name occasionally used for blood-sucking horse-flies and clegs (see *Tabanidae*).

WHEAT BULB FLY. *Hylemyia coarctata* or *Leptohylemyia coarctata*, a small black fly of the family Anthomyidae, a major agricultural pest. In appearance it is similar to a house fly but a little smaller. It lays its eggs in the soil and the ensuing maggots burrow into the centres of new shoots of wheat, barley, rye etc.

WHEAT JOINTWORM. The larvae of the chalcid wasp *Harmolita tritici* which burrows into the stems of wheat and is an agricultural pest in North America.

WHEAT MIDGE. A name for a number of gall-midges of the family Cecido-myidae whose larvae attack young wheat shoots. One of these, *Sitodiplosis mosellana*, is a destructive pest in Europe and North America.

WHEAT SAWFLY. Any of a large number of sawflies that lay their eggs in young wheat stems; genera include *Cephus, Dolerus, Pachynematus* etc.

WHEAT-STEM BORER. See *Wheat Sawfly*.

WHEAT-STEM SAWFLY. See *Wheat Sawfly*.

WHEEL BUG. *Arilus cristatus*, a large American Assassin Bug (see *Arilus*).

WHIRLIGIG BEETLE. See *Gyrinidae*.

WHITE ADMIRAL. *Limenitis camilla*, a handsome nymphalid butterfly found throughout Europe and Asia as far as Japan but rather rare in Britain. The wings are brown with a broad white band across each. The larvae feed on honeysuckle (*Lonicera*).

WHITE ANT. A name commonly but incorrectly used for termites (see *Isoptera* and *Termes*).

WHITE-BANDED GRAYLING. *Pseudochasara anthelea*, a satyrid butterfly from the Balkans and Middle East, similar in general appearance to the other graylings but with broad white bands across the wings.

WHITE-BELTED HOVER-FLY. *Volucella pellucens*, a two-winged fly of the family Syrphidae resembling a large bee in shape and size. The colouring is black with a white band across the front of the abdomen. It lays its eggs in the nests of wasps, the larvae scavenging and sharing the food of their host.

WHITE BUTTERFLIES. See Pieridae.

WHITE ERMINE MOTH. See *Ermine Moth*.

WHITE-FACED BURROWING BEE. *Andrena albicans*, a species of mining bee about 1 cm. long, black or brown with yellowish hairs on the thorax and abdomen and on the head of the male; the female has white hairs on the face. She lays her eggs in cells in the ground, a ball of honey and pollen being placed in each as food for the developing larvae.

WHITEFLY. A name for a number of small homopterous plant-lice of the family Aleurodidae having the body covered with fine white, powdery wax. Like the aphids which are closely related to them, they suck the juice from leaves, young shoots and fruit and smother the surface with a sticky secretion of honeydew. The best known are the Cabbage Whitefly *Aleurodes proletella* and the Greenhouse Whitefly *Trialeurodes vaporariorum*. The latter, which has spread all over the world from Central America, attacks tomatoes, cucumbers and other greenhouse plants. It can to a large extent by controlled by the introduction of an appropriate chalcid wasp (*Encarsia*).

WHITE-FRINGED WEEVIL. *Graphognathus leucoloma*, originally from Argentina, now a major pest on a wide range of plants in Australia (see also *Naupactis* and *Pantomorus*).

WHITE-LEGGED DAMSELFLY. *Platycnemis pennipes*, a common European damselfly with a thin body about 4 cm. long. The male is predominantly greenish-blue and black; the female more yellowish green. The legs of both sexes are pure white, and the male has the tibiae of the middle and hind-legs enlarged.

WHITE LETTER HAIRSTREAK. *Thecla W-album* or *Strymonidia W-album* (see *Strymonidia*).

WHITE L-BUTTERFLY. *Polygonia L-album*, a nymphalid butterfly very similar to the Comma Butterfly but slightly larger and having on the underside of each hind-wing a small white L-shaped line instead of the comma (see *Polygonia*).

WHITE-LINED GRASSHOPPER. *Stenobothrus lineatus* also called the Stripe-winged Grasshopper, a small, short-horned species about 2 cm. long with a green head and thorax, a brownish abdomen and elytra with a white longitudinal stripe and a white spot near the tip of each.

WHITE-LINED SPHINX MOTH. *Deilephila lineata*, a common hawk-moth of North and South America having a wing-span of about 10 cm., brownish with a wide reddish band across each wing and with the veins of the fore-wings lined with white. The larvae feed on vines, Virginia creeper etc.

WHITE-MARKED TUSSOCK MOTH. *Hemerocampa leucostigma*, a widespread North American moth of the family Lymantriidae whose handsome caterpillar is black and yellow striped with a red head and with four tussocks of dense white hairs and three pencils of long black hairs.

WHITE MOUNTAIN BUTTERFLY. See *Oeneis*.

WHITE PINE WEEVIL. *Pissodes strobi* and related species: small reddish brown, long-snouted weevils whose larvae burrow beneath the bark of pine trees destroying the cambium.

WHITE SATIN MOTH. *Stilpnotia salicis* or *Leucoma salicis*, a smooth, all white, European moth of the family Lymantriidae with a wing-span of about 5 cm. The caterpillars are brightly coloured with black, red, yellow and white marks. They feed on poplar and willow and sometimes occur in such large numbers that they may completely defoliate a tree.

WHITE-SHOULDERED HOUSE MOTH. *Endrosis sarcitrella*, a small nightflying moth, one of the Microlepidoptera, having a mottled wing-pattern of grey and brown with the front of the thorax white. The larvae are scavengers, feeding on vegetable refuse in birds' nests, farm buildings, mouse-holes etc.

WHITE SPECK RINGLET BUTTERFLY. *Erebia claudina*, a satyrid butterfly from the high Alps, resembling the other ringlet butterflies in general appearance but the male has six white dots on the underside of the hind-wing near the margin (see *Ringlet Butterflies*).

WHITE-SPOTTED MOLE BEETLE. *Anthribus albinus* or *Platystomus albinus*, a Central European member of the family of Broad Weevils (Anthribidae): a flattened, dark brown and white insect with long antennae and a short broad snout. Its larvae develop under the bark of dead or dying trees.

WHITE-SPOTTED SAWYER. See *Monochamus*.

WHITE-STOCKINGED BLACK FLY. *Simulium venustum*, a common simuliid or buffalo-gnat of North America; a blood-sucking insect distinguished by its white-banded legs. It transmits protozoan parasites of poultry (see *Simuliidae*).

WHITE-TAILED DRONE-FLY. *Eristalis intricaria*, a hover-fly of the family Syrphidae resembling a small blackish-brown bee with a white-tipped abdomen. The aquatic larva is a 'rat-tailed' maggot, *i.e.* it breathes with a very long, telescopic tail-siphon by means of which it can reach the surface of the pond (see *Drone-fly* and *Rat-tailed Maggot*).

WHITE WAVE MOTH. *Deilinia pusaria*, a geometrid moth of the subfamily Ennominae, white with a faint grey, wavy line across each wing. The larvae are green and stick-like; they feed on alder, birch and sallow and pupate in silken cocoons.

WILLOW BEAUTY. *Cleora rhomboidaria*, a geometrid moth of the subfamily Ennominae varying in colour but generally greyish brown with a pattern of darker, wavy, transverse lines. The males have wide comb-like antennae. The brown, stick-like larvae feed on privet, lilac, ivy, birch and many other trees and shrubs.

WILLOW FLY. *Nemoura cinerea*, a small, mottled brown stonefly (Plecoptera) common near ponds and streams on chalk downland.

WILLOW GALL. A number of different insects produce galls on willow leaves and shoots. The best known are the terminal rosette-galls produced by the midge *Rhabdophaga rosaria* and the red bean-shaped galls produced on the leaves by the sawfly *Pontania proxima* (see *Bean-gall Sawfly* and *Rosette-galls*).

WILLOW HERB HAWK-MOTH. See *Proserpinus*.

WILLOW LEAF BEETLES. A name for several small beetles of the family Chrysomelidae of which the adults and larvae feed on willow leaves. *Galerucella lineola* is pale yellowish brown and about 5 mm. long; *Phyllodecta vulgatissima*, slightly smaller, is a shiny metallic blue; *Phyllodecta vitellinae* is a shiny bronze colour.

WILLOW AND POPLAR SCALE. *Chionaspis salicis*, a scale insect of the family Coccidae whose cast-off skins have the appearance of tiny, white, mussel-shell shaped scales on the bark of willows and poplars (see *Coccidae*).

WILLOW SAWFLY. A name used for many species of sawflies that attack willow leaves.

WILLOW WOOD MIDGE. *Helicomyia saliciperda*, a tiny reddish-brown gall-midge of the family Cecidomyidae whose minute larvae bore into leaves and stems of willow. Since the eggs are often laid in a chain formation, a number of larvae living together may make long pupating chambers beneath the bark.

WILLOW WOODWASPS. Members of the family Xiphydriidae, especially *Xiphydria prolongata*: symphytous Hymenoptera similar in general appearance to the better known Giant Woodwasp *Urocerus gigas* but much smaller and with a shorter ovipositor. They attack deciduous trees such as willow and alder but never conifers. Eggs are laid under the bark and the larvae tunnel inwards for a short distance.

WINDOWED BEE-FLY. *Thyridanthrax fenestralis*, a hairy, two-winged fly of the family Bombylidae resembling a small bee with a long pointed proboscis held stiffly in front. The body is black with yellowish-brown hairs; the wings are densely black except for a clear point near the tip and clear spots or 'windows' in the black area. The larva is a parasite in the larvae of other insects.

WINDOW FLY. (1) *Scenopinus fenestralis* and related species: small black, two-winged flies that are not very active and often rest on windows of outhouses or other buildings. The larvae live among rubbish or refuse and prey upon the larvae of clothes moths or other insects.

(2) *Anisopus fenestralis*, a small, fragile midge with rather broad, mottled wings. The larvae live in damp places.

WINGS. Most insects have two pairs of wings, one pair on the mesothorax and the other on the metathorax. In Diptera only the former are functional for flying, the latter being reduced to small balancers or *halteres*. Wings are formed from enlarged folds of epidermis and cuticle which grow out from the thorax. When complete the upper and lower surfaces of a wing are fused together except along the lines of the veins which may contain tracheae and blood-vessels. A wing may be membranous and transparent, as in bees, wasps, flies etc. or it may be thickened and hardened to form an elytron or tegmen, as in the case of the fore-wings of beetles, grasshoppers, cockroaches etc. The surface of a wing may be completely smooth, as in dragonflies, or covered with fine hairs as in caddis flies. The hairs may be modified to form scales. In mosquitoes these scales are only located along the lines of the veins. In butterflies and moths the whole wing is densely covered with scales of various shapes, sizes and colours which give the distinctive wing-pattern of each species (see also *Flight, Frequency of Wing-beat, Wing-veins* and *Venation*).

WING-BEAT. See *Frequency of Wing-beat*.

WING-BUD. A small fold of epidermis growing out from the thorax of a nymph or of a pupa, eventually to become the wing of the adult insect.

WING-CASE (WING-COVER). See *Elytron* and *Tegmen*.

WINGLESS INSECTS. See *Flightless Insects*.

WING-PAD. See *Wing-bud*.

WING-SCALES. See *Scales*.

WING-VEINS. Narrow sclerotized tubes between the upper and lower epidermis of an insect's wing. Circulation of the blood or haemolymph takes place along these and in many cases also they mark the positions of tracheal tubes. In most insects some of the veins are situated in furrows (*concave veins*) or on ridges (*convex veins*), which thereby stiffen the membrane like a fan of pleated paper. Primitive insects such as mayflies and dragonflies usually have a complex network of veins. In more specialized insects the number is usually reduced and each species is characterized by a definite number and arrangement (see *Venation*).

WINTER GNAT. A name for a number of non-bloodsucking insects resembling small crane-flies that 'dance' in large numbers on warm winter days. The best-known genus is *Trichocera* (*q.v.*).

WINTER MOTH. *Operophtera brumata* or *Cheimatobia brumata*, a well known pest of fruit and other trees: a member of the family Geometridae, with flightless females which crawl up the trunks of the trees. Grease-banding is used against these and other flightless moths (see *Operophtera*).

WIREWORMS. The larvae of Click Beetles (Elateridae): yellowish, worm-like, short-legged larvae that live in the ground for several years feeding on roots, tubers and especially young seedlings planted in rows. They are a cause of considerable loss to agricultural crops. (See also *Click Beetle*.)

WITCH HAZEL CONE-GALL. See *Hormaphis*.

WITCH HAZEL LEAF-ROLLER. *Episimus argutanus*, a tortricid moth

343

whose larvae make cone-like nests by rolling the leaves of the American Witch Hazel *Hamamelis virginea.*

WOHLFAHRTIA. A two-winged fly whose maggots were formerly used by physicians for cleaning up decayed tissue and bacteria in wounds.

WOOD ANT. A name for many woodland species of ants, particularly of the genus *Formica. Formica rufa,* the European Wood Ant, is dark brown with a reddish brown thorax and legs. The workers are about 6 mm. long; the males and females about 9 mm. They are widely distributed and live in very large dome-shaped nests made of pine needles or other vegetable matter. Many thousands may live in one nest (see *Ant* and *Formica*).

WOOD-BORERS. Wood-boring is carried out by many insects either to obtain food or as a means of protecting the eggs and the developing larvae and pupae. The habit is developed most conspicuously in Coleoptera, some Hymenoptera and the larvae of some Lepidoptera. The boring action may be performed by the jaws (as in beetles, weevils, larvae of moths etc.) or by the ovipositor (as in sawflies, woodwasps etc.). Very few insects possess the enzyme *cellulase* which is necessary to digest the cellulose of the cell-walls; the furniture beetle *Anobium* and some longhorns have it. Termites and many other wood-boring insects have an intestinal flora or fauna to do this for them. Others can eat only the sugars and other cell-contents after breaking down the cell-walls by mastication. (See also *Bark Beetles, Death Watch Beetle, Weevil, Cossidae, Siricidae* and *Wood-eaters.*)

WOOD-BORING COCKROACH. See *Cryptocercus.*

WOOD-BORING WASP. A name for several species of the genus *Trypoxylon*: slender solitary wasps that make their nests in the stems of shrubs and stock them with spiders as food for the developing larvae.

WOOD CARPET MOTH. *Epirrhoe rivata,* a small geometrid moth of the subfamily Larentiinae having wings banded with light and dark brown. The larvae are stick-like and feed on plants of the family Rubiaceae.

WOOD CRICKET. *Nemobius sylvestris*: the smallest British cricket about 1 cm. long, brown, with short flap-like elytra and no hind-wings. It lives among dead leaves. In Britain it is found only in the extreme south, particularly in the New Forest.

WOOD DOR BEETLE. *Geotrupes sylvaticus* (= *stercorosus*), a blue-black shiny dung-beetle with a rounded body similar to that of the common Dor Beetles but much smaller. It lives in dung of catttle, horses or other animals in wooded districts.

WOOD-EATERS. Wood consists chiefly of the two substances *cellulose* and *lignin.* Although some insects can apparently digest cellulose, only a few can digest lignin by direct enzyme action. The breaking down of both these substances can, however, be performed by the action of certain specific bacteria, fungi and protozoa which are normally present in the soil. Many insects feed on damp wood that is already decaying; these are in fact feeding largely on fungi. Insects such as termites and wood-boring beetles that feed on fresh wood often have a dilated hind-gut containing a vast assortment of micro-organisms that live and breed there in a state of symbiosis and provide the necessary enzymes to break down the wood. Without these the insects, in most cases, would find it impossible to survive.

WOODLAND BROWN BUTTERFLY. *Lopinga achine,* a brown satyrid butterfly found in shady woods all over Central and Northern Europe and

Asia as far as Japan; characterized by four or five large, yellow-ringed eye-spots on both sides of the fore- and hind-wings. The larvae feed on various grasses.

WOODLAND GRASSHOPPER. *Omocestus rufipes*, a European short-horned grasshopper about 15 mm. long, of a greenish brown colour with orange-red on the underside of the abdomen and on the legs.

WOODLAND GRAYLING. *Hipparchia fagi*, a European satyrid butterfly of a smoky brown colour with a broad, whitish band along each wing; having a large and a small ring-spot on each fore-wing and a small one on each hind-wing. It is found chiefly in beech woods; the larvae feed on grasses.

WOODLAND GROUND BEETLE. *Carabus sylvestris*, a common carnivorous beetle of the family Carabidae; stoutly built, about 3 cm. long, black with a purplish or greenish sheen. The wing-cases are punctured with three rows of tiny holes.

WOOD LEOPARD MOTH. See *Leopard Moth*.

WOOD NYMPH. A name for a number of satyrid butterflies of North America, generally dark brown with one or two white-centred black eye-spots on each fore-wing. *Satyrus alope* is the largest species (see *Satyridae*).

WOOD-RAT FLEA. *Histricopsylla gigas*, the largest known flea, about 5 mm. long, found in the nests of the North American Wood-rat *Neotoma floridana*. It has the distinction of holding the world's record for flea-jumping: 32 cm. along and 17 cm. high.

WOOD SATYR. See *Wood Nymph*.

WOOD TIGER BEETLE. *Cicindela sylvatica*, a carnivorous beetle about 18 mm. long having dark brown, elongated elytra each marked with three curved lines of pale yellow. It lives chiefly on sandy heaths (see *Tiger Beetles*).

WOOD TIGER MOTH. See *Parasemia*.

WOODWASP. See *Siricidae*.

WOOD WHITE. *Leptidea sinapis*, a greenish white pierid butterfly smaller than the Cabbage Butterfly and without the black spots which characterize the latter. It is found in woodlands all over Europe where the larvae feed on leguminous plants.

WOOL CARDER BEE. *Anthidium manicatum*, a fairly large, brown striped bee of the family Megachilidae, named from its habit of stripping the woolly coating off some plants and using it to line its nest.

WOOLLY APHID. *Eriosoma lanigerum*, a small plant-louse, originally a native of America but now a world-wide pest of apple trees. Like other aphids it reproduces parthenogenetically in large numbers and sucks the juice of the tree, particularly on the trunk and branches, causing scabs and gnarled excrescences. Unlike most aphids, instead of secreting honeydew it exudes a white waxy substance forming a mass of woolly threads under which large numbers of the insects are protected.

WOOLLY BEAR. A densely hairy brown caterpillar, the larva of any moth of the family Arctiidae, particularly those of the Tiger Moths.

WORKERS. Among social insects such as bees, ants, wasps and termites, the workers are sterile individuals which build the nest, fetch and store food and feed the other members of the colony; they far outnumber all the other castes. In the case of bees the workers develop from fertilized eggs, the larvae being given a diet of nectar and pollen only. If given a more complete diet of 'royal jelly' which has been partly predigested and concentrated, the same larvae may become queen bees. Worker Hymenoptera are always sterile females but worker (and soldier) termites are sexually immature individuals of either sex (see *Castes*).

WYEOMYIA. A genus of mosquitoes whose larvae live in the liquid contained in pitcher plants in Central and South America.

X

XANTHOPHYLL. The yellow pigment of leaves which is sometimes absorbed by insects; it is present, for instance, in the skins of caterpillars such as those of the Cabbage White Butterfly and in the cocoons of silkworms.

XANTHOPTERIN. A yellow pigment derived from *pteridine*, found in the bodies of wasps and in the wings of certain butterflies (see *Pterin Pigments*).

XANTHORHOE. See *Silver-ground Carpet Moth* and *Twin-spot Carpet Moth*.

XENOPSYLLA. *Xenopsylla cheopis*, the Indian Rat-flea that transmits bubonic plague.

XENOS. A genus of Strepsiptera whose larvae and wingless females are parasitic in wasps and cause *stylopization* (*e.g. Xenos vesparum*). See *Strepsiptera*.

XESTOBIUM. *Xestobium rufovillosum*, the Death-watch Beetle, a brown wood-boring beetle about 6 mm. long belonging to the family Anobiidae: a notoriously destructive pest of old buildings (see *Death-watch Beetle*).

XIPHYDRIIDAE. Alder and willow woodwasps: a family of Hymenoptera allied to the larger woodwasps (Siricidae). In the British species the head and thorax are black, flecked with white and there is a distinct neck; the abdomen is black with the middle segments red. Eggs are laid in slits in the bark and the larvae tunnel into the wood.

XIXUTHRUS. *Xixuthrus heyrovskyi*, a large brown longhorn beetle from the Fiji Islands; one of the world's largest species about 13 cm. long. It is probably now extinct owing to the fact that the long, fat larvae are edible and were considered a great delicacy by the natives.

XORIDES. *Xorides filiformis*, a European and Asiatic ichneumon fly about 18 mm. long, black with a red abdomen and with white-banded antennae. It lays its eggs in the bodies of Capricorn Beetle larvae (*Pyrrhidium*).

XYELIDAE. A primitive family of woodwasps usually less than 5 mm. long whose short-legged maggot-like larvae develop in young male pine-cones; the adults feed on pollen from catkins of birch and other trees.

XYLENA. See *Sword-grass Moth*.

XYLEUTES. *Xyleutes boisduvali*, the Giant Australian Goat Moth: a member of the family Cossidae, light grey with a heavy body and a wing-span of over

25 cm. The larvae bore into tree trunks where they may spend a year or more developing.

XYLOBORUS. A genus of Ambrosia Beetles, pinhole borers of the family Scolytidae that tunnel into wood and take in fungi which they cultivate on a prepared bed of excreta and wood-dust to provide food for the developing larvae (see *Scolytidae* and *Ipinae*).

XYLOCAMPA. A genus of noctuid moths including the Early Grey (*Xylocampa areola*), a small moth with an elaborate wing-pattern of smoky grey and dark brown. The moth is common in woodlands where it rests by day on tree trunks etc. and is well camouflaged. The larvae feed on honeysuckle (*Lonicera*).

XYLOCOPIDAE. Carpenter-bees: large bees, usually dark violet or black in colour, which burrow into timber. They are widely distributed in all parts of the world but are not native to Britain. *Xylocopa violacea*, the Blue Carpenter Bee, is a native of Central and Southern Europe. It is about 25 mm. long, glossy black with dark brown, opaque wings. It makes its nest in old timber.

XYLODREPA. A genus of carrion beetles of the family Silphidae. *Xylodrepa quadripunctata*, the Four-spot Carrion Beetle, is an oval-shaped beetle about 12 mm. long with light greyish yellow elytra having two black spots on each. It lives in deciduous woods and hunts caterpillars.

XYLOPHAGA. A general name for any wood-eating insects.

XYLOPHAGUS. A genus of flies (Diptera), with larvae living in decaying wood.

XYLOTA. A genus of hover-flies (Syrphidae) whose short-tailed larvae live in moist decaying wood. *Xylota segnis* is a common European species about 15 mm. long, black with a reddish banded abdomen.

XYLOTHRECHUS. *Xylothrechus aceris*, the Gall-making Maple Borer: a North American longhorn beetle of the family Cerambycidae. Since beetles of this family are primarily wood-borers, this species is exceptional in making galls.

Y

YELLOW ANT. A name given to several species of ants but particularly to *Acanthomyops flava*, a small European species with light brown body and yellow legs. It is common in fields and meadows where nests are made in the form of elongated mounds always directed east and west. As the ants increase in number they extend the nest in an easterly direction, always occupying the new end which is drier.

YELLOW-BANDED RINGLET BUTTERFLY. *Erebia flavofasciata*, a satyrid butterfly from the rocky slopes of the high Alps; reddish brown with a wide, curved, pale yellow band on the underside of each hind-wing. The larvae feed on coarse grasses (see *Satyridae*).

YELLOW-BANDED SKIPPER. *Pyrgus sidae*: a small butterfly of the family Hesperiidae, smoky brown with a pattern of spots in white or cream; the underside of the hind-wing has two broad, irregular bands of yellow bordered with thin brown crenated lines. It is found in Central and Eastern Europe and Asia Minor; the larvae feed on mallow.

YELLOW BUTTERFLIES. A group of butterflies of the family Pieridae whose wings contain yellow *pterin* pigments derived from uric acid. The Brimstone Butterfly *Gonepteryx rhamni* and the Clouded Yellow *Colias croceus* are the best known.

YELLOW DUNG-FLY. See *Dung-fly*.

YELLOW EMPEROR MOTH. See *Imperial Moth*.

YELLOW FEVER MOSQUITO. *Aedes aegypti*, a tropical culicine, mosquito the chief carrier of the yellow fever virus in Central Africa and Central America. It is also, however, widely spread in areas where yellow fever does not yet occur. A few other species of *Aedes* can carry the disease if conditions are right.

YELLOW-HORNED MOTH. *Polyploca flavicornis* or *Achyla flavicornis*, one of the Lutestring Moths (Polyplocidae): a greenish grey moth with three pairs of black wavy lines across the fore-wings. The thorax and abdomen are fat, light grey and very hairy. The legs are short with leaf-like appendages on the first pair and spurs on the hind pair. The larvae feed on birch (see *Polyplocidae*).

YELLOW JACKET. A colloquial name sometimes used for any of the yellow and black wasps.

YELLOW-LEGGED CLEARWING. *Sesia vespiformis*, a clearwing moth of the family Sesiidae resembling a wasp about 25 mm. long. The thorax is black with a yellow stripe on each side; the abdomen is banded with black and yellow, the male having a black tuft of hair at the hind-end and the female a yellow tuft; the legs are also yellow and black.

YELLOW-LEGGED CONOPS. *Conops flavipes*, a thick-headed fly of the family Conopidae about 1 cm. long, black with yellowish legs and with three thin yellow bands on the abdomen. The insect resembles a hover-fly but is less active. Its larvae are parasites in bees.

YELLOW-LEGGED PHILONTHUS. *Philonthus flavipes*, a small, predatory rove beetle of the family Staphylinidae about 6 mm. long, black with short, bright red elytra and reddish yellow legs. It is usually found under stones near streams.

YELLOW-LEGGED TORTOISESHELL. *Nymphalis xanthomelas*, an Eastern European and Asiatic butterfly very similar to the Large Tortoiseshell but having the middle and hind-legs yellowish brown instead of black. The larvae feed on willows.

YELLOW MEADOW ANT. *Lasius flavus*, one of the commonest European ants about 4 mm. long, light yellowish brown with paler yellow legs. It makes its nest in the form of grass-covered mounds and spends most of its life below ground. It 'farms' green aphids for the sake of the honeydew which they secrete.

YELLOW-NECKED TERMITE. *Calotermes flavicollis*, a southern European species of termite of which the 'soldiers' have greatly elongated heads nearly half the length of the body (see *Isoptera* and *Castes*).

YELLOW OPHION. *Ophion luteus*: a large ichneumon fly about 18–20 mm. long, a common European species which often flies into houses at dusk. It is pale orange-yellow with a long, very narrow waist and a flattened abdomen. The whole body is often bent roughly into an S-shape. The female differs from those of most ichneumons in not having a long ovipositor. The larvae are parasites in the caterpillars of noctuid moths.

YELLOW PLANT LOUSE. See *Paramyzus*.

YELLOW SHELL MOTH. *Euphyia bilineata*, a common carpet moth of the subfamily Larentiinae, yellowish grey with several irregular transverse lines of brown or black. It is common in hedgerows where the green larvae feed at night on grasses, dock, chickweed and other low plants.

YELLOW-TAIL MOTH. *Euproctis similis*, a common tussock moth of the family Lymantriidae, pure white except for the tip of the abdomen which is bright golden-yellow. The larva is brightly coloured red, white and black with numerous long, black, irritant hairs. It feeds on hawthorn leaves and pupates in a yellow silky cocoon.

YELLOW UNDERWING MOTH. A name for several noctuid moths all having the hind-wings bright yellow or orange with a black border. The Large Yellow Underwing, *Noctua pronuba* or *Triphaena pronuba*, has a wing-span of about 6 cm. The fore-wings are narrow and are marked with greyish brown and white; the hind-wings are orange with a very broad black border. The larvae are light grey-brown and feed on a variety of plants. Other species include the Lesser Yellow Underwing (*Euschesis comes*), Lunar Yellow Underwing (*Euschesis orbona*), Least Yellow Underwing (*Triphaena interjecta*), Broad-bordered Yellow Underwing (*Triphaena fimbria*), Lesser Broad-bordered Yellow Underwing (*Triphaena ianthina*) etc.

YEW GALL-GNAT. *Cecidomyia taxi*, a common gall-gnat whose larvae produce galls in the terminal buds of yew (*Taxus baccata*).

YPONOMEUTIDAE. Formerly spelled *Hyponomeutidae*. A family of Ermine Moths, generally white or greyish flecked with black. The caterpillars are hairy and live, a large number together, in dense silken webs which may cover entire branches of trees. Within these webs they feed and may completely strip a tree of its leaves. *Yponomeuta padella* attacks the Bird-cherry (*Prunus padus*); other species attack apple and other fruit trees.

YPSOLOPHA. A genus of moths of the superfamily Tinaeoidea which, although grouped with the Microlepidoptera, are larger than most. They have hook-tipped fore-wings, fringed hind-wings, spurred hind-legs, long thin antennae, long palps and reduced tongues. *Ypsolopha dentella* is a brown and yellow species whose larvae feed on honeysuckle (*Lonicera periclymenum*); *Ypsolopha lucella* is a larger, paler species whose larvae feed on the Spindle Tree (*Euonymus europaeus*).

YUCCA MOTH. *Tegeticula alba* or *Pronuba yuccasella*, a small white moth of North America upon which the Yucca plant is absolutely dependent for its pollination (see *Pronuba*).

Z

ZAPATER'S RINGLET BUTTERFLY. *Erebia zapateri*, a satyrid butterfly from the mountains of Spain; dark brown with a much paler, broad yellow band near the outer edge of each fore-wing, this band forming a background for two tiny black rings.

ZARHOPALUS. A genus of minute parasitic wasps of the family Encyrtidae that lay their eggs in the bodies of aphids.

ZEBRA CATERPILLAR. The yellow and black striped caterpillar of the North American noctuid moth *Ceramica picta*; a common garden pest in parts of the United States.

ZEBRA SWALLOWTAIL. *Papilio marcellus* or *Papilio ajax*, also called the Papaw Swallowtail: a handsome North American butterfly ranging from the Appalachians to the Rocky Mountains. It has a span of about 8 cm. and is characterized by broad vertical bands of dark brown and translucent white across both wings. There are several seasonal forms which were formerly thought to be different species. The summer form has very long tails on the hind-wings. The caterpillars feed on leaves of the Papaw tree *Carica papaya*.

ZELLER'S SKIPPER. *Borbo borbonica*, a small dark brown butterfly of the family Hesperiidae having pointed front-wings each with a row of translucent white spots. It is found near the sea coasts of Spain and North Africa.

ZENILLIA. *Zenillia vulgaris*, a very common black, hairy tachinid fly about 6 mm. long whose larvae are parasites in various caterpillars.

ZERYNTHIA. *Zerynthia polyxena*, a small papilionid butterfly from Southern Europe, the Mediterranean and the Middle East; light yellow with an elaborate black pattern on both wings and a row of triangular red marks along the edges of the hing-wings. The caterpillar is reddish yellow with tufts of bristles; it feeds exclusively on Birthwort (*Aristolochia clematitis*).

ZETOPHLOEUS. *Zetophloeus pugionatus*, a large beetle from Madagascar belonging to the family Brenthidae, known as Long Beetles. The whole insect is very long and narrow, the head and snout being larger than the rest of the body. It lives behind the bark of trees.

ZEUGLOPTERA. An alternative name for Micropterygidae (*q.v.*), minute primitive moths with biting mouth-parts. The name is used when they are regarded as not being true Lepidoptera.

ZEUZERA. See *Leopard Moth*.

ZICRONA. *Zicrona caerulea*, the Blue Bug: a small, shiny metallic blue shieldbug about 4 mm. long, commonly found on chalk or sandy soil.

ZOOTERMOPSIS. A genus of termites that live in damp wood in the forests of western Canada and the United States.

ZORAPTERA. A small group of insects apparently related to book-lice and sometimes placed in the order Psocoptera. They live in decaying wood or sometimes in termite colonies. They comprise both winged and wingless individuals but little is known of their life.

350

ZOROTYPUS. The principal genus of the small and little known order Zoraptera (*q.v.*).

ZÜNZLER. A name taken from the German and sometimes used as a general term .to denote various moths of the family Pyralidae, *e.g.* the Indian Meal Moth (*Plodia*), the Mediterranean Flour Moths (*Ephestia* and *Pyralis*) etc.

ZYGAENIDAE. Burnet Moths and Forester Moths, a family of brightly coloured, day-flying moths with long fore-wings, large bodies covered with short hairs, and long tongues. Burnet Moths are usually greenish black with red spots; Foresters have bright green fore-wings and white hind-wings. European species include the Six-spot Burnet (*Zygaena filipendulae*), the Bloodwort Burnet (*Zygaena laeta*) and the Green Forester (*Procris statices*). Larger species are to be found in the tropics, one of the most beautiful being the Indian *Erasmia sanguiflua* which has a wing-span of 10 cm. and is coloured blue and brown with a violet sheen and with white spots.

ZYGENTOMA. A suborder of Thysanura (bristle-tails) including the Silverfish (*Lepisma*) and the Firebrat (*Thermobia*) (see *Thysanura*).

ZYGOPTERA. Damselflies: a group of dragonflies with slender bodies and narrow-based wings which are held vertically above the abdomen when at rest. The hind-wings are not markedly different from the fore-wings, as they are in true Dragonflies (Anisoptera). The nymphs of damselflies have three elongated caudal gills at the hind-end of the abdomen. (See also *Odonata*).

CLASSIFICATION OF INSECTS

SINCE there are probably over a million species of insects and these are divided into several hundred families it is not surprising that the tables of classification given by various authors differ from one another in many respects. There are 29 Orders of insects or according to some authorities 32, depending upon whether certain groups are regarded as single Orders or are subdivided. The following is a list of the Orders generally recognized:

1. Protura.
2. Collembola.
3. Diplura.
4. Thysanura.
5. Ephemeroptera.
6. Odonata.
7. Dictyoptera.
8. Isoptera.
9. Zoraptera.
10. Plecoptera.
11. Notoptera (Grylloblattodea).
12. Cheleutoptera (Phasmida).
13. Orthoptera.
14. Embioptera.
15. Dermaptera.
16. Psocoptera.
17. Mallophaga.
18. Anoplura.
19. Thysanoptera.
20. Hemiptera (Rhynchota).
21. Coleoptera.
22. Neuroptera.
23. Mecoptera.
24. Trichoptera.
25. Lepidoptera.
26. Diptera.
27. Siphonaptera (Aphaniptera).
28. Strepsiptera.
29. Hymenoptera.

These Orders may be grouped together into subclasses, divisions, superorders or other categories in a number of different ways depending upon what features are considered to be of most significance. The characteristics that are generally taken into account are:

(a) Degree of metamorphosis including presence or absence of a pupal stage.
(b) Mode of development of wings.
(c) Structure of wings and arrangement of veins.
(d) Feeding habits and structure of mouth-parts.
(e) Comparison of the biology of present-day Orders with what can be deduced about that of extinct groups.

The first four Orders in our list are primitive wingless insects that undergo no metamorphosis. They are known as *Apterygota* or *Ametabola*. All the other Orders show some degree of metamorphosis and are therefore called *Metabola*. Since these either have wings or have lost them during the course of evolution they may also be called *Pterygota*. Orders 5–20 in our list show partial metamorphosis but have no pupal stage and are known as *Hemimetabola*. In some systems the name Hemimetabola is restricted to Mayflies and Dragonflies and the rest are called *Heterometabola*. Orders 21–29 undergo complete metamorphosis and pass through a pupal stage. These are known as *Holometabola*.

When we consider the mode of development of the wings we find that the Hemimetabola acquire wing-buds which are visible externally at an early stage and grow larger with each successive instar. These are therefore called *Exopterygota*. On the other hand the Holometabola show no external signs of wings until they pupate. This is because wing-buds have been developing internally in

352

pockets and only become visible when they are extruded at the time of pupation. These insects are therefore called *Endopterygota*.

An alternative system of naming the principal groups, while taking into account a number of features, emphasizes particularly the structure and venation of the wings. According to this system Ephemeroptera (mayflies) and Odonata (dragonflies) are known as *Palaeoptera* because their wing-structure is most like that of the earliest known insects. Their wings cannot be folded and their venation consists merely of a simple unspecialized network. All other winged insects are known as *Neoptera* because their venation shows some degree of specialization and the wings can be folded when in repose. In Orders 7–15 of our list the wings contain numerous veins with some specialization and loss of cross-veins. This group is called *Polyneoptera*. Orders 16–20 are known as *Paraneoptera*. They are in many ways like the Polyneoptera but are of much more recent evolutionary origin. The remaining Orders (21–29), *i.e.* the Holometabola, all show considerable reduction in the number of veins and a very definite arrangement for each species. They include such insects as bees, butterflies, two-winged flies and beetles. All these are known as *Oligoneoptera*.

IT SHOULD BE EMPHASIZED that these systems are not mutually exclusive, as they are all based on a consideration of many different aspects of structure, development or evolution. A preference for stressing some features more than others will determine which nomenclature is used.

We may summarize the foregoing facts in the following four systems.

System A.
Ametabola.	Orders	1–4.
Hemimetabola.	,,	5–20.
Holometabola.	,,	21–29.

System B.
Ametabola.	Orders	1–4.
Hemimetabola.	,,	5–6.
Heterometabola.	,,	7–20.
Holometabola.	,,	21–29.

System C.
Apterygota.	Orders	1–4.
Exopterygota.	,,	5–20.
Endopterygota.	,,	21–29.

System D.
Apterygota.	Orders	1–4.
Palaeoptera.	,,	5–6.
Polyneoptera.	,,	7–15.
Paraneoptera.	,,	16–20.
Oligoneoptera.	,,	21–29.

The detailed but far from complete classification given below is based on System B. but alternative group-names are given in parenthesis. We have included all the Orders and the principal Suborders, but below this level it must be realized that the world of insects contains MANY HUNDREDS OF FAMILIES. It is impossible to list these in the short space available and we have contented ourselves with arranging alphabetically some of the better known families in each Order. Except in the larger Orders we have not attempted to group the families into superfamilies or other categories. Nor have we defined or described

CLASSIFICATION OF INSECTS

them, as such definitions and descriptions of families are to be found in the main part of the dictionary. Wherever possible, however, we have given the names of one or two well known insects in each group.

PHYLUM. ARTHROPODA.

CLASS. INSECTA (Hexapoda).

SUBCLASS 1. AMETABOLA (Apterygota). Primitive wingless insects without metamorphosis.
   Order 1. PROTURA. The most primitive insects. *e.g. Eosentomon.*
   Order 2. COLLEMBOLA. Springtails. *e.g. Sminthurus.*
   Order 3. DIPLURA. Two-tailed Bristle-tails. *e.g. Japyx.*
   Order 4. THYSANURA. Three-tailed Bristle-tails, Silverfish. *e.g. Lepisma.*

SUBCLASS 2. METABOLA (Pterygota). Winged or secondarily wingless insects.

DIVISION 1. HEMIMETABOLA (Palaeoptera, Exopterygota).
Insects with incomplete metamorphosis without a pupal stage. The adults have a primitive network of veins in the wings.
   Order 5. EPHEMEROPTERA. Mayflies.
   Order 6. ODONATA. Dragonflies.
      Suborder 1. Zygoptera. Damselflies.
      Suborder 2. Anisoptera. True Dragonflies.

DIVISION 2. HETEROMETABOLA (Exopterygota, Polyneoptera and Paraneoptera).
Insects have a varying degree of metamorphosis without a pupal stage. Wings able to be folded; having numerous veins but with some degree of specialization.
   Order 7. DICTYOPTERA. (Formerly classed with Orthoptera.)
      Suborder 1. Blattodea. Cockroaches.
      Suborder 2. Mantodea. Praying Mantids.
   Order 8. ISOPTERA. Termites.
   Order 9. ZORAPTERA. Minute louse-like insects. *e.g. Zorotypus.*
   Order 10. PLECOPTERA. Stoneflies.
   Order 11. NOTOPTERA (Grylloblattodea). A small order of wingless insects intermediate between cockroaches and crickets.
   Order 12. CHELEUTOPTERA (Phasmida). Stick Insects and Leaf Insects.
   Order 13. ORTHOPTERA. Grasshoppers etc.
      Suborder 1. Ensifera.
      Principal Families:
         Tettigoniidae. Long-horned grasshoppers and Bush Crickets.
         Gryllidae. Crickets.
         Gryllotalpidae. Mole-crickets.
      Suborder 2. Caelifera.
      Principal Families:
         Acrididae. Short-horned Grasshoppers.
         Tetrigidae. Groundhoppers.
         Locustidae. Locusts.
   Order 14. EMBIOPTERA. Web-spinners. *e.g. Embia*
   Order 15. DERMAPTERA. Earwigs.

354

Order 16. PSOCOPTERA. Book-lice etc.
Order 17. MALLOPHAGA. Biting Lice. Bird-lice. *e.g. Menopon.*
Order 18. ANOPLURA. Sucking Lice. *e.g.* Human Louse *Pediculus.*
Order 19. THYSANOPTERA. Thrips.
Order 20. HEMIPTERA (Rhynchota). Bugs and plant-lice.
  Suborder 1. Homoptera.
    Principal Families:
      Aphididae. Greenflies etc.
      Cercopidae. Frog-hoppers.
      Cicadidae. Cicadas.
      Coccidae. Scale-insects and Mealy-bugs.
      Fulgoridae. Lantern Flies.
      Cicadellidae. Leaf-hoppers.
      Membracidae. Tree-hoppers.
  Suborder 2. Heteroptera.
    Principal Families:
      Cimicidae. Bedbugs.
      Coreidae. Squashbugs.
      Corixidae. Small Water Boatmen.
      Gerridae. Pondskaters.
      Miridae. Capsid Bugs.
      Nepidae. Water Scorpions.
      Notonectidae. Backswimmers (Water Boatmen).
      Pentatomidae. Shieldbugs.
      Reduviidae. Assassin Bugs.
      Tingidae. Lacebugs.

DIVISION 3. HOLOMETABOLA (Endopterygota, Oligoneoptera).
Insects with complete metamorphosis including a pupal stage. Wings have a reduced number of veins and are often highly specialized.
Order. 21. COLEOPTERA. Beetles.
  Principal Families:
    Anobiidae. Furniture Beetles.
    Buprestidae. Splendour Beetles.
    Cantharidae. Soldier Beetles.
    Carabidae. Ground Beetles.
    Cerambycidae. Longhorn Beetles.
    Chrysomelidae. Leaf-beetles and Flea-beetles.
    Cicindelidae. Tiger Beetles.
    Coccinellidae. Ladybirds.
    Curculionidae. Weevils.
    Dermestidae. Skin Beetles.
    Dynastidae. Rhinoceros Beetles, Hercules and other 'giants'.
    Dytiscidae. Carnivorous Water Beetles.
    Elateridae. Click Beetles.
    Gyrinidae. Whirligig Beetles.
    Hydrophilidae. Herbivorous Water Beetles.
    Lampyridae. Glow-worms and Fireflies.
    Lucanidae. Stag Beetles.
    Meloidae. Oil Beetles and Blister Beetles.
    Necrophoridae. Burying Beetles.
    Scarabaeidae. Chafers, Scarabs, Dung Beetles.
    Scolytidae. Pinhole Borers, Bark Beetles.

Staphylinidae. Rove Beetles, Devil's Coach-horse.
Tenebrionidae. Flour Beetles, Mealworm Beetles.
Order 22. NEUROPTERA.
 Suborder 1. Megaloptera.
 Principal Families:
  Sialidae. Alder-flies.
  Raphidiidae. Snake-flies.
 Suborder 2. Planipennia.
 Principal Families:
  Chrysopidae. Green Lacewings.
  Hemerobiidae. Brown Lacewings.
  Myrmeleontidae. Ant-lions.
Order 23. MECOPTERA. Scorpion-flies.
Order 24. TRICHOPTERA. Caddis Flies.
Order 25. LEPIDOPTERA. Butterflies and Moths.
 Suborder 1. Homoneura (Jugatae).
 Families:
  Micropterygidae. Tiny moths with biting mouth-parts.
  Hepialidae. Swift Moths.
 Suborder 2. Heteroneura. All other butterflies and moths.

(**N.B.** The distinction between butterflies and moths is an artificial one, no longer used in formal classification, but as a matter of convenience we have grouped the following families into these two categories.)

MOTHS. Principal families:
 Arctiidae. Tiger Moths, Footman Moths.
 Bombycidae. Silkworm Moths.
 Cossidae. Goat Moths.
 Drepanidae. Hook-tips.
 Geometridae. Loopers, Carpet Moths, Pugs etc.
 Lasiocampidae. Eggars, Lackeys, Drinkers etc.
 Lymantriidae. Tussock Moths, Vapourer, Yellow-tail etc.
 Noctuidae. Owlets, Yellow Underwings.
 Notodontidae. Prominent Moths, Puss Moth.
 Psychidae. Bagworm Moths.
 Pterophoridae. Plume Moths.
 Pyralidae. Grain Moths, Meal Moths.
 Saturniidae. Emperor Moth, Giant Silkworm Moths, Atlas Moth.
 Sesiidae. Clearwing Moths.
 Sphingidae. Hawk-moths.
 Tineidae. Clothes Moths.
 Tortricidae. Leaf-rollers.
 Zygaenidae. Burnet Moths.

BUTTERFLIES. Principal Families:
 Acraeidae. African transparent-winged butterflies.
 Amathusiidae. Very large Asiatic and Australian butterflies.
 Brassolidae. Owl Butterflies. South America.
 Danaeidae. Milkweed and other large butterflies, mostly tropical.
 Erycinidae. Duke of Burgundy Fritillary and others, mostly South American.
 Heliconiidae. Large, brightly coloured, South American.

Hesperiidae. Skippers.
Ithomiidae. South American transparent-winged.
Lycaenidae. Coppers, Blues, Hairstreaks.
Morphidae. Large iridescent blue butterflies from South America.
Nymphalidae. Fritillaries and Aristocrats. Peacock, Red Admiral, Tortoiseshell etc.
Papilionidae. Swallowtails, Birdwings, Apollo etc.
Pieridae. Whites and Yellow Butterflies.
Satyridae. Browns, Graylings.
Order 26. DIPTERA. Two-winged Flies.
Suborder 1. Nematocera.
Principal Families:
Bibionidae. St. Mark's Fly.
Cecidomyiidae. Gall-midges.
Ceratopogonidae. Biting Midges.
Chironomidae. Non-biting midges and gnats.
Culicidae. Mosquitoes.
Mycetophilidae. Fungus Gnats.
Sciaridae. Fungus Gnats.
Simuliidae. Black Flies.
Tipulidae. Crane-flies.
Suborder 2. Brachycera.
Principal Families:
Asilidae. Robber Flies.
Bombyliidae. Bee-flies.
Tabanidae. Horse Flies, Gadflies.
Suborder 3. Cyclorrhapha.
Series. Aschiza.
Principal Families:
Syrphidae. Hover Flies.
Phoridae. Hump-backed Flies.
Series. Pupipara.
Principal Families:
Hippoboscidae. Forest Flies, Sheep Keds.
Nycteribiidae. Bat Flies.
Series Acalypterae (Acalyptrata).
Principal Families:
Agromyzidae. Leaf Miners.
Drosophilidae. Fruit Flies.
Ephydridae. Shore Flies.
Sciomyzidae. Marsh Flies.
Trypetidae. Fruit Flies.
Series Calypterae (Calyptrata).
Principal Families:
Anthomyiidae. Flower Flies.
Calliphoridae. Blowflies.
Gastrophilidae. Bot Flies.
Muscidae. House Flies.
Oestridae. Warble Flies.
Sarcophagidae. Flesh Flies.
Tachinidae. Parasitic Flies.
Order 27. SIPHONAPTERA (Aphaniptera). Fleas.
Order 28. STREPSIPTERA. Minute parasitic insects. *Stylops.*

CLASSIFICATION OF INSECTS

Order 29. HYMENOPTERA. Bees and Wasps etc.
  Suborder 1. Symphyta.
    Principal Families:—
      Siricidae. Woodwasps.
      Tenthredinidae. Sawflies.
  Suborder 2. Apocrita.
    Principal Families:—
      Apidae. Hive Bees.
      Bombidae. Bumble Bees.
      Chalcididae. Parasitic Wasps.
      Cynipidae. Gall-wasps.
      Formicidae. Ants.
      Ichneumonidae. Ichneumon Flies.
      Megachilidae. Leaf-cutting Bees.
      Pompilidae. Spider-hunting Wasps.
      Sphecidae. Hunting Wasps, Digger Wasps.
      Vespidae. Social Wasps.

BIBLIOGRAPHY

BAER, J. G. *Animal Parasites*. (Weidenfeld & Nicolson, 1971.)
BORRADAILE, L. A., POTTS, F. A., EASTHAM, L. E. S. and SAUNDERS, J. T. *The Invertebrata*. (4th Edition with insect section revised by Prof. Eastham.) (Cambridge, 1967.)
BRITISH MUSEUM (Natural History). Miscellaneous leaflets on insects of economic importance.
BUCHSBAUM, RALPH. *Animals without Backbones*. (Chicago University Press, 1938.)
BURTON, JOHN. *The Oxford Book of Insects*. (Oxford, 1968.)
BUTLER, C. G. *The World of the Honey Bee*. (Collins, 1962.)
CHAPMAN, R. F. *The Insects: Structure and Function*. (E.U.P.)
CHINERY, MICHAEL. *A Field Guide to the Insects of Britain and Northern Europe*. (Collins, 1973.)
CHRYSTAL, R. NEIL. *Insects of the British Woodlands*. (Warne, 1937.)
COLYER, C. N. and HAMMOND, C. O. *Flies of the British Isles*. (Warne, 1968.)
CORBET, P. S., LONGFIELD, C. and MOORE, N. W. *Dragonflies*. (Collins, 1960.)
CROMPTON, JOHN. *The Hunting Wasp*. (Collins, 1948.)
DAGLISH, ERIC FITCH. *Name this Insect*. (Dent, 1952.)
DRIMMER, FREDERICK (Editor). *Illustrated Encyclopaedia of Animal Life*. (Odhams, 1964.)
FITTER, R. and M. *Dictionary of British Natural History*. (Penguin, 1967.)
FORD, E. B. *Butterflies*. (Collins, 1967.)
FORD, E. B. *Moths*. (Collins, 1972.)
FROST, S. W. *Insect Life and Insect Natural History*. (Dover, New York, 1959.)
GOODDEN, ROBERT. *Butterflies*. (Hamlyn, 1971.)
GROVE, A. J. and NEWELL, G. E. *Animal Biology*. (Univ. Tutorial Press.)
HALL, CHARLES A. *Pocket Book of British Butterflies & Moths*. (A. & C. Black, 1938.)
HENDERSON, I. F. and W. D. *Dictionary of Biological Terms*. Revised by J. H. Kenneth. (Oliver & Boyd, 1963.)
HIGGINS, L. G. and RILEY, N. D. *A Field Guide to the Butterflies of Britain and Europe*. (Collins, 1970.)
HIRONS, M. J. D. *Insect Life of Farm and Garden*. (Blandford Press, 1966.)
IMMS, A. D. *General Textbook of Entomology* (9th. Ed.) (Methuen, 1970.)
IMMS, A. D. *Insect Natural History*. (Collins, 1947.)
IMMS, A. D. *Outlines of Entomology*. (Methuen, 1944.)
LAROUSSE. *Encyclopaedia of Animal Life*. (Hamlyn, 1967.)
LINSENMAIER, WALTER. *Insects of the World*. (McGraw-Hill, 1972.)
MARSHALL, J. F. *British Mosquitoes*. (British Museum, Nat. Hist. 1938.)
MATTHEWS, L. H. and MAXWELL KNIGHT. *The Senses of Animals*. (Museum Press, London, 1963.)
MILNE, L. J. and M. *The Senses of Animals and Man*. (André Deutsch, 1962.)
OLDROYD, HAROLD. *Collecting, Preserving and Studying Insects*. (Hutchinson, 1970.)

BIBLIOGRAPHY

OLDROYD, HAROLD. *Elements of Entomology.* (Weidenfeld & Nicolson, 1968.

OLDROYD, HAROLD. *Insects and their World.* (Brit. Mus. Nat. Hist. 1966.)

OLDROYD, HAROLD. *The Natural History of Flies.* (Weidenfeld & Nicolson, 1964.)

PARKER, T. J. and HASWELL, W. A. *Textbook of Zoology.* (Revised Lowenstein) (Macmillan, 1961.)

PENNAK, R. W. *Collegiate Dictionary of Zoology.* (Ronald, New York, 1964.)

ROSS, HERBERT H. *A Textbook of Entomology.* (John Wiley, New York, 1965.)

ROTHSCHILD, LORD. *A Classification of Living Animals.* (Longmans, 1964.)

ROYAL ENTOMOLOGICAL SOCIETY. *Handbooks for the Identification of British Insects.*

SANDARS, EDMUND. *An Insect Book for the Pocket.* (Oxford, 1951.)

SHORT, J. R. T. *Introduction to Applied Entomology.* (Longmans, 1963.)

SIMON, HILDA. *Insect Masquerades.* (Fredk. Muller, London, 1969.)

STANEK, V. J. *Pictorial Encyclopaedia of Insects.* (Hamlyn, 1969.)

STEPHENSON, E. M. and STEWART, C. *Animal Camouflage.* (Black, 1955.)

WIGGLESWORTH, SIR VINCENT B. *Insect Physiology.* (Methuen, 1966.)

WIGGLESWORTH, SIR VINCENT B. *The Life of Insects.* (New American Library, 1968.)

WIGGLESWORTH, SIR VINCENT B. *Principles of Insect Physiology.* (Methuen, 1956.)

WINKLER, J. R. and BOHAC, V. *A Book of Beetles.* (Spring Books, London, 1964.)

WOOD, GERALD L. *Guinness Book of Animal Facts and Feats.* (Guinness, London, 1972.)